Portfolio Management
Theory and Application

McGraw-Hill Series in Finance

Archer and Kerr: *Readings and Cases in Corporate Finance*
Ball and Kothari: *Financial Statement Analysis*
Beaver and Parker: *Risk Management: Problems and Solutions*
Bergfield: *California Real Estate*
Blake: *Financial Market Analysis*
Bowlin, Martin, and Scott: *Guide to Financial Analysis*
Brealey and Myers: *Principles of Corporate Finance*
Brealey, Myers, and Marcus: *Fundamentals of Corporate Finance*
Chew: *The New Corporate Finance*
Coates: *Investment Strategy*
Cottle, Murray, and Block: *Security Analysis*
Doherty: *Corporate Risk Management: A Financial Exposition*
Dubofsky: *Options and Financial Futures: Valuation and Uses*
Edmister: *Financial Institutions: Markets and Management*
Edwards and Ma: *Futures and Options*
Farrell: *Systematic Portfolio Management*
Francis: *Investments: Anaysis and Management*
Francis: *Management of Investments*
Garbade: *Securities Markets*
Gibson: *Option Valuation: Analyzing and Pricing Standardized Option Contracts*
Hayes and Habbard: *Investment Banking*
Heck: *The McGraw-Hill Finance Literature Index*
Ibbotson and Brinson: *Investments Markets: Gaining the Performance Edge*
James and Smith: *Studies in Financial Institutions: Commercial Banks*
Johnson: *Financial Institutions and Markets: A Global Perspective*
Kau and Sirmans: *Real Estate*
Kester and Luehrman: *Case Problems in International Finance*
Kohn: *Financial Institutions and Markets*
Lang: *Strategy for Personal Finance*
Levi: *International Finance: The Markets and Financial Management of Multinational Business*
McLoughlin: *Principles of Real Estate Law*
Martin, Petty, and Klock: *Personal Financial Management*
Peterson: *Financial Management and Analysis*
Riehl and Rodriguez: *Foreign Exchange and Money Market*
Robertson and Wrightsman: *Financial Markets*
Rothstein: *The Handbook of Financial Futures*
Schall and Haley: *Introduction to Financial Management*
Silverman: *Corporate Real Estate Handbook*
Sirmans: *Real Estate Finance*
Smith: *The Modern Theory of Corporate Finance*
Williams, Smith, and Young: *Risk Management and Insurance*

Portfolio Management

Theory and Application

SECOND EDITION

James L. Farrell, Jr.

Chairman
Farrell-Wako Global Investment Management, Inc.

Adjunct Professor
New York University

Chairman
The Institute for Quantitative Research in Finance

With the collaboration of

Walter J. Reinhart

Finance Professor
Loyola College in Maryland

Irwin McGraw-Hill

Boston, Massachusetts   Burr Ridge, Illinois   Dubuque, Iowa
Madison, Wisconsin   New York, New York   San Francisco, California
St. Louis, Missouri

Irwin/McGraw-Hill

A Division of The **McGraw·Hill** Companies

PORTFOLIO MANAGEMENT
Theory and Application

This book is printed on acid-free paper.

2 3 4 5 6 7 8 9 0 DOC DOC 9 0 9 8 7

ISBN 0-07-020082-3

This book was set in Times New Roman by Publication Services, Inc.
The editors were Michelle E. Cox and Judy Howarth;
the production supervisor was Leroy A. Young.
The cover was designed by Karen K. Quigley.
Project supervision was done by Publication Services, Inc.
R. R. Donnelley & Sons Company was printer and binder.

Library of Congress Cataloging-in-Publication Data

Farrell, James L.
    Portfolio management : theory and application / James L. Farrell,
Jr. with the collaboration of Walter J. Reinhart. — 2nd ed.
        p.   cm. — (McGraw-Hill series in finance)
    Rev. ed. of: Guide to portfolio management. c1983.
    Includes bibliographical references and index.
    ISBN 0-07-020082-3
    1. Portfolio management.   I. Reinhart, Walter J.   II. Farrell,
James L. Guide to portfolio management.   III. Title.   IV. Series.
HG4529.5.F37   1997
332.6—dc20   96–22194

ABOUT THE AUTHOR

JAMES L. FARRELL, JR., CFA, who received a B.S. from the University of Notre Dame, an M.B.A. from the Wharton School, and a Ph.D. from New York University (NYU), has had over 25 years experience as a security analyst, applied financial researcher, and portfolio manager at major financial institutions, including College Retirement Equities Fund (CREF) and Citibank. Dr. Farrell pioneered a systematic approach to stock selection based on the concept of "alpha" and employed a stategy built around this approach to manage portfolios of U.S. equities at an investment counseling firm that he founded in 1980. Dr. Farrell has since expanded the use of the alpha strategy by applying it to international markets. As chairman of Farrell-Wako Global Investment Management (FWGI), he now manages both U.S. domestic equity portfolios and those of foreign equity markets.

Since 1976, Dr. Farrell has served as chairman of the Institute for Quantitative Research in Finance, also known as the "Q" Group. The "Q" Group is a cooperative organization comprising a wide variety of investor-type organizations, all of whom are interested in expanding the state of the art of investment management. The "Q" Group includes as its members many of the leading practitioners in the area of quantitative approaches to investing. The Group conducts semiannual seminars, where practitioners and academics discuss evolving theories and applied techniques for investing.

Dr. Farrell has served as an adjunct professor of finance at both NYU and Columbia University, where he taught courses in portfolio management. He has written extensively on such portfolio management topics as asset allocation, security valuation, portfolio analysis, and international investing. In addition to successfully implementing the alpha strategy for managing portfolios, Dr. Farrell has written and lectured on the merits of this approach for introducing greater discipline and structure in the investment process. His early research and writing on factor analysis and homogenous stock groupings anticipated the current strong interest in equity style analysis as a way of managing portfolios and evaluating their performance.

To My Wife, Cyrille
and Our Children, Jim, Barbara, and Catherine

CONTENTS

PART 3 **Security Valuation and Risk Analysis**

P A R T 4   Asset Class Management

PREFACE

This book has a primary focus on portfolio management. It covers the theoretical under-pinnings as a basis for a better understanding of its relevance in managing portfolios. As a practitioner, I emphasize the application of theory to practice.

While there is a natural connection between theory and portfolio practice, it is not seam-less. Much of the theory that is relevant to practice was, in fact, developed more than 25 years ago. However, only in the last 10 years have the concepts developed much earlier begun to be put into practice on a wide scale. In fact, a great deal of innovative work in broadening the application of theory is being done by researchers, analysts, and portfolio managers at investment firms.

This book is divided into six parts. The first part, composed of Chapter 1 alone, de-scribes the forces that are leading to a greater discipline and structure in the practice of portfolio management. Part One also describes the organizational structure of the portfo-lio management industry and outlines some of the key concepts underlying the practice of portfolio management.

Part Two comprises Chapters 2, 3, and 4 and describes both portfolio theory and capital market theory. Asset allocation and portfolio analysis are two prime applications of these theories and are illustrated in these chapters.

Part Three, comprising Chapters 5, 6, and 7, focuses on bond and stock evaluation. Managers attempting to outperform a benchmark need to understand the forces that give value to securities so as to be able to discriminate between under- and overvalued securities when constructing an actively managed portfolio.

Part Four, comprising four chapters, covers the equity portfolio management process. Chapter 8 describes the way in which a disciplined stock valuation approach can be devel-oped into a strategy that fits the active/passive framework, while Chapter 10 describes the relevance of equity style management to portfolio management. In Chapter 11 I describe how the principles of portfolio management can be transported from the U.S. market to international markets. Chapter 9 focuses on asset allocation, both from a strategic and a tac-tical perspective, and describes the patterns of return that portfolios generate as differing rebalancing strategies are employed.

Part Five focuses on the use of derivatives in portfolio management. Chapter 12 covers futures before options are covered in Chapter 13, because the concepts underlying futures are more intuitive and the uses of these instruments are a more natural adjunct for port-folio management strategies. Options are more complex but have many portfolio strategy applications. Equally important, the principles underlying option valuation have broad im-plications in understanding the basic principles of such strategies as portfolio insurance and tactical asset allocation. Furthermore, option valuation principles are being applied more extensively in the area of bond valuation, and that is why I include Chapter 14 on bond management in this part of the book.

Part Six comprises a single chapter, Chapter 15, on portfolio evaluation. This evaluation serves as a review of much of what was covered in the prior chapters, because a portfolio evaluation process should evaluate those aspects of a strategy and investment process that are significant in generating returns or exposing the investor to risk. As such, performance measurement might also be considered as a preview of what should be covered in portfolio management.

In all, I think that the book provides a compact yet comprehensive overview of the practice of portfolio management. In describing theory I have tried to keep the description as brief as possible by focusing on the critical underlying elements while appealing to intuition as much as possible. Correspondingly, there are some specialized areas such as futures and options that can undergo quite extensive description in more specialized books. I cover these subject areas more succinctly to focus on the most essential aspects of their use as well as how they relate in the overall portfolio management picture.

While there are many fine finance and investment books in the marketplace, I think that this book distinguishes itself in several ways. First, the book focuses on portfolio management, whereas most others combine portfolio management with descriptions of other aspects of the field of finance and investments. As both a practitioner and an (albeit part-time) academic, I have emphasized and tried to maintain a tone of practical application throughout. In that regard I have tried to introduce practical application of theory quickly, as for example the discussion of asset allocation as a practical application of portfolio theory in Chapter 2. Also, each chapter has extensive description and examples of how portfolio management applies.

In addition to its practical tone, the book has several distinctive aspects. First, there is an emphasis throughout on the role of active portfolio management with regard to stock selection, style management, international investing, bond management, and asset allocation. At the same time, the book emphasizes the need to control risk when managing actively; hence the notion of active/passive strategies. In addition, the book stresses rigorous valuation methods, based on both traditional and more modern concepts, as the best way of identifying opportunities to enhance return in the portfolio management process. Correspondingly, the book provides ways of converting the theoretical notions from portfolio theory and capital market theory into practical ways of analyzing the risk exposure of a portfolio. Finally, the book not only describes the use of CAPM-based methods of analyzing performance but also describes the return attribution methods that are more illuminating and commonly used among practitioners.

An instructor's manual is available to teachers using the book. The instructor's manual contains chapter overviews and outlines, answers to the questions and problems, and test questions with suggested answers.

ACKNOWLEDGMENTS

I want to thank the following reviewers who contributed to the revision of this book by providing me with helpful comments and suggestions: W. Brian Barrett, University of Miami; W. Scott Bauman, Northern Illinois University; Paul Bolster, Northeastern University; William Dukes, Texas Tech University; M. E. Ellis, St. John's University; James Greenleaf, Lehigh University; Charles Jones, North Carolina State University; Robert Kleiman, Oakland University; Jeffrey M. Mercer, Northern Illinois University; Daniel Page, Auburn University; Hun Park, University of Illinois; Steve Swidler, The University of Texas at Arlington.

James L. Farrell, Jr.

PART ONE

Introduction

CHAPTER 1

━━━━━━━━━━━━━━━━━━━━━━━━━━━━━━━

Systematic Portfolio Management

INTRODUCTION

The goal of portfolio management is to assemble various securities and other assets into portfolios that address investor needs and then to manage those portfolios so as to achieve investment objectives. The investor's needs are defined in terms of risk, and the portfolio manager maximizes return for investment risk undertaken.

Portfolio management consists of three major activities: (1) asset allocation, (2) shifts in weighting across major asset classes, and (3) security selection within asset classes. Asset allocation can best be characterized as the blending together of major asset classes to obtain the highest long-run return at the lowest risk. Managers can make opportunistic shifts in asset class weightings in order to improve return prospects over the longer-term objective. For example, a manager who judges the outlook for equities to be considerably more favorable than that for bonds over the forthcoming year may well desire to shift from bonds to equities. Also, managers can improve return prospects by selecting securities that have above-average expected return within the individual asset classes.

We begin this chapter by describing how the growing availability of financial and economic data, quantitative tools, and underlying financial theory have facilitated the task of developing strategies and investment techniques for addressing investor needs. We then go on to describe how portfolio managers interact with primary investors and other participants in the process when fulfilling the functions of portfolio management. We conclude the chapter by illustrating how two critical underlying features of financial markets—trade-off between risk and return, and the concept of market efficiency—relate to the main activities of portfolio management.

INVESTMENT MANAGERS

A multitude of investment management organizations offer portfolio management services to clients including individual investors, mutual funds, endowments, large pension plans, life insurance, casualty insurance, and banks. It is estimated that there are more than 1000 of these investment organizations, ranging in size from one- to three-person "boutique" managers, providing specialized portfolio management services to a small clientele niche, to major full-line organizations, providing a full array of portfolio management services to a broad range of clientele types. Organizations differ greatly in their approach to investment analysis and portfolio management as well, displaying many different investment styles. Organizations may use explicit or implicit procedures and may be relatively controlled or uncontrolled. Many may deal with uncertainty only obliquely, some may utilize inconsistent estimates in the process, and others may use statistical models to estimate risk.

Investment organizations differ not only in size and degree of specialization but also in their approaches to investment analysis and portfolio management. On the whole, however, the business of portfolio management has tended toward greater structure and discipline in the investment process and toward greater use of systematic approaches to investing. Those organizations at the forefront in implementing systematic approaches to portfolio management have gained market share at the expense of other firms, in large part because they have been more effective in addressing client needs and achieving investment objectives.

FORCES FOR CHANGE

Table 1-1 presents the three forces that have been most important in the development and growth of the systematic approach to investment management. Perhaps the major force has been the development of strategies, models, and techniques based on powerful financial and economic theories that began emerging 40 to 50 years ago. The corresponding growth of financial and economic data bases, the rapid evolution of computer hardware and software, and the development of powerful statistical tools provided the means for testing and implementing these investment models and techniques.

THEORY AND APPLICATION

Table 1-2 shows the five most significant theoretical breakthroughs in financial research. These theories are simple in concept, yet quite powerful. Most important, they have had a profound impact on the practice of investment management, as the list of applications relevant to each theory illustrates.

From portfolio theory, for example, comes the practice of formally determining an asset allocation. Virtually every major plan sponsor undertakes such an evaluation, either alone or with the help of an investment plan consultant who has developed a model for properly positioning plan assets. The principles of portfolio theory have also provided both impetus and framework for global investment analysis.

Capital market theory, by providing an operationally useful framework for assessing risk-return trade-offs, has inspired the development of an objective basis for portfolio

TABLE 1-1
Forces for change

I. Theoretical breakthroughs
II. Development of data bases
III. Tools of analysis
    Statistical
    Computer, communications, and software

TABLE 1-2
Theoretical breakthroughs leading to systematic techniques for investment management

Theory	Application
Portfolio theory	Asset allocation
	Global investing
Capital market theory	Risk-return trade-off
	Portfolio analysis
	Performance measurement
Security valuation	Dividend discount model
	Market line
Market efficiency	Active/passive
	Multiple valuation model
Derivative securities valuation	Protective put
	Portfolio insurance
	Index futures

analysis and has improved methods of measuring the performance of funds. Investment managers and major plan sponsors as well as leading consultants have applied these methods to improve objective setting and control of the investment process.

Theoretical developments in security valuation have led to models such as the dividend discount model (DDM) and the security market line, which allow investors to make objective comparisons of individual securities and asset classes. Research into the efficiency of the market has led to the development of both active and passive approaches to investing and has also encouraged the development of more powerful methods of valuation. Finally, derivative securities valuation models have spawned a variety of option- and future-related strategies, which have broadened the scope of investing.

DATA BASES

These five theoretical breakthroughs provide an invaluable framework for investors attempting to analyze the structure and dynamics of financial markets. They have also been a prime motivating force in the development of financial and economic data bases. Those data bases (the development of price and return data for common stocks in the early 1960s, for example) have in turn been instrumental for testing the efficacy of the theories as well as for developing new theories and analytical techniques. In retrospect, it is remarkable that objective data on stock returns were first developed less than 30 years ago, primarily because of the impetus of emerging theory.

Since the development of price and return data on common stocks, data bases covering many types of financial and economic measures and indicators have proliferated. There is now a surfeit of data in some areas, while other areas, such as real estate and some international markets, call out for more and better data. The rapid development of computer technology and high-speed electronic communications has provided the means of delivering the data as well as of manipulating them efficiently.

The data bases can be used in innumerable ways: in testing, as inputs to models, or in the service of a better understanding of the market and its individual components. A

TABLE 1-3
Financial and economic data bases

Data types
Market values
Returns
Fundamental (earnings, dividends, etc.)
Economic (GNP, CPI, etc.)
Combination (P/E, yields, etc.)

Period of analysis
Current-contemporaneous
Historic
Expectational

Security type
Individual security
Sector/industry
Market
Asset classes

comprehensive listing and description of the data bases and their uses lies far beyond the scope of this book. Instead, we will list some of the major data bases and discuss some suggestions as to how one might use these to illustrate the interrelationships between data bases and portfolio management.

Table 1-3 classifies data sources according to various criteria and illustrates the many ways investors use data. Historical data provide perspective, whereas current data are needed for ongoing operations, and expectational data offer enhanced analytical insights. Data on individual securities are important in their own right and can also be aggregated into broader measures of interest. Investors may wish to evaluate such data by sector or industry (for example, comparing the energy sector with the durable goods sector) or by market (comparing the U.S. market with the Japanese market, for example) or by asset class (stocks, say, versus bonds or bills).

TOOLS OF ANALYSIS

Given the theoretical framework and appropriate data, statistical techniques, computers, and software provide the "tools of analysis." These tools represent a third vital component of what might be considered a three-part foundation for systematic portfolio management. They provide the basis for an objective and efficient evaluation of whether financial and economic data are useful in the portfolio management process. Statistical techniques and computer software also provide the means for testing the efficacy of newly developed strategies and techniques of portfolio management. Finally, they allow for efficient evaluation of the success of portfolio management, whether systematic or not, in achieving performance objectives.

Table 1-4 provides an illustrative selection of some statistical techniques. Regression analyses are used to test the viability of approaches as well as to develop structures for models. Multivariate analytical techniques, such as factor analysis and discriminant analysis, are helpful tools for evaluating the behavior of prices, economic data, or other fundamental

TABLE 1-4
Tools of analysis

Statistical and Other Quantitative Methods

Regression and variations
Multivariate analysis
   Factor analysis
   Discriminant analysis
Time series analysis
   ARCH models
   ARIMA models

Computational power and speed

PC workstation
Software
Electronic communications

---

factors essential to assessing the structure of financial markets. Sophisticated time-series analysis originated with Box-Jenkins and the associated ARIMA models. More recent innovations in this area include ARCH (autoregressive heteroscedastic) models, which provide a means of assessing the stability of the structure of models and thereby offer insights into modeling patterns of change over time.

Computer technology has evolved to the point where PCs and workstations offer considerable processing power at relatively low cost. Software development has progressed apace, facilitating the effective use of computers to operate relatively complex statistical and mathematical procedures and manipulate large amounts of data. Finally, the general availability of electronic communication facilitates the rapid delivery of data and enables more efficient data processing.

PARTICIPANTS

Several groups other than professional portfolio managers are important participants in the portfolio management process. Portfolio investors represent a primarily important grouping. These range from small individual investors to giant plan sponsors that include such major groupings as corporate pension plans, state and local pension plans, endowments, and foundations. Investment consultants constitute a third grouping that provides advisory services to major investment plan sponsors and high–net worth individuals in setting goals, asset allocation, and selection of investment managers. Correspondingly, these and other more specialized services represent a fourth grouping that evaluates the performance of investment managers.

While portfolio investors are ultimately responsible for all components of the decision-making process, the most appropriate focus for investors will be goal setting. Because of the critical importance of the asset allocation decision and the structure of the investment business in the United States, many major portfolio investors assume responsibility for this phase of the portfolio decision-making process. This is a relatively recent phenomenon, having evolved from the mid-1970s and given impetus by the severe market decline of 1973–1974 along with the introduction of the Employee Retirement Income Security Act (ERISA), which defined prudent behavior on the part of plan sponsors and managers.

Previously, investment managers had been delegated responsibility for asset allocation as well as other phases of investment decision making. Outside of the United States, investment managers continue to assume this overall decision-making responsibility, but it is likely that overseas plan sponsors will increasingly assume asset allocation responsibility.

In making the asset allocation decision, major portfolio investors employ the services of investment management consultants. These are organizations that specialize in not only advising on asset allocation but other critical aspects, such as setting of goals and selection of investment managers. As specialists, investment consultants have developed sophisticated procedures and programs that provide a structural approach to the asset allocation determination. Also, they have the benefit of experience across a variety of plans, providing added insights into the asset allocation process.

For the security selection phase of the investment process, as well as for active weighting shifts across asset classes, the large majority of portfolio investors use outside investment managers. The outside managers retained for security selection are often specialists at managing within a broad asset class, such as equity specialists or bond specialists. Within a broader asset class, there can be further subdivision and managers that focus on that investment aspect as a specialty. Again, investment consultants often provide critical input in advising portfolio investors in the selection of managers. Consultants develop large data bases on individual managers and continuously evaluate managers, so they are in a position to match managers to the investors' needs.

The widespread availability of specialty managers and the continuing evolution of differing types has led to the use of a multitude of investment managers by many major investors. This, in turn, creates problems of selecting individual managers so as to avoid redundancy as well as of coordinating the individual managers to optimize the total program. Again, consultants and some specialty organizations provide advice and some structured analytical techniques to aid in designing and operating a multimanager program over time. Correspondingly, the proliferation of differing types of specialty managers compounds the performance evaluation task. There is need to diagnose more aspects of the investment

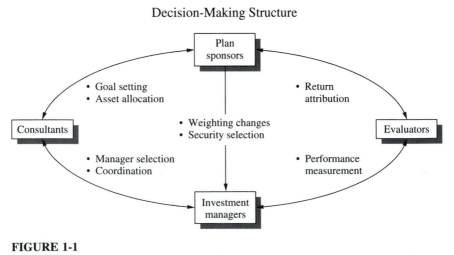

FIGURE 1-1
Decision-making structure.

process through procedures known as return attribution, which will be discussed in the final chapter of this book.

Figure 1-1 illustrates the investment decision-making structure that we described as typifying the U.S. environment. Note that the diagram shows the responsibilities of each of the participants with regard to each of the components of the decision process as well as the interrelationship in the decision structure. Decision-making responsibilities are shared, and there are many interrelated advisory relationships in this decentralized structure.

This rather complex decision-making structure contrasts with a simple structure that characterized the U.S. environment prior to the 1970s and that continues to be representative of the situation outside the United States. In this simplified structure a single investment manager, or at most a small group of managers, assumes responsibility for all aspects of the investment process. This evolution into a more complex structure has in turn had a profound impact on the form and the way that portfolio management is conducted in the United States and will have a similar impact on the investment business as the structure evolves in other countries.

ASSET CLASSES

As noted in the introduction, developing the appropriate asset allocation is a critical phase of the portfolio management process. Table 1-5 shows a breakdown of asset classes available for portfolio construction by the participants in the portfolio management process. Equities, bonds, and money market instruments are major asset categories that are large, are generally highly marketable, and have traditionally been used extensively by long-term portfolio investors. Real estate is a large investment category, but it has received relatively limited direct investment from portfolio investors because of its lack of liquidity, the difficulty in

TABLE 1-5
Asset classes for portfolio investment

Common stocks
    Domestic equities
        Large-capitalization
        Small-capitalization
    International equities
        Major-country markets
        Emerging markets
Bonds
    Governments and agencies
    Corporates
        AAA-rated
        Baa-rated
        High-yield (junk) bonds
    Mortgage-backed securities
    International bonds
Money market instruments
    Treasury bills
    CDs and commercial paper
    Guaranteed investment contracts (GIC)
Real estate
Venture capital

valuing the investment, limited understanding of its risk character, and relatively high cost of management. Venture capital is a smaller and potentially highly rewarding category, but suffers from the same problems as real estate: lack of liquidity, difficulty of valuation, and high cost of management. Furthermore, risk for venture capital is difficult to appraise but is almost certainly quite substantial; as a result, venture capital is a category used only to a limited extent even by the relatively small number of investors active in the area.

Note that the overall equity classification is subdivided into several categories that port- folio investors consider relevant when assembling a portfolio. Because of differing price behavior, it is becoming more usual to distinguish between large- and small-capitalization stocks when evaluating the domestic (U.S.)-based portion of the equity allocation. Although definitions vary, stocks with capitalization of $1 billion and less are usually considered to fall in the small-capitalization category. There is a growing interest in international invest- ing, primarily in major country markets such as Japan and the United Kingdom. More in- vestors, however, are evaluating emerging markets such as Thailand and Mexico, and these are usually considered as a separate category of international investing.

It is also usual to subdivide the bond classification into several categories for greater per- spective in asset allocation. Because of their unimpeachable credit standing, governments— also referred to as treasuries—represent a distinct category. Corporate bonds represent an- other category and are usually classed according to varying degrees of credit quality or risk. The highest-quality corporates are AAA-rated bonds, with Baa bonds representing the low- est threshold of institutionally acceptable quality. The high-yield or "junk" bond category carries significant credit risk but has appeal for certain investors. Mortgage-backed secu- rities have been a rapidly growing category that has appeal to certain investors. Finally, international bonds have appeal for diversification purposes as well as potential in inflation- hedging programs.

Money market instruments are a third major classification that offers investors flexi- bility in developing an asset allocation, especially for shorter-term repositioning activities. Treasury bills represent the highest-quality subcategory, as well as a highly liquid one, in this short-term classification. Certificates of deposit (CDs) and commercial paper carry some credit risk but offer higher returns than T-bills and are also generally quite marketable. Guar- anteed Investment Contracts (GICs) are short- to intermediate-term instruments, issued by insurance companies, that offer a guaranteed fixed return over a fixed maturity period. The GICs offer generally higher returns than alternative instruments, albeit with credit risk, and while short-term interest rates were high, these were quite appealing to investors, especially in the case of defined-contribution plans.

RISK-RETURN TRADE-OFF

In selecting asset classes for portfolio allocation, investors need to consider both the return potential and the riskiness of the asset class. It is clear from empirical estimates that there is a high correlation between risk and return measured over longer periods of time. Furthermore, capital market theory, which we describe in Chapters 3 and 4, posits that there should be a systematic relationship between risk and return. This theory indicates that securities are priced in the market so that high risk can be rewarded with high return, and conversely, low risk should be accompanied by correspondingly lower return.

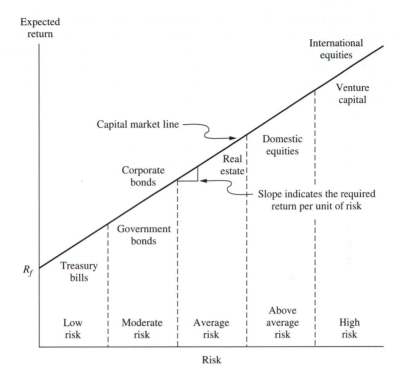

FIGURE 1-2
Relationship between risk and return.

Figure 1-2 is a capital market line showing an expected relationship between risk and return for representative asset classes arrayed over a range of risk. Note that the line is upward-sloping, indicating that higher risk should be accompanied by higher return. Conversely, the capital market relationship can be considered as showing that higher return can be generated only at the "expense" of higher risk. When measured over longer periods of time, the realized return and risk of the asset classes conform to this sort of relationship.

Note that Treasury bills are positioned at the low end of the risk range, consistent with these securities' generally being considered as representative of risk-free investing, at least for short holding periods. Correspondingly, the return offered by T-bills is usually considered as a basic risk-free return. On the other hand, equities as a class show the highest risk and return, with venture capital at the very highest position on the line, as would be expected. International equities, in turn, are shown as higher risk than domestic equities. Bonds and real estate are at an intermediate position on the capital market line, with real estate showing higher risk relative to both corporate and government bonds.

MARKET EFFICIENCY

We noted that there is a capital market relationship indicating a trade-off between risk and return across differing asset classes. Given an asset allocation, major investors should then expect to earn a return commensurate with the chosen asset mix: Allocations toward high-risk assets should be expected to earn high returns, whereas those positioned toward low-risk assets would be expected to earn low returns. In order to add value (increase returns) beyond that given by the basic asset mix, investors can (1) shift weightings across the major asset classes, (2) select securities of above-average attractiveness within the asset class, or both. The opportunity to add value in either way, in turn, depends on the degree of security market mispricing, which is a function of the efficiency of the market.

An *efficient market* is one in which price corresponds to value (price *reflects* value), and a perfectly efficient market is one in which price corresponds to value at all times. Prices change only when new information becomes available, and by the nature of an efficient market, new information is unanticipated. Because information is unanticipated, it will arrive randomly and thereby generate for securities a price pattern that will have the characteristics of a random series. Thus, one of the ways that researchers infer the efficiency of a market is by testing for randomness of security price changes over time.

Basic assumptions for efficiency are that there is an objective equilibrium value for a security and that price will gravitate toward this equilibrium value. This, in turn, implies that investors are rational, at least on average, so that their activities of buying and selling will move the price toward the intrinsic value of the security. Furthermore, we would expect that the speed of adjustment to equilibrium would depend on the availability of information and the competitiveness of the market. Highly competitive markets with many well-informed participants should show quite rapid adjustments to equilibrium, whereas those with fewer participants and a lesser flow of information might experience a fairly slow adjustment to equilibrium.

Researchers have, in turn, offered objective definitions as to the degree of efficiency of a market that take the following three forms: (1) the weak form, (2) the semistrong form, and (3) the strong form. The weak form asserts that current prices fully reflect the information implied by the historical sequence of prices; in other words, an investor cannot enhance his or her ability to select stocks by knowing the history of successive prices and the results of analyzing them in all possible ways. The semistrong form of the hypothesis asserts that current prices fully reflect *public* knowledge about the underlying companies (including, for example, earnings, dividends, public announcements by management, and other widely reported statements), and therefore efforts to acquire and analyze this knowledge cannot be expected to produce superior results. The strong form asserts that even those with privileged information cannot often make use of it to secure superior investment results.

While initial results of testing for market efficiency were generally supportive of the hypothesis, more recent research has uncovered notable instances of inefficiency, which have become known as *market anomalies.* Furthermore, the degree of market efficiency is not a constant over time. For example, it is well known that profit opportunities were rather common in the options and futures markets as those first developed, but over time much of the mispricing has been dissipated. Correspondingly, we would expect efficiency to vary across markets and types of securities. For example, we might expect the U.S. stock market to be more efficiently priced than other world markets, but even within the U.S. market we might expect to find small-cap stocks less efficiently priced than large-cap stocks. Finally, we might expect securities to be less efficiently priced where there is great complexity or a relatively limited flow of information. Our view is that markets are rational and that securities prices reach equilibrium over time, but that even well-developed and active markets are unlikely to be perfectly efficient.

It is important that participants in the investment decision-making structure develop an informed viewpoint as to the efficiency of the market. For investors, market efficiency is a critical consideration in determining what resources will be committed to active efforts in changing asset class weightings and security selection. Market efficiency is also a prime determinant for investment managers in developing strategies and designing the investment process. Investment consultants need to have an informed viewpoint so as to advise investors properly as well as select managers. Performance evaluators as well as consultants need to appraise the significance of investment performance in the context of the efficiency of the market.

CONCLUSION

The portfolio management industry in the United States has evolved over the last two decades into a structure with several distinct groupings of highly professional participants. This structure developed because it best matches participants with their prime responsibilities in the differing phases of the decision-making process while facilitating the use of a greater level of investment expertise at all stages in the process. At the same time, the greater structural complexity and increased scope of interaction among the various participants compounds the need for coordinating and monitoring the differing elements of the structural process.

Although the current structure differs from the past, the critical components of the investment decision process remain the same. Investors need to establish goals and be aware of the capital market trade-off in developing an asset allocation that best meets the return target at an acceptable level of risk. Furthermore, all the participants need to develop a viewpoint as to the efficiency of the market. This view will, in turn, influence the extent to which resources are devoted to seeking higher returns from either (1) asset class weighting changes or (2) security selection. Finally, we have seen that the systematic approach to portfolio management can greatly facilitate the design and execution of strategies related to these decision components.

SELECTED REFERENCES

Brinson, Gary, Randolph Hood, and Gilbert Beebower: "Determinants of Portfolio Performance," *Financial Analysts Journal,* July–August 1986, pp. 39–44.

Brinson, Gary, Randolph Hood, and Gilbert Beebower: "Determinants of Portfolio Performance," *Financial Analysts Journal,* May–June 1991, pp. 40–48.

Cootner, Paul: *The Random Character of Stock Market Prices,* MIT Press, Cambridge, Mass., 1974.

Fama, Eugene F.: "Efficient Capital Markets: A Review of Theory and Empirical Work," *Journal of Finance,* May 1970, pp. 383–417.

Farrell, James L. Jr.: "Systematic Portfolio Management: Evolution, Current Practice and Future Direction," "*Financial Analysts Journal,* September–October 1993, pp. 12–16.

Hagin, Robert: *Modern Portfolio Theory,* Dow Jones–Irwin, New York, 1979.

Ibbotson, Roger G. and Carol Fall: "The United States Market Wealth Portfolio," *Journal of Portfolio Management,* Fall 1979.

Lorie, James H., P. Dodd, and M. H. Kimpton: *The Stock Market: Theories and Evidence,* Irwin, Homewood, Ill., 1985.

Malkiel, Burton G.: *A Random Walk Down Wall Street,* Norton, New York, 1985.

QUESTIONS

1. Indicate what the major activities of portfolio management are.
2. What is systematic portfolio management, and what are the forces of change propelling its implementation?
3. What are major theories that have most influenced the evolution of portfolio management? Cite some examples of the practical application of these theories.
4. In what ways are data bases utilized, and how can these be helpful in the portfolio management process?
5. What role do quantitative techniques and computer technology play in the portfolio management process?
6. What are major groupings of participants, and how do they interact in the portfolio management process?
7. What are the major asset classes available for portfolio construction, and how do they differ?
8. What is the notion of a risk-return trade-off, and why is it important?
9. What is the concept of market efficiency, and why is it important to the various participants?
10. What is the single factor most important for ensuring efficient capital markets?
11. Describe the differences between the weak, semistrong, and strong forms of the efficient market hypothesis.

PART TWO

Portfolio Construction and Analysis

Constructing the portfolio and analyzing its characteristics are basic activities for professional portfolio managers. In constructing a portfolio, the underlying concept is diversification across individual securities so as to minimize the impact of adverse results from a few securities. Portfolio theory provides both a theoretical justification for diversification and an analytical framework for assembling individual securities in such a way as to achieve proper diversification.

Capital market theory is a logical extension of the need to assess risk within the context of a portfolio. When viewed in this way, what matters is the component of risk that is common to all securities. The other part, which is specific to an individual security, is irrelevant, because it can be diversified away. The common, or systematic, component is measured by the well-known *beta* (β), which is a gauge of the sensitivity of a security to movements in the market. Capital market theory demonstrates that systematic risk is what should be rewarded, and empirical results show that higher-risk securities have, in fact, earned higher returns over longer periods than lower-risk securities. Portfolio managers should be aware of this risk-return trade-off when assembling classes of assets in an asset allocation or when considering individual securities for inclusion in a portfolio.

The theoretical development of capital market theory has, in turn, spawned a whole body of analysis, which many refer to as *portfolio analysis*. Capital market theory emphasizes the importance of monitoring the systematic risk level of a portfolio as well as the degree of diversification of the portfolio. Many organizations and services that provide what might be termed "portfolio diagnostics" have been developed. These diagnostics derive a beta measure to assess the market risk exposure of the portfolio as well as other measures to assess the degree of diversification of the portfolio.

While the general market has a powerful effect on securities, other systematic effects also have impact on securities and have been termed *extramarket correlation*. In this phenomenon, subgroups of securities (for example, energy stocks or defense stocks) show a high degree of co-movement within a grouping but independent movement across groups.

Research shows that the major stock groupings show this homogenous stock group behavior. Portfolio diagnostics services have thus supplemented the basic beta model of risk with other indicators, known as *factors,* that allow the manager to evaluate exposure to the risk of extramarket correlation. This diagnostic has been exceptionally valuable to large plan sponsors, who typically employ many investment managers with differing "styles" of investing to allow them to evaluate risk exposure and coordinate the total investment effort.

In this part we describe approaches to portfolio construction as well as portfolio analysis. We begin in Chapter 2 by describing the theoretical approach for constructing portfolios; we then illustrate how it has found practical application in asset allocation (blending asset classes together into an appropriate portfolio mix). In Chapters 3 and 4 we describe the basis for capital market theory from two different aspects. In addition, we describe in Chapter 3 a simplified method that has found practical application for assessing the major risk characteristics of a portfolio, and we then go on to describe in Chapter 4 a more complete method that allows the evaluation of more aspects of portfolio risk exposure.

CHAPTER 2

Portfolio Construction

INTRODUCTION

Portfolio construction can be simply viewed as a matter of selecting securities to include in a portfolio and then determining the appropriate weighting: proportional representation of the securities in the portfolio. The Markowitz model indicates that the proper goal of portfolio construction should be to generate a portfolio that provides the highest return at a given level of risk. A portfolio having this characteristic is known as an *efficient portfolio* and has generally been accepted as the paradigm of optimal portfolio construction.

In addition, the Markowitz model provides an explicit and disciplined process, known as *optimization*, for constructing portfolios that attain the goal of being efficient. This optimization process has found extensive application by major plan sponsors as they attempt to determine the best mix of major asset classes for the portfolio. This process is known as *asset allocation* and is practicable because the number of major asset classes to be considered is by nature limited. When the universe of securities under consideration expands beyond such a limited number, the Markowitz optimization process is impractical, and alternative approaches, which we describe in the next two chapters, need to be employed.

Since the Markowitz model provides the underlying concepts for efficient portfolio construction as well as the foundation for other aspects of portfolio analysis, we devote a considerable portion of this chapter to describing the Markowitz model. In this regard, we cover the concepts of efficient portfolios and diversification, which are basic to portfolio construction. We also describe the basic inputs needed to implement the Markowitz efficient portfolio construction process, as well as the impacts that variations in these inputs can have on the resulting risk-return characteristics of the portfolio. We then go on to illustrate how the Markowitz process can be applied in practice by describing its use in generating an asset allocation.

PORTFOLIO CONSTRUCTION PROCESS

The portfolio construction process can be broadly characterized as comprising the following phases. First, the universe of securities eligible for selection needs to be defined. For most

17

plan sponsors the focus has been on the major asset classes of common stocks, bonds, and money market instruments. More recently, these investors have been incorporating international stocks and nondollar bonds to provide a global perspective, and some have included real estate and venture capital to further broaden the scope of investing. Although the number of asset classes to consider remains limited, the number of securities within these various classes can be quite substantial. For example, managers of common stocks would generally have at least 200 securities in their universe, with the average somewhere around 400 to 500, and some at 1000 or more.

Investors also need to develop expectations with regard to the return potential, as well as the risk exposure, of individual securities and broad asset classes. Furthermore, it is important that these estimates be explicitly stated so as to facilitate a comparison of the attractiveness of the securities and asset classes across the universe. The worth of the resulting portfolio for investing will depend heavily on the quality of these estimated security inputs. Given the importance of this phase, we devote Part Three of this book to describing valuation models and techniques for generating risk-return expectations for securities and asset classes.

The third phase of the process, the actual optimization, entails a selection of individual securities and a proper weighting of these in the portfolio. In blending securities together to form the desired composite, it is necessary not only to consider the risk-return characteristics of each of the securities but also to evaluate how these are likely to interact over time. As noted, the Markowitz model provides both the conceptual framework and analytical tools for determining the optimal portfolio in a disciplined and objective way.

MARKOWITZ MODEL

Markowitz's pioneering work on portfolio analysis is described in his 1952 *Journal of Finance* article and subsequent book in 1959. The fundamental assumption underlying the Markowitz approach to portfolio analysis is that investors are basically risk-averse. This means simply that investors must be compensated with higher return in order to accept higher risk. Consequently, given a choice, for example, between two securities with equal rates of return, an investor will select the security with the lower level of risk, thereby rejecting the higher-risk security. In more technical terms, this assumption means that investors maximize expected utility rather than merely trying to maximize expected return. Utility, a measure of satisfaction, considers both risk and return.

The assumption of investor risk-aversion seems reasonable and is bolstered by evidence. First is Markowitz's own observation that investors typically hold diversified portfolios. If investors were not risk-averse, the logical course of action would be merely to hold the single security promising the highest return so as to maximize expected return. Further evidence that investors are risk-averse is the fact that they purchase various types of insurance, such as life, health and accident, and auto. Individuals who purchase insurance are willing to pay to avoid future uncertainty; that is, they want to avoid the risk of a potentially large future loss even if the cost (premium) exceeds the expected payoff of the insurance. Finally, as we show in the latter part of this chapter, securities with different degrees of risk differ in their return realized over time, with higher risk accompanied by higher return. This is evidence that investors require a higher return in order to accept higher risk.

Presuming risk-aversion, Markowitz then developed a model of portfolio analysis that can be summarized as follows. First, the two relevant characteristics of a portfolio are its expected return and some measure of the dispersion of possible returns around the expected return; the variance is analytically the most tractable.[1] Second, rational investors will choose to hold efficient portfolios—those that maximize expected returns for a given degree of risk or, alternatively and equivalently, minimize risk for a given expected return. Third, it is theoretically possible to identify efficient portfolios by the proper analysis of information for each security on expected return, variance of return, and the interrelationship between the return for each security and that for every other security as measured by the covariance. Finally, a computer program can utilize these inputs to calculate the set of efficient portfolios. The program indicates the proportion of an investor's fund that should be allocated to each security in order to achieve efficiency—that is, the maximization of return for a given degree of risk or the minimization of risk for a given expected return.

CONCEPT OF EFFICIENCY

The notion of efficiency can be best illustrated by means of Figure 2-1. The vertical axis refers to expected return; the horizontal axis refers to risk as measured by the standard deviation of return; and the shaded area represents the set of all the possible portfolios that could be obtained from a given group of securities. A certain level of return and a certain risk will be associated with each possible portfolio. Thus, each portfolio is represented by a single point in the shaded area of the figure.

Note that the efficient set is represented by the upper left-hand boundary of the shaded area between points A and B. Portfolios along this efficient frontier dominate those below the line. Specifically, they offer higher return than those at an equivalent level of risk or,

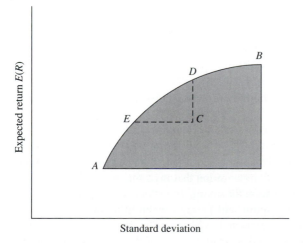

FIGURE 2-1
The portfolio possibility set.

---

[1] It should be noted that here, as well as throughout the book, we use expected returns and expected variance, because we are dealing with the future. Usually, historical information is used to generate the expected values. As we all know, actual outcomes may differ from the expected.

alternatively, entail less risk at an equivalent level of return. For example, note that portfolio C, which does not lie on the efficient boundary, is dominated by portfolios D and E, which do lie on the efficient boundary. Portfolio D offers greater return than portfolio C at the same level of risk, whereas portfolio E entails less risk than portfolio C at the same level of return.

Rational investors will thus prefer to hold efficient portfolios—that is, ones on the line and not those below it. The particular portfolio that an individual investor selects from the efficient frontier depends on that investor's degree of aversion to risk. An investor who is highly averse to risk will hold a portfolio on the lower left-hand segment of the frontier, whereas an investor who is not too risk-averse will hold one on the upper portion. In more technical terms, the selection depends on the investor's risk-aversion, which might be characterized by the nature and shape of the investor's risk-return utility function.

SECURITY AND PORTFOLIO RETURN

Because return and security valuation are interrelated, we begin this section by discussing some principles of valuation. First, we note that securities derive value from the cash flow they are expected to generate. Securities include all investments, such as debt instruments, common stock, options, futures, preferred stock, real estate, and collectibles. Since the cash flow will be received over future periods, there is need to discount these future flows to derive a present value or price for the security. Assuming that we are valuing the security over a single holding period (say, a year), we can illustrate the process of valuation with a particularly simple model:

$$P_0 = \frac{\text{Cash flow} + P_1}{(1 + k)} \tag{1}$$

The model indicates that the present value (or alternatively, current price) P_0 of the security is the cash flow (e.g., dividends or coupons) received over the period plus the expected price at the end of period P_1, discounted back at the rate k. Note that the value of the security is positively related to the cash flow and expected future price of the security. The current price will be higher as the cash flow or future price is expected to be higher; the current price will be lower as the cash flow or future price is expected to be lower. On the other hand, the value of the security is inversely related to the discount rate k, so the current price will be lower as the discount rate is higher and will be higher as the discount rate is lower.

The discount rate is alternatively referred to as a *required return, R,* and is composed of two elements: (1) a risk-free return R_f and (2) a risk premium B. The risk-free return, in turn, is generally considered to comprise a real return component and an inflation premium. The real return R_r is the basic investment compensation that investors demand for forgoing current consumption; that is, the compensation for saving. Investors also require a premium to compensate for inflation, and this premium will be high when inflation is expected to be high and low when the inflation rate is expected to be low. The real return and inflation premium are a basic return demanded by all investors, so the risk-free return is a return component that is required of all securities.

The risk premium is made up of the following elements: (1) interest rate risk, (2) purchasing power risk, (3) business risk, and (4) financial risk. We will see in a later section of this chapter that securities differ in their exposure to these risk elements. As a result, the premium or return that investors require to compensate for risk will differ across securities as the perceived exposure to the risk elements is high or low for the security.

By rearranging the equation, we can solve directly for the discount rate k. In this form it is usual to also think of the discount rate as a return expected by investors, that is, an expected return $E(R)$:

$$k = E(R) = \frac{\text{Cash flow} + (P_1 - P_0)}{P_0} \tag{2}$$

Note that this equation indicates that expected return is directly related to cash flow and expected end-of-period price. When the cash flow and end-of-period price are expected to be high, the rate of return will be high as well, whereas a cash flow and end-of-period price that are expected to be low would result in a low expected rate of return. On the other hand, the equation indicates that the expected return is inversely related to the current price of the security. When the current price is low, the expected return will be high, whereas a high current price would result in a low expected return. Changes in current security prices, when expected cash flow and end-of-period prices remain the same, thus provide a way for securities to adjust to provide returns required by investors.

We can also use Equation (2) for calculating the return earned on a security over a past period (realized return), only this time we would insert a realized value for the cash flow and an actual ending-period price rather than expected values of these variables.[2] In calculating the return for, say, a common stock, it is helpful to think of the realized return as consisting of a yield component—dividend divided by beginning-of-period price D/P_0—and a capital gain component, which is the percentage change in price $[(P_1 - P_0)/P_0]$ over the period:

$$\text{Return} = \frac{D}{P_0} + \frac{P_1 - P_0}{P_0} \tag{3}$$

As an example, we assume that a stock was selling at $50 a share at the beginning of the period (P_0), paid a $2 dividend ($D$), and sold at $54 at the end of the period (P_1). We then calculate the return realized over the period, which we assume to be a year, as follows:

$$\text{Return} = \frac{\$2}{\$50} + \frac{\$54 - \$50}{\$50} = 0.04 + 0.08 = 0.12 = 12\%$$

The calculation shows that the realized return of the stock, 12 percent, was derived from a 4 percent yield component and from an 8 percent capital gain. When discussing returns, the calculations, which result in decimals, can be converted to percentages by multiplying by 100.

An efficient portfolio (or any portfolio, for that matter) is described by the list of individual securities in the portfolio as well as by the weighting of each security in the portfolio. The estimated or expected return of the portfolio is, in turn, merely a weighted average of the expected returns of the individual securities of which the portfolio is composed. Calculation of the expected return can be most easily illustrated for a two-security portfolio. Using

---

[2] We might note that the realized return and expected return will be the same when the realized cash flow and end-of-period price are the same as the expected value of these variables. While it would be unusual for these values to be the same over any single period, we might expect that over time, realized returns and expected returns would tend to correspond. This is the basis for use of previous realized returns as proxies for expectations.

TABLE 2-1
Return, variance, and standard deviation

Year	Return, $R_1\%$ (1)	Deviation, $R_1 - \bar{R}$ (2)	Deviation^2, $(R_1 - \bar{R})^2$ (3)
1	5	-10	100
2	15	0	0
3	25	$+10$	100

$$\text{Average return } \bar{R} = \sum_{i=1}^{N} \frac{R_i}{N} = 15\%$$

$$\text{Variance of return} = \text{Var}(R) = \sum_{i=1}^{N} \frac{(R_i - \bar{R})^2}{N} = 67\%$$

$$\text{Standard deviation of return } S = \sqrt{\text{Var}(R)} = 8.2\%$$

W_i to represent the security's proportion of the portfolio and $E(R_i)$ the expected return, the expected return of the portfolio R_p is calculated as follows:

$$R_p = E(R_p) = W_1 E(R_1) + W_2 E(R_2) = \sum_{i=1}^{2} W_i E(R_i) \tag{4}$$

For example, stock A constitutes 60 percent of the portfolio with an expected return of 15%, and Bond B constitutes 40 percent with an expected return of 10%:

$$R_p = (0.6)(0.15) + (0.4)(0.10) = 0.09 + 0.04 = 0.13 = 13\%$$

Measuring Risk

In addition to determining the rate of return, it is also important to assess the risk or uncertainty that may be associated with earning the return. The variance of return and standard deviation of return are alternative statistical measures that are proxies for the uncertainty or risk of return.[3] These statistics in effect measure the extent to which returns are expected to vary around an average over time. Extensive variations around the average would indicate great uncertainty regarding the return to be expected.

Table 2-1 illustrates calculation of the variance and standard deviation for the returns realized over a three-year period for a hypothetical stock. The first column shows the year-by-year returns and the average return of 15 percent over the three-year period. The second column shows the deviations of the individual-year returns from the average, and the third column shows the squaring of these deviations. Squaring puts all the deviations in absolute (positive) terms and has other useful statistical properties. The variance is merely the average of the squared deviations, as can be seen from the variance formula:

$$\text{Var}(R) = \sum_{i=1}^{N} \frac{(R_i - \overline{R})^2}{N} = \frac{200}{3} = 67\% \tag{5}$$

---

[3] An alternative definition of uncertainty might be the probability of an adverse outcome.

TABLE 2-2
Calculating the covariance

Year	Return R_1 (1)	Deviation $R_{1i} - \overline{R}_1$ (2)	Return R_2 (3)	Deviation $R_{2i} - \overline{R}_2$ (4)	Product of deviations (2) × (4)	Combined returns $(R_1 + R_2)/2$ (6)
1	5	−10	25	+10	−100	15
2	15	0	15	0	0	15
3	25	+10	5	−10	−100	15
	$\overline{R}_1 = 15$		$\overline{R}_2 = 15$		−200	15

$$\text{Covariance} = \text{Cov}(R_1 R_2) = \sum_{i=1}^{N} \frac{(R_{1i} - \overline{R}_1)(R_{2i} - \overline{R}_2)}{N} = \frac{-200}{3} = -67\%$$

$$\text{Correlation} = \rho_{12} = \frac{\text{Cov}(R_1 R_2)}{S_1 S_2} = \frac{-67\%}{(8.2)(8.2)} = -1$$

Note that the dimension of the calculated variance is the return squared, which is, of course, economically meaningless.[4] Hence, we would normally take the square root of the variance to obtain the standard deviation S, which also measures the variability of the distribution and has the further advantage of being set out in terms of return. Despite the difference in dimensions, both risk measures can be used interchangeably to rank the relative riskiness of securities; that is, if security A is riskier than security B in terms of variance, it will also be riskier in terms of standard deviation.

Risk in a Portfolio Context

While standard deviation and variance measure the riskiness of a security in an absolute sense, there is also need to consider the riskiness of a security within the context of an overall portfolio of securities. The riskiness of a portfolio will thus depend on how a security blends with the existing securities and contributes to the overall risk of a portfolio. The *covariance* is a statistic that measures the riskiness of a security relative to others in a portfolio of securities. In essence, the way securities vary with each other affects the overall variance, hence the risk, of the portfolio.

Table 2-2 illustrates the calculation of the covariance for a two-asset portfolio with equal weights. The first column shows the year-by-year returns of the security used in Table 2-1 to illustrate the calculation of the variance and standard deviation, while the third column shows the returns of a second hypothetical security. Note that the pattern of returns for the second security is merely the reverse of the first, so that each will have the same average return and standard deviation of return. Columns 2 and 4 show the deviations of the returns of each security from the average return, and Column 5 shows the product of these deviations (Column 2 times Column 4). The average of the products of these deviations is the return $\text{Cov}(R_1 R_2)$.

---

[4]Technically the divisor in this formula should be $n - 1$. This is to adjust for the loss of one degree of freedom in the calculation. For simplicity of exposition, we have avoided this adjustment here and in the other illustrations in this section.

$$\text{Cov}(R_1 R_2) = \frac{1}{N} \sum_{i=1}^{N} (R_{1i} - \overline{R}_1)(R_{2i} - \overline{R}_2) = \frac{-200}{3} = -67\% \qquad (6)$$

In this case the calculated covariance is a large negative value. This is because the deviations of the two securities are consistently opposite; that is, the securities moved counter to
each other consistently. In contrast, if the two securities had moved consistently in tandem,
the deviations would have been in the same direction and the covariance would have been
positive. An intermediate case would be where the securities moved in tandem in some periods and counter to each other in other periods. This pattern would result in a covariance
of lower value, as the deviations would offset each other.

Note that like the variance, the covariance is expressed as percent squared. For this
and other reasons the covariance is difficult to interpret, at least for practical application.
To facilitate interpretation, it is therefore useful to standardize the covariance. Dividing the
covariance between two securities by the product of the standard deviation of each security
produces a variable with the same properties as the covariance but scaled to a range of -1 to
$+1$. The measure is called the *correlation coefficient*. Letting ρ_{12} represent the correlation
between securities 1 and 2, the correlation coefficient can be defined as

$$\rho_{12} = \frac{\text{Cov}(R_1 R_2)}{S_1 S_2} = \frac{-67}{(8.2)(8.2)} = -1 \qquad (7)$$

In this instance the correlation coefficient is -1, which indicates that the two securities
are perfectly negatively correlated, as might be expected because the two securities consistently moved opposite to each other. Generally, negative correlation, and hence negative
covariance, is desirable in a security, because such securities have great risk-reducing potential in a portfolio context. In this sense they are low-risk. The last column in Table 2-2
illustrates this by showing that a combination of the two securities (equally weighted in a
portfolio) would display constant year-by-year returns. Putting these negatively correlated
securities together completely eliminates risk while maintaining the same level of return.
The second security, while showing risk when viewed by itself, is a highly desirable risk-
reducing (in this case risk-eliminating) security. In pragmatic settings it is difficult to find
negatively correlated securities.

As may be deduced from the foregoing, the variance (or risk) of a portfolio is not simply
a weighted average of the variances of the individual securities in the portfolio. There is
also need to consider the relationship between each security in the portfolio and every other
security as measured by the covariance of return. The method of calculating the variance of
a portfolio can again most easily be illustrated for a two-security portfolio. Using $\text{Var}(R_1)$
to represent the variance of each security, $\text{Cov}(R_1 R_2)$ to represent the covariance between
the two securities, and W_i to represent the proportion that each security represents in the
portfolio, the calculation of the portfolio variance $[\text{Var}(R_p)]$ is as follows:

$$\text{Var}(R_p) = W_1^2 \text{Var}(R_1) + W_2^2 \text{Var}(R_2) + 2W_1 W_2 \text{Cov}(R_1 R_2) \qquad (8)$$

In words, the variance of the portfolio is the weighted sum of the variances of the individual securities plus twice the covariance between the two securities.[5] We can, in turn, use this

---

[5] As a matter of interest, although the formula refers to a portfolio of only two securities, it has great generality,
since a group of securities can be considered a single security in analyzing the problems of portfolio management.

TABLE 2-3
Security covariance and portfolio variance

	Return	S	Variance
Stock 1	.10	0.40	.16
Stock 2	.10	0.40	.16

$$W_1 = 0.5 \quad W_2 = 0.5 \quad \sum_{i=1}^{2} W_i = 1.00$$

$$R_p = \frac{1}{2}(.10) + \frac{1}{2}(10) = .10$$

$$\begin{aligned} \text{Var}(R_p) &= W^2 \text{Var}(R_1) + W^2 \text{Var}(R_2) + 2W_1 W_2 \rho_{12} S_1 S_2 \\ &= (0.25)(0.16) + (0.25)(0.16) + 2(0.5)(0.5)\rho_{12}(0.4)(0.4) \\ &= 0.08 + 0.08\rho_{12} \end{aligned}$$

simple expression to begin to examine the effect on overall portfolio risk of adding securities with differing covariance characteristics. We will then go on to examine the more general case of adding many securities to the portfolio and the effect on portfolio risk. This analysis should provide perspective on the effectiveness of diversification in controlling portfolio risk.

Diversification

To begin to understand the mechanism and power of diversification, it is important to consider the impact of covariance more closely. We can do this most directly by redefining the covariance formulation in the following way:

$$\text{Cov}(R_i R_j) = \rho_{ij} S_i S_j \tag{9}$$

In this form the covariance is equal to the correlation coefficient between two securities times the standard deviation of each security. Holding standard deviation constant, this says that the higher the correlation between two securities, the higher the covariance and the higher the risk of the portfolio. Conversely, the lower the correlation, the lower the covariance and hence the lower the overall risk of the portfolio.

This illustrates the power of diversification. Adding extra securities, especially those with a lower covariance, should be an objective in building portfolios. Only in the case of +1 correlation will the risk of the portfolio remain the same. In all other cases the overall risk of the portfolio is reduced. In order to see more specifically how different values of covariance or correlation can affect the variance of a portfolio, it will be useful to consider the data shown in Table 2-3.

Table 2-3 shows expected return, standard deviation, and variance data for two hypothetical stocks. Note that both stocks have expected returns of 10 percent and identical standard deviations S (and hence variances). Each stock has a weight of 50 percent in the portfolio to account for 100 percent of the portfolio weight; that is, the portfolio is fully

---

For example, if we are interested in understanding what the addition of a security does to the variance of an existing portfolio, we can think of the existing portfolio as a single security. This simple formula therefore has great analytical power.

invested. Given the data, the expected return of the portfolio R_p works out to 10 percent, as shown in the first line below the data. The next two lines show the variance formula along with the inserted values to illustrate the calculation. The final line shows that the variance of the portfolio depends on the value of the correlation coefficient.

Security Correlation and Portfolio Risk

The correlation coefficient measures the extent to which the two stocks move together and varies in value from $+1$ to -1 with a midpoint of zero. A correlation coefficient of $+1$, indicating perfectly positive correlation between the two stocks, is illustrated by the upward-sloping line in Figure 2-2a. For example, bearish new information concerning security A would result in lowered expectations for security B as well. The downward-sloping line in Figure 2-2b illustrates a correlation coefficient of -1 and indicates perfectly negative correlation between the two stocks. In this instance, bearish new information about security A would increase expectations for security B. Finally, the random scatter of plots in Figure 2-2c illustrates a pattern of zero correlation, or independence, between the two stocks. New information on security A, whether bearish or bullish, would have no effect on security B.

Figure 2-3 illustrates the way that the returns of the two securities (A and B) might fluctuate over time when the correlation is perfectly positive and when it is perfectly negative. When the two securities are perfectly positively correlated, the dotted line representing the return pattern of security B would lie on top of the solid line representing the return of security A, as illustrated in part a of the figure. In this case, where securities move perfectly in tandem ($\rho_{12} = +1$), the portfolio variance is $0.16[\text{Var}(R_p) = 0.08 + 0.08(1) = 0.16]$. In this case, the variance of the portfolio is a weighted average of the variances of the two securities and is the same as the variance of an individual security. Diversification provides no risk reduction, only risk averaging, and is therefore not a productive activity when securities are perfectly positively correlated.

On the other hand, when the two securities are perfectly negatively correlated, the dotted line representing the return pattern of security B would move directly opposite to the solid line representing the return of security A, as illustrated in part b of the figure. In this case, where securities move counter to each other ($\rho_{12} = -1$), the variance of the portfolio

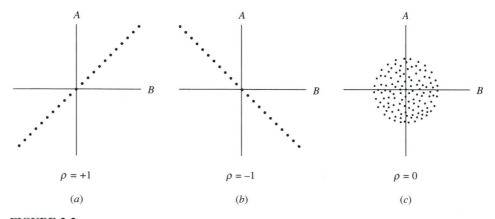

$\rho = +1$ $\rho = -1$ $\rho = 0$

(a)   (b)   (c)

FIGURE 2-2
Correlation of returns between securities A and B.

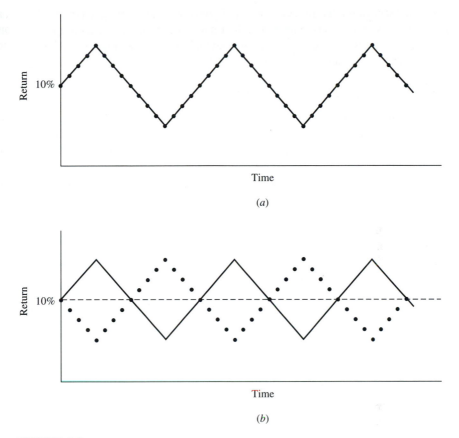

FIGURE 2-3
Security correlation and portfolio variance. (*a*) Perfectly positive correlation; (*b*) perfectly negative correlation.

is zero [Var(R_p) = 0.08 + 0.08(−1) = 0]. This is illustrated by the horizontal dashed line in part *b* that indicates an average return of 10 percent with no period-by-period fluctuations. Here diversification immediately eliminates risk and is a highly productive activity when securities are perfectly negatively correlated. Unfortunately, in pragmatic settings perfect negative correlation is rare; it is found only in certain arbitrage situations, such as the simultaneous purchase and short sale of a security traded in two different markets.[6]

If the correlation between the two securities is zero (ρ_{12} = 0), the variance of the portfolio is 0.08[Var(R_p) = 0.08 + 0.08(0) = 0.08]. The portfolio variance in this case is less than that of a single security (0.16). While Figure 2-3 does not illustrate this case specifically, we could visualize the resulting portfolio line, which would show fluctuation, but of a lesser amplitude than that of the line represented by a single security. Diversification

---

[6]A similar situation is the simultaneous purchase of a convertible bond and short sale of the common stock. Other arbitrage situations include writing a put and simultaneously buying an equivalent call, or having a long and short position in nearly identical futures contracts traded on two different exchanges. All such positions presume a temporary price disequilibrium, which, corrected through convergence, will bring profit to the arbitrageur.

reduces risk and is a productive activity when securities show zero correlation. From the foregoing, we may infer that diversification reduces risk in all cases except that in which $\rho = +1$. Thus, diversification is a useful activity in pragmatic settings.

Adding Securities to Eliminate Risk

This third case can further illustrate the power of diversification. First, note the general formula for the variance of a portfolio:

$$\text{Var}(R_p) = \sum_{i=1}^{N} W_i^2 \text{Var}(R_i) + \sum_{\substack{i=1 \\ i \neq j}}^{N} \sum_{j=1}^{N} W_i W_j \text{Cov}(R_i R_j) \tag{10}$$

The formula says that the variance of a portfolio is a weighted average of the variance of the individual securities plus the covariance between each security and every other security in the portfolio. If securities have zero correlation, and hence zero covariance, the second term goes to zero, and the expression reduces to

$$\text{Var}(R_p) = \sum_{i=1}^{N} W_i^2 \text{Var}(R_i) \tag{11}$$

Assume for purposes of illustration that only securities with zero covariance are available, that each security has the same variance (as shown above), and that equal amounts are invested in each security.

$$\text{Var}(R_p) = \sum_{i=1}^{N} \left(\frac{1}{N}\right)^2 \text{Var}(R_i)$$

$$= N \left(\frac{1}{N}\right)^2 \text{Var}(R_i)$$

$$\text{Var}(R_p) = \frac{1}{N} \text{Var}(R_i)$$

$$S_p = \frac{S_i}{\sqrt{N}} \tag{12}$$

Using this formula and assuming, as in the example, that the individual securities have standard deviations of (0.4 percent), the data in Table 2-4 show how the risk (standard deviation) of the portfolio declines as zero-correlated securities with identical standard deviations are added to the portfolio. Risk is reduced to less than 10 percent of that of a single-stock portfolio when 128 securities are in the portfolio and to less than 2 percent of the original risk when 510 are included. As the number of securities added becomes larger and larger (approaches infinity, in technical terms), the standard deviation of the portfolio approaches zero.

The principle here is that if there are sufficient numbers of securities with zero correlation (zero covariance), the portfolio analyst can make the portfolio risk arbitrarily small. This is the basis for insurance, which explains why insurance companies attempt to write many individual policies and spread their coverage so as to minimize overall risk. It also has direct relevance in providing a benchmark for assessing the extent to which diversification

TABLE 2-4
Portfolio risk and number
of securities (zero correlation)

Number of securities	Standard deviation of portfolio return, %
1	40.0
2	28.3
8	14.1
16	10.0
32	7.1
128	3.5
510	1.8

can be effective in reducing risks for equity investors. The next section discusses empirical evidence concerning the usefulness of diversification in reducing risk.

Systematic and Diversifiable Risk

When dealing with U.S. stocks, eliminating risk entirely through diversification is not possible. Virtually no stocks show negative or even zero correlation. Typically, stocks show some positive correlation—above zero—but less than perfectly positive (+1). Empirically, it seems that the typical correlation coefficient for U.S. stocks is between 0.5 and 0.6; that is, if we sampled at random any two stocks out of the total stock universe, we would likely find that the correlation coefficient calculated for the two stocks was between 0.5 and 0.6. As a result, diversification (adding securities to a portfolio) results in some reduction in total portfolio variance but not in complete elimination of variance.

There have been several studies of the effectiveness of diversification in reducing portfolio risk. One by Fisher and Lorie provides perhaps the best illustration of the process. They looked at all listed stocks and randomly sampled from this list to build portfolios ranging from one stock to 500 stocks. Stocks within the portfolios were weighted equally. These simulations allowed the researchers to see how the variance of a portfolio was reduced as stocks were added to the portfolio. Correspondingly, it also showed how quickly the effect of adding stocks exhausted the power of diversification.

Table 2-5 shows some representative statistics from the study. The first column shows the size of portfolios analyzed. These range from one-stock portfolios to portfolios of more

TABLE 2-5
Portfolio size—risk and return

Portfolio size	Average return, %	Standard deviation, %	Diversifiable risk, %	Market-related risk, %
1	9	40.0	45	55
2	9	32.4	38	62
8	9	25.6	20	80
16	9	24.0	12	88
32	9	23.6	8	92
128	9	22.8	2	98
Index fund	9	22.0	0	100

Source: Fisher, Lawrence, and James H. Lorie: "Some Studies of Variability of Returns on Investment in Common Stocks," *Journal of Business,* April 1970, pp. 99–134.

than 100 stocks. Note that the one-stock portfolios on average provided a return of 9 percent; in other words, the average return for stocks was 9 percent. This average remained the same for all sizes of portfolios. However, the risk decreased with an increase in the size of portfolio. Hence, one can reduce risk and hold return constant through diversification. In particular, note that the standard deviation of a one-stock portfolio (or average standard deviation for an individual stock) was 40 percent, whereas the standard deviation of a large (128-stock) portfolio was 22.8 percent, or little more than half that of an individual stock.

We see, however, that the effects of diversification are exhausted fairly rapidly. Most of the reduction in standard deviation takes place by the time that the portfolio reaches 16 or 32 stocks. In sum, adding securities to a portfolio reduces risk because securities are not perfectly correlated (+1); however, the effects of this process are exhausted quite rapidly, because securities are in fact rather highly correlated (0.5 to 0.6). This is in contrast to the theoretical results in Table 2-4, which show the portfolio risk continuing to decline when securities have zero correlation. There are benefits to diversification, but in practice they are limited.

The fifth column in Table 2-5 indicates that one component of total risk (standard deviation) is market-related. This portion is in turn a function of the correlation of the portfolio with the overall market and is derived by multiplying the correlation coefficient of the portfolio with the market by the standard deviation of the portfolio, and then dividing this calculated value by the total risk of the portfolio. For example, an individual security with a correlation coefficient of 0.55 with the market and a standard deviation of 40 percent has a market-related risk of 22 percent [(0.55)(40%) = 22%]. Dividing this calculated value by the total risk of the security of 40 percent results in a 55 percent market-related proportion of total risk. The table shows that market-related risk increases as a proportion of the portfolio risk as the size of the portfolio increases; large portfolios are more highly correlated with the market.

Because market-related risk affects all securities and cannot be diversified away, it is also referred to as *systematic risk*. Risk that is unexplained by the market is known as *diversifiable* or *unsystematic risk*. A small portfolio of, say, one or two stocks has a lot of diversifiable risk. A large portfolio has relatively little diversifiable risk. A perfectly diversified fund—an index fund—will reflect only market-related, or systematic, risk. The last column of Table 2-5 shows diversifiable risk decreasing with portfolio size.

These important concepts are illustrated in Figure 2-4. The chart shows total portfolio risk declining as number of holdings increases. Increasing diversification tends to result

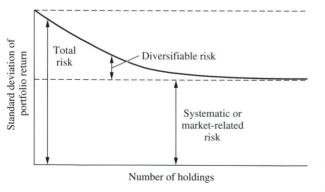

FIGURE 2-4
Diversification and systematic risk.

in only systematic or market-related risk. The remaining variability reflects the fact that the return on nearly every security depends to a degree on the overall performance of the market. Consequently, the return on a well-diversified portfolio is highly correlated with the market, and its variability or uncertainty is basically the uncertainty of the market as a whole. Investors are exposed to market uncertainty no matter how many stocks they hold.

The foregoing analysis has implications both as to the sort of risk that should be rewarded in the marketplace and as to the relevant measure of risk for securities and portfolios. In particular, since diversification provides a relatively easy way of eliminating a "deadweight loss" (diversifiable or unsystematic risk) from the portfolio, it seems reasonable that the marketplace is unlikely to reward it. It will only reward systematic risk, which investors cannot eliminate. Accordingly, this implies that the relevant measure of risk is systematic risk, which in turn has implications on input required, calculations, and asset management. (This will be covered further in Chapter 3.)

RISK-RETURN AND WEIGHTING CHANGES

To illustrate how the risk-return character of a portfolio changes as we vary the weighting of securities in the portfolio, we use the data shown in Table 2-6 for two hypothetical stocks. Panel A shows the expected returns and standard deviations for each of the stocks. Note that stock A has both a higher expected return and standard deviation than stock B to illustrate a trade-off between risk and return. Also, for purposes of illustration, we assume that the correlation between the two stocks is (1) +1.0 to represent perfect correlation; (2) 0 to represent independence; or (3) + 0.5 for a correlation that is approximately in line with the average correlation between stocks in the United States. Using this data in Panel B, we calculate the expected return and risk for a portfolio of these two stocks over a range of portfolio weights for each of the three correlation assumptions. In making these calculations we assume that the portfolio is fully invested and that the weight of stock A is W, so the weight of stock B is $(1 - W)$.

Panel B of Table 2-6 shows the calculated risk and return data for these portfolios, where the weight of stock A ranges in increments of 0.20 from 0 percent to 100 percent,

TABLE 2-6
Risk-return portfolio trade-off varying portfolio weights

Panel A			
	Expected return	Standard deviation	Correlation assumptions
Stock A	15%	24%	+1.0, 0.0, +0.5
Stock B	12%	18%	

Panel B						
Portfolio weighting:						
Stock A (W)	0	20	40	60	80	100
Stock B ($1 - W$)	100	80	60	40	20	0
Expected return	12.0	12.6	13.2	13.8	14.4	15.0
Standard deviation						
Corr = 1.0	18.0	19.2	20.4	21.6	22.8	24.0
Corr = 0.5	18.0	17.3	17.7	19.0	22.0	24.0
Corr = 0.0	18.0	15.2	14.4	16.1	19.5	24.0

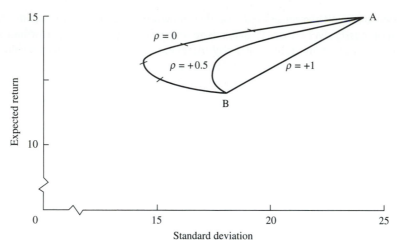

FIGURE 2-5
Risk-return portfolio trade-off, varying portfolio weights.

with the corresponding weight of stock B ranging down from 100 percent to 0 percent. The third row in panel B shows the expected return for the portfolio and indicates that the portfolio consisting of 100 percent of stock A has the highest return and the portfolio consisting of 100 percent of stock B has the lowest expected return. Other combination portfolios show intermediate levels of return, as would be expected from the basic character of the component stocks. The bottom three rows show the calculated portfolio standard deviation for each of the three correlations. This illustrates how portfolio variance changes as the security weightings vary.

For ease of comparison, Figure 2-5 shows a plot of the varying risk-return trade-off of the two stock portfolios at each of the three assumed correlation levels. Note that there is a direct linear trade-off of risk and return, as evidenced by the upward-sloping straight line when the assumed correlation is perfectly positive ($\rho = 1$). On the other hand, there is a curvilinear relationship and a lesser level of risk for the portfolios when the correlation is zero and at +0.5. This illustrates the general principle that there is productive diversification and risk reduction when correlation is less than perfectly positive. Correspondingly, there is a more favorable risk-return trade-off at a correlation of zero than at a +0.5 correlation level, again illustrating the potential gains from diversification as correlation is lower. If we could find securities with a perfectly negative correlation (-1.0), it would be theoretically possible to construct a two-asset portfolio with zero variance.

SHORT SELLING

In the previous section we assumed that the weighting of individual securities in the portfolio was positive, or at least no less than zero. In a formal optimization problem, this is stated as a *nonnegativity constraint* on individual securities, and it means that selling securities short is precluded from the portfolio solution. This, of course, is consistent with conventional institutional practice, where short selling is restricted either by regulation or by traditional behavior. The majority of individual investors and other types generally refrain from short selling, and short selling is a small share of total activity, reflecting this overall behavior.

However, some potentially rewarding investment strategies employ short selling as a significant component of the process. Such strategies are consistent with the underlying principles of portfolio theory. Having an ability to sell short expands the effective opportunity set for analysis by a substantial degree. Again, this should allow an investor to develop a better risk-return combination than if short selling were restricted or precluded from consideration. We will describe one such strategy that is related to stock selection in detail, when we discuss stock selection in Chapter 8.

In the meantime, it is useful to illustrate the impact of short selling on portfolio characteristics by extending the previous analysis to include that activity. For this purpose, we again use the two hypothetical stocks with the same underlying return and standard deviation characteristics as in the previous section. We begin the analysis by first assuming a correlation of 0.5 between the two stocks; this is again in line with the average degree of correlation across all stocks in the market. We also analyze for the case of a 0.8 correlation between stocks, which would be a level of correlation representative of that between participants in the same industry or general economic sector. Companies in the drug industry or energy sector would be examples of pairs of such companies.

Figure 2-6 shows the effect on the portfolio's expected return when we vary the proportions (W and $1 - W$) invested in stocks A and B. When the proportion invested in stock A varies from zero to 1 (so that the weighting in stock B varies from 1 to zero), the portfolio expected return increases from 12 percent (stock B's expected return) to 15 percent (stock A's expected return), and again would represent the return pattern under a nonnegativity constraint. When short sales are allowed, our strategy would be to sell stock B short (lower expected return) and invest the proceeds of the stock sale in stock A (higher expected return) to increase the expected portfolio return. For example, when W is 2.0 and $(1 - W)$ is -1, expected portfolio return increases to 18 percent $[2 \times 0.15 + (-1) \times 0.12]$. At this point

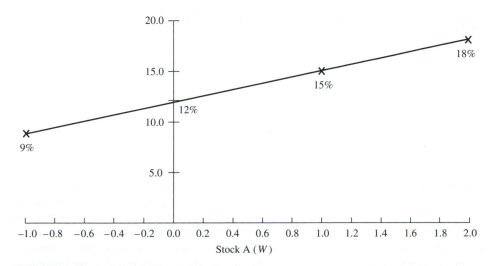

FIGURE 2-6
Expected return and varying portfolio weights.

TABLE 2-7
Risk-return portfolio trade-off varying portfolio weights, short selling allowed

Stock A (W)	Stock B (1 − W)	Expected return	Standard deviation	
			Corr = 0.5	Corr = 0.8
−1.00	2.00	9.00	31.70	22.10
−0.80	1.80	9.60	28.20	20.60
−0.60	1.60	10.20	24.90	19.30
−0.40	1.40	10.80	22.00	18.40
−0.20	1.20	11.40	19.60	18.00
0.00	1.00	12.00	18.00	18.00
0.20	0.80	12.60	17.80	18.40
0.40	0.60	13.20	17.70	19.40
0.60	0.40	13.80	19.00	20.60
0.80	0.20	14.40	22.00	22.20
1.00	0.00	15.00	24.00	24.00
1.20	−0.20	15.60	27.20	22.80
1.40	−0.40	16.20	30.60	28.20
1.60	−0.60	16.80	34.30	30.50
1.80	−0.80	17.40	38.10	32.80
2.00	−1.00	18.00	42.00	35.30

the value of stock A is twice the equity in the account. This extreme position is financed in part by selling stock B short in an amount equal to the portfolio's net worth. We could reverse the process by selling stock A short and reinvesting in stock B, and the left part of the chart shows the impact of this activity. As expected, it results in a lower return of only 9 percent $[(-1) \times 0.15 + 2 \times 0.12]$.

While portfolio return increases as we sell shares in the lower-returning stock B short and reinvest the proceeds in stock A, portfolio risk increases as well. Table 2-7 illustrates this by showing calculated portfolio variance using both correlation assumptions of 0.5 and 0.8 over a range from 0 percent to 200 percent invested in stock A. Note that within the 0 to 100 percent range, the variance first decreases with the initial diversification in stock A and then increases as the portfolio again becomes concentrated in stock A and again is undiversified to illustrate the workings of diversification as noted before. Note also that the portfolio variance is consistently higher for the 0.8 correlation portfolio than at 0.5 correlation over this range as would be expected.

Note that, over the illustrated range from 100 percent to 200 percent investment in stock A when short selling is allowed, portfolio standard deviation increases under either correlation assumption. Notice, however, that portfolio standard deviation is lower as the correlation between stocks is higher (0.8 versus 0.5) over this illustrated range of 100 percent to 200 percent. This illustrates a general principle that short selling is more beneficial (less risky) the higher the correlation between securities. It is preferable to have the security that is sold short not only do less well but also move in line with the security that is held long. As a result, short selling is likely to be most productive when executed with respect to securities with similar characteristics; a particularly noteworthy example is short selling of stocks within an industry or economic sector where characteristics are likely to be similar.

TABLE 2-8
Full variance-covariance model selection universe and requisite inputs

Universe size (N)	Return (N)	Variance (N)	Covariance $\dfrac{(N)(N-1)}{2}$	Total $2N + \dfrac{(N)(N-1)}{2}$
			Inputs	
2	2	2	1	5
3	3	3	3	9
4	4	4	6	14
5	5	5	10	20
10	10	10	45	65
100	100	100	4950	5150
200	200	200	19900	20300
500	500	500	124750	125750
1000	1000	1000	499500	501500

REQUIRED MODEL INPUTS

In order to use the Markowitz full covariance model for portfolio construction, the investor must obtain estimates of the returns and the variances and covariances of returns for the securities in the universe of interest. To estimate the expected return and variance of a two-stock portfolio, five estimates are needed: expected return for each stock; variance of return for each stock; and the covariance of return between the two stocks. Generalizing to the case of N stocks, there would be need not only for N return estimates and N variance estimates but also $N(N-1)/2$ covariance estimates, for a total of $2N + [N(N-1)/2]$ estimates. For example, analyzing a set of 200 stocks would require 200 return estimates, 200 variance estimates, and 19,900 covariance estimates, for a total of 20,300 estimates. Note that the task of estimation is increased considerably by the need to consider explicitly the interrelationship among securities as represented by the covariance. Table 2-8 illustrates how input estimates vary for selected universe sizes.

While the Markowitz model is the most comprehensive one, it has found relatively little use in solving practical problems of analyzing universes with large numbers of securities, mainly because of the overwhelming burden of developing input estimates for the model. As noted, analysis of a universe of 200 stocks, which would be considered as below average in size for equity managers, would require 20,300 different estimates. The task of collecting the estimates for 20,300 statistics is further complicated by the fact that few individuals are capable of estimating such sophisticated measures as variances and covariances. Also, the quantity of required data can tax the memory capacity of even the largest computers when the number of securities gets large.

Furthermore, the coordination of this data-gathering procedure presents difficulties. Most securities research departments are organized so that specialists are assigned to the coverage of an individual industry or a small group of industries. In turn, this specialization means that analytical personnel generally have little knowledge of the characteristics of industries other than their assigned industry; thus, obtaining estimates of relationships across industries is difficult. For example, the electronics specialist is likely to find it difficult to assess the degree of co-movement between his assigned industry and others, such as the food or chemical industries.

Index models circumvent the difficulty of dealing with a great number of covariances by providing a simplified method of representing the relationships among securities. There are essentially two types of index models: single-index and multi-index. The single-index model is the simplest and might be thought of as being at one extreme point of a continuum, with the full covariance Markowitz model at the other. Multi-index models might be regarded as an intermediate point on this continuum. In the next chapter we will discuss the single-index model, including the capital asset pricing model. We will then cover the multi-index model in Chapter 4.

ASSET ALLOCATION

While the full variance-covariance model of Markowitz has found relatively little application with regard to evaluating large universes of securities, it has nevertheless been used with great regularity and with a high rate of success in the practical field of asset allocation, whose objective is to obtain a blend of asset classes that provide a high return at an acceptable level of risk to the investors. Portfolio managers, especially large institutional investors such as corporate and public pension plans, foundations, and endowment funds, use asset allocation extensively to develop the most appropriate mix of assets to meet the investment goals of the plan. The objective of the process is thus perfectly consistent with the Markowitz notion of an efficient portfolio.

Furthermore, the mean-variance portfolio approach can be used for this purpose, because the problem of developing inputs is manageable. The reason is that the number of asset classes that will be included in the analysis is limited by nature. When determining an asset allocation, many organizations deal with only three classes of assets: (1) common stocks, (2) long-term bonds, and (3) money market instruments. For that case there is need for three return and variance estimates, as well as three estimates of the correlation among the asset classes—all a manageable task. Other organizations expand the analysis to include international equities and real estate, but virtually none consider more than eight or ten classes for the analysis. For an analysis of eight asset classes, there would be need for eight return and variance estimates as well as 28 correlation estimates—a difficult yet feasible task of estimation.

In addition relatively good historic data exist on returns, variances, and correlations for such asset classes as common stocks, long-term bonds, and short-term money market instruments. These data have provided good perspective on the historic risk-return behavior of these asset classes. This in turn has helped researchers develop ways of modeling and projecting returns and asset risk characteristics into the future. We will describe such methods in greater detail in Chapter 9, when we discuss the very important subject of asset allocation. In the meantime, it is useful to describe in some detail the nature and character of the data that have been generated with respect to the well-researched asset classes of common stocks, bonds, and money market instruments. In subsequent chapters we shall comment on the status of generally less well-researched asset classes, such as international stocks.

Risk-Return Characteristics of Asset Classes

It is useful to calculate returns and measure risk for asset classes over various past intervals. First, this helps evaluate the behavior of the asset class over different economic episodes, such as the business cycle. Second, returns measured over sufficiently long periods may be taken as representative of the returns that investors may have expected to earn over the period. This may in turn be useful in establishing some benchmarks as to what returns investors might be expecting to earn in the future. Finally, availability of realized return and risk measures can be used to compare the performance behavior across asset classes.

Several researchers, most notably Ibbotson and Sinquefeld, have in fact calculated the realized return and standard deviation of return over past periods for four asset classes: common stocks, corporate bonds, Treasury bills, and long-term government bonds. They not only wished to see how these securities performed over various time periods but also wanted to assess how the returns on differing asset classes related to the relative riskiness of the asset class. Correspondingly, they wished to determine the real return earned on the various asset classes over the period.

To determine the real return on assets, Ibbotson and Sinquefeld obtained inflation rates and compared these with the nominal returns on assets.[7] A way to assess the risk-return relationship among assets is to establish a hierarchy of risk and return and compare across the various asset classes. For example, Treasury bills would be considered the least risky of the asset classes, and we could compare the return earned on these assets with inflation to determine real return. Long-term government bonds entail greater risk than Treasury bills, and we might characterize the added return to compensate for this risk as a *liquidity premium.* Long-term corporate bonds carry a credit risk not incurred by governments, and we might designate the extra return earned by corporate over government bonds as a default premium. Finally, common stocks can be compared with the least risky assets (Treasury bills) to determine a risk premium for investing in this most risky of the asset classes.

Table 2-9 shows the rates of return and standard deviation of return for each of the asset classes, as well as the inflation rate, over the 67-year period from 1926 to 1993. Note that common stocks provided the highest return over the period, and showed the highest standard deviation of return, while Treasury bills earned the least return and exhibited the lowest variability, with government and corporate bonds showing intermediate risk-return character. Inflation averaged 3.1 percent over the period; using this rate to adjust the nominal

---

[7]The nominal return R on a security, conceived as real return and compensation for inflation I, can be related as follows:

$$1 + R = (1 + R_r)(1 + I)$$

The real return can then be derived as

$$1 + R_r = \frac{1 + R}{1 + I}$$

By cross-multiplying this equation we obtain

$$R_r = R - I - R_r I$$

which reduces to the following analytically useful approximation when R_r and I are small:

$$R_r = R - I$$

TABLE 2-9
Realized return, inflation, real returns, and risk premiums (1926–1993)

	Realized return, %	Real return, %	Liquidity premium	Default premium	Risk premium, %	Standard deviation of return, %
Common stock	10.3	7.2	—	—	6.6	20.5
Long-term corporate bonds	5.6	2.5	—	0.6	—	8.4
Long-term government bonds	5.0	1.9	1.3	—	—	8.7
Treasury bills	3.7	0.6	—	—	—	3.3
Consumer Price Index (inflation)	3.1	—	—	—	—	—

Source: SBBI Yearbook, Ibbotson Associates, Chicago, 1994.

rate of return would have resulted in a lower real return in all asset classes. The real return for stocks over the period was 7.2 percent, while the real return for Treasury bills was only 0.6 percent. The two long-term bond categories showed real returns of 1.9 and 2.5 percent over the period.

Comparing returns across classes, we can assess the differing premia earned for accepting risk over the period. Note that long-term government bonds earned 5.0 percent and Treasury bills 3.7 percent, indicating a realized liquidity premium of 1.3 percent over the period. Long-term corporate bonds earned 5.6 percent; as compared with the 5.0 percent return for governments, they provide a default premium of 0.6 percent over the period. Finally, common stocks earned 10.3 percent, to provide a risk premium of 6.6 percent for these riskiest of the assets compared with the least risky asset, Treasury bills. As a matter of interest, comparing returns in this fashion is especially helpful when formally determining an asset allocation, which will be described in the next section.

Generating the Efficient Frontier

To demonstrate the application of asset allocation, we first proceed to generate a frontier of efficient mixes of asset classes. For this purpose we will consider three major asset classes: common stocks, long-term bonds, and money market instruments. These are the securities commonly used by portfolio managers and major investors, either as a complete list of classes for consideration or as essential classes within more extended groupings of asset classes. These can thus be representative of the sort of actual results produced from an asset allocation while at the same time being clear enough in application to illustrate the process.

As noted before, we need inputs for the asset classes; in this instance, we need returns and variances for each of the three classes, as well as correlation relationships that require three estimates. We devote a considerable portion of Chapter 9, on asset allocation, to describing ways of developing inputs for an asset allocation, both because of the importance of this activity, as well as the differing techniques that one might use. For purposes of simplicity of demonstration, we will refer to the historical data that we reviewed in the prior section and assume that the returns and risk characteristics shown by the three asset classes over the longer period reviewed, 1926–1993, are representative of future activity. Again, as part of our analysis in Chapter 9, we will evaluate that kind of assumption.

TABLE 2-10
Risk-return data (1926–1993)

Asset class	Mean returns	Standard deviation	Correlation		
Common stock	12.3%	20.5%	1.0	—	—
Long-term bonds	5.4%	8.7%	0.114	1.0	—
Treasury bills	3.7%	3.3%	−0.5	0.24	1.0

Table 2-10 shows the realized return and standard deviation of return for each of the three asset classes, as well as the correlation across those asset classes shown over the 1926–1993 period. Given these inputs, we can use a mathematical program that is constructed to generate the efficient set of portfolios. It is known as a *quadratic optimization program* and is available from commercial vendors as well as at university and other research sites. We have chosen not to describe the detailed mathematical background and modeling necessary to develop such a program; other books and articles offer excellent, albeit technical, descriptions and are cited as references to this chapter.

Instead, we will focus on providing a conceptual background for the model; illustrate its application by way of its most important use in asset allocation; and only summarize it as follows. Essentially, the program is constructed to minimize the risk of a portfolio at a given level of return—that is, develop the efficient portfolio at a given return level (say, for example, at 5 percent, 10 percent, or 20 percent). The program develops minimum-risk portfolios at different levels of return, in each case specifying the asset classes and their weighting in the portfolio at that level of return.[8] Proceeding in this fashion, the program develops a series of portfolios, differing in risk and return, that trace out an efficient frontier, which is plotted in Figure 2-7.

Table 2-11 shows the risk and return characteristics as well as asset class weightings for five portfolios that correspond to points 1, 3, 5, 7, and S&P 500 in the efficient frontier shown in Figure 2-7. Portfolio 1 has the lowest risk but also the lowest return. Note that it is heavily weighted in the lowest-risk asset class—Treasury bills—as might be expected. On the other hand, the S&P 500 portfolio at the extreme of the frontier is entirely weighted in equities. As a result, this portfolio offers the highest expected return, along with the highest risk. Portfolio 5 has intermediate risk and return characteristics and also shows less extremes in terms of asset class weightings: it has a more balanced asset mix.

In evaluating the desirability of portfolios along the efficient frontier, many investors prefer to think more intuitively, in terms of the probability of loss, or failure to meet a target return, rather than the mean-variance characteristics of the portfolio. Fortunately, we can transform the return–standard deviation parameters of an optimized portfolio into a probability-of-loss framework if we assume that returns are normally distributed. For example, a portfolio with a mean return of 9% and standard deviation of 12%, such as portfolio

---

[8]Generally the maximum-return portfolios are generated at each risk level subject to the constraint that the portfolio be fully invested or, alternatively, that the weights of the individual securities in the portfolio sum to 1. The return, risk, and covariance inputs for the securities are constants and are not changed by the portfolio analysis. The weights of the securities are the variables that the portfolio analysis adjusts in order to obtain the optimum portfolios. By varying these weights the portfolio's expected return and risk are varied. However, as the weights are varied, the restriction that the portfolio be fully invested cannot be violated.

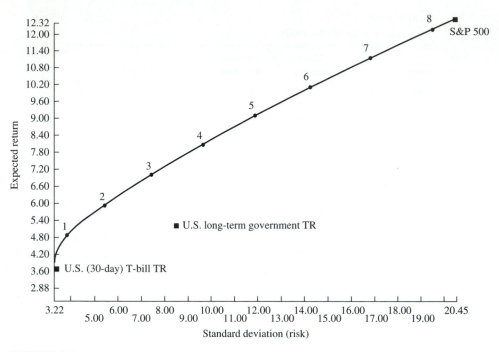

FIGURE 2-7
Efficient frontier, 1926–1993 (U.S. assets only).

5, would have 83 percent of the distribution above a return of -3% (above one standard deviation from the mean), or alternatively 17 percent below -3%. Figure 2-8 illustrates the distribution; these probabilities can be simply read from a normal distribution table.

Typically, target returns for investors might be set to avoid either an excessive loss or, for that matter, any negative return, and they would be expressed as the probability of the return being below zero over the period. Alternatively, some investors are concerned about earning a real rate of return matching or exceeding the rate of inflation over the period and might set, for example, a 3% target if that was the expected inflation rate. Furthermore, investors typically think in terms of meeting or exceeding such targets with an 80 percent

TABLE 2-11
Risk-return efficient frontier

	1	3	5	7	S&P 500
Asset class weighting (%)					
Common stock	12.50	32.90	53.30	81.00	100.00
Long-term bonds	11.60	27.00	42.40	19.00	0.00
Treasury bills	75.90	40.10	4.30	0.00	0.00
Total	100.00	100.00	100.00	100.00	100.00
Expected return (%)	5.00	7.00	9.00	11.00	12.30
Standard deviation (%)	3.90	7.60	12.00	16.90	20.50
Probability of loss (%)	10.0	17.9	22.7	25.8	27.4

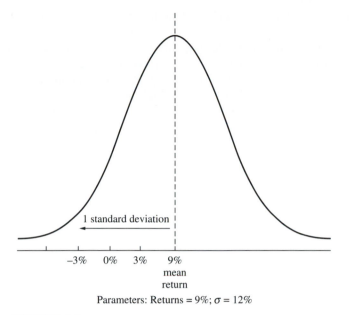

1 standard deviation

−3%   0%   3%   9%
mean
return

Parameters: Returns = 9%; σ = 12%

FIGURE 2-8
Probability-of-loss portfolio return distribution.

or 90 percent probability or, similarly, facing only a 10 percent or 20 percent probability of failing to meet the target.

Figure 2-8 illustrates this mode of analysis graphically by showing the bell-shaped distribution of returns for the medium-risk portfolio 5 from the efficient frontier shown in Table 2-11. The figure shows the mean return of 9% and return of −3%, which is one standard deviation below the mean, along with threshold returns of 0% and 3%. At a 3% target level, 70 percent of the return distribution is above 3% (or $\frac{1}{2}$ standard deviation below the mean), so the complement is a 30 percent probability of underperforming the target. Correspondingly, the zero-loss target is $\frac{3}{4}$ standard deviation below the mean, with 77 percent of the distribution above that level, for a probability of loss of 23 percent. The bottom line of Table 2-11 shows the loss probabilities associated with each of the optimized portfolios.

In Appendix A we illustrate a mode of analysis known as shortfall analysis, which elaborates on this basic probability-of-loss notion and provides a structured way of evaluating the desirability of portfolios across the efficient frontier. In the next section we cover a utility-based method of evaluating portfolios from the efficient frontier.

Risk Aversion

As noted in the introduction to this chapter, investors will select portfolios from the efficient frontier in keeping with their degree of aversion to risk. Those investors with a high degree of risk aversion will select portfolios with low risk, as measured by a low variance (standard deviation) of expected return. On the other hand, those with a higher tolerance for risk (low degree of risk aversion) will select portfolios that have a higher expected return, despite an associated higher variance (standard deviation) of expected return. By way of illustration, the investor with a high degree of risk aversion would likely select a low-risk portfolio like that illustrated by point 1 or 2 on the frontier in Figure 2-7. The investor with a higher tolerance for risk would likely select a portfolio like point 7 or 8 on the efficient frontier in Figure 2-7.

On a more conceptual basis, the selection of a portfolio would be a matter of maximizing the investor's expected *utility*. This, in turn, entails deducing what trade-off of risk and return constitutes utility for the investor. Following classical economic analysis, indifference curves (IDCs) are developed showing the magnitude and form of the risk-return trade-off in a mean-variance framework. Figure 2-9a presents IDCs for an investor. Along these curves the investor is indifferent to the risk-return trade-off. Once these indifference curves are known, the optimum portfolio to select is one on the efficient frontier that is tangent to the indifference curve that is highest in risk-return space. This is illustrated in Figure 2-9b.

While the conceptual framework is clear, practical application is far more difficult, because it is virtually impossible to model the complete pattern of indifference curves of an investor, and highly difficult even to come up with approximation for the trade-off between risk and return. One such approximation that has been developed and provides some perspective on the problem is known as the *certainty equivalent return* approach.

We can briefly describe the approach as follows. First, we assume that a risk-averse investor will penalize the expected rate of return of a risky portfolio by a certain percentage to account for the risk involved. The greater the risk the investor perceives, the larger the penalty. We can formalize this notion of a risk-penalty system by assuming that each investor

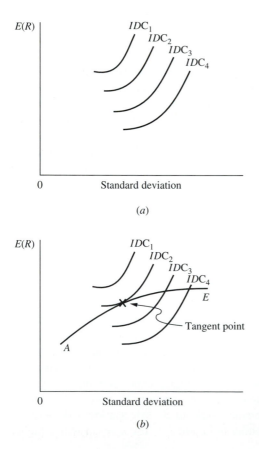

FIGURE 2-9

Portfolio selection. (*a*) Indifference curves for a risk-averse investor; (*b*) portfolio selection at point of tangency.

can assign a utility rank to competing investment portfolios, based on the expected return and risk of those portfolios. Portfolios receive higher utility for higher expected return and lower value for higher risk. One function that is employed assigns to a portfolio with an expected return $E(R)$ and variance of return σ^2 the following utility:

$$U = E(R) - \tfrac{1}{2}A\sigma^2 \tag{13}$$

where U is the utility value and A is an index of the investor's aversion to taking on risk.

Equation (13) is consistent with the notion that utility is enhanced by expected return and diminished by risk. The extent to which variance lowers utility depends on A, the investor's degree of risk aversion. Note that for an investor who is not averse to risk and is thus indifferent to risk, the coefficient A would be zero, and utility would be the same as the expected return of the portfolio. For the more realistic case of risk aversion, the size of A and, hence, the penalty will be greater as the degree of risk aversion increases.

As a benchmark for comparison, note that the utility provided by a risk-free portfolio is simply the rate of return on the portfolio, because there is no penalty for risk (variance is zero). Because we can compare utility values to the rate offered on risk-free investment when choosing between a risky portfolio and a safe one, we may interpret a portfolio value as its *certainty equivalent rate of return* (CERR) to an investor. Alternatively, the certainty equivalent rate of a portfolio is the rate that risk-free investments need to offer with certainty to be considered equally attractive to the risky portfolio.

Because of the difficulty of directly assigning a risk aversion parameter to an investor, the certainty equivalent approach has found limited practical application in allowing an investor to select a portfolio from the efficient frontier. It can, however, be useful in deducing the risk aversion of an investor when one knows his or her existing portfolio holdings. For example, we can use the certainty equivalent approach to deduce the risk aversion of an investor who holds a portfolio that is fully invested in common stocks, or correspondingly, an investor who holds a more balanced portfolio such as the 60/40 stock mix that is typical of many major pension funds.

This method is illustrated by means of Figure 2-10, which shows an efficient frontier along with two portfolios: (1) an all-stock portfolio (S) and (2) a portfolio (M) with a balanced mix of 60 percent stocks and 40 percent bonds. We can deduce the risk aversion by

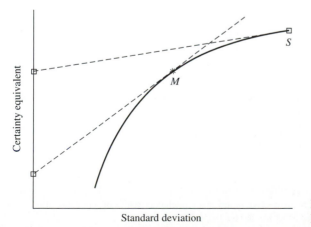

FIGURE 2-10
Efficient frontier, certainty equivalent.

simply drawing a line tangent to the portfolio of interest on the efficient frontier and extending it back to the vertical axis. The point of tangency represents the risk-return trade-off for the portfolio, while the point of intersection with the vertical axis represents the certainty equivalent return.

Note that the line tangent to portfolio S intersects the vertical axis at a relatively high level, whereas the line tangent to portfolio M intersects at a lower level. We would, of course, expect that the all-stock portfolio, which marks the highest risk-return point on the efficient frontier, to require the relatively highest certainty equivalent for investors with a relatively low degree of risk aversion. Correspondingly, the slope of the line is steeper for intermediate-risk portfolio M, resulting in a lesser certainty equivalent return for investors with a higher degree of risk aversion. After deducting the risk-return trade-off, we can then determine what portfolio changes can be made to maintain this trade-off. We illustrate this approach in the following section.

Expanding Asset Classes

As noted previously, the initial focus of investors in asset allocation has been on three major asset classes: common stocks, bonds, and money market instruments. This focus was due not only to the importance and familiarity of these asset classes but also to the availability of data on their risk-return characteristics. More recently, investors have broadened their scope for including other asset classes in an allocation. This, of course, is a natural extension of the principles deriving from portfolio theory, where the larger the universe of securities under consideration, the greater the potential opportunity to develop improved diversification.

Adding asset classes, especially those that have favorable covariance characteristics, has become a goal of more and more investors and portfolio managers. Some of the asset classes that investors have prominently added for asset allocation consideration include international equities and bonds as well as real estate. Other asset classes that might be considered small and nonstandard, yet receive serious consideration by some investors, include venture capital, gold, and other commodities. The ongoing development of better data bases for these asset classes has made the broadening of the asset universe a more feasible goal of the asset allocation process.

To illustrate the impact of expanding the asset class universe, we add the international equity class to our three major asset classes. In the past, major plan sponsors have carried relatively low weightings of international equities (generally less than 5 percent) in the asset mix. More recently, however, a strong trend has developed toward increasing this international equity exposure in the plan, with estimates that the average exposure will increase to the 15 to 20 percent level over the next three to five years. This trend is being propelled by the favorable diversification opportunities offered by international equities as well as the potential for high growth offered by selected international countries.

As inputs to the optimization, we again use historical data for returns, variances, and correlations for the same 1926 to 1993 period as in the previous analysis.[9] Table 2-12 shows these data for the international equity class, as well as domestic stocks, bonds, and T-bills. Note that the international stock class showed slightly higher returns along with greater

---

[9]Data for returns on international equities are available back to 1970 and up to 1993. To link that period with the longer 1926 to 1993 period, we assume that the relative return and risk characteristics of international equities would have been the same for the full period as for the shorter 1970–1993 period.

TABLE 2-12
Risk-return data, four asset classes

Asset class	Mean Return	Standard deviation	Correlation			
International stocks	15.5%	30.3%	1.0	—	—	—
U.S. stocks	12.3%	20.5%	0.56	1.0	—	—
Long-term bonds	5.4%	8.7%	0.22	0.14	1.0	—
Treasury bills	3.7%	3.3%	−0.25	−0.05	0.24	1.0

volatility than domestic stocks over the period. The correlation between domestic and international stocks was relatively low, and the bonds and T-bills show virtually no correlation with international stocks over the period.

Figure 2-11 shows the plot of the efficient frontier, while Table 2-13 shows the risk-return characteristics, as well as asset class weightings for five portfolios from the efficient frontier generated by the augmented optimization. The format is the same as before, except that international equities are included. Note that the lowest-risk portfolios are heavily weighted in T-bills as before, but the medium- and higher-risk portfolios carry significant weightings in international equities, first at the expense of the bond weighting and then replacing domestic equities. The weighting for international equities is especially notable at the higher risk level because of their diversifying potential and their returns comparable to domestic equities.

Figure 2-12 shows the efficient frontier of portfolios graphically, including international equities along with the three-asset class frontier that we developed previously using the same inputs. Note that the international equity–augmented frontier line lies above the original frontier, thus dominating the three-asset class optimization. This dominance was especially notable at higher return levels, where higher equity return would be achieved with less addition to risk because of the relatively lower correlation of international stocks. This comparison illustrates that the general case of expanding the universe of securities—in this case, asset classes—is productive in enhancing the risk-return trade-off.

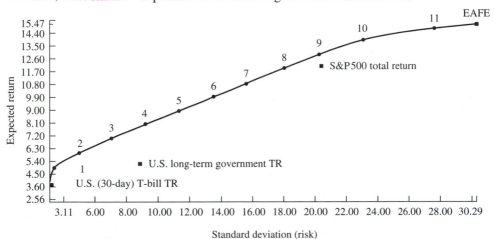

FIGURE 2-11
Efficient frontier.

TABLE 2-13
Risk-efficient frontier

	1	3	5	7	9
Asset class weightings (%)					
International stocks	5.8	11.4	14.2	19.7	28.4
U.S. stocks	5.8	19.7	33.7	47.6	60.8
Long-term bonds	5.1	14.4	23.7	29.4	5.5
Treasury bills	83.3	68.9	54.5	25.7	0
Total	100.0	100.0	100.0	100.0	100.0
Expected return (%)	5.0	7.0	9.0	11.0	13.0
Standard deviation (%)	3.6	7.0	11.2	15.5	20.1

The figure also shows the median risk-return portfolio (60/40 stock-bond mix), designated M(0) and plotted on the domestic-only frontier. An investor with the risk aversion imputed from the certainty equivalent approach described in the prior section, would maintain that same level by selecting a portfolio from the augmented frontier and designated M(1). This portfolio is the tangency point of a line parallel to, but higher than, the one tangent to the domestic-only frontier. Both lines show the same risk-return trade-off, but the line tangent to the foreign-augmented frontier provides a higher CERR than the domestic-only frontier, illustrating the gain in investor utility from expanding the selection universe.

World Market Portfolio

The potential risk-return enhancement from expanding the selection universe has, in turn, led to the concept of a "world market" portfolio. Figure 2-13 shows the aggregate size and composition by asset class of such a portfolio, which comprises cash equivalents, fixed-

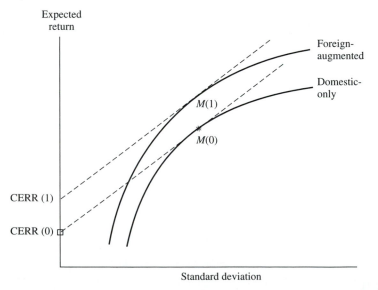

FIGURE 2-12
Efficient frontiers: domestic-only and foreign-augmented.

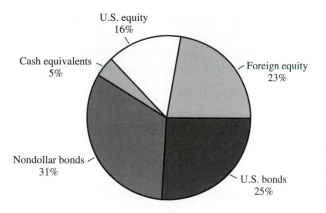

FIGURE 2-13
Global investable capital markets. (*Source:* Brinson Partners, Inc.)

income securities, and common stocks and is a *world* portfolio because it includes foreign as well as domestic (U.S.) securities. The assets represented include the major classes generally available for investment and are ones we will describe in some detail in later chapters of this book.

The world portfolio of investable capital markets aggregated $33,000 billion as of the end of 1993. Note that the cash equivalents represented a relatively minor portion of the portfolio. Long-term bonds represented 55.7 percent of the portfolio, with foreign securities representing a greater portion than domestic securities. Common stocks constituted 39.5 percent of the total, with U.S. stocks representing a lesser portion than foreign stocks. Foreign securities—both fixed-income and common stock—represented 54.1 percent of the world portfolio, indicating that foreign investing should be an important consideration when undertaking an asset allocation. Although real estate is a large category, and venture capital can offer high potential return, we exclude these asset classes because they are not readily marketable assets.

The world market portfolio, in turn, has use in asset allocation as well as performance achievement. This type of portfolio serves the purpose of spurring investors into developing representation across all asset classes to develop efficiently diversified portfolios. In another sense, it provides a way of assessing to what extent an investor's portfolio positioning might diverge from a well-diversified standard. For those investors pursuing more active and aggressive strategies that focus on concentrating investment in a relatively few asset classes, these divergences can be significantly large. Correspondingly, the world market portfolio can be considered as a benchmark or standard for performance measurement; the challenge for managers is at least to equal and preferably to exceed the performance of this standard. This concept is growing as a practical standard among pension plan and other large money management sponsors, as well as on the part of managers and consultants.

CONCLUSION

Portfolio theory, as embodied in the Markowitz model, provides a conceptual framework for much that is to follow in this book, as well as an analytical approach that has direct practical application. For example, it is often stated that diversification is the only "free lunch" in portfolio management. Analytically, we have seen that adding securities to a portfolio can result in reduced risk with no loss of return; this is an operational guideline that has consistently proven its usefulness in practice. The principle of diversification is also an insight that provides the basic foundation for models of equilibrium in the market, some of which we will cover in later chapters. Finally, the Markowitz model has direct practical application for developing an asset allocation as well as providing some analytical principles for global investing.

APPENDIX A
CHOOSING THE EFFICIENT PORTFOLIO

Shortfall Constraint Approach[10]

When viewing portfolio risk as a minimum return that will be exceeded with some specified probability, some refer to this as a "shortfall constraint" approach. To illustrate this approach, we assume an investor is willing to assume a 10% probability of loss associated with an investment. For an example portfolio with an 8% expected return and standard deviation of 10%, 10% of the distribution is that segment more than 1.282 standard deviations, or 12.82% below the 8% expected return. In turn, a −4.82% return (8% minus 12.82%) represents the 90 percent threshold for this portfolio, and represents what some refer to as a "shortfall constraint."

We can, in turn, illustrate how this concept of a shortfall constraint can be generalized to a universe of all possible portfolios, each having its own distinct return distribution. First, we continue to assume that portfolio distributions are normal and that the "shortfall constraint" is a probability of loss of 10 percent (also probability of gain of 90 percent). As a consequence, any normal distribution with expected return $E(R_p)$ and standard deviation σ_p has only a 10% probability of a return that falls $1.282\,\sigma_p$ below $E(R_p)$. For our illustrative portfolio there was a 90 percent probability of returns exceeding −4.82%. As a general matter, all portfolios that have a 90 percent probability of exceeding a −4.82% return are those with a combination of expected returns and standard deviations such that

$$R_p - 1.282\,\sigma_p = -4.82\%$$

Figure 2-A1 is a risk-return diagram illustrating that the shortfall constraint plots as a straight line with slope 1.282 and Y-axis intercept of −4.82%. All portfolios lying on or above this line have a 90 percent probability of exceeding the −4.82 percent return minimum, while portfolios that lie below this line will not exceed a return of −4.82 percent with 90 percent confidence. As one would expect, the minimum return for a given confidence level will increase as the expected return increases (holding the standard deviation constant) and will decrease as the standard deviation increases (holding the expected return constant).

Assessing risk as the probability of failing to earn a minimum return can further be helpful in selecting the optimal portfolio from an array of portfolios representing the efficient frontier. This is because the shortfall restriction essentially provides information regarding the risk tolerance of the investor. By formally introducing the shortfall probability as a

---

[10]This approach was developed and described by Leibowitz, Martin, and Roy Henriksson, "Portfolio Optimization with Shortfall Constraints: A Confidence-Limit Approach to Managing Downside Risk," *Financial Analysts Journal,* March–April 1989, pp. 34–41. This appendix follows that analysis.

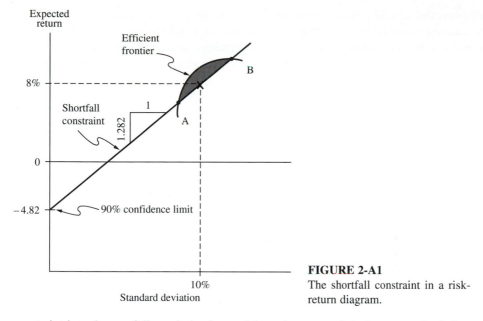

FIGURE 2-A1
The shortfall constraint in a risk-return diagram.

constraint into the portfolio optimization problem, the range of choice across the full array of efficient portfolios can be narrowed to those that are most relevant to the investor. That is, the constraint allows the investor to focus on that segment of the frontier that best fits his or her degree of risk aversion. The probability of target shortfall, therefore, can be thought of as a risk tolerance assessment tool (when coupled with another measure of risk).

Figure 2-A2 illustrates this process of selecting an optimal portfolio in conjunction with a shortfall constraint. It shows an efficient frontier of portfolios along with the short-

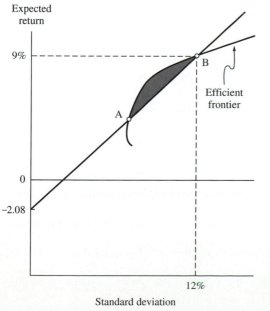

FIGURE 2-A2
Influence of the allowable shortfall.

fall constraint of a 90 percent probability of exceeding a -4.82% return. Note again that the shortfall constraint segments the combination of expected returns and risk. Portfolios to the right of the line violate the constraint; their realized returns do not exceed -4% with 90 percent confidence. Portfolios to the left of the line actually satisfy a higher 90 percent confidence limit than -4.82%.

At the same time, only portfolio risk-return trade-offs on or below the efficient frontier are feasible. As Figure 2-A2 shows, the set of feasible portfolios satisfying a shortfall constraint is limited. The set of portfolios to be considered for selection in the optimization decision is limited to the shaded area of portfolios that both are feasible and also satisfy the specified shortfall constraint. In this case, the investor would select a portfolio from the segment ranging from point A to point B, as these represent the optimal portfolios available. In this illustration, and in other cases, the use of the shortfall constraint reduces the array of choice to a more manageable range. We should note, however, that the constraint may be either too severe, so as to preclude the possibility of any choice, or too loose, so as to maintain much, if not all, of the efficient frontier as a range of choice.

SELECTED REFERENCES

Best, M., and R. Grauer: "The Sensitivity of Mean-Variance Efficient Portfolios to Changes in Asset Means: Some Analytical and Computational Results," *Review of Financial Studies,* 1991.

Booth, David, and Eugene Fama: "Diversification Returns and Asset Contributions," *Financial Analysts Journal,* May–June 1992, pp. 26–32.

Brealey, Richard A.: *An Introduction to Risk and Return from Common Stock Prices,* MIT Press, Cambridge, MA, 1969.

Chopra, V., and W. Ziemba: "The Effect of Errors in Means, Variances, and Covariance on Optimal Portfolio Choice," *Journal of Portfolio Management* 19, 1993, pp. 6–11.

Dybig, Philip: "Short Sales Restrictions and Kinks on the Mean-Variance Frontier," *Journal of Finance,* March 1984, pp. 239–244.

Elton, Edwin J., and Martin J. Gruber: "Estimating the Dependence Structure of Share Prices— Implications for Portfolio Selection," *Journal of Finance,* December 1973, pp. 1203–1232.

———: *Modern Portfolio Theory and Investment Analysis,* John Wiley & Sons, New York, 1991.

Evans, John L., and Stephen H. Archer: "Diversification and the Reduction of Dispersion: An Empirical Analysis," *Journal of Finance,* December 1968, pp. 761–67.

Fisher, Lawrence, and James H. Lorie: "Rates of Return on Investments in Common Stocks," *Journal of Business,* January 1964, pp. 1–21.

———: "Rates of Return on Investments in Common Stocks: The Year-by-Year Record, 1926–1965," *Journal of Business,* July 1968, pp. 291–316.

———: "Some Studies of Variability of Returns on Investment in Common Stocks," *Journal of Business,* April 1970, pp. 99–134.

Gibbons, M., S. Ross, and J. Shanken: "Test of the Efficiency of a Given Portfolio," *Econometrica* 57, 1989, pp. 1121–1152.

Green, R., and B. Hollifield: "When Will Mean-Variance Efficient Portfolios Be Well Diversified?" *Journal of Finance* 47, 1992, 1785–1809.

Harlow, W.V.: "Asset Allocation in a Downside-Risk Framework," *Financial Analysts Journal,* September–October 1991, pp. 28–40.

Haugen, B., and N. Baker: "The Inefficiency of the Value-Weighted Index," *Journal of Portfolio Management,* 1989, pp. 42–55.

Ibbotson, Roger, and Laurence Siegel: "The World Market Wealth Portfolio," *Journal of Portfolio Management,* Winter 1983, pp. 5–17.

Ibbotson, R., L. Siegel, and K. Love: "World Wealth: Market Values and Returns," *Journal of Portfolio Management,* Fall 1985, pp. 4–23.

Ibbotson, Roger G., and Rex A. Sinquefeld: *Stocks, Bonds, Bills, and Inflation: The Past (1926–1976) and the Future (1977–2000),* Financial Analysts Research Foundation, Charlottesville, VA, 1977.

Jobson, J.D.: "Estimating the Mean-Variance Efficient Frontier: The Markowitz Criterion Is Not Enough." Presented to the Q Group, Fall Seminar, 1994.

Jorion, P.: "Portfolio Optimization in Practice," *Financial Analysts Journal,* 1992, pp. 68–74.

———: "Bayesian and CAPM Estimators of the Means: Implications for Portfolio Selection," *Journal of Banking and Finance,* 1991, pp. 717–727.

———: "Bayes-Stein Estimation for Portfolio Analysis," *Journal of Financial and Quantitative Analysis,* 1986, pp. 279–292.

Liebowitz, Martin, and Roy Henriksson: "Portfolio Optimization with Shortfall Constraints: A Confidence-Limit Approach to Managing Downside Risk," *Financial Analysts Journal,* March–April 1989, pp. 34–41.

Lewis, Alan: "A Simple Algorithm for the Portfolio Selection Problem," *Journal of Finance,* March 1988, pp. 71–82.

Lorie, James H., and Mary T. Hamilton: *The Stock Market: Theories and Evidence,* Richard D. Irwin, Homewood, IL, 1988.

Markowitz, Harry: "Portfolio Selection," *Journal of Finance,* March 1952, pp. 77–91.

———: *Portfolio Selection: Efficient Diversification of Investments.* John Wiley & Sons, New York, 1959.

Merton, R.C.: "An Analytic Derivation of the Efficient Portfolio Frontier," *Journal of Financial and Quantitative Analysis* 7, 1972, pp. 1851–1872.

Michaud, R.: "The Markowitz Optimization Enigma: Is Optimized Optimal?" *Financial Analysts Journal,* 1989, pp. 31–42.

Modigliani, Franco, and Gerald Pogue: "An Introduction to Risk and Return," *Financial Analysts Journal,* March–April 1974, pp. 68–80.

Perold, A.F.: "Large-Scale Portfolio Optimization," *Management Science* 30, pp. 1143–1160.

Sharpe, William: " Imputing Expected Security Returns from Portfolio Composition," *Journal of Financial and Quantitative Analysis* 9, 1974, pp. 463–472.

———: *Portfolio Theory and Capital Markets,* McGraw-Hill, New York, 1970.

———: "Risk, Market Sensitivity and Diversification," *Financial Analysts Journal,* January–February 1972, pp. 74–79.

QUESTIONS AND PROBLEMS

1. Refer to the data in Table 2-3. Calculate the expected return and variance of the portfolio, assuming that the portfolio weights are 0.75 for security 1 and 0.25 for security 2, that the expected return of security 1 is 18 percent and the standard deviation is 0.60, and that the correlation between the two securities is 0.5.
2. Refer to the data in Table 2-4. Calculate the standard deviation of the following portfolios: four stocks, nine stocks, twenty-five stocks, thirty-six stocks, and forty-nine stocks.
3. Determine the number of inputs needed to analyze a 250-stock universe and a 70-stock universe using the Markowitz full-covariance model.
4. Describe the concept of efficiency.
5. Describe the process of diversification and its benefits. Also, comment on the different components of individual security and portfolio risk.

6. Refer to Table 2-6 and calculate the expected return and standard deviation of the portfolio when the correlation between the stocks is -0.3 and then -1.0.

7. Refer to Table 2-7 and compute the standard deviation assuming a correlation of 0.0 and -1.0.

8. What is the asset allocation, and how is the Markowitz full-covariance model appropriate for this activity?

9. Explain nominal returns, real returns, and risk premium and how these differ across asset classes.

10. Describe the characteristics of the output from a portfolio optimization. What are the minimum-risk and maximum-risk portfolio compositions?

11. How is the probability of loss relevant as a measure of risk for optimal portfolios?

12. Refer to portfolio 5 in Table 2-11 and determine the minimum return or maximum loss target for an investor desiring to exceed that with a 90 percent probability.

13. Explain the notion of a certainty equivalent return and how it relates to selecting an optimal portfolio.

14. How can the certainty equivalent approach provide useful information in a practical sense?

15. Explain how expanding the universe of securities under consideration can be helpful in improving the risk-return trade-off.

16. How can the certainty equivalent approach be helpful in selecting the "optimal" portfolio from this expanded frontier of portfolios?

17. Explain the concept of a "world portfolio." How has this found practical application?

18. What is the relationship between the covariance and the correlation coefficient? Why is the correlation coefficient considered more useful?

19. Discuss why the concepts of covariance and diversification are closely related.

20. How can short selling increase a portfolio's expected return?

21. The mean annual return for the S&P 500 over the 1926–1993 period was 10%. Given no other information, would you use this figure as a forecast of the return for the S&P 500 over the next year? Are there any reasons why you might want to adjust your forecast up or down from 10%?

22. With respect to the prior question, would you have as much confidence in your forecast for the S&P index as you would in your forecast for any individual stock?

23. Based on the data in Table 2-9, what would you estimate to be the probability of losing money in stocks or bonds next year?

24. Over the 1926–1993 period, the worst return for stocks was -43.3%, but the CPI was also down at -9.5%. In 1974, stocks also showed a severe decline of 26.5%, but the CPI showed an increase of 12.2%. Which was a worse year for stock investors?

25. Listed below are the annual returns generated by IBM stock for the 10 years 1969–1978. Calculate the mean annual return and the standard deviation of these returns. Also, calculate the covariance and the correlation coefficient for the returns of IBM and those of the S&P 500 returns for this time period.

	Annual returns, %	
	IBM	S&P 500
1969	16.98	−8.50
1970	−11.36	4.01
1971	7.64	14.31
1972	21.12	18.98
1973	−22.14	−14.66
1974	−30.01	−26.48
1975	37.68	37.20
1976	28.27	23.84
1977	1.76	−7.18
1978	13.93	6.56

26. Use the following data to calculate the variance and standard deviation for a portfolio containing stocks 1 and 2:

$$\rho_{1,2} = 0.75 \qquad \sigma_1 = 10 \qquad \sigma_2 = 20$$

$$W_1 = \tfrac{2}{3} \qquad W_2 = \tfrac{1}{3}$$

27. Given the following ex post data for stocks X, Y, and Z, calculate all the unique covariances and correlation coefficients.

	Annual returns, %		
	X	Y	Z
1990	6.2	−9.5	26.5
1991	3.6	−11.7	−12.3
1992	4	13.8	2.6
1993	2.4	−5.3	10.5
1994	0.2	9.5	9.2

CHAPTER 3

Capital Market Theory and Applied Portfolio Analysis

INTRODUCTION

Whereas the Markowitz model is the foundation for portfolio analysis, the capital-asset pricing model (CAPM) is the model for capital market theory. The Markowitz model is *normative*—it shows how investors ought to behave. Capital market theory, on the other hand, is *positive*. Given that investors behave in the fashion suggested by Markowitz, there are implications for (1) the behavior of security prices, (2) the sort of risk-return relationship that one would expect, and (3) the appropriate measure of risk for securities. The section discussing diversification in the previous chapter attempted to develop some of those implications in an informal fashion. The CAPM is a general equilibrium model that attempts to provide more explicit answers for those implications.

This chapter begins by outlining the major assumptions underlying capital market theory (CMT). It then goes on to describe the two main components of CMT: (1) the capital market line (CML) and (2) the security market line (SML). We will then discuss use of the SML in determining the appropriate expected return for stocks, along with its role as a benchmark for appraising the relative valuation of stocks. It needs to be recognized that in practice the SML and the CAPM are used interchangeably. For the most part CAPM is employed because of the pricing implications. After describing these uses, we will review the empirical evidence on the CAPM to see how well the model conforms to pragmatic-world market behavior.

In the second part of the chapter we will describe the single-index model, which is the empirical counterpart of the theoretical CAPM as well as an index simplification for implementing the Markowitz model. We will then illustrate how this model can be used as a practical method for analyzing the structure and important characteristics of a portfolio. We conclude by showing how financial researchers and commercial portfolio analysis services have elaborated on the basic single-index model in the quest for better estimates of betas for securities and portfolios.

54

CAPM ASSUMPTIONS AND IMPLICATIONS

Table 3-1 lists the assumptions that are usually made in deriving CMT. Note that because CMT builds on the Markowitz model, it automatically makes the assumptions that are necessary for that model of portfolio analysis. In particular, it assumes that investors (1) are risk-averse, expected-utility maximizers, (2) choose their portfolios on the basis of the mean and variance of return, and (3) have a one-period time horizon that is the same for all investors. As noted before, these assumptions imply that investors will diversify and will want to select portfolios from somewhere on the efficient frontier. The CAPM, as a general equilibrium model with implications regarding the behavior of security prices, makes a stronger statement, however, and hence needs other, stronger assumptions.

The bottom part of Table 3-1 lists those additional assumptions. Note that one of these is that a risk-free asset exists and that borrowing and lending at the risk-free rate are unrestricted. In portfolio parlance, "risk-free" means certainty of outcome (expected variance equals zero), *not* free of all risk. Treasury bills are risk-free in nominal terms and are usually taken as a proxy for a risk-free asset, but there is question whether in an inflationary environment there is such a thing as a risk-free asset—that is, there will be uncertainty of real return. After developing the model on the assumption of a risk-free asset, we will then examine the effect on the model of relaxing this particular premise.

Another assumption of CMT is that investors have homogeneous expectations regarding the means, variances, and covariances of security returns. This assumption suggests that every investor has an identical view of the prospects for each security. This, in turn, allows us to derive the model in a relatively straightforward fashion as well as to develop implications that are relatively unambiguous. Actually, the model can be derived assuming only that there is a "considerable consensus" by investors regarding future prospects; however, the derivation then becomes more complex, and the implications less clear, than when homogeneous expectations are assumed.

The model's additional assumptions of no taxes or other market imperfections, such as transaction costs, are needed to make possible the arbitrating of "mispriced" securities, thus forcing an equilibrium price. When the assumption of no taxes is relaxed, the question arises as to whether high-dividend stocks offer higher pretax returns than low-dividend stocks of equivalent risk. This has been a subject of considerable theoretical debate and empirical testing. Evidence to date indicates that the effect, if it exists at all, is likely to be small, perhaps 50 basis points or less. Correspondingly, the existence of transaction costs means

TABLE 3-1
Assumptions for capital market theory

Common to both the Markowitz model and CMT:
1. Investors are risk-averse, expected-utility maximizers.
2. Investors choose portfolios on the basis of their expected mean and variance of return.
3. Investors have a single-period time horizon that is the same for all investors.

Additional assumptions:
4. Borrowing and lending at the risk-free rate are unrestricted.
5. Investor expectations regarding the means, variances, and covariances of security returns are homogeneous.
6. There are no taxes and no market imperfections, such as transaction costs mispriced by an amount equal to transaction costs.

that securities can potentially be mispriced by an amount equal to transaction costs. This effect is also likely to be relatively minor, because transaction costs are small relative to the price of securities; that is, estimates for a typical common stock are on the order of 50 to 100 basis points.

The implications of these assumptions are that there is a CMT consisting of a CML and an SML or CAPM. The CML provides the framework for determining the relationship between expected return and risk for portfolios of securities. Correspondingly, it indicates the appropriate measure of risk for a portfolio. The CAPM provides the framework for determining the relationship between expected return and risk for individual securities as well as for portfolios. The CAPM also indicates the appropriate measure of risk for securities. It will be useful to cover the CML first, as it provides a foundation for better understanding of the CAPM, which in turn has broader application in understanding the risk-return trade-off in the marketplace.

Lending and Borrowing

The CML is usually derived on the assumption that there exists a riskless asset available for investment. It is further assumed that investors can borrow or lend as much as desired at the risk-free rate R_f. Given this opportunity, investors can then mix risk-free assets with a portfolio of risky assets M to obtain the desired risk-return combination. Letting W represent the proportion invested in risk-free assets and $1 - W$ the proportion invested in the risky asset, we can use a formula like the one in the previous chapter (see page 33) to calculate the expected return on the combination or portfolio R_p:

$$E(R_p) = WR_f + (1 - W)E(R_m) \qquad (1)$$

The top panel of Table 3-2 uses this formula to calculate expected returns associated with three investor options: (1) mixing lending with risky assets, (2) investing only in the risky asset, and (3) mixing borrowing with risky assets. The lending example in the top panel of Table 3-2 assumes that the investor apportions half his funds to the risk-free asset ($W = 0.5$) and the other half to the risky asset. The leverage example assumes that the investor borrows (negative lending, or $W = 0.5$) at the risk-free rate and invests half again as much in the risky asset. The intermediate example assumes exclusive investment ($W = 0$) in risky assets. Figure 3-1 presents a pictorial representation of the CML, and the three investor options.

Note that lending provides the lowest return at 7.5 percent, borrowing the highest at 12.5 percent, and exclusive investment in the risky asset an intermediate return at 10 percent. While borrowing increases expected return and lending reduces expected return, there is a trade-off in increased and decreased risk. Intuitively, when one invests in risk-free *and* risky assets, the total risk of the portfolio is less than that of the risky set alone (portfolio A in Figure 3-1). Conversely, when one borrows to buy additional risky assets, the total risk of the portfolio increases over that of the risky set alone. The latter case is commonly known as *financial leverage* (portfolio B in Figure 3-1).

We can again use the formula in Chapter 2 (page 38) for calculating the variances of a portfolio to indicate the nature of the trade-off. In particular, if we let W represent the proportion of the portfolio in the risk-free asset and $1 - W$ the risky asset, the variance of the portfolio [$\text{Var}(R_p)$] is

$$\text{Var}(R_p) = W^2 \text{Var}(R_f) + (1 - W)^2 \text{Var}(R_m) + 2W(1 - W)\rho S_f S_m \qquad (2)$$

TABLE 3-2
Risk-return for differing combinations of borrowing and lending

		Return		
Proportion in Risk-free asset W	**Risk-free return** R_f, %	**Proportion in risky asset** $1 - W$	**Risky return** R_m, %	**Portfolio return** R_p, %
0.5	5	0.5	10	7.5
0	5	1.0	10	10.0
−0.5	5	1.5	10	12.5

	Risk	
Proportion in risky asset $1 - W$	**Standard deviation of return** S_m, %	**Portfolio risk** S_p, %
0.5	20	10
1.0	20	20
1.5	20	30

		Risk-return trade-off		
Portfolio return R_p, %	**Risk-free return** R_f, %	**Risk premium** $R_p - R_f$, %	**Portfolio risk** S_p, %	**Factor of proportionality** $(R_p - R_f)/S_p$
7.5	5.0	2.5	10	.25
10.0	5.0	5.0	20	.25
12.5	5.0	7.5	30	.25

Note that only the second term of the equation $(1 - W)^2 \mathrm{Var}(R_m)$ has a positive value. The value of the first term is zero because the return on the riskless asset has zero variance; the third term has a value of zero because the return on the riskless asset has a standard deviation of zero. It is also true that the variance of the portfolio of risky assets is a given value. Thus the variance of the combination portfolio depends exclusively on the proportion which is invested in the risky asset or, equivalently, the proportion invested in the risk-free asset. The formula for determining the risk of a combined portfolio of risky and risk-free assets can be expressed as a standard deviation S_p, as in the following:

$$\sqrt{\mathrm{Var}(R_p)} = S_p = (1 - W)S_m \tag{3}$$

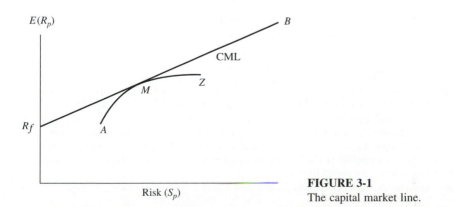

FIGURE 3-1
The capital market line.

Since the risk associated with the combination is directly proportional to the position in the risky asset, we show, in the middle panel of Table 3-2, the risk values associated with the three alternative versions of investing in the previous example: (1) investing half the funds in a risk-free asset, (2) investing exclusively in risky assets, and (3) borrowing and investing half again as much in the risky portfolio. Note that the risk of 30 percent is greatest for the borrowing alternative, with the greatest return, and is least, at 10 percent, for the lending alternative that had the lowest return. Investing exclusively in risky assets provided both intermediate risk and return.

In fact, returns are proportional to risk, as illustrated by the calculation at the bottom of Table 3-2, which shows that the factor of proportionality is calculated by subtracting the risk-free rate from the return and dividing by the risk (standard deviation). Note that the factor of proportionality is 0.25, indicating that one unit of return is accompanied by four units of risk.

The Capital Market Line

The possibility of lending and borrowing changes the original efficient frontier to the straight line $R_f MB$, as shown in Figure 3-1. This line, rising from the interest rate R_f on the vertical axis and tangential to the curve at point M, sets out all the alternative combinations of the risky portfolio M with risk-free borrowing and lending.[1] The segment from point R_f to point M includes the mixed portfolios of risky and risk-free securities. Levered portfolios (combinations of M with risk-free loans) are represented by points along the line beyond point M.

Since, according to the CMT, all investors have identical (homogeneous) expectations, they will all observe a risk-return diagram such as that illustrated in Figure 3-1. Accordingly, every investor will seek to construct a portfolio consisting of the risk-free asset and portfolio M. Because all investors hold the same risky portfolio, then for equilibrium it will include all risky securities in proportion to their market value. If this were not true, prices would adjust until the value of the security was consistent with its proportion in portfolio M. This portfolio of all risky assets is referred to as the *market portfolio*.[2]

Given that all investors hold portfolio M, Tobin[3] observed that the investment decision is made. Tobin further noted that the only decision left was how to finance the investment in M. The separation of investment and financing decisions is known as *Tobin's separatability theorem*. The form of financing (i.e., the amount of R_f) is based on the investor's aversion to risk. Those with a high risk aversion will include more R_f and be a lender. Others with less risk aversion will borrow and purchase more M.

The investor can now attain any point along the line $R_f MB$ by combining the portfolio of risky assets M with the risk-free asset R_f or by leveraging the portfolio M by borrowing

---

[1] Note that the portfolio of risky assets, represented by point M, has the property of maximizing the angle formed when a straight line is drawn from point R_f to any point on the curve. Portfolio M is, therefore, the one that provides the maximum return per unit of risk (standard deviation), and in essence the CML is a new efficient frontier.

[2] The market portfolio is a critical notion underlying the CML and the CAPM. Work by Roll casts doubt not only on the possibility of identifying such a portfolio and of conducting valid tests of the explanatory capacity of the model but also on application of principles of the CAPM in practice. One of the merits of the alternative theory of asset pricing, the arbitrage pricing theory (APT), to be discussed later in the chapter, is that it does not depend on the existence or identifiability of a market portfolio.

[3] Tobin, James: "Liquidity Preference as Behavior towards Risk," *Review of Economic Studies*, February 1958, pp. 65–85.

and investing the funds in *M*. Portfolios on line $R_f MB$ are preferred to portfolios between *A* and *M* and between *M* and *Z*, since they offer greater return for a given level of risk. These portfolios, except portfolio *M*, dominate those exclusively made up of risky assets.

The line $R_f MB$ formed by the action of all investors mixing the market portfolio and the risk-free asset then becomes the capital market line (CML). Mathematically, the CML can be described in terms of the risk-free rate and the return on the market portfolio:

$$E(R_p) - R_f = \frac{E(R_m) - R_f}{S_m} S_p \tag{4}$$

In words, this equation says, that for a portfolio on the CML the expected rate of return in excess of the risk-free rate is proportional to the standard deviation of that portfolio.[4] The slope of the CML has been called the *price of risk*. As Equation (4) shows, it is the constant of proportionality and equals the difference between the expected return on the market portfolio and that on the risk-free security $(E(R_m) - R_f)$ divided by the difference in their risks $(S_m - 0)$. The slope is the additional expected return for an additional unit of risk, or reward per unit of risk.

We can refer to data from the 1926–1993 period to develop a crude benchmark for what the price of risk might have been over that 67-year period. In particular, the return on the market over that period was 10.3 percent, while the standard deviation of the market was 20.6 percent. Using the 3.7 percent return on Treasury bills as a proxy for the risk-free rate and plugging these values into the formula would have indicated a slope of approximately $\frac{1}{3}$. Investing in the market portfolio would provide a reward of 6.6 percent (10.3 − 3.7) for bearing a risk corresponding to a standard deviation of 20.6 percent, or a 1 percent return for every 3 percent of risk assumed over the period.

The CML thus provides a risk-return relationship and measure of risk for efficient portfolios—that is, for those that plot on the line representing the efficient frontier. In particular, it indicates that the appropriate measure of risk for an efficient portfolio is the standard deviation of return for the portfolio S_p. It also indicates that there will be a linear relationship between the risk as measured by the standard deviation and the expected return for these efficient portfolios. The formulation for this risk-return relationship is given in Equation 3.

THE SECURITY MARKET LINE/CAPITAL ASSET PRICING MODEL

The CML shows the appropriate measure of risk and the risk-return relationship for efficient portfolios, but it does not show those for inefficient portfolios or individual securities. Sharpe in his study shows that the analysis can be extended to a related but not identical

---

[4]This formula can be derived by first rearranging the equation (2) for the standard deviation of portfolio return from

$$S_p = (1 - W)S_m$$

to obtain $(1-W) = S_p/S_m$ and $W = 1-S_p/S_m$, and then substituting these expressions in Equation (1) for expected return:

$$R_p = WR_f + (1 - W)R_m$$

Simplifying, we obtain equation (3).

measure of risk:[5] the familiar beta concept—a measure of risk that applies to all assets and portfolios, whether efficient or inefficient. In addition, Sharpe provides the SML/CAPM, which specifies the relationship between expected return and risk, again for all assets and portfolios, whether efficient or inefficient. However, his derivation is fairly complex, so we will provide a more direct and intuitive derivation of the SML/CAPM. For ease of presentation, we will refer to this concept as the CAPM.

The CAPM can be most effectively derived by referring to the section on diversification in Chapter 2. Recall that the total risk of a security as measured by the standard deviation S_i is essentially composed of two components: systematic risk and diversifiable risk. We saw that the diversifiable component could be reduced as we added securities, or diversified the portfolio, thereby increasing the proportion of systematic risk in the portfolio. Correspondingly, we saw that when diversification increases, so does the correlation of the portfolio with the market. We concluded from this discussion that the systematic component is the relevant one both for measuring risk as well as for determining the risk-return relationship.

To measure the systematic risk of a security or portfolio, we simply multiply the correlation coefficient between the security or portfolio and the market portfolio, ρ_{im}, by the standard deviation of the security or portfolio, S_i. For a portfolio that is perfectly diversified, the systematic component will be equivalent to total risk, because the correlation between the portfolio and the market is perfectly positive ($\rho_{im} = +1$), so that $\rho_{im}S_p = S_p$. In this case the measure of risk is the standard deviation, and the CML, which employs the standard deviation, is the appropriate measure of the risk-return relationship.

For portfolios that are less than perfectly diversified or for individual securities, however, systematic risk and total risk will not be equivalent, because the portfolios and individual securities are less than perfectly correlated with the market. For example, the typical individual security will have a correlation coefficient with the market of 0.55. With a standard deviation of 40 percent, the systematic risk of the typical security will be 0.55 × 40 percent = 22 percent, or little more than half the total risk. The SML, which uses systematic risk as its risk measure, is the appropriate risk-return relationship for securities and for portfolios that are less than perfectly diversified; that is,

$$E(R_i) - R_f = \frac{E(R_m) - R_f}{S_m}\rho_{im}S_i \qquad (5)$$

This relationship says that the expected return of a security in excess of the risk-free rate is proportional to the systematic risk of the stock. Note that the left-hand side of the equation is identical to the CML and that the factor of proportionality on the right-hand side is the price of risk. The CAPM and CML differ only in the measure of risk: systematic risk for the CAPM and total risk for the CML. However, it is important to recognize that one is not a linear or simple transformation of the other.

By using the definition of the correlation coefficient $\mathrm{Cov}(R_iR_m)/(S_iS_m)$ and rearranging terms, the CAPM can be restated as

$$E(R_i) - R_f = \frac{\mathrm{Cov}(R_iR_m)}{\mathrm{Var}(R_m)}[E(R_m) - R_f] \qquad (6)$$

---

[5]Sharpe, W. F.: "Capital Asset Prices: A Theory of Market Equilibrium under Conditions of Risk," *Journal of Finance*, September 1964, pp. 425–442.

Note that the coefficient on the right-hand side of equation (6) is the same as the beta of the stock, so that we can restate the equation in its more familiar form as

$$E(R_i) = R_f + \beta_i[E(R_m) - R_f] \tag{7}$$

It will be useful to note at this point that for all practical purposes the beta coefficient in the equation of the SML is the same as the beta of the market, or single-index, model. As a result, for application and testing of the relationship, researchers and practitioners ordinarily use the single-index model as the empirical counterpart of the theoretical SML. We will describe this model and how it is used to generate beta estimates, along with its practical application in portfolio analysis, in a later section of this chapter.

Risk-Return Relationship

When the equation of the CAPM is plotted in expected return–beta coordinates, it yields a straight line, as shown in Figure 3-2. Note that the vertical axis refers to expected return, while the horizontal axis uses beta rather than standard deviation as the measure of risk. The line is determined by the return on the risk-free asset (which has, by definition, a beta of zero) and the expected return on the market (which has a beta of 1.00, also by definition). In equilibrium all securities and portfolios will plot along the CAPM, whether efficient or inefficient.

Since all securities are expected to plot along the CAPM, the line provides a direct and convenient way of determining the expected return on a security. In particular, each beta level might be regarded as representing a risk class, and all securities that fall in that risk class would be expected to earn a return appropriate for that class. Presuming that we know the beta of the security, we can directly use the CAPM formula to solve for the expected return or, alternatively, use the CAPM graph to generate an expected return for the security.

To illustrate this, Table 3-3 shows some market data along with data for two hypothetical securities A and D. Note that the risk-free rate is assumed to be 5 percent and the expected market return 12 percent, to provide an expected market-risk premium of 7

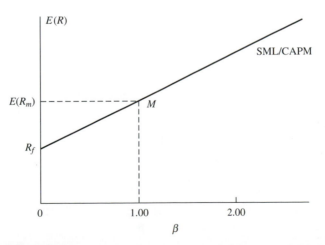

FIGURE 3-2
Security market line/capital asset pricing model.

TABLE 3-3
Capital Asset Pricing Model (CAPM)

	Expected return E(R)	Risk-free rate R_f	Beta β_i	Market-risk premium $[E(R_m) - R_f]$
Market	12.0	5	1.00	7
Security A	13.4	5	1.20	7
Security D	10.6	5	0.80	7

percent. Security A has a beta of 1.20, while security D has a beta of 0.80. Given market data and the beta for a security, the expected return can be calculated by means of the SML equation given in the body of the table, where security A has an expected return of 13.4 percent and security D an expected return of 10.6 percent.

Alternatively, one can derive an expected return for the security graphically, as illustrated in Figure 3-3, in which the CAPM is derived from the market data in Table 3-3. Once this and the beta values are known for the security, one can plot the securities and read off the expected return from the vertical axis. For example, security A, with a beta of 1.20, has an expected return of 13.4 percent, while security D, with a beta of 0.80, has an expected return of 10.6 percent. The expected returns are, of course, the same as those in Table 3-3 by formulation.

As a matter of interest, we might use the CAPM graph to classify securities. Those with betas greater than 1.00 and plotting on the upper part of the line, such as security A, will be classified as aggressive, while those with betas less than 1.00 and plotting on the lower part of the line, such as security D, will be classified as defensive. Aggressive securities would be expected to earn above-average returns, whereas defensive securities would be expected to earn below-average returns, as can be seen in the CAPM graph.

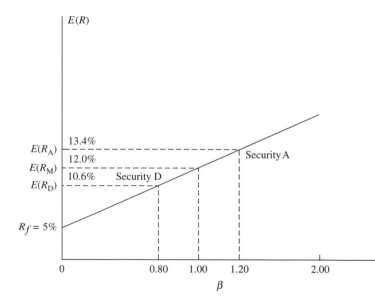

FIGURE 3-3
Capital asset pricing model.

Undervalued and Overvalued Securities

The CAPM also provides a framework for evaluating the relative attractiveness of securities. In particular, high-risk stocks are expected to offer high returns because of their risk. The question is whether they are offering returns more or less than proportional to their risk. Conversely, low-risk stocks are expected to offer lower returns by virtue of a lower risk level. Again the question is whether they are offering returns more or less than proportional to their risk.

Figure 3-4 illustrates how the CAPM provides an explicit framework for this appraisal. The figure shows a hypothetical market line with nine securities plotted relative to it. Note that securities A, B, and C plot above the line, securities X, Y, and Z below the line, and securities M, N, and O on the line. At the same time, securities A, M, X plot at a beta level of 0.80; B, N, and Y plot at a beta of 1.00; and C, O, and Z at a beta of 1.20. Each of the three sets of securities is in the same risk class, of which there are three: high, low, and average.

In the market-line context, stocks that plot above the line presumably are undervalued (attractive) because they offer a higher expected return than stocks of similar risk. Stocks A, B, and C, which plot above the line, are undervalued relative to their beta class. The current prices of these stocks are too low, and we can see from the simple rate of return formulation that they would have to rise—leading to above-average performance—to raise the denominator and lower the required return of the stock:

$$E(R_i) = \frac{E(P_1) - P_0 + \text{dividend}}{P_0} \tag{8}$$

On the other hand, a stock is presumably overvalued (unattractive) when it is expected to produce a lower return than issues of comparable risk. Stocks X, Y, and Z, which plot below the line, are overvalued relative to their beta class. The current prices of these stocks are too high, and in this case we can see from the rate of return formulation that they would have to fall—leading to below-average performance—to lower the denominator and thereby raise the return of the stocks.

Stocks M, N, and O, which plot on the line, are appropriately valued in the context of the CAPM market line. These stocks are offering returns in line with their riskiness. The

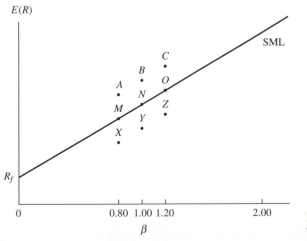

FIGURE 3-4
The CAPM and security valuation.

prices of these stocks are "right," and one would expect average stock performance, since they are neither undervalued nor overvalued.

Thus, stocks plotting off the market line would be evidence of mispricing in the marketplace. There are, in turn, three major reasons for mispricing in the securities market. The first is transaction costs, which may reduce investors' incentive to correct minor deviations from the CAPM. The cost of adjustment may be greater than or at least equal to the potential opportunity presented by the mispricing. Second, investors subject to taxes might be reluctant to sell an overvalued security with a capital gain and incur the tax. Finally, imperfect information can affect the valuation of a security. Misinformation could be either positive or negative and may have an impact on current prices.

Figure 3-5 is an idealized illustration of how the CAPM would look when actual market conditions are as we just described. In this case securities would not all be expected to lie exactly on the CAPM; therefore, in practice the CAPM is a band instead of a thin line. The width of this band varies directly with the imperfections in the market.

As may be surmised, the CAPM has practical implications as a means of identifying undervalued and overvalued securities. Chapter 5 will describe how this method has been implemented and the results of using this framework to identify relatively attractive stocks. The results demonstrate the usefulness of these techniques of portfolio management while also offering some evidence of the degree to which there may be mispricing in the market place. Misinformation could be either positive or negative and may have an impact on current prices.

Empirical Tests

It will be useful at this point to describe how the CAPM equation (5) has been tested empirically and thereby illustrate how well actual market data has conformed to the risk-return relationship suggested by the CMT. The test results should provide perspective on which assumptions of the model are most severely compromised.

The risk-return relationship described by Equation (5) (the CAPM) is an *expected,* or *ex ante,* relationship. The returns referred to in the model are expected returns, while the beta

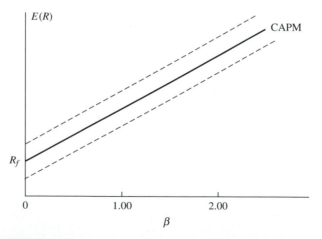

FIGURE 3-5
Capital asset pricing model—presence of market imperfections.

to which it refers is derived from expected covariances and expected variances of returns. This risk-return relationship is forward-looking rather than backward-looking and should embody investors' expectations. Ideally then, in testing the relationship one would like to have data on expected returns and expected beta values for individual securities or portfolios of securities. Expectations, however, are difficult to observe, especially with respect to the risk attributes of securities and portfolios of securities.

In testing the relationship, researchers have thus relied on realized, or historical data. The assumption here is that if enough observations are available in a test, investors' expectations will be aligned with realizations. That assumes that realizations will be representative of expectations. For example, researchers would derive returns over, say, the most recent ten-year period and assume that these realized values were representative of expectations over that period.

After obtaining returns, researchers calculate betas by regressing the returns of individual securities or groups of securities against the returns of some market index. This procedure is within the context of the single-index model that will be described in the latter part of this chapter. Once the betas have been calculated, they can be plotted against the return of individual securities or groups of securities. For this purpose the average return of the security or group of securities, realized over the period of the study, is taken as representative of the return-beta relationship.

Figure 3-6 is a risk-return diagram illustrating this for a hypothetical set of securities. Note that the figure shows the plots of the beta-return values for each of the securities as well as a line fitted to the plotted points. The equation for fitting the line to the plots is the following:

$$\text{Return} = \gamma_0 + \gamma_1 \beta + u \tag{9}$$

In testing the risk-return relationship, researchers are concerned with assessing how well this fitted line conforms to the theoretical CAPM. If the fitted line conforms perfectly with the theoretical, it should show the following characteristics. First, the line should be

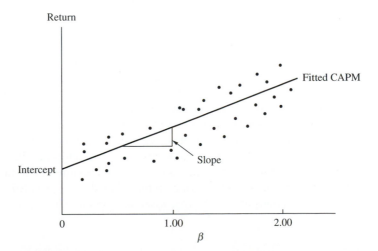

FIGURE 3-6
Empirically fitted capital asset pricing model.

upward-sloping, thereby verifying that securities or portfolios with higher systematic risk earned higher returns than those with lower risk, at least over longer periods of time. On average there should be a linear relationship between beta and return, verifying that other "nonsystematic" factors are not important in determining returns. Finally, the constant term, or intercept, in the equation (γ_0) would be expected to equal the risk-free rate (R_f). Correspondingly, the slope of the line (γ_1) would be expected to equal the average market-risk premium ($R_m - R_f$) during the period studied.

AMENDED CAPM

As there have been numerous tests of the CAPM (SML) relationship along the lines just described, discussion of the various techniques for testing and of the results of the tests would be interesting in itself. However, reporting such analyses and results would require considerable space and would not be appropriate to the intention of this book. For our purposes it is most useful to summarize and comment on the specific findings with regard to the three desired characteristics of the empirical CAPM just described. First, the anticipated positive risk-return relationship has generally been found to be upward-sloping when studied over longer periods of time. Over shorter intervals, however, the relationship was not necessarily upward-sloping. There were periods when the relationship was unclear as well as periods when it in fact sloped downward. That was generally the case during bear-market periods, when the realized risk premium in the market was negative even though a positive relationship is more likely to be realized over longer periods. At the same time, tests of the linearity of the relationship showed that factors other than risk were not important in explaining realized returns; the CAPM was in fact linear.

On the other hand, tests showed that the line did not intercept the vertical axis at the risk-free rate, thus indicating a potential deficiency in one of the main assumptions of the CAPM.[6] Specifically, the assumptions of the existence of a risk-free asset and of investors' ability to borrow and lend freely at that rate may not be a valid representation of the workings of the marketplace. Furthermore, casual observation suggests that those assumptions may be the most questionable ones used in the model.

To begin with, investors generally cannot borrow and lend at the same rate. Financial intermediaries charge a higher rate than the rate at which they lend; the spread incorporates a profit margin and a premium to compensate for the credit risks of the borrower. Borrowers thus pay a higher rate than they would receive for lending or investing funds.

Moreover, in an inflationary environment there is no such thing as a risk-free investment. Due to their certainty of outcome, Treasury bills have normally been cited as a reasonable proxy for a risk-free asset. These instruments are free of credit risk and, because of their short-term nature, are virtually free of interest rate risk. Treasury bills are in fact essentially riskless in nominal terms—but not in real terms. They are subject to the *purchasing power risk,* which becomes more severe as the rate of inflation becomes more intense.

Black, realizing this problem and observing empirical evidence, amended the CAPM to accommodate these violations of the risk-free asset assumption. His analysis indicated

---

[6]We should also note that the slope of the line has been shown to be flatter than it should be, implying that the realized risk premium for the market is lower than expected.

that it was possible to substitute for the risk-free asset an asset that he referred to as a *zero-beta* asset or portfolio. Such a portfolio is designed to have a return that has no correlation with the market. The amended CAPM has a structure similar to the original, but it has the zero-beta return (R_z) rather than the risk-free rate (R_f) in the equation:

$$E(R_i) = E(R_z) + \beta_i[E(R_m) - E(R_z)] \tag{10}$$

Figure 3-7 illustrates the amended CAPM (amended SML). Note that the intercept of the line, designated R_z, would be at a higher level than the risk-free rate, designated R_f.[7] The fact that the intercept is higher in the amended model also means that the line will slope less than with a risk-free asset. We would also expect the slope of the line to vary over time as the return on the zero-beta factor fluctuated. All this is, of course, more in line with the previously discussed empirical results, implying that the Black zero-beta model offers a better explanation of the risk-return relationship than the pure version of the CAPM.

Adjusting for Taxes

As noted at the outset, the simple form of the CAPM is derived ignoring the presence of taxes. The implication of this assumption is that investors are indifferent about whether the income they receive is in the form of capital gains or dividends and that all investors hold the same portfolio of risky assets. Taxes, however, are a fact of life, and, more importantly for pricing securities, capital gains are taxed in general at a lower rate than dividends. We might then expect that investors with different tax status would hold different portfolios of risky assets even when expectations about pretax returns for those portfolios were the same. Correspondingly, we would expect equilibrium prices for those assets to differ from what they would be if taxes did not matter.

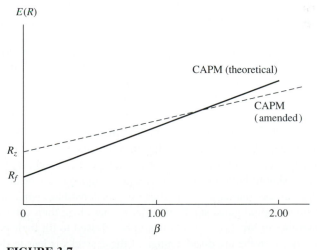

FIGURE 3-7
Capital asset pricing model, theoretical and amended.

---

[7]The zero-beta factor, while not correlated with the market, would be expected to have some variation associated with it, unlike a risk-free asset, which would have no variance.

Michael Brennan was the first researcher to formally consider the impact on capital asset prices of differential tax rates on capital gains and dividend income.[8] In developing a tax-adjusted model, Brennan made the usual assumptions used in deriving the simplified form of the CAPM but also assumed that dividend yields are certain. Allowing for the impact of differential taxes, the return on any asset or portfolio is given by the following tax-adjusted CAPM:

$$E(R_i) = R_f(1 - T) + \beta_i[E(R_m) - R_f - T(D_m - R_f)] + TD_i \qquad (11)$$

where $T = \dfrac{T_d - T_g}{1 - T_g}$

T_d = economywide average tax rate on dividends
T_g = economywide average tax rate on capital gains
D_m = dividend yield on market portfolio
D_i = dividend yield on the stock

Note in Brennan's model that if the tax rate on dividend income equals the tax rate on capital gains, the tax adjustment parameter $T = 0$, and this model reduces to the simple form of the CAPM. If there are differential taxes, expected return depends linearly on beta as in the simple form of the CAPM, but the market return must be adjusted for the impact of taxes on the dividend yield of the market portfolio. In addition, the expected pretax return of the security or portfolio becomes a function of a second variable: the dividend yield of the security or portfolio adjusted by the tax factor effect parameter T.

When dividend income is, on average, taxed at a higher rate than capital gains (as in the U.S. economy), the tax adjustment parameter T is positive, and expected pretax return is an increasing function of dividend yield. High-yield stocks would be expected to offer higher pretax returns than low-yield stocks of the same systematic risk. Correspondingly, the expected return will be higher as the differential tax rate between dividend income and capital gains is higher: the T parameter becomes larger as the tax differential increases. The fact that expected pretax return increases as dividend yield rises is intuitively appealing, because the larger the fraction of return paid in the form of dividends, the more taxes the investor will have to pay, and the larger the pretax return required.

If securities are priced according to the tax-augmented expression, it follows that investors should weight their portfolio holdings toward or away from dividend yield according to their tax bracket. That is, investors should still hold widely diversified portfolios that resemble the market portfolio, except that they will now be tilted in favor of those stocks in which the investor has a comparative advantage. For example, investors in high income tax brackets should hold a lesser percentage of high-yield stocks in their portfolio than the percentage of the market portfolio these stocks constitute, while they should hold more low-yield, high–capital gains stocks in order to maximize their after-tax return. Correspondingly, investors in low tax brackets would be advised to tilt their portfolios toward high-yield stocks, because the tax disadvantage of these stocks is less to them than it is to the average stockholder.

---

[8]Brennan, Michael: "Taxes, Market Valuation, and Corporate Financial Policy," *National Tax Journal* 25, 1970, pp. 417–427.

Such a *yield tilt* strategy may have some potential for increasing after-tax returns, but following such a strategy introduces a cost in terms of additional nonmarket risk. That is, a tilted portfolio will most likely have more nonmarket (residual) risk than a portfolio that is well diversified across all yield levels. For example, many high-yield stocks are those of regulated public utilities, and their prices tend to move together over and above common movements with the level of the overall stock market. Similarly, low-yield "growth" stocks also tend to move together. The investor thus needs to determine whether the potential additional return from following the yield tilt strategy is worth incurring the added nonmarket risk.

However, there is debate as to the magnitude or even the presence of a tax effect in the pricing of securities. The special tax status of certain institutional investors and the counterbalancing tax strategies available to investors tend to offset the impact of taxes on the return to investors, thus reducing the tax effect on the pricing of securities.[9]

Whether these counterbalancing forces are powerful enough to eliminate a tax effect is essentially an empirical question. Some studies by competent researchers indicate the existence of this effect, while other studies by equally competent researchers indicate no significant tax impact in the pricing of capital assets. Furthermore, even those studies that support the existence of a tax effect also show that the magnitude of the effect is rather limited in the pricing of stocks, perhaps on the order of 30 basis points per annum. Executing a yield tilt strategy would thus seem to depend primarily on the strength of the investor's personal conviction as to the presence of a tax factor.

Role of the Market Portfolio

While empirical results are generally consistent with some sort of risk-return trade-off in the marketplace, Richard Roll has directed some fundamental criticism at the relevance of these tests in affirming the CAPM as the appropriate model for describing this trade-off.[10] This criticism is aimed at one of the critical notions—the concept of a market portfolio—underlying CMT and the CAPM. Recall that the market portfolio is one that contains all the securities in the universe by their proper weights. This portfolio should, in turn, be an ex ante efficient portfolio—that is, it should offer the highest expected return at the expected risk level.

Researchers have generally taken it for granted that the market portfolio must be an efficient portfolio, but that assumption becomes the crux of Roll's analysis. To begin with, Roll demonstrates that choosing the incorrect portfolio or index as proxy for the market can lead to misestimates of the systematic risk of individual securities and portfolios and hence result in an inappropriate estimate of the CAPM. Roll notes that this misestimation error is not of the usual statistical sort but rather is a basic bias that cannot be corrected by the use of more powerful statistical tools. The error can only be avoided by properly identifying what the ex ante efficient market portfolio is.

---

[9]Miller, Merton, and Myron Scholes: "Dividends and Taxes," *Journal of Financial Economics,* December 1978, pp. 333–364.

[10]Richard Roll: "A Critique of the Asset Pricing Theory as Tests. Part I: On Past and Potential Testability of the Theory," *Journal of Financial Economics* (March 1977), pp. 129–176.

Roll indicates, however, that identifying this portfolio is a highly difficult if not in fact impossible task, because it requires some mechanism or ability to capture investor expectations. We noted before the difficulty of assessing expectations—much less appropriately putting them into a proper framework. As a result, Roll contends that empirical tests that have been conducted are not, in fact, tests of the CAPM. Furthermore, because of the virtual impossibility of identifying the ex ante efficient market portfolio, Roll contends that it is unlikely that CMT and the CAPM can be tested empirically.

The observation by Roll that no unambiguous test can be achieved because of the difficulty of identifying the market portfolio exactly is technically correct. However, it is not so clear that the criticism is of practical significance. To begin with, many empirical studies of the relationship over differing time frames that have in fact all virtually affirmed the risk-return relationship. Furthermore, even those studies that have used substantially different methodologies have also affirmed the relationship.

In view of this particular criticism, recent studies have attempted to assess the sensitivity of the relationship to the use of differing market indexes. These studies have constructed various indexes as market proxies using diverse asset classes, such as stocks, bonds, real estate, and durable goods, combined in varying proportions. We might note that these indexes, as is typical of almost any kind of broad index, are highly correlated to each other. The results of these tests using the various market proxies have been virtually the same, regardless of the market index, and in line with previous empirical studies that affirmed the risk-return relationship. From these initial tests it appears that misestimation of the market proxy may have limited practical significance. Investors can obtain usable estimates of market-risk parameters (betas) and gauge the risk-return relationship by using a generally representative market index, such as the S&P 500, or a more comprehensive one such as the Wilshire 5000.

THE SINGLE-INDEX MODEL

As we have seen, the CAPM is a simple yet elegant model that has profound implications for the general equilibrium of security prices. In this sense, despite its limitations, the CAPM has evoked great interest on the part of financial researchers assessing the behavior of market prices. As we have also seen, the CAPM can have practical use in providing a standard for security evaluation. Alternatively, it can provide a benchmark for assessing security pricing disequilibrium and, as such, a guideline to profitably selling and purchasing securities, as we will demonstrate later.

In addition to use as a benchmark for valuation, the CAPM has highly important implications with respect to portfolio analysis. By demonstrating that systematic risk is the critical component of risk for a security or portfolio, it emphasizes the need to focus on the appraisal of the level of systematic risk, or, alternatively, market risk, of a security or portfolio. Correspondingly, it indicates the relative "unimportance" of nonsystematic risk, because that component of risk can be diversified away in a portfolio. In highlighting only two components of risk to be considered, the model reduces the number of statistical inputs required and greatly simplifies the analysis of a portfolio of securities.

Although the CAPM has behavioral and practical implications, it needs to be converted into an empirically usable form for research and evaluation purposes. Fortunately, the *single-index model* is a reasonably direct analog of the security market line (SML) and is commonly used as a means of testing the CAPM as well as developing practical applications of the theoretical framework. The form of the two models is quite similar; the CAPM is expressed in terms of expected relationships—both risk and return—whereas the single-index model is a statistical model for representing a return-generating process.

The basic notion underlying the single-index model is that all stocks are affected by movements in the general market. When the general market index is rising strongly, stocks in general will tend to rise in response to this market movement. Conversely, when the general market index is falling precipitously, stocks in general will tend to decline accordingly. Furthermore, this general market movement or market factor is assumed to be the systematic force that acts on all stocks. Other effects are presumed to be specific or unique to the individual stock and diversified away in a portfolio.

We can best illustrate this co-movement of stocks with a market index by referring to the scatter diagram in Figure 3-8. The vertical coordinate represents the rate of return on the security or portfolio of interest. In this case we will use a portfolio called the OMEGA Fund to illustrate the relationship. The horizontal axis shows the rate of return for the S&P 500, which is used here to represent the return on the market portfolio.

In preparing the diagram, we first computed quarterly returns for the S&P 500 and the OMEGA Fund over the 1975–1993 period (72 returns). We then plotted these returns on the diagram as follows. If for example, during one quarter OMEGA earned a 10 percent return and the S&P 500 earned 7 percent, we would move up the vertical axis to 10 percent and across the horizontal axis to 7 percent and plot a point. All 72 returns were plotted in this way so that they lined up on the chart as shown in Figure 3-8.

The plots indicate a systematic relationship between the return on the OMEGA Fund and the return on the market. We described this relationship by fitting a line to these points, using the single-index model, also known as the market model. The model is a simple linear regression identifying return on a security, or portfolio in this case, as the dependent variable R_i, and the S&P 500 return R_m, representing the market, as the independent variable. It is expressed as

$$R_i = \alpha_i + \beta_i R_m + e_i \qquad (12)$$

The beta parameter β in the single-index model is the same as the slope of the fitted line in the scatter diagram in Figure 3-8. It measures the responsiveness of the security or fund to the general market and indicates how extensively the return of the portfolio or security will vary with changes in the market return.

In turn, the beta coefficient is defined as the ratio of the security's covariance of return with the market $[\text{Cov}(R_i R_m)]$ to the variance of the market $[\text{Var}(R_m)]$ and can be calculated as follows:

$$\beta_i = \frac{\text{Cov}(R_i R_m)}{\text{Var}(R_m)} = \frac{\rho_{im} S_i S_m}{S_m S_m} = \frac{\rho_{im} S_i}{S_m} \qquad (13)$$

In the instance shown in Figure 3-8, the portfolio had a standard deviation of 21 percent and the market a standard deviation of 18 percent over the eighteen-year period. At the same time, the correlation between the two returns was +0.94. The portfolio's beta can then be calculated with Equation (6):

$$\beta_p = \frac{(0.94)(21\%)}{18\%} = 1.10 \qquad (14)$$

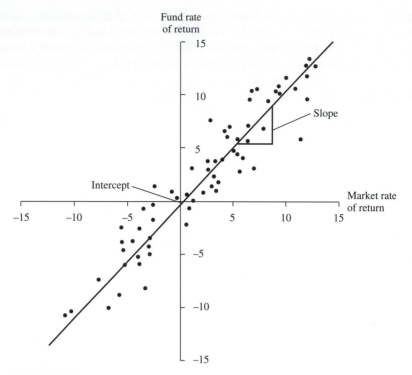

FIGURE 3-8

Scatter diagram for the single-index model. $R_f = \alpha + \beta R_m + e_i$ where R_f = fund return, R_m = S&P 500 return, and β = market sensitivity.

The calculated beta of 1.10 indicates that the fund is 10 percent more sensitive to the market than a fund with a beta of 1.00. For example, when the market goes up 10 percent, we can expect this fund to go up 11 percent, and when the market declines 10 percent, we can expect the fund to decline 11 percent.

The alpha parameter α is the intercept of the fitted line and indicates what the return of the security or portfolio would be when the market return is zero. For example, a security or portfolio with an alpha of +2 percent would earn 2 percent even when the market return was zero, and it would earn an additional 2 percent at all levels of market return. Conversely, a security or portfolio with an alpha of −2 percent would lose 2 percent when the market return is zero, and would earn 2 percent less at all levels of market return. The positive alpha thus represents a sort of bonus return and would be a highly desirable aspect of a portfolio or security, whereas a negative alpha represents a penalty to the investor and is an undesirable aspect of a portfolio or a security. In this case, the OMEGA Fund's intercept was virtually zero, indicating that the portfolio provided neither a bonus return nor a penalty for the investor. In the next chapter we will see more clearly the significance of the alpha value, and in Chapters 6, 7, and 8 we will discuss ways of estimating alphas for individual securities.

The final term in Equation (12), e, is the unexpected return resulting from influences not identified by the model. Frequently referred to as *random* or *residual* return, it may take on any value, but over a large number of observations it will average out to zero. It is further assumed that these residual returns are uncorrelated between securities; that is, once the market effect has been removed from the security, there should be no significant correlation between securities. In other words, this assumption means that the only systematic effect influencing returns on stocks or portfolios is a general market effect. It should be recognized that this is the underlying premise and procedure of the CAPM.

Measuring Risk and Return

Using the single-index model specification, we can express the expected return of an individual security as

$$E(R_i) = \alpha_i + \beta_i E(R_m) \tag{15}$$

The return of the security is thus a combination of two components: (1) a specific return component represented by the alpha of the security; and (2) a market-related return component represented by the term $\beta_i(E(R_m))$. The residual return disappears from the expression because its average value is zero; that is, it has an expected value of zero.

Correspondingly, the risk of the security $[\text{Var}(R_i)]$ becomes the sum of a market-related component and a component that is specific to the security, as illustrated by the following:

$$\text{Var}(R_i) = \beta^2 \text{Var}(R_m) + \text{Var}(e) \tag{16}$$

$$\text{Total risk} = \text{market-related} + \text{specific risk}$$

The market-related component of risk is sometimes referred to as *systematic risk,* as it is common to all securities. This risk systematically affects all securities. The specific risk component is also referred to as *diversifiable risk,* since it is unique to the security and can be reduced as securities are added to a portfolio.

In calculating risk and return of a portfolio we can use similar formulas and aggregate across the individual securities to measure those aspects of the portfolio. In particular, the expected return of the portfolio becomes a weighted average of the specific returns (alphas) of the individual securities plus a weighted average of the market-related returns $\beta_i E(R_m)$ of the individual securities. Defining $\alpha_p = \sum_{i=1}^{N} W_i \alpha_i$ as the portfolio alpha and $\beta_p = \sum_{i=1}^{N} W_i \beta_i$ as the portfolio beta, we can directly represent portfolio return as a portfolio alpha plus a portfolio beta times expected market return, as shown:

$$E(R_p) = \alpha_p + \beta_p E(R_m) \tag{17}$$

Because of the assumption that securities are related only through a common market effect, the risk of a portfolio is also simply a weighted average of the market-related risks of individual securities plus a weighted average of the specific risks of individual securities in the portfolio. Again using $\beta_p = \sum_{i=1}^{N} W_i \beta_i$ to represent the portfolio beta, we can express portfolio risk as

$$\text{Var}(R_p) = \beta_p^2 \text{Var}(R_m) + \sum_{i=1}^{N} W_i^2 \text{Var}(e_i) \tag{18}$$

Note that the diversifiable risk component W_i^2 will become smaller as securities are added to the portfolio. This is because, according to the single-index model, these risks are uncorrelated. The reduction thus becomes similar to the example in Table 2-4, which illustrates how variance is reduced when securities are uncorrelated and have equal weight in a portfolio. The effect would be the same in this case, except that we are dealing with one component, diversifiable risk, rather than total risk. The market-related component in this case

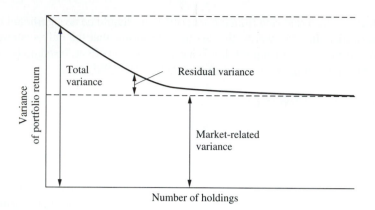

FIGURE 3-9
Single-index model and the market-related and residual risk
components of total risk.

would remain unaffected by the addition of extra securities, because systematic risk is the
component that cannot be reduced by diversification. Figure 3-9 illustrates this, again within
the context of the single-index model.

Applying the Single-Index Model

Table 3-4 illustrates use of the single-index model to calculate expected return and variance
for a hypothetical portfolio of four securities: (1) Merck, a drug company, to represent a
rapid-growth security; (2) Bethlehem Steel, to represent a cyclically oriented security; (3)
Kellogg, a food company, to represent a stable type of security; and (4) Chevron, to represent an energy-oriented security. The table shows the weighting of these companies in
the hypothetical portfolio; the weights sum to 1.00 to represent a portfolio fully invested in
stocks. It also shows basic input data: alphas, betas, and residual variances for calculating
portfolio return and variance.

The upper formulation in the table illustrates calculation of the portfolio return. Note
that we have set the alpha values of the individual stocks at zero, as we are assuming no
special information regarding the relative attractiveness of the individual stocks. (In Chapter 8 we will discuss explicit ways of estimating alpha values for stocks.) In this case the
weighted average alpha of the portfolio is simply zero. The betas of the individual stocks
have been estimated with historical data, and the projected market return is 11 percent, a
reasonable approximation of the consensus of expectations at the end of 1993. The weighted
average beta of the portfolio is 1.02, and using the projected market return of 11 percent results in a market-related return of 11.2 percent. With an expected alpha of zero, the expected
return of the portfolio is entirely market-related and is also projected at 11.2 percent.

The lower formulation in the table illustrates calculation of the portfolio variance.
Since the standard deviation of the market over the 1975–1993 period was 18 percent (or,
alternatively, its variance was 324 percent^2), we will assume that this historical figure is
appropriate for projection into the future. The specific risk estimates for each of the stocks
are also historically derived. The bottom line shows the market-related risk calculated from
the weighted portfolio beta and the projected market variance, along with the weighted average of the specific risk of the individual stocks. Note that the specific risk of the portfolio

TABLE 3-4
Portfolio risk and return, single-index model

Security	Weighting	a$_i$	B$_i$	Var(e)
Merck	0.25	0	1.20	446^2
Bethlehem Steel	0.25	0	1.09	653
Kellogg	0.25	0	0.89	579
Chevron	0.25	0	0.89	310
Portfolio value	1.00	0	1.02	124^2

1. $E(R_p) = \alpha_p + \beta_p + E(R_m)$

$\qquad = 0 + 1.02(11\%)$

$\qquad = 11.2\%$

2. $Var(R_p) = \beta_p^2 Var(R_m) + \sum_{i=1}^{n} W_i^2 Var(e)$

$\qquad = (1.02)^2(324) + 124\%$

$\qquad = 337\%^2 + 124\%^2$

$\qquad = 461\%^2$

Source: Terry Jenkins, I.T.S. Associates, Inc., Cambridge, Mass.

is less than that of any of the individual stocks. This is, of course, consistent with the single-index model's assumption of being able to diversify specific risk by adding securities to the portfolio.

Analyzing Portfolio Risk and Return

Index models provide particularly useful insights into analyzing the risk-return characteristics of a portfolio, because they allow one to categorize the sources of risk and return into individual, identifiable components. According to the single-index model, the components of return can be considered as (1) market-related and (2) security-specific. Correspondingly, there are risks associated with each of these return components, and again according to the single-index model, we determine that (1) the beta coefficient β_m is a general measure of exposure to market risk; (2) the residual risk Var(e) measures the uncertainty of earning the specific return.

Since the general market effect is a predominant source of return and risk for a portfolio, managers should be concerned with monitoring the exposure of the portfolio to this source of risk. Portfolio managers need to determine whether the portfolio positioning is consistent with longer-run policy targets or is appropriate for current market conditions. For example, if the outlook for the market were judged to be especially favorable, the manager might well desire to take advantage of this by raising the portfolio beta above its current level. Conversely, if the forecast were for a declining market, the appropriate strategy would be to lower the beta from its current level. Finally, if the manager were uncertain of the direction of the market and wished to hedge against this uncertainty, then the appropriate strategy would be to keep the portfolio beta in line with the market beta of 1.00 and maintain a neutral posture toward the market. (We will have more to say about this in Chapters 8 and 9.)

Finally, the single-index model indicates that the measure of security-specific return is the alpha value and that this is desirable when positive and undesirable when negative. Correspondingly, the measure of the uncertainty associated with earning the specific return is the variance of the residual; this will be large when the portfolio is poorly diversified and small when the portfolio is well-diversified. Portfolio managers should therefore endeavor to construct the portfolio in such a way that the resulting alpha is positive and large, but they should also be aware of the amount of residual risk that is incurred in constructing such a portfolio. The lower the nonmarket risk, the greater the certainty of attaining the positive alpha; the greater the nonmarket risk, the lower the certainty of attaining the positive alpha.

As a result, the goal should be to construct a portfolio with a high positive alpha while minimizing nonmarket risk, so as to develop a portfolio with high alpha per unit of risk. Portfolio optimization techniques, in fact, provide a way of formally determining from a security universe the combination and weighting of securities that provide the portfolio with optimal risk-return characteristics. We will describe the inputs needed to apply these techniques and outline the general method of generating such optimal portfolios in the next chapter.

Applied Portfolio Analysis

Meanwhile, by way of actual practical illustration, we can gain perspective on how this sort of analytical model helps investment managers align portfolio characteristics to conform to investment objectives. In this regard, we should note that one of the requirements that systematic investment management has introduced and emphasized in the development of portfolio strategies is the need to express investment objectives in terms of explicit risk and return parameters. Furthermore, it is usual practice to express these objectives with respect to a comparison benchmark. Obviously, the choice of an appropriate benchmark becomes an important consideration. Correspondingly, the benchmark becomes the direct means or standard of evaluating success in meeting the investment objective.

To illustrate this method of portfolio analysis by way of actual practice, we display in Table 3-5 a set of objectives and control parameters for an equity portfolio strategy that emphasizes adding incremental return within the context of below-average risk and is executed with success by a systematic investment manager over a period of years. The S&P 500 index is the benchmark, with the return objective of meeting or exceeding the S&P 500 return by 2 percent along with above-average consistency over time. In addition, the manager does not wish to assume market timing risk, so the portfolio beta is controlled in a range from 0.95 to 1.05 to be in line with that of the market.

TABLE 3-5
Investment strategy objectives

Portfolio risk control parameters	
Investment objective:	Outperform with consistency
Benchmark:	S&P 500 Index
Expected excess return:	2%
Cash position	Limit 10%
Market risk (beta) target:	0.95–1.05
Residual risk target:	Less than 5.0%

Correspondingly, the objective for portfolio residual risk is low with a target standard error of 5.0% or less. Also, referred to as *tracking error,* a low standard error helps ensure that the portfolio will move in line with (track) the benchmark S&P 500 index.

Table 3-6 shows a listing of individual common stocks along with other relevant attributes for a portfolio constructed to meet the investment performance objectives just outlined. Note that the stocks are listed alphabetically for convenience of illustration, but other categorizations provide more perspective, as we will see later. The 68 stocks listed are regarded as major stocks that are representative of the S&P 500 and may be thought of as a subset of that index. The table also shows the portfolio weighting of each of the stocks, with the weights by individual stock ranging between 0.7 percent and 2 percent. There is relatively little concentration by individual issue. These individual stock weightings aggregate to a total of 98 percent, indicating a fully invested equity portfolio, as shown at the bottom of the table. Cash, representing a negligible 2 percent, provides transaction flexibility.

Note that the table also shows the betas of the individual stocks, to provide a measure of market risk for each of the stocks. These betas are designated as "fundamental" betas to indicate a specialized approach for deriving this measure. We will explain the meaning and importance of this measure in the next section of this chapter. Using the individual stock weightings and these beta values, we can simply create a weighted average beta to represent the portfolio beta. Note that the portfolio beta aggregates to 1.05, again as shown at the bottom of the table. This, of course, is in line with the objective of controlling market risk with a value in line with that of the S&P 500.

In a similar fashion we can develop an alpha value for the portfolio, by simply taking a weighted average of the individual alpha values for each of the stocks shown on the table. The alpha values shown on the table for each of the stocks are "forecast" alphas as opposed to alphas developed from a historical regression procedure. We will illustrate the process for developing these alphas along with its importance in Chapter 8. Note that the weighted average alpha (portfolio alpha) is 4 percent and exceeds the performance target of 2 percent.

At the same time, note that the residual standard error of the portfolio is 3.7 percent and is within the control parameter of 5.0 percent that was indicated at the start as a guideline. Again, due to the single-index model assumption of uncorrelated individual stock residuals, we can obtain this value for the portfolio as simply a weighted average of the standard errors of the individual stocks (these standard errors are not shown on the table). With a total of 68 stocks and showing relatively equivalent weighting across the portfolio, it is not surprising that the standard error is relatively small. As a matter of comparison, the standard error of this portfolio is less than 10 percent of that for our four-stock example portfolio in Table 3-4. This relatively small standard error in turn offers greater confidence that the portfolio alpha will be realized over time. Empirically, an alpha-to-standard-error ratio exceeding 0.5 is a strong indicator of performance; in this case, the ratio is 1.33.

On balance, this portfolio meets the performance objective and the control parameter established as part of the strategy. Presuming that the expected return for the S&P 500 was 11 percent, we would expect this portfolio to generate a return of 13 percent (11 percent market return plus 2 percent plus alpha) on average over time. At the same time, we would expect the portfolio to track the performance of the S&P 500 with a relatively small error. The portfolio market risk is in line with the S&P 500, and the standard error is relatively

TABLE 3-6
Portfolio risk-return structure

Stock	Portfolio weighting	Forecast alpha	Fundamental beta
1. AlliedSignal Inc.	1.38	3.7	1.02
2. Armstrong World Inds.	1.20	4.8	1.18
3. Ashland Oil Inc.	1.43	6.9	0.87
4. Barnett Bks Inc.	1.02	7.3	1.25
5. Bristol Myers Squibb Corp.	1.59	2.1	0.93
6. Cabletron Sys. Inc.	1.21	2.4	1.26
7. Capital Cities ABC Inc.	1.66	3.3	1.04
8. Caterpillar Inc. Del.	1.50	4.6	1.22
9. CBS Inc.	1.07	5.2	1.03
10. Chrysler Corp.	1.57	7.1	1.08
11. CMS Energy Corp.	1.44	8.6	0.51
12. Coastal Corp.	1.41	2.5	0.78
13. Colgate Palmolive Co.	1.66	3.6	1.02
14. Columbia Gas System	1.39	4.1	0.62
15. Compaq Computer Corp.	1.38	5.3	1.46
16. Computer Assoc. Intl.	1.88	1.8	1.39
17. Dana Corp.	1.28	7.4	1.08
18. Deere & Co.	0.82	2.3	0.76
19. Eaton Corp.	1.49	4.3	1.11
20. Equifax Inc.	1.78	8.2	0.93
21. Federal Express Corp.	1.14	2.7	1.29
22. Federal Natl. Mtg. Assn.	1.52	3.5	1.24
23. First Chicago Corp.	1.56	1.5	1.26
24. First UN Corp.	1.36	6.3	1.02
25. Ford Mtr. Co. Del.	1.64	1.2	0.99
26. Gap Inc. Del.	1.06	6.2	1.22
27. General Mtrs. Corp. CL H	1.07	5.1	0.74
28. Goodyear Tire & Rubber	1.29	4.5	1.17
29. Harris Corp. Del.	2.06	1.1	1.29
30. Hercules Inc.	1.80	3.3	1.15
31. IBP Inc.	1.63	2.2	0.87
32. Illinova Corp.	1.24	4.3	0.55
33. Intel Corp.	1.64	5.2	1.37
34. International Bus. Mach.	1.60	5.5	1.01
35. ITT Corp.	1.46	4.1	1.03
36. Johnson & Johnson	1.62	3.7	1.10

low. Correspondingly, we would expect incremental performance—positive alpha—to be delivered with relative consistency.

FUNDAMENTAL ATTRIBUTES

In addition to evaluating the market risk exposure of the portfolio as measured by beta, many managers desire to evaluate the portfolio with respect to fundamental attributes. Some of the commonly used attributes include *P/E* ratio, price-to-book-value ratio, earnings growth rate, dividend yield, and market capitalization. These are the sort of variables that managers

TABLE 3-6
(continued)

Stock	Portfolio weighting	Forecast alpha	Fundamental beta
37. Keycorp New	1.35	2.1	1.02
38. Kroger Co.	1.62	3.5	1.26
39. Lockheed Corp. Del.	1.67	4.1	0.74
40. Loral Corp.	1.67	5.6	0.80
41. Louisiana Pac. Corp.	1.47	6.6	1.19
42. Mallinckrodt Group Inc.	1.13	5.7	1.08
43. Maytag Corp.	1.41	1.3	1.26
44. MBNA Corp.	1.49	3.7	1.13
45. McDonnell Douglas Corp.	1.81	2.1	0.72
46. Mead Corp.	1.63	1.1	1.15
47. Micron Technology Inc.	1.37	0.9	1.57
48. Midwest Res. Inc.	1.18	6.2	0.31
49. Monsanto Co.	1.93	0.8	1.15
50. Morton Intl. Inc.	1.52	5.6	1.06
51. Paccar Inc.	1.09	2.1	1.12
52. Phelps Dodge Corp.	1.54	2.5	1.03
53. Philip Morris Cos. Inc.	1.86	6.1	0.90
54. Phillips Petr. Co.	1.55	4.7	0.83
55. Procter & Gamble Co.	1.65	1.7	1.02
56. Reebok Intl. Ltd.	1.65	6.6	1.53
57. Rohm & Haas Co.	1.47	5.3	1.21
58. Safeway Inc.	1.76	4.0	1.29
59. Schering Plough Corp.	1.96	3.8	1.12
60. Shawmut Natl. Corp.	0.96	2.7	1.15
61. Signet Bkg. Corp.	1.56	4.6	1.39
62. Sprint Corp.	1.69	2.2	0.81
63. Tenneco Inc. New	1.38	5.1	0.83
64. Texas Instrs. Inc.	1.13	6.7	1.40
65. U.S. Healthcare Inc.	1.76	4.4	1.32
66. Unocal Corp.	1.07	3.5	0.79
67. Whirlpool Corp.	1.09	6.1	1.32
68. Worthington Inds. Inc.	1.70	1.1	1.02
Cash	2%	—	0
	100%	4.0%	1.05

Standard error: 3.7%

consider when appraising the return potential and riskiness of an individual stock, so it is natural to view the overall portfolio in this context. Also, these represent the kinds of descriptor variables that investors use to characterize portfolio managers as to whether they are oriented toward large-capitalization or small-capitalization stock investing, or whether they are growth stock or "value" stock investors.

Just as with the portfolio beta, we can use the same cross-sectional approach to calculate the portfolio measure for the fundamental attribute of interest. One way to assess the growth positioning of a portfolio is to calculate a weighted average of the projected five-year growth rates for companies in the portfolio and compare that to the weighted average growth rate of companies in the index as a measure of exposure relative to the benchmark average. Correspondingly, value is commonly considered to be the complement of growth, because high growth is usually accompanied by higher valuation, whereas low growth is usually accompanied by lower valuation. In addition, many investors compare the weighted *P/E* of the portfolio to that of the benchmark as a way of assessing the valuation positioning of the portfolio.

Table 3-7 illustrates the exposure of the stock portfolio to the attributes of growth and value by comparing the distribution of its weightings in five distinct growth rate and *P/E*

TABLE 3-7
Equity sector analysis

U.S. target fund	Number of assets	Market value	Percent of total	Percent of S&P 500	Percent difference from S&P 500
Beta sectors:					
1. 0.0–0.9	16	2,436,450.00	22.46	32.61	−10.15
2. 0.9–1.1	19	3,125,182.25	28.81	28.68	0.13
3. 1.1–1.3	24	3,826,442.45	35.27	28.67	6.61
4. 1.3–1.5	7	1,132,491.70	10.44	8.34	2.10
5. Above 1.5	2	327,100.00	3.02	1.69	1.32
	68	10,847,666.40	100.00	100.00	
Yield sectors:					
1. Above 8.0	1	128,537.50	1.18	1.18	0.00
2. 5.0–8.0	3	508,587.50	4.69	12.64	−7.95
3. 3.0–5.0	16	2,428,012.50	22.38	27.35	−4.97
4. 0.0–3.0	42	6,860,572.65	63.24	52.57	10.67
5. 0.0	6	921,956.25	8.50	6.25	2.24
	68	10,847,666.40	100.00	100.00	
Growth sectors:					
1. 0.0–8.0	8	1,320,537.50	12.17	16.48	−4.31
2. 8.0–12.0	29	4,384,368.45	40.42	42.65	−2.23
3. 12.0–16.0	23	3,930,300.00	36.23	27.78	8.45
4. 16.0–20.0	7	1,081,491.70	9.97	10.01	−0.04
5. Above 20.0	1	130,968.75	1.21	3.08	−1.87
	68	10,847,666.40	100.00	100.00	
P/E sectors:					
1. 0.0–8.0	4	668,362.50	6.16	3.63	2.53
2. 8.0–12.0	21	3,032,298.70	27.95	12.00	15.95
3. 12.0–16.0	22	3,687,800.00	34.00	24.07	9.93
4. Above 16.0	21	3,459,205.20	31.89	53.86	−21.98
5. N/A	0	0.00	0.00	6.44	−6.44
	68	10,847,666.40	100.00	100.00	
Capitalization sectors:					
1. Above 5.0 ($bil)	28	4,654,129.20	42.90	77.67	−34.76
2. 1.0–5.0	39	6,064,999.70	55.91	21.16	34.75
3. 0.5–1.0	1	128,537.50	1.18	1.00	0.19
4. 0.1–0.5	0	0.00	0.00	0.18	−0.18
5. 0.0–0.1	0	0.00	0.00	0.00	0.00
	68	10,847,666.40	100.00	100.00	

segments to that of the benchmark S&P 500 index. Note that the portfolio is weighted relative to the index in the lower two segments of growth but is overweighted in stocks growing at 12 percent or better. Correspondingly, the portfolio is underweighted in the two highest *P/E* brackets but overweighted in the lower three brackets. The portfolio is showing a somewhat anomalous configuration of exposure to high growth despite a below-average *P/E*, which may be indicative of success in purchasing above-average growth at a reasonable valuation.

The table also shows how the distribution of the portfolio beta differs from the S&P 500, with a heavier concentration in above-median-beta stocks than the S&P 500 and a lesser proportion in the lowest-beta (0.0–0.9) bracket. At the same time, the portfolio is underweighted relative to the S&P 500 in the two above-average dividend yield brackets. With an average yield that is less than that of the S&P 500, the portfolio will be subject to risk from changing interest rates: Higher yield helps buffer volatility deriving from interest rate changes, as we demonstrate analytically in later chapters. This relatively greater interest rate sensitivity of the portfolio is, in turn, reflected in the somewhat above-average beta for the portfolio.

Finally, note from the table showing the market capitalization distribution that the portfolio is positioned almost entirely in the two highest market capitalization brackets with virtually no representation, either absolutely or relative to S&P 500, in the lower three brackets. At the same time, the portfolio shows a below-average exposure in the highest market capitalization bracket, resulting in an overall below-average capitalization size relative to the S&P 500 average. This below-average capitalization size, however, derives from the essentially equal weighting of individual holdings in the portfolio, as opposed to a weighting in proportion to capitalization. In comparison, the capitalization weighting scheme for the S&P 500 results in a preponderance of very large companies dominating the index. Generally, the top 50 companies in the S&P 500 represent approximately 50 percent of the weighting; so that 10 percent of the companies by number represent about 50 percent of the value weight.

Table 3-8 shows some additional measures of market capitalization that provide alternative perspective on the relative positioning of the portfolio. Note that the dollar-weighted and arithmetic averages for the portfolio are almost the same (9.5 billion versus 9.05 billion), whereas the dollar-weighted average of $21.8 billion is considerably greater than the arithmetic average of $6.7 billion for the S&P 500. Correspondingly, the market value for the median company in the portfolio exceeds that of the S&P 500, as does the arithmetic average for the portfolio ($9.05 billion versus $6.7 billion for the S&P 500). From these data, we might deduce that the portfolio will be representative of the performance of a select group of large-capitalization stocks, whereas the S&P 500 Index indicates changes in the aggregate market value of stocks represented by the index.

TABLE 3-8

	U. S. Target Fund	S&P 500
Dollar-weighted average	9.5	21.79
Market cap, arithmetic average	9.05	6.71
Market cap, median	4.32	3.56
Smallest stock	1.45	0.06
Largest stock held	53.26	84.72

Measuring Beta

It should be apparent from the preceding discussion that beta is a critically important concept. We have seen that it is the fundamental measure of risk as derived from the Security Market Line (SML) or CAPM of the CMT. Correspondingly, it is a critical element of the single-index model. For assessing risk, determining the risk-return trade-off, conducting a portfolio analysis, and many other practical applications, properly measuring the beta of individual securities and portfolios is essential.

Although estimating betas using the single-index model framework is straightforward, there are alternative ways of treating the input, and these variations can lead to significant differences in calculated betas. Choice of a market proxy is a major consideration; many use the S&P 500, but others can justifiably use proxies such as the Wilshire 5000, NYSE Index, or the Russell 3000. In addition, there can be differences in the period over which the calculations are made. While many use a five-year period for the analysis, others will use longer or shorter periods with justification. Other portfolio managers require the period of analysis to span two market cycles, to encompass two periods of rising and falling markets, and call this a market cycle beta. Finally, the interval of measurement can differ; some opt to use daily data to help increase the precision of measurement, rather than the more commonly used monthly or quarterly data.

A more serious problem in developing estimates of beta is that of measurement error. We noted in an earlier section that the market factor generally accounts for less than one-half the risk of a stock, generally averaging around 25% of the total. As a result, there can be substantial overestimation as well as underestimation of the betas of individual securities, a phenomenon that has been noted often in practice. It is important to recognize that this is less of a problem in a portfolio, where errors of overestimation for some stocks tend to be offset by errors of underestimation for other stocks.

Financial researchers, along with some commercial services that provide betas for securities, employ statistical adjustment techniques to compensate for errors in estimating the individual security betas. The general concept is that there is a tendency to overestimate the betas of high-beta stocks and to underestimate the betas of low-beta stocks. In subsequent periods we would observe a tendency of betas of securities to regress toward a mean of 1.0, the average of all securities. That is, high-beta stocks would tend to show a lower beta in a subsequent period, and low-beta stocks would show a higher beta in the subsequent period. One particularly simple yet practicable formula used by Merrill Lynch to adjust betas for measurement error is the following:

$$\beta_a = 0.66\beta_h + 0.34\beta_m \qquad (18)$$

This equation simply indicates that the adjusted beta of a stock (β_a) is a weighted average of its historically measured beta (β_h) and an adjustment factor that moves the adjusted beta toward the average beta (β_m) of the market. The empirically derived weighting, two-thirds to the historically measured beta and one-third to the average beta, provides an adjustment that has been shown to reduce estimation error in subsequently observed betas. Table 3-9 gives an example of the sort of adjustment to beta of some selected securities.

Fundamental Beta

Correspondingly, measured betas have shown instability over time, both at the individual security level and the portfolio level, with some degree of frequency. Betas calculated over

TABLE 3-9
Adjusted betas

Stock	Historic beta	Adjusted beta	Beta change
1. Texas Instruments	1.66	1.43	−0.23
2. Compaq	1.45	1.29	−0.16
3. Fannie Mae	1.38	1.24	−0.14
4. Caterpillar	1.28	1.17	−0.11
5. GM	1.22	1.14	−0.08
6. IBM	1.07	1.04	−0.03
7. International Paper	0.99	0.99	—
8. Procter & Gamble	0.93	0.94	0.01
9. GTE	0.84	0.88	0.04
10. Hershey	0.81	0.86	0.05
11. Bristol-Myers	0.80	0.86	0.06
12. FPL	0.78	0.84	0.06
13. Exxon	0.72	0.81	0.09

one historic period, using whatever variety of statistical approaches, often show a significant difference in a subsequent period. Instability of betas over time should not be surprising; as a matter of fact, we should expect at least some changes in betas for individual securities. Companies go through stages of growth and maturity; some change their financial policies significantly, and others pursue differing business diversification strategies. All or any of these or other changes should lead to shifts in the risk posture of the company and, hence, be reflected in a changing beta.

An approach that has conceptual appeal and has met with success is to introduce fundamental variables into the process of determining betas for individual securities. For example, companies paying high dividends and providing relatively high dividend yields would be expected to be less risky than low-dividend-yield firms. Correspondingly, firms with high debt-to-equity ratios—highly leveraged firms—would be expected to be more risky than firms with low debt in the financial structure. Firms with a highly liquid balance sheet would be expected to be less risky than firms with a low-liquidity position. Finally, those companies with high operating leverage, and subject to large earnings variability, would be viewed as more risky than firms with a stable earnings pattern.

In addition, it would be expected that the economic sector would have an impact on the level of riskiness of a firm, as illustrated by the data in Table 3-10. This data shows a classifi-

TABLE 3-10
Risk of major stock groupings

Group	Beta
Growth	1.24
Cyclical	1.11
Stable	0.90
Energy (oil)	0.85

Source: Farrell, James L., Jr.: "Analyzing Covariation of Return to Determine Homogeneous Stock Groupings," *Journal of Business,* April 1974, pp. 186–205.

cation of stocks into four broad market sectors—growth, cyclical, stable, and energy—along with the calculated beta for each of the sectors. Note that the growth and cyclical sectors show above-average betas, and we might expect that an individual company within either classification would also exhibit an above-average beta. On the other hand, we would expect that companies within either the stable or energy category would show a below-average beta, in line with that of the category.

In addition, the industry classification of a company should have a bearing on the beta characteristic of the stock of that company. For example, the air transport and electronics industries are high-risk by nature, and measured betas for these industries generally range from 1.50 to as high as 2.00. Conversely, the electric utility industry, which has low risk characteristics, generally shows measured betas closer to 0.5. Knowledge that a company is in the air transport or electronics industry would predispose one to estimate that its beta is in the 1.5–2.0 range, whereas a company in the electric utility industry would be preconditioned to have a beta closer to 0.5.

Using this approach to adjust the beta, we combine the historical beta with the fundamental characteristics of a company as well as its classification with respect to industry and sector affiliation. We can use an equation of the following generalized form to generate an adjusted beta (β_a) for individual stocks:

$$\beta_a = a + \beta_h + cI + d_1E + d_2Q + d_3Y + d_4L \tag{19}$$

This equation illustrates that the beta of the security (β_a) is a function of the historic beta (β_h) adjusted by its industry affiliation (I) and other fundamental determinants, including earnings stability/instability (E), financial leverage (Q), dividend yield (Y), and balance sheet liquidity (L). For example, a company in a less risky industry would have its beta adjusted down, whereas participation in a higher-risk industry would result in an upward adjustment. Companies with high earnings stability, low debt/equity ratios, high dividend yield, and high liquidity would experience a downward adjustment to beta. Those companies with unstable earnings, high debt, low dividend yield, and low liquidity would have upward-adjusted betas.

The previously described equation is a very general description of a model first proposed and tested by Barr Rosenberg and used commercially by BARRA, a consulting firm, to generate "fundamental" beta estimates. The actual model used by BARRA is much more elaborate in detail, consisting of some 101 elements, referred to as fundamental descriptors, with regular parameter updating, using a generalized least-squares version of multiple-regression analysis. Assessing which beta model is best awaits more definitive tests, but results to date indicate that the BARRA model offers an improvement over many alternative beta estimation procedures. As a result of both test results and conceptual appeal, betas generated by this process have gained relatively widespread acceptance as reliable inputs for purposes of portfolio analysis.

Forecast Betas

In prior sections we have shown how the market model can be used as a practical means of estimating betas for use as indicators of systematic risk, as well as market risk measures for purposes of portfolio analysis. We have also described how differing statistical techniques can be used to refine basic market data or, in combination with fundamental data, to refine estimates of beta for improved measures of that critical measure of risk. We should also note that for each of the approaches described, the reliance has been historic data, market, fundamental, or a combination of these. The result is a historically derived beta, but for those using fundamental data or refined statistical techniques, the estimated beta is an improved measure.

It is useful, however, to attempt to generate forecasts of beta as a measure of risk, just as organizations typically attempt to generate forecasts of returns for securities. As noted, we observe and expect some instability of betas for securities, because the underlying riskiness of the company changes over time on a cyclical or secular basis for a variety of reasons. Properly anticipating such changes provides the basis for generating superior risk measures, but also allows opportunities for return enhancement.

Figure 3-10 reproduces a security market line to help illustrate how return opportunities can arise from anticipating changes in the riskiness of securities. The chart shows two hypothetical stocks differing in risk, as measured by current betas of 1.00 for stock M and 1.20 for stock N. Each offers return in line with its risk and thus plots on the market line, similar to the situation shown previously in Figure 3-4, which illustrated stocks offering fair value.

The riskiness of each stock is projected to change in the direction illustrated by the dashed lines in Figure 3-10. In the case of stock M, we project that the riskiness will increase in the future from the current historically measured level of 1.00 to the 1.20 level in the future. Correspondingly, we project that the riskiness of stock N will decrease from its current above-average level of 1.20 to an average level of 1.00 in the future.

With a change in riskiness, we anticipate, in keeping with the framework of the SML, that the expected return of each stock should change as well. In the case of stock M, investors

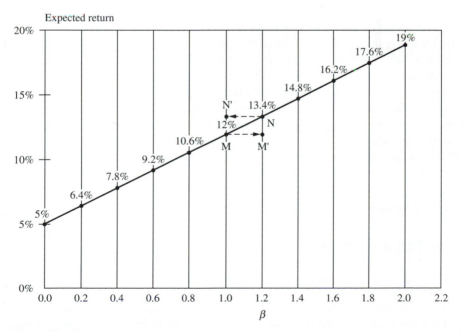

FIGURE 3-10
Forecasting betas.

should expect to earn 13.4% in the future, compared to 12.0% currently expected, while the opposite should occur with regard to stock N, whose investors would expect to earn 12% rather the current 13.4%. As a process of adjusting to these new expected risk-return levels, stock M should undergo a period of underperformance to correct a situation of overvaluation with respect to its new risk level. Conversely, stock N should exhibit overperformance to correct its undervaluation at the projected risk level.

The process of stock price adjustment is thus analogous to that illustrated previously, differing in that the situation of disequilibrium arises from a predicted change in riskiness, rather than anticipation of below- or above-average returns at a given risk level. Just as in forecasting stock returns, forecast of risk (beta) requires a model as well as analytical input. Unlike models for returns, however, there has been relatively little developmental effort in determining a practically usable model for forecasting, and correspondingly little analytical experience in developing risk estimates. There is, however, significant opportunity to add value in an investment process by a complementary effort to forecast risk as well as return.

CONCLUSION

General equilibrium theory such as the CMT, along with models like the CML, SML, and CAPM, not only allow improved understanding of market behavior, but also provide practical benefits. First, such models focus investor attention on the importance of systematic risk (market risk) and the need to control that important risk element; correspondingly, they emphasize the need to monitor the valuation of the overall market. Second, they stress that there is a relationship between risk and return and provide an operational framework for this in terms of the SML or CAPM. Investors should be aware that seeking only high return is not sufficient, that risk needs to be considered as well. Finally, the SML/CAPM provides a benchmark for the evaluation of the relative attractiveness of securities. Correspondingly, the SML/CAPM can provide a standard for evaluating manager performance, because it provides an explicit framework for determining risk-adjusted performance.

Furthermore, we have seen that the single-index model provides a simple yet illuminating empirical model for taking advantage of the insights of the SML. Use of an index model such as the single index allows a focus on the critical aspects of a portfolio and, as we will see later, provides a practical mechanism for evaluating performance in a risk-adjusted mode. This model thus provides the initial basis for the practical implementation of the many aspects of portfolio analysis. In turn, it also provides the foundation for the development of even more illuminating index models, which will be described in the next chapter.

SELECTED REFERENCES

Black, Fischer: "Capital Market Equilibrium with Restricted Borrowing," *Journal of Business,* July 1972, pp. 444–455.

Black, Fischer, Michael C. Jensen, and Myron Scholes: "The Capital Asset Pricing Model: Some Empirical Tests," in Michael C. Jensen (ed.), *Studies in the Theory of Capital Markets,* Praeger, New York, 1972.

Breeden, D.T.: "An Intertemporal Asset Pricing Model with Stochastic Consumption and Investment Opportunities," *Journal of Financial Economics* 7, 1979, pp. 265–269.

———: "Consumption, Production, and Interest Rates: A Synthesis," *Journal of Financial Economics* 16, 1986, pp. 3–39.

Callahan, Carolyn, and Rosanne Mohrs: "The Determinants of Systematic Risk: A Synthesis," *The Financial Review,* May 1989, pp. 157–182.

Chan, Louis, and Josef Lakonishok: "Are the Reports of Beta's Death Premature?" *Journal of Portfolio Management,* Summer 1993, pp. 51–62.

Chance, Don: "Empirical Estimates of Equivalent Risk Classes and the Effect of Financial Leverage on Systematic Risk," *The Financial Review,* Fall 1981, pp. 12–29.

Elton, Edwin J., and Martin J. Gruber: "Estimating the Dependence Structure of Share Prices— Implications for Portfolio Selection," *Journal of Finance,* December 1973, pp. 1203–1232.

Evans, John L., and Stephen H. Archer: "Diversification and the Reduction of Dispersion: An Empirical Analysis," *Journal of Finance,* December 1968, pp. 761–767.

Fama, Eugene F.: " Risk, Return and Equilibrium: Some Clarifying Comments," *Journal of Finance,* March 1968, pp. 29–40.

———and K. French: "Common Risk Factors in the Returns on Stocks and Bonds," *Journal of Financial Economics,* February 1993, pp. 3–56.

Fama, E.F., and J.D. MacBeth: "Risk, Return, and Equilibrium: Empirical Tests," *Journal of Political Economy,* May–June 1973, pp. 607–636.

Fouse, W., and W. Jahnke, and B. Rosenberg: "Is Beta Phlogiston?" *Financial Analysts Journal,* January–February 1974, pp. 70–80.

Francis, Jack C.: *Investments: Analysis and Management,* 3d ed., McGraw-Hill, New York, 1980.

Fuller, Russell Jr.: "Capital Asset Pricing Theories—Evolution and New Frontiers," Monograph no. 12, Financial Analysts Research Foundation, Charlottesville, VA, 1981.

Grinold, Richard: "Is Beta Dead Again?" *Financial Analysts Journal,* July–August 1993, pp. 28–34.

Jensen, M.C.: "Risk, the Pricing of Capital Assets and the Evaluation of Investment Portfolios," *Journal of Business,* April 1969, pp. 167–247.

———: "Capital Markets: Theory and Evidence," *Bell Journal of Economics and Management Science,* Autumn 1972a, pp. 357–398.

Lys, Thomas, and Jowell Sabino: "Research Design Issues in Grouping-Based Tests," *Journal of Financial Economics,* December 1992, pp. 355–388.

Modigliani, Franco, and Gerald Pogue: "An Introduction to Risk and Return," *Financial Analysts Journal,* March–April 1974, pp. 68–86.

Reilly, Frank, and David Wright: "A Comparison of Published Beta," *Journal of Portfolio Management,* Spring 1988, pp. 64–69.

Roll, R.: "A Critique of the Asset Pricing Theory's Tests," *Journal of Financial Economics,* March 1977, pp. 129–176.

Rosenberg, Barr: "Prediction of Common Stock Betas," *Journal of Portfolio Management,* Winter 1985, pp. 5–14.

Rosenberg, Barr, and James Guy: "Beta and Investment Fundamentals," *Financial Analysts Journal,* May–June 1976, pp. 60–72.

Rudd, Andrew, and Barr Rosenberg: "The 'Market Model' in Investment Management," *The Journal of Finance,* May 1980, pp. 597–606.

Schwert, William: "Stock Market Volatility," *Financial Analysts Journal,* May–June 1990, pp. 23–34.

Sharpe, William F.: "A Simplified Model for Portfolio Analysis," *Management Science,* January 1963, pp. 277–293.

———: "Capital Asset Prices: A Theory of Market Equilibrium under Conditions of Risk," *Journal of Finance,* September 1964, pp. 425–442.

———: *Investments,* Prentice-Hall, Englewood Cliffs, NJ, 1978.

———: *Portfolio Theory and Capital Markets,* McGraw-Hill, New York, 1970.

————: "Risk, Market Sensitivity and Diversification," *Financial Analysts Journal,* January–February 1972, pp. 74–79.

Sharpe, W.F., and G.M. Cooper: "Risk-Return Classes of New York Stock Exchange Common Stocks, 1931–1967," *Financial Analysts Journal,* March–April 1972, pp. 46–54.

Thompson, D.J.: "Sources of Systematic Risk, in Common Stocks," *Journal of Business,* April 1976, pp. 173–188.

Tobin, James: "Liquidity Preference as Behavior towards Risk," *Review of Economic Studies,* February 1958, pp. 65–85.

Treynor, Jack L.: "Toward a Theory of Market Value of Risky Assets," unpublished manuscript, 1961.

Vasicek, O.A., and J.A. McQuown: "The Efficient Market Model," *Financial Analysts Journal,* September–October 1972, pp. 71–84.

QUESTIONS AND PROBLEMS

1. Compare the assumptions needed for Markowitz's portfolio policy theory with those necessary for capital market theory.
2. Explain the concept of an efficient portfolio.
3. Explain how the existence of unlimited borrowing and lending opportunities allows one to change the form of the efficient frontier.
4. Why is the existence of a market portfolio a critical notion underlying the capital asset pricing model?
5. Why doesn't the standard deviation of return provide a suitable measure of risk for individual securities and inefficient portfolios?
6. Why is systematic risk the relevant component for individual securities and inefficient portfolios?
7. When is systematic risk equivalent to total risk?
8. If a security plots above the security market line, is it under- or overvalued?
9. If a security plots below the security market line, does its price need to rise or fall in order to plot back on the line?
10. What are some reasons why securities might plot off the security market line?
11. Explain why riskless borrowing and lending may not be a practically valid assumption and how that potential deficiency changes the risk-return relationship indicated by the security market line.
12. Explain how the existence of differential taxes would change the risk-return relationship of the capital asset pricing model.
13. Outline a strategy that investors might follow if taxes do in fact have an effect on the pricing of stocks.
14. List some arguments why taxes may not in fact affect the pricing of stocks.
15. Refer to Table 3-2. Compute the returns to the three investors, assuming that the market return is 5 percent and then 2 percent.
16. Assume that the market price of risk is one-third, that the risk-free rate is 9 percent, and that the standard deviation of market return is 21 percent; then determine the expected return on the market.
17. Assume that the risk-free rate is 9 percent and the expected return of the market is 15 percent. Graph the security market line and indicate where securities that are aggressive would plot and where those that are defensive would plot.
18. Security J has a beta of 0.70, while security K has a beta of 1.30. Calculate the expected return for these securities, using security market line data from the preceding problem.
19. Portfolio K pays a dividend of $2, sells at a current price of $50, and is expected to sell at $52 at the end of the year. It has a beta of 1.10. Refer to Table 3-3 and determine at what price the portfolio should sell to be in equilibrium with portfolios A and D.

20. Assuming that the tax rate on dividend income is 40%, while the tax rate on capital gains is 28%, calculate the tax factor T in the tax-adjusted CAPM.

21. Assume that differential taxes matter; using the same tax rates on dividend income and capital gains as in the preceding problem, determine the expected return for a stock with a beta of 1.20 and a dividend yield of 6 percent. Assume that the expected market return is 15 percent and the dividend yield is 4 percent, while the risk-free rate is 8 percent.

22. Determine the expected return for a stock with a beta of 0.90 and a yield of 2 percent where differential taxes matter. Assume the same data as in the preceding problem.

23. Given the following information and the assumption of the single-index model, what is the co-variance between stocks 1 and 2? $B_1 = 0.90$; $B_2 = 1.10$ and variance of the market index is 0.04.

24. Assume that the standard deviation for the market is 18 percent, and for an individual stock 40 percent, and that the correlation between the stock and market is 0.5. Calculate the beta of the stock.

25. Refer to the data in Table 3-4. Calculate the expected return and risk of the portfolio with the single-index model formulation using the following portfolio weights: Merck (0.40), Bethlehem Steel (0.15), Kellogg (0.15), and Chevron (0.30).

26. Describe some of the deficiencies of the CAPM both from a theoretical and empirical perspective.

27. What are the practical problems in estimating betas for stocks?

28. Describe some of the procedures that portfolio analysts use to reduce the margin of error in esti-mating betas.

29. A portfolio consists of five stocks with the following yields: 3.1%; 2.2%; 0.5%; 5.6%; and 6.6%. Calculate the portfolio yield assuming that each stock is equally weighted and then calculate the yield assuming that the weighting is as follows: 0.20, 0.25, 0.35, 0.10, and 1.0.

30. The risk of an efficient portfolio to an investor is measured by the standard deviation of the portfo-lio's returns. Why shouldn't the risk of an individual security be calculated in the same manner?

31. Assume the following information on the market, the risk-free rate, and two stocks:

	Expected return	Correlation with market	Standard deviation
T-bill rate	4%	0.00	0.00
S&P 500 index	11%	1.00	15.00
Stock A	14%	0.70	25.00
Stock D	9%	0.40	20.00

(a) Draw the SML.
(b) Calculate the betas of the stocks.
(c) Plot the stocks relative to the SML.
(d) What are the alphas of the stocks?

32. Is an investor who owns any portfolio of risky assets other than the market portfolio exposed to some unique risk?

33. Using monthly returns over the past five years, we calculate a beta of 1.30 for a stock. What would be the adjusted beta, using standard techniques?

34. How might you estimate an ex-ante beta?

35. Graph a typical characteristic line. Graph a typical security market line. Explain the difference between the two lines and how they are related.

36. The S&P 500 is frequently used as the market index in the market model (and as a proxy for the "market portfolio" in the CAPM). Identify two other possible choices for a market index.

37. Is it possible for a security to have a very high standard deviation of returns and a low beta? Explain.

38. Graph a typical security market line and indicate where the overpriced and underpriced securities would plot. Also, indicate where the aggressive and defensive securities would plot.

39. Define, in words, the following: (a) market risk, (b) total risk, (c) unsystematic risk, (d) systematic risk.

40. A mutual fund has over $1 billion in assets invested in more than 100 securities. How would you expect the total risk of this fund to be divided between systematic and unsystematic risk?

41. Pick your favorite stock, collect 36 months of price and dividend data, and compute monthly returns and the mean and standard deviation of these returns. For the same stock, compute its beta by using the S&P 500 as the market index. Is your favorite stock an "aggressive" or "defensive" security?

42. For your favorite stock (see Problem 41), compute its beta based on the first 18 months of data and then recompute its beta based on the last 18 months of data. Did the stock's beta change over this time period? If the beta did change, are you aware of any reason that may have caused this to occur? (For example, did the company make an acquisition, issue substantial amounts of new debt, etc.?) Finally, if the stock's beta did change, do you believe that the change is significant, or just due to random sampling error?

43. Assume that the standard deviation of the returns for the market index is 20%. Given the information below, compute the betas for Stock A and Stock Z. Explain why Stock Z has a lower beta, even though it has a higher σ.

	Stock A	Stock Z
σ_i	25%	50%
ρ_{im}	0.60	0.20

44. In the market model, $r_{it} = \alpha_i + \beta_i r_{mt} + e_{it}$:
    (a) Which is the dependent variable?
    (b) Given $\sigma_i^2 = 100$ and $\text{Cov}(i, m) = 100$, then calculate β_{im}. Would you classify this stock as defensive or aggressive?
    (c) If $\rho_{im} = 0.8$, what is the standard deviation of stock i?

CHAPTER 4

Arbitrage Pricing Theory/
Multi-Index Model

INTRODUCTION

In the previous chapter we described capital market theory and the capital asset pricing model as a model of equilibrium pricing behavior that has practical usefulness in providing (1) a measure of systematic risk, (2) a benchmark for security valuation, and (3) a standard of performance measurement. The model is, however, based on several assumptions, some of which may appear quite unrealistic and have led a significant number of investors to question the validity of the model as well as its practical utility. Correspondingly, the necessity and difficulty of correctly identifying a market that is "efficient" have led to fundamental criticism concerning the ability either to test the CAPM empirically or to implement it in a practical sense.

Part of the rationale in developing the CML, and later the CAPM, was that all securities are related to a single underlying factor that could explain systematic risk. In addition, the unsystematic, or firm-unique, risk was diversifiable in a portfolio. A benefit of the CAPM and other single-index models is simplicity and reduced input requirements. Given the set of assumptions and the criticisms of single-index models, including the CAPM, a reasonable next step would be to (1) reduce the assumptions and (2) recognize that more than one factor may affect security prices. Thus, a multi-index model is a logical way to proceed in developing a portfolio model that can be implemented to provide useful information in making portfolio decisions. We will first discuss a specific multi-index model (arbitrage pricing) and then move on to a general discussion of multi-index models.

Arbitrage pricing theory (APT) is based on fewer and perhaps more palatable assumptions than the CAPM and generates an equilibrium model that is remarkably similar to the CAPM. The basic underlying notion of the APT is the *law of one price:* Two securities that are the same in risk and return class cannot sell at different prices. Also, the APT bases its derivation on an index model—generalized multi-index model—of the return-generating process, whereas in CMT the return-generating model—the single-index model—is employed only as a means of testing and implementing the security market line (SML) relationship. The fact that APT generates a market relationship similar to the CAPM provides an alternative and reinforcing analysis that supports the notion of an objective equilibrium risk-return relationship in the market.

We begin this chapter by describing the APT model. We will indicate its underlying assumptions, describe its derivation, and illustrate its use in evaluating pricing behavior in the market and other applications. We then go on to describe the multi-index return-generating model that underlies the APT and how that model enhances the basic insight of the single-index model in portfolio analysis. We will conclude the chapter by showing how the multi-index model framework can be used as a practical means of evaluating the risk-return structure of a portfolio.

ARBITRAGE PRICING THEORY

S. Ross developed an alternative model of equilibrium in securities markets, known as arbitrage pricing theory (APT).[1] The model does not depend critically on the notion of an underlying market portfolio. Instead, it derives returns from the properties of the process that generates stock returns and employs arbitrage to define equilibrium. Under certain circumstances APT derives a risk-return relationship identical to the SML/CAPM. We will thus begin this chapter by covering the APT, both for the additional perspective it offers in studying the equilibrium process and for the reinforcement it provides to the existence of a risk-return relationship in the marketplace.

It is useful to begin describing the APT by indicating the assumptions on which it is based and comparing these with the assumptions used in developing the CAPM. Like the CAPM, the APT assumes that (1) investors have homogeneous beliefs, (2) investors are risk-averse utility maximizers, and (3) markets are perfect, so that factors like transaction costs are not relevant. In contrast to the CAPM, the APT does not assume (1) a single-period investment horizon, (2) that there are no taxes, (3) that investors can freely borrow and lend at the risk-free rate, or (4) that investors select portfolios on the basis of the mean and variance of return.

An additional assumption that the APT makes and one that is basic to that model of equilibrium concerns the process of generating security returns. In particular, the APT assumes that security returns are linearly related to a set of indices representing those underlying factors that give rise to returns on stocks. In fact, when returns are generated by a single factor (the general market effect) we will see that the APT model produces a relationship like the CAPM. We should note, however, that the market portfolio plays no special role in the APT; that is, the market portfolio may or may not be one of the factors influencing security prices. The following equation illustrates the general form of the model, assuming that there are several underlying factors generating returns for the securities:

$$R_i = \alpha_i + \beta_{i1}I_i + \beta_{i2}I_2 + \cdots + \beta_{ik}I_k + e_i \tag{1}$$

This equation is a multi-index generalization of the single-index model. As with the single-index model, the alpha parameter (α) represents the expected level of return of the stock when all indices have a value of zero. The indices representing the underlying factors are

[1]Ross, S.: "Return, Risk and Arbitrage," in I. Friend and J. Bicksler (eds.), *Risk and Return in Finance,* Ballinger, Cambridge, 1976.

designated as I, and the beta (β) parameters are sensitivity coefficients with respect to the indices. Again, higher values of beta coefficients indicate greater sensitivity, whereas lower values indicate lesser sensitivity of the stock return to a particular index.

Unfortunately, APT does not specify the number or type of factors that are important in determining security returns. We might surmise that fundamental elements such as interest rates, inflation, real economic growth, risk premium relationships, and changes would be important underlying determinants of returns. Alternatively, we might assess that proxies such as a market index (representing a general market effect) or the market capitalization of a security (as a representative of the liquidity characteristic) would be important in explaining security returns. Assessing these explanatory factors is a significant problem that we will deal with later in this chapter and in other parts of this book as well.

Finally, the equation includes an error term, which is specified to have the same characteristics as before. In particular, it is expected to average zero $[E(e) = 0]$ over time, as well as to be uncorrelated across securities $[E(e_i, e_j) = 0]$, as is true with the single-index model specification. It is especially important that the indices in the model fully capture the intercorrelation across securities, thereby ensuring that the specification of uncorrelated residuals is fulfilled. This is because in deriving the APT model, an underlying assumption is that one can reduce this error term to zero through diversification. That is, by building a portfolio with a large number of securities, the error term can be eliminated (reduced to insignificance), and the focus can then be on evaluating the responsiveness of the portfolio to changes in the factor indices.

APT Model

Assuming that the factor model, Equation (1), is descriptive of the return-generating process, Ross uses an arbitrage argument to develop a model of equilibrium pricing. Since illustration of this derivation would be excessively complex and would not serve our purposes, we will omit it (those interested may refer to Ross's articles listed at the end of this chapter). Instead, we will assume that the market portfolio is the single factor R_1 generating returns and show only the final form of the risk-return relationship, derived from the APT and expressed in terms of the APT notation:

$$E(R_i) = R_z + b_1 \lambda \qquad (2)$$

Note that, like the CAPM, the APT risk-return relationship is linear. Since the APT does not assume an ability to borrow and lend freely at the risk-free rate, the R_z that is directly derived from this model could represent either a risk-free return (if available) or the zero-beta return that was derived by Black for the amended version of the CAPM. The λ term represents the risk premium associated with the market $E(R_m) - R_z$. The b coefficient measures the responsiveness of the security to changes in the market factor and thus represents a measure of the systematic risk of the security. As noted before, the expression is equivalent to, or at least empirically indistinguishable from, the CAPM when, and if, the market is the sole factor.

If there is only a single factor (the market), the APT pricing relationship is a straight line on a graph of expected return, $E(R_i)$, and systematic risk with respect to factor 1 (the market), as shown in Figure 4-1. Note that there are three plots, A, D, and U, representing three portfolios with no diversifiable risk. Portfolio A has above-average risk ($\beta = 1.20$), while D has below-average risk ($\beta = 0.80$), and U has average risk ($\beta = 1.00$). Portfolios

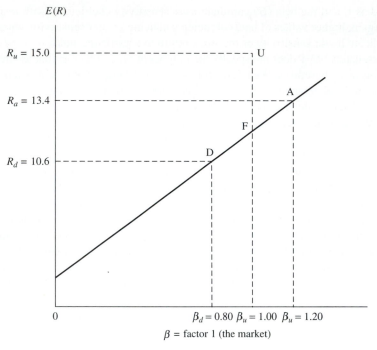

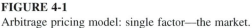

FIGURE 4-1
Arbitrage pricing model: single factor—the market.

A and D are giving returns proportional to their risk (13.4 and 10.6 percent, respectively) and are therefore fairly priced. Portfolio U is offering a greater return (15.0 percent) than would be warranted by its risk and is therefore undervalued.

Process of Arbitrage

Portfolio U thus presents a profit opportunity, which we can convert into a riskless arbitrage. For example, to construct portfolio F with the same risk as portfolio U, an investor could apportion half his investment to portfolio A and the other half to portfolio D. Since the risk of the resulting combination is simply a weighted average of the risks of the individual components ($\frac{1}{2} \times 0.80 + \frac{1}{2} \times 1.20$), the risk of the combination would be 1.00. Correspondingly, the return of the combination would be a weighted average of the returns of the components ($\frac{1}{2} \times 10.6\% +$

TABLE 4-1
Undertaking a riskless arbitrage

	Investment	Return	Risk (β)
Portfolio U	+$1000	+$150	1.0
Portfolio F	− 1000	− 120	−1.0
Arbitrage portfolio	0	$ 30	0

$\frac{1}{2} \times 13.4\%$), or 12 percent for the combination. This return would be in line with the portfolio's riskiness, as illustrated in Figure 4-1, but less than the 15 percent offered by portfolio U.

The data in Table 4-1 illustrate how we can convert the return differential between two portfolios of equal risk into a riskless arbitrage. For example, an investor could sell $1000 of portfolio F short, obtain the proceeds, and invest the $1000 long in portfolio U. Note that this transaction involves no net cash outlay by the investor, as shown by the zero net investment in the arbitrage portfolio. Correspondingly, there would be no risk undertaken, because the two portfolios have identical risk and the process of buying and short selling equal amounts nets to a zero-risk position. Portfolio F represents an arbitrage portfolio with a beta of zero and a positive return to the investor of $30.

Since an investor can obtain a return with no investment and no risk, the investor (or investors) will continue to engage in this arbitrage. This activity of selling portfolio F (and hence portfolios A and D) short would drive down the price of portfolios A and D, while the activity of buying portfolio U would drive up its price. Again using our simple return equation, we can see that the return on portfolios A and D will increase as the price declines (the denominator decreases), and that the return on portfolio U will decrease as the price increases (the denominator increases):

$$E(R) = \frac{P_t - P_0 + \text{dividend}}{P_0} \qquad (3)$$

This activity continues until the return on portfolio U equals that of portfolio F. All three portfolios—A, D, and U—will then lie on a line, thus illustrating how the arbitrage process keeps the risk-return relationship linear. Note that this process of arbitrage might just as well be considered in the context of the CAPM as the process preventing securities from diverging from that line. As before, however, we would expect that the presence of imperfections such as transaction costs, taxes, and imperfect information means that securities plot only within a band around the line rather than on it.

Extramarket Factors

Analyzing the APT model in terms of a single factor is useful in providing a clearer perspective on the linkage between arbitrage and equilibrium as well as allowing a more direct way of comparing this model to the CAPM. It is useful, however, to also evaluate the APT model using two factors, so as to provide perspective on the relationship between a multi-index model and models of market equilibrium like the APT and CAPM. In addition, the preponderance of empirical research on stock return behavior indicates that it is likely that more than one factor is important in explaining returns.

As noted, the general market factor is a prime effect used to explain stock returns, both because of its direct theoretical connection with the CAPM and because stock returns are importantly linked to market indices that are used as proxies for such an effect. Another factor that has both conceptual appeal and empirical support is the relationship of liquidity and stock returns. Liquidity in this sense means the cost to transact quickly, either buying or selling. For example, the need to sell a house quickly would likely require a significant price concession by the seller, and we generally characterize real estate as a low-liquidity asset class. Correspondingly, stocks of large companies are generally easier to buy and sell than those of small companies, and portfolio managers will normally use size of company as a proxy for liquidity.

While investors differ in their need for liquidity—some will consider it of great importance and others of relatively minor importance—it is likely that on balance, liquidity is a desirable characteristic for securities and will command a premium (or penalty for illiquidity). As a result, we would expect securities with low liquidity to offer a higher return as a liquidity premium than securities with high liquidity. In evaluating the pricing relationship for securities, we would thus need to relate the expected return of each security in a universe to both its liquidity and its relationship to a general market factor. The following two-factor version of the APT model describes such a relationship:

$$E(R_i) = R_z + b_1\lambda_1 + b_2\lambda_2 \tag{4}$$

This equation says that the expected return on a security $E(R_i)$ is again a function of a risk-free return (zero-beta), and the return now relates to the sensitivity to two factors rather than only one factor. We again define λ_1 as the risk premium for the market factor and b_1 as the sensitivity coefficient of the return to the market factor. The expression includes a second risk premium λ_2 for the liquidity factor, and b_2 is the sensitivity coefficient of the return to liquidity. As compared to the single-factor version of the APT model, the zero-beta factor R_z indicates the return on a typical security with both zero market risk and zero liquidity risk.

Pricing Relationship

To illustrate use of Equation (4) as an equilibrium pricing model, we make the following assumptions. To begin, we can again assume that the expected return on the market factor is 12 percent and the risk free rate is 5 percent, so that the risk premium for the market factor is 7 percent $((R_m - R_z) = \lambda_1 = 12\% - 5\%)$. Correspondingly, we assume that the expected return on the liquidity factor is 8 percent and, also using 5 percent as the risk-free return, derive a risk (liquidity) premium of 3 percent $((R_L - R_z) = \lambda_2 = 8\% - 5\%)$ for that factor. Using these assumed inputs, Figure 4-2 graphically shows the two-factor APT pricing relationship, along with two hypothetical stocks plotted relative to the pricing relationship.

Note that the figure is three-dimensional, because expected returns are related to two characteristics of securities and the pricing relationship is now represented as a plane rather than a line. Factor 1 shown on the graph represents the market risk factor: that is, the slope of the plane in the market risk direction. It indicates the additional return per unit of market risk if other attributes (in this case liquidity) are held constant. Factor 2 on the graph is the liquidity factor and is the slope of the plane in the liquidity direction. It represents the additional return required as liquidity decreases, or alternatively the increase in the liquidity premium, holding other attributes (in this case market risk) constant.

The figure thus illustrates that for a given level of market risk, less liquid securities have a higher expected return—liquidity premium—than more liquid securities. Correspondingly, for a given level of liquidity, securities with higher market risk have higher expected returns than those with lower market risk. In addition, there are securities with various levels of market risk and liquidity that provide the same level of expected return $E(R_i)$.

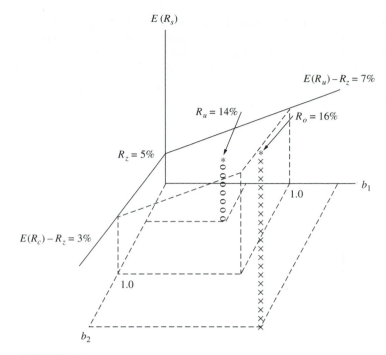

FIGURE 4-2
Market and liquidity risk-return relationship.

Security Valuation

To appraise the valuation positioning of a security (whether it is under-, over-, or fair-valued), now we need to gauge it with respect to two dimensions, and the two securities plotted in Figure 4-2 allow us to do that. Note that stock U offers an expected return of 14 percent and plots above the plane, while stock O offers an expected return of 16 percent and plots below the plane. Stock U has a beta of 0.8 with respect to the market factor, indicating below-average market risk exposure, and with a beta of 0.5 on the liquidity factor exhibits below-average exposure to liquidity risk. Conversely, stock O has a beta of 1.20 with respect to the market factor indicating above-average market risk exposure, and with a beta of 1.5 on the liquidity factor exhibits above-average exposure to liquidity risk.

Using the APT pricing relationship $[E(R_i) = R_z + b_1\lambda_1 + b_2\lambda_2]$, we derive an equilibrium expected return of 12.1 percent for security U. This return is composed of the risk-free rate (zero-beta) of 5 percent plus compensation for exposure to the market risk factor of 5.6 percent $[b_1(R_M - R_z) = 0.8(12 - 5)]$ along with compensation for exposure to the liquidity risk factor of 1.5 percent $[b_2(R_M - R_z) = 0.5(8 - 5)]$. However, showing an expected return of 14 percent, we would consider the security undervalued given its market and liquidity risk exposures. The security price should adjust upward relatively (outperform) to sell in line with other stocks of comparable risk and therefore have the expected return for U decrease to 12.1 percent.

Correspondingly, we can derive an expected equilibrium return of 17.9 percent for stock O. This return is also composed of the risk-free rate (zero-beta) of 5 percent plus compensation for exposure to the market risk factor of 8.4 percent [$b_1(R_M - R_z) = 1.2(12 - 5)$] along with compensation for exposure to the liquidity risk factor of 4.5 percent [$b_2(R_M - R_z) = 1.5(8 - 5)$]. With an expected return of 16.0 percent, we would consider the security overvalued given its market and liquidity risk exposures. The price of this security should adjust downward relatively (underperform) to sell in line with other stocks of comparable risk and have the expected return for 0 increase to 17 percent.

Arbitrage Process

We can illustrate the process of adjusting the equilibrium for both securities within the context of the APT framework as follows. First, by the law of one price, two securities portfolios that have the same risk cannot sell at different expected returns. In this situation it would pay arbitrageurs to buy security U and sell an equal amount of security (E) with the same risk characteristics and offering an equilibrium return of 12.1 percent. Buying security U and financing it by selling security E short would guarantee a riskless profit with no investment and no risk.

The top panel data in Table 4-2, showing the results of an investor selling $1000 of security E short and buying $1000 of security U, illustrates the process. Note that the arbitrage portfolio involves zero investment and has no systematic risk: the factor betas net to zero, yet earn $190 profit. We would expect arbitrage to continue until stock U plots on the plane and shows the appropriate equilibrium return.

The process of arbitrage would work similarly to correct the overvaluation of security O. In this case, the procedure would be to sell stock O short and use the proceeds to purchase a portfolio of equivalent risk but providing an equilibrium return. Again, we would end up with an arbitrage portfolio with no investment and no systematic risk, yet offering a positive return. The data in the bottom panel of Table 4-2 illustrate this and would indicate a continuance of arbitrage until stock O plots on the plane and shows the appropriate equilibrium return.

TABLE 4-2
Arbitrage and security price corrections

	Undervalued security (U)			
	Initial cash flow	**End-of-period cash flow**	b_{i1}	b_{i2}
Security E	+1000	−1210	−0.8	−0.5
Security U	−1000	1400	0.8	0.5
Arbitrage portfolio	0	190	0	0
	Overvalued security (O)			
	Initial cash flow	**End-of-period cash flow**	b_{i1}	b_{i2}
Security O	+1000	−1600	−1.20	−1.50
Security E	−1000	1790	1.20	1.50
Arbitrage portfolio	0	190	0	0

Comparing Equilibrium Models

It is useful to conclude this part of the chapter on equilibrium pricing models by comparing the APT and CAPM models when the security return generating process is a multi-index (factor) model. Recall that we previously showed that with only one index (factor), in particular the market effect, the resulting form of the APT was similar to the CAPM of the capital market theory. Similarly, we can briefly show that the APT and CAPM are consistent even when returns are generated by more than one index (factor). To illustrate, we again use the two-factor version of the multi-index model with a riskless security:

$$E(R_i) = R_F + b_{i1}\lambda_1 + b_{i2}\lambda_2 \tag{5}$$

Note that we can define the λ_j as the excess return on a portfolio with a b_{ij} of 1 on an individual index and a b_{ij} of zero on all other indices. Assuming that the CAPM holds as the equilibrium model for all securities, as well as portfolios, the equilibrium return on each λ_j is then given by the CAPM so that

$$\lambda_1 = \beta_{\lambda 1}[E(R_M) - R_F] \quad \text{and} \quad \lambda_2 = \beta_{\lambda 2}[E(R_M) - R_F]$$

Substituting these values back into Equation (5) results in the following expression:

$$E(R_i) = R_F + b_{i1}\beta_{\lambda 1}[E(R_M) - R_F] + b_{i2}\beta_{\lambda 2}[E(R_M) - R_F]$$

Simplifying, we then obtain

$$E(R_i) = R_F + (b_{i1}\beta_{\lambda 1} + b_{i2}\beta_{\lambda 2})[E(R_M) - R_F]$$

We can further define β_i as a linear combination of the two factors $(b_{i1}\beta_{\lambda 1} + b_{i2}\beta_{\lambda 2})$ to obtain expected return being priced by the CAPM:

$$E(R_i) = R_F + \beta_i[E(R_M) - R_F] \tag{6}$$

The APT solution with multiple factors appropriately priced can be consistent with the CAPM, just as we have shown in the case of a one-factor model. In Appendix A, Jack Treynor describes an alternative approach for showing consistency between the two models of Capital Market equilibrium.

Although the APT and CAPM can be shown to be consistent under certain strong assumptions, there is considerable debate among researchers as to which of the two, APT or CAPM, is the appropriate model of pricing equilibrium. Assessing the comparative value of the two models is essentially an empirical question, and there have been many attempts at resolving this one with many types of empirical tests. Unfortunately, both models are inherently quite difficult to test, and the many tests conducted to date have been unable to verify which of the two models is superior. It is unlikely that a definitive test of the relative efficacy of these two models will be derived in the near future, and given the inherent difficulties it may in fact be an impossible task.

Fortunately, determining the superiority of either model is not of great practical consequence. Each model provides a powerful underlying reason for equilibrium in the market. In the case of APT it is arbitrage, whereas for the CAPM it is diversification and the merits of holding efficient portfolios. In addition, the bulk of empirical evidence seems to indicate that the risk-return relationship generally corresponds to a form like the SML/CAPM, with the strength of the relationship improved as portfolios enlarge and the measurement covers extended time periods. For our purpose, we have assumed that there is a tendency for security prices to gravitate toward an equilibrium relationship like the CAPM, and we view the fact that two differently derived models both develop a CAPM expression as complementary and reinforcing evidence for our working assumption.

MULTI-INDEX PORTFOLIO ANALYSIS

We now turn from the relationship of index models to models of equilibrium pricing to further evaluate the role of index models in portfolio analysis. As noted in the prior chapter, index models have a particularly important usage in analyzing the critical aspects of a portfolio. In Chapter 3 we illustrated the analytical approach using the single-index model. The single-index model is, however, an oversimplification. There is strong empirical evidence that several important factors affect the returns of securities rather than only a single predominating effect, as is assumed for a single-index model. As a result, investors are best served with a multi-index model rather than a single-index model when analyzing a portfolio of securities.

In applying the multi-index model, there is, however, first a need to identify what the significant factors affecting the returns of securities are. One obvious factor is the market effect, and that is commonly used as one of the factors in a multi-index model. There is less agreement, however, as to what other factors should be included to supplement a general market effect, or what factors should be employed if, in fact, a general market effect is not utilized in the model.

Assessing the appropriate factors is a matter of both analytically determining those effects that might theoretically have important impact on returns and then using statistical approaches to assess these determinants. We suggested previously that a liquidity factor might be a useful supplement to the general market effect. Other factors that could easily be incorporated are industry effects or general effects of stock groupings (such as energy, stable, cyclical, or growth stocks). To assess the significance or importance of these effects, multivariate statistical tools such as cluster and factor analysis can be highly important in identifying the cross-sectional patterns of price behavior of groupings of stocks.

More fundamentally, one might propose that such underlying factors as inflation, real economic growth, interest rates, exchange rates, or risk premium changes would have a significant impact in determining the returns of securities. While these sorts of variables have a great deal of theory and logic to recommend them, verifying whether and to what extent or how these factors affect security price (and hence returns) represents a considerable econometric problem. This is because of the substantial difficulty of linking real economic and financial market behavior. Also, there are significant leads and lags, which are likely to be quite variable as well, between economic events and the response of security prices. As a matter of interest, connecting these variables is one of the most daunting tasks of empirically testing the APT model.

As a result, we have chosen to illustrate the process of portfolio analysis and a multi-index model with indices that were developed from a multivariate statistical analysis of the behavior of stock prices. In addition to a general market effect, this analysis showed that the groupings of growth, cyclical, stable, and energy stocks were important in explaining returns. These groupings not only provided an objective basis for determining index inputs to the model but also have favorable statistical properties (Appendix B at the end of this chapter describes these). We will thus begin our illustration of multi-index portfolio analysis

TABLE 4-3
Sources of equity risk

Source	% of risk
General market	30
Market sector: growth, cyclical, stable, energy	15
Industry affiliation	10
Specific	45
Total	100

using these indices and then describe an alternative commercial approach that has practical application and widespread usage.

The Multi-Index Model

In applying the single-index model the assumption is that the general market factor is the only systematic effect operating across all securities. There are, however, factors that have impact across subclasses of securities and create correlation in addition to that of the general market. These other factors are considered to be extramarket correlation. For example, stocks that are expected to grow at above-average rates (growth stocks) tend to perform well or poorly as a group. Correspondingly, classes of cyclical, stable, and energy stocks tend to show similar group behavior. Finally, stocks classified into traditional industries, such as the steel or drug or food industry, tend to perform well or poorly as a group. We will analyze this phenomenon of stocks performing as a group in more detail in Chapter 10.

Meanwhile, Table 4-3 shows the major sources of risk and the percentage of the total risk of a typical stock that can be explained by these factors. Note that there are four sources of risk rather than just the two (general market effect and a unique factor) that are assumed in the single-index model. The additional two sources—a broad market sector effect and an industry effect combined—explain 25 percent of the total risk of a stock, or almost as much as that accounted for by the general market effect. Failure to account for these extra market sources of correlation can lead to errors in estimating the risks of individual securities as well as to problems in generating truly efficient portfolios when undertaking portfolio analysis.

The most direct way to accommodate these extra factors is the multi-index model. The concept here simply augments the single-index model with additional indices that account for these extramarket effects. For example, if we wished to account for group effects, we would construct indices of growth, cyclical, stable, and energy stocks and incorporate these four indices along with an index for the general market effect in a multi-index model. A multi-index model incorporating the market effect and the four extramarket effects takes the following form:

$$R_i = \alpha_i + \beta_m R_m + \beta_g R_g + \beta_c R_c + \beta_s R_s + B_e R_e + e_i \tag{7}$$

The model says that the return on the stock is a function of five factors: (1) general market factor R_m, (2) growth factor R_g, (3) cyclical factor R_c, (4) stable factor R_s, and (5) energy factor R_e. The alpha parameter has the same general meaning as in the single-index model: It is the return expected when the return on all five factors is zero. The residual term e_i has the same properties as in the single-index model.

The beta coefficients attached to the five indices have the same meaning as in the single-index model; that is, they indicate what a 1 percent change in the index will do to the return of the stock. For example, if the beta coefficient for the growth index were 2.0, this would indicate that a 1 percent increase in the growth index would result in a 2 percent increase in the stock's return. The residual term e is more likely to meet the specification of being uncorrelated with the residual of other stocks, because the multi-index model ensures that extramarket as well as general market sources of correlation are removed from the stock returns. As a result, once these factors are removed, we expect there to be no systematic effect operating across securities and the residual returns to be uncorrelated.

A multi-index model of this type can be employed directly, but it is most easily used for computing risk and selecting optimal portfolios if the indices are uncorrelated (independent). Generally, however, raw return indices will contain a combination of factors. For example, an index representing growth-stock returns would contain an effect from the general market as well as the growth-stock effect; that is, the general market factor has impact on all stocks. Therefore, the general market factor should be removed from the growth-stock index so that it will be possible to focus exclusively on the impact of the growth effect on stocks.

Appendix B describes techniques of adjusting indices for the general market factor to convert them into an independent form. Using these techniques of adjusting for the general market factor, a growth index, for example, becomes an index of the difference between the actual return on growth stocks and the return that would be expected given the rate of return on the stock market R_m. Similarly, β_g becomes a measure of the sensitivity of the return on the stock to this difference. Correspondingly, we can think of β_g as the sensitivity of the stock's return to a change in the return to growth stocks when the rate of return on the market is fixed at zero.

Measuring Risk and Return

Given these multi-index model specifications, we can express the expected return of an individual security $E(R_i)$ as

$$E(R_i) = \alpha_i + \beta_m E(R_m) + \beta_g E(R_g) + \beta_c E(R_c) + \beta_s E(R_s) + \beta_e E(R_e) \tag{8}$$

The return of the security is thus a combination of three components: (1) a specific return component represented by the alpha of the security, (2) a market-related component represented by the term $\beta_m E(R_m)$, and (3) four extramarket components as represented by the extramarket terms in the equation. The residual term again disappears from the expression (as in the single-index model) because its average value is zero; that is, it has an expected value of zero.

Correspondingly, the risk of the security, $\text{Var}(R_i)$, becomes the sum of (1) a market-related component, (2) a component that is a combination of the four extramarket factors, and (3) a component that is specific to the security, as illustrated by the following formulation:

$$\begin{aligned} \text{Var}(R_i) = {} & \beta_m^2 \text{Var}(R_m) + \beta_g^2 \text{Var}(R_g) + \beta_c^2 \text{Var}(R_c) \\ & + \beta_s^2 \text{Var}(R_s) + \beta_e^2 \text{Var}(R_e) + \text{Var}(e) \end{aligned} \tag{9}$$

In calculating the risk and return of a portfolio we can use similar formulas and aggregate across the individual securities to measure those aspects of the portfolio. In particular, the expected return of the portfolio becomes a weighted average of the specific returns (alphas) of the individual securities plus a weighted average of the market-related returns plus a weighted average of the extramarket-related returns. Defining $\alpha_p = \sum_{i=1}^{n} W_i \alpha_i$ as the portfolio alpha, $\beta_{pm} = \sum_{i=1}^{n} W_i \beta_{im}$ as the market beta of the portfolio, and $\beta_{pk} = \sum_{i=1}^{n} W_i B_{ik}$ as the sector betas for the portfolio, we can represent portfolio return as a portfolio alpha plus the market and sector betas times their respective expected returns:

$$E(R_p) = \alpha_p + \beta_{pm}E(R_m) + \beta_{pg}E(R_g) + \beta_{pc}E(R_c) + \beta_{ps}E(R_s) + \beta_{pe}E(R_e) \qquad (10)$$

Because we constructed the market and four extramarket indices to be independent of one another, we can express portfolio risk as simply a weighted average of the market-related risk of individual securities plus a weighted average of the extramarket risk plus a weighted average of the specific risk of individual securities in the portfolio. Using $\beta_{pm} = \sum_{i=1}^{n} W_i \beta_{im}$, to represent the market beta of the portfolio and $\beta_{pk} = \sum_{i=1}^{n} W_i \beta_{ik}$ to represent the sector betas, we can express portfolio risk as

$$\text{Var}(R_p) = \beta_{pm}^2 \text{Var}(R_m) + \beta_{pg}^2 \text{Var}(R_g) + \beta_{pc}^2 \text{Var}(R_c)$$

$$+ \beta_{ps}^2 \text{Var}(R_s) + \beta_{pe}^2 \text{Var}(R_e) + \sum_{i=1}^{N} W_i^2 \text{Var}(e_i) \qquad (11)$$

Note that the diversifiable risk component becomes smaller as securities are added to the portfolio, while the extramarket risks do not. Because the single-index model incorporates these risks into the specific risk component and thus implicitly assumes that they are diversifiable, it will generally understate the magnitude of diversifiable risk in a portfolio. We will be able to see this in the following example.

Applying the Multi-Index Model

Table 4-4 illustrates use of the multi-index model for calculating the expected return and variance for a hypothetical portfolio of the same securities used in the single-index example in Table 3-4. Recall that we used four representative securities: (1) Merck, as a growth company; (2) Bethlehem Steel, as a cyclically oriented company; (3) Kellogg, as a stable company; and (4) Chevron, as an energy-oriented company. The table shows the weighting of the stocks in this hypothetical portfolio. Note that the portfolio is heavily weighted in the growth sector (Merck) and the energy sector (Chevron), with only nominal weighting in the stable (Kellogg) and cyclical (Bethlehem Steel) sectors. The portfolio might be characterized as concentrated rather than diversified with respect to the market sectors.

The upper formulation in Table 4-4 illustrates calculation of the expected portfolio return. Note that we have again set the alpha values of the individual stocks at zero, so that the weighted average alpha of the portfolio is simply zero. The market betas of the stocks are the same used in the single-index example, as is the expected return of 11 percent for the market index. The weighted average beta to the portfolio is 1.04 and again, using the 11 percent return projection for the market, results in a market-related return of 11.4 percent for the portfolio.

The betas of the individual stocks with the nonmarket indices were also estimated using historical data. Note that each of the four has a significantly positive beta coefficient with

TABLE 4-4
Portfolio risk and return, multi-index model

Security	Weighting w_i	α_i	β_{im}	β_{ig}	β_{ic}	β_{is}	β_{ie}	Var(e), %
Merck	0.45	0	1.20	0.98	−0.62	−0.20	−0.28	233^2
Bethlehem Steel	0.05	0	1.09	−0.26	0.98	−0.29	−0.24	448
Kellogg	0.10	0	0.89	−0.41	−0.60	0.74	−0.58	385
Chevron	0.40	0	0.89	−0.63	−0.32	−0.21	1.24	81
Portfolio value	1.00	0	1.04	0.15	−0.42	−0.11	0.30	65^2

1. $E(R_p) = \alpha_p + \beta_{pm}E(R_m) + \beta_{pg}E(R_g) + \beta_{pc}E(R_c) + \beta_{ps}E(R_s) + \beta_{pe}E(R_e)$

$= 0 + 1.04(11\%) + 0.15(1\%) + (-0.42)(-2\%) + (0.11)(-1\%) + 0.30(2\%)$

$= 13.1\%$

2. $\text{Var}(R_p) = \beta_{pm}^2\text{Var}(R_m) + \beta_{pg}^2\text{Var}(R_g) + \beta_{pc}^2\text{Var}(R_c) + \beta_{ps}^2\text{Var}(R_s) + \beta_{pe}^2\text{Var}(R_e) + \sum_{i=1}^{4} w_i^2\text{Var}(e)$

$= (1.04)^2(324) + (0.15^2)(137) + (-0.42)^2(193) + (-0.11)^2(149) + (0.30)^2(94) + 65\%^2$

$= 347\%^2 + 48\%^2 + 65\%^2$

$= 460\%^2$

Source: Terry Jenkins, I.T.S. Associates, Inc., Cambridge, Mass.

respect to its assigned classification; that is, the beta coefficient is a statistical criterion for classification to a group. For example, Merck's beta with the growth index is 0.98, Bethlehem Steel's beta with the cyclical index is 0.98, Kellogg's with the stable index is 0.74, and Standard Oil of California's with the energy group's index is 1.24. At the same time, note that the stocks are generally uncorrelated or negatively correlated with other indices, as indicated by low or negative beta values. We have assumed that the return on the nonmarket indices for the period ahead will be 1 percent for the growth index, −2 percent for the cyclical index, −1 percent for the stable index, and 2 percent for the energy group's index. Given these return estimates and the portfolio betas for these indices, the incremental return from these nonmarket sources would be 0.15 percent for growth, 0.84 percent for cyclical, −0.11 percent for stable, and 0.60 percent for energy. Thus, nonmarket sources would add 1.7 percent in return and result in a total expected return of 13.1 percent for the portfolio.

The lower formulation in Table 4-4 illustrates calculation of the portfolio variance. Note that we have used the same estimate for the variance of the market as we used in the single-index example. The estimates of the variances of the nonmarket variances are historically derived. The residual variance estimates are also historically generated, but in this instance they reflect the removal of both market and group effects; hence they will be smaller than those shown for the single-index model. On the bottom line the market-related risk, nonmarket-related risk, and the weighted average specific risk of the portfolio aggregate to a total portfolio risk of 460 percent. The specific risk component can be reduced further by adding more securities to the portfolio, but the extramarket risk will remain if the weights of the portfolio in the four sectors remain the same.

Figure 4-3 is a chart similar to Figure 3-9 that illustrates this effect more clearly. In contrast to Figure 3-9, which shows two components of risk, this figure shows three:

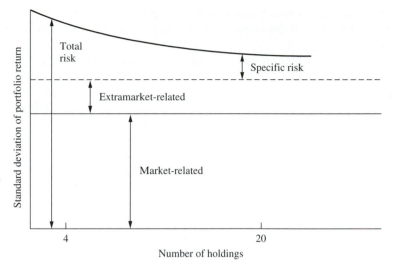

FIGURE 4-3
Market-related, extramarket-related, and specific risk.

extramarket-related, market-related, and specific. These three risk components are shown for a portfolio of four stocks and another of twenty stocks. Both portfolios are constructed with the same weightings in the four market sectors (growth, cyclical, stable, and energy) as the example in Table 4-4.

Note that, as in the previous illustration (Figure 3-9), the specific risk declines as securities are added to the portfolio—that is, as the portfolio increases from four to 20 securities. However, the extramarket risk remains, as will typically be the case with portfolios concentrated in the major sectors. For those portfolios that are weighted more evenly in the sectors, the nonmarket component of risk will be less. This is because these portfolios will be better hedged or diversified with respect to this risk component.[2]

Composite Attribute Models

To further illustrate use of multi-index models in relation to analyzing the characteristics of a portfolio, we first describe an alternative model for portfolio analysis and then demonstrate its application. The model is based on fundamental and technical attributes of a security as well as the industry affiliation of a security. It is an elaboration on the basic model developed by the BARRA organization and widely disseminated commercially for estimating beta values of securities. The model is sometimes referred to as a mixed model, because the single-index model is used as a starting point and a second model is constructed to estimate the nonmarket characteristics, or what is termed the extramarket covariance, of securities.

---

[2]In a large diversified portfolio these extramarket effects tend to cancel out. In particular, a well-diversified fund can be characterized as one where the fund weighting in groupings of growth, cyclical, stable, and energy stocks, as well as of major industries, is generally in line with weightings of those groups and industries in the overall market. For example, if the energy group represents 20 percent of the overall market and the fund is weighted accordingly, then there will be no differential risk to the fund from that risk factor. In this example the extramarket effect tends to cancel out, as the weighting of the groups is not too divergent from that of the market.

The model, however, can be considered within the general category of multi-index models where the first index is the market and other indices are used to explain extramarket covariance.

Within the context of this model, the nonmarket risk or total residual risk is composed of two major components: (1) extramarket covariance and (2) specific risk. The second component or specific risk is, as the term implies, unique to the individual security and is what remains after market risk and extramarket covariance are removed. It has the same meaning as it does within the context of the single-index model and can be diversified away similarly, because it is again assumed to be uncorrelated across securities. The extramarket covariance component, however, cannot be so easily diversified away, because of its interrelationship across groups of securities. This component is further classified into two categories: (1) composite attribute and (2) industry affiliation.

Table 4-5 shows the six attributes that are used by BARRA to estimate this component of extramarket covariance. These six attributes are, in turn, composites of individual attributes of securities such as *P/E*, yield, debt-equity ratio, and share turnover. Overall, some 114 separate attributes need to be considered with respect to the category classification. Choice of particular aspects and formulas for combining simple attributes of security are usually based on economic analysis of historic data and may vary between portfolio managers.

Using these composite attributes, one can evaluate the structure of a portfolio along several dimensions: (1) size, (2) financial risk, (3) growth aspects, (4) earnings variability,

TABLE 4-5
Attributes in the BARRA E1 factor model

1. Index of market variability:
    Historical beta estimate
    Historical sigma estimate
    Share turnover, quarterly
    Share turnover, 12 months
    Share turnover, five years
    Trading volume/variance
    Common stock price (1n)
    Historical alpha estimate
    Cumulative range, one year

2. Index of earnings variability:
    Variance of earnings
    Extraordinary terms
    Variance of cash flow
    Earnings covariability
    Earnings/price covariability

3. Index of low valuation and unsuccess:
    Growth in earnings/share
    Recent earnings change
    Relative strength
    Indicator of small earnings/price ratio
    Book/price ratio

Tax/earnings, five years
Dividend cuts, five years
Return on equity, five years

4. Index of immaturity and smallness:
    Total assets (log)
    Market capitalization (log)
    Market capitalization
    Net plant/gross plant
    Net plant/common equity
    Inflation adjusted plant/equity
    Trading recency
    Indicator of earnings history

5. Index of growth orientation:
    Payout, last five years
    Current yield
    Yield, last five years
    Indicator of zero yield
    Growth in total assets
    Capital structure change
    Earnings/price ratio
    Earnings/price, normalized
    Typical earnings/price ratio, five years

Source: Rudd, Andrew, and Henry K. Clasing, Jr.: *Modern Portfolio Theory: The Principles of Investment Management,* Dow Jones–Irwin, Homewood, Ill., 1982, p. 114.

(5) market variability, and (6) low valuation/unsuccess. For example, one could evaluate the portfolio positioning with respect to a financial risk characteristic of the represented companies relative to that same characteristic as represented by a benchmark of the general market such as the S&P 500. One could measure whether the portfolio positioning is in line with the market or above or below average with respect to the market and to what extent it diverged from the market average. Presumably, divergence from the average introduces extramarket covariance, whereas positioning in line with the market would reduce that aspect of nonmarket risk to zero.

As noted, the second component of extramarket covariance is reflected in the industry affiliation of a security, and we could easily appraise the positioning of the portfolio with respect to industry classification using this approach (or others for that matter). The measure of nonmarket risk exposure, again, would be the divergence of the portfolio industry weighting with respect to that of the market. A weighting in line with the market would mean no extramarket risk with respect to the industry, and an above- or below-average weighting with respect to the industry would result in extramarket risk. For example, if the market weighting as represented by, say, the S&P 500 index was 7 percent in international oils, a portfolio weighting of 7 percent would represent no risk exposure, but a weighting of 11 percent (over) or 3 percent (under) would result in extramarket covariance risk.

APPLIED PORTFOLIO ANALYSIS

To illustrate this mode of analysis and compare with a single-index model, we can again use the portfolio analysis example from the previous chapter. Recall that the objective of the example portfolio strategy was to earn above-average return with a low tracking error

TABLE 4-6
Industry distribution

Industry	Portfolio weighting	Industry	Portfolio weighting
Banks	9.02	Broad casino	1.91
Chemicals—petrol and industrial	7.49	Steel	1.70
Electronic components	5.61	Computers—micro	1.68
Health care—drugs	5.05	Railroad	1.56
Computers—main and mini	4.96	Multiple industry	1.54
Mining	4.47	Petroleum—international	1.54
Retail—food stores	3.71	Security and commission brokerage	1.53
Forest and paper products	3.65	Time sharing and software	1.53
Chemicals—specialty	3.63	Utilities—electric	1.40
Defense	3.60	Air transportation	1.39
Tobacco	3.57	Hospital supply and management	1.38
Farm machinery	3.53	Insurance—property and casualty	1.33
Food and related	3.28	Aluminum	1.26
Aircraft	3.25	Retail—general merchandise	1.24
Motor vehicles and parts	3.24	Business equipment and service	1.16
Capital equipment	3.19	Household—major appliances	1.11
Health care—general	3.07	Insurance—life	1.10
Utilities—gas and pipeline	3.00	Furniture and furnishings	1.08
Computers—peripherals	2.86	Petroleum—Canada	0.83
Petroleum—domestic	2.65	Petroleum—services	0.67

relative to a broad market index, which for purposes of this strategy was deemed to be the S&P 500 index. The means of achieving this was by keeping the market risk in line with the S&P 500 or controlling the portfolio beta at 1.00 and keeping the standard error of residual return of the portfolio at 4.5 percent or less. (These objectives are set forth in Table 3-5.)

Table 4-6 shows a breakdown of the 67 portfolio holdings as classified into industry categories. The weightings range from a 9-percent position in banks to a low weighting of 0.67 percent in petroleum services. There are 40 different industries represented, indicating that the portfolio is broadly diversified along this dimension.

The portfolio industry holdings, however, are not weighted exactly in line with the S&P 500 industry weightings, and some industries are not represented at all in the portfolio. This divergent weighting and nonrepresentation introduces some residual risk (extramarket covariance) to the portfolio that is not measured when using a single index model specification. Similarly, divergences of the portfolio from the S&P 500 positioning along the six composite attributes will introduce a second source of extramarket covariance not captured by the single index model.

Table 4-7 shows the portfolio nonmarket risk in total as well as the way it is subdivided into three categories: (1) composite attribute; (2) industry-related; and (3) specific risk. The table also shows how the portfolio ranks relative to the market with respect to the six composite attributes. For purposes of comparison, the ranking is in terms of percentiles, with the market positioned at the 50th percentile (i.e., at the average) and the extremes represented by the first and 100th percentiles. The portfolio positioning with respect to each of the six attributes is close to that of the market: The portfolio ranging from a low percentile of 45 for the size attribute and a high of 57 for the market variability attribute. As a result, the portfolio reflects little extramarket covariance from this source, as represented by a value of 3.0% shown on the table.

Correspondingly, the portfolio shows relatively little industry-related extramarket covariance, as reflected in the relatively low value of 1.0 percent. This is not surprising, given that the portfolio is well represented across a large number of industries—40 in total—and that the weighting of the industries in the portfolio is generally in line with that of the S&P 500 representation (weighting not shown here). Finally, the residual or specific risk component of the portfolio is 1.5% and is a relatively small total, as would again be expected

TABLE 4-7
Portfolio nonmarket risk

Total nonmarket risk	4.5%
Specific risk	1.5%
Extramarket covariance	3.0%
Industry-related	1.0%
Composite risk attribute	2.0%

Composite risk attributes	S&P 500	Portfolio
Market variability	50	57
Earnings variability	50	49
Low valuation and unsuccess	50	51
Size	50	45
Growth orientation	50	53
Financial risk	50	48

for a portfolio with a large number of stocks—67 in this case—and with individual stock weightings of 2% or less.

In total, the three nonmarket components aggregate to 4.5%, which is within the guide-line objective of 5.0%. Note, however, that the total risk of the portfolio derived from this multi-index analysis is greater than obtained from the single-index evaluation, which showed a portfolio residual risk of 3.5%, or only 75% of the more comprehensive total. This is, of course, an expected result, as the single-index analysis ignores the extramarket com-ponents of industry risk and attribute risk, which constituted 67% of the total nonmarket risk. Ignoring this extramarket risk naturally understates the residual risk of the portfolio or, alternatively, overstates the diversification level.

ANALYZING PORTFOLIO RISK AND RETURN

Index models provide particularly useful insights into analyzing the risk-return character-istics of a portfolio, because they allow one to categorize the sources of risk and return into individual, identifiable components, as shown in Figure 4-4. The figure shows that the com-ponents of return can be considered as (1) market-related, (2) group-related, or (3) security-specific. Correspondingly, there are risks associated with each of these return components, and we see that (1) the beta coefficient β_m is a general measure of exposure to market risk; (2) the relative weighting of the groups with respect to the market indicates exposure to group risk or, alternatively, extramarket covariance; and (3) residual risk $\text{Var}(e)$ measures the uncertainty of earning the specific return.

Since the general market effect is a predominant source of return and risk for a portfolio, managers should be concerned with monitoring the exposure of the portfolio to this source to determine whether the portfolio positioning is consistent with longer-run policy targets or is appropriate for current market conditions. For example, if the outlook for the market were judged to be especially favorable, the manager might well desire to take advantage of this by raising the portfolio beta above its current level. Conversely, if the forecast were for a declining market, the appropriate strategy would be to lower the beta from its current level. Finally, if the manager were uncertain of the direction of the market and wished to hedge against this uncertainty, then the appropriate strategy would be to keep the portfolio beta

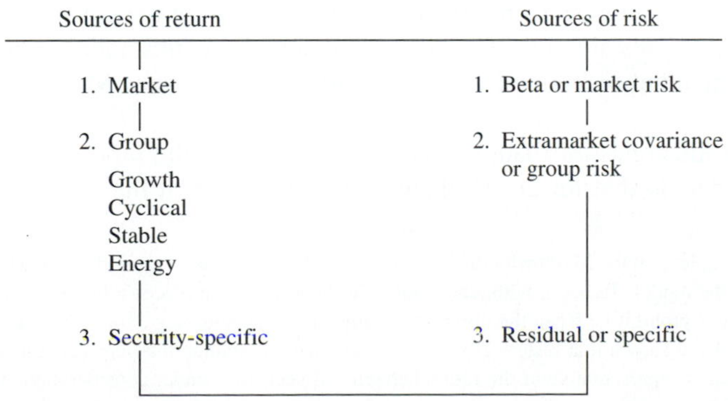

Sources of return	Sources of risk
1. Market	1. Beta or market risk
2. Group	2. Extramarket covariance or group risk
Growth	
Cyclical	
Stable	
Energy	
3. Security-specific	3. Residual or specific

FIGURE 4-4
Components of risk and return.

in line with the market beta of 1.00—that is, maintain a neutral posture toward the market. (We will have more to say about this in Chapters 8 and 9.)

In addition, it is important that the manager evaluate the exposure of the portfolio to the group component to determine whether the positioning in growth, cyclical, stable, and energy stocks is appropriate for current market conditions. There may be periods when an individual group is judged to be particularly attractive, and the manager may desire to tilt the portfolio toward that grouping by weighting it more heavily in the portfolio. Conversely, a certain grouping may be deemed to be particularly unattractive, and the manager would then tilt away from the grouping by weighting it less heavily in the portfolio. When the manager has no opinion about the attractiveness of the groups, then the strategy would be to hedge against the risk of adverse group moves by weighting the groupings in line with their position in the overall market. (We will illustrate this more specifically in the discussion of homogeneous stock groupings in Chapter 10.)

Finally, index models indicate that the measure of security-specific return is the alpha value and that this is desirable when positive and undesirable when negative. Correspondingly, the measure of the uncertainty associated with earning the specific return is the variance of the residual; this will be large when the portfolio is poorly diversified and small when the portfolio is well-diversified. Portfolio managers should therefore endeavor to construct the portfolio in such a way that the resulting alpha is positive and large, but should also be aware of the amount of residual risk that is incurred in constructing such a portfolio. The lower the nonmarket risk, the greater is the certainty of attaining the positive alpha; the greater the nonmarket risk, the lower is the certainty of attaining the positive alpha.

As a result, the goal should be to construct a portfolio with a high positive alpha while minimizing nonmarket risk, so as to develop a portfolio with high alpha per unit of risk. Portfolio optimization techniques, in fact, provide a way of formally determining from a security universe the combination and weighting of securities that provide the portfolio with optimal risk-return characteristics. We now turn to describing the inputs needed to apply these techniques and outline the general method of generating such optimal portfolios.

Generating the Efficient Frontier

Index models not only provide insights into the sources of risk and return for a portfolio; they also facilitate the generation of a set of efficient portfolios. This is because both single- and multi-index models provide a simplified way of representing the covariance relationships among securities. This simplification, in turn, results in a substantial reduction in inputs compared to the number required when using the full-covariance Markowitz portfolio selection model.[3]

Table 4-8 illustrates this data reduction by comparing the input requirements for the two-index models to that for the Markowitz model. Note that the single-index model al-

---

[3] In an attempt to implement the Markowitz full-covariance model, some have resorted to using historically derived data as inputs to the model. To begin with, calculating the historical data places a burden on computer capacity that becomes almost prohibitive when the universe becomes more sizable (e.g., above 500 securities). More importantly, studies have shown that historically derived variance-covariance matrices contain substantial random variations that are not representative of the future behavior of securities under consideration. These errors of estimation can lead to a significant misrepresentation of the variance-covariance matrix and hence of the efficient frontier of portfolios. Those errors have been shown to be severe enough that the full-covariance model becomes inferior to the simplest alternative model.

TABLE 4-8
Data inputs for portfolio selection models

Model	Data inputs for 100-security universe			
	Return	Variance	Covariance	Total
Markowitz	100	100	4950	5150
Single-index	101	101	100	302
Multi-index	105	105	500	710

lows the most substantial reduction in inputs. This is because in the single-index model for portfolio analysis only three estimates need to be made for each security to be analyzed: specific return α_i, measure of the responsiveness to market movements β_i, and variance of the residual term e_i. This is at the cost of two additional inputs: (1) an estimate of the market return $E(R_m)$ and (2) an estimate of the variance of the market $\text{Var}(R_M)$. In the general case of N securities, there would be need for $3N + 2$ estimates. For a universe of 100 stocks, there would be need for 302 estimates, compared with the 5150 estimates required when using the Markowitz full-covariance model.

Note that the multi-index model also provides for a substantial reduction in inputs, but less than that of the single-index model. This is because there is need for seven estimates for each security to be analyzed: specific return α_i; measure of responsiveness to the market β_m and to the four nonmarket factors β_g, β_c, β_s, and β_e; and the variance of the residual return $\text{Var}(e)$. In addition, there would be need for estimates of the return of the market and four nonmarket indices along with estimates of the variances of each of those indices. In the general case of N securities, there will be need for $7N + 10$ estimates. The net requirement for an analysis of 100 securities is 710 estimates, or less than one-seventh of the 5150 required by the Markowitz model for analysis of the same size universe.

Given estimates of returns, variances, and covariances for the securities in the universe under consideration, the efficient set of portfolios is generated by means of the same *quadratic programming* routine that we used to develop an asset allocation in Chapter 2. For purposes of equity selection the program also develops minimum-risk portfolios at different levels of return, in this case specifying the securities and their weighting in the portfolio at that level of return.[4] Proceeding in this fashion, the program develops a series of portfolios differing in risk and return that trace out an efficient frontier similar to the one illustrated by the curve *AEDB* shown in Chapter 2 (see Figure 2-1).[5]

Table 4-9 shows a portfolio generated in the course of a comparative study of the single-index and multi-index portfolio selection models and is illustrative of the output from this process. Note that the table lists 38 individual securities and their weightings in the portfo-

---

[4] Generally the maximum-return portfolios are created at each risk level subject to the constraint that the portfolio be fully invested or, alternatively, that the weights of the individual securities in the portfolio sum to 1. The return, risk, and covariance inputs for the securities are constants and are not changed by the portfolio analysis. The weights of the securities are the variables that the portfolio analysis adjusts in order to obtain the optimum portfolios. By varying these weights the portfolio's expected return and risk are varied. However, as the weights are varied, the restriction that the portfolio be fully invested cannot be violated.

[5] We generally find portfolios increasing in number of securities as we move down the frontier from point B to point A. This is in line with the concept of diversification and variance reduction, discussed in a previous section.

lio. For example, American Home Products has a weight of 2.3 percent in the portfolio, while Sears has a weight of 7.1 percent and Eastman Kodak a weight of 7.2 percent. The weights total 100 percent, indicating that the portfolio is fully invested. The expected return for the portfolio is 14 percent and the standard deviation 18 percent, as shown in the table subhead. The portfolio consists mainly of typical institutional-type names, for which different weightings have been determined so that the expected return is maximum for that level of risk.

Test of Portfolio Selection Models

The usefulness of the portfolios generated by the quadratic programming routine will depend on the quality of the inputs to the process—on the quality of the estimated returns for the securities in the universe. (We will have more to say about this in Chapters 6, 7, and 8.) It also depends on the accuracy of the risk estimates, namely, the estimates of the variances and covariances of returns of securities in the universe of interest.

While index models are simplifications that facilitate the process of portfolio analysis, the trade-off in simplicity may be a less than adequate representation of the risk across the security universe. We have already seen that the single-index model omits consideration of nonmarket sources of risk, and omission of this significant source of additional risk could lead to serious misestimation of the frontier of efficient portfolios. The multi-index model allows incorporation of this additional source of risk and should result in a better representation of the efficient frontier while still economizing on the inputs to the model.

In order to evaluate the relative effectiveness of the single-index and multi-index models in generating an efficient set of portfolios, the author conducted an empirical test. A 100-stock universe was used, and inputs were developed based on returns over the 1961–1969 period with both the single-index and multi-index formulations. Once these inputs had been developed, two sets of efficient portfolios were generated: one based on single-index model inputs and the other based on multi-index model inputs.

Figure 4-5 charts the position of the full set of efficient portfolios generated by the two portfolio selection models: single-index and multi-index.[6] Note that the efficient frontier for the multi-index model is above and to the left of the single-index model frontier for all but extremely high and low risk-return levels. The multi-index model provides higher return at the same level of risk and thus dominates the single-index model over a wide range of returns. This dominance of the multi-index model over the single-index model confirms the expected superiority of the multi-index model in generating efficient portfolios.

Evaluation of the performance of these portfolios over an ex post period (1970–1974) showed that the multi-index model portfolios were consistently superior to the single-index model portfolios. In particular, the multi-index model portfolios consistently provided higher returns than the single-index portfolios at equivalent levels of risk. In fact, the multi-index model portfolios outperformed standard market indices and a sample of mutual funds over the same period. All tests seemed to verify that the multi-index model should be the preferred model for practical portfolio analysis.

---

[6]The efficient set is constructed of curves that are all convex toward the expected return axis. This is because securities have correlation coefficients between positive unity and negative unity. Only perfectly positively correlated securities will generate linear combinations of risk and return; under no circumstances will a portfolio possibility locus curve away from the expected return axis.

TABLE 4-9

Portfolio composition: expected return 14%; standard deviation 18%

Stock	Portfolio weight
Alcoa	1.5
American Can	2.9
American Home Products	2.3
Borg Warner	2.6
Burlington	2.2
Chesebrough Pond	1.2
Columbia Gas Systems	5.0
Campbell Soup	0.6
Deere	1.2
Eastman Kodak	7.2
Federated Department Stores	5.2
Gulf Oil	3.2
Georgia-Pacific	0.8
Gillette	1.3
Goodyear Tire & Rubber	3.7
Honeywell	1.6
International Business Machines	4.5
International Paper	3.4
International Telephone & Telegraph	1.0
Kellogg	0.3
Coca-Cola	2.6
Krattco	1.0
Minnesota Mining & Manufacturing	3.1
Merck	5.6
National Cash Register	0.3
Nalco Chemical	2.1
Procter & Gamble	3.2
R. J. Reynolds	1.1
Sears, Roebuck & Co	7.1
Standard Oil of California	2.7
Sunbeam	0.5
Square D	0.1
Shell Oil	5.9
Timken	2.1
TRW	1.9
Texaco	6.3
Union Oil of California	1.7
Exxon	0.9
Total	100.0

Source: Farrell, James L., Jr.: "The Multi-Index Model and Practical Portfolio Analysis," Occasional Paper no. 4, Financial Analysts Research Foundation, Charlottesville, Va., 1976, p. 43.

Before concluding, we should note that the quadratic programming routine for generating the efficient frontier is something of a "black box" approach. It is difficult to trace the inner workings of the programming routine and hence ascertain the reasons for the inclusion and weighting of a security in a portfolio. Elton and Gruber developed techniques that enable

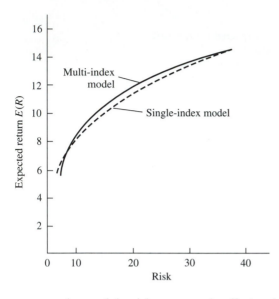

FIGURE 4-5
Ex ante efficient frontier: single-index and multi-index models. (*Source:* Farrell, James L., Jr.: "The Multi-Index Model and Practical Portfolio Analysis," Occasional Paper no. 4, Financial Analysts Research Foundation, Charlottesville, Va., 1976.)

one to understand the risk-return trade-offs that determine the suitability for inclusion of a security in an optimal portfolio.[7] Furthermore, these techniques are sufficiently simplified that the optimal weighting of securities in the portfolio can be easily calculated by means of a hand calculator. At the same time, the resulting portfolio composition is identical to that derived from the use of the more elaborate portfolio selection algorithms that require a large-scale computer for the solution. We illustrate the use of the simplified technique of determining an efficient portfolio in the appendix to Chapter 10.

CONCLUSION

Arbitrage pricing theory uses a different economic logic yet derives an equilibrium model of security pricing that is equivalent to the capital asset pricing model. By providing a complementary means of developing equilibrium, APT provides further justification that the CAPM is at least approximately valid. This is, of course, significant because of the many critically important uses of the CAPM as (1) a model for distinguishing between systematic and diversifiable risk, (2) a benchmark for security valuation, and (3) a standard for performance measurement.

Furthermore, the fact that APT is based on the law of one price makes it intuitively appealing and useful for the insights it offers in such other important areas as derivative securities valuation (as we will see in later chapters). Another appealing aspect of the APT is that it demonstrates how one can go from a multi-index model of security returns to a description of equilibrium, and thus it has a natural relationship to that most important model of practical portfolio analysis. In that regard, we have seen that the multi-index model is most useful for practical portfolio analysis because it combines the simplicity and insights of the single-index model with the potential total analytical power of the full variance-covariance model.

---

[7]Elton, Edwin, Martin Gruber, and Manfred Padbury: "Simple Criteria for Optimal Portfolio Selection," *Journal of Finance,* December 1976, pp.1341–1357.

APPENDIX A
RELATING THE CAPM TO APT

By Jack L. Treynor*

Two common complaints about CAPM are repeated in many textbooks:

1. Evidence that it takes more than one factor to explain the shared or systematic risk in securities refutes the CAPM.
2. In demonstrating that the risk premium on an asset depends only on its systematic factor loadings, APT provides investors with a result of great practical value that the CAPM does not provide.

It may not be coincidental that some of the same books that make the first complaint do not actually discuss the CAPM. Some discuss the market model, and some discuss (usually without attribution) the Vasicek-McQuown pricing model. Both of the latter build on William Sharpe's Diagonal Model paper, which suggested (following up on a footnote in Harry Markowitz's book) that systematic risk could usefully be accounted for by a single factor.

Vasicek and McQuown argued as follows: Assume a single systematic risk factor, such that residual risks are uncorrelated both with this factor and each other. By taking appropriately long positions in some securities and appropriately short positions in others, the individual investor can hedge away all systematic risk. Thus the investor will not bear it unless it competes successfully with residual risk for inclusion in the portfolio. But if the investor includes enough positions (long *or* short) in the portfolio, he or she can drive its residual risk to zero. Now suppose residual risk is priced. Then it offers an infinite reward-to-risk ratio. In order for market risk to compete successfully with residual risk, it must offer an infinite expected return. Otherwise the investor will choose not to hold any systematic risk, and the market will not clear.

The market model takes the assumptions of the Diagonal Model and the result of Vasicek and McQuown and concludes that actual, ex-post systematic return—surprise plus risk premium—in every asset will be proportional to the asset's market sensitivity. Thus both Vasicek and McQuown and the market model assume a single systematic factor. But neither of these is the CAPM: the CAPM in its various forms (Sharpe, Treynor, Lintner, Mossin, Black) makes no assumption about factor structure. In particular, it does not make the one-factor Diagonal Model assumption that Vasicek and McQuown and the market model make.

Actually, a CAPM that abandons the assumptions of homogeneous expectations (as did Lintner) and riskless borrowing and lending (as did Black) does not make many *other* assumptions. All it *does* assume is that asset risk can be adequately expressed in terms of variances and covariances (with other assets), that these measures exist, that investors agree on these risk measures, and that they can trade costlessly to increase expected portfolio return or reduce portfolio variance, to which they are all averse. Short selling is permitted.

Thus, there is nothing about factor structure in the CAPM's *assumptions*. But there is also nothing about factor structure in the CAPM's *conclusions*. Factor structure is about surprise—the nature of correlations between surprises in different assets. In the Diagonal

---

*Jack L. Treynor of Treynor Capital Management is one of the researchers credited with developing Capital Market Theory and is the pioneer, along with Fischer Black, of the theory of active/passive management.

Model, all correlation is accounted for by a single factor. In richer, more complex factor structures, correlations in asset surprise can be due to a variety of pervasive, marketwide influences.

But the conclusion of the CAPM—that an asset's *expected* return for risk bearing is proportional to its covariance with the market portfolio—makes no assertions about the *surprise* in that asset's return. Because expected return and surprise are mutually exclusive elements in *ex post,* actual return, no conflict between the CAPM and factor structure is possible.

This point is the key to the second complaint. In order to demonstrate that APT's principal conclusion—that an asset's risk premium depends only on its systematic factor loadings—also holds for the CAPM, we can assume a perfectly general factor structure without fear of any problems with either the assumptions of the CAPM or its conclusions.

Consider a market in which *absolute* surprise x_j for the ith asset obeys

$$x_i = \sum_j \beta_{ij} u_j + e_i$$

where u_j are the systematic factors in the market and e_i is a residual unique to the ith asset. The absolute surprise x for the market as a whole is simply the sum of absolute surprises for the individual assets:

$$x = \sum_i x_i = \sum_{ij} \beta_{ij} u_j + \sum_i e_i$$

Now the CAPM asserts that any risk premium in the ith asset depends only on its covariance with the market—i.e., on the expectation of the product

$$\left(\sum_j \beta_{ij} u_j + c_i\right)\left(\sum_{hk} \beta_{hk} u_k + \sum_h e_h\right)$$

Bearing in mind that the u's and e's are surprise and assuming that all covariances between e's and between u's and e's are zero, we have for this expectation

$$E\left[\sum_{jhk} \beta_{ij}\beta_{hk} u_j u_k + e_i^2\right]$$

or

$$\sum_j \beta_{ij}\left[\sum_{hk} \beta_{hk}\sigma_{jk}^2\right] + s_i^2$$

where

$$\sigma_{jk}^2 = E[u_j u_k]$$

and

$$s_i^2 = E[e_i^2]$$

We see that an asset's covariance with the market portfolio (absolute surprise with absolute surprise) has two terms—one for systematic factors and one for the asset's unique surprise. A key issue is the relative size of these two terms.

We can, of course, make all the covariance terms in the systematic part zero by choosing a set of factors that are orthogonal. Then the covariance expression becomes

$$\beta_{i1} \sum_h \beta_{h1}\sigma_{11}^2 + \beta_{i2} \sum_n \beta_{n2}\sigma_{22}^2 + \cdots + s_i^2$$

Among the many possible choices of orthogonal factors, we can choose one in which only one factor correlates with the market portfolio. Assign the factor index to the factors so that it has the value one for that factor. Then the first term in the bracketed expression is the variance term for that factor. Ignore for the moment the other systematic terms and focus on the first and last terms in the covariance expression:

$$\beta_{i1} \sum_h \beta_{h1}\sigma_{11}^2 + \cdots + s_i^2$$

Factor the respective terms into standard deviations

$$(\beta_{i1}\sigma_1)\left(\sum_h \beta_{h1}\sigma_1\right) + \cdots + (s_i)(s_i)$$

and consider the first term. Because all the terms involving factor variances are positive, this term represents a lower limit on the size of the systematic contribution. One factor reflects the absolute factor weight of the asset, the other the absolute factor weight of the market portfolio. The former is of the same order of magnitude as the standard deviation of the asset's unique risk; the latter is orders of magnitude larger. (All the systematic risk in the market portfolio's absolute gain or loss is reflected in the market's factor weight. By contrast, the unique risk in the second term is that for a single asset.)

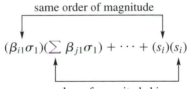

same order of magnitude

$$(\beta_{i1}\sigma_1)(\sum \beta_{j1}\sigma_1) + \cdots + (s_i)(s_i)$$

orders of magnitude bigger

But this means that the systematic product is orders of magnitude larger than the unique product. The sum of *all* the systematic products is of course even bigger still.

The left term in the covariance expression is orders of magnitude smaller than the right term. The only exceptions are assets with little or no systematic risk. Of course, such assets have tiny covariances with the market, hence tiny risk premiums according to the CAPM, and because they have no systematic risk, they have no risk premium under APT.

According to the CAPM, therefore, the left term is orders of magnitude more important to the covariance of the typical asset with market than the right term in determination of an asset's risk premium. Drop the right-hand term. The expression within brackets has a different value for each of the systematic factors. However, it *does not depend on i*—the index that distinguishes among individual assets. What is *outside* the brackets is the factor loadings β_{ij} for the ith individual asset on the factors u_i in the factor structure. However, this is the principal conclusion of APT—that an asset's risk premium should depend only on its factor loadings. Any corollaries that flow from this APT result also flow from the CAPM.

One of the differences between APT and CAPM is the less restrictive assumption of the APT (risk arbitrage). Another difference is specification by CAPM of how systematic factors should be priced in relation to each other. The expression in brackets in the first term is, to some constant of proportionality, the price of risk. The value of the expression, hence that price, is generally going to be different for different factors. APT cannot specify the value of this expression, hence how factors will be priced in relation to each other.

What the APT *does* do is weaken the assumptions necessary to reach this conclusion. APT appeals to the older, better established tradition of arbitrage arguments exemplified by Modigliani and Miller's 1958 paper. APT joins the idea of specifying security risk in terms of a factor structure (Farrar's 1960 doctor's thesis at Harvard, Hester and Feeney's contemporaneous work at Yale) with Modigliani and Miller's arbitrage argument. Some may argue that, in effect, APT substitutes systematic risk *factors* for Modigliani and Miller's risk *classes*.

Others may argue instead that the real provenance of APT is not Modigliani and Miller, but Vasicek and McQuown, with multiple risk factors substituted for the latter's single risk factor.

APPENDIX B
CONVERSION OF CORRELATED INDICES
INTO UNCORRELATED (INDEPENDENT) INDICES

This appendix outlines the method for converting correlated indices into a set of uncorrelated (independent or orthogonal) indices. We will assume for purposes of illustration that there are two indices: a general market index and an index of growth stocks. We would expect the growth-stock index to contain the general market effect as well as the growth-stock effect, because the general market factor affects all stocks. The intent in this case is to remove the general market factor and focus exclusively on the growth-stock effect. Defining R_m as the market return and R_g as the growth-stock return, we can represent the return on a stock as

$$R_i = \alpha + \beta_m R_m + \beta_g R_g + e$$

We can further assume that the return on the growth-stock index is linearly related to the return on the market and express it as follows:

$$R_g = c + DR_m + u$$

This can then be inserted into the prior expression:

$$R_i = a + B_m R_m + B_g(c + DR_m + u) + e$$

When we rearrange the expression, it becomes

$$R_i = (\alpha + \beta_g c) + (\beta_m + \beta_g D)R_m + \beta_g u + e$$

The first parenthesized expression is a constant; the second, $(\beta_m + \beta_g D)$, indicates the impact of a change in the market return R_m on the security return; both the direct effect β_m and the indirect effect through the growth-stock return $\beta_g D$ are included. The term u is now an index of the difference between the return on growth stocks and that expected given the return on the market; that is, it represents incremental return. The combined term $\beta_g u$ indicates the effect of a deviation of the growth-stock return from its predicted relationship with the market R_m. The term e, as usual, measures the specific risk of the stock.

SELECTED REFERENCES

Amihud, I., and Haim Mendelson: "Liquidity and Stock Returns," *Financial Analysts Journal,* May–June 1986.

Berry, Michael, Edwin Burrmeister, and Marjorie McElroy: "Sorting Out Risks Using Known APT Factors," *Financial Analysts Journal,* March–April 1988, pp. 29–42.

Black, Fischer: "Estimating Expected Return," *Financial Analysts Journal,* Sept–Oct 1993, pp. 36–38.

Brown, Stephen: "The Number of Factors in Security Returns," *Journal of Finance,* December 1989, pp. 1247–1262.

Burrmeister, Edwin, and Kent Wall: "The Arbitrage Pricing Theory and Macroeconomic Factor Measures," *The Financial Review,* February 1986, pp. 1–20.

Carroll, Carolyn, and John Wei: "Risk, Return, and Equilibrium: An Extension," *Journal of Business,* October 1988, pp. 485–500.

Chen, Nai-fu: "Some Empirical Tests of the Theory of Arbitrage Pricing," *Journal of Finance* 38, December 1983, pp. 1392–1417.

Chen, Nai-fu, Richard Roll, and Stephen Ross: "Economic Forces and the Stock Market," *Journal of Business* 59, July 1986, pp. 386–403.

Cohen, Kalman, and Jerry Pogue: "An Empirical Evaluation of Alternative Portfolio Selection Models," *Journal of Business,* April 1967, pp. 166–193.

Connor, Gregory, and Robert Korajczyk: "A Test for the Number of Factors in an Approximate Factor Model," *Journal of Finance,* September 1993, pp. 1263–1291.

Dybrig, Philip, and Stephen Ross: "Yes, the APT is Testable," *Journal of Finance,* September 1985, pp. 1173–1188.

Eleswarapu, V., and Marc Reinganum: "The Seasonal Behavior of the Liquidity Premium in Asset Pricing," *Journal of Financial Economics,* December 1993, pp. 373–386.

Elton, Edwin J., and Martin J. Gruber: *Modern Portfolio Theory and Investment Analysis,* John Wiley & Sons, New York, 1991.

Farrell, James L., Jr.: "Analyzing Covariation of Returns to Determine Homogenous Stock Groupings," *Journal of Business,* April 1974, pp. 186–207.

——: "The Multi-Index Model and Practical Portfolio Analysis," Occasional Paper no. 4, Financial Analysts Research Foundation, Charlottesville, VA, 1976.

Gehr, Adam: "Test of the Arbitrage Pricing Model," Research Report no. 88, Institute for Quantitative Research in Finance, 1979.

King, Benjamin: "Market and Industry Factors in Stock Price Behavior," *Journal of Business,* January 1966, pp. 139–190.

Lehmann, Bruce and David Modest: "The Empirical Foundations of the Arbitrage Pricing Theory," *Journal of Financial Economics,* September 1988.

Reinganum, Marc: "Abnormal Returns in Small Firm Portfolios," *Financial Analysts Journal,* March–April 1981, pp. 52–57.

Roll, Richard, and Stephen Ross: "The Arbitrage Pricing Theory Approach to Strategic Portfolio Planning," *Financial Analysts Journal,* May–June 1984, pp. 14–29.

Ross, S.: "Return, Risk and Arbitrage," in I. Friend and J. Bicksler (eds.), *Risk and Return in Finance,* Ballinger, Cambridge, 1976.

——: "The Arbitrage Theory of Capital Asset Pricing," *Journal of Economic Theory,* December 1976.

Shanken, Jay: "The Arbitrage Pricing Theory: Is It Testable?" *Journal of Finance* 37, 1982, pp. 1129–1140.

——: "Multi-Bet CAPM or Equilibrium APT?: A Reply," *Journal of Finance,* September 1985, pp. 1189–1196.

———: "Nonsynchronous Data and the Covariance Factor Structure of Returns," *Journal of Finance,*
      June 1987, pp. 221–231.
Sharpe, William F.: "Capital Asset Prices: A Theory of Market Equilibrium under Conditions of Risk,"
      Journal of Finance, September 1964, pp. 425–442.
———: "Factors in NYSE Security Returns: 1931–1979," *Journal of Portfolio Management,* Summer
      1982, pp. 5–19.
———: *Investments,* Prentice-Hall, Englewood Cliffs, NJ, 1978.
———: *Portfolio Theory and Capital Markets,* McGraw-Hill, New York, 1970.
Stambaugh, R.: "On the Exclusion of Assets from Tests of the Two-Parameter Model," *Journal of
      Financial Economics,* November 1982, pp. 237–268.
Stoll, Hans, and R. Whaley: "Transaction Costs and the Small Firm Effect," *Journal of Financial
      Economics* 12, 1983, pp. 57–79
Treynor, Jack: "In Defense of the CAPM," *Financial Analysts Journal,* May–June 1993, pp. 11–13.
Trycinka, Charles: "On the Number of Factors in the Arbitrage Pricing Model," *Journal of Finance,*
      June 1986, pp. 347–368.

QUESTIONS AND PROBLEMS

1. Compare the assumptions for deriving the APT model to those for the CAPM.
2. Refer to Table 4-4. Weight each of the securities equally (0.25), and calculate the expected return and risk of the portfolio.
3. Compare the assumption of uncorrelated residuals when using the single-index model and the multi-index model.
4. What is extra-market covariance and how is it important in constructing a portfolio?
5. Determine the number of inputs needed to analyze a 350-stock universe using the Markowitz full-covariance model. Compare with inputs needed for a single-index and a five-index model.
6. In what significant ways does APT differ from the CAPM?
7. What is meant by the term "arbitrage profit"?
8. Compare and contrast the beta coefficient from the characteristic regression line with the sensitivity coefficient (or factor loading) in the APT.
9. Compare the advantages and disadvantages of APT and the CAPM. When would the risk-return relationship of the APT be equivalent to that of the security market line?
10. Suppose you used a two-index model to estimate the following relationship for the percentage return on stock Z:

$$r_Z = 0.5 + 0.8r_m + 0.2L + \ell_Z$$

where r_m represents the percentage return on the market index and L represents the unexpected change in liquidity.
   (a) If the market return is 10% and the unexpected change in liquidity is 3%, what return would you expect for stock Z?
   (b) What change in stock Z's return would you expect if there were to be no change in L and a 5 percentage point decrease in r_m?
11. Write the formula for the variance of a portfolio, assuming that a two-factor model has been used to explain returns and that the covariance between the factors is zero. Also, write the general expression for the portfolio's residual variance.
12. Compute the variance of stock Y using the two-index model with a market index and a liquidity index and the following information: Stock Y's market beta = 1.10 and liquidity beta = 0.50; market index variance = 0.08; liquidity index variance = 0.10; stock Y's residual variance = 0.03.

13. Why would you want to compute portfolio variance by a single- or multi-index model rather than by the Markowitz model?

14. Using a two-factor model (market and liquidity), we have the following data on two stocks:

	Market beta	Liquidity beta	Residual variance
Stock 1	0.8	0.2	0.4
Stock 2	1.2	0.4	0.6

Variance of market $= 0.12$; Variance of liquidity $= 0.10$
Covariance between residual 1 and 2 $= 0.02$
Covariance between M and $L = 0$

(a) Compute the variance of stock 2.

(b) Compute the market beta and liquidity beta for an equally weighted portfolio of stocks 1 and 2.

(c) Compute the variance of this portfolio assuming no residual covariance and then adding the residual covariance as given.

PART THREE

Security Valuation and Risk Analysis

We noted before that there is a capital market relationship that implies a trade-off between risk and return across differing asset classes. Given an asset allocation, major investors should then expect to earn a return commensurate with the chosen asset mix: Allocations toward high-risk assets should be expected to earn high returns, whereas those positioned toward low-risk assets would be expected to earn low returns. To add value (increase returns) beyond that given by the basic asset mix, investors can (1) shift weightings across the major asset classes; (2) select securities of above-average attractiveness within the asset class; or both. In this third part of the book, we concentrate on the second option: selecting securities within an asset class.

Security valuation is a critical activity for portfolio managers pursuing active strategies that attempt to add value against a performance benchmark. Good valuation is important in identifying securities that are attractive and hence candidates for inclusion in a portfolio. Conversely, valuation should help identify unattractive securities that should be avoided or, if held, sold from a portfolio. Furthermore, objective valuation measures are most helpful, because they can facilitate a comparison of candidate securities in common units across a universe. As the universe becomes larger, the need for objective valuation becomes even greater.

Pursuit of active strategies, entailing valuation, implies that the portfolio manager assumes that these will be productive in adding value above a passive benchmark. In turn, the opportunity to add value from security appraisal depends on the degree of security mispricing in the market. Correspondingly, whether securities are properly priced or mispriced depends on the efficiency of the market.

We take the view that there is mispricing in the market and therefore that there are opportunities to add value relative to a performance benchmark. However, we also think that the task of identifying such opportunities is difficult and that the activity entails risk, which needs to be considered as well. As a result, portfolio managers need to employ rigorous analysis and a disciplined investment process in order to be successful.

In the following chapters we describe differing approaches to the valuation of securities as well as the perspectives that these methods provide in better understanding the fundamental nature of security risk. Chapter 5 describes approaches to the valuation of bonds and how these approaches are applied in practice, as well as the measures derived for analyzing risk. In Chapter 6 we describe the ways that the classic dividend-discount model (DDM) can be used to evaluate common stocks. Chapter 7 describes simplifications of the DDM and other models that facilitate the practical implementation of common stock valuation.

CHAPTER 5

Bond Valuation and Risk Analysis

INTRODUCTION

As with other securities, valuation of bonds is important for determining the relative attractiveness of bonds in a comparison universe. Valuation is also important in providing a perspective on the exposure of differing types of bonds to a basic source of risk: variation in interest rates. Credit risk is another source that is important in determining the expected return for bonds, and understanding how this risk factor is priced is important in assessing the attractiveness of bonds with differing characteristics. The purpose of this chapter is to describe approaches to the valuation of bonds and how these are applied in practice, as well as the measures derived for analyzing risk.

We begin this chapter with a description of the underlying model that is basic to an understanding of valuation theory. We then go on to describe how this model is structured to value bonds and generate expected returns for bonds. The model is also useful in providing perspective on the way bonds with differing characteristics respond to variation in interest rates, which is the prime source of risk for bonds. The well-known duration measure is related to this analysis and provides a compact expression for exposure to interest rate risk. We describe this measure as well as its related convexity measure and how these are used in practical bond analysis. For long-term bond investors, reinvestment rate risk is critical, and we demonstrate how this risk can impact the results of such bond portfolios. We conclude by examining how bonds vary with respect to credit risk across the quality spectrum and require additional return above that of "riskless" government bonds.

VALUATION THEORY

All investments, including fixed-income and common stocks, derive value from the cash flow they are expected to generate. Because the cash flow will be received over future periods, there is need to discount these future flows to derive a present value or price for the security. At the most general level, then, the value of any security can be established as the present value of a future stream of cash flows, as described by the following formula:

$$P_0 = \sum_{t=1}^{T} \frac{CF_t}{(1 + k)^t} \qquad (1)$$

The model indicates that the present value or, alternatively, current price P_0 of the security is the cash flow (CF) (either dividends or coupons) received over the time horizon T, discounted back at the rate k. Note that the value of the security is positively related to the cash flow. The current price will be higher as the cash flow is expected to be higher, whereas the current price will be lower as the cash flow is expected to be lower. On the other hand, the value of the security is inversely related to the discount rate k. Current price will be lower as the discount rate is higher and will be higher as the discount rate is lower. In addition, we need to recognize that k is a direct measure of risk.

The discount rate is alternatively referred to as a required return R and is composed of two elements: (1) a risk-free return R_f and (2) a risk premium β_i. The risk-free return is, in turn, generally considered to comprise a real return component and an inflation premium. The real return R_r is the basic investment compensation that investors demand for forgoing current consumption; that is, the compensation for saving. Investors also require a premium to compensate for inflation, and this premium I will be high when inflation is expected to be high and low when the inflation rate is expected to be low. Since the real return and inflation premium are a basic return demanded by all investors, the risk-free return is a return component that is required of all securities.

The risk premium is made up of the following elements: (1) interest rate risk, (2) purchasing power risk, (3) business risk, and (4) financial risk. We will see in a later section of this chapter that securities differ in their exposure to these risk elements. As a result, the premium or return that investors require to compensate for risk will differ across securities as the perceived exposure to the risk elements is high or low for the security.

Valuation of a Perpetuity

It is useful to begin describing how Equation (1) can be used to value different types of securities by discussing the special case of valuation of a perpetuity. Recall that a perpetuity pays out a fixed amount over an indefinitely long period. An example is the British consol, a bond with no maturity date, which carries the obligation of the British government to pay a fixed coupon perpetually. Appendix A illustrates how we can reduce a model of the same form as Equation (1) to the simplified form:

$$k = \frac{CF}{P} \qquad (2)$$

In order to recast that expression into the form of a valuation model, we would simply rearrange the equation to solve for a price P rather than the rate of return, as shown in the table:

$$P = \frac{CF}{k} \qquad (3)$$

This expression says that the price P or present value of the perpetuity is simply the fixed cash flow CF, either coupon or dividend, capitalized by the discount rate k, which represents the required return on the security. This equation has particular relevance to the valuation of such special bonds as the British consol and to the broader class of preferred stocks that are generally committed to pay out a fixed dividend amount over an indefinitely long period. For example, for a preferred stock that paid a dividend (cash flow) of $6 and had a required return or alternatively a discount rate k of 0.12, we could use Equation (3) to calculate a value of $50:

$$P = \frac{\$6.00}{0.12} = \$50$$

Although perpetuities such as preferred stocks are a limited class of securities, evaluation of this security type is nevertheless instructive for the broader classes of bonds and common stocks. Bonds are similar to perpetuities in that they pay out a fixed amount of cash flow per period, but they differ in that they generally have a finite life. On the other hand, common stocks have an infinite life, like perpetuities, but they differ in that cash flows are not fixed. As a matter of interest, the expression for valuing a common stock is similar in form to that of Equation (3), with the difference being a modification to take account of the fact that cash flows to the common stock are expected to grow over time.

Bond Valuation

We covered the valuation of a perpetuity first, because of the insights it provides into valuing common stocks and bonds. We now cover bond valuation because bonds are easier to evaluate than stocks, mainly because the benefits that the bondholder expects to receive from holding a bond to maturity are better specified. Analyzing this problem should in turn provide useful insights into the problem of stock valuation.

The cash flow from bonds consists of the coupon payments C, which are generally fixed, and the principal F, which is also usually set by contract. The period over which the coupons are to be paid and the maturity date t for the principal are ordinarily established by terms of the bond indenture. One can use the following valuation model to solve for the price P_b or the discount rate k, which is generally referred to as the *yield to maturity* (**YTM**):[1]

$$P_b = \frac{C}{1 + k} + \frac{C}{(1 + k)^2} + \cdots + \frac{C}{(1 + k)^t} + \frac{F}{(1 + k)^t} \qquad (4)$$

Since we generally know the price of the bond and are interested in determining the yield to maturity, bond valuation becomes a problem of solving for an internal rate of return (IRR). To expedite this process, bond yield tables are available, just as there are present-value tables for solving those problems. Table 5-1 shows a page from a bond yield book to illustrate the format of these tables. Moreover, hand calculators equipped with the appropriate financial routines are convenient and provide quick solutions to problems. In Chapter 14 we illustrate how bond managers use the alternative present value format to derive a price (value) for a bond using cash flows and assumed discount rates (k's) as inputs.

When the current price of the bond is $1000, it is selling at par (100%), and calculating its yield to maturity is simply a matter of dividing the coupon by the par value.[2] For example,

---

[1] Bond interest is ordinarily fixed and paid semiannually, and a more general formulation would indicate semiannual compounding. However, for ease of exposition, we will assume only annual payments and hence ignore the effect of semiannual compounding. In addition, we will ignore variable-rate instruments and bonds that have alternative payments at maturity.

[2] When price differs from par, the effective yield on a bond has two components: (1) the annual coupon rate and (2) the appropriate annual amount of the total discount added to (or premium subtracted from) the coupon rate.

TABLE 5-1
Bond yield table

7% Coupon Rate Yield	Years and months							
	10-6	11-0	11-6	12-0	12-6	13-0	13-6	14-0
4.00	125.52	126.49	127.44	128.37	129.29	130.18	131.06	131.92
4.20	123.58	124.46	125.33	126.18	127.01	127.83	128.63	129.41
4.40	121.68	122.48	123.27	124.04	124.79	125.53	126.26	126.96
4.60	119.81	120.54	121.25	121.94	122.62	123.29	123.94	124.57
4.80	117.98	118.63	119.27	119.29	120.50	121.09	121.67	122.24
5.00	116.18	116.77	117.33	117.88	118.42	118.95	119.46	119.96
5.20	114.42	114.94	115.43	115.92	116.39	116.86	117.31	117.74
5.40	112.70	113.14	113.57	114.00	114.41	114.81	115.20	115.58
5.60	111.00	111.38	111.75	112.11	112.47	112.81	113.14	113.46
5.80	109.34	109.66	109.97	110.27	110.57	110.85	111.13	111.40
6.00	107.71	107.97	108.22	108.47	108.71	108.94	109.16	109.38
6.10	106.90	107.14	107.36	107.58	107.79	108.00	108.20	108.39
6.20	106.11	106.31	106.51	106.70	106.89	107.07	107.24	107.41
6.30	105.32	105.50	105.67	105.83	105.99	106.15	106.30	106.45
6.40	104.54	104.69	104.83	104.97	105.11	105.24	105.37	105.49
6.50	103.76	103.89	104.01	104.12	104.23	104.34	104.45	104.55
6.60	103.00	103.09	103.19	103.28	103.37	103.46	103.54	103.62
6.70	102.24	102.31	102.38	102.45	102.51	102.58	102.64	102.70
6.80	101.48	101.53	101.58	101.62	101.67	101.71	101.75	101.79
6.90	100.74	100.76	100.78	100.81	100.83	100.85	100.87	100.89
7.00	100.00	100.00	100.00	100.00	100.00	100.00	100.00	100.00
7.10	99.27	99.25	99.22	99.20	99.18	99.16	99.14	99.12
7.20	98.54	98.50	98.45	98.41	98.37	98.33	98.29	98.25
7.30	97.83	97.76	97.69	97.63	97.57	97.51	97.45	97.40
7.40	97.12	97.03	96.94	96.85	96.77	96.70	96.62	96.55
7.50	96.41	96.30	96.19	96.09	95.99	95.89	95.80	95.71
7.60	95.71	95.58	95.45	95.33	95.21	95.10	94.99	94.88
7.70	95.02	94.87	94.72	94.58	94.44	94.31	94.19	94.07
7.80	94.34	94.16	94.00	93.84	93.68	93.54	93.39	93.26
7.90	93.66	93.47	93.28	93.10	92.93	92.77	92.61	92.46

if the coupon were $100, the yield to maturity would be $100 divided by $1000, or 0.10, which is 10 percent. If the current price were below $1000, it would be selling at a discount, and the calculated yield to maturity for the bond would be greater than 10 percent in the case of a $100-coupon bond. For example, if the term to maturity were three years and the current price were $952, the yield to maturity using Equation (2) would be 12 percent:

$$P_b = \frac{100}{1.12} + \frac{\$100}{(1.12)^2} + \frac{\$1100}{(1.12)^3}$$

$$\$952 = \$89 + \$80 + \$783$$

If the current price were over $1000, then the bond would be at a premium, and the calculated yield to maturity would be less than 10 percent in the case of a $100 coupon bond.

TABLE 5-1
(continued)

7% Coupon Rate Yield	Years and months							
	10-6	11-0	11-6	12-0	12-6	13-0	13-6	14-0
8.00	92.99	92.77	92.57	92.38	92.19	92.01	91.84	91.67
8.10	92.32	92.09	91.87	91.66	91.45	91.26	91.07	90.89
8.20	91.66	91.41	91.17	90.94	90.73	90.51	90.31	90.12
8.30	91.01	90.74	90.48	90.24	90.00	89.78	89.56	89.35
8.40	90.36	90.07	89.80	89.54	89.29	89.05	88.82	88.60
8.50	89.72	89.42	89.13	88.85	88.59	88.33	88.09	87.86
8.60	89.08	88.76	88.46	88.17	87.89	87.62	87.36	87.12
8.70	88.45	88.12	87.80	87.49	87.20	86.92	86.65	86.39
8.80	87.83	87.48	87.14	86.82	86.52	86.22	85.94	85.67
8.90	87.21	86.84	86.49	86.16	85.84	85.53	85.24	84.96
9.00	86.60	86.22	85.85	85.50	85.17	84.85	84.55	84.26
9.10	85.99	85.59	85.22	84.86	84.51	84.18	83.86	83.56
9.20	85.39	84.98	84.59	84.21	83.86	83.51	83.19	82.88
9.30	84.79	84.37	83.96	83.58	83.21	82.86	82.52	82.20
9.40	84.20	83.76	83.35	82.95	82.57	82.20	81.86	81.52
9.50	83.61	83.16	82.73	82.32	81.93	81.56	81.20	80.86
9.60	83.04	82.57	82.13	81.71	81.30	80.92	80.55	80.20
9.70	82.46	81.98	81.53	81.10	80.68	80.29	79.91	79.56
9.80	81.89	81.40	80.94	80.49	80.07	79.67	79.28	78.91
9.90	81.33	80.83	80.35	79.89	79.46	79.05	78.65	78.28
10.00	80.77	80.26	79.77	79.30	78.86	78.44	78.04	77.65
10.20	79.67	79.13	78.62	78.14	77.67	77.23	76.82	76.42
10.40	78.58	78.03	77.50	76.99	76.51	76.06	75.63	75.21
10.60	77.52	76.94	76.39	75.87	75.38	74.91	74.46	74.04
10.80	76.48	75.88	75.31	74.77	74.26	73.78	73.32	72.88
11.00	75.45	74.83	74.25	73.70	73.17	72.68	72.20	71.76
11.20	74.44	73.81	73.21	72.64	72.10	71.59	71.11	70.66
11.40	73.45	72.80	72.19	71.61	71.06	70.54	70.04	69.58
11.60	72.48	71.82	71.19	70.59	70.03	69.50	69.00	68.52
11.80	71.53	70.85	70.21	69.60	69.03	68.49	67.98	67.49
12.00	70.59	69.90	69.24	68.82	68.04	67.49	66.97	66.48

Source: Expanded Bond Values Tables, Desk Edition, Financial Publishing Company, Boston, 1970, p. 734.

For example, if the term to maturity were again three years and the current price were $1052, the yield to maturity using Equation (2) would be 8 percent:

$$P_b = \frac{100}{1.08} + \frac{\$100}{(1.08)^2} + \frac{\$1100}{(1.08)^3}$$

$$\$1052 = \$93 + \$86 + \$873$$

We can further use the bond valuation model, Equation (4), to demonstrate two elementary but important features of bonds as an investment medium. First, their prices vary inversely with changes in interest rates: If market interest rates k go up, prices P_b decline. Second, the amount of price variation necessary to adjust to a given change in interest rates is a function of the number of years to maturity. In the case of long-maturity bonds, a change in the discount rate k is cumulatively applied to the entire series of coupon payments C, and the payment on principal at maturity is discounted at the new rate for the entire number of years yet to run on the obligation. The net result is a relatively large price change. Short-maturity bonds, however, show only modest changes in price in response to a change in interest rates, because the new discount rate k is applied to only a few coupon payments and similarly applies to principal for only a short period of time. Current prices of long-term bonds are more variable with respect to given interest rate changes than those of short-term bonds.

Table 5-2 illustrates this for two hypothetical bonds differing only in term to maturity: one is a three-year bond, and the other is a six-year bond. Note that when the rate of interest (yield to maturity) is 10 percent, both bonds sell at $1000. However, when the rate of interest moves to 11 percent, the price of the long-term bond declines by 4.7 percent to $953, while the shorter-term bond declines by only 2.6 percent to $974. The longer-term bond is in fact more sensitive to interest rate movements than the shorter-term bond.

Figure 5-1 illustrates this relative interest rate sensitivity more dramatically. The figure shows a perpetuity with a $100 coupon (with values calculated by inserting differing interest rates into Equation (3)) and a three-year bond with a $100 coupon (calculated as illustrated in Table 5-3). Note that the perpetuity shows a much greater variation in value than the short-term bond as interest rates vary over a range of 7 percent to 13 percent. Long-term bonds are characteristically more sensitive to interest rate changes than short-term bonds; that is, long-term bonds generally have greater exposure to interest rate risk.

Bond Pricing Theorems

We have seen from the prior section that the bond valuation model not only provides a way of deriving an expected return for bonds but also allows the analyst to test how bonds in general respond to changing interest rates and how this response will vary according to the individual bond's (1) par value, (2) coupon, and (3) years to maturity. The model thus provides an analytical method for evaluating the exposure of bonds to one of

TABLE 5-2
Maturity and interest rate sensitivity

	Bond A	Bond B
Term to maturity	3 years	6 years
Current price	$1,000	$1,000
Coupon	$100	$100
Yield to maturity	10%	10%
Present value at 11% interest rate		
Year 1	$90	$90
Year 2	81	81
Year 3	803	73
Year 4		66
Year 5		59
Year 6		584
Total	$974	$953
Change in price, %	−2.6	−4.7

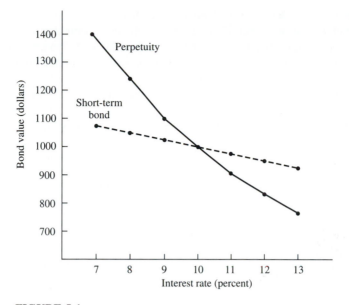

FIGURE 5-1
Values of long-term bonds: 10 percent coupon rates at different
market interest rates.

the fundamental determinants of bond risk—interest rate risk—and explicitly illustrates
the link between return and risk analysis. Furthermore, comprehensive analysis by Burton
Malkiel showed that we can usefully summarize bond response characteristics according to
the following five general principles of bond pricing behavior in an environment of changing
interest rates:[3]

TABLE 5-3
Interest rate sensitivity

	Security A	Security B	Security C
Current price	$1,000	$1,000	$1,000
Cash flow			
Year 1	0	400	100
Year 2	0	400	100
Year 3	1331	400	1100
Yield to maturity, %	10	10	10
Present value at 11% interest rate			
Year 1	$ 0	$360	$ 90
Year 2	0	325	81
Year 3	972	292	803
Total	$972	$977	$974
Change in price, %	−2.8	−2.3	−2.6

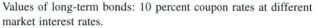

[3] These principles, also known as theorems, were first derived and proven from the basic bond pricing equation by
Burton G. Malkiel: "Expectations, Bond Prices, and the Term Structure of Interest Rates," *Quarterly Journal of
Economics,* May 1962, pp. 197–218.

1. Bond prices will move inversely to interest rate changes.
2. For given change in the level of interest rates, changes in bond prices are greater for longer-term maturities: bond price variability is directly related to term to maturity.
3. A bond's sensitivity to interest rate changes increases at a diminishing rate as the time remaining until its maturity increases.
4. The price changes resulting from equal absolute increases in yield are not symmetrical. More specifically, for any given maturity, a decrease in yields causes a price rise that is larger than the price loss that results from an equal increase in yields.
5. The percentage change in a bond's price due to a change in its yield will be smaller if its coupon rate is higher. Bond price volatility is thus related to coupon.

In addition, the bond valuation model has been used to develop other measures of the sensitivity of bond prices to interest rate changes. These measures, known as duration and convexity, allow an assessment of bond price behavior along other dimensions and provide more explicit ways of gauging the exposure of a bond to interest rate risk. These measures have found extensive use among practitioners, especially with regard to investors focusing on bond management. We describe these measures and their application in the next few sections.

DURATION

We noted in Chapter 2 that all securities are exposed to interest rate risk and that longer-term securities are more vulnerable to this risk than short-term securities. Table 5-2 and Figure 5-1 show this and indicate that maturity of a security provides a gauge of its sensitivity to interest rate risk. That gauge is, however, an imprecise one.

To begin with, a maturity measure ignores interim cash flows to the bond and focuses only on the final payment at maturity. Coupon payments (interim cash flows) are important to interest rate risk, and it is well known that bonds with higher coupons are less sensitive to interest rates than those with lower coupons. In essence, the investor receiving the higher coupon in effect recoups the investment sooner, by means of the faster payback of cash flows, than the investor in a bond with a lower coupon.

Table 5-3 illustrates the maturity deficiency for three hypothetical securities, all with the same three-year maturity. Each currently sells at $1000 and has a yield to maturity of 10 percent; however, the patterns of cash flow differ substantially. Security A pays the entire cash flow at the end of the period; it is a discount bond. Security B pays out its cash flow evenly over the three-year period, somewhat like a mortgage. Security C is the same $100-coupon bond from the previous example and illustrates the pattern of cash flow associated with a coupon bond.

The table shows the effect on the prices of the three instruments of an increase in interest rate from 10 percent to 11 percent. Note that security A, the discount bond, declines the most—by 2.8 percent—as its cash flow is deferred the longest. On the other hand, security B, which pays out an even flow of cash, shows the least decline in price, as it provides the earliest payback of investment. Security C, the coupon bond, as might be expected, shows an intermediate price decline of 2.6 percent.

Despite the same maturity, the three securities show different sensitivities to interest rate changes. Maturity alone would have provided little insight into the relative vulnerability of the three securities to the interest rate risk. Duration, however, is a measure that allows one to evaluate the relative exposure to interest rate risk of securities with differing patterns of cash flow, because it specifically takes into account both interim and final cash flow payments to the security (it gives precision to bond pricing theorem 5).

Figure 5-2 illustrates the basic notion of the duration measure, using the hypothetical security with a level cash flow over the three years. Note that this hypothetical security would have an average life of two years, as shown in the top panel of the figure. A more refined measure of the life of the cash flow would, however, take account of the present value of the flows. In this case the objective would be to calculate the average time point by weighting each payment by the present value of the payment rather than simply the flow of raw dollar amounts. This measure of the time to each payment weighted by the present value of that payment is termed *duration, d*; it is illustrated in the bottom panel of the figure. Note that because earlier payments have higher present value than later payments, the duration will be less than the average life.

Computation of the duration of a bond is similar to computation of a bond price. The formula for computing duration d is

$$d = \left[1\frac{C_1}{(1 + k)} + 2\frac{C_2}{(1 + k)^2} + 3\frac{C_3}{(1 + k)^3} + t\frac{(C_n + F)}{(1 + k)^t} + \right]/P \qquad (5)$$

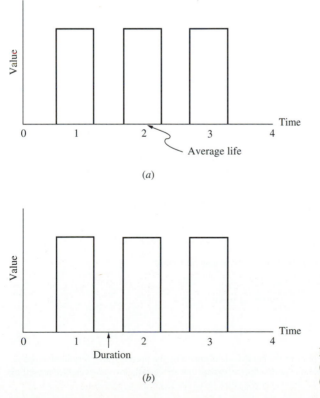

(a)

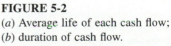

(b)

FIGURE 5-2
(a) Average life of each cash flow;
(b) duration of cash flow.

TABLE 5-4
Calculating the duration of a bond

$$d = \left[1\left(\frac{C_1}{K_1}\right) + 2\left(\frac{C_2}{K_2}\right) + 3\left(\frac{C_3}{K_3}\right)\right]/P$$

Bond A (discount)

$$d = \left[1\left(\frac{0}{1.10}\right) + 2\left(\frac{0}{1.21}\right) + 3\left(\frac{1331}{1.331}\right)\right]/1000$$

$$= [1(0) + 2(0) + 3(1000)]/1000 = \frac{3000}{1000} = 3 \text{ years}$$

Bond B ("mortgage")

$$d = \left[1\left(\frac{400}{1.10}\right) + 2\left(\frac{400}{1.21}\right) + 3\left(\frac{400}{1.33}\right)\right]/1000$$

$$= [1(364) + 2(331) + 3(301)]/1000 = \frac{1929}{1000} = 1.9 \text{ years}$$

Bond C (coupon)

$$d = \left[1\left(\frac{100}{1.10}\right) + 2\left(\frac{100}{1.21}\right) + 3\left(\frac{1100}{1.33}\right)\right]/1000$$

$$= [1(90) + 2(81) + 3(827)]/1000 = \frac{2733}{1000} = 2.7 \text{ years}$$

Notice that Equation (5) consists of setting out the series of cash flows and weighting each flow by the time period in which it occurs. The cash receipts include coupon C and redemption F, while the time weights go from 1 to t. Finally, the sum of these time-weighted cash flows is divided by the price P, obtained by using Equation (4).[4]

Table 5-4 uses Equation (5) to calculate the durations of our three hypothetical securities. Note that discount bond A has a duration of three years, which is the same as its maturity. Zero-coupon discount bonds have a duration equal to their maturity, because the entire cash flow is received at the end of the holding period. On the other hand, securities that make interim payments have durations that are shorter than their maturity. Therefore, coupon bond C has a duration of 2.7 years, which is, of course, less than its three-year maturity. Bond B with its level cash flow has an even shorter duration, 1.9 years, because it pays even more before maturity.

---

[4]We can see this by showing the formula for duration in a more general format:

$$d = \frac{\displaystyle\sum_{t=1}^{T} \frac{C(t)}{(1+k)^t}}{\displaystyle\sum_{t=1}^{T} \frac{C_t}{(1+k)^t}}$$

Note that the denominator is merely the price of the bond as determined by the present-value formulation, Equation (4). The numerator is also a present-value concept of price, except that all the cash flows are weighted according to the length of time to receipt.

Duration and Interest Rate Sensitivity

The most obvious superiority of duration over maturity as a measure of how long investors must wait for their money shows up in measuring sensitivity of bond price to changes in yield: duration gives precision to bond pricing theorem 2. It is generally true that for two bonds with different maturities a 1 percent change in yield will produce a larger price change in the bond with the longer maturity. That is not true, however, if the bonds have different coupons, as we have just seen, and in any case there is no neat relationship between maturity and price sensitivity. Duration, instead, gives a closer measure:

$$\text{Percent change in price} = \frac{-\text{Duration} \times \text{change in yield}}{1 + \text{yield}} \qquad (6)$$

To illustrate, we can use coupon bond C from Table 5-4. Recall that we calculated a duration of 2.7 years for the coupon bond, and we can again assume an increase in interest rates from 10 percent to 11 percent. Using these inputs for the bond, we derive an expected price change

$$\frac{\Delta P}{P} = -d\left(\frac{\Delta k}{1 + k}\right) = -2.7\left(\frac{0.01}{1.10}\right) = -2.5 \text{ percent}$$

This compares with the actual price decline of 2.6 percent calculated in Table 5-2. The difference arises from the fact that the duration-derived measure works best when gauging relatively small changes in interest rate and loses precision as the change in interest rate becomes larger. The assumed change of 1 percent—100 basis points—would be a relatively large change over a short period. Alternatively, we might deduce that the analysis works best when evaluating prospective changes in interest rate and price over shorter intervals, say, over a one- to six-week forecasting period.[5]

Table 5-5 shows duration values for bonds of varying maturities with coupons at three different interest rates: 12, 14, and 16 percent. Note that bonds of longer maturity generally have greater duration than bonds of shorter maturity.[6] For example, at the 14 percent interest rate level, a twenty-year bond paying a 10 percent coupon has a duration of 6.98, while the ten-year bond has a duration of 5.68 and the five-year bond a duration of 3.71. At the same time, note that duration is lower at higher levels of interest rates than at lower levels. For example, the twenty-year bond with a duration of 6.98 at the 14 percent interest rate level has a duration of 7.74 at the 12 percent interest rate level but a duration of 6.30 at the 16 percent level.

It will be instructive to conclude this section by relating this analysis of duration back to our earlier discussion of the components of risk for securities in this chapter.

---

[5] As the formula for calculating duration shows, duration itself changes when yield changes. A rise in yield shortens duration. So duration is a precise measure of price sensitivity to yield change only for very small yield changes. A large yield change will change the duration and the sensitivity. The sensitivity of duration to yield changes is an interesting measure, the usefulness of which is largely unknown.

[6] Duration increases at a diminishing rate as maturity increases, because of the effect of discounting back to present value, which becomes more pronounced at higher discount rates. In some instances the duration of very-long-term bonds is actually less than that of shorter-term bonds, again because of the effect of discounting back to present value.

TABLE 5-5
Duration, coupon rate, and YTM

Years to maturity	Coupon			
	6%	8%	10%	12%
Yield = 12%				
1	0.93	0.92	0.92	0.92
5	4.05	3.91	3.78	3.68
10	6.61	6.23	5.95	5.73
15	7.96	7.46	7.13	6.88
20	8.53	8.05	7.74	7.52
Yield = 14%				
1	0.92	0.92	0.91	0.91
5	3.98	3.83	3.71	3.6
10	6.33	5.95	5.68	5.46
15	7.37	6.91	6.59	6.37
20	7.65	7.24	6.98	6.8
Yield = 16%				
1	0.91	0.91	0.9	0.9
5	3.91	3.76	3.63	3.53
10	6.05	5.68	5.41	5.2
15	6.8	6.38	6.09	5.89
20	6.86	6.51	6.3	6.15

Source: John Rountree, "Duration, an Easily Calculated Risk Measure," Kidder, Peabody & Co., New York, Mar. 24, 1980.

There we noted that securities with a greater interest rate risk should carry a higher premium or discount rate in a valuation framework than securities with less exposure to interest rate risk. The analysis in this section has indicated that securities with longer durations are more sensitive to interest rate changes than securities with shorter durations. We would thus expect longer-duration securities to carry greater discount rates (all other risk factors being equal) than shorter-duration securities to compensate for this greater risk.[7]

---

[7]We should note that duration has limitations as a risk measure. First, duration relates change in price, not changes in rate of return, to yield change. For some purposes this may not matter much. Second, duration relates price change to change in the yield of a particular bond, not to changes in interest rates generally. The price of a bond with a ten-year duration and a yield of 8 percent will move 0.9 percent if the yield corresponding to a twenty-year duration changes by 1 basis point; and the price of a bond with a five-year duration and a yield of 7 percent will change by 0.45 percent if the yield changes by 1 basis point. But one cannot conclude that the risk exposure to interest rate changes is twice as great for the ten-year bond, unless two yields can be expected to change by the same amount. In general, long rates fluctuate less than short rates, and the ten-year-duration bond has less than twice as much risk exposure to interest rate changes as the five-year-duration bond. How much less involves a subjective estimate of the relative magnitude of probable interest rate changes across the yield curve.

CONVEXITY

As illustrated in the previous section, interest rates and bond prices can be linked through duration in a linear relationship to provide a usefully accurate approximation of bond price changes, especially for "small" changes in interest rates. This relationship, however, loses precision as the interest rate changes become large, because the actual relationship between bond prices and interest rates is curvilinear. We can demonstrate the curvilinear relationship by recognizing that the price of a bond will increase a greater amount from a decrease in interest rates than it will decrease in price from an equivalent rise in rates (see bond pricing theorem 4). This asymmetry in price responsiveness is known as *convexity:* Bond percentage price change approximates a convex function rather than a linear function of changes in the interest rate.

Figure 5-3 illustrates the impact of convexity on price–yield relationships by comparing the duration-based estimate of bond price changes and the derived price changes for a

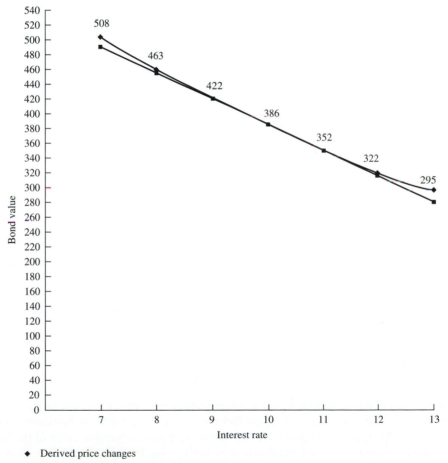

◆ Derived price changes
■ Linear approximation

FIGURE 5-3
Price–yield to maturity relationship, 10-year zero-coupon bond.

ten-year zero-coupon bond priced with a yield to maturity of 10%. The dashed line on the diagram represents the plotted prices derived for the bond at differing interest rates over the range from 7 percent to 13 percent; we used the same procedure to derive these as in the prior illustration of a three-year coupon bond and a perpetuity in Figure 5-2. Note that the plotted line is curvilinear, illustrating the convex nature of the relationship between the price of the bond and interest rate changes.

As noted before, zero-coupon bonds have a duration that is simply the same as their maturity, so the duration for our example bond is ten years, or the same as its maturity. The solid line in the figure is a plot of the duration estimate of price changes, and as noted it is a linear relationship that is tangent to the derived price line at the current 10 percent yield to maturity. Note that there is a divergence between the duration-based estimate and derived bond price at interest rates above and below the 10 percent rate, becoming larger as the interest rate diverges further from 10 percent. This is, of course, because the estimated linear relationship will lie below the curvilinear bond price at interest rates other than 10 percent.

Adjusting for Convexity

In order to adjust for the errors due to convexity, we can augment the basic duration interest sensitivity equation, Equation (7), with a term for convexity. This added term will capture effects from changes in interest rates not reflected in duration. The bond price–interest rate sensitivity equation simply becomes the following form to incorporate convexity (cv) along with duration:

$$\frac{\Delta P}{P} = -d\left(\frac{\Delta k}{1 + k}\right) + cv\left[\frac{\Delta k}{1 + k}\right]^2 \tag{7}$$

Note that the equation is quadratic in form and enables us to represent the bond price–interest rate relationship more fully. The first term, which is duration-related, represents the slope of the line and provides the first-order effects of an interest rate change. The second term, which is convexity-related, is a quadratic term representing the curvature of the line and reflects the second-order effects of an interest rate change. Mathematically, the duration term is the first derivative of the bond price–interest rate relationship with respect to interest rate, whereas the convexity term is the second derivative for interest rates. The formula for duration (d) is as defined before; the formula for the convexity term cv is the following:

$$cv = \left(\frac{1}{2}\right)\frac{\sum_{t=1}^{T}\frac{t(t + 1)C_t}{(1 + k)^t}}{P_0}$$

As in the case of duration, deriving the convexity value is a matter of weighting cash flows (C)—coupons and face value—by a time factor $t(t + 1)$, as shown in the numerator of the expression. This value is in turn divided by the current price or present value of the bond (P_0), and the whole expression standardized by multiplying by the constant of one half.

We can illustrate the use of estimating a bond price reaction to interest rate changes by using the 10 percent zero-coupon bond. For illustrative purposes we assume a 100 basis point decline in interest rates, from 10 percent to 9 percent. With this interest rate decline the bond would increase from a current price of $386 at the 10 percent YTM to a price of $422 at the 9 percent YTM for a percentage increase of 9.33%.

We can compare this derived price change to a formula-estimated price change with a two-stage calculation. First we calculate the duration-related impact of the interest rate change, and then we add the convexity-related effect. Using the duration/interest rate sensitivity expression, Equation (6), we obtain an impact for a ten-year duration of

$$-d\left(\frac{\Delta k}{1 + k}\right) = -(10)\left(\frac{-0.01}{1.10}\right) = 0.0909 \qquad \text{or } 9.09\%$$

As expected from our prior discussion, this change is less than the derived price change of 9.33 percent. This underestimate of price change of 0.24 percent mainly represents the convexity impact as indicated by the following calculation of the bond convexity:

$$cv = \left(\frac{1}{2}\right)\frac{\frac{t(t + 1)C_T}{(1 + k)^T}}{P_0} = \left(\frac{1}{2}\right)\frac{\frac{10(11)(1000)}{(1.10)^{10}}}{\$386} = 55$$

Combining the convexity estimate with the interest rate change, we obtain a convexity-related change for the bond of

$$cv\left[\frac{\Delta k}{(1 + k)}\right]^2 = 55\left[\frac{-0.01}{1.10}\right]^2 = 0.0045$$

Using this convexity adjustment along with the duration-based estimate in the augmented formula, we obtain a total estimated price change for the bond of

$$\text{Price change} = -d\left(\frac{\Delta k}{1 + k}\right) + cv\left(\frac{\Delta k}{1 + k}\right)^2$$

$$= 0.0909 + 0.0045 = 0.0954 \qquad \text{or } 9.54\%$$

Table 5-6 shows the derived price of the example 10 percent zero-coupon bond, along with the duration-based estimate, convexity adjustment, and total estimated price at other interest rate levels. Note that at interest rates that diverge less from 10 percent, the duration-based estimate is usefully close to the derived price. The convexity adjustment becomes relatively more important at more divergent interest rates and combines with the duration estimates to provide a closer approximation of the derived price. As would be expected, the total estimated price, including duration and convexity, tracks the derived price over

TABLE 5-6
Derived and estimated prices, 10-year zero-coupon bond

Interest rate (1)	Interest rate (2)	Bond price (3)	Duration estimator (4)	Price less duration (5)	Convexity-augmented estimate (6)	Price less total estimate (7)
7%	-300	508	491	17	507	1
8%	-200	463	456	7	463	0
9%	-100	422	421	1	423	1
10%	0	386	386	0	386	0

the range of interest rates. The total price estimate reflects the curvilinear nature of the relationship.

Determinants of Convexity

Table 5-7 is a matrix of computed convexity values for bonds differing in coupon as well as maturity. In calculating these values, we assumed that the prevailing rate of interest or yield to maturity for all the bonds was 10 percent. Note that the calculated convexity values for these bonds was consistently larger as the maturity of the bonds was greater. For example, the convexity of the 20-year 10 percent coupon bond was 210, or 14 times the convexity of the five-year 10 percent bond. Correspondingly, the convexity value was consistently lower at higher coupon levels than at lower coupon levels. For example, the convexity of the 20-year 10 percent coupon was only 15 percent of the convexity of the zero-coupon 20-year bond.

As further visual perspective on the way that convexity varies by maturity, it is useful to refer back to Figure 5-1. Recall that we illustrated the response of bond prices to interest rates for two hypothetical bonds: (1) a three-year bond, to represent a short-maturity bond, and (2) a perpetuity, to represent a long-lived fixed-income instrument. Note that the plotted relationship for the perpetuity shows a pronounced curvature, vividly illustrating the convex nature of the bond price–interest rate relationship for this long-lived security. Correspondingly, the plotted price–interest rate relationship for the three-year bond is virtually a straight line, showing only a moderate curvature and hence minimum convexity for this short-term security.

As may be surmised from these illustrations, the degree of curvilinearity—convexity— of the bond price–interest rate relationship increases with the maturity of the security. Short-term bonds show moderate convexity, whereas long-term bonds show greater convexity. Furthermore, convexity will increase as the coupon of the bond is lower, and conversely will be lower as the coupon is higher. Finally, at lower interest rate levels convexity will be greater than when interest rates are higher. Alternatively, the bond price–interest rate relationship is more convex at the lower-interest-rate segment of the curve, as may be deduced by inspection of the graph of the bond in Figure 5-3 or the perpetuity in Figure 5-1.

Duration will as a general rule then provide a better estimate of bond price changes for securities with shorter maturities and higher coupons than for securities with lower coupon rates and longer maturity. In both cases, the estimate based on duration will be better in a high-interest-rate environment than in a low-interest-rate economic environment. In virtually all cases the duration-only–based estimate will provide a useful estimate of bond price changes when the interest rate change is small. As a practical matter, changes in interest rates over short time periods (such as, for example, one month) are virtually always less

TABLE 5-7
Determinants of convexity: coupon and maturity

Maturity	Coupon	
	Zero	10%
5-year	15	7.3
10-year	55	12.3
20-year	210	31.2

than 100 basis points in magnitude. Bond managers can and should be updating the duration estimates on their bonds and portfolios at least that frequently.

Applying Convexity Analysis

In positioning a portfolio with respect to maturity, bond managers have traditionally used three approaches: maturity-concentrated, laddered, and barbell portfolios. As the name implies, maturity-concentrated portfolios are utilized when the manager has a definite interest rate opinion. For example, a manager who expects interest rates to fall would concentrate on long-term maturities (or durations), because the price of these bonds will increase the most. Conversely, expectation of a rise in interest rates would lead to a concentration on short-term bonds to protect against a decline in bond prices.

Laddered and barbell portfolios are illustrated in Table 5-8. Note that the 15- and 10-year laddered portfolios have maturities evenly spaced so that the same amount matures and is invested each year. This maturity structure provides average returns over an interest rate cycle and implies no interest rate forecast on the part of the portfolio manager. In comparison, the barbell structure includes both short- and long-term bonds with no funds invested in intermediate-term bonds, as illustrated by two barbell configurations in the table. A barbell-structure portfolio purportedly has greater liquidity than laddered portfolios, because of the heavier concentration of short-term bonds, and higher returns when the yield curve is upward-sloping, because more funds are invested in long-term bonds.

The barbell structure can also provide a particularly appealing structure when the yield curve is flat; yields are virtually the same for every maturity. Figure 5-4 illustrates such a yield curve structure on August 30, 1989. By overweighing at both extremes of the maturity spectrum, short- and long-term, it is possible to enhance returns over a laddered portfolio or one that is concentrated in intermediate-term bonds. One of the reasons for this enhancement potential is convexity. Recall from our prior discussion that, with interest rate

TABLE 5-8
Examples of laddered and barbell structures for a $20 million portfolio

Years to maturity	15-year laddered	10-year laddered	50–50 barbell	70–30 barbell
1	1,333,333	2,000,000	2,000,000	2,800,000
2	1,333,333	2,000,000	2,000,000	2,800,000
3	1,333,333	2,000,000	2,000,000	2,800,000
4	1,333,333	2,000,000	2,000,000	2,800,000
5	1,333,333	2,000,000	2,000,000	2,800,000
6	1,333,333	2,000,000	0	0
7	1,333,333	2,000,000	0	0
8	1,333,333	2,000,000	0	0
9	1,333,333	2,000,000	0	0
10	1,333,333	2,000,000	0	0
11	1,333,333		2,000,000	1,200,000
12	1,333,333		2,000,000	1,200,000
13	1,333,333		2,000,000	1,200,000
14	1,333,333		2,000,000	1,200,000
15	1,333,333		2,000,000	1,200,000
	$20,000,000	$20,000,000	$20,000,000	$20,000,000

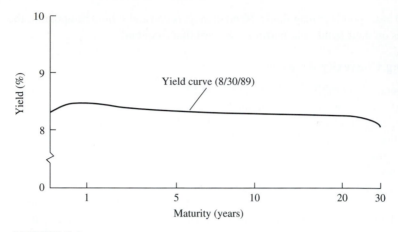

FIGURE 5-4
Flat yield curve, prompting our "barbelled" strategy.

changes, bond prices follow an upward-sloping curvilinear (convex) path and that this effect is most pronounced for longer-term bonds.

To illustrate, we can compare two portfolios with the same duration—for example, five years—but very different compositions. One way to create a portfolio with a five-year duration is to buy only five-year-duration bonds, thus creating a concentrated portfolio. An alternative is to put half the portfolio in T-bills and the other half in long-term bonds, which for our illustration we consider to be ten-year-duration bonds. With this 50/50 short-long allocation, we produce a barbelled portfolio with a five-year duration (0.50 × 0 duration + 0.50 × 10-year duration).

The solid line in Figure 5-5 shows the price response of bonds over the full duration range (0 to 10 years), assuming that the yields on all bonds fall by 100 basis points; that is, the whole yield curve shifts down by one percentage point. When interest rates fall by 100 basis points, the value on the five-year bond, or concentrated portfolio, will be 105.09. The value on the long bond will rise to 110.88, but the value of the short-term paper will stay at 100. Thus, the value on the barbelled portfolio, with a 50/50 weighting, will be 105.44 and is halfway between the two duration extremes. The difference between the value of

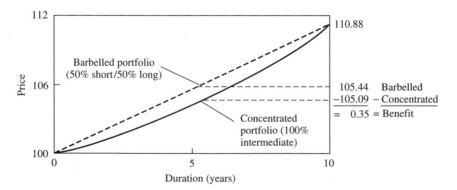

FIGURE 5-5
Barbelled portfolios capture the benefit of convexity. (Source: Francis H. Trainer, Jr., Sanford C. Barnstein & Co.)

these two portfolios (105.44 − 105.09 = 0.35) is the result of convexity. Correspondingly, this differential value is the benefit from barbelling the portfolio—the performance edge that barbelled portfolios have over concentrated ones when interest rates decline. Normally, when the yield curve is upward-sloping, this 35-basis-point differential is overwhelmed by the give-up in yield on short securities. However, when the yield curve is flat, the contribution from convexity gives the barbelled portfolio the overall advantage.

Of course, the reverse is also true: If interest rates are expected to increase, a barbelled portfolio would not be advisable. A concentrated portfolio would show a smaller price decline than a barbelled portfolio of the same duration. Thus, it is important for the portfolio manager to have a forecast of the general trend—increase or decrease—of interest rates before deciding on the structure of the bond portfolio.

REINVESTMENT RATE RISK

Bond managers who pursue strategies that entail trading bonds prior to maturity are primarily concerned with price changes of the bonds in the portfolio over the holding period. Price changes represent both the potential opportunity and the risk for such managers. On the other hand, managers who pursue a buy-and-hold policy are primarily concerned with coupon payments, which are the primary sources of return to that type of manager. The major risk for the buy-and-hold manager derives from the need to reinvest these coupon payments (which are received twice a year) over the life of the bond at the same or higher yield to maturity as provided by the current structure of interest rates.

We can most easily illustrate this *reinvestment rate risk,* or inability to earn the same *interest-on-interest* as implied by the current interest rate structure, by means of the data shown in Table 5-9. The table shows that a five-year 9 percent bond will provide $450 of coupon income and $1000 of maturing principal over its five-year life; however, in order to achieve a *compound* growth rate of 9 percent in asset value over the five-year period, the original $1000 would have to reach a cumulative value of $1553; that is, an incremental dollar return of $553. This $103 gap in return has to be overcome through the accumulation of interest-on-interest. As Table 5-9 shows, this amount of interest-on-interest will be achieved when coupon reinvestment occurs at the same 9 percent rate as the bond's original yield to maturity. At lower reinvestment rates the interest-on-interest will be less than the amount required, and the growth in asset value will fall somewhat short of the required target value of $1553. Naturally, at higher reinvestment rates the cumulative value will be greater than required.

TABLE 5-9
Realized return from a five-year 9% par bond over a five-year horizon

Reinvestment rate, %	Coupon income	Interest-on-interest	Total return	Realized compound yield, %
0	$450	$ 50	$450	7.57
7	450	78	528	8.66
8	450	90	540	8.83
9	450	103	553	9.00
10	450	116	566	9.17
11	450	129	579	9.35

Source: Martin Leibowitz, Salomon Brothers, New York, October 1979.

TABLE 5-10

Magnitude of interest-on-interest to achieve compound yield of 9% par bonds of various maturities

Maturity in years	Total return	Interest-on-interest at 9% reinvestment rate	Interest-on-interest as % of total return
1	$ 92	$ 2	2.2
2	193	13	6.5
3	302	32	10.7
4	422	62	14.7
5	553	103	18.6
7	852	222	26.1
10	1,412	512	36.2
20	4,816	3,016	62.6
30	13,027	10,327	79.3

Source: Martin Liebowitz, Salomon Brothers, New York, October 1979.

Table 5-10 shows that the magnitude of the reinvestment rate risk increases as the maturity of the bonds in the portfolio increases. In particular, it shows the percentage of the total return of the bond that is represented by interest-on-interest. Note that for a one-year bond the interest-on-interest component represents 2 percent of the total, whereas for the five-year bond used in Table 5-9 the interest-on-interest component represents close to 20 percent of the total return. For twenty-year bonds it represents 62.6 percent, and for thirty-year bonds it represents 79.3 percent of the return, or the major component of total return. Interest-on-interest is thus a negligible to only moderate risk factor for shorter-term bonds, but for longer-term bonds it is the major risk consideration.

Reinvestment Risk Control

While the reinvestment rate risk constitutes a major problem in closely achieving any assured level of target return, there are ways of limiting the risk.[8] Using the same five-year 9 percent bond, Table 5-11 shows the total return and its components—coupon income, capital gain or loss, and interest-on-interest—earned over investment horizons ranging from one to five years and for three assumed interest rates: 7, 9, and 11 percent. The capital gains and losses as well as the interest-on-interest are calculated on the assumption that the interest rate moves immediately to the level shown in the rows after purchase of the bond at the beginning of the period. The bond prices are established, and the reinvestments are at these same rates over the remainder of the period.

Note that when the interest rate declines to 7 percent, the interest-on-interest component drops below the level that would have been earned if the rate had stayed at

---

[8] We should note that most bonds are issued with a call provision. This provision gives the issuing corporation the right to redeem the outstanding bonds at a specified price either immediately or after some future date (deferred call). The price is usually a few dollars more than par value and represents a premium to compensate for the privilege of the call; however, this feature presents a future problem to bond investors, because when interest rates decline, the issuing corporation will be inclined to call the existing bonds and refund with a new issue at the lower interest rates. The bondholder will then be faced with the problem of reinvesting the proceeds from the called bond at the lower prevailing interest rate. Moreover, even if the bonds are not called immediately, the existence of the call provision will limit the upside move in the bond to the call price, as investors will assume the bonds will eventually be called.

TABLE 5-11
Realized return from a five-year 9% par bond over various horizons

Reinvestment rate and yield-to-maturity at horizon, %		Horizon period			
		1 year	3 years	4.13 years	5 years
	Coupon income	90	270	372	450
7	Capital gain	68	37	16	0
	Interest-on-interest	2	25	51	78
	Total return	160	331	439	528
	Realized compound yield	15.43%	9.77%	9.00%	8.66%
9	Capital gain	0	0	0	0
	Interest-on-interest	2	32	67	103
	Total return	92	302	439	553
	Realized compound yield	9.00%	9.00%	9.00%	9.00%
11	Capital gain	−63	−35	−16	0
	Interest-on-interest	2	40	83	129
	Total return	29	275	439	579
	Realized compound yield	2.89%	8.26%	9.00%	9.36%

Source: Martin Liebowitz, Salomon Brothers, New York, October 1979.

9 percent. Offsetting this, however, is a capital gain that would be earned from the rise in prices attendant on the yield decline. For example, sale of the bond at the end of year 3 after the rates declined to 7 percent would provide a capital gain of $37, which would more than offset the lower interest-on-interest earnings ($25 versus $32 that would have occurred if rates on bonds had remained at 9 percent). Conversely, if interest rates rose to 11 percent, the interest-on-interest earnings component would rise above the level that would have been earned at 9 percent. Counterbalancing this, however, would be a capital loss that would be incurred if the investor sold at the lower prices before maturity. If the investor held the bond to maturity, there would, of course, be no capital loss, because the price would move to par. Under this circumstance, the total return on the bond due to greater interest-on-interest earnings would have been greater by $26 ($129 less $103) than if the interest rate had remained at 9 percent.

Table 5-11 thus illustrates that lower interest rates lead to increased returns over the short term through price appreciation, but they lead to reduced returns over the longer term through reduced interest-on-interest. For periods between the short term and the longer term, we find that two conflicting forces provide some compensation for each other, with the one force (interest-on-interest) growing stronger and the other force (capital gains) growing weaker with time. As a matter of fact, we can see from the table that there is an intermediate point in the five-year horizon—4.13 years—where the decrease in capital gain is precisely offset by interest-on-interest. Furthermore, it is the same point in terms of years whether interest rates decline to 7 percent, rise to 11 percent, or remain at 9 percent.

We should also note that 4.13 years represents the duration of the 9 percent coupon bond. Recall from earlier in this chapter that duration is an average life based on the present value of each of the bond's cash flow payments, coupons as well as principal. For the hypothetical case of a pure discount bond (a zero-coupon bond) the duration will coincide with its maturity. Since zero-coupon bonds have no cash flows before maturity, they are free from the problem of coupon reinvestment. A 4.13-year zero-coupon bond priced to yield 9 percent would always provide the target return over its maturity period no matter how interest rates may change. Discount bonds are thus ideal for achieving target rates of return.

Immunization

Alternatively, a technique known as *immunization* allows one to protect the portfolio against the "disease" of changing rates even when dealing with coupon bonds. It allows one to lock in a specific rate of return (as well as dollar return) over a specified time period. Immunization depends on the concept of duration for ensuring that the portfolio is structured in such a way that any capital losses (or gains) from interest rate changes will be offset by gains (or losses) on reinvested return. Duration allows this, simply because a coupon bond with a given duration is similar mathematically to a zero-coupon bond having a maturity equal to that of duration. For example, as shown in Table 5-11, a 9 percent target return over a 4.13-year period could be achieved by either a 4.13-year zero-coupon discount bond having a 9 percent yield or a five-year 9 percent par bond, because both bonds have the same duration—4.13 years.

Immunization can be a useful investment application for programs in which an exact amount of funds is to be delivered at a well-defined terminal period. For example, an endowment plan might need $10 million to be available at the end of five years to fund a building program. Presuming the going interest rate was 9 percent, to achieve the objective of providing a target return of 9 percent over a five-year period, the bond manager should choose a bond having a duration of five years rather than a maturity of five years. To obtain a duration of five years in a 9 percent par bond, it turns out that one would need a maturity of around 6.3 years. Table 5-12 shows how such a bond will indeed achieve the required growth in asset value to provide the guaranteed return of 9 percent compounded semiannually.

Although immunization is a rather elegantly appealing procedure, it may not be appropriate and may even be suboptimal for investment programs with less certain payoffs or terminal periods. Furthermore, actual implementation of the technique may be much more involved than our illustration because of the likely violation of some simplifying assumptions. The most significant of these concerns the special and simplified manner in which yield curve shifts. Unfortunately, this special yield curve shift does not represent the many varieties of shifts that are encountered in practice. Immunizing against these other shifts requires many other refinements that we have not discussed here, although the basic principles remain the same.[9] Several commercial services and money management organizations have in fact applied the principles of immunization along with refinements to solve practical problems of bond management.[10]

---

[9]G. O. Bierway, G. Kaufman, R. Schweitzer, and A. Toevs, "The Art of Risk Management in Bond Portfolios," *Journal of Portfolio Management* (Spring 1981). Different assumptions about the shape of the yield curve, and the direction and magnitude of unexpected interest rate changes, lead to different immunizing durations. But Bierway et al. found that the portfolio with an immunizing duration based on the simplest assumptions immunizes almost as well as more complex strategies and appears to be the most cost-effective.

[10]Gifford Fong Associates and Salomon Brothers have done extensive and innovative work in this area. Gifford Fong Associates offers money managers a computer package for executing an immunization strategy.

TABLE 5-12
Realized return from 6-year, 4-month 9% par bond over a 5-year horizon

Reinvestment rate and yield to maturity at horizon	Coupon income	Capital gain	Interest-on-interest	Total $ return	Realized compound rate
7%	$450	$25	$78	$553	9.00%
8	450	13	90	553	9.00
9	450	0	103	553	9.00
10	450	−13	116	553	9.00
11	450	−26	129	553	9.00

Source: Martin Leibowitz, Salomon Brothers, New York, October 1979.

RISK PREMIUM

Government bonds are subject only to interest rate and purchasing power risk. Corporates are subject not only to those risks but to business and financial risk as well. The yields on corporates are thus determined by these credit risks as well as the basic factors that are critical in determining the yield on "riskless" government bonds. The difference in yields on corporates to compensate for this added risk is known as a risk premium. It can be expressed as a yield spread, or difference, between the yield on corporates and the yield on default-free government bonds.

Correspondingly, there is a spectrum of risk or quality differences within the corporate sector as corporate bonds vary in exposure to business and financial risks. Investment rating services attempt to calibrate these quality differentials and to provide their opinions on the relative safety of corporate bonds. Two rating systems in general use are those of Moody's Investment Services and Standard & Poor's. The general ratings, or ranks, assigned to corporate bonds under each of these systems are stratified as shown in Table 5-13.

Bond ratings are designed essentially to rank issues in order of the probability of *default*—that is, inability to meet interest or sinking-fund payments or repayment of principal. Thus, AAA (or triple-A) bonds are those judged to have a negligible risk of default and, therefore, to be of highest quality. AA (or double-A) bonds are also of high quality but are judged not to be quite so free of default risk as triple-A bonds. Bonds rated A and BBB (Baa is Moody's designation) are generally referred to as medium-quality obligations,

TABLE 5-13
Corporate bond quality ratings

Moody's	Standard & Poor's	Quality designation
Aaa	AAA	Highest quality
Aa	AA	High quality
A	A	Upper medium grade
Baa	BBB	Medium grade
Ba	BB	Speculative elements
B	B	Speculative
Caa	CCC-CC	Default possible
Ca	C	Default, some recovery possible
C	DDD-D	Little recovery possible

with the BBB possessing a higher risk of default than the A. These top four grades, AAA through BBB, are considered *investment-quality.* Bonds that do not fall within the first four rating categories are believed to contain a considerable speculative element. Such bonds, designated as *high-yield* ("junk") bonds, fall into classifications of BB (Moody's Ba) or lower. Portfolio managers generally do not invest in bonds with speculative elements unless the objective of the portfolio indicates speculative investing.

We can illustrate the difference in yields due to quality or risk differences by means of data shown in Figure 5-6. This figure shows the yields on government bonds, Aaa corporates, and Baa corporates over the 1964–1993 period. The yield on governments represents the return on a riskless bond, while the yield on Aaa corporates reflects business and financial risk as well. The Baa yield represents the return on a bond of investment quality but subject to significantly greater credit risk than Aaa corporates.

Note that Aaa corporates provided a higher yield than governments, as would be expected, with the difference or risk premium averaging around 70 basis points over the 1964–1993 period. Correspondingly, Baa corporates provided a yield that was consistently in

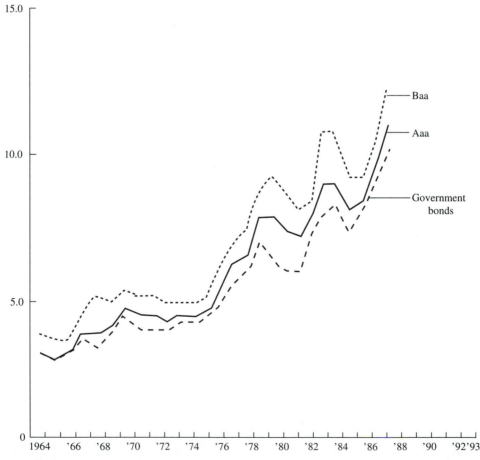

FIGURE 5-6
Yield spreads—treasuries and Aaa and Baa corporates.

excess of Aaa corporate yield, averaging about 115 basis points for the full period. There was consistently a premium paid for credit risk both across, as well as within, security classes over the period.

Table 5-14 shows that the spread or premium fluctuated over the time period, seemingly in line with cyclical fluctuations in the economy. In particular, it appears that the spread was widest at the troughs of economic cycles—1981–82, 1987, and 1990–1991—and narrowest at the peak. This would seem reasonable, remembering that perceived credit risk and potential bankruptcy would be greatest at the trough and least severe at the peak of the economic cycle.

Credit Quality Determinants

There are essentially four fundamental financial factors that can be used to assess the credit quality of a corporation. Perhaps the prime measure of credit quality is the level and trend

TABLE 5-14
Bond yield table, %

Year	20-year Treasury bonds	Aaa	Baa	Yield spread of Aaa and Treasuries	Yield spread of Aaa and Baa
1964	4.18	4.44	4.81	0.26	0.37
1965	4.5	4.68	5.02	0.18	0.34
1966	4.76	5.39	6.18	0.63	0.79
1967	5.59	6.19	6.93	0.6	0.74
1968	5.88	6.45	7.23	0.57	0.78
1969	6.91	7.72	8.65	0.81	0.93
1970	6.28	7.64	9.12	1.36	1.48
1971	6	7.25	8.38	1.25	1.13
1972	5.96	7.08	7.93	1.12	0.85
1973	7.29	7.68	8.48	0.39	0.8
1974	7.91	8.89	10.63	0.98	1.74
1975	8.23	8.79	10.56	0.56	1.77
1976	7.3	7.98	9.12	0.68	1.14
1977	7.87	8.19	8.99	0.32	0.8
1978	8.9	9.16	9.94	0.26	0.78
1979	10.18	10.74	12.06	0.56	1.32
1980	12	13.21	15.14	1.21	1.93
1981	14.18	14.23	16.55	0.05	2.32
1982	10.61	11.83	14.14	1.22	2.31
1983	12	12.57	13.75	0.57	1.18
1984	11.69	12.13	13.4	0.44	1.27
1985	9.5	10.16	11.58	0.66	1.43
1986	7.81	8.49	9.97	0.68	1.48
1987	9.07	10.11	11.29	1.04	1.18
1988	9.08	9.57	10.65	0.49	1.08
1989	8.08	8.86	9.82	0.78	0.96
1990	8.25	9.05	10.43	0.8	1.38
1991	7.05	8.31	9.26	1.26	0.95
1992	7.04	7.98	8.81	0.94	0.83
1993	6.07	6.93	7.69	0.86	0.76

Sources: "An Analytical Record of Yields and Yield Spreads," Salomon Brothers, New York, and Federal Reserve Bulletins.

TABLE 5-15
Comparative bond data

	Bristol Myers	Control Data
Industry	Drugs	Office equipment
Rating	Aaa	Baa
Long-term debt	$120 million	$165 million
Interest coverage	18.7 times	5.5 times
Debt/total capitalization	8%	9%
Net working capital/debt	7 times	2.4 times
Net income/total assets	17.9%	9.1%

of *fixed-charge coverage,* which is the ratio of *earnings* before income taxes to fixed interest charges. In stable industries, earnings coverage of two or more times interest charges may be regarded as adequate, whereas in industries subject to wide fluctuations in earnings a coverage of three, four, or more times may be required for a good rating. In industries sensitive to the business cycle, coverage of fixed charges under recession conditions is the most significant ratio.

The second factor is the level of *long-term debt* in relation to *equity,* where debt includes both the amount shown on the balance sheet and the amount represented by off-balance-sheet obligations, such as lease obligations. An analysis of the corporation's capital structure provides a measure of asset coverage. Again, higher debt-to-equity ratios can be accepted for companies in stable industries than for those operating in industries more exposed to the cycling of the economy.

Third, there is the debtor's *liquidity* position, current and prospective. Some companies may appear to have satisfactory earnings and capital, yet the holders of their bonds or preferred stocks may doubt whether enough cash will be on hand to pay debts when they come due. One ratio that is particularly useful is that of *net working capital* to *long-term debt.* The reasoning here is that net working capital is the permanent portion of working capital and is appropriately financed with longer-term obligations—long-term debt—whereas equity, which is the only truly permanent source of capital, finances the other, less "liquid" portion of corporate assets. Generally, a ratio of 1 is satisfactory for industrial companies.[11]

Finally, the size and competitive position of the company within its industry are important in assessing credit quality. Generally, there is a good reason to have much greater confidence in the long-term continuity of companies that are of substantial size and competitive leaders in their industry. Although size alone does not guarantee a profitable level of operations, seasoned firms that are dominant in their industry naturally tend to be better able to withstand adversity.

We can best illustrate how differences in these factors affect the credit quality of corporate bonds by means of data in Table 5-15 for two companies: Bristol Myers and Control Data. The fundamental data shown are interest coverage, debt-to–total capitalization ratio, the net working capital–to-debt ratio (as a measure of liquidity), and the return on assets (as a measure of basic profitability). It also shows the industry affiliation of the company, as well as the rating of the company's bonds by Moody's Investor Service.

---

[11] While the ratio is generally useful for industrial companies, the ratio of net working capital to long-term debt is not relevant for utilities, because of their small overall working-capital positions and large long-term debt financing.

Note that the Bristol Myers bond is rated Aaa, but the Control Data bond is rated Baa, indicating that the rating service views the Bristol Myers bond as having significantly higher credit quality than the Control Data bond. The reasons for the difference in ratings can be fairly easily discerned from the fundamental credit factors. In particular, Bristol Myers had a significantly higher fixed-charge coverage; a somewhat lower debt-to–total capital ratio; a better liquidity position, as evidenced by a higher net working capital–to-debt ratio; and higher profitability. In addition, Bristol Myers is a leading factor in the pharmaceutical industry, whereas Control Data generally holds a secondary position in the field of office equipment.

FUNDAMENTAL SOURCES OF RISK

We noted in an earlier section of this chapter that four factors have traditionally been considered important in determining the degree of risk, and hence the discount rate (k) required, of a security: interest rate risk, purchasing power risk, business risk, and financial risk. We also saw analytically in this chapter that the changing level and structure of interest rates are a prime source of risk for high-grade bonds—specifically, government bonds. At this point let us evaluate the impact that this interest rate factor and the other risk factors have on the level of the discount rate for bonds in general. This discussion should be helpful not only in understanding historical risk-return relationships but in assessing the extent to which these factors will affect the risk and return of assets in the future. Furthermore, this discussion should help us understand the underlying fundamentals of more quantitative measures of risk.

Interest Rate Risk

Interest rate risk is the variability in return caused by changes in the level of interest rates. All market interest rates tend to move up or down together in the long run. These changes in interest rates affect all securities to some extent and tend to affect all of them in the same way, because the value of a security is the present value of the cash flow of the security. Since the market rate of interest is a component of the discount rate used in calculating present values of securities, all security prices tend to move inversely with changes in the level of interest rates (refer back to Equation (1) to see this inverse relationship). Longer-term securities, in turn, show greater variability in price with respect to interest rate changes than shorter-term securities.

We can refer to the underlying characteristics of securities for help in assessing the relative vulnerability of the different security classes to the interest rate risk. In particular, we would expect cash equivalents to be less vulnerable to interest rate risk than long-term bonds. We would further expect long-term bonds, which might have a maturity of twenty years, to be less vulnerable than preferred stocks, which have a perpetual life. Earlier in this chapter we described the duration measure, which allows a more precise characterization of exposure of securities to interest rate risk.

Purchasing Power Risk

Nominal returns contain both a real return component and an inflation premium to compensate for inflation anticipated over an investment holding period. Inflation rates vary over

time, however, and investors do not always correctly anticipate changes in the rate of inflation. This results in an additional factor that might be termed unanticipated inflation, which
can cause the realized return of securities to diverge from what was anticipated when the
rate of inflation was at the expected level. We can most directly illustrate this effect on
security returns by restating our formula for calculating the expected return of a security:

$$\text{Expected return} = \frac{\text{Cash flow} + (P_1 - P_0)}{P_0}$$

For fixed-income securities such as bonds, whose cash flows (coupon payments) are fixed,
the only way that the return can be adjusted to compensate for an increase in inflation is a
decline in price. The decline in price reduces the denominator and increases the numerator
in the equation and hence increases the expected return on the security. Conversely, when
there is an unanticipated decrease in the rate of inflation, we would expect returns to be
lower. This would be accomplished by an increase in the price, thus raising the denominator
and lowering the return expected in the future.

Bonds and other fixed-income securities, such as preferred stocks, are thus highly vulnerable to accelerating inflation—that is, purchasing power risk. On the other hand, fixed-
income securities would be highly desirable investments during a deflationary period or a
period of decelerating inflation. In fact, we will see in Chapter 9 that the basic merits of
fixed-income securities in an asset allocation scheme are as a hedge against deflation.

Business Risk

Business risk is the uncertainty of income flows that is caused by the nature of a firm's
business. It can be measured by the distribution of the firm's operating income over time.
That is, the more variable the operating income, the greater the business risk; the less variable, the lower the risk. Business risk is divided into two categories: internal and external.
Internal business risk is associated with operating conditions that can be managed within
the firm, and it is reflected in the operating efficiency of the firm. *External* business risk
is associated with operating conditions imposed on the firm by circumstances beyond its
control, such as the political and economic environment in which it operates.

Business risk is included as a factor in the evaluation of securities to recognize that the
stream of earnings expected by the investors may not materialize—a possibility that may
adversely affect the value of the future stream of benefits they expect to receive. In the case
of fixed-income securities the presence of business risk, as measured by deviation from expected earnings, may impair the firm's ability to meet its interest or amortization payments.
The more variability in operating income, the greater is the chance of bond default. In an
extreme case it could mean bankruptcy for the firm and total loss to the bondholder.

Naturally, government bonds are not subject to business risk at all, and good-quality
corporate bonds are subject to it only to a limited extent. Low-quality bonds (high-yield, or
"junk," bonds) can be much more subject to this type of risk. High-grade bonds generally
have little premium built into the expected return for this potential risk, while lower-grade
bonds carry a higher premium. In the extreme, junk bonds require a premium return ap-
proaching that required of equities but in the form of current yield; hence the designation
"high-yield" bonds.

Financial Risk

Financial risk arises from the introduction of debt into the capital structure of a corporation. It is usually measured by the percentage of debt as compared with equity in the capital structure—that is, the debt-to-equity ratio. Since the existence of debt means the obligation to pay fixed financing charges (interest payments) there is a risk that earnings may be insufficient to meet these obligations. This would, of course, have an unfavorable impact on bondholders, who would forgo the expected interest earnings on their investment and could suffer the consequences of default and possible complete loss of their investment. Furthermore, the increased variability of earnings associated with the presence of fixed charges *compounds* the uncertainty beyond that due to the basic business risk of the company.

Common stocks of companies that finance with debt are naturally subject to this risk, which increases directly with the proportion of debt in the capital structure. This risk might also reflect back on the bonds of the corporation that finances too heavily with debt: the more extensive the debt, the lower the quality of the debt. High-grade bonds of corporations that finance with prudent amounts of debt would be subject to this risk only to a limited extent, and government bonds, again, would not be subject to it at all. Bonds used to finance leveraged buyouts (LBOs) are commonly known as junk bonds because the predominant component of such highly leveraged transactions (HLTs) becomes bonds, typically constituting 80–90% of the total. Financial risk in these cases is extreme, and the premium return required is again like that on an equity but in the form of current yield—high-yield bond. In contrast, the extra return required for high-grade bonds of prudently capitalized corporations is limited.

Exposure to Risk Components

It will be useful at this point to use the data shown in Table 5-16 to assess the extent of each of four major bond classes' exposure to the four sources of risk: interest rate, purchasing power, business, and financial risk. Note that the table shows four bond classes: (1) Treasury bills, to represent a short-term security of the highest quality; (2) 20-year government bonds, to represent a long-term security of the highest quality; (3) 30-year AAA corporate bonds, to represent long-term corporates of high quality, and (4) high-yield, or junk, bonds.

The first four columns represent the four components of risk. Exposure to risk is rated on a scale of 5, where 1 means no exposure, 5 represents maximum exposure, and 3 represents average exposure. A rating of 2 indicates below-average exposure to a risk component, while a rating of 4 represents above-average exposure. The fifth column in the table shows the sum of the ratings in each row across, providing a measure of overall exposure to the

TABLE 5-16
Risk-return relationship

	Interest rate (1)	Purchasing power (2)	Business (3)	Financial (4)	Total risk (5)
Treasury bills	1	2	1	1	5
Long-term government bonds	3	5	1	1	10
AAA corporate bonds	3	5	2	2	12
Junk bonds	2	4	4	5	15

risk components. This aggregation is merely an attempt to provide relative rankings of the securities with respect to risk exposure and should not be construed as a precise ordering.

Note that Treasury bills are exposed only to purchasing power risk, and even there only to a limited degree. Treasury bills are often used as proxies for risk-free securities, and their ranking as the least exposed to the components of risk provides some insight into why this is so. Long-term governments show a somewhat greater overall exposure to risk components, mainly deriving from an average exposure to the interest rate risk and maximum exposure to the purchasing power risk. AAA corporates are similarly exposed to the interest rate and purchasing power risks as long-term governments are, but they also exhibit a moderate degree of exposure to business and financial risk. Junk bonds show extreme exposure to financial risks and high exposure to business and purchasing power risk. Because of high current coupons and yields, duration and interest rate risk exposure are less for junk bonds.

The summed ratings across risk categories provide an aggregate measure of the riskiness of individual bond classes. Note that Treasury bills show the lowest aggregate score, at 5, and junk bonds total the highest, at 15. The resultant ranking of bond classes is one that would generally conform to investors' perception of the relative riskiness of these bond classes: T-bill lowest and junk bond highest. Furthermore, the relative returns earned by these differing bond classes over longer periods are generally in line with their riskiness.

While risk and return are generally aligned over longer periods, performance for the individual bond categories can vary considerably over shorter periods, depending on the existing economic environment. For example, Treasury bills performed relatively well during the period of accelerating inflation and rising interest rates from 1970 to the early 1980s, because of low exposure to purchasing power and interest rate risks. Long-duration, high-quality bonds did well after 1981, when inflation subsided (disinflation) and interest rates declined substantially over an extended period. In comparison, junk bonds performed less well over the same period, offering less capital gains potential because of a shorter duration. Correspondingly, junk bonds performed quite poorly in the late 1980s and early 1990s, when bankruptcy risk became prominent, but they performed quite well in 1993, when credit conditions improved.

CONCLUSION

This chapter has dealt with the underlying theory of valuation models. We have seen that these models provide a way of explicitly developing returns for bonds. Furthermore, we have seen that these models allow us to develop a greater understanding of how fundamental sources of risk, such as interest rate, inflation, business, and financial risks, affect the risk-return characteristics of bonds. Developing explicit returns and understanding the risk-return characteristics of securities are, of course, critically important as inputs for generating portfolios of securities that are optimal in terms of risk and return.

APPENDIX A
GENERAL FORMULA FOR A PERPETUITY

We can show the general formulation for calculating a perpetuity by first writing out the cash outlay P and the inflow pattern CF for the hypothetical security in the form of an IRR problem:

$$1000 = \frac{300}{(1+k)} + \frac{300}{(1+k)^2} + \frac{300}{(1+k)^3} + \cdots + \frac{300}{(1+k)^t} \qquad \text{(A)}$$

When we multiply both sides of Equation (A) by $(1 + k)$, we obtain

$$1000(1+k) = 300 + \frac{300}{(1+k)} + \frac{300}{(1+k)^2} + \cdots + \frac{300}{(1+k)^{t-1}} \qquad \text{(B)}$$

Subtracting Equation (A) from Equation (B), we obtain

$$1000(1+k) - 1000 = 300 - \frac{300}{(1+k)^t} \qquad \text{(C)}$$

As the investment horizon becomes longer (i.e., as t approaches infinity), $300/(1+k)^t$ approaches zero because the denominator becomes ever larger. We end up with

$$1000k = 300$$

$$k = \frac{\text{CF}}{P} = \frac{300}{1000} = 30\% \qquad \text{(D)}$$

SELECTED REFERENCES

Altman, E.: "Financial Ratios, Discriminant Analysis and the Prediction of Corporate Bankruptcy," *Journal of Finance,* September 1968, pp. 589–609.

———: "The Anatomy of the High-Yield Bond Market," *Financial Analysts Journal,* July–August 1987, pp. 12–25.

———: "Defaults and Returns on High-Yield Bonds Through the First Half of 1991," *Financial Analysts Journal,* November–December 1991, pp. 67–77.

———: "Defaulted Bonds: Demand, Supply and Performance 1987–1992," *Financial Analysts Journal,* May–June 1993, pp. 55–60.

Bierwag, G. O., George Kaufman, and Alden Toevs: "Duration: Its Development and Use in Bond Portfolio Management," *Financial Analysts Journal,* July–August 1983, pp. 15–37.

Blume, Marshall, and Donald Keim: "Lower-Grade Bonds: Their Risks and Return," *Financial Analysts Journal,* July–August 1987, pp. 26–33.

———: "Realized Returns and Defaults on Low-Grade Bonds: The Cohort of 1977 and 1978," *Financial Analysts Journal,* March–April 1991, pp. 63–72.

Chua, Jess: "A Closed-Form Formula for Calculating Bond Duration," *Financial Analysts Journal,* May–June 1984, pp. 76–78.

Fabozzi, Frank, and T. Dessa Fabozzi: *Bond Markets, Analyses and Strategies,* Prentice-Hall, Englewood Cliffs, NJ, 1989.

Fama, E. F.: "Short-Term Interest Rates as Predictors of Inflation," *American Economic Review,* June 1975, pp. 269–282.

Fisher, Lawrence: "Determinants of Risk Premiums on Corporate Bonds," *Journal of Political Economy,* June 1959, pp. 217–237.

Fong, Gifford: *Bond Portfolio Analysis,* Monograph 11, Financial Analysts Research Foundation, Charlottesville, VA, 1980.

Grier, Paul, and Steven Katz: "The Differential Effects of Bond Rating Changes among Industrial and Public Utility Bonds by Maturity," *Journal of Business,* April 1976, pp. 226–239.

Hickman, W. Braddock: *Corporate Bond Quality and Investor Experience,* National Bureau of Economic Research, New York, 1958.

Homer, Sidney, and M. L. Liebowitz: *Inside the Yield Book,* Prentice-Hall, Englewood Cliffs, NJ, 1972.

Hopewell, Michael H., and George G. Kaufman: "Bond Price Volatility and Term to Maturity: A Generalized Respecification," *American Economic Review,* September 1973, pp. 749–753.

Kessel, Reuben: "The Cyclical Behavior of the Term Structure of Interest Rates," Occasional Paper 91, National Bureau of Economic Research, New York, 1965.

Macauley, F. R.: *The Movement of Interest Rates, Bond Yields and Stock Yields in the United States since 1856.* National Bureau of Economic Research, New York, 1938.

Malkiel, Burton: "Expectations, Bond Prices, and the Term Structure of Interest Rates," *Quarterly Journal of Economics,* May 1962, pp. 197–218.

Pinches, George E., and Kent A. Mingo: "A Multivariate Analysis of Industrial Bond Ratings," *Journal of Finance,* March 1973, pp. 1–18.

Pinches, G. E.: "Factors Influencing Classification Results from Multiple Discriminant Analysis," *Journal of Business Research,* December 1980, pp. 429–456.

Pogue, Thomas F., and Robert M. Soldofsky: "What's in a Bond Rating?" *Journal of Financial and Quantitative Analysis,* June 1969, pp. 201–228.

Reilly, Frank, and Rupinder Sidlus: "The Many Uses of Bond Duration," *Financial Analysts Journal,* July–August 1980, pp. 58–72.

Reilly, Frank, G. Werehi Kao, and David Wright: "Alternative Bond Market Indexes," *Financial Analysts Journal,* May–June 1992, pp. 47–58.

QUESTIONS AND PROBLEMS

1. Assume there is a bond paying an $80 coupon with a term to maturity of three years. Calculate the yield to maturity when the bond sells at (a) par, (b) $800, and (c) $1100.
2. Assume there are two bonds paying a $100 coupon, but one has a term to maturity of four years and the other a term to maturity of seven years. Determine the price of the bonds when the yield to maturity is 8 percent. Then determine the price of the two bonds when the yield is 12 percent, and calculate the percentage change in price from the prior yield.
3. Determine the duration for the following securities:
    (a) a bond due to pay $1200 (interest and principal) at the end of four years and selling at $900
    (b) a bond paying a $100 coupon, selling at $800, and having a maturity value of $1000 in four years
    (c) a "mortgage" type of security making level payments of $500 per annum over a life of four years
    (d) a preferred stock selling at $560 and paying a dividend of $4 per share
4. Determine the expected price change for each of the securities in the preceding problem associated with a 0.10 percent change in the required return (discount rate) of each.
5. Explain the key differences between terms in each of these sets:
    (a) nominal rate, real rate of return
    (b) yield to maturity, coupon rate
    (c) duration, term to maturity
    (d) discount, premium
    (e) inflation premium, risk premium.
6. Explain why and how price volatility of bonds is affected by duration.
7. Explain why yield spreads change and how variations in yield spreads can be incorporated into the management of a bond portfolio.

8. From Level I, 1984 CFA Exam:
   Assume a $10,000 par value zero-coupon bond with a term to maturity at issue of 10 years and a market yield of 8 percent.
   (a) Determine the duration of the bond.
   (b) Calculate the initial issue price of the bond at a market yield of 8 percent.
   (c) Twelve months after issue, this bond is selling to yield 12 percent. Calculate its then-current marked price. Calculate your pretax rate of return, assuming you owned this bond during the 12-month period.
9. Suppose you purchase one of each of the following bonds:

	Annual coupon	Face value	Internal yield	Years to maturity
Bond 1	$85	$1,000	10%	2
Bond 2	0	$1,000	9%	1

   (a) Compute the internal yield of the portfolio of bonds.
   (b) Show how you would proceed to get the Macaulay duration of this portfolio.
10. What does duration measure?
11. What does immunization mean?
12. Assume you have a liability with three required payments:

   $3000 due in 1 year
   $2000 due in 2 years
   $1000 due in 3 years

   (a) What is the Macaulay duration of this liability at a 20 percent rate of interest?
   (b) At a 5 percent rate of interest?
13. CFA Examination I:
    Rank the following bonds in order of descending duration. Explain your reasoning (no calculations required). [10 minutes]
    (a) 15% coupon, 20-year, yield-to-maturity at 10%
    (b) 15% coupon, 15-year, yield-to-maturity at 10%
    (c) Zero-coupon, 20-year, yield-to-maturity at 10%
    (d) 8% coupon, 20-year, yield-to-maturity at 10%
    (e) 15% coupon, 15-year, yield-to-maturity at 15%
14. CFA Examination I:
    You are asked to consider the following bond for possible inclusion in your company's fixed-income portfolio:

Issuer	Coupon	Yield-to-maturity	Maturity	Duration
Wiser company	8%	8%	10 years	7.25 years

   (a) 1. Explain why the Wiser bond's duration is less than its maturity.
       2. Explain whether a bond's duration or its maturity is a better measure of the bond's sensitivity to changes in interest rates. [4 minutes]
   (b) Briefly explain the impact on the duration of the Wiser Company bond under each of the following conditions: [6 minutes]
       1. The coupon is 4% rather than 8%.
       2. The yield-to-maturity is 4% rather than 8%.
       3. The maturity is seven years rather than ten years.

15. A 9-year-old bond has a yield of 10% and a duration of 7.194 years. If the market yield changes by 50 basis points, what is the change in the bond's price?

16. Find the duration of a 6% coupon bond making annual coupon payments if it has 3 years until maturity and has a yield to maturity of 6%. What is the duration if the yield to maturity is 10%?

17. CFA Examination Level 1, 1985:
Rank the following bonds in order of descending duration:

Bond	Coupon (%)	Time to maturity (years)	Yield-to-maturity (%)
A	15	20	10
B	15	15	10
C	0	20	10
D	8	20	10
E	15	15	15

18. A 3.0 percent coupon Treasury bond that has 16 years until its maturity date yields 3.0 percent so that it is priced to sell at its par value of $10,000. (*a*) If the market interest rate rises by 100 basis points from a starting point where the YTM equals 3.0 percent, how much will the bond's price change? (*b*) If the market interest rate falls by 100 basis points from a starting point where the YTM equals 3.0 percent, how much will the bond's price change? (*c*) Which of the bond pricing theorems describes what your calculations have documented?

19. Why must the duration of a coupon-bearing bond always be less than the time to its maturity date?

20. Rank order the following bonds in terms of duration. Explain the rationale behind your rankings. (You do not have to actually calculate the bonds' durations. Simple logical reasoning will suffice.)

Bond	Term to maturity	Coupon interest rate	Yield-to-maturity
1	30 years	10%	10%
2	30	0	10
3	30	10	7
4	5	10	10

21. Consider a bond with 3.5 year duration. If its yield to maturity increases from 8.0% to 8.3%, what is the expected percentage change in the price of the bond?

22. Explain why "immunization" permits a bond investor to be confident of meeting a given liability on a predetermined future date.

23. Why does $D(\Delta r)$ not provide the exact percentage change in bond price for a given change in yield to maturity?

24. What is the realized yield to maturity for a 10%, 5-year debenture bought at par if the bondholder fails to reinvest the coupons?

25. What is the realized yield to maturity of a 10%, 10-year bond bought at par if the reinvestment rate is 8% for the life of the bond?

26. From Level III, 1983 CFA Exam:
The ability to immunize a bond portfolio is very desirable for bond portfolio managers in some instances.
   (*a*) Discuss the components of interest rate risk. In other words, assuming a change in interest rates over time, explain the two risks faced by the holder of a bond.
   (*b*) Define immunization and discuss why a bond manager would immunize his portfolio.
   (*c*) Explain why a duration-matching strategy is a superior technique to a maturity-matching strategy for the minimization of interest rate risk.

27. What is a yield spread, and how do investors utilize yield spreads to assess default risk?
28. A credit rating is a precise measurement of a bond's default risk. Comment.
29. On May 20, 1983, the following yields to maturity existed for long-term bonds on a certain date:

U.S. government	10.38%
Aaa corporate	10.69%
Aa corporate	10.99%
A corporate	11.48%
Baa corporate	11.74%

(a) What were the yield spreads for Aaa, Aa, A, and Baa corporate bonds on this date, based on the U.S. government rate?
(b) If economic conditions subsequently improved, would you expect any change in these yield spreads, and if so, why?

30. From Level II, 1983 CFA Exam:
Quality ratings on bonds are very important because they not only indicate creditworthiness but also have a significant impact on market yields. Therefore, it is important to be aware of the variables that influence the bond ratings assigned and also the cyclical pattern in the quality of bonds issued.
(a) Set forth four major determinants of the ratings assigned to bond issues, and explain why and how each of these determinants affects the ratings.
(b) Discuss why you would expect a cyclical pattern to the quality of bonds issued. Explain the implication of this cyclical pattern for bond portfolio management.

31. Junk bonds are often viewed by investors as having financial characteristics much more akin to those of common stocks than to high-grade corporate bonds. Why?
32. What is convexity, and how does it relate to the problem of managing bonds?
33. Describe how you would adjust for the effects of convexity when evaluating the responsiveness of bonds to changing interest rates.
34. Assume a 20-year zero-coupon bond with a yield to maturity of 7.5%. Calculate the price response from a decline in rates of 50 basis points. Compare that price response to that derived from a duration and convexity estimate.
35. What are the major determinants of convexity, and how do these determinants affect the bond's convexity?
36. Describe approaches that bond managers have used in constructing portfolios.
37. What kinds of interest rate environements are most appropriate for these differing approaches?
38. There has been an unanticipated decline in inflation from 4% to 3%. What is the likely impact on a five-year zero-coupon bond yielding 7%?
39. Interest rates show a 100-basis-point increase. Indicate the relative impact on government bonds and junk bonds. Explain.

CHAPTER 6

Applying Valuation Model Methods

INTRODUCTION

This chapter begins by discussing the underlying theory of equity valuation models. It then describes how these models can be and have been applied to solve practical problems of stock evaluation. To begin with, we will see that the valuation model needs to be specialized for the particular kind of company being analyzed, because companies differ significantly in operating characteristics. Some companies have highly stable earnings patterns, whereas others have erratic or cyclical patterns of earnings. Similarly, some companies are expected to show a strong pattern of growth in earnings, whereas most others will grow more or less in line with the economy. These differing operating patterns in turn require modification of the basic dividend capitalization model in order to accommodate the differences properly. We will discuss what these modifications are and how they apply to the different kinds of companies.

We will also see that no matter what variation of the model is used, there is a critical need to ensure that inputs to these models are developed as carefully as possible. Poorly developed or inappropriate inputs will degrade the performance of even the most elegantly constructed model. Developing appropriate inputs is the responsibility of the fundamental analyst, and the greater the skill and effort of the analyst in developing the inputs, the better the performance of the model will be. Therefore, we will illustrate this process by describing a framework that analysts would typically use to develop inputs for a valuation model. We will also describe examples of how the framework can be used.

The final part of the chapter describes a framework for considering the risk and return of common stocks simultaneously. It is, in fact, the empirical counterpart of the security market line (SML) described in a theoretical context in Chapter 3. We will first show how the market line is constructed in practice. In the process it should become clear that this framework provides an explicit link between valuation theory and models of the risk-return relationship (like the SML and APT) that grow out of portfolio and capital market theory. Once we have described how the line is constructed, we will illustrate the three major uses of the market line: (1) assessing the relative valuation level of the market, (2) assessing the risk-return trade-off in the equity market, and (3) identifying relatively undervalued and overvalued individual securities.

STOCK VALUATION MODELS

Stock valuation is more difficult than bond valuation. Both the cash flow stream (interest) and time horizon (maturity) are well specified in the case of bonds, but these factors need more careful consideration in the case of stocks. To introduce the subject of stock valuation, then, it will be appropriate to consider what constitutes return for a stock, first for a one-year horizon and then for an infinite horizon. We will see that the fundamental determinant of value for a stock is the same for an investor with a short or a long horizon. To begin with, recall that the formula for holding-period returns to determine stock returns for an investor with less than an infinite investment horizon is

$$k = \frac{D + P_1 - P_0}{P_0} \tag{1}$$

In words, this says that return k is dividends paid D plus any change in price $P_1 - P_0$ over the period (assumed to be one year in this case), divided by the initial price P_0. Restating this formula in terms of the familiar present-value format, we obtain

$$P_0 = \frac{D}{1 + k} + \frac{P_1}{1 + k}$$

This says that the current price is a function of dividends to be paid at the end of the year, plus the price of the stock at year end discounted back at the rate k. In the case of an investor with a longer horizon, we can restate the formula more generally as follows:

$$P_0 = \sum_{t=1}^{T} \frac{D_t}{(1 + k)^t} + \frac{P_T}{(1 + k)^T} \tag{2}$$

As the investor's horizon gets longer—as T approaches infinity—the second term becomes insignificant. At infinity the second term goes to zero, so that we are left with expected return consisting entirely of the dividend flow. Expected return is then determined by solving the following equation for k:

$$P_0 = \sum_{t=1}^{T} \frac{D_t}{(1 + k)^t} \tag{3}$$

This formula demonstrates that for an investor with an infinite horizon (or, for practical purposes, anyone with a sufficiently long time perspective) the fundamental determinant of stock value is the dividend flow. We can also deduce less directly that the flow of dividends is the fundamental determinant even for an investor with a relatively short horizon, who buys with the intention of selling. The reason is that the price received when the investor sells the stock will be determined by what other investors perceive as the expected flow of dividends in the future.

It should be noted that this same analysis applies whether the stock is currently paying dividends or not. In the case of a non–dividend-paying stock, as typified by very high-growth stocks, the stockholder with a less than infinite horizon expects to obtain his sole return by selling the stock at a higher-than-current price. Again, this selling price is a function of the projected dividends to be paid out at some future time. Thus, ultimately, the dividend is what determines the value of a corporation for an investor with a short- or long-term perspective. We will illustrate this analysis again in a more rigorous format in a later section.

Dividend Capitalization Model

The preceding section indicated that the relevant cash flows are dividends for stocks and coupon payments for bonds. It also indicated that the relevant time horizon for stocks is perpetual, whereas for bonds it is finite and set by terms of the bond indenture. Despite these differences, we can still state the basic stock valuation model in the same general IRR form used for bond evaluation (see Equation 5-4). Using P as stock price, D as dividend, k as the discount rate for stocks, and t as the time period over which the dividends are received, we can express the stock model as

$$P = \frac{D_1}{1 + k} + \frac{D_2}{(1 + k)^2} + \frac{D_3}{(1 + k)^3} + \cdots + \frac{D_t}{(1 + k)^t} = \sum_{t=1}^{T} \frac{D_t}{(1 + k)^t} \qquad (4)$$

This model is the generalized version of the *dividend capitalization model.* In this form, however, it is unsuitable for practical application, as one would have to develop estimates of the individual cash flows, or dividends (D_1, D_2, etc.), over a very long period—in theory, to infinity. Since this is obviously impossible, modifications—simplifications, if you will—of this model must be developed in order to implement it for practical purposes of stock valuation.

We discuss two simplifications of the model that are, in fact, suitable for practical application and sufficiently flexible to accommodate the various types of common stock available. In this regard, two types are needed in order to accommodate the two major categories of common-stock dividend growth: (1) normal, or generally average, growth and (2) supernormal, or generally above-average, growth. In this section we cover the modification of the model for normal or generally average dividend growth, along with the assumptions involved; then, in subsequent sections, we will discuss the modification for supernormal growth companies and the reasons it is needed. We will also illustrate how investors can develop suitable inputs for these models and develop data for use in portfolio construction.

As noted, the most basic simplification of the dividend capitalization model applies to the case of normal growth. Developed by several authors, it is now probably most closely associated with Gordon. In developing the model a couple of key assumptions are made: that dividends grow at a constant rate g over an infinite time horizon and that the discount rate k is greater than the growth rate g. By making the first assumption, we can eliminate the necessity of considering the dividends year by year over time. In this case we apply a growth rate to an initial dividend, and the dividend rate at a particular year becomes the initial dividend compounded out to a future value at that date. We can then convert the generalized form of the dividend capitalization model to the following form:

$$P = \frac{D_0(1 + g)}{(1 + k)} + \frac{D_0(1 + g)^2}{(1 + k)^2} + \frac{D_0(1 + g)^3}{(1 + k)^3} + \cdots + \frac{D_0(1 + g)^t}{(1 + k)^t}$$

$$= \sum_{t=1}^{T} \frac{D_0(1 + g)^t}{(1 + k)^t} \qquad (5)$$

We can then use applicable techniques for converting cash flow streams that continue at a constant rate over an infinite time—that is, perpetual annuities or perpetuities—into a simpler form. The application of these techniques is described in greater detail in Appendix A to this chapter. Meanwhile, applying these techniques to Equation 2 and making the assumption $k > g$ reduces the model to the desired simpler form shown below.[1]

$$P = \frac{D}{k - g} \tag{6}$$

This simplified form of the dividend capitalization model is the version that is applicable to the problem of valuing companies that are growing at normal or average rates. Put into words, the model says that the value of a stock is equal to its year-ahead forecasted dividend per share D capitalized by the difference between the company's discount rate k and its growth rate g. For example, if a company was expected to pay $2 in dividends and was growing at a rate of 5 percent, and if the appropriate discount rate for that company was 9 percent, the price of the stock would be

$$P = \frac{2.00}{(0.09 - 0.05)} = \$50$$

STOCK VALUE AND DIFFERING MODEL INPUTS

It is useful to redefine some of the terms of the dividend capitalization model, both for help in understanding the factors that create differences in values (prices) and for greater ease of practical implementation. To begin with, we can define E as earnings and b as the retention rate for earnings, so that $1 - b$ becomes the dividend payout ratio. We can then regard dividends as the payout ratio $1 - b$ times the earnings level E. Correspondingly, when we define r as the rate of return on retained earnings, we can multiply this by the retention rate b to obtain a growth rate.[2] Inserting these new definitions into the model, we have

---

[1] This assumption is necessary, for if g is greater than k, all values become infinite, and if g is almost equal to k, all values become too large to be meaningful.

[2] We can analytically show that $g = rb$, as follows. First, we assume that the firm will maintain a stable dividend policy (keep its retention rate constant) and earn a stable return on new equity investment I over time. Since growth in earnings arises from the return on new investments, we can represent earnings at a given time as

$$E_t = E_{t-1} + rI_t$$

Since the firm's retention rate is constant, then

$$E_t = E_{t-1} + rbE_{t-1} = E_{t-1}(1 + rb)$$

Growth in earnings is the percentage change in earnings, or

$$g = \frac{E_t - E_{t-1}}{E_{t-1}} = \frac{E_{t-1}(1 + rb) - E_{t-1}}{E_{t-1}} = rb$$

Since a constant proportion of earnings is assumed to be paid out each year, the growth in earnings equals the growth in dividends, or

$$g_E = g_D = rb$$

In estimating the return on retained earnings, one can assume that the return on investment will be similar to the returns on total investment. Value Line regularly publishes the historical return on net worth as well as one-, two-, and five-year forecasts of this return. Using this data and the estimated retention rate, one can develop a projected growth rate. We illustrate this more fully in subsequent sections.

$$P = \frac{(1-b)E}{k-br}$$

In turn, we can convert this model into a price/earnings (P/E) ratio model simply by moving the earnings variable to the left-hand side of the equation (dividing both sides by E):

$$P/E = \frac{(1-b)}{k-br}$$

Put into in words, this model says that the P/E ratio is equal to the dividend payout rate $1-b$ divided by the difference between the discount rate k and the growth rate g (as represented by the retention rate b times the return on retained earnings r). We can use this model to analyze the effects of changes in the fundamental input on the P/E ratio. We can best illustrate this for a hypothetical security that pays a \$2 dividend out of \$4 in earnings per share (target payout rate of 50 percent), shows a 14 percent rate of return on investment, and has a growth rate of 7 percent and a discount rate of 12 percent. The P/E ratio with these inputs would be 10, as shown below.

$$P/E = \frac{(1-b)}{(k-br)} = \frac{0.50}{0.12-(0.5)(0.14)} = 10$$

Table 6-1 shows the effect on the P/E ratio of varying the discount rate and rate of return on retained earnings of the company, holding the payout rate constant. The numbers in the left-hand column of the table show the range of discount rates considered, and the numbers at the tops of the other columns represent different rates of return on retained earnings—that is, different growth rates of the company. Each number in the body of the table shows the P/E ratio at its column's rate of return on retained earnings and at its row's discount rate.

Note that the P/E ratio varies directly with the return on retained earnings of the company. For example, at the 12 percent discount rate, the P/E ratio is 8.3 when the return is 12 percent, 10 when the return is 14 percent, and 12.5 when it is 16 percent. All other things being equal, highly profitable companies sell at higher P/E ratios than companies with lower profits. On the other hand, the P/E ratio of a company varies inversely with its discount rate. For example, at the 14 percent profitability level, the P/E is 25 when the discount rate is 9 percent, 12.5 when it is 11 percent, and 8.3 when it is 13 percent. Companies with high discount rates should sell at lower P/E ratios than those with lower discount rates.

It is important to recognize that this inverse relationship is linked to the risk concepts we discussed earlier. With higher risk we anticipate higher discount rates and, therefore, lower P/E ratios. All else the same, an investor should be willing to pay more for a dollar's

TABLE 6-1

P/E ratio as a function of the return on retained earnings and the discount rate

Discount rate k	Rate of profitability r				
	12	13	14	15	16
9	16.7	20.0	25.0	33.3	50.0
10	12.5	14.3	16.7	20.0	25.0
11	10.0	11.1	12.5	14.3	16.7
12	8.3	9.1	10.0	11.1	12.5

worth of earnings for the safer expected cash flow. The more uncertain the flow, the less you should be willing to pay for it.

Price/Earnings Ratio and the Discount Rate

Note, finally, that there are two instances in which the *P/E* ratio would be an appropriate indicator of the discount rate for a stock. In one obvious instance the company pays out all its earnings as dividends, so that the earnings variable becomes identical to a dividend variable and the *P/E* ratio is the same as a price/dividend ratio. In terms of our formulation, the retention rate *b* would be zero, and the *P/E* ratio is then equal to the reciprocal of the discount rate:

$$P/E = \frac{(1 - b)}{k - br} = \frac{(1 - 0)}{k - (0)r} = \frac{1}{k}$$

In the second instance the company can only reinvest earnings at the discount rate. This indicates the absence of high return growth opportunities and is the classic finance case known as *expansion,* in which the growth rate is expected to be only average. In terms of our formulation, if the return on reinvested earnings is equal to the discount rate ($r = k$), the *P/E* ratio is then equal to the reciprocal of the discount rate:

$$P/E = \frac{(1 - b)}{k - br} = \frac{(1 - b)}{k(1 - b)} = \frac{1}{k}$$

In Table 6-1, we can see that when the stock has average reinvestment opportunities, as indicated by a return rate *r* and discount rate *k* both equal to 12 percent, the *P/E*, in the bottom left-hand portion of the table, is 8.3. The *E/P* ratio (the inverse of the *P/E*) in this case is also 12 percent and is therefore an appropriate estimate of the actual discount rate. In the presence of high return rate opportunities, the *E/P* ratio would, however, be lower than the discount rate for stocks. For example, at a *P/E* ratio of 10, the simple inverse estimate of the discount rate would be 10 percent, but the table shows that the *E/P* ratio of 10 percent would underestimate the discount rate for a stock with a profitability rate of 14 percent by two percentage points. The true discount rate should be 12 percent, as shown in the left-hand column of the table. In these cases—generally for most stocks—a model that considers growth, such as the dividend discount model, must be used.

Dividend Capitalization Model: Simplified Form

To this point we have analyzed the dividend capitalization model as a way of determining a price or value for a stock. Generally, however, the variable of most interest to investors is the discount rate *k* for the stock. This is because the price of the stock can readily be found, and variables such as the current dividend and the growth rate can be estimated, albeit with varying degrees of ease. We can use the simplified form of the dividend capitalization model for this purpose by rearranging it into a suitable form for estimating the discount rate *k*, as shown below.

$$k = \frac{D}{P} + g \tag{7}$$

This equation states that the discount rate *k* for a stock is a function of two variables: the dividend yield, which is the year-ahead dividend *D* divided by the stock price *P*, and the growth rate of the dividend g. Estimating the dividend and the growth rate of the dividend can be facilitated by first redefining these variables. Defining E as earnings and $1 - b$ as a payout rate, dividends can be thought of as a function of a payout rate and an earnings level $D = (1 - b)E$. Further defining b as a retention rate and r as a return on equity, or a measure of profitability, we can think of the growth rate of the dividend as a function of the retention rate and return on equity, $g = br$. Using these alternative definitions, the equation for determining the discount rate becomes

$$k = \frac{(1 - b)E}{P} + br \qquad (8)$$

Note that in this form, generating inputs thus becomes a task of developing estimates for the following variables: the level of earnings E; the retention rate b or, alternatively, the payout rate $1 - b$; and the basic level of profitability r. The retention or payout rate is a policy variable established by the management of the company. It can be assessed by gauging the behavior of the corporation from past payouts of earnings or, more directly, from the stated policy of the corporation; for example, the management may have a policy of paying out 50 percent of earnings over a longer period of time. Estimating the level of earnings E and the productivity of retained earnings r is, however, a function of the fundamental analyst.

Table 6-2 shows a particularly useful framework that a fundamental analyst can use in the assessment of the earnings level and the return on reinvested earnings of the corporation. The top row of the table shows that the level of earnings per share of the company is a function of five variables: (1) profit margin, (2) capital turnover, (3) a financial leverage factor, (4) a tax rate effect, and (5) level of book value. The exact definition of these variables is shown at the bottom of the table. Note that the multiplication of the first four variables produces the rate of return, which is the earnings per share divided by the book value per share, as shown in the second row of the figure. Also note that the rate of return of the company will be high when the capital turnover is high, profit margins are high, the tax rate is low, and leverage is high and positive. Conversely, the rate of return of the company will be low when the capital turnover is low, profit margins are low, the tax rate is high, and leverage is low. The earnings level will also vary directly with the rate of return on equity and will be correspondingly higher or lower as the book value of the company increases or decreases, respectively.

Book value increases as earnings are retained and will be higher or lower depending on the retention rate b. The retention rate interacts with the rate of return on retained earnings

TABLE 6-2

Fundamental factors in corporate profitability

$$\text{EPS} = M \times T \times L \times U \times B$$

$$\text{Return } r = \text{EPS}/B = M \times T \times L \times U$$

where M = the ratio of net operating income to sales
$\quad\quad\ T$ = the turnover ratio, defined as the ratio of sales to total tangible assets
$\quad\quad\ L$ = the extent to which the return on equity has been raised by the use of leverage, i.e., using debt together with equity
$\quad\quad\ U$ = the after-tax rate $U = (1 - t)$, where t is the tax rate
$\quad\quad\ B$ = the book value per share

TABLE 6-3
Retention, rate of return, and growth

	Company A	Company B
Book value per share B	10.00	10.00
Rate of return on equity r	18%	12%
Earnings per share $B \times r$	1.80	1.20
Retention rate b	2/3	1/3
Retained earnings $b \times$ EPS	1.20	0.40
Earnings on retained earnings $r \times$ RE	0.216	0.048
New level of earnings	2.016	1.248
Growth rate of earnings	(2.016/1.80) − 1 = 12%	(1.248/1.20) − 1 = 4%
Sustainable growth br	12%	4%

to produce growth $g = br$. The growth in book value, and hence in earnings and dividends, will be higher as the rate of retention and return on retained earnings increase. Conversely, it will be lower as the rate of retention and return on retained earnings decrease. While there are other sources of growth, it is especially helpful to think of growth in terms of retention and rate of return on retained earnings, since over the long term this is the only sustainable source of growth for the firm. In fact, some have referred to it as *sustainable growth,* since other potential sources of growth are, by their nature, limited in the extent to which they can change, and hence do not represent sustained, or recurring, sources of growth.[3]

The contribution of earnings retention and investment return to growth can be specifically illustrated by comparing two hypothetical corporations, as shown in Table 6-3. Company A has a return on investment of 18 percent and retains two-thirds of its earnings (one-third payout), whereas company B has a return on investment of 12 percent and retains one-third of its earnings (two-thirds payout). The table shows that company A's earnings will grow by $0.216, or 12 percent, over the next year, whereas company B's earnings will grow by $0.048, or 4 percent, over the next year. These are, of course, the same percentage changes that are implied by the sustainable growth calculation br for both companies. As expected, high return and retention lead to high growth and low return and retention lead to low growth.

Estimating the Discount Rate

We can most easily illustrate the use of the dividend capitalization model in developing a discount rate by estimating the discount rate, or expected return, of the market as a whole. To begin with, the model should be applicable to the total market, since the market is simply an aggregation of individual stocks; if the model applies to the individual components, it should apply to the total. Furthermore, in dealings with an aggregate rather than an individual stock, errors in measuring inputs tend to cancel out; that is, overestimates tend to be offset by underestimates. There is, in effect, an automatic smoothing or normalizing of the data

---

[3]Growth of equity per share has two principal sources: (1) the sale of new stock at a price higher than the existing book value per share; and (2) the plowing back of earnings into the business—that is, paying out only a portion of net income in cash dividends to common stockholders and retaining and reinvesting the balance. Of these two sources, the second is far and away the most important for most companies.

that makes the data more suitable for direct use in the simplified version of the dividend capitalization model.

Table 6-4 shows some relevant valuation data for a fairly representative index of the U.S. equity market: Standard & Poor's Composite Index of 500 Stocks (the S&P 500). This table shows, for the five-year period of 1989–1993, data on earnings, payout ratios, return on investment, and retention rate times the return on investment. Note that the payout ratio averaged 50 percent but fluctuated over the period, whereas the return on investment decreased from 18.1 to 16.0 percent, averaging 14.9 percent for the period.

The 1993 retention rate and return on investment imply a sustainable growth of 8.5 percent. The value of the S&P 500 averaged between 429 and 471 during 1993, and the dividend was $12.70, giving a yield of 2.8 percent. Combining this yield with a sustainable growth of 8.5 percent indicates a discount rate, or expected return, of 11.3 percent for the S&P 500. Of course, this is an average and will differ across companies due to differences in risk, as we will see later in the chapter.

Table 6-4 also compares this current "expected" return of 11.3 percent with that earned by stocks over the 67-year period of 1926–1993. Though the absolute return is now higher than that realized over the 1926–1993 period, it is not necessarily higher when inflation is taken into account. In particular, the 10.3 percent return was earned over a period when the rate of inflation averaged 3.1 percent, providing a real return of 7.2 percent (10.3 percent less 3.1 percent) for stocks. In the five-year period of 1989–1993 inflation averaged 3.9 percent. This figure would imply a real return on stocks of 7.4 percent (expected return of 11.3 percent less underlying inflation of 3.9 percent).

Despite the fact that the current expected nominal return on stocks is different from the past average, the current "expected" real return on stocks is fairly close to that earned over the longer term. This apparent relative stability in real return might, in turn, be helpful in developing a forecast of future return on stocks. In particular, one might build a return forecast by adding the estimated inflation rate and the real return.

Besides application to the overall market, the simplified form of the model is also appropriate for use with certain types of companies that we might characterize as stable and more

TABLE 6-4
The S&P 500—expected return

Year	Earnings E	Payout ratio $1 - b$	Return on investment r	Dividends D	Retention rate b	Growth rate br
1989	24.65	44.8%	18.06%	11.05	0.55	9.9%
1990	23.55	51.4%	15.91%	12.32	0.49	7.8%
1991	20.34	59.8%	10.66%	12.20	0.40	4.3%
1992	22.49	54.7%	13.67%	12.38	0.45	6.2%
1993	26.64	47.2%	16.04%	12.70	0.53	8.5%

Expected return $= [(1 - b)E/P] + br = 2.8\% + 8.5\% = 11.3\%$

Inflation rate	3.9%
Expected real return	7.4%
Realized return 1926–1978	10.3%
Inflation	3.1%
Realized real return	7.2%

Source: Standard and Poor's Security Price Index Record, Standard and Poor's Corporation, New York.

mature. For such companies, the earnings patterns as well as retention rates and returns on investment are fairly stable over time. This is because their investment opportunities, which are a prime consideration in setting the retention rate, are fairly constrained and their basic profitability is pretty constant over time.

As a result, developing the inputs and applying them to the model are fairly straightforward tasks in the case of mature, stable companies. For example, we might use the simplified form of the dividend capitalization model to estimate the expected return for Kellogg. At year-end 1993 Kellogg was selling at $57 and paying a dividend of $1.40, to provide a yield of 2.5 percent. The company's sustainable growth rate was 9.0 percent. Combining these two inputs would indicate an expected return of 11.5 percent for the company.

Though the formula is useful in cases like that of Kellogg, it must be modified substantially to deal with companies that have a highly cyclical operating pattern, such as General Motors (GM), or companies that are expected to show exceptionally high rates of earnings growth, such as Microsoft. The problem with cyclical companies is one of casting the inputs in a suitable form for use in the model. The problem with high-growth companies is that the simplified form of the model is not suitable for use, making an alternative form necessary. We will describe this form in a later section of this chapter. Meanwhile, we will describe the problems that must be overcome in analyzing cyclical companies.

Cyclical Companies

The basic problem in using the valuation model for cyclical companies is to normalize the earnings of the company: in other words, "to adjust the earnings of the company to what they would be at the midpoint of an economic cycle."[4] The purpose is to abstract the earning power of the company from abnormal economic influences such as recession or boom. This concept emanates from Graham and Dodd, who describe it extensively in their textbook *Security Analysis.*

We can most easily describe this concept by referring to Figure 6-1, which shows the idealized earnings trend of a hypothetical cyclical company. The vertical axis is a scale indicating the earnings level, and the horizontal axis is a time line starting at year zero. Note that the earnings line fluctuates up and down regularly, depicting the cyclical earnings pattern of the company. Note also that while the line fluctuates, it shows an upward trend over time, indicating a basic growth rate for the company's earnings. The objective of the normalization procedure is, in effect, to smooth out the fluctuating pattern of earnings in order to determine what the earnings are at a normal level, such as that designated "normal earnings" by point *n* on the graph. Another objective is to discern the trend or sustainable rate of earnings growth as depicted by the slope of the dashed line fitted to the fluctuating earnings line. Once we have done this, we have earnings and growth-rate data suitable for input to the valuation model.

The method of normalizing earnings can best be illustrated by the analytical framework shown in Table 6-2, where the earnings per share of a company are expressed as a function of five variables: (1) profit margin, (2) capital turnover, (3) a financial leverage factor, (4) tax rate effect, and (5) level of book value. This framework shows that earnings can change as a result of changes in any of the variables. However, changes in the first four variables—

---

[4]Graham B., D. Dodd, and S. Cottle, *Security Analysis.* 4th ed., McGraw-Hill, New York, 1962.

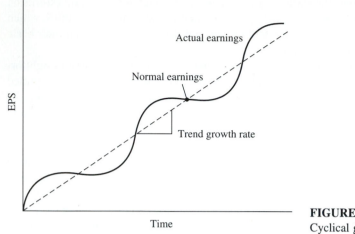

EPS

Actual earnings

Normal earnings

Trend growth rate

Time

FIGURE 6-1
Cyclical growth pattern.

margin, turnover, leverage, and tax effect—cannot be relied upon to sustain growth over a long period of time. Specifically, changes in margin will occur, but upward moves will be limited by competition in the market. Similarly, changes in turnover are almost inevitable, but plant capacity, or the state of technology, will limit the volume of sales relative to capital. Also, the degree of leverage available to a company is limited, either by the willingness of creditors or by the prudence of management. Tax cuts are, of course, a very limited source of growth.

In any one period, changes in these four variables may be critical in determining the level of earnings. Over time, however, the variables will have a tendency to fluctuate around some normal value. These fluctuations will depend on the nature of the industry, the level of the economy, or management discretion, especially with regard to taxes and debt. As has been noted, the fluctuations will be negligible and the need to analyze them limited for a stable company such as Kellogg. On the other hand, for a highly cyclical company such as GM, changes in these variables can be quite sizable, prompting the need for in-depth analysis of these changes. For the more cyclically oriented companies we need to determine the normal levels for margins, turnover, leverage, and taxes, and then multiply them together to obtain a normalized rate of return. Given a normalized rate of return r and a normal retention rate b, we can compute a sustainable growth rate g for normalized earnings per share (EPS) as $g = br$.

Application of Technique

Perhaps it will be helpful to use GM's operating record over the 1973–1974 period—one of severe recession actually stretching into 1975—as a prime example of this kind of analysis. During such a period auto sales are especially adversely affected, resulting in a highly negative effect on turnover and profitability variables. Specifically, fewer sales and a fairly constant capital investment cause a decline in the turnover ratio. Also, fewer sales adversely affect unit costs, leading in turn to a shrinkage in profit margins. The decline in profitability from these two sources is further compounded by a certain amount of debt in capital struc-ture, so that there is a reversal in leverage. In 1974, earnings were below normal owing to

TABLE 6-5
Normalizing earnings—General Motors

	M	×	T	×	L	×	U	=	r	×	B	=	EPS
1974 actual values	5.8		1.54		1.5		0.57		7.7%		$42.8		$3.27
Historical values													
1971	13.40		1.54		1.70		0.52						
1972	14.00		1.66		1.50		0.51						
1973	12.90		1.75		1.60		0.53						
Three-year average	13.40		1.63		1.60		0.52						
1974 normal values	13.4		1.63		1.60		0.52	=	18.1%		$42.8		$7.75

these factors. Actual reported earnings were $3.27 as compared with 1971–1973 earnings of between $7 and $8.

Table 6-5 shows the normalized 1974 GM earnings. The first row gives the actual 1974 earnings along with actual values of the five variables: margin M, turnover T, leverage L, taxes U, and book value B. The middle part of the table shows the values of the variables for the prior three years, 1971–1973, along with an average of the variables over those three years. Averaging the three years of data smooths out cyclical influences and, hence, develops normal values for the variables.

We should note, however, that there are alternative and superior ways of developing normal values for the basic profitability variables. To begin with, we could evaluate the relationships over several business cycles rather than only one, since a twelve-year period might provide more representative figures. Another, possibly preferable, way to focus on specific years in which the economy, and presumably the company, were operating at a "normal" level and use these values as typical or representative. In either case, historical values should be used only as an initial guideline, and the typical, or "normal," values of the past should be adjusted where there may have been a fundamental change. For example, the significant change in the relative price of gasoline and the increasing competition from auto imports may well have changed the fundamental profitability of the auto industry. Professional fundamental analysts would incorporate those kinds of changes into their evaluation of the prospective profitability of the company.

Meanwhile, we use the three-year average to illustrate the normalization process. The final row in Table 6-5 shows the four "normal" values for the variables multiplied together to obtain a "normal" return of approximately 18 percent.[5] Using this return and the same book value of $42.8 indicates that earnings of GM would have been $7.75 if 1974 had been a "normal" year. GM has a policy, or at least a tradition, of paying out approximately two-thirds of its earnings, producing a retention rate b of one-third. Since GM's normalized return on investment r is about 18 percent, sustainable growth g is on the order of 6 percent— that is, $g = br$, $\frac{1}{3}(18$ percent$) = 6$ percent.

---

[5]Note that in this example we have merely been applying historical relationships and not adjusting for future changes in company fundamentals. In particular, the shift to smaller cars is bound to have some effect on the basic profitability of the industry. Some professional analysts believe that this means that GM's profitability has shifted downward to something like 15 percent from the historical 18 percent. One should amend the analysis to account for these changes. Also, the analysis in this section should be considered merely illustrative.

TABLE 6-6
Discount rate—General Motors

$$E(R) = \frac{(1 + b)E}{P} + br$$

$$= \frac{\left(\frac{2}{3}\right)7.75}{30} + \frac{1}{3}(18\%)$$

$$= 17.2\% + 6.0\% = 23.2\%$$

Once these growth and earnings factors have been assessed, we can then apply them directly to the simplified formulation of the dividend capitalization model illustrated in Table 6-6. Inserting the $7.75 computed as normal earnings and the normal dividend payout of two-thirds gives a dividend of $5.15. Relating this to $30—the price at which GM stock was selling as of the end of 1974—indicates a yield of 17.2 percent, which represents only a potential, not actual, yield. With a sustainable growth of 6 percent, this formulation would then provide an expected return of 23.2 percent.

However, we should consider this return only approximate instead of assuming that the company immediately reaches the computed normalized earnings level. It might ordinarily take a cyclical company such as GM two to three years to come out of the trough of an economic cycle and reach its normal earnings level. The assumption of a premature return to normal gives the estimated return an upward bias. Use of a more elaborate formulation, such as the one illustrated in the next chapter, would eliminate the bias and show that the "true" expected return should be 22 percent rather than the previous estimate of 23.2 percent. The simplified model we have shown is useful for purposes of exposition, but for purposes of practical application, use of the more elaborate formulation would be warranted.[6]

GROWTH STOCKS AND THE TWO-STAGE GROWTH MODEL

The most obvious case in which the simplified valuation formula cannot be used to estimate the discount rate for stocks is that of a rapidly growing company. Such companies are unable to conform to the main assumptions used in deriving the simplified form of the dividend capitalization model. Recall that in developing this model, we made two critical assumptions: (1) that the growth rate was constant over an infinitely long period and (2) that the discount rate k was greater than the growth rate g. Constant growth was needed to simplify the dividend progression over time, and the second assumption was necessary to avoid an infinite or negative stock price.

High-growth companies are unlikely to fulfill either of these assumptions. In particular, these companies can be characterized as growing at quite rapid rates relative to general

---

[6]We thus obtain an estimate that is approximately equal to the estimate obtained from the more elaborate formulation. This estimate is somewhat higher because it assumes an earlier flow of higher dividends than other formulations. The bias here is, however, less severe than if one used only a current dividend rate and a sustainable growth in line with the basic profitability of the company—that is, 6 percent. In this case the estimate would have been only 16 percent for expected return. Whether this would have been more appropriate cannot be determined definitively. We do know, however, that GM doubled in price during 1975, outperforming most stocks and giving some credence to the higher estimated return.

economic growth. Quantitatively, these companies would be classified as growing at rates of 15–30 percent, compared with the growth rate of 8–9 percent that was shown to be representative of the current S&P 500 and that might be used as a benchmark for the growth rate of the "nongrowth" stocks. Companies growing at these quite rapid rates of 15–30 percent are unlikely to conform to the assumption of a discount rate that is greater than the growth rate.

At the same time, we cannot assume that this rapid growth will remain constant; we should anticipate a transition to a more normal pace (in line with general economic growth) at some stage. No company could normally be expected to maintain an abnormally high pace of growth. The mere compounding effect of such growth would at some stage result in the company becoming such a large proportion of the economy (if not the total economy itself) that there would be no further prospects of growth. For example, IBM, a premier growth company, showed an earnings growth rate of 18 percent from 1945 to 1980. If the company continued this relative pace of growth and U.S. aggregate corporate profits grew at the historical rate, IBM profits would represent approximately 60–70 percent of aggregate corporate profits in fifteen years. Though possible, continuation of this sort of growth seemed highly unlikely. In fact, IBM's growth rate declined significantly in the 1980s and into the early 1990s.

One convenient way of representing a pattern of growth proceeding at a quite rapid pace in the initial stages and then declining to a rate more in line with the general corporate average is the two-stage growth model. It is the most direct elaboration of the simplified form of the dividend capitalization model. Other multistage elaborations are more complex and allow greater flexibility in the practical application of valuation techniques, but since they are based on the framework of the two-stage growth model, analysis of this model is instructive with regard to more complex elaborations. In addition, the two-stage growth model can be used in developing appropriate valuations for growth stocks, as we will illustrate in this and the following section. For those interested in the multistage growth model, the development and application of this model are described in Chapter 7.

Figure 6-2 illustrates the general pattern of growth assumed by the two-stage growth model to accommodate the expected slowdown in corporate growth. Essentially, the model

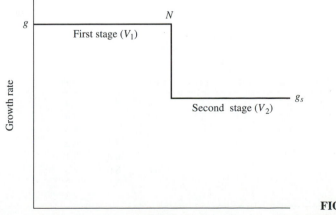

FIGURE 6-2
Two-stage growth model pattern.

presupposes that dividends grow at rate g, which represents the rate associated with super-normal growth, for N periods. It then assumes that the company grows at a rate g_s, which is in line with that of the general corporate average, sometimes referred to as a standard share rate, from $N + 1$ to infinity.

As a matter of interest, it would appear that a 10 percent rate of growth is an approximately representative estimate of the current rate of growth of a standard stock. It is in line with the sustainable growth estimate derived in Table 6-4 for the S&P 500, which might be a useful proxy for a standard share. It is also approximately equal to the rate of growth in dividends for the recent 1975–1990 periods. Table 6-7 shows the rate of dividend growth in the S&P 500 over various periods from 1950 to 1990.

The price of the stock thus becomes a function of two dividend flows: (1) the flow from period 1 to N, which we will call V_1, and (2) the flow from period $N + 1$ to infinity, referred to as V_2. The total value, or price, P of the stock is then a sum of the two flows:

$$P = V_1 + V_2 \tag{9}$$

The two streams can be evaluated by using the techniques for appraising dividend flows, which we covered in earlier sections of the chapter. The V_1 component, in particular, can be evaluated by using the most generalized version of the dividend capitalization model. Using D to represent the beginning dividend, g the growth rate during the period of abnormal growth, N the period of abnormal growth, and k the discount rate, which is constant over the period, the value for the first stage of growth becomes

$$V_1 = \frac{D(1 + g)}{1 + k} + \frac{D(1 + g)^2}{(1 + k)^2} + \frac{D(1 + g)^3}{(1 + k)^3} + \cdots + \frac{D(1 + g)^N}{(1 + k)^N} = \sum_{i=1}^{N} \frac{D(1 + g)^i}{(1 + k)^i}$$

To estimate the value of the flow from year $N + 1$ to infinity, we can use the same procedure for simplifying a sum of dividends as was used before to derive the simplified form of the dividend capitalization model. We should note, however, that the initial dividend for applying the procedure is at period N rather than period 1 and has a future value $D(1 + g)^N$, which is discounted back at $(1 + k)^N$ to give it a present value. We again make the standard assumption of constant growth at the rate g_s, which is reasonable since we have assumed that growth was only in line with the corporate average at that time and that the

TABLE 6-7
Rate of growth (%) in dividends of the S&P 500

				To				
From	1955	1960	1965	1970	1975	1980	1985	1990
1950	2.2	2.8	4.2	3.9	3.7	4.9	4.9	5.4
1955		3.4	5.2	4.4	4.1	5.4	5.3	5.9
1960			6.9	4.6	4.3	5.9	5.7	6.3
1965				2.9	3	5.6	5.5	6.2
1970					3.2	7	6.3	7.1
1975						10.8	8.0	8.3
1980							5.1	7.2
1985								9.3

Source: Standard & Poor's Security Price Index Record, Standard and Poor's Corporation, New York.

discount rate was the same in the second stage as in the first stage of the valuation process. We thus have the following expression for the second-stage value:

$$V_2 = D\frac{(1 + g)^N(1 + g_s)}{(1 + k)^N(k - g_s)}$$

The following equation shows the model for valuing growth stocks as a combination of two components: (1) V_1, representing the period of above-average growth, and (2) V_2, representing the period in which the stock has begun to grow at a rate equivalent to that of the average stock:

$$P = \qquad V_1 \qquad + \qquad V_2$$

$$= \sum_{i=1}^{N} \frac{D(1 + g)^i}{(1 + k)^i} + D\frac{(1 + g)^N}{(1 + k)^N}\left(\frac{1 + g_s}{k - g_s}\right) \tag{10}$$

Finally, we should note that this formulation is also useful in illustrating that the price of a stock in the future is a function of the projected flow of dividends into the future. In particular, note that the V_2 component of the expression can be considered the discounted price at the rate k of the share at the end of period N; this, in turn, is a function of the flow of dividends expected beyond that time. As a result, an investor with a shorter horizon selling stock at time N realizes return as a combined flow of dividends over the holding period and a value P_N at the end of the holding period N:

$$P = \sum_{i=1}^{N} \frac{D(1 + g)^i}{(1 + k)^i} + \frac{P_N}{(1 + k)^N} \tag{11}$$

Note that we are discounting the price P_N that the investor receives at the end of the holding period N (future value) at the rate $1 + k$ to derive its present worth to the stockholder. This thereby demonstrates that the dividend capitalization model is equivalent as a perpetual flow of dividends or as a flow of dividends and a terminal price, which, in turn, is based on a perpetual flow of dividends. The model is thus helpful for illustrating in a more rigorous fashion the discussion in earlier sections of the chapter of how dividends give value to a stock for an investor with either a short- or a long-term horizon.[7]

Valuing a Growth Stock

We give the following as an example of the use of the two-stage model for valuing a growth stock. Assume that the growth rate for a hypothetical company in its period of above-average growth is 20 percent per annum and, for purposes of illustration, that the rate lasts for five years. Beyond the fifth year, we then make the (heroic) assumption that the rate of growth immediately declines to 10 percent, so that from the sixth year onward the company grows at that rate. The rate of 10 percent is presumed to be in line with the growth rate of

---

[7]In this analysis we are assuming that the discount rate k for the stream of dividends in both stages is constant. However, one might well make the case that the risks of the dividend streams differ in the two periods; that is, the risk associated with high dividend growth in period 1 might be considered greater than in period 2. As a result, use of a different discount rate for the two periods would be warranted. We only mention this as a possible refinement, but we will not pursue it further.

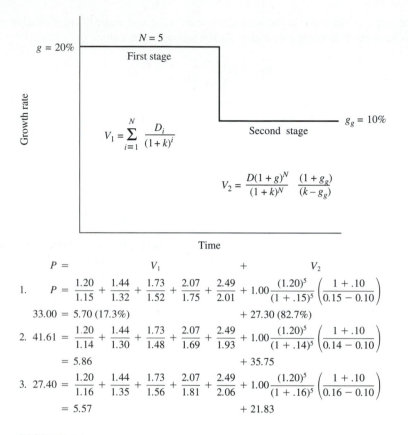

The graph shows:

$g = 20\%$

$N = 5$

First stage

$g_g = 10\%$

Second stage

Growth rate (vertical axis)

Time (horizontal axis)

$$V_1 = \sum_{i=1}^{N} \frac{D_i}{(1+k)^i}$$

$$V_2 = \frac{D(1+g)^N}{(1+k)^N} \cdot \frac{(1+g_g)}{(k-g_g)}$$

$$P = \qquad V_1 \qquad + \qquad V_2$$

1. $$P = \frac{1.20}{1.15} + \frac{1.44}{1.32} + \frac{1.73}{1.52} + \frac{2.07}{1.75} + \frac{2.49}{2.01} + 1.00\frac{(1.20)^5}{(1+.15)^5}\left(\frac{1+.10}{0.15-0.10}\right)$$

$33.00 = 5.70\ (17.3\%) \qquad\qquad\qquad + 27.30\ (82.7\%)$

2. $$41.61 = \frac{1.20}{1.14} + \frac{1.44}{1.30} + \frac{1.73}{1.48} + \frac{2.07}{1.69} + \frac{2.49}{1.93} + 1.00\frac{(1.20)^5}{(1+.14)^5}\left(\frac{1+.10}{0.14-0.10}\right)$$

$= 5.86 \qquad\qquad\qquad\qquad + 35.75$

3. $$27.40 = \frac{1.20}{1.16} + \frac{1.44}{1.35} + \frac{1.73}{1.56} + \frac{2.07}{1.81} + \frac{2.49}{2.06} + 1.00\frac{(1.20)^5}{(1+.16)^5}\left(\frac{1+.10}{0.16-0.10}\right)$$

$= 5.57 \qquad\qquad\qquad\qquad + 21.83$

FIGURE 6-3

Two-stage growth model pattern.

an average, or standard, stock. Analysts typically assume that this is the appropriate terminal (final) rate to use in the application of the two-stage or multistage model.

Figure 6-3 is similar to Figure 6-2, except that it illustrates the growth pattern with data pertinent to the hypothetical company of this example that paid a dividend of $1 last year. The graph shows the standard two-stage growth formulation, and the input data for this example is inserted into the formulation below. When the discount rate for the stock is assumed to be 15 percent, the price of the hypothetical stock is $33. We can see here that the first stage of growth—the V_1 component—provides a value of $5.70 (17.3 percent of the total), whereas the second stage of growth—the V_2 component—provides a value of $27.30 (82.7 percent of the total). Note that the future value, or price, of the stock would be $55 in the end of the 5th year, but when discounted back to present value it becomes $27.30, as noted above.

Though solving for a price, or present value, provides a useful illustration of how the formulation works, ordinarily we would know the price of the stock from generally available market quotes and would be interested in determining the discount rate. Knowing the price, we then solve for the discount rate by using the trial-and-error method or by resorting to standard computer routines. As shown in the calculations at the bottom of Figure 6-3, when

TABLE 6-8
Two-stage growth model—effect of rate and duration of growth in first stage on stock price

Rate of growth, %	Duration of growth (years)						
	3	5	7	10	12	15	20
10	$22	$22	$ 22	$ 22	$ 22	$ 22	$ 22
15	25	27	29	32	34	37	42
20	28	33	38	46	53	63	84
25	32	40	49	67	81	108	170
30	36	48	64	96	125	184	347
40	44	68	104	192	287	522	1405

the price is $33, the discount rate is 15 percent; at a price of $41.61 the discount rate is lower (14 percent); and at a price of $27.75 it is higher (16 percent).[8] This illustrates that the discount rate moves inversely to the price, just as in the simplified formulation.

Table 6-8 shows the effect that variations in the rate of growth and duration of growth inputs at a fixed discount rate of 15 percent have on the value of the stock. Note that when the rate of growth in a five-year growth period increases (for example, from 20 percent to 30 percent), the price increases to $48, but a decrease in the rate to 10 percent reduces the price to $22. As a matter of interest, note in the latter case that the first- and second-stage growth rates are identical; that is, g becomes a constant, so that valuation can be carried out with the simplified form of the dividend capitalization model. When the length of superior growth (20 percent) increases, for example, from five to seven years, the price increases to $38, and when it is reduced from five to three years, the price declines to $28. Higher and longer growth thus leads to higher prices, while lower and shorter growth leads to lower prices.

As a final note, when estimating dividends and growth rates for the two-stage growth models, we can usefully employ the same sort of analytical techniques described earlier with regard to the simplified version of the dividend capitalization model. The major additional requirement for developing inputs to this model is to assess the duration of the superior rate of growth; that is, the length of the first stage of superior growth must be estimated. One framework for helping to assess this transition from rapid to more normal growth is the industrial life cycle, as depicted in Figure 6-4.

The industrial life cycle is a representation of an industry's life as it goes through three distinct stages of growth. The initial pioneering stage, the investment maturity stage, and the stability stage are characterized by varying growth patterns in sales and earnings as the industry is born, matures, and stabilizes over time in the competitive economic environment. The investor might use this to determine the period of superior growth by ascertaining where the company of interest stands with respect to this cycle. For example, a company still in the pioneering stage of development would be expected to have a longer duration of superior growth than one that has entered the expansion phase of development.

While the life cycle theory provides this framework, we should note that it is not without deficiencies. First, the theory is a highly idealized and subjective view of how industries

---

[8] We should note that because of rounding, many of these values will not work out precisely if one uses a hand calculator.

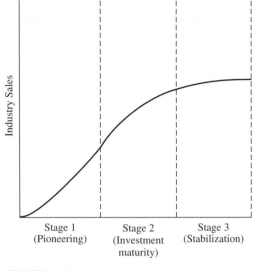

FIGURE 6-4
The industrial life cycle.

grow and mature. Second, there is no guarantee that a specific industry will systematically pass through the four stages described by the theory. Finally, there is nothing inherent in the theory that provides a way of identifying in advance when an industry will pass from one stage to another.

THE MARKET LINE TECHNIQUE

We conclude this chapter by discussing the empirical counterpart to the security market line (SML). It is a technique that provides not only a way of simultaneously considering risk and return, but also an explicit link between the theory of valuation and valuation models and the more formal models of the relationship between risk and return (like the SML and APT) growing out of portfolio theory and capital-market theory. It is thus appropriate that we cover this approach here as a way of connecting the material on valuation in this chapter with the prior discussion of risk in Chapters 3 and 4.

A number of investment organization types have implement the market line approach, since it is perhaps the simplest and most direct way of explicitly considering risk and return for equities. In the following, we describe generally how the market line has been implemented as a tool of analysis by such organizations. First we will describe how the line is constructed; then we will discuss its three main uses: (1) for evaluating the overall attractiveness of the market, (2) for assessing the relationship between risk and return in the equity market, and (3) for evaluating the relative attractiveness of individual stocks.

In using the market line approach, the organization would need to develop return estimates and risk measures for each of the individual stocks in its universe. To ensure that the included securities are representative, many organizations will monitor a universe of, say, the largest 1000 companies. Using such a universe would necessitate the development of 1000 pairs of risk-return estimates. We can most easily illustrate the nature of these estimates by focusing on 15 companies that are representative of the 1000 companies being monitored. Table 6-9 shows risk and return estimates for each of these 15 companies along with ticker symbols that will be useful for identifying the securities when they are graphed.

To begin with, the return estimates are generated according to the same dividend discount model approach that we have been describing in this chapter. However, standard practice is to use a three-stage variant of the model, which is described in the next chapter, rather than the more simplified forms previously discussed. With respect to inputs, there is need for analysts covering the various companies in the universe to develop explicit dividend forecasts. Given these dividend estimates and using the three-stage model, returns are generated like those shown for the 15 companies in the table. Note that the estimated return ranged from a low of 11.3 percent for Ralston to a high of 16.7 percent for Raychem.

As noted before, a risk estimate for each of the companies in the universe must also be developed. This risk estimate might simply be a beta using, for example, monthly returns over the last five years and calculated in the way that was illustrated in Chapter 3. Alternatively, we could use statistical techniques, such as those suggested by Blume, to adjust for the tendency of betas of securities to gravitate toward a mean of 1 over time. Finally, we could also use such data as income and balance sheet ratios to adjust for changes in the fundamental riskiness of the company.

For ease of comparison, we can group companies into five sectors according to riskiness: the 10 percent riskiest in the fifth sector, the next 20 percent in the fourth, the next 20 percent

TABLE 6-9

Selected stocks—Wells Fargo market line: expected return-risk sector, 1976

Company	Ticker symbol	Expected return	Risk sector
Above average–expected return stocks			
Raychem	RYC	16.7	5
Great Lakes Chemical	GLC	15.3	4
Deere	DE	14.6	3
IBM	IBM	14.4	2
Mobil Oil	MOB	14.2	1
Average–expected return stocks			
Data General	DGN	13.8	5
AMR	AMR	13.7	4
Medtronic	MED	13.5	3
Bethlehem Steel	BS	12.9	2
Texas Utilities	TXU	12.1	1
Below average–expected return stocks			
Nike	NKE	12.3	5
Disney	DIS	12.1	4
Xerox	XRX	11.7	3
Unocal	UCL	11.7	2
Ralston	RAL	11.3	1

in the third, the next 20 percent in the second, and the 30 percent least risky in the first. The first sector has the highest percentage of companies because the larger and presumably more significant companies are in this lowest risk category, and the fifth sector contains the smallest percentage because the smaller and less significant companies are in the highest risk category. The table shows three companies and their return estimates for each of the five sectors. Raychem, Data General, and Nike are in the highest-risk sector, while Mobil Oil, Texas Utilities, and Ralston are in the lowest.

Given risk and return estimates like those in Table 6-9 for each of the companies in the universe, we could then plot them on a risk-return diagram, as illustrated in Figure 6-5. The vertical axis refers to return, the horizontal axis refers to risk, and the numbers from 1 to 5 just above the axis and in the body of the chart represent midpoints of the risk sectors. The numbers at the bottom of the lines extending down from the horizontal axis are beta values that bracket the risk sectors. Note that in this case the chart shows the risk-return plots of the 15 stocks shown in Table 6-9. For example, plotting Raychem would be a matter of moving up the vertical axis to 16.7 percent and then across the horizontal axis to the midpoint of risk sector 5. Raychem is a high-risk stock offering a high return, as indicated by its plot on the diagram. The other 14 stocks are similarly plotted on the diagram.

If we did this for all 1000 stocks in the universe, we would have a great number of plots to which we could fit a line. We would, in fact, use statistical techniques—namely, regression techniques—to fit the line to these plots. The line on the chart in Figure 6-5 has been fitted by regression techniques to the plots for the 1000 companies, and it is the

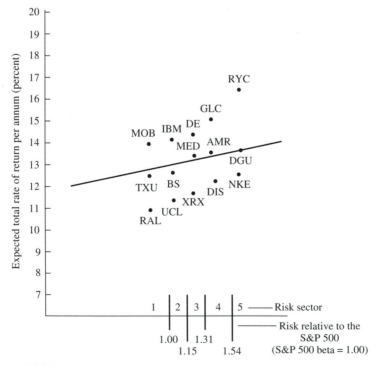

FIGURE 6-5
Security market line.

market line based on the estimates of analysts. Standard practice is to update the line at least monthly to incorporate any changes in inputs as well as to reflect the impact of changes in stock prices on the position of the line.

Market Line Uses

As noted before, the market line has several uses. We can best illustrate its dual use in monitoring the attractiveness of the overall market and assessing the risk-return trade-off in the equity market by referring to Figure 6-6. It is a risk-return diagram showing the position of the market line at three different dates—September 1982, September 1987, and December 1993—based on inputs for generating expected returns and expected risks at those dates. The 1987 line reflects the peak of a bull market and prior to the crash, the 1990 lines reflect the bottom of a bear market, and the 1993 line represents an intermediate market

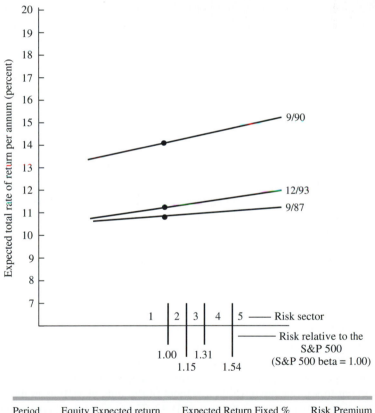

Period	Equity Expected return	Expected Return Fixed %	Risk Premium
9/87	11.2	10.7	4.5
9/90	14.1	10.0	4.1
12/95	11.3	7.0	4.3

FIGURE 6-6
Security market line, historical high and low, 1987–93. *Source:* Vestek, Mellon Capital.

level. The level of the line reflects the general attractiveness or unattractiveness of stocks based on expected returns; the slope of the line reflects the risk-return relationship in the market, allowing the investor to assess the relative attractiveness of high- versus low-risk stocks.[9]

The bottom left-hand portion of Figure 6-6 shows the expected returns of the stocks along with the returns of AAA corporate bonds at each of these three dates. The data allows us to compare equity returns with returns on a high-quality fixed-income instrument, so that we can derive a premium over the return on corporate bonds. For example, in 1993 the expected premium over bonds was 4.3 percent, simply the difference between the expected return of 11.3 percent on stocks and the return of 7.0 percent on bonds. We can then compare this with the premium provided by stocks over longer periods of time to help us assess the relative attractiveness of stocks. For this purpose, we can refer to the data from the Ibbotsen-Sinquefeld study in Chapter 2, which indicated that stocks earned approximately a 4–5 percent premium over long-term corporates over the 67-year period 1926–1993.

Note that stocks were offering a return of 11.2 percent at the September 1987 high level, compared with the 14.1 percent offered in the market trough of September 1990. While the 1987 return was in line with the 10 percent earned on average over the 1926–1993 period, the premium over bonds of 0.5 percent was below the longer-term average of 4–5 percent. On the other hand, in the 1990 market low, the risk premium on stocks of 4.1 percent was in line with the long-term average. Also, inflationary forces were peaking at that time, so that the real return on stocks was expected to expand over the subsequent period.

Also observe that the market line in 1987 was rather flat. There was little premium for assuming greater risk in the equity market: low-beta stocks were offering virtually the same return as high-beta stocks. This contrasts with the situation in 1990, when higher-beta stocks were offering significantly greater returns than lower-beta stocks, as was evidenced by the steep upward slope of the market line at that time. This information can be highly useful, both in making better asset allocation decisions and in structuring the equity portion of the portfolio advantageously. For example, a market line in the position shown for 1987 in Figure 6-6 might indicate the efficacy of shifting from equities to fixed-income securities and perhaps restructuring the equity portion of the portfolio toward lower-beta stocks. Conversely, a market line positioned similarly to the 1990 line might indicate the advantage of shifting more heavily toward equities and perhaps restructuring the equity portion of the portfolio toward higher-beta stocks.

We should note that stocks in general, and especially high-risk stocks, in fact proved to be unattractive in September 1987. This is shown in Figure 6-6 by the upward movement of the market line as prices dropped and the upward rotation of the line until December 1990 as prices of high-risk stocks dropped even faster than the average. Conversely, stocks in general, and especially high-risk stocks, proved to be quite attractive in December 1990. We can again see this in the downward movement of the line, as well as in the downward rotation of the line to its position at the end of 1993. This occurred as stock prices rose in general, and high-risk stocks rose even faster than the average.

---

[9]The market line extends only over the range of risk-return estimates for securities in the universe of interest. Since no security in the universe had betas of zero or even close to zero, the line does not extend to the vertical axis. As a result, it shows no intercept, but one could easily extend the line to gauge the location of the intercept.

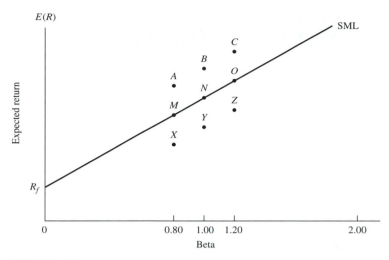

FIGURE 6-7
The market line and security valuation.

Evaluation of Individual Securities

As noted before, the market line is used to assess the relative attractiveness of individual stocks.[10] Recall from Chapter 3 that in the SML context, high-risk stocks are expected to offer high returns by virtue of their risk level, whereas low-risk stocks are expected to offer low returns, again, by virtue of their risk level. The question is whether the stock—low-risk or high-risk—is offering returns more or less than are proportional to its risk. Figure 6-7, which reproduces Figure 3-4 in Chapter 3, illustrates the framework for this analysis. In particular, it shows that hypothetical stocks X, Y, and Z are overvalued, stocks A, B, and C are undervalued, and stocks M, N, and O are appropriately valued in the market line context.

We can now illustrate this analysis by using the data in Table 6-9, which shows the 15 stocks used to demonstrate the construction of the market line. Note that these 15 stocks were grouped into three broad classes in terms of expected return: (1) above average, (2) average, and (3) below average. Also, each of the five stocks in each group represents one of the risk classes. The group at the top of the table shows above-average returns for their risk class and are therefore plotted above the forecasted market line.[11] The group at the bottom of the

---

[10]We should note here that the market line we are using as a benchmark for security selection is fitted to the individual risk-return plots by means of a regression equation, similar to the way that researchers have fitted ex post data in testing the SML relationship (see Chapter 3). The fitted relationship here differs from that used by researchers to test the SML relationship in that the risk-return plots are forecast (ex ante) values for these variables rather than historically derived. Use of ex ante variables is, of course, more in keeping with the SML, which, as we have noted, is an ex ante rather than an ex post relationship. Presumably, one might well use this data to develop superior tests of the relationship than have been possible in the past; however, developers of this technique have not emphasized this use and have used it, rather, primarily as a means of improving portfolio management.

[11]The line we are using here is fitted to the ex ante risk-return values for individual stocks. This is a good property when using the line for stock selection, as the least-squares regression technique generally results in a distribution where half the points (individual stocks) will be above the line and the other half below the line. As a result, one obtains a measure, or benchmark, of the relative attractiveness of stocks that does not depend on the movements of

TABLE 6-10
Above-average return portfolio—risk objective of 1.08

Stock	Weight	Beta	Expected return %
Raychem	0.08	1.65	16.70
Great Lakes Chemical	0.09	1.40	15.30
Deere	0.17	1.25	14.60
IBM	0.26	1.05	14.40
Mobil Oil	0.40	0.85	14.20
Above-average return portfolio	1.00	1.08	14.60
Market line portfolio	—	1.08	13.20
Return differential	—	—	1.40

table shows below-average returns and are thus plotted below the market line. Finally, the group in the middle of the table shows about average returns for their risk class and are plotted above the market line.

Ideally, we would prefer to construct a portfolio of stocks from those that plot above the market line. To ensure maximum return at a given risk level, we used the simplified portfolio optimization techniques developed by Elton and Gruber and illustrated in the appendix to Chapter 10.[12] Use of these techniques provides us with the weightings for the five stocks of above-average attraction shown in Table 6-10.

Note that the portfolio has a weighted average (expected) return of 14.6 percent, along with a portfolio beta of 1.08, and would therefore plot above the market line illustrated in Figure 6-8. This portfolio would be offering a return 1.4 percentage points greater than that of a portfolio plotted on the market line—in other words, a portfolio constructed of stocks of only average attraction. In the language of the capital asset pricing model (CAPM), the portfolio would have a positive expected alpha.

the market; that is, presumably those above the line will outperform those below the line regardless of the direction of the market.

An alternative way to use the line would be to assess the risk-free rate, determine the expected return on the overall market, and then connect the two points to form the forecast market line. The line constructed in this way would not, however, ensure that an equal number of stocks would plot above and below the line. In fact, it is likely that unequal numbers will plot above and below, so the relative positioning of the stocks would depend on the forecast of the risk-free return and the market return.

As a result, determining the relative attractiveness of stocks would depend not only on the quality of the inputs in estimating the risk and return of individual stocks, but also on the accuracy of the forecast of the risk-free rate and the market return. For those who possess some capability in forecasting these returns, the use of the market line in the latter way may well be preferable. However, for those who do not wish to forecast market returns, either for lack of predictive accuracy or for avoidance of extra risk, the approach that we have outlined in the body of this chapter seems more appropriate. In fact, we will see in Chapter 8 that this process works quite well within the context of an investment process that is primarily oriented toward achieving superior overall performance by focusing exclusively on stock selection.

[12]Recall that this method of generating an optimum portfolio relies on the assumption that the single-index model is an appropriate description of the return-generating process for stocks. We have seen, however, that this model is an oversimplification, and a multi-index model that more adequately describes the return-generating process is needed to solve the portfolio selection problem most satisfactorily. For ease of exposition, however, we have used the single-index model.

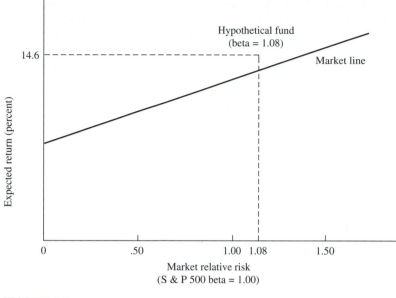

FIGURE 6-8
Risk-return diagram.

Realizing this hoped-for positive excess return would depend, in practice, on whether there was actual mispricing in the marketplace or whether the existence of securities plotting off the market line merely represented (1) misestimated returns for individual securities, (2) a mistaken risk measure, or both. As may be deduced from the discussion on estimating inputs to the valuation model and the attendant difficulties, there are bound to be errors emanating from this source. Moreover, our earlier discussion also indicated that beta is an incomplete measure of risk, so that it, too, is often a cause of error. Despite these potential errors, we can still develop some perspective on the degree of mispricing as well as the opportunity for developing above-average performance by measuring the actual performance of this kind of strategy over time. We will discuss ways of measuring this, as well as the results of the evaluation, in the Chapter 8.

EXTRAMARKET FACTOR

As noted in Chapter 4, another effect, besides the general market factor, that has both conceptual appeal and empirical support in explaining stock returns is the relationship of liquidity and stock returns. In evaluating the pricing relationship for securities, we would thus need to relate the expected returns of each security in a universe to both its liquidity and its relationship to a general market factor. The following two-factor return-generating model describes such a relationship:

$$R_i = a + b_1 R_M + b_2 L$$

This equation says that the return on a stock (R_i) is a function of its sensitivity to two factors rather than only one factor, as in the case of the market model. We define (b_1) as the sensitivity coefficient of the stock to the market factor (R_M) and (b_2) as the sensitivity coefficient of the stock return to the liquidity factor (L). As compared to the single-factor market model, the (a_i) parameter represents the return on a stock with both zero market risk and zero liquidity risk.

To estimate this relationship, we can use multiple regression, as compared to the simple regression used in estimating the single-factor market model. We again use a stock market index like the S&P 500 as a proxy for the general market factor. As a proxy for the liquidity of a stock, it is usual to use the size of the company as measured by its market capitalization. More precisely, the log of the market capitalization of the company is used as the liquidity factor in the multiple regression. To illustrate and compare the single-index and two-index analysis, we can again use the DDM-derived expected returns for the same universe of 1000 stocks as used previously in the market line analysis from a prior section of this chapter.

Using these inputs, Figure 6-9 graphically shows the two-factor pricing relationship along with two hypothetical stocks plotted relative to the pricing relationship. Note that the figure is three-dimensional, because expected returns are related to two characteristics of securities, and the pricing relationship is now represented as a plane rather than a line. Factor 1 shown on the graph represents the market risk factor and is the slope of the plane in the market risk direction. It indicates a required additional return of 7% per unit of market risk, holding liquidity constant. Factor 2 on the graph is the liquidity factor and is the slope of the plane in the liquidity direction. We show the additional return required as liquidity decreases, or, alternatively, the increase in the liquidity premium, holding market risk con-

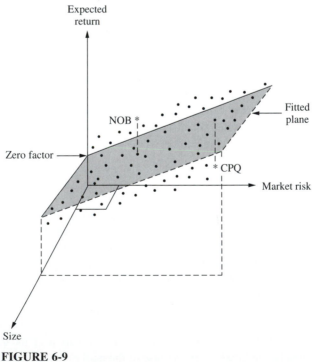

FIGURE 6-9
Factor pricing relationship.

stant. In this case, the fitted relationship indicates a slope of 3% with respect to size or an additional return of 3% for a unit decrease in size.

Two-Factor Stock Valuation

To illustrate use of the market plane in evaluating the relative attractiveness of individual stocks, we show two stocks: Compaq (CPQ) and Norwest Bank (NOB) plotted with respect to the plane. Note that this illustration is similar to that shown in an earlier chapter (Figure 4-2) and is used to illustrate stock valuation with a two-factor market plane. In this instance, we are using derived DDM stock returns, as well as estimated market sensitivities and liquidity sensitivities for the two stocks, along with a fitted market plane using stock returns, market betas, and size inputs as of September 30, 1992.

In appraising the valuation positioning of a stock—whether under-, over-, or fair-valued—we now need to gauge it with respect to two dimensions, and the two stocks plotted with respect to the market plane allow us to do that. Note that NOB offers an expected return of 14% and plots above the plane, while CPQ offers an expected return of 15% and plots below the plane. NOB has a beta of 0.8 with respect to the market factor, indicating below-average market risk exposure, and, with a beta of 0.9 on the size factor, exhibits below-average exposure to liquidity risk. Conversely, CPQ has a beta of 1.3 with respect to the market factor, indicating above-average market risk exposure, and, with a beta of 1.1 on the size factor, exhibits above-average exposure to liquidity risk.

Using the two-factor pricing relationship $[E(R_i) = R_z + b_1 R_m + b_2 S]$, however, we derive a required return of 13.3% for NOB. This return is composed of the zero-beta rate R_z of 5% plus compensation for exposure to the market risk factor of 5.6% $[b_1(R_M - R_Z) = 5.6]$ along with compensation for exposure to the liquidity risk factor of 2.7% $[b_2(R_M - R_Z) = 2.7]$. Currently, showing an expected return of 14%, the stock would be considered undervalued, given its market and liquidity risk exposure. The stock price should adjust upward relatively (outperform) to sell in line with other stocks of comparable risk.

Correspondingly, we derive a required return of 17.4% for CPQ. This return is also composed of the zero-beta rate R_z of 5% plus compensation for exposure to the market risk factor of 9.1% $[b_1(R_M - R_Z) = 9.1]$ along with compensation for exposure to the liquidity risk factor of 3.3% $[b_2(R_M - R_Z) = 3.3]$. With an expected return of 15%, the stock would be considered overvalued, given its market and liquidity risk exposures. The price of this stock should adjust downward relatively (underperform) to sell in line with other stocks of comparable risk.

CONCLUSION

In this chapter, we have discussed the practical problems of using valuation models to develop explicit returns for common stocks. We have also emphasized the importance of developing inputs of the highest quality for the valuation model and illustrated a framework of analysis for developing such inputs. We concluded by showing how the outputs of such a valuation model could be cast in a risk-return framework that has use with regard to both overall market valuation and individual stock selection. We will see in a subsequent chapter that this method has been used as a component of an actual on-line stock selection process that has, in fact, been shown to have facility in distinguishing between attractive and unattractive stocks.

APPENDIX A
SIMPLIFYING THE DIVIDEND CAPITALIZATION MODEL

In simplifying the dividend capitalization model, two critical assumptions are made. The first is that dividends will grow at a constant rate g over a long period of time—in theory, to infinity. This allows us to restate the basic dividend capitalization model, Equation (4), as

$$P = \frac{D(1 + g)}{1 + k} + \frac{D(1 + g)^2}{(1 + k)^2} + \frac{D(1 + g)^3}{(1 + k)^3} + \cdots + \frac{D(1 + g)^T}{(1 + k)^T} \qquad \text{(A-1)}$$

Converting this full equation into a more useable model becomes similar to the process used to illustrate the return on an annuity. First, multiplying by $[(1 + k)/(1 + g)]$ we obtain

$$\frac{P(1 + k)}{1 + g} = D + \frac{D(1 + g)}{1 + k} + \frac{D(1 + g)^2}{(1 + k)^2} + \cdots + \frac{D(1 + g)^{T-1}}{(1 + k)^{T-1}} \qquad \text{(A-2)}$$

Next we subtract Equation A-1 from Equation A-2 to eliminate the middle terms and to obtain

$$\frac{P(1 + k)}{1 + g} - P = D - \frac{D(1 + g)^T}{(1 + k)^T} \qquad \text{(A-3)}$$

Simplifying, we then obtain

$$P(k - g) = D \left[1 - \frac{(1 + g)^T}{(1 + k)^T} \right] \qquad \text{(A-4)}$$

At this point, we make the second critical assumption, which is that the expected return is greater than the expected growth rate of the dividend—that is, $k > g$. Making this assumption allows us to eliminate the complex term on the right-hand side in the brackets. For example, if $g = 1$ and $k = 2$, this term would be $(\frac{2}{3})^T$, and as T approaches infinity, the term would approach zero. When this term disappears and $D = D_0(1 + g)$ is defined as the year-end dividend, this expression simplifies to Equation (10) in the body of the chapter:

$$P = \frac{D}{k - g} \qquad \text{(A-5)}$$

To recapitulate, the analysis is based on two key assumptions. The first, constant growth of the dividend, allows us to simplify the stream of dividend payments. The second, $k > g$, allows us to reduce the expression to its final simplified form. The second assumption is also critical so that the equation does not give nonsense results. If k equals g, the equation contains a zero denominator and yields an infinite price; if k is less than g, a negative price results. When either of these two conditions is present, modification of the model is necessary. This will be treated in Chapter 7.

SELECTED REFERENCES

Babcock, G.: "The Concept of Sustainable Growth," *Financial Analysts Journal,* May–June 1970, pp. 108–114.
———: "The Roots of Risk and Return," *Financial Analysts Journal,* January–February 1980, pp. 56–63.
Bajaj, M. and A. Vijh: "Dividend Clienteles and the Information Content of Dividend Changes," *Journal of Financial Economics,* August 1990, pp. 193–220.

Bauman, W. Scott: "Investment Returns and Present Values," *Financial Analysts Journal,* November–December 1969, pp. 107–118.

Baylis, R. and S. Bhirud: "Growth Stock Analysis," *Financial Analysts Journal,* July–August 1973, pp. 63–71.

Bernstein, Peter L.: "Growth Companies vs. Growth Stocks," *Harvard Business Review,* September–October 1956, pp. 88–95.

Black, Fischer: "A Simple Discounting Rule," *Financial Management,* Summer 1988, pp. 7–11.

Brennan, Michael and Eduardo Schwartz: "Evaluating Natural Resource Investments," *Journal of Business* 68, 1985, pp. 135–158.

Brigham, Eugene F. and James L. Pappas: "Duration of Growth, Changes in Growth Rates, and Corporate Share Prices," *Financial Analysts Journal,* May–June 1966, pp. 157–162.

———and Myron J. Gordon: "Leverage, Dividend Policy, and the Cost of Capital," *Journal of Finance,* March 1968, pp. 85–104.

Chen, Kung and Thomas Shimeroda: "An Empirical Analysis of Useful Financial Ratios," *Financial Management,* Spring 1981, pp. 51–60.

Christie, William: "Dividend Yield and Expected Returns: The Zero-Dividend Puzzle," *Journal of Financial Economics,* November–December 1990, pp. 96–126.

Cohen, J., E. Zinbarg, and A. Ziekel: *Investment Analysis and Portfolio Management,* Richard D. Irwin, Homewood, IL, 1987.

Durand, David: "Growth Stocks and the Petersburg Paradox," *Journal of Finance,* September 1956, pp. 305–315.

Fairfield, Patricia: "P/E, P/B and the Present Value of Future Dividends," *Financial Analysts Journal,* July–August 1994, pp. 23–31.

Farrell, James L., Jr.: "The Dividend Discount Model: A Primer," *Financial Analysts Journal,* November–December 1985, pp. 16–25.

Fouse, W.: "Risk, Liquidity and Common Stock Prices," *Financial Analysts Journal,* May–June 1976, pp. 35–45, and January–February 1977, pp. 40–45.

Gordon, Myron: *The Investment, Financing, and Valuation of the Corporation,* Richard D. Irwin, Homewood, IL, 1962.

Graham, B., D. Dodd, and S. Cottle: *Security Analysis,* 4th ed., McGraw-Hill, New York, 1962.

Higgins, Robert: "Sustainable Growth Under Inflation," *Financial Management,* Autumn 1981, pp. 36–40.

Kathari, S. and Jay Shanken: "Stock Return Variation and Expected Dividend," *Journal of Financial Economics,* April 1992, pp. 177–210.

Leibowitz, Martin and Stanley Kogelman: "The Franchise Factor for Leveraged Firms," *Financial Analysts Journal,* November–December 1991, pp. 29–43.

——— and ———: "Franchise Value and the Growth Process," *Financial Analysts Journal,* January–February 1992, pp. 53–62.

——— and ———: "Inside the P/E Ratio: The Franchise Factor," *Financial Analysts Journal,* November–December 1990, pp. 41–54.

Miller, M. H. J. and F. Modigliani: "Dividend Policy, Growth, and the Valuation and Shares," *Journal of Business,* October 1961, pp. 411–433.

Modigliani, F. and M. H. Miller: "The Cost of Capital, Corporation Finance and the Theory of Investment; Corporate Income Taxes, and the Cost of Capital: A Correction," *American Economic Review,* June 1958, pp. 433–443.

Molodovsky, Nicholas, C. May, and S. Chottiner: "Common Stock Valuation: Theory and Tables," *Financial Analysts Journal,* March–April 1965, pp. 104–123.

Olson, Gerard and Douglas McCann: "The Linkages between Dividends and Earnings," *The Financial Review,* February 1994, pp. 1–22.

Pilotte, Eugene: "Growth Opportunities and the Stock Price Response to New Financing," *Journal of Business,* July 1992, pp. 371–394.

Porter, Michael: "Industry Structure and Competitive Strategy: Keys to Profitability," *Financial Analysts Journal,* July–August 1980, pp. 30–41.

————: *Competitive Advantage: Creating and Sustaining Superior Performance,* Free Press (Macmillan), New York, 1985.

Price, Lee: "Choosing Between Growth and Yield," *Financial Analysts Journal,* July–August, 1979, pp. 57–67.

Rappoport, Alfred: "The Affordable Dividend Approach to Equity Valuation," *Financial Analysts Journal,* September–October 1986, pp. 52–58.

Richards, Verlyn and Eugene Loughlin: "A Cash Conversion Cycle Approach to Liquidity Analysis," *Financial Management,* Spring 1980, pp. 32–38.

Treynor, Jack: "The Investment Value of Plant," *Financial Analysts Journal,* March–April 1994, pp. 12–18.

Wendt, Paul E.: "Current Growth Stock Valuation Methods," *Financial Analysts Journal,* March–April 1965, pp. 91–103.

QUESTIONS AND PROBLEMS

1. A common stock sells at $50, pays a $4 dividend that grows at the rate of 4 percent, and has a required return of 11 percent. Determine the expected price change for this security associated with a 0.10 percent change in the required return (discount rate) of each.

2. A common stock pays out 40 percent of its earnings, which are expected to be $3 at year-end. The return on retained earnings is 15 percent, and the required return on stock is 14 percent. Determine the *P/E* ratio.

3. The return on retained earnings for the stock is now expected to be 18 percent rather than 15 percent, but the required return is also expected to increase to 16 percent. Determine the *P/E* ratio for the stock assuming the earnings and payout ratio remain unchanged.

4. A common stock is earning $2 and pays out $0.80 in dividends. The required return on the stock is 16 percent, and the projected growth rate in dividends is 9 percent. Inflation increases from 9 percent to 11 percent. Determine the change in stock price assuming (*a*) no ability to adjust for the increased inflation and (*b*) a 75 percent adjustment to the change in inflation.

5. Assume that, because of increased competition and energy price changes, GM's normal profit margin is now 11 percent. Calculate GM's normalized rate of return for 1974, as well as its normal earnings and projected sustainable rate of growth.

6. Calculate the sustainable growth for a company that has a policy of paying out 40 percent of its earnings and has shown the following financial characteristics over the past three years.

Year	M	I	L	V
1992	8%	1.9	1.30	0.55
1993	12	2.6	1.60	0.45
1994	10	2.1	1.30	0.50

7. Determine the discount rate for a company paying a $1 dividend that is expected to grow at a rate of 30 percent per annum for the next five years and then grow at a rate of 10 percent beyond that period. Assume a 16-percent discount rate (required return) for the stock.

8. Determine the discount rate for the company in the previous problem using the previously determined price, but assume that the period of superior growth is (*a*) three years and (*b*) seven years.

9. Assume that a stock is expected to grow at a rate of 25 percent over the next five years and then decline over the next three years (years 6 through 8) to a growth rate of 10 percent. Determine the price of the stock that is currently paying a $1 dividend and has a 17-percent discount rate.

10. Determine the discount rate for the stock in the previous problem, but assume the company is now expected to grow at a rate of 30 percent for five years and then decline to a growth rate in line with the economy (10 percent) over the next five years (years 6 through 10). Use the previously determined price.

11. Determine the optimum portfolio weights for the companies in Table 6-7 using the Elton and Gruber method, as shown in Appendix A to Chapter 10, but assume that Raychem has an expected return of 18.5 percent, Great Lakes Chemical a return of 17 percent, and Gulf Oil a return of 13.7 percent.

12. Give three potential applications of security market lines.

13. A market forecasting department estimates that the slope of the SML will increase over the next six months and then stabilize at the steeper slope. What does this imply about the performance of high-beta stocks over (a) the next six months? (b) for the time period after the next six months?

14. We estimate the following ex ante security market line:

$$R_i = 6\% + 5\% B_{im}$$

(a) What is the estimated price of risk?
(b) What is the ex ante alpha for a stock with a beta of 1.1 and an expected return of 13 percent?

15. Why might the constant growth dividend discount model not be useful for evaluating individual common stock prices?

16. The Gordon model assumes that $r > g$. Why is this a necessary assumption?

17. XYZ Corp. paid a $3 dividend, which is expected to grow at a 6 percent rate for the foreseeable future. If investors require a 12 percent return to purchase XYZ stock, what is a good estimate of the price of the stock?

18. Western Holdings Inc. recently paid a $1 dividend, which is expected to grow at a 6 percent rate for the next 3 years. What is a good estimate of the current stock price if investors require a 10 percent return to purchase shares of Western Holdings and expect the stock price to be $15 at the end of 3 years?

19. If the current price of Western Holdings is $10 and expectations with respect to dividends and price at the end of 3 years are the same as in Question 3, what is the return investors require to purchase Western Holdings at its current price of $10?

20. (This question is based on the 1987 CFA Examination, Level I):
Using the data provided, discuss whether the common stock of United States Tobacco Company is attractively priced based on at least three different valuation approaches. (*Hint:* use the asset value, DDM, and earnings multiplier approaches.)

	U.S. Tobacco	S&P 500
Recent price	$27.00	290
Book value per share	$6.42	
Liquidation value per share	$4.90	
Replacement costs of assets per share	$9.15	
Anticipated next year's dividend	$1.20	$8.75
Estimated annual growth in dividends and earnings	10%	7.0%
Required return	13.0%	
Estimated next year's EPS	$2.40	$16.50
P/E ratio based on next year's earnings	11.3	17.6
Dividend yield	4.4%	3.0%

21. (This question is based on the 1988 CFA Examination, Level I):

The Tenant Company, founded in 1870, has evolved into the leading producer of large-sized floor sweepers and scrubbers, which are ridden by their operators. Its latest dividend per share was $.96, its earnings per share were $1.85, and its ROE was 16.9%.

(*a*) Based on these data, calculate a value for Tennant common stock by applying the constant growth dividend discount model. Assume that an investor's required rate of return is a five percentage point premium over the current risk-free rate of return of 7%.

(*b*) To your disappointment, the calculation that you completed in part (*a*) results in a value below the stock's current market price. Consequently, you apply the constant growth DDM using the same required rate of return as in your calculation for part (*a*), but using the company's stated goal of earning 20% per year on stockholders' equity and maintaining a 35% dividend payout ratio. However, you find that you are unable to calculate a meaningful answer. Explain why you cannot calculate a meaningful answer, and identify an alternative DDM that may provide a meaningful answer.

22. (This question is based on the 1986 CFA Examination, Level I.):

You are a portfolio manager considering the purchase of Nucor common stock. Nucor is the preeminent "mini-mill" steel producer in the United States. Mini-mills use scrap steel as their raw material and produce a limited number of products, primarily for the construction market. You are provided the following information:

Nucor Corporation

Stock price (Dec. 30, 1985)	$53.00
1985 Estimated earnings	$4.25
1985 Estimated book value	$25.00
Indicated dividend	$0.40
Beta	1.10
Risk-free return	7.0%
High grade corporate bond yield	9.0%
Risk premium—stocks over bonds	5.0%

(*a*) Calculate the expected stock market return. Show your calculations.

(*b*) Calculate the implied total return of Nucor stock.

(*c*) Calculate the required return of Nucor stock using the security market line model.

(*d*) Briefly discuss the attractiveness of Nucor based on these data.

23. Discuss the simplifying assumptions that underlie the discounted cash dividends valuation models. What problems, if any, may arise from using such simplifications?

24. Does an increase in a firm's growth rate g always mean an increase in its intrinsic value? Explain.

25. Can factors which are external to the firm, such as national economic conditions, affect the intrinsic value of a share of stock? Explain why or why not.

26. (From Level II, 1983 Exam):

The following set of data was provided to Bernice Star in order that she might determine the relative attractiveness of Humana's common stock.

As of the 1982 year-end, the S&P 500 Index was at 140, and estimates for 1983 show earnings at $16.50, and the dividend at $7.40.

(*a*) DuPont's projected growth in earnings is in excess of that expected for the S&P 500; its current yield is higher than that for the S&P 500; and DuPont's projected growth in earnings is not much below that for the Hospital Management Industry Composite. Briefly comment

	Humana	Hospital management industry composite (a)	DuPont (b)
Current market price	$45	$41	$40
1983 Estimates:			
Earnings per share	$2.80	$2.90	$5.00
Dividend per share	0.80	0.65	2.40
Projected annual growth rate for 1983–87:			
Earnings per share	30%	26%	20%
Dividend per share	45%	30%	10%
Beta	1.50	1.60	1.20

(a) Equally weighted data for American Medical International, Hospital Corporation of America, Humana, Lifemark, and National Medical Enterprises.
(b) DuPont selected as representative example of company adversely affected by recession of 1981–1982, and presumably to benefit from anticipated recovery in general business activity beginning in 1983.

on why DuPont is selling at a slight discount to the S&P 500 price-earnings multiple and at a substantial discount to the price-earnings ratio for the Hospital Management Industry Composite.
(b) Briefly comment on why a dividend growth valuation model is a more appropriate method of valuing the S&P 500 and DuPont than the Hospital Management Industry Composite and Humana.

27. (CFA Examination II June 1981):
The value of an asset is the present value of the expected return from the asset during the holding period. An investment will provide a stream of returns during this period, and this stream of returns needs to be discounted at an appropriate rate to determine the asset's present value. A dividend valuation model such as the following is frequently used.

$$P_i = \frac{D_1}{(k_i - g_i)}$$

where P_i = current price of common stock i
  D_1 = expected dividend in period 1
  k_i = required rate of return on stock i
  g_i = expected constant growth rate of dividends for stock i

(a) Identify the three factors that must be estimated for any valuation model, and explain why these estimates are more difficult to derive for common stocks than for bonds.
(b) Explain the principal problem involved in using a dividend valuation model to value
  1. Companies whose operations are closely correlated with economic cycles.
  2. Companies that are of giant size and are maturing.
  3. Companies that are of small size and are growing rapidly. Assume all companies pay dividends.

28. The constant growth model is an overly simple means of valuing most corporations' stocks. However, a number of market analysts believe it is a useful means of estimating a fair value for the stock market as a whole. Why might the constant growth DDM be a more reasonable valuation tool for the market in aggregate as opposed to individual stocks?

29. A publicly held venture capital investment firm is currently paying a dividend of $2 per share on earnings of $4 per share. Its stock is selling for $200 per share. Stocks of similar risk are priced to return 15 percent. What kind of return on equity could explain investors' willingness to pay a price equal to 50 times earnings on this stock?

30. A financial analyst one remarked: "Even if your dividend estimates and discount rate assumption are correct, dividend discount models identify stocks that will produce positive alphas only if other investors eventually come to agree with the DDM's valuation conclusions." Is this statement current? Why or why not?

CHAPTER 7

Equity Valuation Models: Simplifications and Applications

INTRODUCTION

This chapter continues our discussion of the valuation of equity securities. It builds on the previous discussion of the DDM, which described ways to apply that model for valuation, and it uses the security market line and security market plane approaches, which in turn depend on the DDM for generating expected return values. We now turn to describing simplified approaches to valuation that are derived from the basic DDM approach but provide alternative, and in many cases more practically feasible, ways of valuing equities.

We begin the chapter with a general review of those characteristics that are desirable in a valuation model and the sort of uses that are most important for practical application of these models. We then go on to describe the kinds of generalized approaches that have been developed to solve practical problems of valuation and comment on their strengths and deficiencies in application. After that discussion, we will specifically describe several major kinds of simplified models that have been derived from the basic DDM and the ways that these DDM elaborations have been applied. In the final sections of the chapter we will describe how the DDM-based valuation approach can be used to develop better insights into understanding the riskiness of equities as well as how to assess changes in the underlying risk that can create potential return opportunities.

Though valuation is a prime focus in investment-oriented books, it is equally important for its relevance to portfolio management and its interrelation with risk. Understanding valuation is important because of its perspective on risk, which is a prime focus of portfolio management. In addition, developing return inputs is a critical part of the process of actively managing portfolios and adding value through stock selection, industry rotation, or tactical asset allocation. Finally, the techniques of valuation that are described here have direct relevance because they are critically important underlying ingredients for the success of a stock selection strategy that will be described in the next chapter.

USES OF VALUATION MODELS

Active investment management is, in some sense, simply a matter of making comparisons for the purpose of getting more rather than less. The problem is that these comparisons can often be quite difficult. In some cases, the problem is one of comparing across disparate asset classes with quite different financial characteristics. Even within asset classes, the comparisons can be quite testing because companies or industries within a universe of common stocks can differ considerably. Making comparisons is an overwhelming consideration for managers of large, varied pools of assets, but it is also a significant problem even for investors with a more narrow focus.

Security valuation models are a significant aid to the investor in providing a benchmark for comparison. Quantifying with models enables the investor to develop a common standard of comparison, thus facilitating evaluation. In addition, the process of developing inputs and generating security returns requires investors to be explicit. This, in turn, provides a basis for objective evaluation of the process and, hence, a means of improving over time. Finally, use of valuation models can potentially have a beneficial impact in enhancing the analytical effort by making the process more consistent and allowing for a greater coordination of the research effort. This is especially true for larger portfolios where many people—ranging from research analysts to team leaders and portfolio managers—may be involved.

Several rather clear-cut criteria need to be met for a valuation model to qualify as useful in practice. First, the model should be analytically valid by being analytically well-derived and connected to theoretical notions of value. In addition, the model needs to be simple and intuitively appealing. This latter characteristic is most useful in allowing investors to interact with the model by providing useful inputs and allowing tests of sensitivities to variations in model inputs. Along with this, the model should have a pragmatic world application instead of being a theoretically elegant, but abstruse, model. Finally, the model should be global in application and generally applicable across a universe of securities instead of overly specialized to a limited list of companies.

Systematic security valuation has evolved from an approach most closely associated with Graham and Dodd and from the use of such accounting-based notions as the price-earnings ratio to value stocks. Most organizations use some objective measure of value as at least a beginning point for appraising the relative attractiveness of securities. Some organizations focus only on a single aspect of valuation, some use risk and return, and others use a multitude of valuation indicators. The application of these techniques to valuation produces varying degrees of success, which depend greatly on the quality of inputs to the models and the extent of commitment and discipline in execution of the process. In the following section we compare the major valuation approaches that have evolved over time.

EVOLUTION OF SYSTEMATIC SECURITY VALUATION

Graham and Dodd

Most investors would agree that the Graham and Dodd approach pioneered the development of systematic methods of security evaluation. The Graham and Dodd method relies heavily on an examination of accounting statements in establishing an "intrinsic value" for the security. Once an intrinsic value has been established, it can be compared to the current market price of the security to determine whether the security is attractive or unattractive. Graham and Dodd emphasized the need in investing for a "margin of safety," demonstrated by an intrinsic value that is significantly in excess of the current market price of a security. This intrinsic value approach thus has a conservative orientation.

The Graham and Dodd approach has stood the test of time quite well and has been usefully applied over the years. In fact, it might even be said to have had a resurgence of interest in recent years. The so-called school of "value investing" would generally identify itself with the Graham and Dodd approach. Contrarian investing could also be associated with the Graham and Dodd philosophy. Academics and quantitative researchers have used many of the analytical concepts recommended by Graham and Dodd in testing for market anomalies. Notable examples of such tests include tests of the low price-earnings ratio effect, low price-to–book value effects, or screens that use such indicators as net current assets to market price.

The Graham and Dodd approach has a notable attribute of being easily understood but rigorous in application; thus, it has generated a fairly broad degree of useful application. Though it provides a basic framework for evaluation, the approach is not without deficiencies. The Graham and Dodd approach is heavily dependent on accounting data and so suffers from the usual inadequacy of accounting statements to reflect the earning power and asset value of an enterprise accurately. In addition, the basic price-earnings ratio as a measure of worth does not directly accommodate growth prospects of companies and so does not allow easy comparison of companies with differing growth rates. As a result, the Graham and Dodd approach is not generally useful across a complete universe of companies.

The Dividend Discount Model

The dividend discount model is theoretically well derived; it is based simply on the notion of discounting a stream of cash flows that can be compared to a cash outlay or price, and it seems incontestable as a basis of valuation. The discount rate derived in the process provides an explicit rate of return that can be used as a basis of comparison. Furthermore, the model can be applied across a universe of common stocks of differing character. For example, returns can be developed for both high profit/high growth firms and low profit/low growth firms, and the two can be compared.[1] In addition, the returns developed for an asset class such as common stock can be compared to the returns developed by other methods for asset classes such as bonds or real estate as a means of appraising the relative attractiveness of these classes. Though implementation can be complex and generating quality inputs is difficult, institutional managers, investment advisory services, and (more recently, with the advent of low-cost personal computer power) individual investors have successfully applied this model to make such comparisons. However, because risk will vary across the assets, returns should not be the sole criterion.

The security market line technique uses the dividend discount model as a component but also incorporates risk; it integrates valuation methodology and capital market theory into

---

[1]The inadequacies of accounting statements exist because generally accepted accounting principles allow choice in the way financial events are recorded (e.g., seven ways to record inventory), making comparisons across firms and industries difficult.

a practical tool. As described in the previous chapter, the market line has three major uses as a tool for investors. First, the slope of the line provides perspective on what the risk-return relationship is at a point in time and how that might vary as market conditions change. Secondly, the level of the line allows the investor to assess the general attractiveness of the overall market. Finally, the line provides a benchmark for the risk-adjusted attractiveness of individual stocks and, thus, provides a tool for investors in selecting stocks.

In contrast to the dividend discount model, the criterion for stock attractiveness for the market line becomes risk-adjusted excess return or, in the parlance of capital market theory, the alpha value of the stock. Also, the market line approach allows the investor to monitor the impact of varying discount rates on the level and structure of returns in the market. This can be done by observing the shift in level and rotation of the line over time.

Information Coefficient/Multiple Valuation

A more recent development in stock valuation work has been the information coefficient technique. As in the market line approach, the criterion for stock attractiveness is the alpha value of the stock, but this technique uses a different and more flexible methodology for developing an alpha value. In addition to providing an alternative way of developing an alpha value, the information coefficient approach provides a framework for combining disparate sources of information or valuation approaches into a unified composite rating. Combining approaches is important because, empirically, no single valuation approach works well consistently period after period. If individual sources that show predictive power can be found and these sources provide different perspective on stocks (i.e., they are independent), then the combined appraisal from the various sources can provide a more powerful and consistent result than a reliance on any single source. We describe this valuation approach in depth in the following chapter.

THREE-STAGE DDM APPLICATION

As noted in the prior chapter, the three-stage version of the DDM offers a practical means of implementing the DDM method of stock valuation. The first stage of this model variation requires a year-by-year forecast of earnings, usually over a five-year period, and has the benefit of accommodating any impact of the economic cycle on the earnings of a company by either unduly depressing or inflating these earnings. The second stage, a transition period, reflects the natural tapering-down of the growth of a rapidly growing company that may occur over a period ranging from 5 to 20 years, depending on the character of the company. The third stage is the maturity phase, in which all companies are assumed to reach a steady state of growth in line with the overall economy or the average of a broad market index.

Figure 7-1 illustrates the general pattern of growth portrayed by the three-stage model. It shows a hypothetical company that is growing at a rate of 20 percent in the initial period N_g, assumed to last five years, after which the growth rate begins to decline. The model assumes that this growth rate declines linearly over a ten-year period N_d to a 10 percent terminal growth rate. This linear decline means that the growth rate is simply reduced by one percentage point per annum, so the company would grow at a rate of 20 percent in the fifth year, 19 percent in the sixth year, 18 percent in the seventh, and so on until the growth

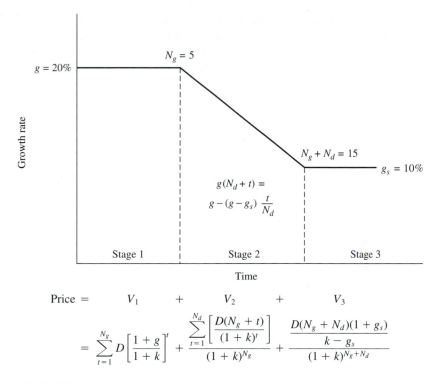

FIGURE 7-1
Three-stage growth model.

rate finally declines to a 10 percent rate in the fifteenth year. The 10 percent terminal growth rate is assumed to be in line with the general corporate average.

The bottom part of Figure 7-1 shows the general formulation for the three-stage model. To illustrate how the formulation can be used to derive an expected return, Table 7-1 shows the calculation for the hypothetical stock illustrated in Figure 7-1. Note that at a price of $33 we derive, by the process of trial and error, an expected return (discount rate) of 16.5 percent. (Recall from the prior chapter that we derived an expected return of 15 percent using the

TABLE 7-1

Calculating the discount rate for the three-stage model

$$V_1 = \frac{1.20}{1.165} + \frac{1.44}{(1.165)^2} + \frac{1.73}{(1.165)^3} + \frac{2.07}{(1.165)^4} + \frac{2.49}{(1.165)^5} = 5.46$$

$$V_2 = \frac{2.96}{(1.165)^6} + \frac{3.49}{(1.165)^7} + \frac{4.09}{(1.165)^8} + \frac{4.74}{(1.165)^9} + \frac{5.45}{(1.165)^{10}} + \frac{6.22}{(1.165)^{11}} + \frac{7.03}{(1.165)^{12}}$$

$$+ \frac{7.87}{(1.165)^{13}} + \frac{8.73}{(1.165)^{14}} + \frac{9.61}{(1.165)^{15}} = 11.29$$

$$V_3 = \left[\frac{10.57}{(0.165 - 0.10)}\right]\left[\frac{1}{(1.165)^{15}}\right] = 16.25$$

Price $= V_1 + V_2 + V_3 = 5.46 + 11.29 + 16.25 = \$33$

two-stage model, so assuming a middle-stage, declining-growth phase adds 1.5 percent to the return of the stock.) Using the formulation in Table 7-1 is tedious, however, because it entails generating the dividend flow and, most importantly, determining the appropriate discount rate by trial and error. Fortunately, computer programs are available that greatly ease the task of calculating discount rates.

The three-stage version of the dividend discount model has several favorable attributes. First, the model is comprehensible, albeit not without a certain degree of complexity. In addition, it should fairly well reflect the theoretical value of a stock. Also, it allows comparisons between high profit–high growth firms and low profit–low growth firms; it also accommodates growth easily and applies across a wide universe of company types. Correspondingly, it provides a mechanism for reflecting the life-cycle nature of differing firms.

At the same time, the model has some significant deficiencies. Because of its complexity and need for a relatively substantial number of inputs, there is the potential for subtle but meaningful biases. In addition, it produces a high degree of sensitivity of results to forecasts far in the future, as may be deduced from our description and illustration of the use of the model. Also, it requires a reasonably high labor intensity to implement the model; proper development of inputs ideally requires training, experience, and professional competence on the part of the analytical team. Finally, interaction with the model and conducting of sensitivity tests using differing inputs are relatively hard.

SIMPLIFYING THE THREE-STAGE MODEL

The H model is a variation on the basic three-stage DDM that simplifies the structure yet retains much of its power for deriving expected return.[2] Because of the simplification, the H model reduces the input burden by eliminating the need for certain input items as well as by making others easier to develop. This, in turn, facilitates sensitivity testing by making it easier to vary the values of the inputs to the model. Correspondingly, the simplified H model variation allows for some analytical insights not readily apparent with the more complex three-stage version of the DDM.

Figure 7-2 illustrates a format used for the two-stage and three-stage versions of the DDM in the structure of the H model. Like the two-stage DDM structure, the H model shows two segments, with the first accommodating above-average growth and the second accommodating an average or standard growth rate. Note also that the H model provides for a taper in the above-average growth rate as does the three-stage model, but it begins with this growth rate tapering immediately. At H years the figure shows that the growth rate is halfway between the above-average rate of growth (g) and the standard rate (g_s), so at $2H$ years the growth rate levels off at the expected long-run normal growth rate for the company.

In terms of formulation, the H model is simply expressed as follows:

$$P = \frac{D}{k - g_s}\left[1 + g_s + H(g - g_s)\right] \tag{1}$$

---

[2]R. J. Fuller and C. C. Hsia, "A Simplified Model for Estimating Stock Prices of Growth Firms," *Financial Analysts Journal* (May–June 1984).

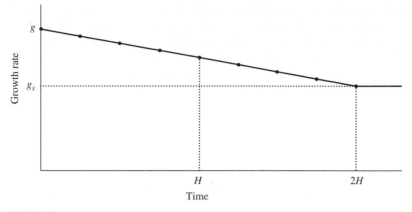

FIGURE 7-2
Dividend growth rate pattern for the H model.

The formulation indicates that the price of the stock (P) is a function of the initial dividend (D), the growth rate both for the initial stage (g) and the second stage (g_s), as well as the estimated half-life (H) for above-average growth; all are capitalized by the difference between the discount rate (k) and the normal growth rate (g_s). Note that the formulation is similar in form to the simplified version of the DDM and, in fact, collapses into that form when (g) is equal to the standard rate (g_s). By a simple rearrangement of the terms in the equation, we can, in turn, develop a more intuitive insight into both the H model and growth valuation in general.

$$P = \frac{D(1 + g_s)}{k - g_s} + \frac{DH(g - g_s)}{k - g_s}$$

Value based on   Premium due to
standard growth rate   superior growth rate

This alternative formulation provides a way of directly measuring the value of above-average growth to the company. The second term shows the premium, or added, value due to growth prospects, and it is often referred to as growth opportunities in other contexts. These opportunities, and the associated value, will be large because the rate of superior growth is higher than the standard rate, and they will be higher because the period of superior growth, as measured by H, is expected to be longer. This premium is then added to the basic value accruing to the company from its standard growth, as derived from the first term in the expression.

In contrast to the three-stage DDM version, we can solve directly for the discount rate (k) when using the H model. Given a current stock price, we simply rearrange the terms from the basic H model formulation to obtain an expected return or discount rate (k) expression:

$$k = E(R) = \frac{D}{P}[(1 + g_s) + H(g - g_s)] + g_s \qquad (2)$$

Note that this expression is quite similar to the simplified form of the DDM that we evaluated in some depth in the previous chapter. In this case, the dividend yield component $D(1+g_s)/P$ is augmented by a term to reflect superior growth and will increase the expected return as

g and H are large. This augmented dividend yield term is then added to the normal growth term, just as in the case of the simplified DDM, to obtain a constant expected return (k).

As noted, the H model will generate results that are very similar to those of the more complex three-stage DDM version when H is halfway through the transition phase (second stage) of the three-stage model. Figure 7-3 illustrates this by comparing the structure of the H model to that of the three-stage dividend discount model. As shown in the figure, H can be interpreted in either of two ways: (1) H is half the amount of time required for the growth rate to change from g to g_s; or in the context of the three-stage model, H is halfway through the stage 2 transition phase.

To illustrate use of the H model and compare its results to the three-stage DDM, we can again use example data for the hypothetical stock in Figure 7-1. Recall that this stock has superior growth g of 20 percent for an initial period of 5 years, which regressed to a standard rate g_s of 10 percent over a 10-year transition period. In terms of our previous figure, point A would be 5 years and point B would be 15 years. Assuming H as the halfway point through the transition period would then result in H being 10 years. Using these estimates as inputs and a discount rate of 16.5 percent, the H model generates a price of \$32.3, calculated as follows:

$$P = \frac{\$1}{0.165 - 0.10}\left[(1.10) + 10(0.20 - 0.10)\right] = \$32.3$$

This derived price is quite close to the \$33 price generated using the three-stage DDM. We can, in turn, decompose the formulation to derive a price component due to standard growth and a component due to growth opportunities. The component due to standard growth is simply

$$\frac{D(1 + g_s)}{k - g_s} = \frac{\$1(1.10)}{0.165 - 0.10} = \$16.90$$

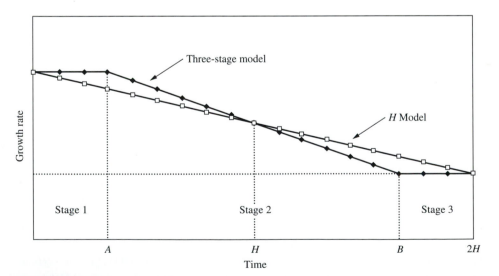

FIGURE 7-3
Three-stage DDM vs. H model growth patterns.

and the price component due to superior growth opportunities is

$$\frac{DH(g - g_s)}{k - g_s} = \frac{\$1(10)(0.20 - 0.10)}{0.165 - 0.10} = \$15.4$$

or somewhat less than half the total stock value.

To further illustrate the use of the H model as a way of developing an expected return for a stock, we can use the same example data as before. In this case, we assume a price and, for illustrative purposes, use \$40 for the hypothetical stock. Using the rearranged formulation, we derive an expected return of 15.25 percent for the stock as follows:

$$k = \frac{\$1}{40}\left[(1.10) + 10(0.20 - 0.10)\right] + 0.10 = 0.1525$$

The H model has many favorable features and would seem to be especially useful for organizations with limited analytical resources, but it is not without drawbacks. First, the model only approximates the return derived from the three-stage model in "most" cases. There may be circumstances where the H model approximation of return or value could be misleading as to the "true" return or value. In addition, the model assumes that the growth rate and dividend values at the beginning of the first stage are representative of those inputs. Companies influenced by cyclical and other abnormal factors would, however, need to adjust for those aberrations. Finally, the model requires an estimate of the half-life—the H factor—and may turn out to be as difficult, if not more so, as developing an estimate of the second stage of the three-stage DDM.

YIELD, GROWTH, AND REVALUATION

We noted in Chapter 6 that a major deficiency of the simplified version of the DDM is that it is not appropriate for valuing stocks growing at exceptionally high rates, because it expects the growth rate used for valuation to persist indefinitely. For high-growth stocks, we expect the current rate to change in a downward direction; conversely, for stocks growing at subpar rates, those growth rates may shift upward under some circumstances.

Presuming a shift in growth rate either up or down, we might also expect a change in valuation to reflect that change. Investors often look at P/E multipliers as an indicator of valuation, and they regard changes in the P/E as changes in the valuation character of a stock. An upward change in the P/E is presumed to reflect improved growth prospects, whereas a downward revision is often regarded as a reflection of lowered growth expectations.

In the context of the simplified DDM, we might view this revaluation as an additional, or third, component of return. With an upward revaluation of the P/E, a stock would experience an additional return, whereas a downward valuation of the P/E would lead to a reduction in return. To reflect this additional return or loss due to any change in the future P/E of a stock, we can add a third component to the simplified DDM to obtain a "three-yield" model:[3]

---

[3] "The Third Yield" is the title of an article by Charles Callard, *Financial Analysts Journal* (Jan–Feb 1968), and is his term for this third component of return. The article describes this simplified method of valuation.

$$E(R) \;=\; k \;=\; \frac{D}{P} + g + \text{RV} \tag{3}$$

This augmented DDM indicates that the return in a stock will be a function of the current dividend yield (D/P), the projected growth rate (g) over the forecasting horizon, and the revaluation return or loss (RV). When there is no change in valuation, the third term becomes zero, and the model is the same as standard simplified "two-yield" DDM. With revaluation, the total return of the stock will be larger when the revaluation is positive and will be lower when the revaluation is downward (negative).

In order to implement this model of valuation, we need to develop three kinds of inputs. As in the case of the simplified DDM, we generate a dividend yield input and develop a growth rate estimate. In contrast to the simplified model, the growth rate forecast is over a finite time horizon of interest that might typically span 5 to 10 years rather than an indefinitely long period. Finally, for the third input we need to develop an estimate of the P/E multiplier for the stock at the end of the horizon for the growth rate forecast. Note that the duration of growth rate forecast and the time for assessing the multiplier valuation need to correspond.

Since the third yield (RV) is the relative growth rate in the multiplier of the stock between the current date and the terminal date of the forecast horizon, we can calculate it by taking the natural log of the ratio of the projected P/E multiplier to the current multiplier and then dividing the natural log of the ratio by the projection period, or holding period, of the stock. As an example, a company selling currently at a 30 P/E is expected to sell at a 15 P/E after a 10-year growth period and would show a ratio of expected to current P/E multiplier of 0.5 and a growth or projection period of 10 years. The natural log of 0.5 is -0.69315, which, divided by 10, becomes -0.069, indicating a negative third yield of 6.9 percent per annum. Presuming a current dividend yield of 1 percent and a projected growth rate of 15 percent over the 10-year period, the indicated investment return is approximately 9 percent per annum: 1 percent dividend plus 15 percent growth minus 7 percent revaluation discount.[4]

To facilitate calculation of the third yield component and to illustrate its potential impact on the total return of a stock, Table 7-2 shows third yield factors for ratios of estimated future multipliers to current multipliers. Note that these ratios range from 5.0 to 0.033 and that there are alternative investment growth durations ranging from 5 to 25 years. The estimated third yield from the prior example can be obtained by finding the negative 6.9 percent per year in the row labeled 0.50 and the column labeled 10 years.

P/B–ROE VALUATION MODEL

The price-to-book value (P/B)–return on equity (ROE) valuation approach has many similarities to the three-yield approach just described. A primary difference is that the P/B–ROE method focuses on book values and explanation of the pricing relative to that measure. Book value has the advantage that investors are familiar with it and use it as an analytical measure

---

[4]The derived return will be "exact" when adding continuously compounded value of the individual components. These values can be generated easily for the second and third yield components, but they can be a problem for the current yield component. Generally, the derivation from this model will be approximate, but not so much that it degrades its usefulness.

TABLE 7-2
Return from multiple change

Expected price multiple divided by current price multiple	Expected duration of the investment				
	5 yrs.	10 yrs.	15 yrs.	20 yrs.	25 yrs.
5.0	32.2%/yr.	16.1%/yr.	10.7%/yr.	8.0%/yr.	6.4%/yr.
4.0	27.7	13.9	9.2	6.9	5.5
3.0	22	11	7.3	5.5	4.4
2.0	13.9	6.9	4.6	3.5	2.8
1.0	0	0	0	0	0
0.50	(13.9)	(6.9)	(4.6)	(3.5)	(2.8)
0.33	(22.2)	(11.1)	(7.3)	(5.5)	(4.4)
0.25	(27.7)	(13.9)	(9.2)	(6.9)	(5.5)
0.20	(32.2)	(16.1)	(10.7)	(8.0)	(6.4)
0.100	(46.1)	(23.0)	(15.5)	(11.5)	(9.2)
0.050	(60.0)	(30.0)	(20.0)	(15.0)	(12.0)
0.033	(68.1)	(34.0)	(22.7)	(17.0)	(13.6)

Source: Charles Callard, "The Third Yield," *Financial Analysts Journal,* Jan–Feb 1968.

in many situations, just as is the case with the earnings and P/E measure. Book value is a more stable benchmark measure than earnings, which in many instances will fluctuate extensively over time. We have seen before that earnings often need to be normalized, which can often be a significant endeavor.

As in the prior case, the P/B–ROE model has an underlying relationship with the DDM and differs from the simplified form of that model in adding a third term to reflect changes in valuation, as in the three-yield model. Using this model, we can express the expected return $E(R)$, or alternatively the required return (k), as a function of the following:

$$E(R) = k = \frac{D}{P} + g_B + RV\left(\frac{P}{B}\right) \tag{4}$$

Note that the yield variable D/P is the same as for the simplified DDM, but the growth variable (g_B) is specified as a growth in book value rather than the dividend. We noted in Chapter 6, however, that one of the useful ways of estimating a growth rate for the dividend is by determining the earnings retention ratio, which is the same as the growth variable in the P/B–ROE model. Finally, the revaluation variable is comparable to the three-yield version, except that the change is with respect to the price-to-book ratio rather than the P/E ratio that we used for illustration in the prior section.

As in the case of the three-yield model, this equation can be used to derive an expected return once input values for the three component variables are determined. Though the model can be used in this way for valuation, it is perhaps more enlightening to provide a different perspective and to make it more tractable for application by converting it into another form. It can be shown[5] that under certain plausible assumptions, a valuation approach relating P/B to ROE is equivalent to the basic form of the model. For purpose of estimating the relationship, the following form is used:

[5] Wilcox, Jerrod, "The P/B–ROE Model," *Financial Analysts Journal* (Jan–Feb 1984), shows this equivalence in describing the model and its use for valuation.

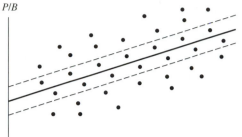

P/B

ROE

FIGURE 7-4
P/B–ROE relationship (June 1992).

$$\log \frac{P}{B} = \alpha + \beta \times \text{ROE}$$

Note that the dependent variable *P/B* is in log form, so the relationship must be estimated using a simple log-linear regression.[6] As usual, the alpha parameter is the intercept and the beta parameter is the slope or estimated additional price for additional return earned on equity. The ROE variable should be the return that the company is expected to earn on equity in the future; it is the same concept as the *r* value that we used in the DDM. For many purposes, especially when evaluating over a large universe, investors use historical values as representative of the ROE to be earned.

To illustrate, we estimated this relationship for a universe consisting of the 600 largest companies and using pricing data as of June 1992. We used book values reported as of the end of 1991 and, to help adjust for cyclical influence and other nonrecurring factors, used an average of the most recent four years' return on equity for each of the companies. The intercept and slope of the line for this cross-sectional relationship are

$$\log \frac{P}{B} = 1.5 + 11.4\text{ROE}$$

Figure 7-4 shows graphically in *P/B*–ROE space the line that was fitted to the 600 stocks using data as described and reflecting prices as of June 1992. Also shown are two dashed lines that bracket the fitted line at plus and minus one standard deviation from the line. Stocks below that lower bound might be considered especially attractive in that they are selling at a *P/B* ratio that is less than warranted, given their ROE. Conversely, stocks above that upper bound might be considered especially unattractive in that they are selling at a *P/B* ratio that is more than warranted given their ROE. This sort of security valuation is directly analogous to that used in the security market line approach, except that the direction of attraction is reversed—there, stocks above the market line are attractive and those below unattractive.

Though this approach and the comparatively similar three-yield approach are useful ways of assessing relative value, they are not without deficiencies. First, they are both highly dependent on the quality of accounting data. Just as earnings can be misleading, for a great

---

[6]The underlying model for this regression equation is $\log(P/B) = -kT + Tr$, where *r* is the return on equity, *T* is the period over which the return is compounded, and *k* is the discount rate as before. The beta parameter in the regression represents *T*, and when we divide (*a/b*), we obtain an estimate of the required return *k*. Alternatively, *k* is the same as the ROE when *P/B* is equal to unity and can be read directly off a graphed relationship.

variety of reasons (such as nonrecurring factors, inappropriate expensing, and an inability to properly portray the economic nature of the firm), reported book values can be misstated for the same reasons and can be especially misleading gauges when there have been periods of strong inflation that cause an understatement of reported values. Though both methods are simplifications, some quite difficult critical assessments need to be made. In the case of the three-yield approach, a terminal P/E needs to be estimated, which can be a daunting task. For the P/B–ROE model, estimating the proper ROE is critical and can also be difficult.

THE Q RATIO

So far we have focused on approaches for valuing expected income and cash flows to assess an appropriate value for the corporation. We might refer to these as income-oriented approaches, as compared to other approaches that we might classify as *asset-oriented,* which focus on directly valuing the assets of the corporation. Though both approaches are ultimately intertwined, because an asset essentially derives value from the cash flow it can generate, the distinction is useful as a means of sharpening the analytical perspective. Furthermore, some valuation approaches are primarily associated with practitioners who are commonly viewed as asset-value-oriented.

Having an alternative valuation approach is important because income-based approaches do not work consistently well over all times and may be particularly deficient in valuing certain kinds of companies, industries, or even broad sectors of the market. A notable example in the United States of a deficiency of income-based approaches occurred during the 1980s, when there was considerable restructuring of corporations through mergers, leveraged buyouts (LBOs), and share buybacks, indicating that their underlying value had not been correctly assessed. In an international context, income-based approaches, such as the DDM and other earnings-based methods, are generally less effective in a market such as Japan. This loss of effectiveness is because of the nature of accounting methods that tend to suppress reported earnings, widespread share crossholdings that complicate the analysis, and tax policies that discourage payment of large dividends by corporations. Asset-based approaches are better suited to the market in Japan.

The q ratio is both a concept and a measure that provides a useful perspective for discussing asset-based valuation. The q ratio approach was devised by Tobin to explain the linkage between the real economy and the financial markets. It is simply defined as the ratio of the market value of the firm, as reflected in the financial markets, to the replacement value of the assets:

$$q = \frac{\text{Market value}}{\text{Replacement value}}$$

It was originally developed as a macroeconomic concept to assess whether additional capital investments by corporations would add to or detract from the market value of the corporation, and thereby provide a signal as to whether or not to invest. With a q ratio below 1, capital investment detracts from the value of the corporation and is not warranted. On the other hand, when the ratio is above 1, then investment is warranted because it would add value to the corporation. Investing would also continue under this circumstance until the q ratio declined to its equilibrium ratio of 1.

The notion also has application to valuation and offers another perspective, which can be shown to be consistent with the DDM, on appraising "growth" opportunities. To illustrate, we can again use a simplified version of the DDM and redefine terms using the retention rate (b), return on assets (r), growth rate (br), and payout rate ($1 - b$), as before. When we express assets as (A), we can then express the simplified dividend discount model as

$$P = \frac{rA(1 - b)}{k - br} \tag{5}$$

We can, in turn, divide by the asset value A, and recognizing that $q = P/A$, we obtain

$$q = \frac{P}{A} = \frac{r(1 - b)}{k - br} \tag{6}$$

We can observe from the expression that when the return on assets (r) is greater than the discount rate or cost of capital (k), q will be greater than 1. This is evidence of true growth and that investment is warranted because it will increase the value of the company. Correspondingly, investment is warranted until the marginal return (r) is equal to the discount rate (k), at which point the q ratio becomes 1. In terms of valuation models, this represents a condition of expansion, where additional investment neither adds to or detracts from the value of the corporation. We comment more on growth and its relation to portfolio management in Chapter 10.

In addition to providing a link between the real economy and financial markets, as well as another perspective on evaluating growth opportunities, the q ratio can represent a standard for asset valuation of individual stocks. As noted, the theoretical equilibrium value of the q ratio is 1, which might also be viewed as a benchmark of fair value. A q above 1 could be viewed as an indicator of overvaluation, depending on the particular stock. Correspondingly, values below 1 could indicate a deficiency of prospects for the company or, alternatively, could be a sign of undervaluation, depending on the particular circumstance. For pragmatic uses, market q's, industry q's, or index q's could be considered the equilibrium value.

To properly assess the valuation status of individual stocks, appraising the replacement value of the company assets is the most critical, though difficult, task. Book value may provide a useful guideline, but this measure is a less than adequate gauge of replacement value. For example, plant and equipment on the books at historic cost may be severely understated in value because of subsequent high inflation. Conversely, plant and equipment may be overstated in value because of obsolescence. Correspondingly, book values do not ordinarily reflect what might be termed "franchise" value. For a consumer product such as Coca-Cola or Hershey, the value of the brand name or franchise will not be fully reflected in the corporate balance sheet. Correspondingly, broadcasting companies that may enjoy quasi-monopolies in an area will not reflect that "franchise" in their balance sheet. There are many other examples of individual companies, or at least industries, that need to be treated on a case-by-case basis.

PRIVATE MARKET VALUE

The private market value concept was applied with significant effect during the "corporate restructuring" period of the 1980s, when many corporations did not reflect their underlying "asset value." Analysts used terms such as "private market value" or "asset value" to denote the true worth of a corporation, or at least the worth to a buyer interested in corporate control. This concept, and analytical approaches to implement it, were generally effective in appraising the worth of corporations during that era. These approaches were especially effective in establishing a value that allowed buyers to finance the purchase of the corporate assets. This financing process provided a "quasi-arbitrage" mechanism for maintaining a floor value for the corporate assets.

To illustrate application of this approach, we describe two complementary methods for establishing a value for corporate assets: (1) direct appraisals of corporate assets, and (2) capitalization of free cash flow. We have selected three companies, representative of disparate industry categories, to illustrate the variety of analytical skills needed to properly appraise the assets of companies with differing business orientations. Furthermore, we review analyses that were derived in an earlier period of the 1980s, when the approach was most successful in identifying misvaluation and the results were most vividly verified by subsequent events.

Table 7-3 shows asset valuation for the three companies using both the direct-appraisal-of-assets method and the capitalization-of-free-cash-flow method. Note that the table shows the market price of the company as of the date of the valuation to allow a comparison with the derived values. Correspondingly, we can compare the value derived from the direct method to that derived from the free cash flow method as alternative means of corroborating the valuation.

Note that each of the companies shows an appraised asset value in excess of the then current market price of the stock. In each of the three cases, the appraisal asset value is built up using the reported book value of the company as a starting point. Some of the standard additions made when adjusting the book value would be excess LIFO inventory reserves, overfunding of the pension plan, deferred tax reserves, and appropriate adjustment for taxes.

TABLE 7-3
Asset valuation appraisal and free cash flow

	Hospital Corp. (HCA)	Associated Dry Goods (DL)	Cummins Engine (CUM)
Current price	$32.00	$68.00	$68.00
Appraisal method			
Stated book value	23.95	41.00	68.62
Book value additions	28.90	52.93	41.45
Book value subtractions	3.65	14.73	—
Restated book value	49.20	93.93	110.07
Restated book market	154%	139%	164%
Capitalized free cash flow			
Pre-tax income	6.45	11.58	16.07
+ Depreciation	2.45	4.65	11.27
Pretax cash flow	8.90	16.23	27.34
− Maint. capital spending	−2.25	−1.73	−9.57
Free cash flow	6.65	14.50	17.77
Multiplier	7.00	6.00	5.50
Capitalized free cash flow	46.55	87.00	97.73
Free cash flow value/price	145%	129%	145%

Some of the standard subtractions from book value would be goodwill or an underfunded pension plan.

In addition to these standard adjustments, the book value needs to be adjusted for asset characteristics that are common to companies in the industry classification or unique to the company. For example, for companies in the retail industry a current appraisal of owned and leased retail space would need to be added to book value. For a company in the extraction industry, a value would need to be placed on resources owned using current values of the commodity being produced. For example, a gold mine property would be valued using the current price of gold, and the book value of a petroleum company would be adjusted by properly appraising the value of the company's oil resources.

As noted, an alternative method for developing an asset value is to calculate a floor value that is based on appraising free cash flows of the company. Here, cash flow is defined as simply pretax income plus depreciation plus interest charges, and it is commonly denoted as EBITD (earnings before interest, taxes, and depreciation). From cash flow, we subtract those capital expenditures and other expenditures needed to maintain the company operations and future cash flow to obtain a surplus, or "free," cash flow.

Free cash flow is important because it provides the management latitude to invest in alternative projects, pay out dividends, or repurchase stock. Alternatively, free cash flow offers an outside buyer latitude to finance a purchase of the company with its own earning power or out of this cash flow. The buyer could purchase the company, simply borrow sufficient funds to finance the purchase, and use the free cash flow to pay down the debt. Assuming an interest rate of 12 percent, the buyer could pay up to 8.3 times free cash flow (or, at a 13 percent rate, could pay up to 7.7 times free cash flow) to purchase the company and still pay off debt at these interest rates. Naturally, buyers would build in some premium for risk in terms of a lower multiplier, depending on the stability of the company or industry of interest. For example, companies in the stable food industry were purchased at higher multiples of free cash flow than more cyclical paper companies during the 1980s restructuring era.

Using this method, Table 7-3 also shows the calculated values for each of the three companies previously evaluated using the direct asset appraisal method. Note that we derive a measure of free cash flow for each of the three companies in the same way, but the capitalization of the free cash flow differs in the multiplier applied. As expected, the multiplier applied to the more cyclical and presumably more risky cash flow of the machinery company is lower than that applied to the more stable and less risky cash flow of the hospital company. The multiplier applied to the retailer is intermediate between the other two, reflecting its level of riskiness.

The bottom part of each section of the table shows the ratio of the derived values for each of the three companies to the then current market prices of the stocks. Note that each of the companies appears undervalued, with ratios greater than 1 (>100 percent), using either valuation approach. Correspondingly, the valuation derived using either method for each of the companies is similar, providing further evidence that the companies might well be undervalued. Indeed, each of these companies showed substantial market price appreciation because of either investor recognition or acquisition by a control buyer.

Though this approach is less appropriate now than during the 1980s, when there was a significantly pervasive undervaluation of corporate assets and credit was more readily available (junk bonds) to finance these transactions, it still is a useful way of estimating a floor value for stocks. Furthermore, the approach has special usefulness in certain international markets, with particular application to Japan. Because of a variety of factors noted previously, income-based valuation is less effective in Japan, whereas asset-based approaches have historically been more appropriate and continue to provide a more useful perspective in that market.

ECLECTIC VALUATION

It is useful at this point to illustrate how the approaches to valuing stocks described in this chapter and the previous one can be used in tandem to evaluate the attractiveness of stocks. For this purpose, we use the appraisals as developed by the Smith Barney research analysts for the grouping of 13 major stocks classified into the drug industry. To evaluate these drug companies, the Smith Barney analysts use three methods that are broadly similar to ones we have described previously and include: (1) a relative P/E-based technique, (2) a dividend discount model (DDM) evaluation, and (3) a cash flow asset valuation method. These three methods offer an objective view of valuation from differing but complementary perspectives that together provide a useful, if somewhat ad hoc, way of assessing the attractiveness of stocks.

The relative P/E-based method used by Smith Barney for evaluating stocks in the drug industry is in the spirit of the three-yield approach described earlier. It entails forecast of earnings over the next 12 months and an estimate of the P/E that will prevail for the stock at the end of the forecast period. Developing a P/E estimate is, in turn, a matter of forecasting the future P/E of a broad index, such as the S&P 500, and then assessing the relationship of the company's P/E to the S&P 500. The current relative P/E is used as a benchmark but is adjusted according to the prospect for growth in the five-year period beyond the year-out forecast. Prospects for improved growth would lead to use of a higher relative P/E, whereas prospects of lower growth would result in application of a lower relative P/E to year-end earnings.

Table 7-4 shows the evaluation of the 13 drug stocks using the relative P/E approved and based on earnings data at the end of September 1992. The table shows the current P/E, current relative P/E, forecast earnings, and forecast relative P/E for each of the companies. It also shows the forecast five-year growth for each over the five-year period beyond September 1993. Using forecast earnings and P/E ratios, the analysts derived a projected price or price objective for each of the stocks. These projected prices can be compared to current prices to calculate a price change or appreciation potential for each of the stocks.

As a second way of evaluating the attractiveness of drug stocks, the Smith Barney research analysts employ a dividend discount model. They use a three-stage version of the DDM that is almost identical in form to the model previously described in this chapter. In executing the model, they develop explicit growth estimates for the first five years as an initial stage, indicate the period and form of decline in the second stage, and finally input growth estimates for the third (steady state) stage. In comparison to our earlier illustration in which we used the current price of the stocks and solved for the discount rate, they developed a discount rate as an input variable. In this way, they could solve for an implied price, or target price, and then compute a percentage change, or appreciation potential, from the current market price.

Table 7-5 shows the results of the DDM analysis of the 13 drug companies. Note that it shows such input variables as the current dividend and the growth rate of the dividend in each of the three stages of the model. Also shown are an earnings growth rate and percent

TABLE 7-4
Drug industry 12-month price appreciation potential (dollars per share)

	Analysts' rating[a]	Current[b]				EPS growth rates[f]		P/E relative	4 Qtr 1993E			Appreciation potential (%)
		May 29 price ($) =	Dec. 1993E EPS ($) ×	P/E ratio	P/E relative	1991–92E (%)	1992–95E (%)		P/E ratio ×	Dec. 1993E EPS ($) =	Price objective ($)	
S&P 500 Index[c]		415.35	27.50[e]	15.1	—	16.7	8.4[e]	—	15.1	—	—	—
8-company drug average[d]	B	61.09	4.49	13.6	0.90	14.6	14.1	1.14	17.2	4.49	77	26
American Home Products	H	75.125	5.65	13.3	0.88	14.7	12.9	1.10	16.6	5.65	94	25
Bristol-Myers Squibb	H	72.375	5.00	14.5	0.96	10.1	14.9	1.15	17.4	5.00	87	20
Glaxo (June)	B	28.250	1.65	17.2	1.14	15.1	22.9	1.60	24.2	1.65	40	41
Eli Lilly	U	66.000	5.65	11.7	0.77	12.2	11.8	0.80	12.1	5.65	68	3
Marion Merrell Dow	U	33.375	2.70	12.4	0.82	18.4	9.9	0.80	12.1	2.70	33	–2
Merck	B	50.375	2.60	19.4	1.28	20.2	18.4	1.70	25.7	2.60	67	33
Pfizer	B	74.625	4.10	18.2	1.21	21.8	22.1	1.65	24.9	4.10	102	37
Rhône-Poulenc Rorer	B	59.375	4.00	14.8	0.98	37.2	21.4	1.40	21.1	4.00	85	42
Schering-Plough	H	52.000	4.15	12.5	0.83	17.9	15.4	1.10	16.6	4.15	69	33
SmithKline Beecham	B	75.375	5.51	13.7	0.91	14.6	15.6	1.15	17.4	5.51	96	27
Syntex (July)	B	38.125	2.95	12.9	0.86	13.8	19.8	1.20	18.1	2.95	53	40
Upjohn (fully diluted)	B	35.000	3.50	10.0	0.66	9.8	9.2	0.80	12.1	3.50	42	21
Warner-Lambert	H	63.250	5.30	11.9	0.79	15.4	11.2	0.80	12.1	5.30	64	1
Wellcome (August)	NR	— in registration —										

Source: Smith Barney. *Note:* Calendar 1993E EPS; Glaxo and Syntex are the average of FY93E and FY94E EPS.
(E) Smith Barney estimates.
[a] B = Buy; H = Hold; U = Underperform; S = Sell; NR = Not rated.
[b] Based on 1993E calendar-year earnings per share. *P/E* relative to the S&P 500 Index.
[c] S&P 500 EPS before write-offs.
[d] Arithmetic average of American Home Products, Bristol-Myers Squibb, Eli Lilly, Merck, Pfizer, Schering-Plough, Upjohn, and Warner-Lambert.
[e] Normalized for the business cycle, S&P 500 1993E EPS are $28.50 and 1992–95E EPS growth rate is 5.5% per year.
[f] Growth rates for U.K. companies are based on EPS measured in sterling, not dollars.

TABLE 7-5
Drug industry dividend discount model valuation^a (dollars per share)

	Analysts' rating^b	May 29 price vs. ($)	Theoretical present value^c ($)	Appreciation potential (%)	Discount rate^d assumption (%)	1991 Div rate ($)	1992–95(E) Growth rate EPS (%)	1992–95(E) Growth rate div(s) (%)	Div payout ratio 1991 (A)	Div payout ratio 1995 (E)	Dividend growth rate assumptions Stage 1 1991–95 (%)	Dividend growth rate assumptions Stage 2 1995–05 (%)	Dividend growth rate assumptions Stage 3 Perp. (%)
S&P 500 Index		415.35	—	—	—	—	10.4	5.1	58.6	48.0	5.1	5.5	5.5
8-company drug average^e	B	61.094	86	41	9.0	1.64	14.2	14.0	47.9	47.5	14.2	9.1	5.5
American Home Products	H	75.125	123	64	8.3	2.38	13.4	13.1	54.6	54.2	13.1	6.9	5.5
Bristol-Myers Squibb	H	72.375	122	68	8.3	2.40	13.7	13.3	60.8	59.8	13.3	6.6	5.5
Glaxo (June)	B	28.250	48	71	9.1	14.0	20.9	23.4	46.1	50.0	23.4	11.1	5.5
Eli Lilly	U	66.000	75	14	9.4	2.00	11.9	12.5	44.4	45.4	10.2	9.3	5.5
Marion Merrell Dow	U	33.375	28	−16	9.2	0.86	11.9	12.5	41.5	42.5	9.8	6.8	5.5
Merck	B	50.375	59	17	8.8	0.77	18.8	19.7	42.1	43.3	20.9	11.3	5.5
Pfizer	B	74.625	77	3	9.6	1.32	22.0	20.7	48.7	46.7	20.6	11.3	5.5
Rhone-Poulenc Rorer	B	59.375	33	−44	11.8	0.45	25.2	42.4	19.9	33.3	42.3	13.7	5.5
Schering-Plough	H	52.000	80	54	8.6	1.27	16.0	16.0	42.2	42.2	16.0	9.9	5.5
SmithKline Beecham	B	75.375	88	16	10.4	15.4	15.4	16.7	32.1	33.6	16.7	13.7	5.5
Syntex (July)	B	38.125	38	−0	10.2	0.83	18.3	17.8	43.9	43.2	17.8	11.6	5.5
Upjohn	H	35.000	33	−5	10.1	1.21	9.3	8.9	42.2	41.5	8.9	8.4	5.5
Warner-Lambert	H	63.250	81	29	8.8	1.76	12.2	11.8	42.3	41.7	11.8	8.7	5.5
Wellcome (August)	NR					— in registration —							

Source: Smith Barney.

(E) Smith Barney estimates.

^aThe dividend discount model calculates the present value of the future stream of dividends. Our model has three stages: Stage 1 (1991–95E) growth rates reflect specific dividend estimates for each year; Stage 2 (1995–2005E) growth rates reflect decline from Stage 1 rate in 1995 to 5.5% in 2005; in Stage 3 (perpetuity), growth rates are 5.5% per year for each drug company and the S&P 500.

^bB = Buy; H = Hold; U = Underperform; S = Sell; NR = Not rated.

^cThe theoretical present value is the price at which the stock would sell if the market fully embraced our projections for dividend growth and discount rate assumptions.

^dThe discount rate is a risk-adjusted rate based on the Capital Asset Pricing Model and utilizing the five-year Treasury note rate. Factors influencing the rate include: earnings declines in the last 10 years, dividend cuts in the last 10 years, and the degree of leverage on the balance sheet.

^eArithmetic average of American Home Products, Bristol-Myers Squibb, Eli Lilly, Merck, Pfizer, Schering-Plough, Upjohn, and Warner-Lambert.

ratio for the dividend in an initial period and at the end of the first stage of growth. The table also shows the discount rate assumed for each of the companies. Note that these vary somewhat from an average, depending mainly on assessed differential degree of riskiness. Given these inputs, the table shows the theoretical price of the stock and the appreciation potential from the current price that is also shown.

As a final way of evaluating the attractiveness of stocks, the analysts derive an "LBO value" for each of the companies. This derivation is very much in line with the capitalization-of-free-cash-flow method that we described in the prior section on private market value. The analysts develop for each of the companies a free cash flow that differs in detail from our prior discussion but is essentially similar. Correspondingly, these analysts use an interest rate (inverse of the multiplier) that differs across companies to capitalize the free cash flow. This derivation provides an estimate of "private market value," or an alternative valuation that might represent a floor value from which a premium or discount from the current price can be calculated.

Table 7-6 shows the derivation of the take-out values for each of the 13 companies. Note that it shows a rather detailed derivation of the free cash that differs somewhat in format from our prior illustration. In addition to the usual additions and subtractions, it also assumes some cash flow savings (additions) from research and development (R&D) and from sales, general, and administrative (SG&A) as well as capital expenditures cost cutting. Given an interest rate assumption, an additional amount of debt that is supportable is derived. To this debt, cash and equivalents are added to derive a buyout price. The table shows a buyout premium (or discount) that provides an appreciation potential from the current price.

Table 7-7 is a summary table showing valuation of the 13 drug companies according to the three types of appraisals: (1) relative EPS growth and P/E valuation, (2) dividend discount valuation, and (3) takeover valuation. Note that the table shows the price target for each of the stocks from each of the appraisal methods, along with the appreciation potential to each target price from the current price. As a crude approximation, we might consider stocks that show high appreciation potential according to all three measures to be attractive because of the consistency of valuation. The next chapter will describe a more explicit way of combining these valuations as well as other valuation types. On this basis, we might consider American Home Products, Bristol-Myers Squibb, Schering-Plough, and SmithKline Beecham to be the most attractive; these are highlighted to indicate this.

VALUATION AND RISK CHANGES

So far we have focused on use of valuation models to develop an improved estimate of the return for a stock, hoping that the better return forecast can lead to an improved ability to differentiate between attractive and unattractive stocks. However, anticipating change in the risk of a stock can also be potentially useful in differentiating between attractive and unattractive securities, because a change in the riskiness of a stock should have a direct impact on the discount rate or expected return of the stock. An increase in the discount rate should lead to a price decline, whereas a decrease would lead to a price increase. A price decline, in turn, raises the expected return, whereas a price increase lowers the expected return.

We can perhaps best illustrate the way that this process works in the context of the security market line and show how changes in security betas affect the expected return $E(R)$ or,

TABLE 7-6

Drug industry takeover valuation analysis of pharmaceutical companies, 1992(E) (dollars in millions)[a]

		AHP	BMY	GLX[b]	LLY	MKC	MRK	PFE	RPR	SGP	SBE[b]	SYN	UPJ	WLA	8-Co.[b] Total
	(1) Revenues	7,646	12,610	8,385	6,363	2,805	10,580	7,677	4,559	4,191	9,158	2,401	3,556	5,585	58,208
Less	(2) Cost of goods sold (excludes depreciation)	2,453	3,065	1,190	1,458	545	2,066	2,035	1,426	786	2,823	320	775	1,637	14,275
Less	(3) R&D and SG&A (less 10% for cost cutting)	2,799	5,455	3,662	2,289	1,157	3,998	3,489	1,949	2,025	3,329	1,191	1,681	2,659	24,395
Less	(4) Interest expense	25	60	131	45	15	80	120	150	80	175	35	31	87	528
Less	(5) Capital expenditures (less 10% for cost cutting)	279	495	866	855	117	900	630	225	329	465	259	270	324	4,082
Equals	(6) Pretax operating cash flow to support additional debt	2,090	3,535	2,536	1,716	972	3,536	1,403	810	972	2,366	596	799	878	14,928
Divide by	(7) Interest rate assumption (%)	6.5	6.5	6.5	7.0	8.0	6.5	7.0	8.0	7.0	7.5	7.0	8.0	8.0	7.1
Equals	(8) Additional debt supportable	32,154	54,385	39,010	24,514	12,144	54,403	20,039	10,119	13,879	31,552	8,516	9,985	10,975	211,373
Plus	(9) Cash and equivalents	4,264	2,058	2,786	962	357	1,633	1,659	160	1,177	1,395	780	425	446	12,624
Equals	(10) Buyout price (8 + 9)[c]	36,418	56,443	41,796	25,476	12,501	56,036	21,698	10,279	15,056	32,946	9,296	10,410	11,421	223,997
Versus	(11) Per share (10/14) ($)	115	109	28	86	44	48	66	75	75	124	41	57	85	80[d]
	(12) Recent price per share ($)	75	72	28	66	33	50	75	59	52	75	38	35	63	61[d]
	(13) Buyout premium (%)[e]	54	50	-2	31	33	-4	-12	26	44	64	8	62	34	31[d]
	(14) Avg. shares out (mils)	315.8	518.6	1503.5	294.9	282.0	1158.9	329.6	137.4	201.5	266.4	225.3	183.8	134.6	3,137.7

Source: Smith Barney.

Note: Calendar 1992E data; Glaxo (FYJune) and Syntex (FYJuly) are the average of FY92E and FY93E data.

(E) Smith Barney estimates.

[a] Except per-share data.

[b] Glaxo and SmithKline Beecham data translated from U.K. sterling into U.S. dollars at the exchange rate of £ = $1.75.

[c] The 8-company total is the sum of American Home Products, Bristol-Myers Squibb, Eli Lilly, Merck, Pfizer, Schering-Plough, Upjohn, and Warner-Lambert.

[d] The 8-company arithmetic average stock price and buyout premium.

[e] Buyout price targets reflect the upside potential of a company that is in play. Until then, a 15–25% discount must be applied to the buyout price to reflect shareholders' minority ownership position, lack of corporate control, and inability to consummate a transaction.

TABLE 7-7
Drug industry summary of price appreciation potentials (dollars per share)

	Analysts' rating[a]	May 29 price ($)	Price targets			Appreciation potentials		
			Rel EPS grth and P/E valuation ($)	Dividend discount valuation ($)	Takeover valuation analysis ($)	Rel EPS grth and P/E valuation (%)	Dividend discount valuation (%)	Takeover valuation analysis (%)
8-company drug average[b]	B	61.09	77	86	80	26	41	31
American Home Products	H	75.125	94	123	115	25	64	54
Bristol-Myers Squibb	H	72.375	87	122	109	20	68	50
Glaxo (June)	B	28.250	40	46	28	41	63	-2
Eli Lilly	U	66.000	68	75	86	3	14	31
Marion Merrell Dow	U	33.375	33	28	44	-2	-16	33
Merck	B	50.375	67	59	48	33	17	-4
Pfizer	B	74.625	102	77	66	37	3	-12
Rhône-Poulenc Rorer	B	59.375	85	33	75	42	-44	26
Schering-Plough	H	52.000	69	80	75	33	54	44
SmithKline Beecham	B	75.375	96	88	124	27	16	64
Syntex (July)	B	38.125	53	38	41	40	-0	8
Upjohn	H	35.000	42	33	57	21	-5	62
Warner-Lambert	H	63.250	64	81	85	1	29	34

Source: Smith Barney.
NA Not Available.
[a]B = Buy; H = Hold; U = Underperform; S = Sell.
[b]Arithmetic average of American Home Products, Bristol-Myers Squibb, Eli Lilly, Merck, Pfizer, Schering-Plough, Upjohn, and Warner-Lambert.

alternatively, the discount rate for the security. Figure 7-5 reproduces a security market line shown in a prior chapter (Figure 3-10) to help illustrate how return opportunities can arise from anticipating changes in the riskiness of securities. The chart shows two hypothetical stocks differing in risk, as measured by current betas of 1.00 for stock M and 1.20 for stock N. Each is offering a return in line with its risk and thus plots on the market line as described in previous chapters.

In the case of stock M, we project that the riskiness will increase from the current historically measured level of 1.00 to the 1.20 level in the future. Correspondingly, we project that the riskiness of stock N will decrease from its current above-average level of 1.20 to an average level of 1.00 in the future. The projected change in risk is illustrated by the dashed lines on Figure 7-5.

With a change in riskiness we anticipate, in keeping with the framework of the market line, that the expected return of each stock should change as well. In the case of stock M, investors should expect to earn 13.4 percent in the future compared to the 12 percent currently expected, whereas the opposite should occur with regard to stock N; investors would expect to earn 12 percent rather than the current 13.4 percent. Table 7-8 illustrates the price impact of these risk changes using the simplified DDM and assumed inputs as shown. Note that the increase in the discount rate for stock M results in a price decline of 16.7 percent, as expected, and the discount rate decrease for stock N results in a 28 percent price increase, also as expected.

The process of stock price adjustment is thus analogous to that illustrated in Chapter 6. The difference is that the situation of disequilibrium arises from a predicted change in riskiness rather than from anticipation of below- or above-average returns at a given risk level. Like forecasting stock returns, forecast of risk (betas) requires a model, as well as analytical input. For such a purpose, it is useful to decompose the risk premium for stocks into the four elements we described in the beginning of Chapter 6 and evaluate how the

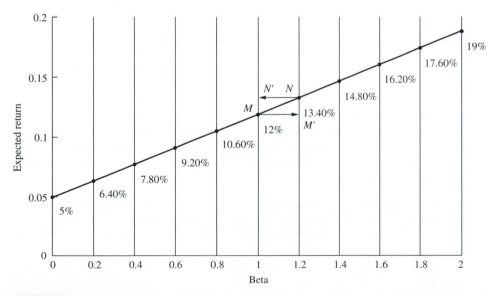

FIGURE 7-5
Forecasting betas.

TABLE 7-8
Discount rate change and stock price change

	Stock M	Stock N
Dividend (D):	$1.00	$1.00
Growth rate (g):	0.05	0.07
Current: $P = \dfrac{D}{k-g}$	at $0.12 = \dfrac{1}{0.12 - 0.05} = \$14.28$	at $0.134 = \dfrac{1}{0.134 - 0.07} = \$15.63$
Projected: $P = \dfrac{D}{k-g}$	at $0.134 = \dfrac{1}{0.134 - 0.05} = \$11.90$	at $0.12 = \dfrac{1}{0.12 - 0.07} = \$20.00$
Price change:	-16.7%	28.0%

discount rate, and hence the expected return of stocks, should respond to changes in these risk elements. The following sections describe some approaches for objectively evaluating the likely impact of changes in these risk elements on stock prices' behavior.

RISKS AND THE DISCOUNT RATE

Interest Rate Risk

It will be useful at this point to analyze those factors that have an impact on the level of the discount rate for stocks: (1) interest rate risk, (2) purchasing power risk, (3) business risk, and (4) financial risk. We can, in fact, analyze interest rate risk within the duration framework, just as we used duration to evaluate the exposure of bonds to this risk. In the case of stocks, dividend payments are presumed to continue over an indefinite period—that is, infinity—so that developing duration for stocks comes within the general category of developing duration for a perpetuity. For perpetuities such as preferred stocks, whose dividend payments are fixed, or British consols (bonds), whose interest payments continue indefinitely, the formula for calculating duration is[7]

$$d = \frac{1}{k} \tag{7}$$

As before, k represents the required return on the security, and the resulting expression is simply the inverse of the required return. Since we are dealing with perpetuities such as preferred and consols, the required return k can be determined by merely observing the current yield of the security. For example, a preferred stock paying a $12 dividend and

---

[7] This expression for duration assumes continuous compounding, and, for purposes of illustrating duration for perpetuities like preferred stocks and common stocks, we will consider that the assumption of continuous compounding is appropriate. When discrete compounding is assumed, the expression for the duration of a perpetuity like a preferred stock is

$$d = \frac{1+k}{k}$$

This expression is only slightly more complex than the one in the text but would tend to obscure the analytical exposition.

selling at \$100 would have a current yield of 12 percent. Assuming that this is representative of the required return on the security, and using Equation 7, we can calculate the duration of the preferred stock as follows:

$$d = \frac{1}{k} = \frac{1}{0.12} = 8.3 \text{ years}$$

The equation for calculating the duration of a common stock is similar, except for the need to recognize that common-stock dividends are expected to grow over the longer term. Again using g to represent the growth rate of the dividend, we can amend the previous equation to account for the expected growth in dividends. The equation for calculating the duration of common stock is then

$$d = \frac{1}{k - g}$$

Note that the denominator of the expression has the same form as that of the dividend capitalization model (see Equation (6) in Chapter 6). Rearranging the dividend capitalization model, we see that

$$D/P = \text{dividend yield} = k - g$$

In words, this says that the dividend yield D/P of the stock is equal to the difference between the required return k and the growth rate g. Substituting for $k - g$, we see that duration for the stock is simply the inverse of the dividend yield:

$$d = \frac{1}{\text{dividend yield}}$$

This, in turn, indicates that stocks with low dividend yields have long durations and are relatively more sensitive to discount rate changes. High-growth stocks are generally characterized by relatively low dividend yields and would be more subject to this risk than low-growth stocks. We would expect high-growth stocks to carry a higher discount rate than lower-growth stocks to compensate for this risk.

We can best illustrate this discount rate sensitivity, or duration effect, by means of the data in Table 7-9. This table shows two stocks, each paying \$1 in dividends and having a discount rate of 10 percent; stock A has a growth rate of 7 percent and stock B has a growth rate of 4 percent. Stock A has a duration of 33.3 years, and stock B has a duration of 16.7 years. When the discount rate increases to 11 percent, the high-growth stock shows a 25-percent decline in price, compared to a 14-percent decline in price for the low-growth stock. Correspondingly, a decrease in the discount rate to 9 percent leads to a 50-percent increase in price for the high-growth stock and a 20-percent price increase for the low-growth stock. The longer-duration stock (33.3 years) thus shows greater variability with respect to discount rate changes than the short-duration stock (16.7 years), as indicated by the preceding analysis.

Because the measure of duration for stocks is similar to the measure of duration for bonds, we can thus compare the duration of stocks and bonds to evaluate the relative riskiness of the two broad security types to interest rate changes. We can use the returns generated by stocks and the returns generated by bonds over the 67-year period 1926–1993 (the same data as shown in Chapter 2) as proxy input data. We can then use Equation (5) in Chapter 5 to calculate bond duration and Equation (8) in this chapter to calculate stock duration.

TABLE 7-9
Sensitivity to discount rate changes

	Stock A	Stock B
Dividend D	$1.00	$1.00
Growth rate g	7%	4%
Discount rate k	10%	10%
Price $= \dfrac{D}{k-g}$	$33.30	$16.70
Duration $= \dfrac{1}{k-g}$	$\dfrac{1}{(0.10-0.07)}=33.3$	$\dfrac{1}{(0.10-0.04)}=16.7$
Discount rate k	11%	11%
Price $= \dfrac{D}{k-g}$	$25	$14.30
Price change	−25%	−14%
Discount rate k	9%	9%
Price $= \dfrac{D}{k-g}$	$50	$20
Price change	50%	20%

Table 7-10 shows the input data and calculated durations for stocks and bonds. Note that over the 67-year period and based on an index of returns of 5 percent for an average maturity of twenty years, the bonds had a duration of twelve years, whereas the stocks showed an average dividend return of 4 percent and a growth rate of 5 percent, indicating a duration of 25 years. At year-end 1993, stocks were yielding 3 percent and showed a duration of 33 years, whereas a high-grade 20-year government bond yielding 8 percent showed a duration of 10 years. Because of their perpetual life and positive growth character, stocks typically show a duration considerably in excess of bonds, which have fixed maturity periods and, of course, no growth characteristics. Stocks should be considerably more responsive to changes

TABLE 7-10
Relative duration—stocks versus bonds

	1926–1993	12/31/93
Bonds		
Average coupon	$5	$8
Maturity	20 years	20 years
Average interest rate	5%	8%
Duration	12 years	10 years
Stocks		
Average dividend	$4	$3
Growth rate	5%	8%
Average discount rate	9%	11%
Duration	25 years	33 years

in real interest rates than bonds are, and correspondingly, they carry a higher premium in the discount rate than bonds do to compensate for this component of risk.

Purchasing Power Risk

It is, however, unclear how responsive stocks should be to changes in nominal interest rates. Nominal rates include both a real interest rate component R and an inflation premium component I and should adjust up or down as the rate of inflation changes. They should increase as the inflation component rises when inflation is high and should decline as the inflation component declines when inflation is low.

Because bond coupons are fixed, bonds should be fully subject to this component of risk. In particular, as the discount rate rises, the price of the bond with a fixed coupon must adjust fully by declining to compensate for the increase in the interest rate. Stocks, however, have an opportunity to offset inflation through an increase in dividends. We can best illustrate this fact by referring back to the basic stock valuation Equation (6) in Chapter 6 and, in this case, augmenting it with an increased dividend growth rate, $1 + I$, to compensate for inflation. Thus

$$P = \frac{D(1 + I)}{k(1 + I) - g(1 + I)}$$

Note that all three variables (dividends, growth, and discount rate) have been augmented with the inflation factor $1 + I$. When inflation increases, the discount rate should be higher by $(1 + I)$ to reflect the higher rate. If the corporate growth rate and dividend increased directly in line with the inflation increase, or by $(1 + I)$, the company would be expected to offset inflation entirely, having no effect on price. In this case, we can factor out the $1 + I$ terms as shown below:

$$P = \frac{(1 + I)D}{(1 + I)(k - g)} = \frac{D}{(k - g)}$$

If, however, the corporation cannot increase its rate of growth in line with inflation or can adjust only partially, there should be a negative effect on stocks. This happens because the discount rate will increase more than the growth rate and dividend level, thus resulting in the application of a net higher discount rate. In the extreme situation where the corporation is completely unable to increase growth in the face of inflation, the dividend becomes almost

TABLE 7-11
Inflation and stock prices

Stock	Zero inflation	5% inflation 100% adjustment	50% adjustment	Zero adjustment
		(1)	(2)	(3)
Dividend	1.00	1.02	1.01	1.00
Growth rate	0.05	0.7010	0.0605	0.05
Discount rate	0.09	0.1118	0.1118	0.1118
Stock price	$25.00	$25.00	$19.69	$16.18
Price change, %	—	—	−$21.00	−$35.00

like a fixed coupon payment. In this case, the stock acts more or less like a bond in bearing the full brunt of an increase in the discount rate.

Table 7-11 illustrates the dividend growth adjustment under three different scenarios: (1) a full dividend growth adjustment to inflation, (2) a partial adjustment—in this case only a 50 percent adjustment to an increase in inflation, and (3) a zero or bondlike adjustment. Note that when inflation increases from 0 percent to 5 percent, stock prices are not affected if growth increases in tandem with inflation; however, stock prices depreciate by 35 percent if there is no adjustment and by 21 percent if there is only a partial adjustment for inflation.

How stocks actually adjust to inflation is essentially an empirical question. Studies indicate that stocks adjust rather fully to inflation over longer periods of time; however, over shorter periods the indications are not so clear. Experience indicates that over some historical periods, stocks have not adjusted fully. For example, they suffered especially severely during the 1973–1977 period, when, in terms of the dividend capitalization model, the change in g lagged behind the change in k. This lag may have been due to tax laws, stickiness in prices, or a multitude of other factors.

Business and Financial Risk

Within the equity market there are varying degrees of exposure to business and financial risk. Companies that are small, hold secondary positions within their industry, have heavy fixed costs and extensive operating leverage, show substantial sensitivity to the business cycle, and demonstrate significant variability in earnings would be expected to have a lot of business risk. Companies in this category that finance heavily with debt would have further significant exposure to financial risk. We would expect such companies to carry the highest discount rates to compensate investors for relatively extensive exposure to these risks.

On the other hand, companies that are large, are leading factors in their industry, have relatively low sensitivity to the business cycle, and show a stable pattern of earnings would be expected to have a lesser degree of business risk. Companies in this category that also have clean balance sheets—that is, financed entirely with equity—would, of course, show no exposure to financial risk. Because of the relatively limited business risk and the absence of financial risk, we would expect the discount rates of these "highest-quality" companies to be significantly lower than those companies in the previous category.

As in the cases of interest rate and purchasing power risk, it is useful to have an analytical framework for understanding the underlying factors contributing to financial and operating risks, so as to be better able to anticipate changes in these major risk components and the impact on stock pricing. Fortunately, there is a reasonably straightforward way of decomposing beta into components of financial and operating risk, based on some theoretically plausible assumptions. First, we assume that the CAPM is valid and also that the proposition of Modigliani and Miller (MM) is valid with respect to the returns expected for a levered firm as compared to an unlevered firm. Then, with the added assumption of risk-free corporate debt, researchers[8] have derived an equilibrium relationship for the equity return of the levered firm L.

[8]Hamada, Robert S. "The Effect of the Firm's Capital Structure on the Systematic Risk of Common Stocks," *Journal of Finance* (May 1972) p. 435–452.

$$E(R) = E(R_u) + [E(R_u) - R_f]\left(\frac{D_L}{S_L}\right)$$

where R_L = equity return to the levered firm L

R_u = equity return of the unlevered firm U, a firm with an asset structure identical to that of firm L

R_f = risk-free return

D_L = total market value of firm L debt

S_L = total market value of firm L equity

This expression indicates that the return to the equity securities of the levered firm L will increase linearly with the debt-to-equity (D_L/S_L) ratio. This result is, in fact, a restatement, within the CAPM framework, of the MM financial irrelevance proposition. To relate this expression to the firm's systematic risk, the CAPM expression for the unlevered firm $E(R_U) = R_f + [E(R_M) - R_f]\beta_U$ can be substituted and then solved for the beta of the levered firm (β_L):

$$\beta_L = \left(1 + \frac{D_L}{S_L}\right)\beta_U$$

The expression indicates that the systematic risk of a levered firm consists of two components: (1) a financial leverage component, D_L/S_L, and (2) an operating risk component, β_U. This result implies an independence of the financing and operating decisions of the firm, which enables us to focus on one or the other of the beta components.

In assessing a change in financial risk and its impact on beta, this analysis would imply that forecasting a change in the debt-to-equity ratio would be a direct indicator of this change. A forecast of a decline in the ratio would imply a decline in the beta, whereas forecast of an increase would imply an increase in beta. Alternatively, we could use a more inclusive measure of financial risk, such as the z-score, and forecast changes in that ratio.[9] Forecast of an increasing z-score would indicate improving financial health that would presumably lead to a decrease in the beta of the stock. On the other hand, forecast of a declining z-score would indicate increasing financial risk that would presumably lead to a decrease in the beta of the stock.

To forecast changes in business risk, proxy measures, such as the variability of operating earnings of the company, might be used. Prospects of increasing variability would presumably indicate an increase in beta, whereas prospect of a decrease in variability would indicate a decrease in beta. The covariability of earnings with a broad index of corporate operating earnings that is an operating earnings beta might also be used as a proxy measure of business risk. Again, an increase in the operating earnings beta would presumably be reflected in an increased stock beta, whereas decrease in the operating earnings beta would be reflected in a lower beta. These two types of measures might proxy for business risk, but a variety of other measures might serve this purpose as well.

---

[9]The z-score is an objective measure of a firm's risk of bankruptcy. We describe this measure more fully in Chapter 14 when we discuss bond management.

CONCLUSION

Valuation is an essential component of the portfolio management process. At the same time, it is a highly difficult, if not daunting, endeavor. We have seen that the most theoretically appropriate approach for equity valuation is the DDM in its three-stage version. Unfortunately, this model is quite difficult to implement due both to the cost, in terms of effort and resources, and to the potential biases and inability to match reality to a greater or lesser degree, depending on the particular case.

We have seen that simplified models make systematic valuation more feasible, but these approaches also have deficiencies. One such deficiency is that these simplifications may lose some of the ability to capture the valuation properly. In addition, these models generally depend heavily on accounting data inputs that are inherently deficient. Finally, these models depend on the important ability to estimate certain inputs that may be smaller in number than DDM but may well be more sensitive to error. On balance, the equity valuation process is a multi-dimensional one that should include several differing approaches to valuation. Fortunately, the information coefficient/multiple valuation approach, which we describe in the next chapter, provides an analytical framework for such an eclectic approach.

APPENDIX A
THE THREE-STAGE DIVIDEND CAPITALIZATION MODEL

Molodovsky, May, and Chottiner (see references) developed the three-stage dividend capitalization model. The two-stage and three-stage dividend capitalization models differ essentially in the way that they allow for a shift in above-normal growth to growth in line with the corporate average. The two-stage model assumes an abrupt one step down in the growth rate. This middle stage offers a generally more realistic way of portraying the real-world pattern of growth and decline than the two-stage model. At the same time, it allows the flexibility of modeling the two-stage pattern where needed by allowing the middle stage of growth to be zero. For these reasons, the three-stage model has been the most popular for practical application.

Figure 7-A1 provides a more elaborate illustration of the model. For ease of exposition, the formula assumes that the initial dividend rate D_0 is \$1. To determine the price of a stock where the dividend differs from \$1, simply multiply the actual dividend by the derived price (or, in this sense, dividend multiplier). Note that the first and third components of the three-stage model are essentially identical to the two-stage model. In particular, the first stage merely represents compounding of the dividend at the supernormal rate and discounting to obtain a value for the supernormal growth phase. The third stage represents the value of the stock when it settles into a growth rate in line with the standard phase. Here the dividend at the end of both the superior and declining growth stages is capitalized and discounted back to present value over both stages.

The three-stage model differs from the two-stage model in requiring a middle segment V_2 to represent the phase when the superior growth rate is declining to that of an average (or standard) stock. The formulation indicates that we take the dividend at the end of the first phase of growth and apply a diminishing growth rate to it over the period of decline. The formulation in the body of Figure 7-A1 shows how to calculate the appropriate growth rate to use for each period of the declining growth phase. For example, in the fifth year of the declining growth phase, the rate of growth would be

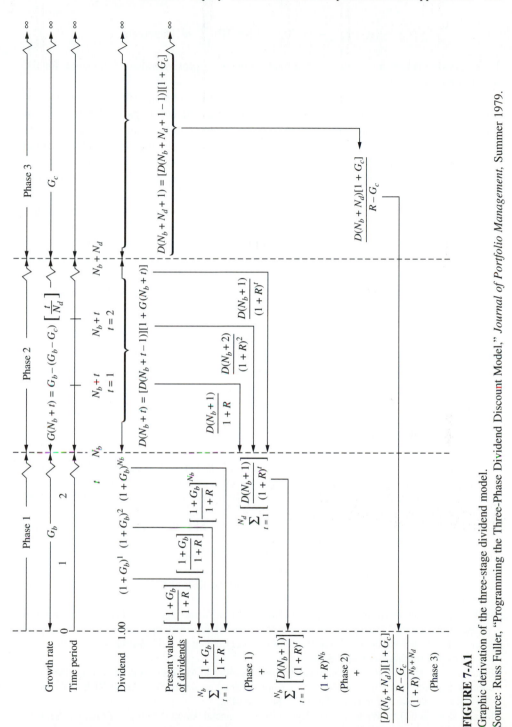

FIGURE 7-A1

Graphic derivation of the three-stage dividend model.

Source: Russ Fuller, "Programming the Three-Phase Dividend Discount Model," *Journal of Portfolio Management*, Summer 1979.

$$g - (g - g_s)\frac{t}{N_d} = 20 - (20 - 10)\frac{5}{10} = 15 \text{ percent}$$

These dividends are in turn discounted back to derive a present value of the stock for the second phase of growth.

Though the formulation representing this model is more elaborate than that for the two-stage model, the burden of estimation is not significantly greater. In particular, for the first stage the method would normally require explicit estimates of the company's dividend for each of the first five years of the planning period, or, alternatively, merely an estimate of the supernormal rate of growth in this initial phase. The second stage would call for an estimate of the rate of growth of the company at the beginning of the period, as well as the number of years over which that rate is expected to decline, to grow in line with the general corporate average. The third-stage input would be an estimate of the rate of growth of the standard share, or, alternatively, the growth rate of the general corporate average.

These kinds of inputs can reasonably be expected because they either are in keeping with the normal tasks of analysts or can be developed by making some standard assumptions. For example, developing explicit dividend estimates for the first stage is a task that can be reasonably expected of an analyst, just as five-year projected income and balance sheet data are the sorts of information that the analyst should be providing as a matter of course. The only major difficulty would be recasting the information in a suitable form for the model. In addition, estimates of the way that above-average rates of growth will taper to be in line with the economy can be facilitated by using some rather simple rules of thumb. Finally, the third-stage model input needs only an estimate based on general economic analysis of the likely rate of general corporate growth.

SELECTED REFERENCES

Beaver, W., P. Ketler, and M. Scholes: "The Association Between Market Determined and Accounting Determined Risk Measures," *Accounting Review,* October 1970, pp. 654–682.

Cohen, J., E. Zinbarg, and A. Zeikel: *Investment Analysis and Portfolio Management,* Richard D. Irwin, Homewood, IL, 1987.

Cowen, Scott, and Jeffrey Hoffer: "Usefulness of Financial Ratios in a Single Industry," *Journal of Business Research,* March 1982, pp. 103–118.

Cusatis, Patrick, James Miles, and Randall Woolridge: "Restructuring through Spin-offs," *Journal of Financial Economics,* June 1993, pp. 293–312.

Fewings, David: "The Impact of Corporate Growth on the Risk of Common Stocks," *Journal of Finance,* May 1975, pp. 525–531.

Franks, Julian, Robert Harris, and Sheridan Titman: "The Postmerger Share-Price Performance of Acquiring Firms," *Journal of Financial Economics,* March 1991, pp. 81–96.

Fuller, Russ: "Programming the Three-Phase Dividend Discount Model," *Journal of Portfolio Management,* Summer 1979, pp. 28–32.

Graham, B., D. Dodd, and S. Cottle: *Security Analysis,* 4th ed., McGraw–Hill, New York, 1962.

Hamada, Robert: "The Effect of the Firm's Capital Structure on the Systematic Risk of Common Stocks," *Journal of Finance,* May 1971, pp. 435–452.

Haugen, R.A., and D.W. Wichern: "The Elasticity of Financial Assets," *Journal of Finance,* September 1974, pp. 1229–1240.

Healy, Paul, K. Palepu, and Richard Ruback: "Does Corporate Performance Improve After Mergers?" *Journal of Financial Economics,* April 1992, pp. 135–176.

Holt, Charles C.: "The Influence of Growth Duration on Share Price," *Journal of Finance,* September 1961, pp. 465–475.

Jahnke, William: "The Growth Stock Mania," *Financial Analysts Journal,* May–June 1973, pp. 65–69.

————: "What's Behind Stock Prices?" *Financial Analysts Journal,* September–October 1975, pp. 69–76.

Jensen, Michael, and Richard Ruback: "The Market for Corporate Control," *Journal of Financial Economics,* April 1983, pp. 5–50.

Johnson, Lewis: "The Role of Convexity in Equity Pricing," *Financial Analysts Journal,* September–October 1992, pp. 69–73.

————: "Equity Duration: Another Look," *Financial Analysts Journal,* March–April 1989, pp. 73–75.

Lang, L., Rene Stulz, and Ralph Walking: "A Test of the Free Cash Flow Hypothesis: The Case of Bidder Returns," *Journal of Financial Economics,* October 1991, pp. 315–336.

Leibowitz, Martin, and Stanley Kogelman: "Resolving the Equity Duration Paradox," *Financial Analysts Journal,* January–February 1993, pp. 51–67.

————, Eric Sorenson, Robert Arnott, and Nicholes Hanson: "A Total Differential Approach to Equity Duration," *Financial Analysts Journal,* September–October 1989, pp. 30–37.

Malkiel, Burton G.: "Equity Yields, Growth, and the Structure of Share Prices," *American Economic Review,* December 1963, pp. 467–494.

————and John G. Cragg: "Expectations and the Structure of Share Price," *American Economic Review,* September 1970, pp. 601–617.

Mitchell, Mark: "The Value of Corporate Takeovers," *Financial Analysts Journal,* January–February 1990, pp. 21–31.

————and Harold Mulhern: "The Stock Price Response to Pension Terminations and the Relation of Terminations with Corporate Takeovers," *Financial Management,* Autumn, 1989, pp. 41–56.

Molodovsky, Nicholas, C. May, and S. Chottiner: "Common Stock Valuation: Theory and Tables," *Financial Analysts Journal,* March–April 1965, pp. 104–123.

Nichols, D.A.: "A Note on Inflation and Common Stock Values," *Journal of Finance,* September 1968, pp. 655–657.

Porter, Michael: "Industry Structure and Competitive Strategy: Keys to Profitability," *Financial Analysts Journal,* July–August 1980, pp. 30–41.

Reilly, F.: "Companies and Common Stocks as Inflation Hedges," *N.Y.U. Bulletin,* 1975–2.

Thompson, Donald: "Source of Systematic Risk in Common Stocks," *Journal of Business,* April 1978, pp. 173–188.

Treynor, Jack: "The Value of Control," *Financial Analysts Journal,* July–August 1992, pp. 6–9.

Wilcox, Jarrod: "The P/B–ROE Valuation Model," *Financial Analysts Journal,* January–February 1984, pp. 58–66.

QUESTIONS AND PROBLEMS

1. What are some desirable characteristics of a valuation model?
2. Using these attributes, compare the dividend discount model to the Graham and Dodd *P/E* approach.
3. Compare the *H* model to the three-stage dividend discount model. What are the similarities and differences?

4. Assume a stock grows at 25 percent for 5 years and then declines to an average rate of 8 percent over a 4-year period. Using these inputs and a 12 percent discount rate, compute the current price by means of the H model.

5. What is the component of return due to superior growth, and what is due to standard growth for the stock described in the previous problem?

6. Compare the results from the previous problem with that derived from the three-stage DDM, and explain the reasons for the difference.

7. In what ways does the "three-yield" model resemble the simplified DDM, and how does it differ?

8. Assume a stock selling at a P/E of 25 with a dividend yield of 1.5 percent is growing at 25 percent per annum but is expected to decline to an 8 percent rate in 5 years and then to sell at 15 times multiple. What is the expected return of the stock?

9. How are the P/B–ROE model and the three-yield model related? What are the advantages and disadvantages of each?

10. A stock is selling below the fitted P/B–ROE line. Should its price rise or fall? Explain.

11. How does the concept of the q ratio relate to common stock valuation?

12. What is the concept of private value, and what are two approaches that allow its practical application?

13. What process helps establish a "floor value" for a stock and then maintains it?

14. Competitive conditions worsen in an industry. Describe the likely impact on the prices of stocks in the industry.

15. The current risk-free rate is 5 percent and the expected return of the market is 12 percent. A stock's riskiness is lessened as its beta has declined from 1.05 to 0.90, but its growth rate has remained the same at 7 percent and its dividend at $2.00. Calculate its likely price change.

16. Refer to Table 7-11 and calculate the price change for a stock that shows a 25 percent adjustment to inflation and then for a 75 percent adjustment.

17. Given your estimate of firm Z's beta of 0.75 from historic data and the fact that the firm has recently increased its total debt ratio from the mean debt ratio for all firms to two standard deviations above mean, what is your estimate of its future beta?

18. Suppose you had computed the beta for First Honest Bank Co. to be 0.95, based on its historical returns. Are there any other adjustments you might want to make to this beta estimate?

19. Using the constant growth dividend discount model, explain how inflation might affect the prices of common stocks.

20. Why do most, if not all, dividend discount models invoke at some point the assumptions of the constant-growth dividend discount model?

21. In general, what do you think might be the relationship between P/E ratios based on reported earnings and the business cycle?

22. Tasty Foods' stock sells for $20 per share, and the most recent dividend was $1.00. An analyst, using the three-phase dividend discount model, estimates that the beginning growth rate of dividends g_a will be 10 percent, but this rate will last for only the first two years ($A = 2$). The growth will then decline to a constant, long-run normal rate of 7 percent ($g_n = 7$ percent) over a three-year transition period ($B = 5; B - A = 3$).

   (a) What is the expected growth rate in year 3; the first year of phase 2; the transition period?

   (b) What are the expected dividends in years 5 and 6?

   (c) If the analyst feels that 12 percent is an appropriate discount rate and given the risk characteristics of the stock, what is the present value of all expected future dividends?

   (d) What is the expected return associated with this stock, given the current market price of $20 and the analyst's estimates of future dividends?

   (e) What is the alpha for Tasty Foods' stock?

23. Using the H model,

   (a) What is the present value of the expected dividends for Tasty Foods in Problem 22?

(b) What is the expected return?
(c) What is the alpha?
24. When using a three-stage growth model, what must an analyst estimate for each security?
25. How has the use of computer programs in conjunction with the three-stage variable-growth dividend valuation model been an improvement over the two-stage model?
26. (a) How are price-earnings ratios calculated?
(b) What are the problems involved in deciding which "earnings" to use in calculating this ratio?
(c) What are relative P/Es and how are they calculated and used?
(d) Why have P/E ratios varied so much during the past 30 years?
27. (This question is based on the 1986 CFA examination, Level II.) You are an investment advisor for a large endowment fund. You are using a basic valuation model that values an asset according to the present value of the asset's expected cash flows and also are using this valuation framework to explain to the fund's trustees how inflation affects the rates of return on stocks. After your presentation, the trustees ask the following:
(a) "If common stocks are attractive for hedging inflation, why did stocks perform so poorly in the 1970s when the inflation rate was increasing?"
(b) "If stocks are attractive inflation hedges, then stock prices should rise the most when inflation increases. So why did stock prices appreciate so much from 1982 to 1986, when the inflation rate was declining?"
Explain your response to each of these questions in the context of this valuation model.
28. You are trying to forecast the expected return on the aggregate stock market for the next year. Suppose the current 1-year Treasury bill rate is 8 percent, the yield to maturity on 20-year Treasury bonds is 9 percent per year, the expected rate of inflation is 5 percent per year, and the expected EPS for the S&P 500 is $30. What is your forecast and why?
29. You are given the following information about two computer software firms and the S&P 400.

	Company A	Company B	S&P 400
P/E ratio	24.00	20.00	12.00
Average annual growth	0.18	0.15	0.07
Dividend yield	0.02	0.03	0.05

(a) Compute the growth duration of each company stock relative to the S&P 400.
(b) Compute the growth duration of Company A relative to company B.
(c) Given these durations, what must you decide in order to make an investment decision?

PART FOUR

Asset Class Management

Figure 1 illustrates a breakdown of the portfolio decision-making process into a hierarchy of critical components. Most broadly, the portfolio management process begins with the determination of the investor's goal for return as well as tolerance for risk in seeking the return objective. Once these have been established, the mix of asset classes that offers the best opportunity to attain the return at a tolerable level of risk must be determined; this is known as the asset allocation phase. A further aspect may involve shifting of the asset mix over time to increase return opportunistically over that provided by a static asset allocation. Finally, there is the security selection aspect, which involves identifying and selecting individual securities or groupings that are most attractively valued.

Of these decision components, the most important for controlling the overall risk and meeting fund objectives is the long-term or strategic asset allocation plan. Strategic asset

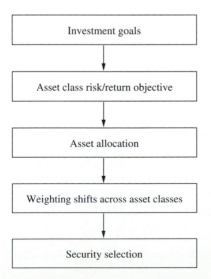

FIGURE 1
Hierarchy of investment decisions.

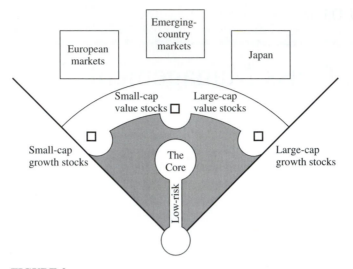

FIGURE 2
The equity playing field. (*Source:* Michael Troutman, "The
Steinbrenner Syndrome and the Challenge of Manager Selection,"
Financial Analysts Journal, March–April, 1991, pp. 37–44.)

allocation entails identifying the included asset classes and the normal weighting of these
assets in the portfolio. Research into the sources of performance of major pension plans
over past periods documents that the strategic asset allocation decision is the prime factor
determining the return realized for the fund.[1]

While many portfolio investors maintain a consistent asset weighting once the allocation is established, others employ a more active approach in changing asset class weightings.
In making these active weighting shifts, a growing number of plan sponsors are relying on
managers known as *tactical asset allocators.* These are specialist managers that utilize objective valuation techniques along with portfolio-rebalancing programs to take advantage of
relative return opportunities across the classes. Other plan sponsors use less structured programs and rely on internal staff, outside consultants, or a combination of the two in making
asset class weighting shifts.

For the security selection phase of the investment process, the large majority of portfolio investors utilize outside managers, generally ones with an investment specialty. In
selecting such managers, major plan sponsors usually assemble a multiple-manager lineup
to achieve the primary objectives of the plan; doing so is sensible given the size of assets
under management. Furthermore, the objective is to develop a mix of managers who can
collectively cover the investment field, just as a baseball team needs a variety of player
types to field a balanced team. Figure 2 illustrates a view of the complete equity manager
team. Note that it builds around a low-risk core of equity holdings, with specialist managers
covering distinct stock categories within both the domestic and international equity markets. Risk control and performance monitoring become especially important to ensure that
such a multiple-manager structure meets the risk/return objectives established for the fund.

---

[1]Brinson, Gary, Randolph Hood, and Gilbert Beebower: "Determinants of Portfolio Performance," *Financial Analysts Journal,* July–August 1986, pp. 39–44.

The following four chapters break down the decision-making process into individual components and describe strategies that are relevant to each of these portfolio management elements. Chapter 8 illustrates how a strategy focused on disciplined valuation methods and systematic portfolio construction techniques can be implemented as a core component of an equity investment plan. Chapter 10 goes on to describe equity-style management and how quantitative techniques can be used to identify relevant styles, as well as how these styles can be blended into the overall equity strategy. As noted, asset allocation is of critical importance in determining the longer-range success of an investment program; so in Chapter 9 we describe ways of determining the long-range strategic asset allocation of the plan as well as ways for managing the asset mix through time with tactical asset allocation methods and other rebalancing alternatives. In Chapter 11, we expand our analysis into a global context and describe strategies that can be used to manage the international equity component of a portfolio.

Disciplined Stock Selection

INTRODUCTION

So far, we have provided basic background and analytical concepts with respect to capital market behavior, portfolio analysis, capital market theory, and valuation models. The next four chapters will build on these concepts, introduce some new ones, and illustrate how these can be applied to practical portfolio management. The first of these chapters are primarily concerned with analyzing the domestic equity investment process and specifically focusing on stock selection (Chapter 8), asset allocation and market timing (Chapter 9), and opportunities associated with major groups (Chapter 10). Chapter 11 introduces and discusses foreign equity investment, building on techniques already described with regard to domestic equity investing but allowing a broadening of the investment horizon.

As noted, this chapter is primarily concerned with stock selection. It begins by describing active and passive strategies of investing, thus providing some perspective for this chapter as well as the next two chapters regarding approaches to equity management in the domestic market. We will then discuss a framework for comparing a disciplined stock selection strategy with other types of strategies, as well as a method of establishing specific objectives for that strategy. We move on to ways of designing the investment process and implementing the strategy and conclude with a discussion of the results of tests and the active implementation of the disciplined stock selection strategy.

ACTIVE–PASSIVE STRATEGIES

Figure 8-1 provides a framework for thinking about investment strategies and is based on analysis from Chapter 2. Note that the diagram is concerned with both risk and return. It indicates that the returns accruing to an individual stock derive from three sources: (1) overall

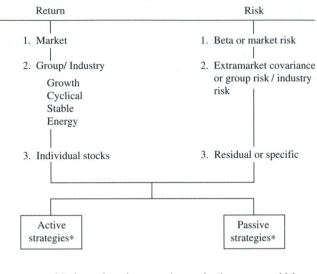

Return	Risk
1. Market	1. Beta or market risk

2. Group/ Industry
 	
    Growth
    Cyclical
    Stable
    Energy
	2. Extramarket covariance
	or group risk / industry
	risk

3. Individual stocks	3. Residual or specific
Active strategies*	Passive strategies*

*Active and passive strategies employ investment vehicles
with specific risk and return characteristics and are designed
to fulfill the differing needs of investors. (The text provides
specific examples of types of investment strategies.)

FIGURE 8-1
Breakdown of types of investment judgments.

market effect, (2) affiliation to the industry or broad market sector,[1] and (3) unique characteristics of the individual security. Correspondingly, risks are associated with each of these components, identified respectively as (1) market risk, (2) group risk, or extramarket covariance,[2] and (3) specific, or residual, risk. In endeavoring to achieve investment objectives, organizations can pursue an active or a passive strategy with respect to each or a combination of these risk-return components.

Organizations that pursue an active strategy with respect to the market component are known as *market timers.* In particular, an organization pursuing such a strategy with a forecast of a rising market would raise the risk of its portfolio either by shifting from cash to stocks, by raising the beta of the equities in the portfolio, or by a combination of both techniques. Conversely, a forecast of a declining market would indicate that the organization should decrease the risk of its portfolio either by shifting to cash from equities, by decreasing the beta of the equities in the portfolio, or by a combination of both techniques. Correspondingly, organizations that wish to maintain a passive stance with respect to market timing should at all times maintain the risk of their portfolios in line with the target for achieving longer-term portfolio objectives.

---

[1]Benjamin King, "Market and Industry Factors in Stock Price Behavior," *Journal of Business,* January 1966, pp. 139–191, showed that an industry effect explained approximately 10 percent of the realized returns of stocks over the 1926–1960 period. James L. Farrell, Jr., "Analyzing Covariation of Returns to Determine Homogeneous Stock Groupings," *Journal of Business,* April 1974, pp. 181–207, showed that a broader-than-industry effect explained an additional 15 percent of the realized returns of stocks over the 1961–1969 period.

[2]Barr Rosenberg, "Extra-Market Components of Covariance in Security Returns," *Journal of Financial and Quantitative Analysis,* March 1974, pp. 263–274.

An active strategy with respect to industries such as broad market sectors has been termed a policy of *group rotation*.[3] Pursuit of such a strategy would entail underweighting or overweighting the group or industry with respect to its weight in the market index and according to whether the outlook for the group has been assessed as favorable or unfavorable. For example, an organization that assessed the outlook for growth stocks as unfavorable and cyclicals as favorable in 1989 would have underweighted the growth component and over-weighted the cyclical component of the market. Again, an organization that decided it had no capacity to forecast in this respect and desired to pursue a passive strategy with regard to this risk-return component would set portfolio weights in the broad market sectors and major industries in line with their weightings in the market index.

Stock selection, an active strategy with respect to individual stocks, is used extensively by investment organizations. Stocks that are identified as most attractive would be over-weighted relative to their weighting in the market index, whereas those considered unattractive would not be held or would be underweighted relative to their position in the index. Organizations typically hold many individual stocks to hedge against the fact that their knowledge of the outlook for individual stocks is at best imperfect. In portfolio analysis, this is known as *diversification*. An organization considering its limited ability, or inability to assess the outlook for individual stocks would logically hold many stocks and weight them in accordance with their weighting in an index. The most efficient way to attain this objective is to create an index fund, which is the ultimate in totally passive strategies.

A STOCK SELECTION STRATEGY

Given this kind of framework for thinking about individual components of the return-generating process for stocks, we can begin to describe more specifically the kinds of investment strategies that an organization might offer, based on combinations of active and passive strategies associated with each component. In this regard, we have chosen to analyze three types of strategies that seem to be general enough to provide perspective on a multitude of variations: (1) remaining totally passive with respect to all three return components—stock, group, and market; (2) remaining passive with respect to market and group components and active with respect to stock selection; and (3) deciding to be active with respect to all three components.

Figure 8-2 illustrates the risk-return characteristics of the three types of strategies. These are labeled (1) totally passive, or index fund, (2) disciplined stock selection, and (3) totally active. The horizontal line is a performance benchmark for return relative to the market; anything above the market return line is an above-average return, and anything under the market return line is a below-average return. The dashed line represents the expected return, relative to the market, associated with each strategy. The height of the bar represents the expected return range or risk associated with that strategy.

Note that the index fund strategy is located at the lower end of the risk-return spectrum because it remains totally passive with respect to return opportunities. An index fund is expected not only to offer no incremental return relative to the index, but also to show relatively little divergence from that neutral performance. At the other extreme, the totally

---

[3] James L. Farrell, Jr., "Homogenous Stock Groupings: Implications for Portfolio Management," *Financial Analysts Journal,* May–June 1975, pp. 50–62.

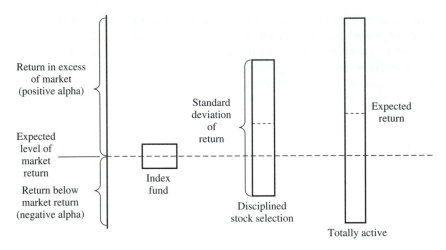

Note: The dashed line across the bar represents the expected return to the strategy, and the height of the bar represents the risk of the strategy as measured by the standard deviation.

FIGURE 8-2

Risk–return characteristics of investment strategies.

active strategy undertakes to take advantage of all three return opportunities: market timing, group rotation, and individual stock selection.[4] If an organization had predictive capability with respect to all three return opportunities, it would earn a return above that of the market or index fund. At the same time it would experience a greater expected return range, or risk, associated with that return. No one's predictions are always right.

The intermediate case actively capitalizes on stock selection capability. It is passive, or neutral, with respect to market and group influence. An organization with predictive capability in stock selection would expect to earn an above-average return—not as much as the totally active strategy but greater than the index fund. At the same time, the organization would expect to experience return variability greater than that of an index fund but less than the totally active strategy. The potential for error is not as great as with the totally active strategy because this strategy does not expose the organization to the risks of the other two return opportunities. We focus on the elements needed to execute the disciplined stock

---

[4]When an organization undertakes an active strategy using both market timing and group rotation, the market risk of the portfolio may, at times, diverge from a beta of 1, a risk in line with the market. An organization that engages in an actual policy of "timing" the market will at times have betas that differ from those of the market. For example, an organization acting on a forecast of a falling market should have a beta of less than 1, but a forecast of a rising market would imply a beta of greater than 1. The diagram in Figure 8-2 assumes that, over a market cycle, the positive-beta divergences will be offset by negative-beta divergences. As a result, this diagram presumes that, over time, the organization's market will average out to that of the market—that is, have a beta of 1 as measured against a broadly representative market index.

For those organizations deliberately pursuing a long-run policy of keeping the market risk of their portfolio above or below the market level, this diagram would be inadequate, because it assumes that the realized return is at the same level as the market risk. When risk differs from the market, the returns earned in excess or below the market may or may not be representative of above- or below-average performance. These returns would have to be adjusted to the experienced risk level of the fund to determine whether the performance had, in fact, been inferior or superior. Chapter 15 discusses techniques for making this adjustment.

selection strategy in the rest of this chapter and then discuss still other elements needed to carry out the totally active strategy in Chapters 9 and 10.

DESIGNING THE INVESTMENT PROCESS

To successfully execute the disciplined stock selection strategy, several critical elements must be present in the investment process. First, the organization needs to ensure that it has predictive capability with respect to individual stock; that is, it must be able to distinguish between relatively attractive and unattractive individual stocks. Thus, the organization needs some method of measuring or assessing predictive capability. It also needs a systematic portfolio construction procedure to ensure that predictions for individual stocks are appropriately built into the portfolio. Finally, operating the system over time means that there will be portfolio rebalancing, as well as transaction costs, associated with that activity. The organization needs to consider the magnitude of transaction costs and develop methods of controlling those costs to avoid a degrading of performance over time.

Figure 8-3 illustrates the necessary elements of the investment process and shows how these fit together to produce the desired strategy. The top of the diagram shows risk on one side and return on the other, similar to the first diagram in this chapter, but this figure is specifically oriented to the stock selection strategy. The middle part of the diagram shows

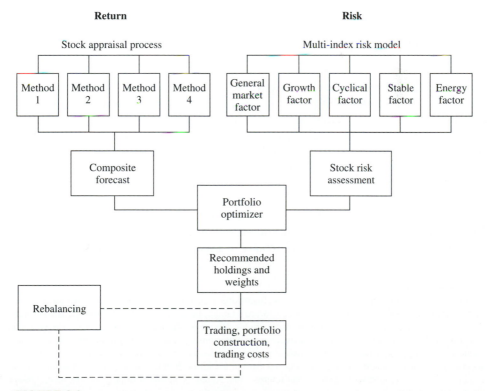

FIGURE 8-3
The equity investment process.

how risk and return can be considered simultaneously to develop an optimum portfolio. The lower part of the diagram illustrates how the process is implemented, and the dashed line extending from the bottom of the diagram indicates that investing over time is a matter of repeating the process.

Note that the return side in Figure 8-3 shows multiple sources—in this case, four—for identifying relatively attractive and unattractive stocks. Use of multiple sources is superior to reliance on a single method of stock selection when individual sources have predictive content and are complementary and not redundant. The block labeled "composite forecast" indicates the need to put these individual forecasts together in an optimum fashion in order to maximize their predictive value. The risk side of the diagram indicates the need for explicit considerations of five major components of risk: general market, growth, cyclical, stable, and energy. We can consider this most effectively by means of a multi-index model, described in Chapter 4.

Given composite return estimates and the multi-index risk model, we can use optimization techniques like those described in Chapter 10 to obtain a portfolio with the highest return at a minimal risk. Once the optimum portfolio has been generated, the securities need to be purchased in the amounts indicated by the optimization model. Trading in securities, however, means incurring transaction costs, and considering these costs and properly controlling them are important to avoid unduly dissipating a performance advantage. This process is especially significant because recycling through the process illustrated in Figure 8-3 and rebalancing the portfolio over time are both necessary.

MEASURING PREDICTIVE ABILITY

As noted before, pursuit of an active strategy of stock selection assumes some ability to identify relatively attractive and unattractive stocks and the need for some method of measuring this stock selection ability. Alternative techniques for measuring predictive ability are available. Perhaps the best one for analyzing stock selection capability is the information coefficient (IC) method. Some of the particular advantages of this method are (1) facility of identifying whether there is consistent ability to select stocks, (2) ease of distinguishing between stock selection capability and the capability of identifying general market and major group moves, and (3) provision of the framework for optimally combining several different sources for selecting stocks.

The method essentially involves correlating outcomes with predictions. The first step in the procedure is to rank the stocks in the universe of interest from relatively most attractive to relatively least attractive.[5] The performance in a succeeding period is then observed, and

---

[5]Ranking securities in a universe means automatically making a judgment of the performance on a relative basis; that is, the performance of a security should be considered relatively better or worse than the average of the universe or the average as represented by, say, a broad market index. We are illustrating a more refined method, where the ranking is within industries, such as the paper industry, or within broad market groupings, such as growth, cyclical, stable, and energy groups. Ranking within groupings allows one to make the assessment against more comparable securities and thereby control for the differing riskiness of securities. In the former case, the resulting ranking might be construed as representing nonmarket returns—that is, returns in excess of or below the market return. To the extent that the latter procedure of grouping controls for the riskiness of securities, the returns might be considered as risk-adjusted excess returns, or alphas.

the stocks in this same universe are ranked from relatively best performing to relatively worst performing.

Table 8-1 illustrates this process more specifically with hypothetical data for 10 companies in the paper industry. The first column shows the analyst's forecast of the relative performance of the stocks in the industry over the prior 12-month period. For example, the table shows that International Paper was forecast to show the best performance (rank of 1) and Crown Zellerbach the worst (rank of 10) over the one-year period. The second column shows the actual performances in terms of companies' rates of return over the 12-month forecast period along with the ranking of the companies by their ex post performances. International Paper was the best performer (+25 percent) and Crown Zellerbach the worst (−5 percent), with the others lining up exactly in concert with their predicted ranking. We can use the following model to measure the relationship between the forecast ranking FR and the actual ranking AR.

$$AR = a + IC(FR) + e \tag{1}$$

This equation says that the actual ranking depends on a constant term a, the forecast ranking FR, the slope IC of the line relating FR to AR, and an error term e with a zero mean and standard deviation. Since the distributions of the two rankings, FR and AR, have identical means and standard deviations, the constant term a, the slope IC, and the standard deviation of error e can be given unambiguous interpretations. Appendix A to this chapter provides further perspective on the meaning of the terms in Equation (1).

In this case, the information coefficient (IC) would be 1, the constant term zero, and the standard deviation of error zero. As might have been deduced from inspection of data, perfect forecasting ability would be indicated. At the other extreme, a complete lack of forecasting ability implies an IC (slope) of zero, a constant term a equal to the average of the ARs, and a standard deviation of error e equal to the standard deviation of the ARs. All sets of ICs between zero and 1, constant terms between AR and zero, and standard errors between the average standard deviation of the ranks and zero imply a level of forecasting ability that is less than perfect but better than random.

Figure 8-4 shows three scatter diagrams that plot actual outcomes against predictions, as well as the measured ICs (information coefficients), to further illustrate different degrees

TABLE 8-1
Predicted ranking versus realized ranking—paper industry

Company	Predicted ranking	Realized return (12 months)	Ex post ranking
International Paper (IP)	1	25	1
Hammermill Paper (HML)	2	20	2
Mead Corp. (MEA)	3	18	3
Westvaco Corp. (W)	4	17	4
Union Camp (UCC)	5	14	5
St. Regis (SRT)	6	11	6
Fort Howard Paper (FHP)	7	8	7
Kimberly–Clark (KMB)	8	4	8
Consolidated Papers (CPER)	9	1	9
Crown Zellerbach (Z)	10	−5	10

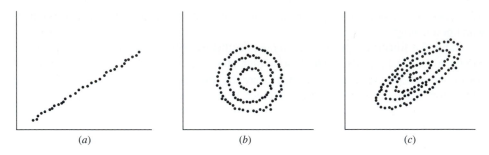

Information coefficients: (*a*) IC = 1.00;   (*b*) IC = 0;   (*c*) IC = 0.15;

FIGURE 8-4

of predictive capability.[6] The first diagram, part (*a*), illustrates a correlation coefficient of +1, which would indicate an ability to anticipate the ex post ranking of stocks perfectly, as was represented by the hypothetical data in Table 8-1. This ability, of course, is highly unlikely in a stock market that is highly competitive and efficient, as most participants would acknowledge. Part (*b*) illustrates the correlation coefficient of zero, which indicates no ability to rank the subsequent performance of stocks. This inability would be consistent with a stock market that is random and very difficult to predict. Part (*c*) represents the intermediate situation of an imperfect degree of forecasting ability as indicated by the 0.15 information coefficient.

The 0.15 information coefficient appears to represent a standard of good performance with regard to stock selection. Several empirical studies that have measured stock selection capability from several different sources (fundamental analyst, valuation models, etc.) document that the capability of individuals is in line with this standard.[7] Among these are the

---

[6]Information coefficients, ICs, are correlation coefficients. When calculating an IC with raw data, the IC is the same as a raw correlation coefficient, and the IC is a rank correlation coefficient when calculating the correlation using ranked data. In theory, the raw correlation coefficient is the slightly better measure. Generally, however, there will be little difference between the resulting correlation coefficients, whether the calculation is based on raw or ranked data; that is, the rank correlation coefficient and raw correlation coefficient will be virtually identical. Furthermore, rank correlation coefficients are easier to calculate and equal the beta coefficient when regressing ranks against ranks, as illustrated in Appendix A to this chapter.

More importantly, with regard to practical application, the rank correlation coefficient is the preferred measure because of the necessity of working with ranked rather than raw data when measuring the predictive capability of an investment process. For a fundamental analyst providing a subjective evaluation of a stock, it is perhaps the only way to obtain some sort of an explicit statement of the relative attractiveness of a security. Even in the case of valuation model data, where the raw predictions are in the form of explicit return predictions, the use of rankings is generally preferable. This process smoothes the data by pulling in extremely high or low return forecasts that are more than likely merely reflective of major forecasting errors.

[7]There are several methods of individual-stock selection that have been subjected to the sort of rigorous analysis that indicates their predictive power. One of the first methods to be analyzed extensively was patterns of insider trading. Research studies, beginning in the early 1960s and more recently updated, have universally indicated that insiders have predictive capability to a statistically meaningful degree. The Value Line stock valuation method has also been subjected to analysis, first by Shelton and then by Black. These researchers demonstrated that the model has facility in identifying mispriced securities and, hence, potential in earning superior returns. Finally, Wells Fargo has evaluated the success of the dividend discount valuation model as cast in the framework of the

market line approach (which was described in the previous chapter), the Value Line time-liness ratings on stocks, insider trading patterns, and several institutions and brokerage an-alytical research departments. Though the figure is relatively small—a lot closer to zero than to +1—it can be quite useful in generating above-average performance, as we will demonstrate in a later section. It is useful, however, only if that level of predictive ability is used within the context of a well-defined investment process, such as the kind that will be described in this chapter. We need to remember that random selection in a well-defined di-versified portfolio should generatee the expected return for the risk undertaken. Successful portfolio management includes positive ICs, which result in superior portfolio performance for the risk undertaken.

COMPOSITE FORECASTING

As noted, predictive capability is available from several different sources, but it is, at best, only modest. Also, no single source provides a constant level of predictive capability over each and every period of time; the capability fluctuates between above-average results and below-average results. Fortunately, the method known as *composite forecasting* has the po-tential of stabilizing predictive capability (reducing the fluctuations) and, at the same time, increasing the power of the predictions. Using multiple sources to stabilize and increase the predictive power of stock selection is analogous to using diversification as a means of reducing the variability of a portfolio from the variability attendant on investing in only a single security.

This method involves putting together separate individual sources to form a multiple source, or composite prediction. It works only when two conditions are present. First, the individual sources must have predictive content—that is, a positive IC; sources without predictive content cannot be used in combination to enhance the forecast. Second, the indi-vidual sources should provide some different perspective on stocks but should not provide information already being provided by another source. In fact, the process works best when the individual sources provide completely independent readings—that is, when they show zero cross-correlation. This concept is similar to the multi-index model introduced in Chap-ter 4, which improved the results of the single-index model (CAPM).

Table 8-2 uses four different sources of stock selection as an example of how the pro-cess of composite forecasting operates. Note that each source has predictive capability, as

---

SML in discriminating attractive from unattractive stocks. This analysis suggests that the method has potential for allowing an organization to earn superior risk-adjusted returns.

Ambachtsheer has also applied the IC method to evaluation of the success of several approaches to selecting individual stocks. He has evaluated the predictive capability of valuation models in this context, with particular emphasis on the Value Line and "market" line methods of stock selection. His studies were consistent with earlier analyses, indicating that both approaches had statistically significant ICs over a reasonably large universe of stocks. His firm, Canavest House, has also evaluated the judgmental capability of analysts from a number of different organizations over a period of years. This monitoring showed that analysts as a group had a modest but statistically significant ability to identify the relative attractiveness of stocks.

Though these studies indicated that some methods of stock selection had predictive content, the degree to which this capability existed could not be regarded as extensive. With regard to studies using the IC method, the measured ICs ranged from about 0.05 to as high as 0.20 when analyzed over reasonable amounts of data. In terms of Figure 8-2, the capability was more on the order of that represented by part (c)—if not less—rather than that represented by part (a).

TABLE 8-2
Stock selection source

Stock selection source	Predictive content (IC)
1	0.10
2	0.10
3	0.10
4	0.10

Composite IC $= [(0.10)^2 + (0.10)^2 + (0.10)^2 + (0.10)^2]^{\frac{1}{2}} = [0.4]^{\frac{1}{2}} = 0.20$

evidenced by a measured IC of 0.10, and, also, that each has equal predictive capability. We are also assuming that each of the sources gives a different perspective on stocks and, for purposes of illustration, that they are independent, the correlation across the sources is zero. As a matter of practical interest, experience has shown that sources like those based on valuation models—both long-term and short-term in orientation—as well as the perspective provided by fundamental analysts, have characteristics that broadly fit these specifications.

Appendix B to this chapter demonstrates that for sources with predictive capability that provide independent readings (uncorrelated with one another), the optimum way of combining them is to weight each source according to its predictive power. Since each of the sources in our example has equal predictive power (IC = 0.10), the optimum way of combining them is to weight them equally in forming the composite forecast. Using all four sources in tandem would result in a composite IC of 0.20, or double the predictive power of 0.10, when relying on only one source. The formulation at the bottom of Table 8-2 shows that the individual ICs combine in proportion to the square of their values, and the resulting composite IC is the square root of the combined total.[8]

When sources of predictive capability are correlated (not perfectly independent), the formula is not so simple, but the principle is generally the same. In this case, the composite IC needs to be adjusted for any dependence, or correlation, across the differing sources of information. The composite IC will be lower as the degree of positive correlation across sources increases, so that if there were positive correlation across the four sources in the example, the resulting IC would be less than 0.20. If the sources in this example were perfectly correlated (or totally redundant), the composite IC would be 0.10, or the same as when only a single source was used. Combining, in this instance, would not be beneficial. As we learned in Chapter 2, combining securities with correlations of +1.00 did not produce diversification benefits. However, with correlation less than perfect, combining securities resulted in higher returns for the same level of risk.

Ambachtsheer and Farrell demonstrated that this composite forecasting approach could be implemented in practice by evaluating two different sources of stock predictions.[9] The

---

[8]The development of linear composite prediction is generally ascribed to J. M. Bates and C. W. J. Granger, "The Combination of Forecasts," *Operations Research Quarterly,* 20, 1969, pp. 451–468. Robert Falconer and Charles M. Sivesind, "Dealing with Conflicting Forecast: The Eclectic Advantage," *Business Economics,* September 1977, pp. 5–11, illustrate the use of composite forecasting with respect to economic data analysis. Keith Ambachtsheer and James L. Farrell, Jr., apply the approach to stock market analysis in "Can Active Management Add Value?," *Financial Analysts Journal,* November–December 1979, pp. 39–47.

[9]Keith Ambachtsheer and James L. Farrell, Jr., "Can Active Management Add Value?" *Financial Analysts Journal,* November–December 1979, pp. 39–47.

TABLE 8-3
Six-month ICs for the long-term and short-term fundamental methods (LTF and STF)

Source	9/73– 3/74	3/74– 9/74	9/74– 3/75	3/75– 9/75	9/75– 3/76	3/76– 9/76	Mean (IC)
LTF	0.12	0.16	0.01	0.13	0.08	0.31	0.135
STF	0.17	0.04	−0.09	0.16	0.11	0.01	0.067
Combined	0.17	0.08	0.00	0.16	0.10	0.30	0.152

Source: Keith Ambachtsheer and James L. Farrell, Jr., "Can Active Management Add Value?" *Financial Analysts Journal,* November–December 1979, pp. 39–47.

first source evaluated was the market line approach to stock selection, which we described in Chapter 6. It is primarily based on a dividend discount valuation model, and to characterize their approach and generalize it, Ambachtsheer and Farrell referred to it as long-term fundamental (LTF). The second source was the Value Line timeliness ratings of stocks, an approach based on relative *P/E* ratios and earnings momentum. To characterize it and contrast it with the LTF approach, the authors referred to it as short-term fundamental (STF).

The top two rows of Table 8-3 show the ICs of the two sources measured at six-month intervals from September 1973 to September 1976. Note that the LTF method shows a positive IC in each interval and averages out to close to 0.15, which is a standard level of good performance. The STF method generally shows positive ICs and averages out to a lower, but still positive, IC. The evaluation indicates that the models do, in fact, have predictive capacity, which is, of course, a necessary condition if these models are to have use in developing above-average performance. In addition, statistical tests indicate that the two models provide generally independent readings on stocks, another necessary condition for usefulness as part of a composite forecasting process.

The third row of Table 8-3 shows the results of combining the LTF and STF methods for use in developing forecasts of individual stock performance. Note that the combined IC averages out to 0.15 for the full period, thereby providing a higher IC than either individual method. Furthermore, the combined IC appears to fluctuate less than the individual methods over the test period. In sum, the results were in line with expectations in terms of increasing predictive ability, as well as seeming to add stability to the capability of the two sources over time.

GENERATING RETURN FORECASTS

Once an organization has assessed that it has predictive capability (a positive IC), it then faces the problem of structuring the analytical process in such a way as to systematically generate return forecasts for each stock in the universe. In doing this, the organization first needs to obtain over- or undervaluation judgments on individual stocks from its security analysis process. These judgments are used whether they result from estimates by individual analysts, a more formal valuation model, or perhaps even other methods of appraisal. These judgments need to be expressed more explicitly as return forecasts or, more properly, as returns apart from those attributable to market and group effects. The final step is to adjust the return forecasts for the degree of predictive capability possessed by the organization– that is, adjust the forecasts for the imperfect predictive accuracy of even the best investment organizations.

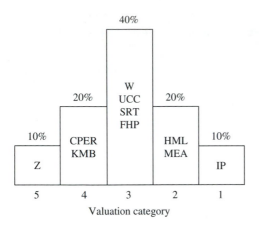

FIGURE 8-5
Allocation rule. (See Table 8-1 for company names represented by letters: e.g., W = Westvaco Corp.)

With respect to the first step in the process—generating judgments of value—the organization needs to ensure that these judgments are unbiased and on the same scale. An extreme example of what the organization will want to avoid is a bias that would result in recommendations of either purchase or sale for all individual stocks. The organization will instead desire to have purchase recommendations in balance with sale recommendations. Also, it will be interested in being able to compare qualitative judgments from a security analyst, such as buy, hold, and sell evaluations, with rate-of-return estimates generated from valuation models. Placing evaluations on the same scale allows comparison across many disparate sources.

To eliminate scale and bias problems, the organization might use a rating scheme, with the ratings serving as proxies for the judged degree of relative over- or undervaluation. The rating scheme could, for example, simply consist of five valuation categories—with 1 the most attractive and 5 the least attractive—and could be applied directly to the selection universe using a simple allocation rule such as the one illustrated in Figure 8-5. The bottom part of the figure applies this rule to the stock-ranking data from Table 8-1. Note that setting up a fixed number of valuation categories eliminates the scale problem, whereas using the simple allocation rule of Figure 8-5 eliminates biases from the judgment process.

GENERATING A RETURN DISTRIBUTION

With knowledge of the cross-sectional distribution of annual stock returns, we can then transform the rating distribution into a return distribution. For example, analysis has shown that in recent years, the standard deviation of residual returns (nonmarket- and nongroup-related) has been on the order of 18 percent with an average value, or expectation, of zero. If returns are normally distributed, two-thirds of all stocks in a typical year will earn returns of between ±18 percent. Alternatively, one-sixth of the stocks will earn returns exceeding 18 percent, and one-sixth of the stock universe will show losses exceeding 18 percent.

We can superimpose the five-point rating scheme on this kind of distribution by first converting the rating points into units of standard deviation from the mean. For this rating distribution, the upper part of Figure 8-6 indicates a standard deviation of 1.1 rating points. Using this standard deviation means that a rating of 5, which is 2 rating points from the mean, is also 1.8 (2 ÷ 1.1) standard deviations from the mean. Similarly, ratings of 4 or 2, which are both 1 rating point from the mean are also 0.9 (1 ÷ 1.1) standard deviations from the mean. Naturally, a rating of 3 would be zero deviations away from the mean.

When we multiply this converted rating by the standard deviation of the return distribution, we obtain the returns illustrated in the middle portion of Figure 8-6. Note that a rating of 1 converts to a return of 32 percent return (1.8 standard deviation times 18 percent standard deviation of return), whereas a rating of 5 converts to a loss of 32 percent (−1.8 standard deviation times 18 percent standard deviation of return). Similarly, a rating of 2

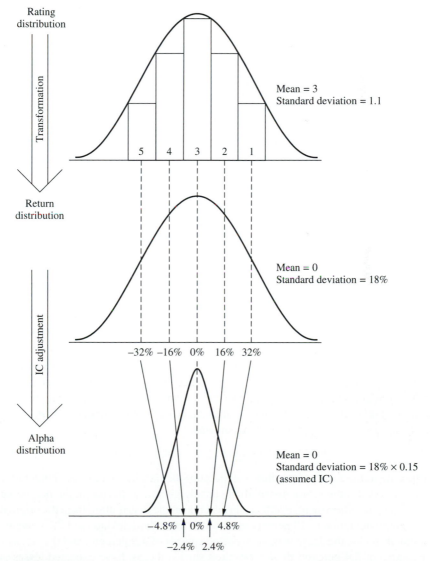

FIGURE 8-6
Rating and return distributions.

becomes a 16 percent return (0.9 times 18 percent), whereas a rating of 4 converts to a loss of 16 percent (-0.9 times 18 percent). A rating of 3, or an average ranking, converts to a zero return as would be expected for this neutral rating. In a sense, this converted return distribution presents the opportunity for explaining these gains and losses, and an organization with perfect forecasting ability (an IC of +1) would be confronted with the total potential of this distribution.

ADJUSTING FOR PREDICTIVE CAPABILITY

As noted before, however, empirical research indicates that predictive capability, with re-spect to individual stocks, is far less than perfect; ICs on the order of 0.15 represent quite satisfactory levels of performance in a highly competitive security market environment. Thus, adjustment of the empirical return distribution for less than perfect predictive capa-bility is needed. An organization can adjust the return distribution for its level of predictive capability by means of the following formula:

$$R = \text{IC(FR)} + e \tag{2}$$

This formula says that the return on the stock R comprises two components: (1) the forecast IC(FR), and (2) the error e in the forecast. The error term has an expected value of zero, $E(e) = 0$, and a variance $e = (1 - \text{IC}^2)\,\text{Var}(R)$. To illustrate the role of the error term in the forecast, we can assume that the standard deviation of stock return is 18 percent, or has a variance of 324, and that the organization has an IC of 0.20. Given the forecast, the stock-return variance R becomes $(1 - \text{IC}^2)\,\text{Var}(R) = (1 - 0.20^2)(324) = 311$.

When the IC has a value of 1, the error term becomes zero; the forecasting ability is perfect, and the actual return is completely explained by the forecast return. On the other hand, when the IC is zero, there is no forecasting ability; the forecast return explains nothing, and the resulting return and error are equivalent. The organization has no opportunity to explain any part of the distribution of returns.

If we assume some level of predictive capability—for example, the 0.15 level, which represents the standard of performance—the formula allows us to see the effect of the IC adjustment for partial predictive capability. Recall, for example, that a stock rated 1, or most highly rated, would have a return equivalent of 32 percent using the historical return distribution. Adjusting the IC to reflect an imperfect degree of forecasting capability would, however, considerably reduce the return that the investor should expect. Using the previous equation and taking its expected value, so that the error term disappears—$E(e) = 0$—we obtain an expected return for the stock, as shown:

$$E(R) = \text{IC(FR)} = 0.15(+32\%) = 4.8\% \tag{3}$$

Adjusting to the levels of predictive capability that are likely to be encountered in ac-tual practice reduces the return distribution considerably, as reflected in the bottom part of Figure 8-6. The IC adjustment, in effect, shrinks the whole distribution from the original one with a standard deviation of 18 percent to one with a standard deviation of 2.7 percent. The highest-rated stocks, the 1s, now have expected returns of 4.8 percent, and the stocks rated 2 have returns of 2.4 percent; the lowest-rated stocks, the 5s, have expected losses of 4.8 percent, and the stocks rated 4 are expected to lose 2.4 percent. Organizations with greater or lesser ICs would be faced with wider or narrower return distributions. An organization with no forecasting capability, or an IC of zero, would be faced with no opportunity range around a mean of zero.

As a further note, the resulting distribution of adjusted returns, as shown at the bottom of Figure 8-6, might be considered as an alpha distribution. These alphas would have the same meaning as the alphas discussed in Chapter 4; that is, they represent returns expected apart from market and group effects and again represent a potential bonus return or penalty, as the case may be. In this case, we generate the alphas in an indirect way, whereas in the case of the market line method, as described in Chapter 6, the alphas represented by the distance above and below the line were generated directly. The approach just described is more flexible, however, in that expectations about stocks from disparate sources can be converted into alphas that are comparable across the sources.

TRANSACTION COSTS

Finally, the organization needs to know the transaction costs and to compare them with the return opportunities facing the organization. Transaction costs include both commissions and the price impact of the transaction—the rise in price when buying or the decline when selling. Wagner and Cuneo evaluated those costs for institutional investors and showed that the round-trip transaction costs (commissions and market impact) were on the order of 3 percent.[10] This study was, however, prior to the removal of fixed commission rates, which has resulted in lower average commission rates, at least for institutional investors. Currently, commission rates average approximately 0.25 percent of the cost of a transaction compared with perhaps 1 percent prior to the demise of fixed commission rates. Assuming that the price impact of transactions averages another 0.25 percent, the cost of a one-way transaction would be about .50 percent, or 1 percent for a round-trip transaction.

Transaction costs represent a hurdle rate that a return opportunity must surpass in order to justify trading. For example, if round-trip transaction costs are 1 percent, a purchase opportunity and a sale opportunity must show a more-than-1-percent spread to justify action. The lower the transaction costs are, the lower the hurdle rate can be; the higher the transaction costs are, the higher the hurdle rate can be.

An organization with a high IC—that is, high predictive capability—would be justified in developing more trades than would an organization with a low IC because the organization with the higher IC would have a greater margin of return for overcoming transaction costs than an organization with a low IC. In other words, the organization with greater predictive capability would have a greater adjusted return distribution than the low-IC organization, as illustrated in Figure 8-6. Consequently, high ICs at a given transaction cost imply high turnover, but low ICs imply low turnover because there is less margin to overcome the cost of transacting. Correspondingly, high transaction costs at a given IC imply that low turnover is optimum, whereas low transaction costs at a given IC imply that higher turnover is justified. Regardless of the IC level, keeping transaction costs low improves the return distribution.

---

[10]Wayne Wagner and Larry Cuneo: "Reducing the Cost of Stock Trading," *Financial Analysts Journal,* November–December 1975, pp. 35–44.

APPLIED COMPOSITE FORECASTING

At this point, we illustrate how the author has used the process just described to assess the relative attractiveness of 800 stocks in a stock selection universe. This universe included only companies with market capitalization in excess of $1 billion, so it is most representative of large institutional-grade stocks. It includes all 500 companies in the S&P market index. The other 300 companies provide exposure to industries, such as the specialty chemical industry, that are not components of the S&P 500 index and allow for a more complete selection.

In monitoring the stock selection universe, we gather information about these 800 companies from four different sources. We continue to rely on the same two broad valuation categories—long-term fundamental and short-term fundamental, as in the original study. The specific models within the categories differ in particular but not in spirit. We have supplemented these with two other stock evaluation categories that are termed (1) trading fundamentals, and (2) analyst judgment. The general category of trading fundamentals includes such information as that provided by share repurchase programs or insider trading patterns; the analyst judgment category monitors the buy-hold-sell recommendations of security analysts. Because each of the four sources has demonstrated predictive content and because statistical measures indicate that the four sources are mutually independent, the sources are well suited for the composite forecasting process described previously in this chapter.

Table 8-4 is from a report that provides a composite ranking and information for each of the 800 companies in the universe with respect to each of the four broad evaluation categories. The companies are classified according to standard S&P 500 industries, which are, in turn, further grouped into one of the four homogeneous stock groupings: growth, cyclical, stable, or energy. In this instance, the report shows companies in three industries (forest products, paper, and paper containers) that are, in turn, classified into the cyclical sector. Companies are ranked within industries according to their alpha value.

The first four columns show the ratings of the companies within each of the four evaluation categories and according to the same five-way ranking scheme described previously. Note, for example, that Westvaco ranks quite high—1—with respect to trading fundamentals and moderately high—2—with respect to both long-term fundamentals and analyst judgmental categories, but it is rated relatively unattractive—4—according to short-term fundamentals. The final column of the table shows the combined rating of the stock converted into a projected excess return, or alpha, using the composite IC and the technique of converting ratings that we have been discussing. As a general rule, stocks with alphas in excess of 3.0 are considered highly attractive, but stocks with alphas below −3.0 are considered highly unattractive.

With regard to the stocks shown in the table, we would consider Westvaco and Kimberly-Clark to be highly attractive because their alphas are positive and large. If we were constructing a portfolio anew or did not currently hold these stocks, we should consider them for inclusion. On the other hand, Georgia-Pacific, Potlatch, Domtar, and Diamond International have quite negative alphas, and we would consider them to be unattractive. We should avoid these, or, if we held these in a portfolio, we should consider replacing them with stocks showing large positive alphas, such as the ones listed above. In considering such a switch, however, the potential pickup in added return should be compared to the cost of the transaction.

In building a portfolio, the first step is to identify the most attractively priced stocks, which generally turn out to be the 120 stocks with the highest positive alphas. Once

TABLE 8-4
Stock universe monitor

	Long-term fundamentals	Short-term fundamentals	Trading fundamentals	Analyst judgment	Alpha
Forest products					
Evans Products	2	3	1	4	2.7
Weyerhaeuser	4	3	2	3	1.0
Boise Cascade	3	4	1	3	0.6
Champion International	2	4	3	3	0.0
Louisiana-Pacific	2	4	3	3	−0.2
Pacific Lumber	3	3	3	3	−0.8
Willamette Industries	2	5	3	3	−1.7
Georgia-Pacific	3	4	3	4	−3.4
Potlatch	3	4	4	3	−4.8
Paper					
Westvaco	2	4	1	2	4.9
Kimberly-Clark	3	3	1	3	4.8
Great Northern Nekoosa	3	3	3	2	2.4
James River	3	3	3	3	0.6
Union Camp	3	3	3	3	0.0
St. Regis Paper	2	4	3	3	0.0
Mead	1	4	5	3	−0.7
Crown Zellerbach	3	4	3	3	−0.8
Hammermill Paper	3	3	4	3	−0.8
Fort Howard Paper	5	1	3	4	−1.9
Consolidated Papers	3	3	3	4	−1.9
International Paper	3	3	4	3	−2.3
Domtar, Inc.	3	5	3	3	−3.1
Paper containers					
Federal Paper Board	3	2	3	3	1.6
Maryland Cup	4	3	3	3	−1.0
Bemis	3	3	4	3	−2.0
Diamond International	5	3	5	4	−7.7

Source: James L. Farrell, Jr., "A Disciplined Stock Selection Strategy," *Interfaces,* October 1982.

identified, they are analyzed to ensure that the basic inputs to the evaluation are valid. We also assess whether there might be an impending change in the basic evaluation inputs that has not been captured in the processing. Finally, we attempt to incorporate into our analysis factors that cannot be structured into a formal evaluation framework. This further analysis usually reduces the list of potential investment candidates. From this reduced list, we then construct the portfolio according to the guidelines and procedures outlined in the following sections of this chapter.

PORTFOLIO CONSTRUCTION

Once the organization has made return forecasts and adjusted them for the level of predictive capability, it then must ensure that these predictions are properly embodied in the portfolio.

TABLE 8-5
Portfolio construction objective

1. Portfolio market risk should be in line with that of the S&P 500.
2. Portfolio should be highly diversified with respect to group/industry risk.
3. Portfolio should have many individual stock judgments with high predictive content working at the same time.

The organization needs in turn to develop a well-defined set of portfolio construction guidelines and carry out the portfolio construction process in a controlled and disciplined fashion. This process is especially important because predictive capability, where it exists, is modest at best and can easily be lost or dissipated at other stages in the investment process.

Table 8-5 shows the broad guidelines that the organization should follow in constructing the portfolio. These three guidelines are consistent with the objective of the strategy, which is to rely on stock selection alone in attempting to attain above-average performance without capitalizing on the opportunities associated with the market and group components of return. The guidelines also conform to the framework of thinking about risk and return that we described in the opening section of this chapter.

Since the objective is to rely exclusively on stock selection, the risk associated with the market and group components of return needs to be controlled. In order to control the risk associated with market timing, the organization should keep the portfolio as fully invested in equities as possible. Alternatively, it should keep the cash position at a minimum; a maximum of 2 percent would seem to be a workable rule. Correspondingly, the organization should keep the beta of the equity portion of the portfolio at 1, or within a range of 0.95 to 1.05, in order to maintain the market risk of the equity portion in line with the market, as measured by an index such as the S&P 500.

To control the risk associated with major groups, the portfolio needs to be well-diversified. In particular, the organization needs to ensure that the portfolio is not over-weighted with respect to a particular group or, alternatively, that it is not tilted too heavily in the direction of one of the major nonmarket factors. Conversely, the organization needs to ensure that the portfolio is not underweighted with respect to the major groups or, alternatively, unduly tilted away from one of the major factors. For example, if energy stocks represented 20 percent of the weighting in the overall market, constructing the portfolio so that this factor had the same representation—neither significantly more nor less—would be important.

The third major requirement, or guideline, for the portfolio construction process is to ensure that the portfolio includes a sufficient number of stocks—say, between sixty and ninety. Holding a sufficient number of stocks helps diversification by reducing specific risk in the fashion analyzed in Chapter 2. Holding a sufficient number of stocks is, however, also consistent with the fact that our predictive ability is going to be modest at best. We expect our judgments—bets, if you will—to work out on average but not with respect to each and every one; our ICs are not $+1$. The greater the number of stocks held means that the averages are more likely to work in our favor.

PORTFOLIO OPTIMIZATION

Once the guidelines have been established, there are two main procedures for implementing the portfolio construction strategy. One is to use more traditional types of constraints, such as industry guidelines, minimum numbers of stocks to include in a portfolio, or maximum size of individual holdings. This approach can work effectively when the objectives are explicitly defined and the process has been specifically delineated, as it has in this instance. Furthermore, it has the merits of being simple and the least costly to operate.

The other approach is to use optimization procedures such as those identified and discussed in Chapter 10. These approaches are more costly—though not prohibitively so—and more complex. Furthermore, it is essential that the procedure used is based on an appropriate model of the risk-return generating process. In this regard, we recommend use of the multi-index, or multifactor, approach that was discussed in earlier chapters. It takes into account those major effects impacting stocks—general market, growth, cyclical, stable, and energy—and, at the same time, provides most of the economy of operation and ease of interpretation of the simplest model of the return-generating process—the single-index model.

Given return estimates and using the multi-index risk model, the optimization procedure works in the following way.[11] It seeks out those stocks having the most favorable returns; at the same time it balances these return opportunities against the riskiness of the stocks. The intent here is to hedge against market and group risks, as well as to reduce specific risk as much as is consistent with the objective of obtaining a high return. The result should be a mix of stocks that best fulfills the objective of the portfolio—that is, to obtain a high return at a minimal risk.

Table 8-6 shows an actual portfolio constructed using optimization techniques and built to conform to the sort of guidelines that we have been discussing in this chapter. The table shows the companies' names and weights in the portfolio.[12] Note that the weights sum to 100 percent, which indicates that the portfolio is fully invested in equities and that the cash position of the portfolio is zero, as is shown at the bottom of the table. This cash position is, of course, consistent with the practical portfolio guideline calling for no more than 2 percent cash in the portfolio.

Note also that the second column of the table shows the beta values of the individual stocks as a measure of their exposure to general market risk. We can obtain a beta value for the overall portfolio by simply using the individual beta value and the weight of the company in the portfolio to calculate a weighted average beta for the portfolio, as was illustrated in Chapter 3. Commonly referred to as a cross-sectional beta, the beta value provides a way of estimating the exposure of the overall portfolio to general market risk at a given point in time. Note that the weighted average, or cross-sectional, beta of the portfolio was 1.03, in line with a practical guideline calling for a 0.95–1.05 beta range for the portfolio. On balance, the portfolio was well-controlled with respect to market risk.

---

[11]Those interested in a more elaborate description of how an optimization technique works should refer to Appendix A in Chapter 10. Using the simplified portfolio techniques of Elton and Gruber, this illustrates the generation of an optimal portfolio. Though the single-index model, rather than the multi-index model, was used in that process, the example should nevertheless illustrate the way that an optimization technique selects securities for inclusion in a portfolio and determines the optimum weightings for these securities.

[12]In generating the portfolio, several weighting constraints were established. One was that no individual security would represent more than 3 percent of the portfolio weighting, with the exception of AT&T, Exxon, and IBM, which represent more than 3 percent weightings in the S&P 500. An additional constraint was that the weightings of the portfolio in the growth, cyclical, stable, and energy groupings would be in line with the S&P 500 weighting. Given these constraints, the objective was to obtain a maximum return while minimizing residual risk (standard error) at a beta level of 1.

254 PART IV: Asset Class Management

TABLE 8-6
Stock selection portfolio

Security	% of portfolio market value	Beta
Aetna Life & Casualty Co.	1.50	1.43
Alcan Aluminum Ltd.	1.00	1.05
Amax, Inc.	0.50	1.13
Amerada Hess Corp.	2.00	1.32
American Home Products	1.00	0.70
AT&T	5.00	0.67
Anheuser–Busch, Inc.	1.00	1.07
Atlantic Richfield	2.00	0.87
Bethlehem Steel	1.00	1.48
Burroughs Corp.	1.50	1.06
Cameron Iron Works	1.00	1.28
Campbell Soup Co.	1.00	0.74
Carnation Co.	1.00	0.98
CBS, Inc.	0.50	1.19
Chase Manhattan Corp.	1.50	1.23
Coca-Cola Co.	1.00	0.78
Conoco, Inc.	2.00	0.86
Digital Equipment Corp.	1.50	1.45
Dow Chemical Co.	1.00	1.08
Emerson Electric	1.00	0.98
Exxon Corp.	5.00	0.83
Federated Department Store	1.00	1.30
Florida Power & Light	1.50	1.05
Foster Wheeler Corp.	1.50	1.36
Gannett, Inc.	1.50	0.95
General Electric	2.00	0.98
General Motors	2.50	1.04
Georgia-Pacific	1.50	1.08
Gulf Oil Corp.	3.00	0.82
INA Corp.	1.00	1.51
Ingersoll Rand	1.00	1.13
IBM	3.50	0.87
Johnson & Johnson	1.00	0.77
Koppers, Inc.	1.00	1.31
Kroger Co.	1.00	0.98
Lone Star Industries	1.00	1.20
R. H. Macy & Co., Inc.	1.50	1.44
Maytag Co.	1.00	0.96
McDonald's Corp.	2.00	1.32
Medtronic, Inc.	0.50	1.47
Melville Corp.	1.50	1.20
Merck & Co., Inc.	1.00	0.84

One way of measuring exposure with regard to group risk is to simply compare the weighting of the portfolio in these major sectors with the weighting of that sector in the overall market. This comparison determines whether there is underweighting or overweighting with respect to the market. The bottom part of Table 8-6 shows the weighting of the portfolio in each of the four major sectors, as well as the weighting of the sectors in the S&P 500, which we are using as a generally acceptable proxy for the market. Note that the portfolio is

**TABLE 8-6
(continued)**

Security	% of portfolio market value	Beta
Midland Ross Corp.	1.00	1.32
Minnesota Mining & Manufacturing	2.00	0.96
Monsanto Co.	1.00	1.18
Motorola, Inc.	0.50	1.32
NCNB Corp.	1.50	1.23
Newmont Mining	1.00	1.16
Northern Natural Gas Co.	1.50	0.96
Owens Illinois	1.00	1.08
Perkin Elmer Corp.	0.50	1.47
Philip Morris, Inc.	2.00	0.73
Phillips Petroleum	2.00	0.92
Revlon, Inc.	1.00	1.07
R. J. Reynolds Industries	1.00	0.50
Rockwell International Corp.	2.00	0.94
Schering Plough Corp.	1.00	1.02
Schlumberger Ltd.	3.00	0.85
Seaboard Coast Line	0.70	1.37
Southern California Edison	1.50	0.84
Southern Railway	0.80	1.00
St. Regis Paper Co.	1.50	1.12
Standard Oil (Ohio)	2.00	1.05
Texaco, Inc.	3.00	0.85
Texas Instruments	0.50	1.31
Thomas & Betts Corp.	0.50	1.10
Union Carbide Corp.	1.00	1.01
United States Fidelity & Guaranty Co.	1.00	1.43
Wang Labs, Inc.	1.00	1.64
Total portfolio	100.00	1.03
Cash	0.0	$R^2 = 0.98$

Portfolio alpha = 3.5 $\qquad$ Standard error 2.2%

Sector	% of portfolio	% of S&P 500
Growth	31	32
Cyclical	23	23
Stable	25	25
Energy	21	20
Total	100	100

well-diversified, or hedged, with respect to group risk; the weights of the portfolio are virtually the same as the weighting in the overall market. The portfolio optimization procedure, of course, ensures the control of this kind of risk most efficiently.

Two other related diagnostics that provide perspective on the overall level of diversification of the portfolio are the coefficient of determination R^2 and the standard error of the portfolio. (Appendix A provides perspective on the meaning of these two portfolio diagnostics.) Both measure how closely the portfolio will move in tandem with the market. A high R^2 and a low standard error indicate that the portfolio will move closely in tandem with the market, whereas a low R^2 and a high standard error indicate that the portfolio will tend to move out of phase with the overall market. As a benchmark, the typical actively managed institutional portfolio will have an R^2 of between 0.90 and 0.93 and a standard error on the order of 7 percent.

Note that the portfolio in Table 8-6 has an R^2 of 0.98 and a standard error of 2 percent, which are well within the guidelines established for diversification of a portfolio that is designed for the stock selection strategy. At the same time, the portfolio is more highly diversified than the typical actively managed portfolio because of the conscious decision to control market and major group risk closely and the intent to hold a reasonably large number of securities in the portfolio. Note that the portfolio contains 69 stocks, which is again within the guidelines. Specific risk is, therefore, controlled, and the opportunity for the weighted-average projected alpha of 3.5 percent (shown as portfolio alpha in the table) to be realized is maximized.

MANAGING THE PROCESS OVER TIME

The final problem is that of managing the process over time. The dashed line leading from the bottom part of Figure 8-3 indicates that this managing involves repeating the procedures that we have been describing in this chapter. In particular, return forecasts for individual stocks are continuing to be generated and are combined with the appropriate weights to develop an updated list of stock-return estimates. Presumably, these estimates will change because of both continual reassessment of the future prospects for companies by the stock selection sources and changes of prices in the marketplace. Optimization with these revised estimates will lead to different recommended portfolio holdings, which, in turn, means rebalancing—portfolio turnover—with the attendant trading and transaction costs. Setting the optimum rebalancing cycle is an important but difficult task. Too-frequent rebalancing and turnover can lead to foregone profits on securities and excessive transaction costs, but an overlong rebalancing cycle can lead to dissipation of gains on formerly profitable holdings. The ideal, of course, would be to set the rebalancing cycle so that securities are sold as they are peaking, in terms of relative performance, and replaced with more highly ranked securities. The optimum period is likely to depend on the types of stock selection method used and the phase of the market cycle. Analysis of the time trend and peaking behavior of the ICs of a source or sources of stock selection may be helpful, but hardly conclusive, in this important, though highly difficult, area.[13]

In this regard, the organization should be especially alert to monitoring the return-estimating process by continuing to monitor the ICs of the separate sources, ensuring that the sources are continuing to provide useful information. Sources will show fluctuating patterns with regard to predictive capability, and the analyst should bear this in mind before eliminating a source that may temporarily show a deterioration in performance. The analyst

---

[13] In the world of public reports regarding the holdings and performance of portfolios (mutual funds), management is forced to consider rebalancing, at a minimum, once a quarter. If the holdings are still appropriate, rebalancing is not needed. At times, with the need to report results on a quarterly basis, long-term holdings that may match the overall objective of the portfolio pose a conflict for the portfolio manager. If the security is expected to perform in the long term, the portfolio manager should not rebalance just because one quarter's results are not as favorable as desired.

should ascertain whether there has been a long-term fundamental deterioration in predictive capability. Concurrently with the monitoring of the individual sources, an analysis of how well the combining process is working should be conducted by measuring whether the sources are continuing to provide complementary information or independent readings. A trend toward redundancy, or too high of an intercorrelation, would call for elimination of the source.

The second major factor to monitor over time is transaction costs, because predictive capability and transaction costs are interrelated. In particular, an organization with predictive capability should act on those predictions in order to take advantage of performance opportunities. The result will be an increase in trading and the attendant transaction costs. With greater predictive ability, the organization should be inclined to trade more and, of course, will be subject to more transaction costs. Failure to account for transaction costs can result in a dissipation of performance and, in the extreme, could lead to subpar performance.

Here, the level of transaction costs should be properly established and monitored over time to ensure that the estimated cost level remains appropriate. For example, if transaction costs prove to be higher than originally estimated, a lower level of turnover would be appropriate at a given level of predictability. Conversely, if transaction costs prove to be less, the organization would have a greater latitude for acting on predictions. Investigating over time how transaction costs have varied across different types of stocks would also be useful. Establishing different trading costs for different classes of securities—for example, using a higher cost for smaller, less liquid stocks than for large, actively traded stocks—might also have merit. Finally, investigating trading strategies that would help minimize those costs might be useful.

PERFORMANCE OF STRATEGY OVER TIME

We conclude this part of the chapter by describing the performance results of a test of the strategy that is described in the same Ambachtsheer and Farrell article "Can Active Management Add Value?" discussed in an earlier section.[14] In testing the strategy, the authors developed three variations, differing only with respect to the source of return estimates. One variant used only the Value Line, or short-term fundamental (STF), stock selection method as a sole source of return inputs. Another variant used the market line, or long-term fundamental (LTF), method as the sole source of return inputs. The third variant used the stock selections generated by combining the two individual sources, STF and LTF, within the composite forecasting framework. The authors compared the performance of the three strategy variants over a three-year period with the S&P 500.

Table 8-7 shows the performance results. Note that all three variants of the strategy outperformed the S&P 500. In addition, the performance advantage of each was directly in line with the predictive content of the information source. The STF method, with the lowest IC of 0.07, showed the least differential—2.2 percent—while the combined source, with the highest IC of 0.15, showed the greatest differential—6.7 percent. Test results showed that "low-quality" predictive information about stocks could be translated into above-average

---

[14]Keith Ambachtsheer and James L. Farrell, Jr., "Can Active Management Add Value?" *Financial Analysts Journal,* November–December 1979, pp 39–47.

TABLE 8-7
Stock selection performance, 9/30/73–9/30/76

Stock selection strategy	Average annual return, %	IC	Differential % Return above S&P 500
Combined stock selection	10.0	0.15	6.7
LTF	9.0	0.135	5.7
STF	5.5	0.07	2.2
S&P 500	3.3	—	0

Source: Keith Ambachtsheer and James L. Farrell, Jr., "Can Active Management Add Value?" *Financial Analysts Journal,* November–December 1979, pp. 39–47.

performance, with the magnitude of the IC indicating the degree of the performance advantage.

Figure 8-7 also shows the performance results from a consistent application (by the author) of the philosophy and techniques of the disciplined stock selection strategy described above to the management of investment funds over the period 1974–1990. Note that the strategy provided a 3.2 percent positive excess return result on average over time. Furthermore, the performance was delivered with consistency and with few periods of underperformance relative to the S&P 500. For long-term investors, the positive alpha result translates into a significantly greater terminal wealth for the investor than provided by the index ($114,307 with the discipline strategy versus $72,396 for the S&P index).

Disciplined Stock Selection (DSS) Strategy vs. S&P 500
Growth of $10,000 (12/31/90)

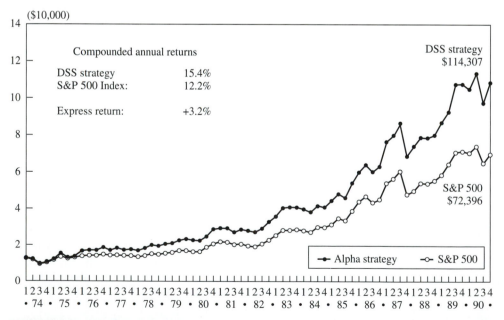

FIGURE 8-7
Disciplined Stock Selection (DSS) strategy vs. S&P 500.

LONG/SHORT STRATEGIES

In addition to the strategies just described, there are others that are natural variations of this basic theme. One category that is growing more important in use is popularly referred to as long/short strategies. These strategies are designed to take advantage of the full array of opportunity offered by the distribution of valuation ratings over a universe of stocks. As the name implies, the investor constructs the portfolio position by "going long" on stocks with high positive alphas and selling short stocks with negative alphas. If the long positions are properly offset by short positions, the result can be a combined position that is neutral with respect to market risk (uncorrelated with the market); hence, it is referred to as a "long-short market-neutral" strategy. The investor will nevertheless earn a positive return from both the positively rated stocks held long and the negatively rated stocks sold short, if the basic valuation process works and the portfolios are properly constructed.

With regard to valuation, we can refer to Figure 8-8 to illustrate the alpha approach to selecting stocks for short selling. Note that the figure is based on the analysis described in a previous section, where we indicated that stocks with high positive alphas, such as Westvaco (+4.9), were attractive for purchase. Correspondingly, stocks with large negative alpha ratings, such as Potlatch (−4.8), are attractive for shorting. These stocks are overvalued and likely to underperform the market.

In selecting negatively rated stocks for shorting, the investor also needs to follow the same portfolio construction guidelines as when selecting positively rated stocks for purchase. The investor does this to match the risk characteristics of the resulting short portfolio as closely as possible to the long portfolio. Keeping the market risk of the two portfolios in line with the guideline of 1.00, or the same as the market, helps protect against a divergence of performance due to different portfolio market exposure. Correspondingly, keeping the short portfolio well diversified to minimize tracking error due to group and individual stock risk would be desirable.

Table 8-8 compares a short portfolio constructed from negatively rated stocks to a long portfolio constructed from positively rated stocks, both using the same market risk and

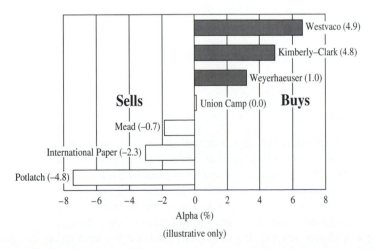

FIGURE 8-8
Expected excess return—selected paper and forest products stocks.

TABLE 8-8
Long and short portfolios: comparative characteristics

Characteristics	Long portfolio	Short portfolio
Market risk (BETA)	1.00	1.00
Sector Diversification:		
Energy	8.9%	10.1%
Financial	14.0	12.5
Utility	11.8	12.6
Technology	15.6	14.3
Basic industry	16.4	14.2
Consumer cyclical	10.6	11.6
Stable consumer	13.0	14.1
Health care	9.8	9.7
Total	100.0	100.0
Number of stocks	53	55
Tracking error	4.50	5.00
Expected alpha	3.50	−4.00

diversification guidelines. Note that both portfolios are fully invested and have virtually identical betas. At the same time, the positioning with respect to major stock market sectors is in line with the market breakdown for both portfolios. Finally, both portfolios have sufficient stocks to reduce the specific risk component to a low level appropriate to controlling tracking error. The two portfolios are virtual mirror images of one another, differing primarily in that the long portfolio is strongly positioned with positive-alpha stocks, as indicated by a weighted-average portfolio alpha of 3.5, while the short portfolio is strongly positioned with negative-alpha stocks, as evidenced by a weighted-average portfolio alpha of −4.0.

In addition to holding stocks long and short in equal dollar balance, the portfolio manager could add an overlay of permanent stock index futures in an amount equal to the invested capital. As a result, the portfolio would have a full equity market exposure at all times, while earning profits from both the long and short positions in addition to profits or losses resulting from the equity market's rise or fall. This compound strategy—futures, shorting, and underlying equity—provides a similar result to the basic disciplined stock selection strategy, except that potential additional profits can accrue from the short position. We will refer to this strategy as long-short "market-enhanced."

RETURN PATTERNS

In this section, we illustrate the steps in initiating the long and short portfolio positions. We also show the resulting long/short "market-neutral" and long/short "enhanced market" portfolio positions, as well as the pattern of returns implied by these strategies. Correspondingly, we indicate the contribution that individual elements make to the overall portfolio return. In showing these return patterns, we make use of the same kinds of payoff diagrams used in Chapter 13 to illustrate the characteristics of option-related strategies.

Figure 8-9 shows several diagrams that illustrate the underlying components and resulting return pattern for the two long/short strategies. Panel (a) in the upper part of the figure shows the pattern of returns for a portfolio of stocks held long. For illustrative

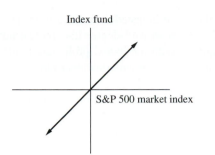

(a) Long an index fund

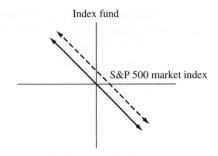

(b) Short an index fund

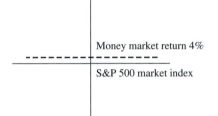

(c) Combined long/short index funds

Long portfolio   10 million
Short portfolio   −10 million
Money market fund   10 million
Net position   10 million

(d) Long/short portfolio positions

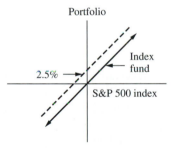

(e) Long an active equity fund

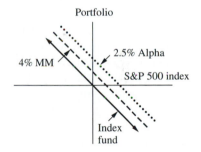

(f) Short an active equity fund

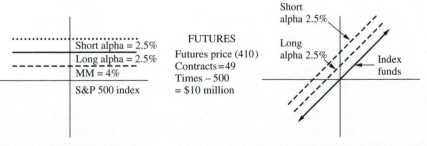

(g) Long/short market neutral position

(h) Long/short enhanced market position

FUTURES
Futures price (410)
Contracts=49
Times − 500
= $10 million

FIGURE 8-9
Patterns of returns—long/short strategies.

purposes, we begin by assuming a $10 million portfolio that is invested as an index fund. The return pattern plotted against the S&P 500 market index shows a 45-degree line, indicating the index fund should move virtually exactly in tandem with the index; profits are made equally to the index in upward moves while losses accrue in line with downward moves in the index.

Panel (*b*) in the upper right-hand portion of the figure shows the return pattern when we sell short an index fund portfolio in the same $10 million amount. It again shows a 45-degree line except that the line is in the opposite direction of the previously diagrammed long portfolio line. When the market declines, profits accrue to the short position, but in an upward market move, the short position incurs losses in tandem with the market move. The diagram also shows a dashed line that is parallel and above the short portfolio return line to represent a constant additional return from investing the proceeds of the short sales; typically, these proceeds are maintained as collateral and invested at a risk-free rate—usually in money market instruments.

Panel (*c*) in the figure shows the resulting return characteristics of the combined long and short portfolios. Note that the combined portfolio shows a constant return over all levels of market return; we use a 4 percent rate to illustrate current money market rates. If a portfolio of stocks is shorted in the same amount against a portfolio held long, market movements are neutralized. This neutralization occurs because the combination of a long portfolio with a positive beta is offset by the equivalently negative beta of a short portfolio, resulting in a beta of zero for the combination. When the market declines, losses on the long portfolio are offset by gains on the short portfolio, and, conversely, with gains in the market, losses on the short position are offset by gains on the long position. Because we illustrate using index funds (portfolios that are mirror images), the matching should be almost exact.

Panel (*d*) in the figure shows the values of the three component positions in the combined long/short portfolio. Note that the initial value of the long position is $10 million, as would be expected. At the same time, the short position shows a negative value of $10 million, indicating a liability for that amount. The third component is the value of the money market account, which is $10 million, that represents the invested amount of the proceeds from the short sales and is a credit that, on settlement, would discharge the obligation of the short sales. Over time, the account would earn at the 4 percent rate that would add to the beginning net value of $10 million.

Though assumption of an index fund as the underlying equity facilitates the exposition, portfolio managers would only pursue these strategies if there was prospect for adding value beyond the return from the initial proceeds of the short sale. To do this, the portfolio manager needs capability to differentiate between attractive and unattractive stocks, as well as portfolio construction techniques that produce underlying portfolios that track the market closely. The panels in the third section of Figure 8-9 illustrate with underlying equity portfolios that are well diversified with marketlike risk characteristics, as described in the prior section.

Panel (*e*) illustrates that when stock selection is productive in identifying undervalued stocks for the long portfolio, the return line will plot above and parallel to the line for an index fund. In this case, we assume from the dashed line in the diagram that active stock selection can add 2.5 percent alpha to the portfolio over time. Correspondingly, panel (*f*) illustrates that when stock selection is productive in identifying overvalued stocks that are suitable for inclusion in the short portfolio, the return line will again plot above and parallel to the line for an index fund. We also assume that stock selection can add 2.5 percent alpha to the short portfolio, which is in addition to the return on the short sale proceeds that are invested in a money market fund; the higher line in the diagram reflects the additional alpha return to shorting overvalued stocks.

Panel (*g*) in the bottom left-hand part of Figure 8-9 shows the resulting investment position when we combine the two active long and short portfolios. Note that the resulting return pattern is similar to that shown in panel (*c*) except that we have added two extra layers of alpha return to the basic money market return. Assuming that we can earn an added 2.5 percent return from both the long portfolio and the short portfolio, we obtain a combined extra return of 5.0 percent to add to the basic money market return of 4 percent. By definition, this alpha return is uncorrelated with the market; each of the three components (two alphas and money market return), as well as the total return of 9 percent, graph as horizontal straight lines in the diagram. Unlike the money market return, however, the alpha return components are not riskless. We discuss the risk exposure posed by long/short strategies in the next section.

Finally, the bottom right-hand section of the figure (panel *h*) shows the return pattern when we augment the combined long/short position with an overlay of futures. For this purpose, we purchase futures contracts in sufficient number to cover the initial portfolio position. Assuming that the current market level for the S&P 500 is 400 and the related future is selling for 410, we can cover the $10 million beginning position by purchasing 49 contracts. The derivation of this purchase quantity is shown in the bottom middle portion of the figure.

With a futures overlay, the return of the combined long/short positions plots as a diagonal line above and parallel to the return line for an index fund held in a long position (same as in panel *a*). The long/short enhanced market portfolio will be above the index line by the combined alphas of the long and short underlying equity portfolios; for our example, this return will be a total of 5 percent (2.5 percent long alpha plus 2.5 percent short alpha). There will be no additional return from the proceeds of the short sales, as there was in the market-neutral strategy. We assume that these earnings will be approximately offset by the added basis implied in the value of the futures contract; this value tends to be in line with the rate on risk-free instrument.

LONG/SHORT RISK

For either the market-neutral or enhanced market strategy, any incremental return derives from the effectiveness of active stock selection in the underlying long/short portfolios in producing positive alphas. Because the market-neutral strategy produces approximately a money market return in the absence of a performance spread between the longs and shorts, the benchmark, or hurdle rate, for the strategy is a money market rate. Correspondingly, an appropriate benchmark for the enhanced market strategy is the S&P 500, because when there is no spread between the longs and shorts, the strategy would produce approximately an S&P 500 return.

At the same time, the performance risk for either of these two strategies is related to the two alpha components of return: long and short. Individually, the risk related to alpha return is residual, or specific stock-related risk. This risk, also known as *tracking error*, is a measure of how much the performance of a portfolio will vary relative to an index over time. For a well-diversified portfolio, tracking error will be relatively low because residual risk

TABLE 8-9

Tracking error of combined portfolio differing correlation assumption

Correlation	Tracking error Long-alpha portfolio	Tracking error Short-alpha portfolio	Covariance	Tracking error Combined long/short
Positive (+1)	0.05	0.05	2(+1)(0.05)(0.05)	0.1
Independent (0)	0.05	0.05	2(0)(0.05)(0.05)	0.0707
Negative (−1)	0.05	0.05	2(−1)(0.05)(0.05)	0

can be reduced through the process of adding securities and controlling industry and sector risk. As illustrated before, the objective in constructing both the long and short portfolios was to reduce this risk equivalently.

When combining long and short portfolios, the investor needs to consider an additional component of risk that emanates from the estimated correlation between the long and short alpha. Table 8-9 illustrates the resulting combined portfolio risk assuming three possible correlation scenarios: (1) perfectly positive (+1.0), (2) uncorrelated or zero correlation, and (3) perfectly negative (−1.0). The illustration also assumes that the tracking error for both portfolios—long and short—is equal and is 5 percent.

When the correlation between long and short alpha portfolios is perfectly positive (+1), the resulting total combined risk is simply twice the tracking errors of the individual long and short alphas, or a total of 0.10. With zero correlation, the same forces of diversification that we described in prior chapters come into play to result in a reduced risk of 0.0707 for the combined portfolio. Finally, negative correlation (−1.0) between the long and short alphas allows a complete elimination of tracking error for the combined portfolio, as the individual alpha variations are mutually offsetting.

Though differing correlation conditions impact the resulting tracking error of the combined long/short portfolio, they also have implications for portfolio return prospects. For example, negative correlation would be a desirable feature for eliminating tracking error from the combined portfolio but would imply that the favorable alpha results from one portfolio would be counteracted by unfavorable alpha results from the other portfolio. Correspondingly, positive correlation would result in little or no reduction in portfolio risk but would imply that the alpha results from both long and short portfolios would be the same. With hedging strategies, positive correlation is a desirable characteristic, as described in Chapter 2.

Table 8-10 shows a two-by-two matrix of portfolio return possibilities that allows us to evaluate the relationship between return prospects and portfolio risk from a different perspective. Over any single period, the alpha return from the portfolio can be either

TABLE 8-10

Portfolio possibilities—long and short

Long-portfolio results	Short-portfolio results Short (+)	Short (−)
Long (+)	+ +	+ −
Short (−)	− +	− −

favorable—designated as ($+$)—or unfavorable—designated as ($-$). The boxes in the figure show the four possibilities for the two portfolios: long and short with respect to alpha results over the period.

Note that the diagonal (upper left-hand box and lower right-hand box) show the possibilities where both portfolios show the same results. Though there is positive correlation between portfolio results in both cases, the combined alpha return is favorable in one case (double plus box) and unfavorable in the other case (double minus box). Over time and with a well-functioning alpha valuation process, we would expect the favorable results to outnumber the unfavorable results. With proper portfolio construction, we would also expect that this would be a consistent pattern over time. Again, as with the IC method, the more favorable results will lead to superior portfolio performance in well-defined diversified portfolios.

In contrast, the off-diagonal boxes show negative correlation between the results for the two portfolios, with either the adverse results of the short portfolio offsetting the long-portfolio's (upper right-hand box) or the long-portfolio adverse results offsetting those of the short portfolio (lower left-hand box). Though these offsetting portfolio movements reduce tracking error over time, these converse results also degrade the combined portfolio return; positive results are offset by negative results. Once again, the most favorable case for this strategy is the one in which the alpha processes for both long and short are predictive and work in tandem over time.

CONCLUSION

This chapter began by describing the main opportunities available to managers of domestic equities: stock selection, group rotation, and asset allocation–market timing. We then emphasized the importance of the need to analyze the investment process, so as to emphasize those areas of strength in the organization through active strategies and to downplay those areas of weakness by using passive investment strategies. We thus introduced the notion of active–passive investment strategies. We then described the components and organizational structure necessary to implement active strategies of stock selection. Finally, we showed that the basic stock selection strategy, or the long/short variations, have potential for adding value with relatively limited risk.

APPENDIX A
DEFINING THE FORECASTING REGRESSION EQUATION

In the simple linear regression model between a dependent variable Y and an independent variable X,

$$Y = a + bX + e$$

the following relationships hold:

$$b = \frac{\text{Cov}(X, Y)}{\text{Var}(X)} = \frac{\rho_{xy}(S_xS_y)}{S_xS_x} = \frac{\rho_{xy}S_y}{S_x} \tag{1}$$

$$a = \bar{Y} - b\bar{x} \tag{2}$$

If the two variables are in no way related, meaning they are uncorrelated, $\rho_{xy} = 0$, then $b = 0$. If $b = 0$, $a = Y$. If the two variables are perfectly related, $\rho_{xy} = 1$, and also have the same mean and standard deviation (we can be sure that they would when using ranked data), then $b = 1$. If $b = 1$, then $a =$ zero.

To provide perspective on the meaning of the error term, note that the total variability of the dependent variable Y can be partitioned into two parts: (1) the part explained by the independent variable X; and (2) the unexplained part, or error. Substituting the regression equation for Var(Y), we obtain

$$\text{Var}(Y) = \text{Var}(a + bX + e)$$

Since Var(a) = 0, and the Var(bx) = b^2 Var(X), this equation becomes

$$\text{Var}(Y) = b^2 \, \text{Var}(X) + \text{Var}(e)$$

$$= \frac{\text{Explained}}{\text{variance}} + \frac{\text{Variance of}}{\text{the error}}$$

When we take the square root of the Var(e), we obtain the standard deviation, a measure commonly referred to as the standard error. This standard deviation provides a measure of the dispersion of individual plots around a regression line, as illustrated graphically in Figure 8-Al. A small standard error would reflect a narrow scatter of plots around the line, indicating a well-defined relationship. In contrast, a large standard error would reflect a wide scatter of plots around the line, indicating a loosely defined relationship.

The standard error is, in turn, related to the coefficient of determination R^2, which is a measure of the portion of the variance explained by the underlying relationship. It is calculated as follows:

$$\frac{\text{Explained variance}}{\text{Total variance}} = \frac{b^2 \, \text{Var}(X)}{\text{Var}(Y)} = R^2$$

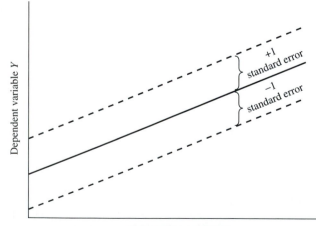

FIGURE 8-A1
Standard error of the regression.

At the same time, the standard error, or variance of the error, measures the portion that is unexplained and is calculated as follows:

$$\frac{\text{Unexplained variance}}{\text{Total variance}} = \frac{\text{Var}(e)}{\text{Var}(Y)} = 1 - R^2$$

APPENDIX B
COMBINING FORECASTS

This appendix illustrates the procedure for the special case of combining forecasts from two different methods, in which each has a positive IC and the two sources are independent (cross-correlation is zero). In this regard, it might be easier to demonstrate the process of combining forecasts by working with forecast errors, or the unexplained portion of realized return. This emphasis is in contrast to the discussion in the body of the study, which focuses on the correlation coefficient, or the explained portion of returns. Error reduction is, however, equivalent to maximizing the correlation by combining.

To begin with, we can designate the two forecasting methods as F_1 and F_2, and we can denote the variance of errors associated with each as $\text{Var}(F_1)$ and $\text{Var}(F_2)$ and the correlation between the errors of the two methods as ρ_{12}. Note that the method with the smaller error would be one with the higher IC. In addition, the objective in combining forecasts is to minimize forecast errors, which, as noted, would be equivalent to maximizing correlation. We can further let k represent the weight of the first method and $1 - k$ represent the weight of the second, where the weights sum to 1, thereby ensuring that the combined forecast is unbiased. The variance of errors in the combined forecast, $\text{Var}(C)$, can then be written as:

$$\text{Var}(C) = k^2 \, \text{Var}(F_1) + (1 - k)^2 \, \text{Var}(F_2) + 2\rho_{12}k(\text{Var}(F_1))^{\frac{1}{2}}(1 - k)(\text{Var}(F_2))^{\frac{1}{2}}$$

Note that the extent of error reduction depends on the correlation between methods, ρ_{12}, as can best be illustrated by analyzing two extreme cases mentioned in the body of the study: zero correlation and perfectly positive correlation between methods. We first assume that the forecasting methods have the same predictive power, or that $\text{Var}(F_1) = \text{Var}(F_2)$. We also assume that both forecasts carry the same weight in the combining formula, or that $k = \frac{1}{2}$. Substituting in the original formulation produces the following expression, where $\text{Var}(F)$ is a general representation of the error from both methods:

$$\text{Var}(C) = \tfrac{1}{2} \, \text{Var}(F) + 2\rho_{12}(\tfrac{1}{4}) \, \text{Var}(F)$$

When the methods are independent, the variance of the combined forecast is one-half that of an individual forecast because the zero correlation, $\rho_{12} = 0$, eliminates the covariance term in the expression. On the other hand, when the correlation is perfectly positive, $\rho_{12} = +1$, the variance of the combined forecast is the same as that of an individual forecast because the covariance term becomes equivalent to the error of an individual forecast.

As noted before, we can also illustrate that weighting of forecasting methods in proportion to their forecasting power is optimum. We can specifically illustrate this optimization by first differentiating the original expression in this appendix with respect to k and then equating to zero, which provides the following expression where the combined error is minimum (combined IC is greatest):

$$k = \frac{\text{Var}(F_2) - \rho_{12} \, \text{Var}(F_1)^{\frac{1}{2}} \, \text{Var}(F_2)^{\frac{1}{2}}}{\text{Var}(F_1) + \text{Var}(F_2) - 2\rho_{12} \, \text{Var}(F_1)^{\frac{1}{2}} \, \text{Var}(F_2)^{\frac{1}{2}}}$$

Where $\rho_{12} = 0$, this reduces to

$$k = \frac{\text{Var}(F_2)}{\text{Var}(F_1) + \text{Var}(F_2)}$$

Note that where each method has equal forecasting power, the errors would be equal and the numerator would be one-half the denominator, which would indicate that equally powerful methods should be weighted equally to obtain the optimal reduction in forecasting error.

SELECTED REFERENCES

Alexander, John: "Earnings Surprise, Market Efficiency, and Expectations," *The Financial Review,* November 1992, pp. 475–502.

Ambachtsheer, Keith P.: "Portfolio Theory and Security Analysis," *Financial Analysts Journal,* November–December 1971, pp. 53–57.

———: "Profit Potential in an 'Almost Efficient' Market," *Journal of Portfolio Management,* Fall 1974, pp. 84–87.

———: "Where are the Customers' Alphas?" *Journal of Portfolio Management,* Fall 1977, pp. 52–56.

———: and James Farrell, Jr.: "Can Active Management Add Value?" *Financial Analysts Journal,* November–December 1979, pp. 39–47.

Amihud, Yakov, and Haim Mendelson: "Liquidity, Asset Prices and Financial Policy," *Financial Analysts Journal,* November–December 1991, pp. 55–66.

Arbel, A., S. Carvell, and P. Strebel: "Giraffes, Institutions and Neglected Forms," *Financial Analysts Journal,* May–June 1983, pp. 57–63.

Arnott, Robert, and William Copeland: "The Business Cycle and Security Selection," *Financial Analysts Journal,* March–April 1985, pp. 26–33.

Bagwell, L.S.: "Dutch Auction Repurchases: An Analysis of Shareholder Heterogeneity," *Journal of Finance,* March 1992, pp. 71–105.

Bates, J.J., and C.W.J. Granger: "The Combination of Forecasts," *Operations Research Quarterly,* 1969, pp. 451–468.

Bidwell, Clinton: "A Test of Market Efficiency: SUE/PE," *Journal of Portfolio Management,* Summer 1979, pp. 453–458.

Black, Fischer: "Yes, Virginia, There Is Hope: Test of the Value Line Ranking System," *Financial Analysts Journal,* September–October 1973, pp. 10–14.

Boot, Arnoud: "Why Hang on to Losers? Diversities and Takeovers," *Journal of Finance,* September 1992, pp. 1401–1423.

Broughton, John, and Don Chance: "The Value Line Enigma Extended: An Examination of the Performance of Option Recommendations," *Journal of Business,* October 1993, pp. 541–569.

Brown, Stephen, and Jerold Warner: "Measuring Security Price Performance," *Journal of Financial Economics,* September 1980, pp. 205–258.

Collins, Bruce, and Frank Fabozzi: "A Methodology for Measuring Transactions Costs," *Financial Analysts Journal,* March–April 1991, pp. 27–36.

Conrad, Jennifer, and Gaustan Kaul: "Long-Term Market Overreaction or Biases in Computed Returns," *Journal of Finance,* March 1993, pp. 39–63.

Dann, Larry: "Common Stock Repurchases: An Analysis of Returns to Bondholders and Stockholders," *Journal of Financial Economics,* June 1981, pp. 113-138.

Davidson, Wallace, and Sharon Garrison: "The Stock Market Reaction to Significant Tender Offer Repurchases of Stock: Size and Purpose Perspective," *The Financial Review,* February 1989, pp. 93–107.

Dimson, E., and Paul Marsh: "An Analysis of Brokers and Analysts Unpublished Forecasts of UK Stock Returns," *Journal of Finance,* December 1984, pp. 257–293.

Falconer, Robert, and Charles M. Sivesind: "Dealing with Conflicting Forecasts: The Eclectic Advantage," *Business Economics,* September 1977, pp. 5–11.

Farrell, James L., Jr.: "Integrating Disciplined Stock Selection into Portfolio Management," Institute for Chartered Financial Analysts, 1984.

———: "The Multi-Index Model and Practical Portfolio Analysis," Occasional Paper no. 4, Financial Analysts Research Foundation, 1976.

———: "A Disciplined Stock Selection Strategy," *Interfaces 12,* October 1982, pp. 3–12, also December 1983 Addendum.

———: "What Is Systematic Stock Selection?" *Journal of Investing,* Summer 1989, pp. 12–20.

Givoly, Dan, and Dan Palmon: "Insider Trading and the Exploitation of Inside Information," *Journal of Business,* January 1985, pp. 69–88.

Grinold, Richard: "Alpha Is Volatility Times Score," *Journal of Portfolio Management,* Summer 1994, pp. 9–16.

———: "Information Analysis," *Journal of Portfolio Management,* Spring 1992, pp. 14–21.

Hand, John, Robert Holthausen, and Richard Leftwich: "The Effect of Bond Rating Agency Announcements on Bond and Stock Prices," *Journal of Finance,* June 1992, pp. 733–752.

Harlow, N.V., and John Howe: "Leveraged Buyouts and Insider Non-Trading," *Financial Management,* Spring 1993, pp. 109–118.

Hodges, Stewart, and Richard Brealey: "Portfolio Selection in a Dynamic and Uncertain World," *Financial Analysts Journal,* March–April 1973, pp. 50–65.

Holthausen, R., and R. Leftwich: "The Effect of Bond Rating Changes on Common Stock Prices," *Journal of Financial Economics,* 17, 1986, pp. 57–89.

Hudson, Carl, John Jahera, and William Lloyd: "Further Evidence on the Relationship between Ownership and Performance," *The Financial Review,* May 1992, pp. 227–239.

Jacobs, Bruce, and Kenneth Levy: "Disentangling Equity Return Regularities: New Insights and Investment Opportunities," *Financial Analysts Journal,* May–June 1988, pp. 18–44.

———: "Long/Short Equity Investing," *Journal of Portfolio Management,* Fall 1993, pp. 52–63.

Jegadeesh, Narasimhan: "Seasonality in Stock Price Mean Reversion: Evidence from the U.S. and the U.K.," *Journal of Finance,* September 1991, pp. 1429–1444.

——— and Sheridan Titman: "Returns to Buying Winners and Selling Losers: Implications for Market Efficiency," *Journal of Finance,* March 1993, pp. 65–91.

Jones, Robert: "Designing Factor Models for Different Types of Stock: What's Good for the Goose Ain't Always Good For the Gander," *Financial Analysts Journal,* March–April 1990, pp. 25–30.

Kim, W., J.W. Lee, and Jack Francis: "Investment Performance of Common Stocks in Relation to Insider Ownership," *The Financial Review,* February 1988, pp. 53–64.

Kong, H.: "Unstable Weights in the Combination of Forecasts," *Management Science,* June 1986, pp. 683–695.

Loeb, Thomas: "Trading Cost: The Critical Link Between Investment Information and Results," *Financial Analysts Journal,* May–June 1993, pp. 39–46.

Lorie, James, and Victor Niederhoffer: "Predictive and Statistical Properties of Insider Trading," *Journal of Law and Economics,* April 1968, pp. 35–53.

Madden, Gerald: "The Performance of Common Stocks After Intensive Trading by Insiders," *The Financial Review,* Spring 1979, pp. 27–35.

McEnally, Richard, and Rebecca Todd: "Cross-Sectional Variation in Common Stock Returns," *Financial Analysts Journal,* May–June 1992, pp. 59–63.

Michaud, Richard: "Are Long–Short Equity Strategies Superior?" *Financial Analysts Journal,* November–December 1993, pp. 44–49.

Newbold, P., and C.W.J. Granger: "Experience with Forecasting Univariate Time Series and the Combination Forecasts," *Journal of the Royal Statistical Society,* 1974, pp. 131–146.

Penman, Stephen: "Insider Trading and the Dissemination of Firms' Forecast Information," *Journal of Business,* October 1982, pp. 179–504.

Perold, A.F.: "The Implementation Shortfall: Paper Versus Reality," *Journal of Portfolio Management,* April 1988, pp. 4–9.

Perold, Andre, and Robert Salomon: "The Right Amount of Assets Under Management," *Financial Analysts Journal,* May–June 1991, pp. 31–39.

Phillips, Susan, and Clifford Smith: "Trading Costs for Market Efficiency," *Journal of Financial Economics,* June 1980, pp. 179–201.

Poterba, J.M., and Lawrence Summers: "Mean Reversion in Stock Prices," *Journal of Financial Economics* 22, 1988, pp. 27–59.

Pugh, William, and John Jahera: "Stock Repurchases and Excess Returns: An Empirical Examination," *The Financial Review,* February 1990, pp. 127–142.

Reinganum, Marc: "The Anatomy of a Stock Market Winner," *Financial Analysts Journal,* March–April 1988, pp. 16–28.

Richardson, Matthew, and Tom Smith: "A Unified Approach to Testing for Serial Correlation in Stock Returns," *Journal of Business,* July 1994, pp. 371–400.

Rozeff, Michael, and Mir Zaman: "Market Efficiency and Insider Trading: New Evidence," *Journal of Business,* January 1988, pp. 25–44.

Senchak, A.J., and John D. Martin: "The Relative Performance of the PSR and PER Strategies," *Financial Analysts Journal,* March–April 1987, pp. 46-56.

Seyhun, Nejat: "The Information Content of Aggregate Insider Trading," *Journal of Business,* January 1988, pp. 1–24.

——: "Insiders' Profits, Costs of Trading, and Market Efficiency," *Journal of Financial Economics,* June 1986, pp. 189–212.

Sheikh, Aamir: "The Behavior of Volatility Expectations and Their Effects on Expected Returns," *Journal of Business,* January 1993, pp. 93–116.

Shelton, John P.: "The Value Line Contest: A Test of the Predictability of Stock Price Changes," *Journal of Business,* July 1967, pp. 251–269.

Singh, Ajai, Mir Zaman, and C. Krishonamurti: "Liquidity Changes Associated with Open Market Repurchases," *Financial Management,* Spring 1994, pp. 47–55.

Tinic, Seha, and Richard West: "Risk and Return: January Versus the Rest of the Year," *Journal of Financial Economics,* December 1984, pp. 561–574.

Treynor, Jack: "Long-Term Investing," *Financial Analysts Journal,* May–June 1976, pp. 56–59.

—— and Fischer Black: "How to Use Security Analysis to Improve Portfolio Selection," *Journal of Business,* January 1973, pp. 66-86.

Wagner, Wayne, and Larry Cuneo: "Reducing the Cost of Stock Trading," *Financial Analysts Journal,* November–December 1975, pp. 35–44.

Wagner, Wayne, and Mark Edwards: "Best Execution," *Financial Analysts Journal,* January–February 1993, pp. 65–71.

Wilcox, Jerrod: "The Effect of Transactions Costs and Delay on Performance Drag," *Financial Analysts Journal,* March–April 1993, pp. 45–57.

QUESTIONS AND PROBLEMS

1. Differentiate between an active and a passive investment strategy.
2. Explain the notion of extramarket correlation.
3. What are the major components of equity returns, and what risks correspond to each?
4. What is the measure of security-specific returns, and what risk is associated with it?

5. How does an investor ensure that the portfolio is hedged (neutralized) against the market timing risk?

6. What is the logical strategy for an investor to pursue who has no skill in evaluating the relative attractiveness of the market, groups, or individual stocks?

7. Briefly explain the kind of risk-return trade-off an investor would anticipate when moving from passive to more active strategies.

8. What purposes do portfolio diagnostics serve in managing a portfolio?

9. What is the difference between a time-series derived beta and cross-sectional beta?

10. What are the statistical measures of the diversification of a portfolio?

11. Explain how adding or subtracting cash can change the beta of a portfolio.

12. Describe the various active strategies that are available for obtaining above-average return, and indicate the passive alternative to these active strategies.

13. An organization needs to assign ratings to stocks from three different industries: 5, 15, and 20 stocks, respectively. Determine how many stocks will be in each of the five rating categories for each of the three industries, using the rule illustrated in Figure 8-5.

14. What are the benefits of composite forecasting, and under what conditions is it appropriate to use this method?

15. An organization evaluates three independent sources of information and assesses each as having an IC of 0.15. It decides to use a composite forecasting method. Determine the combined IC for the organization using the three sources.

16. Refer to Figure 8-6 and assume that the standard deviation of the stock-return distribution is 26 percent and that the organization's IC is now 0.10. Determine the adjusted return distribution for that organization.

17. Discuss the importance of considering transaction costs when rebalancing the portfolio.

18. Outline the basic elements needed to execute an active strategy of stock selection.

19. What is a "long–short market-neutral" strategy, and what components would be needed to implement such a strategy?

20. Assume that stock X had an expected excess return of 4 percent, while stock Y had an expected excess return of −2 percent. What would be the expected excess return on an equally weighted portfolio of the two stocks? How would you improve the portfolio, and what would be the resultant expected return?

21. In a long–short market-neutral portfolio, what are the components of risk, and how do these compare with a standard long-only portfolio?

22. A long portfolio has a beta of 1 with a standard error of 4 percent and alpha of 2 percent; a second portfolio has a beta of 1 as well, a standard error of 3 percent, and an alpha of −1 percent. What are the expected alpha and risk for a combined long–short portfolio of the two portfolios?

CHAPTER 9

Managing the Asset Class Mix

INTRODUCTION

Asset allocation encompasses selection of asset classes, proper blending of these asset classes in a portfolio, and managing this asset mix over time. Determining the asset mix that best suits the risk-return objective of the investor is the most important decision in meeting the longer-range goals of the investment plan. Because of its focus on the longer range, this aspect of the process is also referred to as strategic asset allocation.

Once the longer-range asset mix is established, investors can then attempt to identify asset class pricing discrepancies and change the mix opportunistically over the interim. This aspect is known as *tactical asset allocation* and by nature has a shorter-term orientation. It has the potential for adding value over time but also presents significant risks that must be considered.

Tactical asset allocation may also be considered as one of the ways of managing the asset mix over time. Another way is to simply pursue a buy-and-hold policy for the established asset mix over the planning horizon. A third way is to pursue a strategy of dynamic rebalancing, more popularly known as portfolio insurance. Each of these strategies will create over time a differing pattern of returns that the investor needs to consider in deciding the most appropriate strategy for managing the asset mix.

The purpose of this chapter is to discuss asset allocation and its differing aspects. We begin by describing a structured procedure for strategic asset allocation. The second part of the chapter deals with tactical asset allocation and the ways of implementing this aspect of asset allocation. The third section describes the three ways of managing the asset mix over time and the type of return pattern associated with each of the procedures. The appendix describes the way that the asset allocation process is altered when the liabilities of the investment plan are considered along with the assets.

STRATEGIC ASSET ALLOCATION

The purpose of the strategic asset allocation process is to put assets together in a portfolio in such a way as to maximize return at a level of risk consistent with the investor's objective.

This process involves four key elements. First, the investor needs to determine the assets that are eligible for the portfolio. Second, the investor needs to determine expected return for these eligible assets over a holding period, or planning horizon. Third, once returns have been estimated and risk assessed, the techniques of optimization described in Chapter 2 should be used to find portfolio mixes providing the highest return for each level of risk. The final step is to choose the portfolio (from the efficient frontier) that provides the maximum return at a tolerable risk level.

Since we have described the kinds of assets that are available in the investment universe in Chapter 2, we discuss the other three elements in this chapter, giving special emphasis to determining the expected return and risk for assets of interest to the portfolio manager. There are essentially two methods of estimating the risk-return relationship among securities. The first is to assume that the future will be like the past and to extrapolate this past experience into the future. At the other extreme is the scenario approach, which involves establishing appropriate economic scenarios and then assessing the returns and risks associated with these scenarios. Generally, forecasts using this approach have a three- to five-year planning horizon. Forecasting by extrapolating the past into the future implicitly presumes an infinite planning, or forecasting, horizon. We begin by describing this approach and then cover the more complex scenario approach to forecasting risk-return relationships.

USING THE PAST TO FORECAST THE FUTURE

Since we will first be describing forecasting by the analysis of past data, we have reproduced the returns and risks associated with asset classes in Table 9-1. Note that we are considering only three asset classes: common stocks, long-term bonds, and short-term Treasury bills, which simplifies the analysis and improves the illustration. The returns and risks associated with the assets were developed over the 1926–1993 period. The returns are realized returns and include income and capital gains, whereas the risks are the standard deviation of return and correlation among the asset classes.

Note that stocks showed the highest return, Treasury bills showed the lowest, and bonds showed intermediate return. The risk of the assets as measured by the standard deviation of return was in line with the realized return in which stock returns were the most variable and Treasury bills the least variable. Finally, stocks showed virtually zero correlation over the period with Treasury bills and slightly positive correlation with bonds, whereas Treasury bills showed moderately positive correlation with bonds.

In forecasting, investors will ordinarily assume that the standard deviations and correlations among assets realized over the past will persist in the future. They will, however,

TABLE 9-1
Risk and return characteristics of major asset classes, 1926–1993

Asset class	Return, %	Standard deviation, %	Correlation Stocks	Bonds	Treasury bills
Stocks	10.30	20.50	1.00		
Bonds	5.00	8.70	0.14	1.00	
Treasury bills	3.70	3.30	0.05	0.24	1.00

Source: SBBI, 1994 Yearbook, Ibbotson Associates, Chicago.

TABLE 9-2
Nominal returns, inflation, real returns, and projected returns for major asset classes, %

Asset class	Nominal return (1926–1993)	Inflation rate (1926–1993)	Real return (1926–1993)	Expected inflation 1994	Projected return
Stocks	10.30	3.10	7.20	3.00	10.20
Bonds	5.00	3.10	1.90	3.00	4.90
Treasury bills	3.70	3.10	0.60	3.00	3.60

adjust projected returns for current levels of inflation, as theory and empirical research indicate investors are primarily concerned with real, rather than nominal, returns. Projections then assume that the real return earned in the future will be the same as that earned in the past. Nominal returns projected into the future will differ from past returns by the differences in the assumed future level of inflation and the rates realized in the past.

Table 9-2 shows the inflation rate for the 1926–1993 period, the realized real return for the three asset classes, and projected nominal returns incorporating current levels of inflation. Over the 1926–1993 period, inflation was 3.1 percent, so that the real return on stocks was 7.2 percent, on bonds 1.9 percent, and on Treasury bills close to zero. According to current estimates, inflation was to proceed at a rate of 3 percent, or at a rate virtually identical to the long-range past average. Adding the current inflation rate to the real returns of the past period provides projected nominal returns, only slightly lower than in the past, of 10.2 percent for stocks, 4.9 percent for bonds, and 3.6 percent for Treasury bills.

Subdividing Historical Data

We can develop further insights into projecting past data into the future by subdividing the past 64 years into six natural periods. The first, 1929–1933, was a period of extreme deflation without recovery in the economy. The second, 1934–1938, was also a period of deflation but with prospects of recovery in the economy. The third period, 1939–1945, is an extreme case of a controlled economy, with both prices and interest rates set by regulatory agencies. The fourth, 1946–1965, was an extended period of stable prosperity. In the fifth period, 1966–1980, inflation began to accelerate and real growth slowed. The final period, 1981–1993, was one of disinflation, that is, decelerating inflation.

Table 9-3 shows the performance of stocks, bonds, and Treasury bills over these six periods. The six historical capital market environments with their frequency of occurrence are shown across the top of the table. The frequency of occurrence was determined simply as the percentage of the total 64-year period encompassed by a particular market environment; for example, the market was in an environment of deflation with no hope of recovery for the 5-year period 1929–1933, or 8 percent of the 1929–1993 period. The return realized by the asset classes and the inflation rates over each of the six periods are also shown. Finally, the table shows the real return (nominal return less inflation rate) for each of the asset classes, the inflation premium (CPI rate of change), and the equity risk premium (stock return less Treasury bill return) over each of the six periods.

Note that stocks did poorly during the initial period of deflation with no recovery and during the period of inflation. On the other hand, stocks did quite well during the period of deflation with recovery as well as during the 1946–1965 and 1981–1993 periods, when

TABLE 9-3
Historical capital markets experience, 1929–1993, %

Capital-market environments	Deflation		Controls	Good times	Inflation	Disinflation
	Without recovery	With recovery				
Years	(1929–1933)	(1934–1938)	(1939–1945)	(1946–1965)	(1966–1980)	(1981–1993)
Frequency of occurrence	0.08	0.08	0.11	0.31	0.23	0.20
Average annual returns						
Stocks	−6.70	15.30	11.50	15.00	5.60	14.30
Bonds	6.20	7.80	3.50	2.30	4.60	14.10
Treasury bills	1.90	0.20	0.20	1.90	5.70	7.50
CPI	−5.00	1.30	3.90	2.90	6.00	4.10
Average annual return components						
Real rate	6.90	−1.20	−3.70	−1.00	−0.30	3.40
Inflation premium	−5.00	1.30	3.90	2.90	6.00	4.10
Equity risk premium	−8.60	15.10	11.30	13.10	−0.10	6.80

real economic growth was favorable and inflation moderate. Stocks performed moderately well during the period of controls. Real economic growth and low inflation appear to be favorable environments for stocks, whereas high inflation and low or declining real growth are unfavorable for stocks.

Bonds performed well during the two deflationary periods, showed relatively poor performance during the three periods between 1938 and 1980, and again performed well in the 1981–1993 period of disinflation. In a sense, bonds provide a hedge against slow economic growth and deflation but suffer in a relative sense in other periods. Treasury bills, on the other hand, appear to provide some hedge against inflation, as indicated by their performance in line with the rate of inflation in the period 1966–1980. During other periods, Treasury bills are less attractive relative to both stocks and bonds.

The data illustrate that the performance of broad asset classes can diverge considerably from the longer-term average over shorter time intervals. Economic conditions change, and some of the factors that gave rise to the longer-term average performance may not be relevant at all in the future or may again cause quite wide performance divergences by individual asset classes over shorter intervals. Subdividing historic data can give the analyst perspective in identifying that component of history that is most relevant for the future. Correspondingly, looking at subdivided history in this way may be helpful in identifying likely future economic episodes (scenarios) and the way that these might impact on asset class behavior. Identifying relevant economic scenarios is a key element of the scenario forecasting approach to be discussed in the next section.

SCENARIO FORECASTING

The other major approach to developing returns and assessing risk for securities is the scenario approach. The scenario approach differs from the historical approach with respect to both the analytical difficulty in developing the forecast and the appropriate time horizon for the forecast. To begin with, the scenario approach requires greater analytical effort and forecasting skill than the approach of extrapolating history into the future. The trade-off is, of course, the greater flexibility in dealing with changing environments and, hence, the derivation of more effective forecasts of future returns.

Though forecasting with the historical approach implies an infinite forecasting horizon, the scenario approach requires a more explicit statement of the forecast period. Generally, forecasters will choose an intermediate-term forecasting horizon of, say, three to five years. This time horizon forces planners to look beyond seasonal and cyclical events and focus on sociopolitico-economic trends and their implications for stock prices and interest rates. At the same time, this planning horizon is not as remote as to be beyond the capability of developing some objective and useful forecasts of value.

In addition, this time horizon provides the appropriate perspective for shorter-term portfolio decision making. Once longer-term benchmark yields and price levels for security classes have been established, tactical portfolio decisions flow naturally from the interaction of (1) short-term fluctuations around these benchmark yields and price levels and (2) a predetermined long-term investment plan. In this latter respect, we can differentiate tactical asset allocation—a shorter-term approach—from strategic asset allocation—a longer-term approach to determining and changing the composition of the portfolio. We will discuss tactical asset allocation and its integration with the strategic asset allocation process later in this chapter.

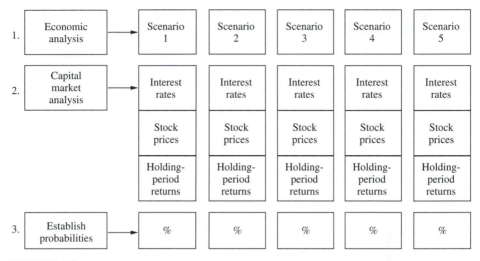

FIGURE 9-1
Scenario forecasting process.

Figure 9-1 illustrates the necessary steps to implement the forecast. The diagram shows that the first step is to identify the possible range of economic environments that could exist. Five scenarios are listed, and the task here is to describe the expected real growth-inflation paths that could occur in each. We should note that the number of scenarios will vary as economic conditions change, as well as according to the disposition of the individual forecaster; the five scenarios listed in the figure should be considered as only illustrative of the process. The next step is to develop for each scenario the implications for interest rates, stock prices, and holding-period returns for each asset class. The third step is to determine the probability associated with the occurrences of each scenario.

Determining Scenarios

As noted before, the number of economic scenarios will vary over time as economic conditions change. It will also vary across different forecasters, as some deal with as few as three and some with as many as a dozen or more. In illustrating the scenario process, we will deal with five, as this number is large enough to be descriptive of the current economic environment but small enough to be analytically tractable. In addition, we noted previously that the economic environment of the past 64 years could be classified into six different episodes. Some of the current scenarios can be compared to these past economic environments for perspective on the likely future behavior of classes of stocks, bonds, and bills.

Table 9-4 shows the five scenarios used to describe the 1994–1998 economic environment. These five scenarios are designated (1) high growth/low inflation, (2) disinflation, (3) deflation, (4) reflation, and (5) stagflation. The table shows the rate of GNP growth and the rate of inflation as measured by the CPI associated with the scenario. It also shows the direction of change in the discount rate, which represents the required return for the risk of the security, according to each of the scenarios. Finally, it indicates the probability of occurrence of each of the scenarios.

Because of a fixed coupon, high-quality bonds would be expected to do well in the deflation and disinflation scenarios, as discount rates decline and bond prices increase to

TABLE 9-4
Possible economic scenarios

Scenario	GNP growth	Inflation rate	Discount rate change	Probability of occurrence
(1) High growth/low inflation	3.50	3.00	Stable	0.35
(2) Disinflation	2.50	2.50	Down	0.30
(3) Deflation	1.00	1.00	Down	0.05
(4) Reflation	3.50	4.50	Up	0.20
(5) Stagflation	2.00	5.00	Up	0.10

reflect lower required returns. Common stocks would be expected to do the best in the high-growth/low-inflation scenario, as this asset class is the only one to benefit directly from improved growth in the economy. Though the reflation scenario would favor stocks the most, performance would be tempered, as higher growth would be offset by an increasing discount rate. In the stagflation scenario, we expect Treasury bills to do best because the yields should adjust in line with inflation. Empirical research indicates that Treasury bills not only move in line with inflation but can in fact predict inflation rates; so that if we observe Treasury bill yields increasing for no "apparent" reason, the increase could be due to expectation of higher inflation. An investor rolling over cash equivalents can thus adjust yield quickly in order to keep returns in line with the current structure of discount rates.

Capital-Market Implications

The upper part of Table 9-5 shows holding-period returns associated with each scenario for each of the asset classes: stocks, bonds, and Treasury bills. Note that Treasury bill returns are generally high when bond returns are low, and vice versa. Bonds are expected to provide a hedge against deflation, but Treasury bills are expected to provide a hedge against inflation. Unsurprisingly, these two assets exhibit contrary return behavior, as they are hedging against contrary economic phenomena—upward and downward changes in the prices of goods and services.

TABLE 9-5
Asset class returns and economic scenarios

Scenario	Asset class return			Probability of occurrence
	Stocks	Bonds	Bills	
High growth/low inflation	17%	8%	4%	0.35
Disinflation/low growth	12	12	2	0.30
Deflation	2	15	1	0.05
Reflation	10	4	5	0.20
Stagflation	4	4	5	0.10
Expected return	12.1	8.4	3.6	1.00
Standard deviation	14.00	7.00	3.00	
Correlation				
Stocks	1.00	—	—	
Bonds	0.20	1.00	—	
Bills	0.05	−0.70	1.00	

Note also that stocks show the greatest absolute and relative return in the high-growth/low-inflation economic scenario. They provide a means of participating, to the greatest extent, in the favorable fortunes of the economy, whereas Treasury bills and bond prospects are, by nature, quite limited. Stocks provide dramatically different returns depending on whether there is a disinflationary or deflationary environment in prospect. According to the disinflationary scenario, stocks would be highly correlated with bonds but, in deflation, would diverge quite sharply from bond performance. Stocks, like Treasury bills, perform moderately well in the reflation environment but show considerably poorer performance in the stagflation environment. On balance, stocks tend to act independently of bonds and Treasury bills.

The bottom part of Table 9-5 shows for each asset class the expected return developed by the scenario approach. This expected return was developed by weighting the return associated with each scenario by the probability of occurrence of the scenario. It is, in other words, simply a weighted average return. The table also shows the standard deviations and correlation coefficients for the three asset classes. The standard deviations and correlation coefficients for the scenario approach are derived by using the usual standard deviation and correlation coefficient formulas along with the probabilities associated with each of the scenarios.

The derived returns and standard deviations shown in Table 9-5 are consistent with an expected risk-return relationship in which common stocks showed the highest return and standard deviation, Treasury bills the lowest, and bonds an intermediate return and standard deviation. In addition, the calculated correlation of 0.20 between bonds and bonds indicates a moderately positive relationship that is consistent with the pattern of returns projected over the forecast period. Finally, the derived moderately positive correlation between stocks and Treasury bills and the strongly negative correlation between bonds and Treasury bills is representative of the contrary response of Treasury bills and the other two asset classes to the differing economic conditions over the forecast period.

Though the return and risk measures generated by the scenario approach has a similarity to the historic relationship shown in Table 9-1, there are some notable differences. First, the returns for common stocks derived from the scenario analysis are significantly higher than the historic experience, but the projected standard deviation is lower. In addition, the projected bond return of 8.4 percent is even more highly divergent from the historic data at almost twice the average of 5.2 percent. Finally, the projected correlation of −0.7 between Treasury bills and bonds is significantly more negative than derived from the historic data.

DETERMINING THE OPTIMUM MIX

The next step in the asset allocation process is to develop mixes of assets that provide optimum risk-return combinations. We can use the portfolio optimization techniques described in Chapter 2 to develop these optimum portfolios.[1] Recall that we need returns, standard deviations, and covariances for the asset under consideration as inputs to these optimization models. For purposes of illustration, we will use as inputs the risk and return statistics developed as a part of the scenario approach.

---

[1] Because there are only a limited number of asset classes and variance and covariance inputs can be readily derived, the full-covariance Markowitz formulation is usually used directly to generate portfolio mixes for an asset allocation.

TABLE 9-6
Optimum portfolios, expected return, asset mix

	Portfolio				
	A	**B**	**C**	**D**	**E**
Expected return	12.1	11.9	11.6	11.3	10.8
Standard deviation	10.9	9.7	8.2	6.7	4.8
Asset mix					
Stocks	85	75	63	50	35
Bonds	5	15	25	25	10
Treasury bills	10	10	12	25	55
Total	100	100	100	100	100
Probability of exceeding 5% return	74	76	79	83	89

Table 9-6 shows five optimum portfolios representing selected risk levels along the efficient frontier.[2] It shows the expected return associated with each portfolio and the risk of the portfolio as measured by the standard deviation. In addition, the table shows the composition of the portfolio—the percentage weighting of each asset class in the portfolio. Finally, it shows the probability of the return on the portfolio not exceeding a certain minimum level. This probability represents a sort of hurdle rate, or threshold, that an investor would presumably be especially concerned about exceeding; for purposes of illustration, we are setting the hurdle rate at 5 percent.

Note that the proportion of stock held in optimum portfolios is directly related to their risk. As risk-return increases, the optimum equity portion increases; the reverse is true with Treasury bills because large holdings are associated with lower-risk portfolios. Bonds have higher weights in medium-risk portfolios than in either high- or low-risk mixes. The highest-risk portfolio has a 0.74 probability of exceeding the 5 percent hurdle rate, and the lowest-risk portfolio has a 0.89 probability of exceeding the hurdle rate.

The final step in the asset allocation process is to choose the portfolio that meets the requirements of the investor. Those investors with a high tolerance for risk would choose the higher-risk portfolio. Presumably, these investors are willing to tolerate a higher probability of not achieving a certain minimum return in order to earn a higher return. On the other hand, those with a lower tolerance for risk would choose the lower-risk portfolio. They are

---

[2]Peter Dietz of Frank Russell Company conducted a study to determine the minimum and maximum percentages of a portfolio that should be represented by stocks and bonds. He obtained historical return data for these asset classes over the 1970–1975 period, formed portfolios with varying mixes of stocks and bonds, and computed the return and risk associated with the portfolio using the historical return data. Dietz calculated this for all combinations of stocks and bonds, varying the time periods to obtain risk and return characteristics for a whole range of portfolios over many differing historical return episodes.

The study showed that portfolios should have a minimum of 35 percent or a maximum of 60 percent in bonds and a minimum of 40 percent and a maximum of 65 percent in stocks to obtain the best reward per unit of risk. Portfolios with bond or stock allocations outside those boundaries had a significantly less favorable reward-risk ratio than those within those bounds. Portfolios that were structured within those bounds had reward-risk ratios that were fairly similar. The study is interesting in cautioning against extreme divergences in asset mix for a portfolio.

presumably more interested in achieving a certain minimum return, as illustrated by their 5 percent level in Table 9-6.

As a final note, we have illustrated the development of a strategic portfolio mix by considering only the universe of asset classes. At the same time, investors such as pension plans, for example, have liabilities that should be considered as well when developing a portfolio mix. This process is known as asset/liability optimization and is described in the appendix to this chapter. The general process for the allocation is similar to the asset-only case, but the recommended mix can differ depending on the character of the liabilities.

TACTICAL ASSET ALLOCATION (TAA)

As noted before, the expected return, standard deviation, and covariance inputs to the asset allocation process are of a longer-term nature, which can be defined here as a period of more than three years; however, these longer-term asset class expectations embody short-term risk-return parameters. In particular, the short-term return—say, the one-year return—will likely diverge above or below the average to be realized over the longer period. In the absence of special information, it is best, however, to proceed as if the year-by-year results will be identical to the longer-term average. For example, if the expected return on stocks is 13 percent over a four-year forecasting period, we would assume that the return realized each year would be 13 percent.

On the other hand, the position can be taken that the investor has special knowledge about the return from an asset class that differs from the average expected over the longer period. The investor can vary the asset mix from the position established on the basis of longer-term projections to take advantage of the short-term forecast. For example, if, for long-term planning purposes, an organization is using the expected 13 percent return on stocks but forecasts a declining market for the coming 12 months, it could use this judgment to reduce its exposure to stocks below a level consistent with its long-term view.

This process of forecasting shorter-term return movements and varying the asset mix accordingly is tactical asset allocation, popularly known as TAA. It is an activist management style, analogous to company or industry group selectivity. It is consciously taking an incremental risk in order to achieve incremental return. Engaging in this activity, however, presumes some sort of predictive capability with respect to market moves. The following section describes how to assess predictive ability and provides a framework for assessing the appropriate amount of risk-taking to obtain the incremental return.

Assessing Predictive Ability

A requisite for engaging in tactical asset allocation (TAA) is some level of predictive ability. The information coefficient (IC) method described in Chapter 8 provides a way of measuring this capability just as it does with respect to measuring stock selection capability. Before describing the application to TAA, we should be aware that actual measurement of predictive accuracy in calling market moves is not easy. Whereas predictive accuracy tests on individual company judgments typically yield as many judgments per measurement period as the size of the stock selection universe, only one market judgment can be made per measurement period. In order to develop as large a sample for market judgments as for individual stocks, many measurement periods must pass. The statistics pertinent to evaluating market timing capability are, in short, much less readily available than those for stock selection. Additionally, comparing differing time periods and making relative judgments about predictive ability are more difficult.

Figure 9-2 shows that measuring TAA capability is a three-step procedure. The first step is to compile an expression of the degree to which the market is over- or undervalued. We can again use the five-point rating scheme: rating 1 represents an extremely undervalued market, which would occur 10 percent of the time; 2 represents a moderately undervalued market, which occurs 20 percent of the time; 3 represents a neutral market, occurring 40 percent of the time; 4 represents a moderately overvalued market, occurring 20 percent of the time; and 5 represents an extremely overvalued market, which occurs 10 percent of the time.

Once these return categories are set, they must be converted into explicit return forecasts. As part of this process, we need to express rating categories in terms of standard deviations from the mean of the rating distribution. For the rating distribution used here, the standard deviation is 1.1 rating points. In this case, a rating of 5 or 1, which are 2 rating points away from the mean, are also 1.8 ($2 \div 1.1$) standard deviations away from the mean. Similarly, a rating of 4 or 2, which are 1 rating point away from the mean, are also

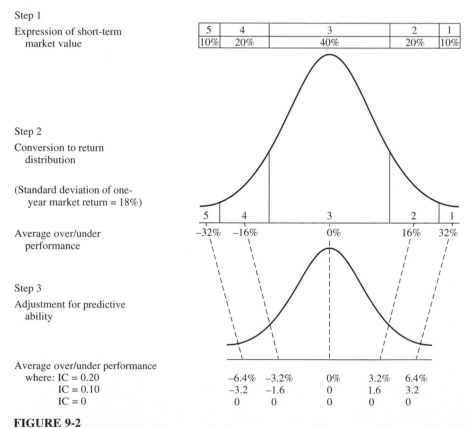

| Step 1 |
| Expression of short-term market value |

| 5 | 4 | 3 | 2 | 1 |
| 10% | 20% | 40% | 20% | 10% |

Step 2

Conversion to return distribution

(Standard deviation of one-year market return = 18%)

| 5 | 4 | 3 | 2 | 1 |
| −32% | −16% | 0% | 16% | 32% |

Average over/under performance

Step 3

Adjustment for predictive ability

Average over/under performance					
where: IC = 0.20	−6.4%	−3.2%	0%	3.2%	6.4%
IC = 0.10	−3.2	−1.6	0	1.6	3.2
IC = 0	0	0	0	0	0

FIGURE 9-2
Evaluating TAA capability.

0.9 (1 ÷ 1.1) standard deviations away from the mean. Naturally, a rating of 3 would be zero deviations away from the mean.

Given the ratings distribution and using a forecast standard deviation of 18 percent for the market, the explicit return forecasts become those illustrated in step 2 of Figure 9-2. These forecasts show that we convert a rating of 1, which is 1.8 standard deviations above the mean, into a 32-percent outperformance (1.8 × 18) and we convert a rating of 5, which is 1.8 below the mean, into a 32-percent underperformance. Similarly, we convert a rating of 2, which is 0.9 standard deviations from the mean, into a 16-percent outperformance (0.9 × 18), and a rating of 4, which is 0.9 below the mean, into a 16-percent underperformance. Naturally, a rating of 3, which is right at the mean of the distribution, converts into a performance that is in line with the longer-term expectation for the market—13 percent in this case. In this regard, note that we are indicating underperformance or outperformance relative to the average expected return for the market over the longer term, which means that a projected rating of 5 converts into an expected return of −19 percent, or 13 percent less the forecast shortfall of 32 percent.

The third step involves adjusting the raw return adjustments for the assessed degree of accuracy in making the return forecast. Some predictive accuracy in turn implies some ability to create a correlation IC between forecast return deviations $F(D)$ and actual return deviations D. This is expressed in the following formula:

$$D = ICF(D) + \text{error} \tag{1}$$

The formula tells us that the return deviation comprises two components: (1) the part explained by the forecast $ICF(D)$ and (2) the error in the forecast, or the remainder. When the ability to predict is perfect, $IC = 1.0$, the error in the forecast is zero, and the actual deviation becomes equal to the forecast deviation—$D = F(D)$. On the other hand, when there is no predictive ability, $IC = 0$, the forecast explains no part of the deviation, and actual deviation is then equal to the error term—$D = e$.

These are, of course, extremes, and as we have noted before, where predictive ability does exist, it is likely to be on the order of 0.10 to 0.20. To illustrate the case of some predictive ability, we will assume that the organization has made an assessment that the market is moderately overvalued—a rating of 4 on our five-way rating scale. This rating, in turn, converts to an expected return deviation of −16 percent. Assuming that the organization has predictive capability on the order of 0.10, the expected deviation $E(D)$ becomes[3]

$$E(D) = ICF(D) = 0.10(-0.16) = -1.6$$

The diagram further illustrates this adjustment for three levels of predictive capability: 0.20, 0.10, and zero. When we adjust for less than perfect predictive capability, the return

---

[3] To further illustrate, we can indicate that the market return R_M will be a function of its long-term expected return (13 percent) and a deviation D around the return:

$$R_M = 13 + D$$

The deviation D has an expected value $E(D)$ of zero and a variance $\text{Var}(D) = 18^2 = 324$. As noted in the body of the chapter, the deviation can be explained as follows:

$$D = ICF(D) + \text{error}$$

The error has an expected value $E(e)$ of zero and a variance $\text{Var}(e) = (1 - IC^2)\text{Var}(D)$. The market variance, given the forecast, then becomes $(1 - IC^2)\text{Var}(D) = (1 - 10^2)(324) = 321$.

forecast divergences become much smaller than indicated by the raw returns. For example, a rating of 5, which converts to a -3.2 percent return, becomes a forecast of -6.4 percent when adjusted for 0.20 predictive capability and -3.2 percent when adjusted for 0.10 predictive capability. Note that zero predictive capability means that low return divergences adjust to a zero forecast return divergence, automatically implying no activity with regard to TAA.

MANAGING MARKET SENSITIVITIES

Presuming some predictive ability and given a market forecast, the organization needs to adjust the portfolio accordingly to take advantage of the forecast. For example, forecast of a rising market would suggest reducing cash, increasing the portfolio beta, or a combination of the two. Conversely, forecast of an overvalued market and, presumably, an impending market decline would suggest increasing cash, decreasing the beta of the portfolio, or, again, a combination of the two. To determine how much adjustment to the portfolio is warranted to take advantage of this extra return opportunity, however, a more formal analytical framework is required, which we can illustrate as follows.

To begin with, we can assume that an investor engaging in market timing would desire to maintain the same trade-off between risk and return as when maintaining the asset mix constant over time—that is, not engaging in market timing. We can express this quantitatively as the desire to maintain a constant ratio of expected return in excess of the risk-free rate to the standard deviation of return. Also known as the Sharpe ratio, it can be expressed as

$$\text{Sharpe ratio} = \frac{\text{expected return} - \text{risk-free rate}}{\text{standard deviation of return squared}} \tag{2}$$

To illustrate, we can again use our long-term expected return of 13 percent and forecast standard deviation of 18 percent for the market, along with an assumed risk-free rate of 6 percent. We will assume that the organization not only bases its longer-term forecast on this data, but also uses it as a forecast for the forthcoming year—that is, the assumed data remains the same year by year. We will call the ratio of return to risk derived from this data the "no special information" ratio and use it as a benchmark. Using the assumed data, the ratio becomes[4]

$$\frac{\text{Long-term expected return} - \text{risk-free rate}}{\text{Standard deviation of return squared}} = \frac{13 - 6}{18^2} = 0.0216$$

To illustrate market timing, we can refer again to the organization that views the market as moderately overvalued. Recall from the prior section that with a predictive accuracy of 0.10, its raw 16 percent deviation forecast $F(D)$ should be adjusted to $0.10(-16)$ for an expected deviation $E(D)$ of -1.6 percent. Given this, the portfolio manager should adjust his beta in such a way as to maintain the "no special information" ratio of excess expected return to variance, which in the example is 0.0216. If we assume that the one-year forecast does not significantly affect the standard deviation, the appropriate new beta level can be approximated by the ratio of the forecast one-year expected return to the "no special

---

[4]This calculation assumes that the stock portfolio has a market sensitivity (beta) of 1 and carries no specific risk.

information" long-term excess expected return:[5]

$$\beta = \frac{E(R_m) - R_f - E(D)}{E(R_m) - R_f} = \frac{13 - 6 - 1.6}{13 - 6} = 0.77 \qquad (3)$$

The formula thus calls for a reduction of the beta for the portfolio from the prior assumed level of 1.00 to 0.77. The formula represents a formal rationale for why an organization that considers the market extremely overvalued is unlikely (and unjustified in doing so) to go to a 100 percent cash position, which reduces the beta to zero. The rather modest adjustment in the beta derives, in turn, from the fact that the return deviation was adjusted for imperfect forecasting ability. It also reflects an intention to incur no overall added risk in pursuit of greater return—that is, maintain the "no special information" ratio of excess expected return to variance.

CYCLICAL BEHAVIOR OF THE MARKET

Table 9-7 shows the performance of the S&P 500 in rising and falling market periods—bull and bear markets, if you will. The table shows the duration of the rising or falling markets and the percentage change in the index over those time spans. Note that since World War II there have been twelve market declines, which, from the late 1960s to the early 1980s, have been more severe and prolonged than in the earlier and latter periods. Correspondingly, the rising, or bull, markets were more prolonged in the earlier and latter periods than in the intervening period. Keep in mind that when these broad market movements occur, virtually all stocks are affected at least to a certain degree. Particularly, in a long bull market, virtually all stocks experience some appreciation, but in a long bear market, virtually all stocks experience some decline.

The changing behavior of the market has relevance to the ease of implementing a strategy of tactical asset allocation. For example, operating with TAA strategies would have been quite difficult during the 1950s and early 1960s. This period of unusually favorable market experience produced returns that were high on average and market declines that were relatively short-lived (averaging only nine months in length, with the longest being fifteen months). Investors attempting to forecast the market and recommending selling would have had to have been quite nimble to successfully time a sale and repurchase in the space of nine months. This problem would have been especially severe for large investors because substantial time is needed to establish positions. On the other hand, the market declines of eighteen months in 1969–1970 and twenty-one months in 1973–1974 were more severe and protracted than in the previous period. Funds attempting to protect against a market decline would have had greater opportunity to successfully time a sale and repurchase over a period of eighteen to twenty-one months than in the nine-month interval of the earlier period.

---

[5]This approximation is so because the required condition is

$$\beta_p = \frac{E(R_m) - R_f + E(D)}{\text{Variance of portfolio}} = \frac{E(R_m) - R_f}{\text{Var}(D)} = \frac{13 - 6}{324} = 0.0216$$

If $\text{Var}(P) = \beta_p^2 \text{Var}(D)$, the equality condition is met by allowing β_p to take on a value equal to the ratio of the forecast risk premium over the "no special information" risk premium.

TABLE 9-7
Major bear and bull markets, 1929–1990, and performance of the S&P 500

Dates	Duration, months	Change, %
Sept. 1929–June 1932	33	−84.80
June 1932–Feb. 1934	20	137.30
Feb. 1934–Mar. 1935	13	−25.70
Mar. 1935–Feb. 1937	23	115.30
Feb. 1937–Apr. 1938	14	−45.30
Apr. 1938–Oct. 1939	18	30.40
Oct. 1939–Apr. 1942	30	−39.20
Apr. 1942–May 1946	49	138.50
May 1946–June 1949	37	−25.30
June 1949–Jan. 1953	43	87.40
Jan. 1953–Sept. 1953	8	−11.10
Sept. 1953–July 1956	34	109.60
July 1956–Dec. 1957	17	−17.30
Dec. 1957–July 1959	19	48.10
July 1959–Oct. 1960	15	−10.10
Oct. 1960–Dec. 1961	14	33.50
Dec. 1961–Oct. 1962	10	−21.70
Oct. 1962–Jan. 1966	39	66.10
Jan. 1966–Oct. 1966	9	−17.30
Oct. 1966–Dec. 1968	26	38.10
Dec. 1968–May 1970	17	−28.60
May 1970–Dec. 1972	18	55.20
Dec. 1972–Sept. 1974	21	−46.60
Sept. 1974–Dec. 1976	27	53.80
Dec. 1976–Mar. 1978	15	−15.10
Mar. 1978–Nov. 1980	32	52.00
Nov. 1980–July 1982	20	−19.00
July 1982–Oct. 1983	15	53.30
Oct. 1983–July 1984	9	−10.00
July 1984–Aug. 1987	37	118.00
Aug. 1987–Dec. 1987	4	−26.80
Dec. 1987–June 1990	30	49.60
June 1990–Oct. 1990	4	−14.80

The impact of differing market environments on the opportunity to use market forecasts profitably is illustrated by the data in Table 9-8, which shows hypothetical fund performance over two peak-to-peak market cycles. The first cycle includes a relatively short bear market (nine months) and should be representative of market forecasting results within the longer-term (1953–1968) favorable equity environment. The second cycle includes the eighteen-month bear market of 1969–1970 and should be representative of potential results in the more difficult equity markets of the 1970s.

First, assume that a fund can position up to 25 percent of its assets in cash and the remainder is invested in equities represented by the S&P 500. Further assume that the fund can act on a forecast of market peaks and troughs (1) with a lead of two quarters, (2) with a lead of one quarter, (3) precisely at the peak or trough, (4) with a lag of one quarter, and (5) with a lag of two quarters. Table 9-8 shows the percentage added to the fund performance

TABLE 9-8
Hypothetical fund performance in two peak-to-peak market cycles, %

	1/1/66–12/31/68		1/1/69–12/31/72	
	Return	Added return	Return	Added return
S&P 500 performance (buy and hold)	23.90	—	29.50	—
Fund performance (cash-equity transfer)				
Two-quarter lead	24.20	0.30	34.70	5.20
One-quarter lead	26.70	2.80	36.00	6.50
Precise positioning	30.40	6.50	44.20	14.70
One-quarter lag	27.70	3.80	38.40	8.90
Two-quarter lag	22.60	−1.30	34.00	4.50

under each of the five lead-lag positioning assumptions for the two peak-to-peak market cycle periods.

Note that the full-cycle return of the S&P 500 was approximately the same in both periods, with the latter period showing a somewhat greater return. A shift from a fully invested position in equities to 25 percent cash at the peak and a redeployment of cash to equities at the market trough would, however, have been relatively more beneficial in the latter cycle than in the earlier one. Cash management would have provided an incremental return of 14.7 percent versus 6.5 percent for the one-quarter lead. In addition, cash management activities would have provided higher returns in the latter cycle than in the earlier cycle under all lead-lag assumptions. Finally, there would have been positive benefits to cash management under all lead-lag assumptions in the latter cycle, whereas in the earlier cycle, the two-quarter lag would have had a negative impact.

FORECASTING THE MARKET

There are any number of techniques for forecasting the market. The particular method, or variety of methods, used depends on the preference of the forecaster. The success in using the technique or techniques depends, in turn, on the skill of the forecaster in interpreting the data. The three major categories of techniques are (1) valuation-based methods, (2) business cycle and monetary indicators, and (3) technical indicators. We will comment on each of these categories and illustrate some specific methods in the rest of this chapter.

Valuation Indicators

One of the more useful kinds of indicators of market value derives from the market line described in Chapter 6. Recall that the market line provides an indication of the overall level of stock prices, as well as of the risk-return trade-off in the market. We can simply compare current market returns with those in other periods to develop some perspective on the current level. It is more useful, however, to compare the current absolute returns with the return on alternative investments, such as bonds and Treasury bills, to develop a relative attractiveness measure commonly referred to as a risk-premium valuation indicator. In addition, we may also want to compare the return with current inflation rates to assess what sort of real return is being offered by stocks and how that return has varied in the past.

We can evaluate the longer-range productivity of the risk premium (expected stock returns less short-term rates) valuation indicator by reference to the data shown in Table 9-9. This table shows the relationship—measured over the 1951 to 1990 period—between the risk premium and subsequent stock returns versus Treasury bills. Note that the risk premium is segmented into seven brackets ranging from a low of 2 percent or less to a high of 10 percent or greater. Also shown are the number of months over the period in which the premium was in a particular bracket. Note that the risk premium exceeded 10 percent for only 10 months of the period and was at the low extreme of less than 2 percent for only 25 months. The risk premium was more frequently observed and evenly distributed across the brackets between 2 percent and 10 percent.

The table also shows the stock returns realized for one, three, and twelve months subsequent to the observed risk premium, as well as the percentage of times that the realized return was positive. Note that when the risk premium exceeded 10 percent, subsequent stock returns were significantly large and positive, with the percentage positive increasing from 80 percent after one month to 100 percent after one year for the period of measurement. Conversely, for months in which the risk premium was low (2 percent or less), the subsequent stock returns were negative and increasingly negative as the time period increased from one month to one year. Correspondingly, the percentage of positive subsequent returns was low, implying a high probability of subpar returns when the risk premium is low.

The data in the table also indicates that there is a strong positive relationship between the size of the risk premium and subsequent stock returns. Realized returns were consistently higher as the risk premium increased, and conversely, the realized returns were lower, or negative, as the risk premium was lower. Using the information coefficient method, we measured the relationship between the risk premium and subsequent one-month returns for the 1981–1990 period to derive an IC of 0.18 that is positive and highly significant.

Market Implied Returns

The scenario framework itself can provide some immediate perspective in evaluating the current attractiveness of the market. Recall that the scenario approach entails determining scenarios, developing the capital-market implications of the scenarios, and assigning the

TABLE 9-9
Risk premium and realized return (1951–1990)

Risk premium range	Number of monthly observations	Average subsequent excess return (stock return less T-bill return)			Percentage of positive excess returns (stock return less T-bill return)		
		1 mo.	3 mo.	12 mo.	1 mo.	3 mo.	12 mo.
> 10%	10	2.5	6.8	26.1	80	80	100
8–9.9	64	1.9	4.8	16.7	66	78	89
6–7.9	102	0.5	2	6.1	57	63	63
5–5.9	64	0.7	1.6	4.8	61	70	67
4–4.9	107	0.4	1.8	2.7	60	64	62
2–3.9	96	−0.1	−1.4	2.8	48	42	60
< 2%	25	−1.8	−1.7	−6.9	32	36	40
Total	468	0.5	1.5	5.7	57	61	66

Source: Robert Arnott and Frank Fabozzi: *Active Asset Allocation,* 2nd ed., Probus Publishing, Chicago, IL, 1992.

probabilities of occurrence of the scenarios. Given this data, we can determine the expected return on assets under consideration; in our example, we determined the expected return of stocks, bonds, and Treasury bills over a four-year holding period.

We can, however, reverse this process by first assessing the expected return for the asset, given current price levels and consensus-input estimates, and then determining what the market seems to be assigning as probabilities to the different scenarios. For example, at year-end 1993, as we indicated previously, the S&P 500 was providing a yield of 3.0 percent. The growth rate implied by current return on equity and retention rate was generally in the 8-percent range, and adding these together (yield plus growth) provided an implied return of 11.0 percent compared with the 12.1-percent return developed from the scenario forecast.

Table 9-10 shows the five economic scenarios described earlier, the return for stocks associated with each scenario, and the probabilities of occurrence that lead to a scenario-related expected return of 12.1 percent for stocks. The final column shows a set of probabilities that may represent the weighting of scenarios implied by the return of 11 percent indicated by the alternative method of forecasting. Note that these implied probabilities give less weight to more-favorable scenarios and greater weight to less-favorable scenarios. If this implied weighting were to seem particularly unreasonable, the course of action might be to increase the stock weights in the portfolio from its longer-term target to take advantage of an apparent undervaluation.

Economic and Technical Indicators

Use of business cycle and monetary indicators to forecast the market is based on the fact that there should be some relationship between economic activity and stock returns. This relationship derives from the fact that dividends and the pricing of dividends are the fundamental source of value for the market. The dividend-paying ability of corporations and the discount rate for dividends should, in turn, be a function of general economic conditions.

Table 9-11 shows the relationship of stock returns to real GNP, inflation (CPI), and profits over the two quite different economic and market environments of the 1953–1968 and 1969–1974 periods. Note that stocks showed an average annual return of 14 percent in the earlier period but an average loss of 3 percent in the latter period. The change in the return behavior of stocks might be attributed to a change in the general economic environment between the two periods. In particular, inflation increased and interest rates rose substantially, increasing the discount rate for dividends. Correspondingly, corporate profitability did not keep pace, leading to a below-average rate of dividend growth.

TABLE 9-10
Stock return and probability of scenario

Scenario	Scenario related return	Original probability of scenario	Consensus probability of scenario
High growth/low inflation	17%	0.35	0.25
Disinflation/low growth	12	0.30	0.35
Deflation	2	0.05	0.10
Reflation	10	0.20	0.20
Stagflation	4	0.10	0.10
Expected return		12.10%	11.05%

TABLE 9-11
Stock returns and economic variables, %

	Compound annual trend	
	1954–1968	1969–1974
S&P 500 (total return)	14.00	−3.40
GNP (real)	3.90	3.20
Inflation (CPI)	1.70	5.60
Dividends	5.70	3.40
Interest rates		
Treasury bills	3.10	6.10
AAA corporates	4.30	7.60

Economic indicators are used to anticipate changes on a shorter-term basis. Some types of economic indicators used in this regard are (1) the rate of change of corporate profits, (2) growth in the real money supply, and (3) the GNP gap. We should note, however, that relating economic data to stock prices on a short-term basis is much more problematic than assessing longer-term relationships because of the leads and lags in the relationships and their variance over time.

Though use of economic indicators has theoretical support, technical indicators are mainly based on empirically derived relationships. One indicator that seems to have been successful in the past is a simple relation of recent returns to past returns on the market. When returns had been high in recent times, the market was likely to regress to a lower level, but the converse was true when returns had been low in the recent period. The framework of a four-year period seems to work best, and this period may be related to the business cycle, which has averaged about four years over time. There are, of course, myriad other technical indicators, but discussing them would be beyond the scope of this book.

COMPOSITE STOCK MARKET FORECASTING

Just as in the case of stock selection reviewed in the prior chapter, individual predictors of stock market performance can be combined into a composite indicator of market performance. Again, one of the conditions for combining indicators is that the individual components have predictive power; that is, the predictors have demonstrated positive ICs. Combining also works best when the individual predictors show a low degree of intercorrelation; optimally the cross-correlation between predictors would be zero or insignificantly different from zero. This concept is similar to the multi-index model introduced in Chapter 4, which improved the results of the single-index model (CAPM).

Two predictors that have been shown to be useful for combining into a composite are (1) the expected real return for stocks and (2) an index of business conditions. The expected real return for stocks is a valuation indicator that adjusts the expected return for stocks for potential inflation to derive a real return expectation. The business conditions index is a composite of individual economic indicators that attempt to capture underlying factors that influence the cyclical behavior of the stock market, such as interest rate changes, monetary policy, liquidity conditions, and earnings changes.

Table 9-12 shows data for these predictors generated by analyzing information from the 1951–1990 period. Note that both predictors showed ICs that were positive and highly

TABLE 9-12
Combining stock market predictors (1951–1990)

Individual predictor:	
Expected real return—stocks	IC = 0.14
Business conditions indicator	IC = 0.25
Cross correlation:	
Expected real return and business conditions	0.01
Combined predictor	IC = 0.28

Source: Robert Arnott and Frank Fabozzi: *Active Asset Allocation,* 2nd ed., Probus Publishing, Chicago, IL 1992.

significant, with the business conditions indicator showing predictive power that was about twice as great as the valuation predictor. The two predictors also showed cross-correlation of 0.01 over the period, indicating a usefully low degree of dependence between the two. When combined, the two-indicator composite showed an IC of 0.28 that was 10 percent higher in predictive power than the higher individual business conditions predictor with an IC of 0.25.

The combining process in this case was productive because the predictors met the conditions of showing high predictive power individually along with a low degree of interdependence; the predictors had close to cross-sectional independence. In combining the two, we derived the optimal weighting for the composite by simple regression to indicate a 0.65 weighting for the business conditions index and a 0.35 weighting for the valuation indicator. This approximate two-to-one weighting relationship is in line with expectations that indicators should be combined in line with the relative predictive power of the indicator; the business conditions indicator was approximately twice as powerful as the valuation indicator.

ASSET MIX MANAGEMENT

In managing an asset mix over time, investors can follow three general approaches. The first is to determine the appropriate asset mix, initiate it, and leave it alone over the appropriate holding period—say three to five years. This approach might be termed a buy-and-hold approach, and it is inactive with respect to rebalancing over time. Investors who have long-term planning horizons and are satisfied with a strategic asset mix might find this the most appropriate way of managing the mix over the holding period. This approach has minimum transaction costs and management fees, but the risk of a poor forecast or no reaction to a changing environment increases.

The other two approaches are active and require periodic rebalancing and attendant transactions for the portfolio over time. One approach—commonly termed constant-mix—is designed to maintain a constant proportionate representation of assets in the portfolio over time. For example, the investor may desire to maintain the stock–bond mix at a consistent 60/40 ratio over time. Maintaining this mix requires periodic rebalancing and transactions as relative asset prices change. Market timing (that is, tactical asset allocation) can be viewed as a variant of a constant-mix approach because it attempts to adjust for relative changes in asset values by redeploying from the higher-valued asset back to the lower-valued asset.

These strategies reallocate based on a valuation appraisal rather than merely a mechanical rule, and they presumably offer greater opportunity to enhance the asset allocation result.

The third general approach to managing a portfolio over time could be termed portfolio insurance. Such approaches are inherently the most dynamic and require the greatest degree of rebalancing and attendant transactions. The intent of these approaches is to provide participation in the high return to the stock market, while at the same time limiting the extent of downside risk. Effectively executing this type of approach can be a significantly practical problem.

In the following sections, we describe and compare these three general approaches to managing the asset mix over time. Each has its own distinctive character and offers certain benefits for an investor. None of the three approaches is, however, clearly superior to the other. We will see that merits of an individual approach depend greatly on the type of market environment encountered and the risk profile of the investor. One approach may be particularly suitable for a period of volatility but might not fit a strongly trending market. Because the market character changes over time, approaches will vary with respect to suitability. Determining the type of market environment likely to transpire is, of course, a daunting task in itself. Investors are probably best served by choosing an approach that fits their longer-term investing style best.

Buy-and-Hold Strategies

A buy-and-hold strategy is characterized by an initial asset mix that is bought and then held over time. These strategies purposely do not undertake active rebalancing programs, regardless of what happens to relative values. They are easy strategies to operate and also to analyze, and they provide perspective on more complex approaches. To illustrate this strategy type and others, we will utilize payoff diagrams similar to ones used to describe the attributes of various option-based strategies. For our purposes, the payoff diagram relates the portfolio performance of the strategy over time to the performance of the stock market over the same period.

Figure 9-3 shows the payoff diagram for a buy-and-hold strategy that has a mix of 60 percent stocks and 40 percent money market instruments (60/40 mix), with a total portfolio value of $100 when the stock market level is $100 as well. Note that the portfolio value increases as a function of stock market value and that the relationship between portfolio value and market value is linear. The slope of the line depends on the amount invested in stocks, and in this case the slope is 0.6; portfolio increases in value by 60 cents for every dollar increase in stock market value. The minimum value for the portfolio is indicated by the intercept, which in this case is a $40 value in money market instruments, and indicates the downside risk for the portfolio (e.g., stock value equals zero).

At the same time, note that the upside potential for the strategy is unlimited; the strategy participates in continued upward movements in the stock market. Correspondingly, the greater the initial percentage invested in stocks, the better the performance of a buy-and-hold strategy will be when stocks outperform money market instruments, and the worse the performance of a buy-and-hold strategy will be when stocks underperform money markets. Finally, note that the relative weighting of the asset classes in the portfolio will change as the market varies over time. At higher market levels the percentage weighting in stocks will be greater, whereas at lower market levels the percentage weighting will be less and is a natural outcome of not rebalancing.

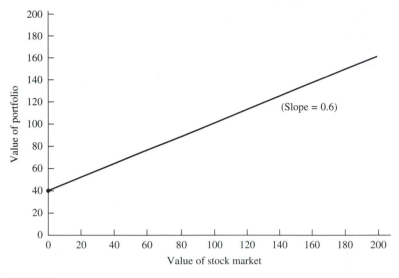

FIGURE 9-3
Payoff diagram, 60/40 stock/money market mix, buy-and-hold strategy.

Constant-Mix Strategy

In contrast to a buy-and-hold strategy, the constant-mix strategy maintains a consistent proportionate representation of assets in the portfolio, as, for example, a 60/40 stock–money market mix. In order to maintain this mix, the investor needs to rebalance the portfolio as the market varies over time. When the market rises in value, the proportionate representation of stocks in the portfolio will rise; so the investor needs to sell stocks as the market rises and reinvest in money markets. Conversely, the investor needs to draw down on the money market assets and reinvest in stocks as the market declines, because stocks will have become a smaller proportion of the portfolio.

Figure 9-4 shows that this process of selling stocks as the market rises and buying stocks as the market declines will result in a payoff pattern that is curvilinear, as compared to the linear payoff pattern for the buy-and-hold strategy. At higher market levels, the constant-mix strategy returns less than the buy-and-hold because the proportion in the higher-return asset has been reduced by the enforced selling of stocks as the market rises. Conversely, the return to the constant-mix strategy is less at lower market levels because of an enforced program of purchasing stocks as the market declines. In other words, in markets that exhibit a strong trend up or down, a constant-mix strategy will be inferior to a buy-and-hold strategy; profits are foregone in the up moves, and losses are compounded on the downside.

However, the constant-mix strategy can be beneficial when the markets are volatile and there are many reversals; upmoves are quickly followed by downmoves, and vice versa. To illustrate, we can assume the market declines from $100 to $80, at which point the constant-mix investor rebalances by buying stock but the buy-and-hold investor does nothing. If the market reverses back to the initial level of $100, the buy-and-hold investor will be in the same position as before, but the constant-mix investor will be at a higher level; the constant-mix investor has added shares to the portfolio through rebalancing at a lower price level and now owns more shares at the current $100 price level than before.

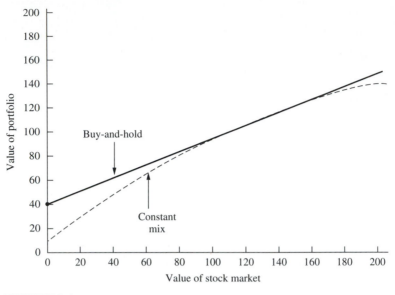

FIGURE 9-4
Payoff diagram, constant-mix strategy, 60/40 mix.

Figure 9-5 illustrates this reversal effect by way of a payoff diagram for both strategies. Line AB shows that the value of the portfolio for the buy-and-hold investor declines to $80 at point B but returns to its original value of $100 when the market rises back to its original level. The buy-and-hold investor simply moves up and down a single straight line in the payoff diagram. Conversely, for the constant-mix investor, the slope of the payoff line will change with each rebalancing that changes the number of shares of stock held. In this instance, both types of investors followed line AB as the market declined, but with additional shares from rebalancing at point B, the constant-mix investor followed the more steeply sloping line BC upward as the market rose.

Portfolio Insurance

A third category of strategies for allocating assets dynamically are those that we might broadly categorize as portfolio insurance–related. One simplified version of portfolio insurance that also has practical implications is known as constant-proportion portfolio insurance (CPPI). It is much simpler to implement than the more well-known option-based portfolio insurance and, for our purposes, is also easier to illustrate. We begin by noting that this simplified portfolio insurance strategy takes the following general form:

$$\text{Exposure to stocks} = m(\text{Total portfolio value} - \text{Floor value})$$

In implementing this strategy, the investor determines a minimum amount that represents a floor value for the portfolio. The difference between the total portfolio value and the floor represents the cushion that effectively provides a protection for the floor value. Constant-proportion portfolio insurance strategies are those with multipliers (m) greater than one. Given a multiplier and floor value, we can determine the exposure or amount to be invested in stocks by way of the formula.

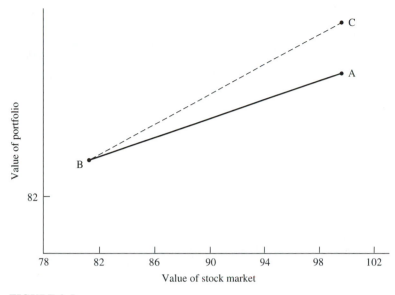

FIGURE 9-5
Constant-mix vs. buy-and-hold 60/40 mix. (*Source:* Andre Perold and William Sharpe: "Dynamic Strategies for Asset Allocation," *Financial Analysts Journal,* Jan–Feb 1988.)

To illustrate, we can assume a portfolio with a value of $100 and a desired floor of $75, so that the initial cushion is then $25. Assuming a multiplier (m) of two, we derive an initial investment in stocks of $50 (2 × $25 cushion) and a resultant 50/50 mix of stocks and money market instruments. Assuming a 20 percent decline in the market from 100 to 80, the investor's stocks will fall from $50 to $40, and the total portfolio value will be $90. At that point, the cushion will be $15 (= $90 − $75), so that the appropriate stock position becomes $30 using the CPPI rule (2 × $15). In order to attain the desired position, the investor needs to sell $10 of stock and invest the proceeds in money market instruments. Conversely, when the market rises, stocks should be bought by reducing the balance in money market instruments.

As with portfolio insurance strategies generally, the CPPI strategy is programmed to sell stocks as they fall and buy stocks as they rise. Under the CPPI strategy, the portfolio is expected to do at least as well as the floor, even in a severely declining market; such a strategy puts more and more into money market instruments as stocks decline, reducing the exposure to stocks to zero as the portfolio value approaches the floor. This, of course, assumes that the investor can rebalance at appropriate times during a market decline. Precipitous declines in the market or lack of liquidity may short circuit these processes and degrade the benefits of such "insurance"-based strategies. An example of such a decline occurred in the market crash of October 1987.

Figure 9-6 shows that the CPPI process can be characterized as a curvilinear one, as again compared to the linear relationship of a buy-and-hold strategy. At market extremes, the CPPI strategy does especially well relative to the buy-and-hold strategy. At high levels of the market, the strategy effectively leverages up on stock (through the multiplier effect) by buying progressively more as the market rises. Conversely, the strategy reduces stock more

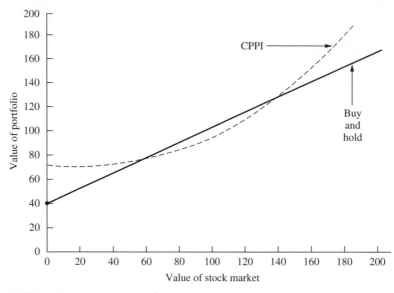

FIGURE 9-6
Payoff diagram: CPPI and buy-and-hold. (*Source:* Andre Perold and William
Sharpe: "Dynamic Strategies for Asset Allocation," *Financial Analysts Journal,*
Jan–Feb 1988.)

rapidly through this multiplier effect as the market declines, which dampens the impact of
the decline compared to a buy-and-hold strategy.

On the other hand, in a trendless or flat market, the CPPI strategy will do relatively
poorly because of market reversals that are generally characteristic of such markets. Reversals are harmful because of the need to sell stock on a market decline but repurchase when
the market rebounds. Correspondingly, a market rise would require a purchase of stock but
a subsequent sale as the market reverts back to its original level. Unlike the constant-mix
strategy, the CPPI strategy will be buying fewer shares at higher prices and selling more
shares at lower prices to result in a lower net portfolio value at the end of such a period.

Strategy Characteristics

Table 9-13 compares the characteristics of the three dynamic asset allocation strategies: (1)
buy-and-hold, (2) constant-proportion, and (3) portfolio insurance along several dimensions.
It shows the rebalancing action required when the market rises as well as when it declines.

TABLE 9-13
Dynamic asset allocation strategies: comparative characteristics

Strategy	Market decline/rise	Payoff pattern	Favored market environment	Degree liquidity required
Buy-and-hold	No action	Linear	Bull market	Little
Constant-proportion	Buy declines Sell rises	Concave	Volatile and trendless	Moderate
Portfolio insurance	Sell declines Buy rises	Convex	Strong trend	High

It also indicates the type of payoff pattern that is descriptive of the strategy. Third, it shows which market environments are favorable or unfavorable for the strategy. Finally, it indicates market liquidity required for effective execution of such strategies.

Note that both constant-proportion and portfolio insurance are active strategies that require action as the market moves, whereas the buy-and-hold strategy by definition requires no action. The buy-and-hold strategy sets up a linear payoff pattern, whereas the two active strategies generate curvilinear patterns. The process of buying stocks on declines and selling on rises results in a concave payoff pattern for the constant proportion strategy, whereas the process of selling on market declines and buying on rises results in a convex payoff pattern for the portfolio insurance strategy.

A strong bull market favors the buy-and-hold strategy as well as the portfolio insurance strategy, which provides greater protection in a downturn. Volatile, trendless markets are most favorable to the constant-proportion strategy but detrimental to portfolio insurance. Buy-and-hold strategies require liquidity only to initiate a position, whereas constant-proportion strategies need liquidity because trading is likely to be persistent over time. Portfolio insurance is by nature likely to require the greatest liquidity.

We can further observe that any strategy giving a convex payoff pattern is representative of the purchase of portfolio insurance, but strategies such as the constant-mix that give concave patterns represent the sale of insurance. Concave and convex strategies may be seen as mirror images of one another on either side of buy-and-hold strategies. A "buyer" of a convex strategy is correspondingly a "seller" of a concave strategy, and vice versa. When the portfolio of one who buys a convex strategy is combined with the portfolio of the seller of that strategy, the result is a buy-and-hold position.

The fact that convex and concave strategies are mirror images of one another implies that the more demand there is for one of these strategies, the more costly its implementation will become and the less healthy it may be for markets generally. Such a development did, in fact, occur during the period prior to the market crash of October 1987, when portfolio insurance strategies became popular and a significant component of the market. These "convex" strategies are inherently volatile and demand significant liquidity because of the trading demanded. Though these strategies did not "cause" the market crash, it is likely that they exacerbated the market turbulence at that period.

CONCLUSION

This chapter has indicated that the portfolio analysis model described in Chapter 2 provides the explicit framework for determining an asset allocation that best meets the longer-term goals of the investor. We have also explained the scenario approach to developing risk-and-return inputs for asset classes. This approach places the heaviest burden of estimation on the user, but it has the greatest potential of providing the most useful input for the analysis; it is an analytical technique that can be applied to many other areas of forecasting.

We then discussed tactical asset allocation, which has a shorter-term orientation with the objective of improving the portfolio return by opportunistically shifting the weighting of the assets from their longer-term allocation. Here we described an analytical framework that explicitly considers our assessed degree of forecasting ability and thereby establishes the proper amount to "bet" on this activity. We further described those analytical tools that might be useful in assessing the relative attractiveness of the overall market. The review in the final part of the chapter showed that tactical asset allocation can also be considered as a natural counterpart to portfolio insurance and, along with a buy-and-hold policy, these represent the three major ways of managing a portfolio mix over time.

APPENDIX A
ASSET/LIABILITY OPTIMIZATION

In the prior sections, we described methods of developing an optimal allocation of assets and illustrated three major asset classes: (1) domestic equities, (2) domestic bonds, and (3) money market instruments. In a sense, development of an allocation by analyzing asset class returns alone is analogous to a focus on the asset side of an investment plan's balance sheet. Investment plans, however, also have obligations that need to be funded by the assets of the plan. These obligations might be construed as representing the liability side of the plan's "balance sheet."

These obligations or liabilities should be well defined and explicitly stated as such for the investment plan. For example, the primary purpose of pension plans is to fund pensions of employees, either currently retired or anticipated to retire at some future date. Actuaries make explicit, albeit not always accurate, estimates of the magnitude of these obligations, which are, in turn, designated and reported as liabilities of the plan. Endowment plans have obligations to fund educational programs and needs over longer periods, and foundations need to provide funding for programs of interest over longer periods as well. Though the obligations of endowments and foundations may be less well defined, more difficult to estimate, and more flexible with respect to the level of funding than in the case of pension plans, these obligations are nevertheless real and represent a kind of liability of the plan.

In those cases in which the asset portfolio is meant to fund a specified liability schedule, such as pension plans, the appropriate portfolio for optimization should comprise both assets and liabilities. The focus then becomes the surplus, which is the difference between the market value of the assets and the present value of the liabilities. As a consequence, both asset returns and liability returns need to be considered in the analysis.[6]

Though the returns and volatility of asset classes such as stocks and bonds are readily apparent with data and empirical studies to document performance, liabilities are also volatile but relatively less apparent.[7] We illustrate this volatility for a hypothetical pension plan that is funding for a mix of 60 percent retired and 40 percent active employees. The ratio of retired to active employees will vary over a wide spectrum depending on the maturity of the plan; mature companies woulld have a higher ratio of retired employees, whereas emerging, rapidly growing companies would have a greater ration of active employees. For this plan, the 60 percent of retired employees is at the higher end of the retired /active spectrum and would be more representative of a mature company.

Figure 9-A1 shows the year-by-year schedule of estimated payments for retirees (both current and projected), for this hypothetical plan from the current time and over a 70-year

---

[6]Martin Leibowitz was the first to indicate the need to consider both and developed the notion of surplus optimization. See Leibowitz, Martin, and Roy Henrikson, "Portfolio Optimization Within a Surplus Framework," *Financial Analysts Journal,* March–April 1988, pp. 43–51.

[7]Leibowitz, Martin, in an article "Pension Asset Allocation through Surplus Management," elucidated this concept of developing these returns.

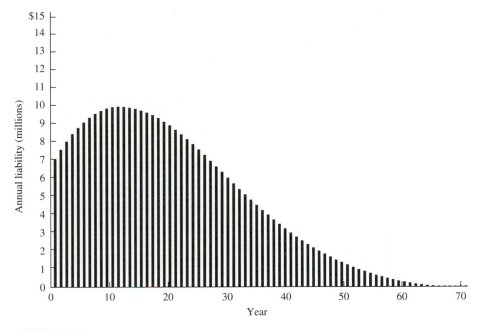

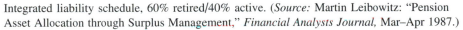

FIGURE 9-A1
Integrated liability schedule, 60% retired/40% active. (*Source:* Martin Leibowitz: "Pension
Asset Allocation through Surplus Management," *Financial Analysts Journal,* Mar–Apr 1987.)

period. Actuaries make these projections based on such factors as (1) the size of the
workforce—both current and expected future level, (2) compensation levels and expected
growth based on productivity and inflation trends, and (3) current and expected benefit
levels.

The present value of this schedule of payments can be determined by discounting it
at an appropriate discount rate, with the total liability varying with the rate of discount.
Figure 9-A2 shows the present value of the liability schedule at various interest rates across
a relevant range. Note that at an 8 percent interest rate, the liabilities of the pension plan
aggregate $100 million. This present-value cost can be interpreted as the dollar amount of
assets required to fund the liabilities fully when invested at the specified interest rate, which
in this illustrative case is 8 percent.

As interest rates change, the aggregate level of liabilities, or alternatively the cost of
the pension payments, will change as well. Again note from Figure 9-A2 that a decline in
interest rates from 8 to 7 percent would result in an $11 million increase in the present-
value cost of these liabilities. This increase constitutes an 11 percent growth in liability
costs. Alternatively, we could refer to this 11 percent rate of increase in costs as a "liability
return." Similarly, increases in interest rates would lead to decreases in liabilities and, hence,
the cost of liabilities.

The liability return represents a return threshold that the assets must match in order to
maintain a given surplus level of assets less liabilities. If the assets and the liabilities are
equal at the beginning of the period, the surplus is zero, and the asset returns must equal
the liability return in order for the asset and liability values to remain even. If the surplus is

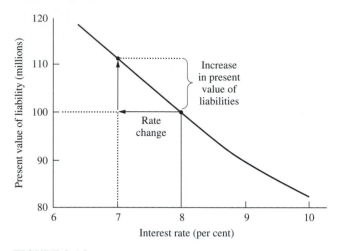

FIGURE 9-A2
Liability return. (*Source:* Martin Leibowitz: "Pension Asset
Allocation through Surplus Management," *Financial Analysts
Journal,* Mar–Apr 1987.)

not zero (if there is a positive surplus or a negative deficit), the asset returns must be equal
in dollar terms to the liability returns in order to maintain a constant dollar surplus. In other
words, for the surplus condition to be preserved, the asset return times the asset base must
equal the liability return times the liability base.

Generally, actuaries discount liability schedules to present value at a rate that is related
to long-term bond rates; as a result, in a period of rising long-term interest rates, pension
plan liabilities will decline due to the fact that they are discounted at higher rates. In such
periods, there will be positive liability returns, whereas in periods of declining interest rates,
there will be negative liability returns because projected liabilities are discounted at a lower
rate. In this framework, the risk to the pension plan is a failure of asset values to match these
liability changes, which is especially so in periods of rapidly declining interest rates when
liabilities show the greatest increase due to the discounting relationship.

Since the risk to a plan is an adverse change in the magnitude of the liabilities, the
ideal "risk-free" asset moves in tandem with changes in plan liabilities. In the case of a
pension plan that has liabilities tied to changes in long-term interest rates, the asset that
moves most closely with changes in "liability returns" are long-term bonds.[8] As a result,
pension plans consider long-term bonds to represent the risk-free asset rather than short-
term Treasury bills or money market instruments, as we assumed in our discussion of an
asset-only optimization.

Figure 9-A3 illustrates the difference between the optimal portfolios generated, depending on whether asset returns are only considered or transformed into their returns
relative to the changes in the value of the relevant liabilities.[9] For this purpose, we consider

---

[8]Technically, the matching instruments should be a portfolio immunized to have the same duration as the liabilities.
For simplicity, we assume that the returns of an appropriate long-term bond will provide the matching asset.

[9]As an analogy,we mignht consider the asset to be one where the investor is required to have a prespecified short
position. The size of the short position (the negative weight) will be the present value of the liabilities.

Panel A   Traditional optimization, 1963–1987

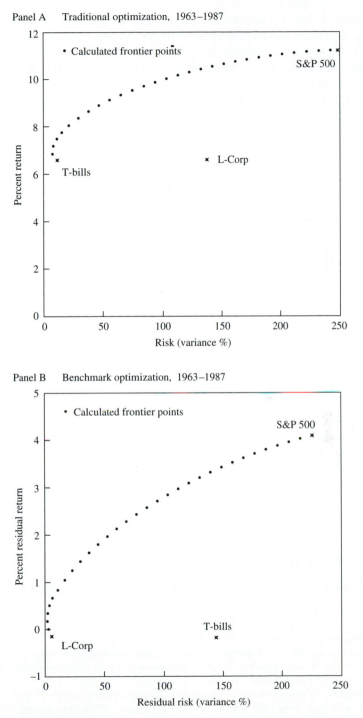

Panel B   Benchmark optimization, 1963–1987

FIGURE 9-A3
(*Source:* Richard Michaud: "Pension Policy and Benchmarks
Optimization," *Investment Management Review,* Spring 1989.)

only three asset classes: (1) common stocks, (2) long-term bonds, and (3) money market instruments. We further assume that common stocks offer the highest expected return and also have the highest risk, as measured by the standard deviation of return. Finally, we assume, somewhat unrealistically but for purposes of illustration, that long-term bonds and money market instruments offer the same expected return.[10]

Panel A in Figure 9-A3 shows an efficient frontier generated by considering risk-return inputs for the three asset classes: stocks, bonds, and money market instruments. Note that the efficient portfolios consist of only stocks and money market instruments. At the lowest risk level money market instruments constitute the total portfolio, but at the highest risk levels equities constitute the total portfolio. Bonds are not part of the efficient mix; money market instruments have the same return as bonds but lower risk, and hence they dominate.

Though money market instruments have the lowest risk in an asset-only optimization, they may well have high risk when liabilities are considered, as illustrated in Panel B of Figure 9-A3. For our example pension fund, long-term bonds or their equivalent become the low-risk asset because this class of assets will match the "returns of the plans liabilities." Money market instruments become more risky because they will not match changes in "liability returns"; the relative riskiness of the two asset classes is reversed. In this case, long-term bonds with a lower risk dominate money market instruments with the same return but higher risk, with respect to liability returns. The efficient frontier now consists of bonds and equities with the low-risk portfolio consisting of bonds alone and the high-risk portfolio again consisting of equities alone. Money market instruments do not enter this solution.

Though we have illustrated asset/liability optimization with respect to the surplus position of pension plans, the concept can be extended to institutions such as thrifts, insurance companies, endowments, and foundation funds in which the liability may not be as well defined. This framework can also be applied to certain managed funds in which performance is determined relative to a well-defined benchmark. As such, the process might well be referred to in a more general sense as "Benchmark Optimization."[11] Whether considered more narrowly as surplus optimization or more generally as benchmark optimization, the procedure is a natural extension of the asset-only optimization framework previously described.

SELECTED REFERENCES

Arnot, Robert, and Frank Fabozzi: *Active Asset Allocation,* 2nd ed., Probus Publishing, Chicago, IL, 1992.

---

[10]Our illustration is with respect to a funded plan where asset value matches liability value so that the plan has a zero surpplus. The analysis needs to be amended somewhat for more of less than fully funded plans. The principles and broad conclusions remain the same.

[11]This term was dubbed by Richard Michaud in an article "Pension Policy and Benchmarks Optimization," *Investment Management Review,* Spring 1989. Michaud indicates that a feature of this approach is the ability to develop optimal asset mix recommendations in an integrated framework that includes capital market expectations, funding status, and stochastic economic linkage between assets and liabilities.

Bakshi, G., and Z. Chen: "Baby Boom, Population Aging, and Capital Markets,"*Journal of Business,* April 1994, pp. 165–202.

Bilsen, John: "The Speculative Efficiency Hypothesis," *Journal of Business,* July 1981, pp. 438–452.

Black, Fischer, and Robert Jones: "Simplifying Portfolio Insurance," *Journal of Portfolio Management,* Fall 1987, pp. 48–51.

Cagan, P.: "Common Stock Values and Inflation—The History Record of Many Countries," *National Bureau Supplement,* National Bureau of Economic Research, New York, 1974.

Campbell, John: "Stock Return and the Term Structure," *Journal of Financial Economics,* June 1987, pp. 373–399.

—— and John Ammer: "What Makes the Stock and Bond Markets? A Variance Decomposition for Long-Term Asset Returns," *Journal of Finance,* March 1993, pp. 3–37.

Chan, Louis: "Consumption, Inflation Risk, and Real Interest Rates: An Empirical Analysis," *Journal of Business,* January 1994, pp. 69–96.

DeBondt, W.F., and R.H. Thaler: "Does the Stock Market Overreact?," *Journal of Finance,* July 1985.

Dietz, Peter: "Setting Objectives and Allocating Assets: The Pension Manager's Dilemma," paper presented at the Spring 1976 seminar of the Institute for Quantitative Research in Finance, Scottsdale, AZ.

Edesess, Michael, and George A. Hambrecht: "Scenario Forecasting: Necessity, Not Choice," *Journal of Portfolio Management,* Spring 1980, pp. 10–15.

Estrella, Arturo, and Gikas Hardouvelis: "The Term Structure as a Predictor of Real Economic Activity," *Journal of Finance,* June 1991, pp. 555–576.

Ezra, D. Don: "Asset Allocation by Surplus Optimization," *Financial Analysts Journal,* January–Febuary 1991, pp. 51–57.

Fama, Eugene: "Stock Returns, Expected Returns, and Real Activity," *Journal of Finance,* September 1990, pp. 1089–1108.

——: "Inflation, Output, and Money," *Journal of Business,* April 1982, pp. 201–232.

—— and Ken French: "Permanent and Temporary Components of Stock Prices," *Journal of Political Economy,* 96–2, 1988, pp. 246–273.

—— and ——: "Dividend Yields and Expected Stock Returns," *Journal of Financial Economics,* October 1988, pp. 3–35.

—— and G. W. Schwert: "Asset Returns and Inflation," *Journal of Financial Economics,* November 1977, pp. 115–146.

Fanning, James: "A Four-Indicator System for Forecasting the Market," *Financial Analysts Journal,* September-October 1971, pp. 49–56.

Farrell, James L., Jr.: "Is Market Timing Likely to Improve Performance?" paper presented at the Spring 1976 seminar of the Institute for Quantitative Research in Finance, Scottsdale, AZ.

——: "Fundamental Forecast and Superior Asset Allocation," *Financial Analysts Journal,* May–June 1989, pp. 32–37.

Ferson, Wayne, and Campbell Harvey: "Sources of Predictability in Portfolio Returns," *Financial Analysts Journal,* May–June 1991, pp. 49–56.

French, K., N. Schwert, and R. Stambrough: "Expected Stock Returns and Volatility," *Journal of Financial Economics,* September 1987, pp. 3–30.

Grant, Dwight: "Market Timing and Portfolio Management," *Journal of Finance,* September 1979, pp. 1119–1131.

Grossman, Sanford: "The Role of Derivatives in Constructing Asset Classes," Institute for Quantitative Research in Finance, Spring Seminar 1994, Palm Beach, FL.

Halvers, Ronald, Thomas Cosimano, and Bill McDonald: "Predicting Stock Returns in an Efficient Market," *Journal of Finance,* September 1990, pp. 1109–1128.

Hill, Joanne, and Frank Jones: "Equity Trading, Program Trading, Portfolio Insurance, Computer Trading and All That," *Financial Analysts Journal,* July–August 1988, pp. 29–38.

Ibbotson, Roger, and Rex Sinquefeld: "Stocks, Bonds, Bills, and Inflation: Historical Returns (1926–1978)," Financial Analysts Research Foundation, Charlottesville, VA, 1979.

Jegadeesh, Narasinkan: "Evidence of Predictable Behavior of Security Returns," *Journal of Finance,* July 1990, pp. 881–898.

Keim, Donald, and Robert Stambraugh: "Predicting Returns in the Stock and Bond Markets," *Journal of Financial Economics* 17, December 1986, pp. 357–390.

Leibowitz, Martin: "Pension Asset Allocation through Surplus Management," *Financial Analysts Journal,* March–April 1987, pp. 29–40.

—— and Rory Henriksson: "Portfolio Optimization Within a Surplus Framework," *Financial Analysts Journal,* March–April 1988, pp. 43–51.

Leuthold, Steven: "Interest Rates, Inflation and Deflation," *Financial Analysts Journal,* January–February 1981, pp. 28–41.

Lindenberg, Eric, and Stephen Ross: "Tobin's q ratio and Industrial Organization," *Journal of Business,* January 1981, pp. 1–37.

Lintner, J.: "Inflation and Common Stock Prices in a Cyclical Context," National Bureau of Economic Research, 1973 Annual Report, pp. 23–36.

Long, J.B.: "Stock Prices, Inflation, and the Term Structure of Interest Rates," *Journal of Financial Economics,* July 1974, pp. 131–170.

MacBeth, James, and David Emanuel: "Tactical Asset Allocation: Pros and Cons," *Financial Analysts Journal,* November–December 1993, pp. 30–44.

——, ——, and Craig Heatter: "An Investment Strategy for Defined Benefit Plans," *Financial Analysts Journal,* May–June 1994, pp. 34–41.

Marsh, Terry, and Robert Merton: "Dividend Behavior for the Aggregate Stock Market," *Journal of Business,* January 1987, pp. 1–40.

Marshall, David: "Inflation and Asset Returns in a Monetary Economy," *Journal of Finance,* September 1992, pp. 1315–1342.

Michaud, Richard: "Pension Policy and Benchmarks Optimization," *Investment Management Review,* Spring 1989, pp. 35–43.

Modigliani, Franco, and Richard Cohn: "Inflation and the Stock Market," *Financial Analysts Journal,* March–April 1979, pp. 22–44.

Nelson, C. R.: "Inflation and Rates of Return on Common Stocks," *Journal of Finance,* May 1976, pp. 22–44.

Perold, Andre, and William Sharpe: "Dynamic Strategies for Asset Allocation," *Financial Analysts Journal,* January–February 1988, pp. 16–26.

Peters, Edgar: "Fractal Structure in the Capital Markets," *Financial Analysts Journal,* July–August 1989, pp. 31–37.

——: "A Chaotic Attractor for the S&P 500," *Financial Analysts Journal,* March–April 1991, pp. 55–62.

Rose, Andrew: "Is the Real Interest Rate Stable?," *Journal of Finance,* December 1988, pp. 1095–1112.

Rozeff, Michael: "Money and Stock Prices: Market Efficiency and the Lag in Effect of Monetary Policy," *Journal of Financial Economics,* September 1974, pp. 245–302.

——: "The Money Supply and the Stock Market," *Financial Analysts Journal,* September–October 1975.

Rubinstein, Mark: "Portfolio Insurance and the Market Crash," *Financial Analysts Journal,* January–Febuary 1988, pp. 38–47.

Schipper, Katherine, and Rex Thompson: "Common Stocks as Hedges Against Shifts in the Consumption or Investment Opportunity Set," *Journal of Business,* April 1981, pp. 305–328.

Schwert, William: "Why Does Stock Market Volatility Change Over Time?," *Journal of Finance,* December 1989, pp. 1115–1145.

Scott, James H.: "Managing Asset Classes," *Financial Analysts Journal,* January–Febuary 1994, pp. 62–69.

Sharpe, William F.: "Integrated Asset Allocation," *Financial Analysts Journal,* September–October 1987, pp. 25–32.

Smith, Rodger, and Thomas Richard: "Asset Mix and Investment Strategy," *Financial Analysts Journal,* March–April 1976, pp. 67–71.

Weigel, Eric: "The Performance of Tactical Asset Allocation," *Financial Analysts Journal,* September–October 1991, pp. 63–70.

QUESTIONS AND PROBLEMS

1. What is tactical asset allocation (TAA)?
2. Compare TAA to strategic asset allocation.
3. Discuss how the fundamental characteristics of asset classes can be useful in devising an asset allocation.
4. What are the three major strategies for managing a portfolio over time?
5. In what way does a TAA strategy qualify as a way of managing a portfolio over time?
6. Assume the following market environments: (a) highly volatile, (b) stable but trendless, (c) bull market with volatility, (d) bear market with volatility, and (e) bull market with low volatility. Describe how each of the three strategies would fare, which would do best, and which would do worst in each of these environments.
7. What is the risk premium approach to forecasting the market direction?
8. How can economic and technical indicators be used to assess the attraction of the market?
9. How can use of multiple inputs be helpful in forecasting the attractiveness of the market?
10. What conditions are necessary in order for a combining of inputs to be productive in forecasting the market?
11. Assume a constant-proportion portfolio insurance strategy. What is the investment in stocks and portfolio mix using a multiplier of three, a portfolio of $100, and floor of $80?
12. What is the appropriate stock position when the market declines by 10 percent and then when it rises by 25 percent?
13. Discuss how market history may be useful in setting probabilities for differing market scenarios.
14. Outline and discuss the major steps in asset allocation.
15. Compare and contrast the historical and scenario approaches to developing input data for asset allocation.
16. Calculate the standard deviation of the rating distribution shown in Figure 9-2. Then calculate the standard deviation assuming that the probability of falling into each of the five rating categories is equal—that is, 20 percent for each.
17. Assume that the standard deviation of the market is 22 percent and the organization has a predictive capability on the order of 0.15 (IC = 0.15). Determine the adjusted return distribution for that organization using the format in Figure 9-2.
18. Assume that the organization in the previous problem determines that the market is moderately undervalued—rates it 2. Determine the appropriate portfolio beta.
19. Describe how the scenario approach can be used as a benchmark for comparing current consensus expectations for market return.
20. Describe how return and risk varied over major asset classes over the long historical period from 1926 to the present.

21. Give a general description of how to use the historical approach to making a forecast.
22. How do forecasters accommodate differing inflation levels when making a forecast?
23. How can subdividing historical data be helpful in making a forecast?
24. Briefly describe the components of a scenario method of forecasting.
25. In what major respects does the scenario approach differ from the historical approach to forecasting?

CHAPTER 10

Equity Investment Styles

INTRODUCTION

Within the equity market, investment managers pursue a variety of investment strategies that have become known as styles of investing. Two of the more popular styles are growth stock investing and nongrowth, or what has become known as value, stock investing. Also, there is a differentiation of style according to the capitalization size of the company, and we commonly see managers conducting strategies that focus on small or mid-sized stocks in addition to major stocks. Finally, we observe classes of managers known as rotators that opportunistically attempt to shift investment focus into the style that promises the best performance at a given time.

These styles are based on the differing behavior of groupings of stocks in the marketplace. Alternatively, such groupings of stocks can be viewed as subcomponents of a broader stock market. The fact that these subcomponents exist presents portfolio managers with the opportunity to develop stagies based on differing stock group behavior. Correspondingly, the availability of a variety of strategies based on stock group behavior presents investors with greater choice but also more complexity in designing an overall investment program.

The purpose of this chapter is to describe investing in the equity market according to style classification (major stock groupings), as well as the implications of this phenomenon for portfolio managers and investors. We begin by describing the two most popular ways of investing according to style differentiation: (1) investing according to size of company, and (2) investing according to growth or value characteristics of stocks. Because style investing is based on the differing behavior of stocks as a group, we describe statistical techniques that can facilitate the proper identification of relevant groupings and the classification of stocks into groupings. Along with these descriptions, we describe how the existence of differing stock groupings has implications both for investment strategies as well as investor behavior.

CLASSIFICATION BY SIZE

Classification of stocks according to size can be justified on the basis of both differing liquidity characteristics and empirical evidence. We noted previously that a premium return appears to accrue to stocks according to the liquidity characteristics of the stocks. Furthermore, the size of the company, as measured by the total market capitalization of the company, appears to be a reasonable proxy for liquidity. Using size as a proxy, we expect small stocks to have the least liquidity and provide a greater return over time than large stocks.

Because of differing liquidity characteristics and other factors as well, small stocks have, in fact, provided a significantly higher return than large stocks. Rolf Banz first documented this phenomenon by calculating the returns over the 1926–1981 period for NYSE-listed stocks, ranked by market capitalization, into the lowest two deciles: 9th and 10th deciles, or the fifth quintile.[1] Ibbotson Associates subsequently updated the performance of these two smallest-capitalization deciles for the period 1982 to 1993. Combining the results of these studies shows this smallest-capitalization quintile of stocks with an average annual return of 12.4 percent over the full 1926–1993 period, compared to a return of 10.3 percent for the S&P 500 for a premium of 2.1 percent for small stocks over the full period. As a matter of interest, the S&P 500 stocks generally rank into the largest deciles (1 to 4) by capitalization and is usually considered as the index most representative of large-capitalization investing.

Though small-capitalization stocks have provided higher returns than large stocks over time, the performance has varied significantly as evidenced by data in Table 10-1 for five subperiods over the recent 30-year period from 1963 to 1993. Small-capitalization stocks outperformed large stocks significantly in the first, third, and fifth subperiods but underperformed substantially in the second and fourth subperiods. Volatility of performance, both absolutely and relative to large stocks, thus characterizes small stocks. Correspondingly, these two sections of the market—large and small—tend to move out of synch with each other. Over the longer 1926–1993 period, the measured correlation between large and small stocks was 0.80, which is a relatively low degree of correlation considering that these sectors are both components of the equity market.

In monitoring the performance of stocks below the size represented by the S&P 500, there are several benchmark indexes. First, the Ibbotson index is a regular updating of the

TABLE 10-1
Large- and small-capitalization stock performance (1963–1993)

Subperiod	Small-capitalization return	Large-capitalization return
1) 1963– 968	30.90%	12.20%
2) 1969–1974	−13.60	−3.40
3) 1975–1983	35.30	15.70
4) 1984–1990	2.60	14.60
5) 1991–1993	29.20	15.60

---

[1]Banz, Rolf W., "The Relationship Between Returns and Market Value of Common Stocks," *Journal of Financial Economics,* vol. 9 (1981), pp. 3–18.

return of the bottom capitalization quintile of stocks for an index originally constructed by Banz/Ibbotson. The Russell 2000 index is another barometer that provides a broader perspective for small-capitalization stock behavior. This index is comprised of the smallest 2000 stocks of an overall Russell 3000 index of the largest 3000 U.S. stocks by capitalization. A third index, the Wilshire 4500, is a subcomponent of the Wilshire 5000, which includes all U.S. stocks. The Wilshire 4500 includes all U.S. stocks except those in the S&P 500 and is thus a comprehensive barometer of equity activity beyond the S&P 500. Finally, the S&P Mid-Cap index of 400 companies spans the spectrum from small- to medium-capitalization companies and is a useful barometer of the performance of companies one tier below the size of the S&P 500. All these indexes tend to be highly correlated with each other but differ in performance behavior from the S&P 500.

COMBINING STRATEGIES

Though small stocks are highly volatile individually and as a class, blending a small-capitalization strategy with a large-capitalization strategy has the potential for improving the risk-return characteristics of an overall investment program. First, small-capitalization stocks exhibit low correlation with major stocks. The measured degree of correlation of 0.80 between large and small stocks is usefully low for purposes of diversification. In addition, there is potential for above-average returns over time from small-cap investing. This return premium derives from the inherently greater riskiness of small stocks; they have both a higher beta as well as liquidity premium. Finally, there is potential for further enhancing returns by applying disciplined valuation procedures to the universe of small-capitalization stocks.

In the following text we describe how one investment counselor constructs an overall equity investment program that combines small-cap and large-cap stocks. For this purpose the organization uses a universe of the largest 3000 stocks in the U.S. marketplace. This universe is essentially the same as the listing of the companies in the Russell 3000 index, which is also composed of the 3000 largest companies by market capitalization.

Table 10-2 shows this universe of 3000 companies broken down into deciles, where decile one represents the largest 300 companies in the universe and decile ten the smallest 300 by market capitalization. It also shows the range of capitalization within each of the deciles. For example, the tenth decile spans a range of $170 million to $195 million in size, and the first decile contains companies of $4.7 billion and larger. This decile also represents 66 percent of the total universe by market capitalization, but the tenth decile represents only 0.7 percent as shown in the third column of the table.

For the large-capitalization strategy, the organization uses the top two deciles, or the largest 600 companies as the selection universe. This largest subsection encompasses companies of $2.1 billion and larger in size, and these two deciles combined represent close to 80 percent of the total market capitalization of the 3000 companies. Those companies that are selected from this universe for inclusion in the portfolio average close to $12 billion in market capitalization.

The selection universe for the small/mid-cap strategy encompasses deciles three through ten, or 2400 companies out of the total 3000. These companies range down from approximately $2 billion to approximately $150 million in size of market capitalization. Representing the other 20 percent of the total universe, this subsection of small-to-medium-size

TABLE 10-2
Disciplined stock selection strategies—selection universe

Market cap decile	Number of companies	Market cap range	% of total market cap	Large-cap strategy	Small/mid-cap strategy
1	300	>$4.7B	66.1	X	
2	300	$2.1–4.7B	13.3	X	
3	300	$1.3–2.1B	7.0		X
4	300	$810M–1.3B	4.3		X
5	300	$570–810M	2.9		X
6	300	$420–570M	2.1		X
7	300	$320–420M	1.6		X
8	300	$250–320M	1.2		X
9	300	$195–250M	0.9		X
10	300	$170–195M	0.7		X
Totals	3000			600	2400

	U.S. stocks	Large-cap strategy	Small/mid-cap strategy
Largest 3000		600	2400
Size range		>$3.0B	$150M–3.0B
Average size		$11.75B	$1.1B

Source: Farrell-Wako Global Investment Management, Inc.

companies becomes a potential completion component for an overall stock selection program. Companies selected from this universe for inclusion in the small- to mid-cap portfolios average slightly over $1 billion in size and typically span across the smallest company deciles to the mid-size company deciles.

Once the largest 600 stocks are classified into the large-capitalization category, and the remaining 2400 as small/mid-capitalization stocks, the organization values the stocks in both the large- and small/mid-cap sections universe, using the same multidimensional approach as described in Chapter 8. As with large-cap stocks, the small-cap stocks are ranked according to derived alpha values. Portfolios of 50 to 70 stocks are then constructed from highly ranked stocks according to the following guidelines.

- Set a beta target of 1.25, which is appropriate for small-capitalization stock investing.
- Set an alpha target of 3 percent, which can be achieved by a disciplined stock selection process.
- Keep the individual issue weighting below 3 percent, which helps minimize the degree of stock-specific risk.
- Eliminate those stocks that fall below a certain valuation threshold.
- Remain fully invested, not attempting to time the market.

Table 10-3 compares the risk-return characteristics of the small/mid-capitalization strategy, the large-capitalization strategy, an optimized combination of the two, and an S&P 500 index fund as a benchmark. Note that the index fund has a beta of 1.00 with a tracking

TABLE 10-3
Risk return profile of strategies

Characteristics	Index fund	Strategy large-cap	Small/mid-cap	Combined 70% large 30% small
Market risk (beta)	1.00	1.00	1.25	1.075
Tracking error (standard error)	0.50	3.50	10.00	5.00
Expected excess return (alpha)	0.00	2.00	3.00	2.20
Expected return (total)	12.00	14.00	16.00	14.60

error of 50 basis points, which might represent the upper bound for well-organized funds. Because index funds incur no added risk (except for minimal tracking error), we expect no incremental return or, alternatively, a zero alpha. Over time, the fund is expected to earn the market return, which for purposes of illustration is projected at 12 percent.

The large-capitalization strategy is constructed to also have a beta of 1.00, as with the index fund, but will experience tracking error from a focus on selecting favorably valued stocks. We expect to earn a positive incremental return (alpha) from this activity of 2 percent, which is additional to the expected market return of 12 percent, for a total expectation of 14 percent. In comparison, the small-capitalization strategy incurs greater market risk and a significantly greater tracking error than the large-cap alpha strategy. For this strategy, we expect to earn a risk premium over time for assuming above-average market risk. Also, we expect to earn a higher alpha of 3 percent from selecting stocks from this larger universe of small-capitalization stocks. Though the small-capitalization strategy is expected to earn the highest overall return of the strategies, it would generally be unsuitable as a sole component of an investment plan because of its large tracking error, which evidences high diversification risk.

However, when we blend the small-cap strategy with the broad-based large-cap strategy, we obtain a more appropriately diversified portfolio with a favorable risk-return profile. We can attain this result by using portfolio optimization procedures as described in previous chapters but with special application to this purpose. In illustrating this application, we make the same assumptions as to projected market returns, expected alphas, betas, and tracking errors for the two strategies as described before. We further assume that the correlation between the two stock groupings—large and small—is 0.80 and in line with past experience.

Table 10-4 shows the results of the optimization using these underlying assumptions. The return-risk column tells us that relying on either strategy alone is less efficient than using a combined strategy. For example, a mix of 90 percent large-cap/10 percent small-cap gives us a return-risk ratio of 0.63—greater than the 0.62 ratio for the large-cap strategy alone. Correspondingly, the risk-return ratio for the small-cap strategy alone of 0.58 is the lowest of the portfolio combination shown, despite offering the highest expected return of 16 percent. Finally, note that the ratio peaks at 0.64, indicating that the optimum mix is 70 percent large-cap/30 percent small-cap. A level of diversification is achieved that makes this strategy a more efficient mix.

TABLE 10-4
A combination strategy small- and large-cap

% invested		Results		
Small-cap	Large-cap	Return	Std. dev.	Return-risk
0%	100%	14.00%	22.70%	0.62
10	90	14.20	22.60	0.63
20	80	14.40	22.80	0.63
30	70	14.60	23.00	0.64
40	60	14.80	23.40	0.63
50	50	15.00	23.80	0.63
60	40	15.20	24.30	0.63
70	30	15.40	25.00	0.62
80	20	15.60	25.80	0.62
90	10	15.80	26.50	0.60
100	0	16.00	27.40	0.58

GROWTH AND VALUE STOCK GROUPINGS

In addition to size, the other major way of differentiating styles is according to growth and value orientation. Mutual fund organizations have traditionally described their investment objectives for a fund in such broad terms as (1) growth and (2) income/growth, which we might also construe as "value." For example, the T. Rowe Price grouping of mutual funds has long been associated with the growth style of investing. Furthermore, they created a fund that stresses investing in emerging growth companies, so that the fund has both a growth and small-capitalization orientation. Correspondingly, the Affiliated group of mutual funds has long been identified with the value (growth/income) style of investing, and we compare its style with that of T. Rowe Price in a later section. At the same time, investment counselors typically portray their investment strategies in such broad terms as growth and value. Such classifications are further reinforced by consultants, plan sponsors, and performance evaluators.

Just as with groupings by size, investors also use fundamental characteristics as a means of classifying stocks into growth and "value" (nongrowth) groupings. For this purpose, growth stocks can be broadly characterized as those expected to grow at superior rates, whereas nongrowth stocks can be characterized as growing at a rate in line with the economy. Since growth expectations are unobservable, we need to resort to proxies to assess the sort of growth that an investor expects for a stock or group of stocks. We have chosen two measures that would best seem to approximate these growth expectations: (1) return on equity times retention rate or sustainable growth and (2) dividend yield.[2]

Sustainable growth is a fairly direct and objective measure of the growth prospect of a company, although it suffers from the usual deficiencies associated with accounting data. On the other hand, dividend yield is a market-determined variable that is not subject to accounting deficiencies. Furthermore, we should expect a negative trade-off between dividend yield and growth, both through companies' earnings retention versus dividend payout and through the pricing of superior growth prospects by the market. The two variables should

---

[2]Recall that in Chapter 6 we described ways of estimating the sustainable growth rate for companies.

thus be complementary, albeit negatively related, for capturing investor expectations for future growth.

Using dividend yield and sustainable growth rate variables, the two stock groupings—growth and nongrowth—are distinguished as follows. First, we expect growth stocks to be characterized by high retention rates and high profitability rates (or some combination of the two), but we expect nongrowth stocks to be characterized by low retention rates or relatively lower profitability. Correspondingly, we expect companies sustaining high growth rates to pay relatively lower dividends and to show even lower dividend yields to the extent that superior growth prospects are built into the price of the stock. Conversely, we expect nongrowth companies to pay higher dividends and be characterized by even higher dividend yields to the extent that the price of the nongrowth stock does not reflect superior growth prospects.

Sustainable Growth–Dividend Yield Characteristics

To illustrate that sustainable growth and dividend yield variables, in fact, distinguish these two groups of stocks, we selected a sample of 354 stocks. These stocks were mainly of large institutional quality and represented approximately 90 percent of the market weighting of the S&P 500. The same companies were also spread over 90 of the S&P 500's 108 industry groupings, thereby providing great diversity as well as encompassing the market portion of the index. We calculated a measure of sustainable growth and a dividend yield for each of the stocks in the sample over the periods 1970–1979 and 1980–1989. These periods serve a function in assessing the stability of the relationships.

Figure 10-1 shows the sustainable growth–dividend yield relationship for growth and non-growth stocks over the 1970–1979 period, and Figure 10-2 shows the same relationship for the 1980–1989 period. The vertical axis refers to the growth rate as measured by the sustainable growth rate (retention times return on equity), and the horizontal axis refers to

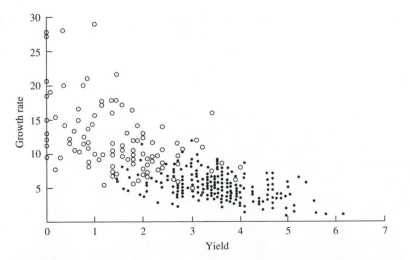

FIGURE 10-1
Growth–yield characteristics (circles = growth; dots = nongrowth), 1971–1979.

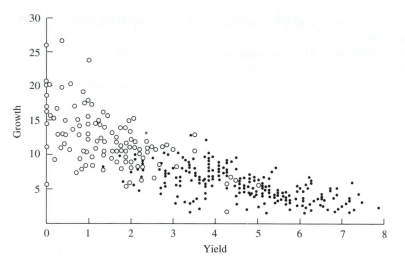

FIGURE 10-2

Growth–yield characteristics (circles = growth; dots = nongrowth), 1980–1989.

the dividend yield. The stocks classified as growth stocks, according to their price behavior in the market, are plotted with circles, and stocks classified as nongrowth (cyclical, stable, or energy) are plotted with dots.

Note that in both figures, most of the growth stocks plot together in the upper left-hand portion of the quadrant, and the majority of the nongrowth stocks plot in the lower right-hand portion of the quadrant. Growth stocks are thus characterized by high sustainable growth and low dividend yield, and nongrowth stocks are characterized by relatively low sustainable growth and relatively high yields. Furthermore, the figures illustrate that growth and dividend yield are negatively related, as might be expected.

For further evaluation of the yield and growth distinctions between stock groups, Table 10-5 shows average values of the variables for the two groups, growth and nongrowth, over

TABLE 10-5

Means and standard deviation for dividend yield and sustainable growth variables for growth and nongrowth stocks

	1970–1979			1980–1989		
	No.	Dividend yield	Sustainable growth	No.	Dividend yield	Sustainable growth
Growth	112	1.57	12.1	124	1.58	12.44
		(0.93)*	(4.87)		(1.06)	(4.18)
Nongrowth	229	3.51	5.41	230	4.7	6.44
		(0.99)	(2.10)		(1.34)	(2.30)
Total	341	2.87	7.61	354	3.61	8.54
		(1.33)	(4.53)		(1.95)	(4.22)

*Numbers in parentheses indicate standard deviation.

Source: James L. Farrell, Jr., George Pinches, and James Scott, "Growth Stock Fundamentals: Implications for Portfolio Management," unpublished paper, 1991.

the 1970–1979 and 1980–1989 periods. Note that the average dividend yield, and the average sustainable growth for the growth and nongrowth groups, are substantially different for both periods of the test. In particular, the sustainable growth rate for the growth group is quite high in relation to the nongrowth group: 2.24 (12.10/5.41) times in the first subperiod and 1.93 (12.44/6.44) times in the second period. Correspondingly, the dividend yield variable for the growth stock group is quite low in relation to the nongrowth group: 0.45 (1.57/3.51) times in the first period and 0.34 (1.58/4.70) times in the second period.

Appendix A describes how a statistical technique known as *discriminant analysis* can be used to classify stocks according to sustainable growth and divided yield characteristics into appropriate groupings.

GROWTH/VALUE PERFORMANCE INDEXES

We have seen from the prior analysis that the fundamental characteristics of growth stocks differ significantly from those of the nongrowth/value groupings. The performance of managers specializing in either growth or value-type stocks will, in turn, be significantly conditioned by the trend in these sectors. As a result, proper evaluation of the performance of such managers requires reference to the overall environment for these particular subcomponents of the overall market. In response to these needs, several major research organizations have developed indexes for growth stocks and value (nongrowth) stocks.

In developing indexes, these organizations typically select an underlying fundamental attribute as the differentiating characteristic for classifying stocks into either of the growth or value categories. One that is commonly used is to simply classify stocks according to the rate of growth of the company, with high-growth stocks being classified into a growth category and slower-growth stocks into a nongrowth or value category. Correspondingly, many others use simplified valuation measures such as *P/E* (price–earnings ratio) or *P/B* (price–book ratio) to classify stocks into growth or value categories. Using such variables, stocks with low *P/E*'s or *P/B*'s would be classified as value stocks, and those with high *P/E*'s or *P/B*'s would be classed in the growth stock category.

Once stocks are classified into a broad category, these organizations have created indexes that show the return earned by such groupings of growth and value stocks over time. These indexes, in turn, provide portfolio managers with information for assessing how major subgroupings of stocks are behaving over time, just as a broad-based index such as the S&P 500 allows perspective on the overall market. Correspondingly, such indexes provide investors with a benchmark for gauging the performance of those investment managers that specialize in managing growth stock or value stock portfolios. Growth stock managers are most appropriately evaluated against a growth stock benchmark, but value stock managers are most appropriately evaluated against a value stock benchmark.

We can illustrate by reference to growth and value indexes that are subcomponents of the S&P 500 and constructed by BARRA—an investment research and consulting organization—in conjunction with Standard and Poor's (S&P). The S&P/BARRA growth and value indexes are constructed by sorting the S&P 500 companies based on their price/book ratios, with the low price/book companies constituting the value index and high price/book companies making up the growth index. Each S&P 500 company is included in either the growth or the value index, and the two indexes each have approximately the same market value. Companies in the growth index tend to be bigger; therefore, it contains

TABLE 10-6
Annual returns, S&P 500–style indexes (1979–1991)

Year	Large-cap growth, %	Large-cap value, %
1979	15.7	21.1
1980	39.4	23.6
1981	−9.8	0.0
1982	22.0	21.0
1983	16.2	28.9
1984	2.3	10.5
1985	33.3	29.7
1986	14.5	21.7
1987	6.5	3.7
1988	11.9	21.7
1989	36.4	26.1
1990	0.2	−6.8
1991	38.4	22.6
Average annual return	16.5	16.6

Source: Standard & Poor's/BARRA.

roughly two-fifths of the S&P 500 companies. These indexes are rebalanced semiannually and when needed.

Table 10-6 shows the annual returns of these growth and value subcomponents of the S&P 500 over the 1979–1991 period. Over the full period, the two indexes showed approximately the same overall return, averaging 16.5 percent for the growth index and 16.6 percent for the value index. The performance of the two indexes, however, diverged significantly in certain years, as well as over extended subperiods within the overall period. Growth stocks outperformed in the 1980 period but significantly underperformed value stocks from 1981 to 1984 and again from 1986 to 1988. Growth stocks again showed significantly better performance from 1989 to 1991.

GROUPING BY PRICE ACTION

Though fundamental characteristics provide a workably useful way of classifying stocks, a more objective way is to analyze the differing price behavior of groupings of stocks in the marketplace. There are statistical techniques that facilitate the direct analysis of stock price behavior to determine or verify that the price action of stocks, in fact, conforms to groupings such as growth and value categories, or other groupings for that matter. These techniques are helpful for both identifying relevant stock groupings and classifying individual stocks into appropriate categories.

We illustrate the application of such statistical techniques to analyze the price behavior of stocks and develop groupings that conform to a common pattern by reviewing the results of a statistical test for relevant stock groupings published by Farrell.[3] This analysis was

---

[3] James L. Farrell, Jr. "Analyzing Covariation of Return to Determine Homogeneous Stock Groupings," *Journal of Business,* April 1974, pp. 181–207.

TABLE 10-7
Definitions and examples of growth, cyclical, stable, and energy stocks

Growth stocks

Earnings of these companies are expected to show a faster rate of secular expansion than the average company.
Examples:
   Electronics companies, such as Hewlett-Packard, Perkin Elmer, AMP, and Texas Instruments
   Office equipment companies, such as Digital Equipment and Wang Labs
   Drug and hospital supply companies, such as Baxter Labs, Becton Dickinson, and Merck

Cyclical stocks

These companies have an above-average exposure to the economic cycle. Earnings would be expected to be
down more than the average in a recession and up more than the average during the expansion phase of the
business cycle.
Examples:
   Metals companies, such as Phelps-Dodge, Asarco, Alcoa, and Bethlehem Steel
   Machinery companies, such as Caterpillar, Ingersoll Rand, Cincinnati Milacron, and Deere
   Building-related companies, such as Johns-Manville and Weyerhaeuser
   General industrial companies, such as Goodyear, International Paper, Square D, Continental Group,
   and Eaton

Stable stocks

These companies have a below-average exposure to the economic cycle. Earnings would be expected to be
down less than the average in a recession and up less than average during the expansion phase of the business
cycle. Earnings of these companies are the most adversely impacted by inflation but fare relatively the best in
periods of decelerating inflation, or disinflation.
Examples:
   Utilities, such as American Electric Power
   Food and beverage companies, such as General Foods, Coca-Cola, and Kellogg
   Retailers, such as Sears and Federated Department Stores
   Banking, insurance, and finance companies, such as Chase Manhattan, Transamerica, and Household
   Finance
   General consumer merchandising companies, such as Gillette, Reynolds, and Procter and Gamble

Energy stocks

Energy companies supply energy to both producers and consumers. The earnings of these companies are
affected by the economic cycle but, most importantly, by trends in the relative price of energy.
Examples:
   Coal companies, such as Pittston and Westmoreland Coal
   Crude-oil producers, such as Pennzoil, General American Oil, and Superior Oil
   Domestic oil companies, such as Shell Oil, Atlantic Richfield, and Union Oil
   International oil companies, such as Exxon, Texaco, and Standard Oil of California

oriented toward determining whether the price action of stocks conformed to the classes of
growth and other nongrowth groupings of cyclical, stable, and energy (oil) stocks.[4] Table
10-7 defines these classes of stocks and gives some examples of the types of companies
represented in these classes.

   To test whether stocks actually grouped accordingly, Farrell first selected a sample of
100 stocks and then developed monthly returns for each of the stocks over the 1961–1969

---

[4]In Farrell's original study, the fourth group was identified as oil; however, subsequent analysis indicates that the
group is more broadly identified as representing an energy effect.

period. It was not possible, however, to work directly with the unadjusted returns because virtually all stocks are correlated with a general market effect. This effect, therefore, needed to be removed, and we needed to see if there was added comovement among stocks that conformed to the classification into growth, cyclical, stable, and energy stocks. (Those who are interested in the technicalities of making this adjustment should read the published material.)

Once returns had been adjusted, a coefficient of correlation between each stock in the sample and every other stock was calculated. Because the sample contained 100 stocks, each being correlated with every other resulted in $100 \times 100 = 10,000$ correlation coefficients. If stocks group according to growth, cyclical, stable, and energy characteristics, we would expect them to be positively and highly correlated within groupings and generally uncorrelated across groups. More specifically, we would expect growth stocks to be highly correlated with other growth stocks but not to be correlated with cyclical, stable, or energy stocks; cyclical stocks to be highly correlated with other cyclical stocks but uncorrelated with growth, stable, or energy stocks; stable stocks to be highly correlated with other stable stocks but uncorrelated with growth, cyclical, or energy stocks; and energy stocks to be highly correlated with other energy stocks but uncorrelated with growth, cyclical, or stable stocks.

This expected pattern of correlation is illustrated by the matrix of correlation coefficients in Figure 10-3. The correlation coefficients within each of the classes of growth, cyclical, stable, and energy stocks are arranged along the diagonal of the matrix. These within-group correlation coefficients should show high and positive values; they are identified by the letter H and a plus sign. The correlation coefficients off the diagonal represent the correlation of stocks between groups (growth with cyclical, cyclical with stable, etc.). These correlation coefficients, which we expect to be low, are identified by the letter L.

	Growth	Cyclical	Stable	Energy
Growth	Growth stocks H+	L	L	L
Cyclical	L	Cyclical stocks H+	L	L
Stable	L	L	Stable stocks H+	L
Energy	L	L	L	Energy stocks H+

FIGURE 10-3
Matrix of correlation coefficients—growth, cyclical, stable, and energy stocks.

Cluster Analysis

To analyze whether the actual correlation matrix, in fact, showed this expected pattern, Farrell used cluster analysis. This technique systematically examines the matrix of correlation coefficients and separates stocks into groups or clusters, within which stocks are highly correlated and between which stocks are poorly correlated. The stepwise nature of this method permits use of a simple, rapid computer program that involves (1) searching the correlation matrix for the highest positive correlation coefficient, (2) combining these stocks to reduce the matrix by one, and (3) recomputing the correlation matrix to include the correlation between the combined stock or cluster and the remaining stocks or clusters.

This process can be illustrated with a specific example. Assume that of all possible stock pairs, two electronics stocks, Hewlett-Packard and Perkin Elmer, were the most highly correlated. The routine would combine these stocks to form a cluster of two stocks, simultaneously reducing the number to be clustered from 100 to 99. It would then search the correlation matrix for the next highest pair of correlation coefficients. Again, for purposes of illustration, assume that AMP, another electronics company, and the Hewlett-Packard/Perkin Elmer cluster were the most highly correlated. AMP and the Hewlett-Packard/Perkin Elmer cluster would then be combined to form a larger three-stock cluster, again simultaneously reducing the number to be clustered by one, from 99 to 98. This iterative routine continues until all positive correlation coefficients are exhausted or until (on the ninety-ninth pass) all 100 stocks form a single cluster.

At each scanning, the stocks are classified into one fewer group than on the previous pass, thus yielding, for example, $100 - 50 = 50$ groups on the fiftieth pass. If the hypothesis that the 100 stocks in the sample could be categorized was correct, by the ninety-sixth pass the four remaining groups should correspond to those hypothesized. Furthermore, all positive correlation coefficients should be exhausted by the ninety-sixth pass, thus terminating the procedure. This, in turn, would indicate not only that the sample data can be explained by four independent groupings, but also that there is a low degree of correlation across stock groupings.

Figure 10-4 provides four diagrams of the results of the cluster routine, showing the stage in which pairs or groups of stocks joined, and the value of the correlation coefficient at that stage. The number of stocks in each cluster is growth 31, cyclical 36, stable 25, and energy (oil) 8. Stocks classified a priori as growth, cyclical, stable, or energy (oil) actually clustered within their allocated groups. All group clusters appeared to contain highly intercorrelated stocks, as final stocks, or groups of stocks clustering into individual groups at relatively high levels of positive correlation: 0.19 for growth, 0.15 for stable, 0.18 for cyclical, and 0.27 for energy (oil). The final four groups were not positively correlated, as evidenced by the fact that the routine terminated on the ninety-sixth pass and that the positive correlation of 0.15 was the lowest positive correlation on the prior (ninety-fifth) pass.[5]

---

[5]In order to test for the persistence of stock groupings, the analysis was updated for later periods, using the same sort of statistical procedures as the ones in Farrell's original study. This updated analysis showed that four clusters were adequate to explain the correlation matrices for the initial and later periods. For both initial and later periods, these clusters were identified as containing growth, cyclical, and stable stocks, with the fourth cluster being more appropriately identified as an energy rather than a more narrowly defined oil group. The cluster results were by and large in line with those from Farrell's original study, indicating the stability of return-determined homogeneous groups over time. Though the updated statistical indicated that the same four stock groupings were appropriate

The statistical test for stock groupings thus illustrates that large well-known S&P 500-type stocks can be grouped into categories of growth, cyclical, stable, and energy stocks. Furthermore, these groups are homogeneous in the sense that stocks within each group show a strong comovement and, at the same time, tend to act independently of other stock groupings. In a sense, these groups can be thought of as representing four different submarkets within the overall domestic equity market. There is, in effect, (1) a growth component, (2) a cyclical component, (3) a stable component, and (4) an energy component. In turn, the existence of these differing markets of homogeneous stock groupings has implications for active and passive portfolio management strategies.

PORTFOLIO CONSTRUCTION/PASSIVE STRATEGY

Homogeneous stock groupings have implications in developing a passive strategy, to which we alluded in Chapter 8. It is useful at this stage to reinforce that earlier analysis and illustrate its importance more completely. In particular, when constructing a portfolio, it is important to compare the fund weighting in the four groupings (growth, cyclical, stable, and energy) with a market average, such as the S&P 500, in order to determine whether the fund is concentrated in a particular area or well diversified relative to the average. A fund proportioned in line with the average ensures against overexposure to poor performance by a particular grouping. If the fund is to outperform the average, it must be heavily concentrated in a grouping with a favorable outlook. (Needless to say, it risks underperformance if the favorable outlook does not materialize.)

The data in Table 10-8 provides a more specific illustration of the use of homogeneous groupings for purposes of portfolio construction. This table shows the weighting of the four groupings of growth, cyclical, stable, and energy (oil) stocks in the S&P 500. In addition, it shows the portfolio structure of two large mutual funds—Affiliated Fund and T. Rowe Price Growth—classified by the four homogeneous groups. Finally, it shows the portfolio betas calculated from monthly data over the 1968–1972 period, as well as the total return performance of the two funds and the S&P 500 between December 31, 1972, and July 31, 1974.

Affiliated Fund was heavily weighted (approximately twice as heavily) relative to the S&P 500 in the cyclical group, but T. Rowe Price Growth was heavily weighted (approximately twice as heavily) relative to the S&P 500 in the growth group. Both funds had approximately the same beta: 1.11 for T. Rowe Price and 1.09 for Affiliated. The performance of the two funds and the S&P 500 was, however, substantially different over the December 31, 1972, to July 31, 1974, period. The S&P 500 declined 29 percent, Affiliated was down 16 percent, and T. Rowe Price was down 42 percent.

---

for explaining the data, we should note that there were instances in which individual stocks switched group affiliation; that is, there was migration of individual stocks across the groupings. This fact was especially true with respect to the growth grouping, in which stocks fell into one of the nongrowth groupings in the latter analysis. This occurrence, of course, should be expected from the fact that the fundamental distinguishing feature of a growth stock is investor expectation of superior growth in earnings and that this superior growth is finite, that is, limited in duration. Once the company has exhausted its opportunities to generate superior growth, we would then expect its price action to conform to that of a nongrowth stock.

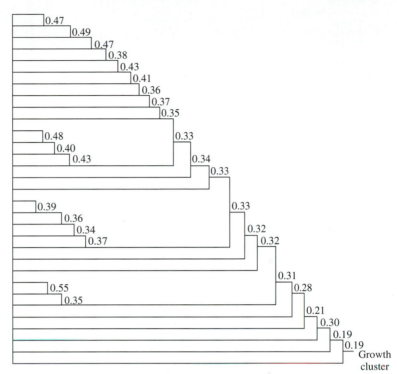

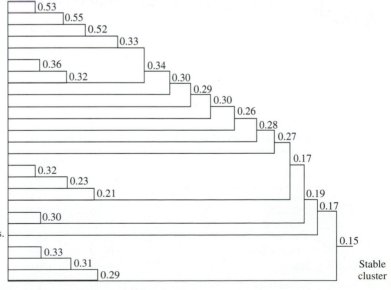

FIGURE 10-4
Cluster diagram.

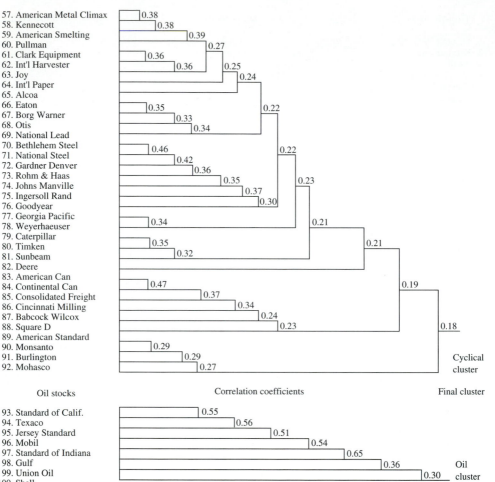

FIGURE 10-4

(*continued*)

TABLE 10-8
Portfolio construction—S&P 500 and mutual funds, %

	S&P 500	Affiliated fund	T. Rowe Price
Stock sector			
Growth	39.80	10.50	80.20
Cyclical	24.00	57.50	8.70
Stable	20.00	18.00	4.10
Energy (oil)	16.20	14.00	7.00
Total	100.00	100.00	100.00
Portfolio beta	1.00	1.09	1.11
Fund performance (12/31/72–7/31/74)	−29.00	−16.00	−42.00

Source: James L. Farrell, Jr., "Homogeneous Stock Groupings: Implications for Portfolio Management," *Financial Analysts Journal,* May–June 1975.

With both funds having betas in excess of 1, they would have been expected to decline by more than the S&P 500 in the bear market of December 31, 1972, to July 31, 1974. Affiliated Fund was down significantly less than the market because cyclical stocks performed especially well over this period (being down only 10 percent). T. Rowe Price underperformed the market and did even worse than expected on a beta-adjusted basis because growth stocks performed especially badly over this period (declining by 42 percent). The data illustrate the merits of both diversifying to avoid the wrong group (growth stocks) at the wrong time and concentrating in the right group (cyclicals) at the right time.

GROUP ROTATION/ACTIVE STRATEGY

Many managed portfolios or funds have a policy of concentrating investments in a particular category of stocks. For example, T. Rowe Price, as noted previously, has a long-standing policy of investing in growth stocks. It does not shift the weighting of the fund over time to different categories of stocks, such as from growth to cyclical. T. Rowe Price has been quite successful with this policy, rewarding long-term holders of the fund with above-average returns. The policy also helps fund holders establish a consistent risk exposure.[6]

An alternative to this philosophy of concentration is to pursue a policy of shifting fund weightings among the four groupings of growth, cyclical, stable, and energy stocks. If the outlook for a particular group is favorable, the strategy would be to give that group more weight in the portfolio than it enjoys in the S&P 500. On the other hand, if the group outlook is unfavorable, the strategy would be to give the group less weight. This policy, which can be termed group rotation, is the active counterpart to the passive strategy discussed in the previous section.[7]

The potential rewards, if we are correct in forecasting the direction of the groups, can be quite substantial. To illustrate these potential rewards, we assumed (1) perfect foresight with respect to groups, (2) total investment in only one of the four groups at a particular time, and (3) no transaction costs. Though these assumptions are obviously unrealistic with respect to real-world portfolio procedures, they are useful for illustrating the potential of group rotation as an investment strategy.

In a study of the returns from group rotation, Farrell assumed that the fund shifted into growth stocks as of December 31, 1970, then into energy (oil) stocks as of June 30, 1971, and finally into cyclicals as of June 30, 1973.[8] Pursuing this strategy over the period from December 31, 1970, to June 30, 1974, would have provided a total return of 97 percent. Over this same period, the S&P 500 stock index provided a return of 4 percent, so that there was a net advantage to group rotation of 93 percent over the period.

An update of the strategy for the period from mid-1974 to the end of 1991 suggested the following shifts. First, the strategy would have been to shift into stable stocks as of June 30, 1974, and hold them until December 30, 1975, when it would have been profitable to shift

---

[6]We should note that T. Rowe Price was one of the premier performers over the 1963–1971 period. It showed an average annual return of 12.6 percent over the period, or 2.7 percentage points better than the average annual return of 9.9 percent for the S&P 500.

[7]Organizations that pursue this strategy are classified by style as "rotators."

[8]James L. Farrell, Jr., "Homogeneous Stock Groupings: Implications for Portfolio Management," *Financial Analysts Journal,* May–June 1975, pp. 50–62.

TABLE 10-9
Returns to investment strategies: group rotation versus buy and hold S&P 500, 1971–1991

Period	S&P 500	Growth stocks	Energy stocks	Cyclical stocks	Stable stocks	Net advantage to rotation
12/70–6/72	21.70%	48.50%				26.80%
6/72–6/73	0.20%		22.50%			22.30%
6/73–6/74	−14.50%			8.50%		23.00%
6/74–12/75	12.40%				45.00%	32.60%
12/75–12/76	24.00%			41.10%		17.10%
12/76–12/80	48.00%		85.0%			37.0%
12/80–12/83	42%				56%	14%
12/83–12/84	6%		17%			11%
12/84–12/85	32%				41%	9%
12/85–12/87	25%			40%		15%
12/87–12/88	17%		28%			11%
12/88–12/91	66%	89%				23%

Source: James L. Farrell, Jr., "Homogeneous Stock Groupings: Implications for Portfolio Management," *Financial Analysts Journal,* May–June, 1975.

back into cyclicals and hold them through 1976; the final shift in the 1970s would have been into energy stocks for the period until 1980. In the 1980s, the positioning would begin with stable stocks in 1981, back into energy stocks for 1984, and then a shift into cyclicals for the 1986–1987 period, when the shift would be into energy stocks for 1988. The final shift would be into growth stocks for the 1989–1991 period.

Table 10-9 shows the detailed breakdown of the group rotation strategy over the full period from December 31, 1970, to December 31, 1991. It shows the returns accruing to each of the favorably positioned groups within the subperiods, as well as the return of the S&P 500 over that period. Note that the favorable group outperforms the S&P 500 by a substantial margin in each of the subperiods. The total return from the group rotation strategy over the full 21-year period would have been over 20% percent per annum in comparison to a return of 11.6 percent per annum on the S&P 500, for a net gain of over 8 percent per annum over this time period.

The previous data and analysis thus indicates that there is substantial opportunity for improving portfolio performance through identifying the appropriate group in an investment strategy of group rotation. To take advantage of these opportunities, we need some predictive capability in assessing the relative attractiveness of the groupings, just as we need predictive capability to engage successfully in stock selection or market timing. Developing an understanding of the fundamental factors that characterize or discriminate between stock groups should be an important step in gaining the ability to successfully anticipate group moves.[9] In the following sections, we describe (1) ways of identifying fundamental factors, (2) methods of determining the relative values of the grouping, and (3) a framework for positioning the groupings in a portfolio to maximize its risk-return characteristics.

---

[9]Developing an understanding of the fundamental factors distinguishing stocks is also important for the following two reasons: (1) to ensure that the groupings or effect will persist over time and (2) to ensure that individual stocks are classified into appropriate groupings.

FORECASTING GROWTH STOCK PERFORMANCE

The relative swings in performance of growth and value stocks present opportunities for active managers to enhance returns over time. Forecast of a relative return advantage to growth stocks would indicate a shift in weighting of the portfolio to this broad sector, whereas anticipation of relative outperformance of "value" stocks would indicate a shift in portfolio weighting toward this broad sector of cyclical, stable, and energy stocks. Portfolio managers might judge the direction of performance of growth stocks relative to other groupings by analyzing any or all of the following underlying factors: (1) the direction of interest rates, (2) the position of the yield curve, and (3) the relative valuation level of the growth and value groupings.

Interest Rate Impact

We have seen in Chapter 6 that common stocks display the longest duration of the major asset classes. This long duration derives from the fact that the cash payments—dividends—are deferred into the future with the expectation that these dividends will grow to an even higher level. Because these longer-range cash flows are discounted at higher rates, the resulting duration will be higher than that of a fixed-income instrument that pays out a higher cash flow (coupon) in the near term.

As we have seen, growth stocks are characterized by even lower initial dividend payments than "value" stocks due to lower payout rates. The lower dividend payments are expected to be compensated for by a faster-than-average growth in the future. With an even longer deferral of cash flow than that for an average common stock, the discounting of the cash payments is greater, resulting in a longer duration for the growth stock class.

Analytically, we can derive a usefully approximate measure of duration for nongrowth ("value") stocks by rearranging the simplified form of the dividend discount model, as illustrated in Chapter 6. Because of the need to account for a varying rate of dividend growth, the simplified dividend discount model is not appropriate for deriving duration estimates for growth stocks. Conventional practice is to use the three-stage dividend discount model to generate the pattern of cash flows, discount these flows and weight them accordingly to derive a duration estimate for the stock of interest, either growth or nongrowth.

Table 10-10 shows duration estimates derived for a sample of growth and nongrowth stocks using the three-stage dividend discount model that provides a generalized method for both types of stocks. Note that the three growth stocks show significantly longer durations than the other seven nongrowth stocks. Intuitively, these durations are reasonable because the growth stock dividend yields are minuscule (0.21 percent) compared to the (3.67 percent) yield of the nongrowth stocks. Also, the nongrowth stocks are positioned in industries, such as oil, electric utilities, steel, and autos, that are mature, slow-growing sectors of the economy.

Interest rate changes should thus have a major impact on growth stock prices and *P/E* ratios. For example, with an interest rate decline, the relative *P/E* of growth stocks, the longest-duration financial asset should expand appreciably. Growth stocks' *P/E*'s act as a "call" on lower interest rates. As the market's *P/E* expands with falling rates, stocks with growth rates above the market average benefit from both the rise in the market's *P/E* and an increasing relative *P/E* for growth.

This expansion occurs for two reasons. First, the market's *P/E* expands because a given rate of growth is worth more when discounted by a lower required return (Figure 10-5). In

TABLE 10-10
Common stock durations

Ticker	Company name	Industry name	Dividend yield	Duration
AMGN	Amgen Inc	Health care—drugs	0.00	29.32
MCD	McDonalds Corp	Restaurant	0.62	31.54
MSFT	Microsoft Corp	Computers—peripherals	0.00	35.93
	Growth stocks		0.21	32.26
AN	Amoco Corp	Petroleum—domestic	3.58	22.99
CAT	Caterpillar Inc Del	Capital equipment	2.34	21.12
CPL	Carolina Pwr & Lt Co	Utilities—electric	5.37	22.98
F	Ford Mtr Co Del	Motor vehicles	4.83	10.24
FNB	First Chicago Corp	Banks	3.56	20.03
GIS	General Mls Inc	Food & related	3.43	24.49
PD	Phelps Dodge Corp	Mining	2.59	18.35
	Non-growth stocks		3.67	20.03

addition, stocks with growth rates greater than the market's get a *P/E* benefit from lower interest rates that is more than the benefit for the overall market. In other words, their relative *P/E*'s expand. In Figure 10-6, the dark lines refer to stocks with varying growth rates, *P/E* is twice that of the market. But if the market *P/E* rises to 20*x* because bond yields fall,ranging from 5 percent to 30 percent. If we take a stock with a 20 percent growth rate, at a market *P/E* of 12.5*x* (bottom axis), the relative *P/E* of that stock (left axis) is 200 percent, i.e., its *P/E* is twice that of the market. But if the market *P/E* rises to 20*x* because bond yields fall,

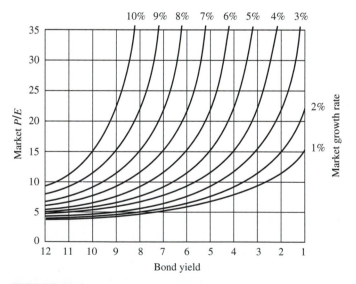

FIGURE 10-5
Market's *P/E* at varying bond yields and growth rates. (*Source:* Edward Kershner, *Portfolio Managers' Spotlight,* Paine Webber, 1995.)

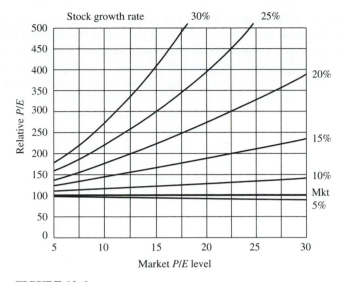

FIGURE 10-6
Relative *P/E* of a stock, given varying growth rates for the stock
and *P/E* levels for the overall stock market. (*Source:* Edward
Kershner, *Portfolio Managers' Spotlight,* Paine Webber, 1995.)

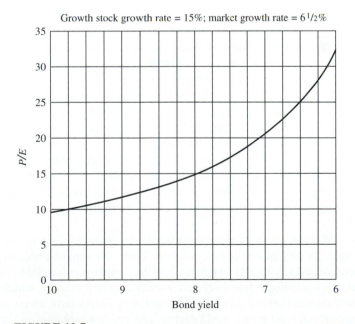

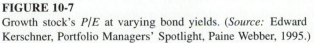

FIGURE 10-7
Growth stock's *P/E* at varying bond yields. (*Source:* Edward
Kerschner, Portfolio Managers' Spotlight, Paine Webber, 1995.)

that same stock will have a relative *P/E* of 275 percent, so the relative *P/E* of this growth stock will have expanded from 200 percent to 275 percent as the market's *P/E* expanded.

Notice that the higher the growth rate of the stock in question is, the greater the expansion in relative *P/E* will be as the market's *P/E* expands. A stock growing at 25 percent (as opposed to the 20 percent used in the previous example) would have a relative *P/E* of about 250 percent when the market's *P/E* is 12.5*x*. If bond yields fell and the market *P/E* rose to 20*x*, its relative *P/E* would expand to 400 percent. This represents a huge 150 percentage-point increase in relative *P/E,* or twice the 75 percent increase in the previous example.

By way of a specific example, Figure 10-7 illustrates a growth stock with a growth rate of 15 percent, more than double the market's growth rate of 6.5 percent. At a bond yield of 8 percent, the stock is worth a *P/E* on normal earnings of 15*x*, but at a bond yield of 6 percent the growth stock's *P/E* expands to 32*x*.

Yield Curve

Data prepared by quantitative strategists at Merrill Lynch, and displayed in Figure 10-8, illustrate that the relative performance of growth and "value" stocks correlate with rates of gain or decline in corporate earnings. When corporate earnings in general are increasing, value stocks tend to do well. During such periods, the high and usually more steady rate-of-earnings growth for the growth class of stocks tends to be less highly valued, leading to a commensurate underperformance. On the other hand, during periods of decreasing corporate-earnings momentum and outright declines in earnings, growth stocks tend to outperform value stocks. The generally more steady and positive-earnings growth for the growth class is then more highly sought by investors.

Because the slope of the yield curve may be an implicit forecast within the financial market of future growth prospects and, thereby, earnings changes, it can also be an indicator of the direction of growth and value stock groupings. For example, if the future is expected to be less robust, then the yield curve will generally take on what is known as an inverted shape, meaning that short-term interest rates are generally higher than long-term bond rates. The curve might become inverted for two reasons. First, the Federal Reserve might have raised short-term interest rates because they fear the risk of inflation. By raising short-term rates, they hope to begin to constrain borrowing power, which will, in turn, slow the economy. Second, long-term investors might buy long-term bonds because they believe that nominal growth rates will be slow or that inflation is not a concern. Such buying would raise the price of bonds but lower their yields. Thus, an inverted curve, whether it be inverted because the Fed has raised short-term rates or because longer-term investors are not fearful of future rising growth and interest rates, generally signals a poor economic environment ahead.

A steep yield curve, or one in which short-term rates are generally lower than long-term bond rates, signals a view of a more robust future. That view could be because the Fed has lowered short-term rates in an attempt to stimulate the economy, or it could be because long-term investors are beginning to fear that future growth may be too strong, which would force interest rates higher as borrowing pressures mounted. If longer-term investors sold bonds because of such fears, bond prices would decline and yields would rise.

If the contentions are that the yield curve is a forecast of future economic conditions and that growth strategies outperform as conditions worsen, we might expect growth stategies

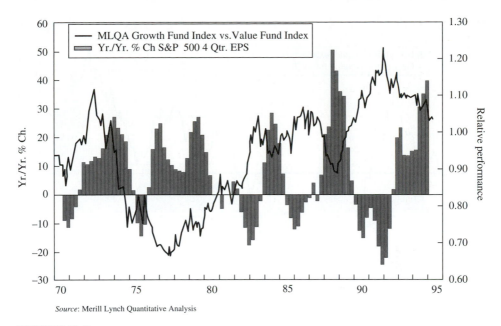

Source: Merill Lynch Quantitative Analysis

FIGURE 10-8
Growth vs. value—relative performance and S&P 500 EPS momentum.

to have outperformed when the yield curve was inverted. If value strategies outperform as conditions improve (whether on a real or nominal basis), value strategies should have worked better when the yield curve was steep.

Figure 10-9 shows that the above-described relationship between growth, value, and the slope of the yield curve appears to hold. The chart compares the relative net asset value of the 18 growth and value mutual funds with the 3-month T-bill to the 30-year T-bond ratio. That ratio being greater than 1.0 indicates that the yield curve is steep and that the bond rate is higher than the bill rate. That ratio being less than 1.0 indicates that the yield curve is inverted and that the bill rate is higher than the bond rate.

The relative fund performance seems to adhere to the description above, although it is not straightforward. The extreme values relating to the slope of the yield curve seem to be more important than the slope itself. There may actually be four phases through which the yield curve changes its slope, and growth and value each seem to outperform during two of them. Starting with a yield curve that is changing from flat to inverted, growth will tend to outperform value because investors realize that the Fed is actually trying to choke off the economic expansion. Next, as the slope changes from extremely inverted to flat, growth will still outperform value because investors now believe that the Fed, realizing that it may have been too restrictive, is beginning to ease short-term interest rates because the economy is beginning to slip into recession. Value will begin to outperform as the slope of the yield curve changes from flat to steep. Here, investors realize that the Fed is now trying to make a concerted effort to stimulate the economy. Value will also outperform as the slope goes from extremely steep to flat, because investors will believe that the Fed is reacting to the strength within the economy and is trying to slow the economic expansion. Value will continue to

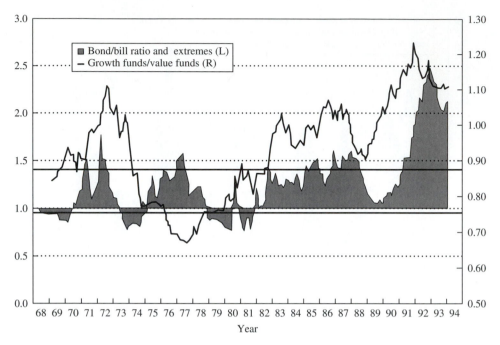

FIGURE 10-9
Extremes of the bond/bill ratio and growth and value investing.

outperform until the slope of the yield curve is flat. Beyond that, we return to the starting phase in this example.

Table 10-11 summarizes the slope of the yield curve and growth and value performance.

Relative *P/E*s

A third way of appraising growth stocks is by looking at the valuation level of this grouping compared to the overall market. Over time the growth group tends to go to extremes in valuation, due to its greater sensitivity to interest rate swings, as well as a tendency toward speculative extremes. Figure 10-10 shows the price-earnings ratio of a grouping of growth stocks relative to the *P/E* of the overall market as measured by the S&P 500 *P/E*. Note that the *P/E* of the growth group approached and exceeded that of the S&P 500 by twice in the 1970–1973 period, often characterized as the era of the "favorite 50" of large high-growth

TABLE 10-11
Growth & value performance and the
slope of the yield curve

Yield Curve	Style Performance	Rationale
Flat to inverted	Growth outperforms	Choking economy
Inverted to flat	Growth outperforms	Overly restrictive
Flat to steep	Value outperforms	Stimulative
Steep to flat	Value outperforms	Too easy

Source: Merrill Lynch quantitative analysis.

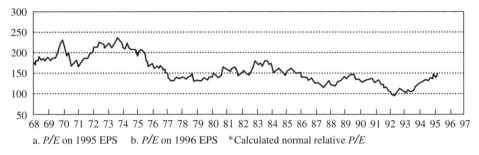

a. *P/E* on 1995 EPS   b. *P/E* on 1996 EPS   *Calculated normal relative *P/E*

FIGURE 10-10
High-growth relative *P/E*. (*Source:* Edward Kerschner, Portfolio Managers' Spotlight, Paine Webber, 1995.)

stocks. Subsequently, the relative *P/E* of the group drifted down in line with the S&P 500, or close to 100 percent of the S&P 500 in the early 1990s.

Valuation can be helpful in appraising the relative attractiveness of this group, especially at extremes such as the early 1970s and the more recent period. For this purpose, an especially simple yet illuminating way to assess this valuation is by means of the payback model developed by Holt based on the two-stage dividend discount model and described in Chapter 6. The Holt model essentially allows us to determine the extent to which a growth stock's relatively higher *P/E* ratio is compensated by a relatively higher growth rate.[10] Assuming that a market average such as the S&P 500 is representative of the *P/E* and growth-rate characteristics of the average stock, we can represent the duration of growth model as follows:

$$\frac{P/E \text{ growth stock}}{P/E \text{ market average}} = \left[\frac{1 + \text{growth rate (growth stock)}}{1 + \text{growth rate (market average)}}\right]^{\text{T}}$$

In words, this equation says that the ratio of the *P/E* ratios of the growth stock and the market average is equal to the ratio of their composite growth rates raised to the *T*th power. For this purpose, the composite growth rates include growth due to reinvested dividends, so that the growth rate is a sort of total return rate. The time period *T* might be considered the period when the higher growth rate of the growth stock "pays back," or offsets, the initial penalty

---

[10]Charles C. Holt, "The Influence of Growth Duration on Share Prices," *Journal of Finance,* September 1962, pp. 465–475, derived an expression for determining the period of superior growth within the framework of the two-stage dividend capitalization model. This expression implies that once the period of of superior growth is completed, the growth stock assumes the characteristics of a nongrowth stock and is priced accordingly; that is, it assumes the same *P/E* as a nongrowth stock. In addition, Holt suggested that the dividend payout of the growth stock increased to that of a nongrowth stock when it completed the period of superior growth. Finally, he postulated that growth and nongrowth stocks were equivalent in terms of riskiness. This assumption implies that the returns to growth and nongrowth stocks should be equalized over time and facilitates the derivation of the years of superior growth estimates. Though this assumption facilitates the derivation of a simplified formulation, we should be aware that growth stocks are as likely to be riskier than average growth stocks. For one thing, growth stocks have greater exposure to interest rate risk and, as a consequence, should generally provide a premium return over the average stock. This assumption introduces a bias in favor of growth stocks into the analysis, but given the fact that the measure is mainly intended as a broad gauge indicator of valuation, the bias is not likely to be a serious impediment to practical application.

of a higher *P/E* ratio. All other things being equal, the shorter this payback period, the more attractive the stock should be, whereas the longer the payback period, the less attractive the stock should be.

In addition to the application to individual stocks, the Holt model can be applied to valuing growth stocks as a class. This analysis is, in fact, particularly enlightening for illustrating the extreme valuation to which growth stocks as a class had risen at the end of 1972. At that time, growth stocks were selling at a *P/E* ratio of 32 times and the total return growth rate implied for the group was 13 percent, whereas the S&P 500 was selling at a *P/E* ratio of 14.0 times with an implied total return growth rate of 9.5 percent. Using the previously noted formulation along with these inputs, we solve for an implied period of superior growth of over 25 years. To use an oft-cited Wall Street aphorism, growth stocks were discounting the hereafter. Growth stock performance subsequent to 1972 was decidedly inferior, underperforming the S&P 500, for example, by 40 percent over the 1973–1977 period.

On the other hand, growth stocks were showing extreme levels of undervaluation in the late 1980s. At that time, growth stocks as a class were selling at a *P/E* ratio of 15 times and the total return growth rate implied for the group was 17 percent, whereas the S&P 500 was selling at a *P/E* ratio of 13 times with an implied total return growth rate of 12 percent. Again using the payback formulation along with this data as inputs, we derive an implied period of superior growth of 3.3 years. As we showed in the prior sections, growth stock performance from 1989 to 1991 was significantly positive, both absolutely and relatively.

FUNDAMENTAL CHARACTERISTICS
OF NONGROWTH GROUPINGS

When attempting to discriminate among nongrowth groupings of cyclical, stable, and energy stocks, directly analyzing the companies' sources of profit would be more useful. One of the fundamental sources of profit is, of course, the price level of the companies' products and services. The general level of prices is set in a macroeconomic context and changes as inflationary forces moderate or intensify. Companies, in turn, differ in their reaction to changes in prices. Those with greater flexibility in pricing their products and services fare better than others during inflationary periods, but other companies fare relatively better during periods of decelerating price changes or when the general level of prices remains stable.

Table 10-12 shows the major categories of industries included within the three groupings of cyclical, stable, and energy stocks. It should be helpful in illustrating the responses of different types of companies to changes in price levels. Note that the energy sector consists of companies that provide the most basic input to the manufacture and consumption of goods and services. On the other hand, the stable sector consists of companies that provide goods and services at the final stage of demand, they primarily market to the consumer. The cyclical sector consists primarily of companies at an intermediate stage of processing, their customers are primarily other companies.

We would, in turn, expect the stable sector to be the most adversely impacted by accelerating inflation. Food, beverage, tobacco, and retailer companies would have difficulty in passing on increased prices to consumers because of the well-known phenomenon of consumer resistance to increased prices during such a period. At the same time, the costs of such companies usually keep pace with inflation, resulting in a squeeze on profit margins. Util-

TABLE 10-12
Industries classified by major sectors

Growth	Cyclical	Stable	Energy
Hospital management	Aluminum	Food processors	Coal
Pollution control	Copper	Beverage	Domestic oil
Cosmetics	Miscellaneous metals	Tobacco	International oil
Drugs	Autos	Household products	Crude-oil producers
Hospital supplies	Auto parts and trucks	Retailers	Oil service companies
Electronics	Building materials	Utilities	
Entertainment	Chemicals	Telephones	
Hotels/restaurants	Containers	Banks	
Computers	Textiles	Insurance	
Newspapers/broadcasters	Tires	Finance	
Specialty chemicals	Electrical equipment		
Growth retailers	Machinery		
	Forest products and paper		
	Steel		
	Railroads		

ities, as regulated entities, encounter lags in adjusting rates or rate allowances that are not fully compensating and consequently suffer during periods of accelerating inflation. Banks, finance companies, and life insurance companies are significant net creditors and, therefore, suffer like other creditors during inflationary periods. Casualty insurance companies, as net creditors, are also exposed and suffer further impairment of underwriting margins when regulatory lags fail to adjust rates fully and promptly for inflationary effects. Conversely, we would expect stable companies to fare relatively well as inflation decelerates and during periods of price stability.

While stable companies would have difficulty passing on rising costs to final demanders—the consumers—cyclical companies, as intermediate producers, would have greater flexibility in this regard. In particular, we would expect cyclical companies to pass on costs to other companies with greater ease when demand for the product is high, capacity is limited, and inflationary pressures are widespread. We would, of course, expect that during periods of relatively slack demand and excess capacity, cyclical companies would have difficulty raising prices, so their profit margins and overall profitability would suffer accordingly.

Energy companies, which supply a primary factor of production, would seem to have the greatest flexibility in pricing their product and passing costs on to customers at either the producer or consumer level. A rising trend in energy prices seems to have the most favorable consequences for profitability and, hence, relative performance. Conversely, a declining trend in energy prices seems to be the most useful indication of declining profitability and, hence, relatively inferior performance by energy-related companies.

Relative Performance of Nongrowth Groupings

An indicator of the relative swings in profitability between stable companies, or final-stage producers, and cyclical companies, or intermediate producers, is the relationship between producer or wholesale prices (WPI) and consumer prices (CPI). In this respect, we can

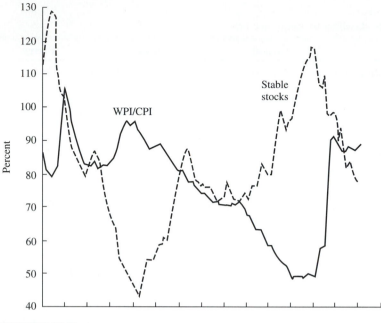

FIGURE 10-11
Stable stocks and the consumer price index.

broadly regard the CPI as representative of the prices that the final-goods producers (stables) receive, the WPI is representative of those companies costs but also indicative of the prices that intermediate producers (cyclicals) receive. As a result, we would expect that the profit margins of final-goods companies would be relatively favorably impacted when the CPI is rising relative to the WPI.

Figure 10-11 plots the returns of the stable grouping, adjusted for general market effects against the WPI/CPI ratio, and Figure 10-12 plots the returns of cyclical companies also adjusted for general market effects against this same ratio. Note that the performance of the stable group moves counter (inversely) to the WPI/CPI ratio, indicating that this group performs well when the ratio is declining but poorly when it is rising, as might be expected from the likely impact on the relative profitability of these companies. Conversely, the performance of cyclical companies is positively related to the WPI/CPI ratio, indicating that this group performs well when the ratio is rising but poorly when it is declining. These performances, again are what we would expect from the likely impact that changes in the ratio should have on the profitability of these companies.

Figure 10-13 shows an index of energy stock returns adjusted for general market effects and plotted against the rate of inflation, which is measured as an average of the previous three years and the year-ahead change in an index of energy prices. Note that the energy stocks performed in line with the relative price index for energy, as would be expected. Energy companies performed especially well during the energy crises of 1970–1972 and 1977–1980, when prices rose at a relatively rapid rate. These companies performed poorly when energy prices relatively declined.

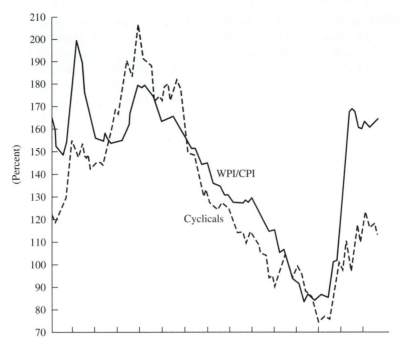

FIGURE 10-12
Cyclical stocks and the WPI to CPI ratio.

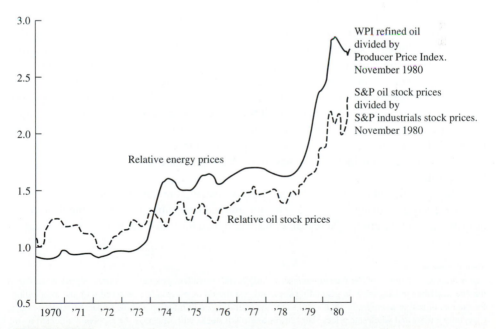

FIGURE 10-13
Energy stocks and the relative price of energy (*Source:* C.J. Lawrence, Inc., New York).

In effect, what we have described here is a sort of stage-of-processing model for understanding the relative performances of the different nongrowth groupings. To a certain extent, the favorable effect of changing prices for one group might adversely impact the performance of another group. For example, rising energy prices would favorably impact oil companies but unfavorably impact the cost structure of intermediate producers, such as chemical companies. We might further expect prices at these various stages of processing to accelerate or decelerate, as the economy moves through the business cycle. For example, over the cycle, the prices of primary products tend to lead those of intermediate products, which in turn lead the prices of final goods.

Given these differing group reactions to changes in the price level or its components, we as portfolio managers would react in the following way to expected changes in prices. A forecast of accelerating inflation would call for an underweighting of stable companies in the portfolio, but a forecast of decelerating inflation would imply an overweighting of these companies. A forecast of increasing energy prices would indicate the relative attractiveness of energy companies and call for an overweighting of this group, but a forecast decrease would call for the opposite reaction. Finally, a forecast of a rising WPI would call for an increased position in cyclicals, but a forecast decrease would imply an underweighted position.

Adjusting Forecasts

If we assume some capability for predicting these group moves either through the kind of analysis that we have just outlined or some other kind, we are faced with the question of determining to what extent the organization should act on these forecasts.[11] In particular, we need to determine to what extent a favorably positioned grouping—one with a positive return forecast—should be overweighted in the portfolio and to what extent the group should be underweighted when an inferior performance is projected. The method of overweighting and underweighting essentially involves applying some of the principles discussed in earlier chapters along with more formal techniques of active-passive portfolio management.

This procedure can be outlined as follows. The first step is to generate forecasts of relative attractiveness for the four groups: growth, cyclical, stable, and energy stocks. The second step is to convert these into explicit forecasts of nonmarket return. The third step is to adjust these forecasts by means of the information coefficient (IC) method for the organization's presumed degree of forecasting capability. Once we have developed the return forecast, we need to consider the riskiness of each group to determine its optimum weighting in the portfolio.

The upper part of Figure 10-14 shows how we can use the same sort of rating technique, described earlier with regard to stock selection and market timing, for expressing the relative attractiveness of the groups. Note that we have assigned the following hypothetical ratings to

---

[11]In estimating the return of the four groupings, we might well consider applying a scenario approach similar to the one described in Chapter 9. In generating scenarios, we should be especially concerned with the implications for the rate of real economic growth, as well as for the overall trend in inflation and the impact of relative prices, especially energy and wholesale prices. The returns to growth stocks will, of course, be especially affected by the trends in real growth, the return to stable stocks will be affected by the overall rate of inflation, the return to cyclical stocks by the trend in wholesale prices, and the returns to energy stocks by the trend in energy prices.

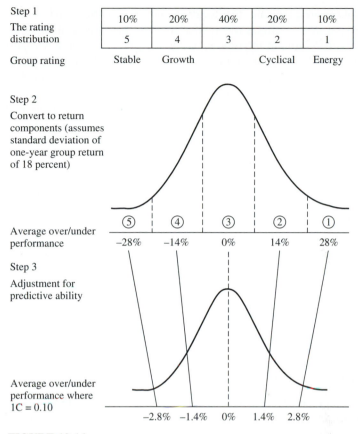

Step 1
The rating
distribution

10%	20%	40%	20%	10%
5	4	3	2	1

Group rating   Stable   Growth   Cyclical   Energy

Step 2

Convert to return
components (assumes
standard deviation of
one-year group return
of 18 percent)

Average over/under
performance

Step 3

Adjustment for
predictive ability

Average over/under
performance where
1C = 0.10

FIGURE 10-14
Forecasting group returns.

the groups: energy stocks are rated 1, or most attractive; cyclical stocks are 2, or moderately attractive; growth stocks are 4, or moderately unattractive; and stable stocks are 5, or least attractive. Even though we only have four groups to rate, the ratings still result in the desired average of 3, indicating an unbiased set of ratings. The standard deviation of the ratings is 1.3.[12]

---

[12]Recall from the previous two chapters that the first step in this process is to convert the rating of a grouping into standard deviations from the mean rating of 3. We do this by dividing the rating by the standard deviation of the rating distribution, which in this case is 1.3. For example, the cyclical group has a rating of 2, which is $1 \div 1.3 = 0.77$ standard deviations above the mean, but the growth group, which has a rating of 4, is 0.77 standard deviations below the mean. Correspondingly, the energy group, which is rated 1, is $2 \div 1.3 = 1.54$ standard deviations above the mean, but the stable group, which is rated 5, is 1.54 standard deviations below the mean. Once the ratings have been converted into standard deviations, we then multiply these by the standard deviation of the return distribution, which in this case is 18 percent. For example, the energy group, which is 1.54 standard deviations above the mean, converts to a return of 28 percent (1.54×18), but the stable group, which is 1.54 standard deviations below the mean, converts to a return of -28 percent. Correspondingly, the cyclical group converts to a return of 14 percent (0.77×18), but the growth group, which is 0.77 below the mean, has a return of -14 percent.

Empirical research indicates that the cross-sectional distribution of group returns, unrelated to general market effects (nonmarket returns), has averaged about 18 percent per annum. So, for two-thirds of the time in any given year—assuming normally distributed returns—the nonmarket-related return of the group will be $+/-18$ percent. Therefore, for one-sixth of the time, the return will be higher than 18 percent, but for another one-sixth of the time, it will be lower than -18 percent.

The middle section of Figure 10-14 shows the mapping of the rating distribution onto the empirical return distribution. Note that a rating of 1 converts to a return of 28 percent for the energy group, a rating of 2 to a 14 percent return for the cyclical group, a rating of 4 to a 14 percent loss for the stable group, and a rating of 5 to a 28 percent loss for the stable group. The center of the distribution is zero, indicating that the average, or expected return, is centered at zero, which would, in effect, be the kind of distribution or opportunity available to a forecaster with perfect predictive capability—an IC of +1.

We know, however, that it is necessary to adjust the distribution for the fact that predictive capability, where it exists, is likely to be imperfect at best. The bottom part of Figure 10-14 shows the adjustment that would be made for a hypothetical forecaster with an IC of 0.10. For this forecaster the expected return for the highest-rated group (energy stocks) becomes 2.8 percent, and for the cyclical group 1.4 percent, whereas the expected loss for the growth group becomes 1.4 percent, and for the stable group 2.8 percent. The standard deviation of this distribution becomes 1.8 percent, compared with the original 18 percent, and represents the degree of shrinkage of the distribution owing to imperfect forecasts.

OPTIMUM WEIGHTING

In order to determine how extensively to overweight or underweight the groups in a portfolio, we need to consider the market and nonmarket risks of the groups, as well as the return opportunities. For example, we would presumably want to overweight the energy group and underweight the stable group in the portfolio to take advantage of the return opportunity and avoid the potential loss. This overweighting and underweighting would add nonmarket risk to the portfolio and could move the portfolio beta to above or below 1, exposing the portfolio to market risk.

Figure 10-15 illustrates the importance of considering both risk and return in developing the optimum weightings of the groups in the portfolio. The solid curve shows the risk and return of various portfolios containing different combinations of the four groups: growth, cyclical, stable, and energy. Point M represents the market portfolio; it contains market proportions of the four groups. Points G and C are portfolios with group weights that diverge from the market portfolio and thus contain "bets" on the groups.

Note that point G provides a higher return and is at a higher risk level than point M. Portfolio G, however, provides a higher return per unit of risk than the market portfolio. The angle of the line extending from R_f, representing the risk-free rate, to point G is greater than the angle of the line extending from R_F to point M Note also that the line is tangent to the curve at point G, indicating that it is at the maximum angle. Any portfolio to the right of point G would provide a less favorable return-risk ratio; the weightings of the groups in these portfolios would be less than optimum.

In fact, as we move to the right along the line, the return-risk ratio becomes even less favorable than that provided by market M. For example, portfolio C, on the line to the right

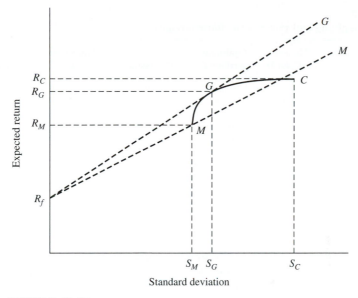

FIGURE 10-15
Optimal group weights.

of G, provides a higher return than either G or M and yet has significantly higher risk, which results in a less favorable return-risk ratio than the market—that is, a line from R_f to point C would have a lesser slope than the line $R_f M$. This information shows that overconcentration in the pursuit of high return leads to an excessive build-up of nonmarket risk.

In order to consider nonmarket risk explicitly and thereby develop an optimal portfolio as illustrated by point G in Figure 10-15, we can again resort to the optimization techniques described in Chapter 2. Appendix B illustrates the way that weights are developed for the groups using the simplified portfolio optimization techniques of Elton and Gruber.[13] As noted before, the merits of these techniques are that they allow the analyst to see explicitly the risk-return trade-offs of assets under consideration and thereby better understand the reasons for the inclusion and weighting of groups in the optimal portfolio.

Because Appendix B describes the application of the optimization technique, we will merely discuss the results of analysis as shown in Table 10-13. The table shows the weightings of the groups in the optimal portfolio, as well as approximate weightings of the groupings in the market which allows a comparison of the divergence of portfolio weighting from the market. Note that optimum portfolio G has greater weighting in the energy and cyclical groups than the market, as might be expected given their relatively favorable rating. At the same time, the growth and stable groups have a zero weighting, which is, of course, less than their weighting in the general market. The portfolio is, in effect, long the energy and cyclical groups and short the growth and stable groups.

Table 10-13 also shows the weighted average return and risk, as measured by the standard deviation of return, for this optimum portfolio, as well as the ratio of the excess return

---

[13] Edwin Elton, Martin Gruber, and Manfred Padberg: "Optimal Portfolios from Simple Ranking Devices," *Journal of Portfolio Management,* Spring 1978, pp. 15–19.

TABLE 10-13
Portfolio weighting and risk-return characteristics

Stock group	Market portfolio M (1)	Optimum portfolio G (2)	Divergence (2) − (1) = (3)	Concentrated portfolio C (4)	Divergence (4) − (1) = (5)
Cyclical	0.25	0.45	+0.20	1	+0.75
Energy	0.20	0.55	+0.35	0	−0.20
Growth	0.30	0.00	−0.30	0	−0.30
Stable	0.25	0.00	−0.25	0	−0.25
Expected excess return	7%		9%		9.80%
Standard deviation of return	18%		21%		26%
Return/standard deviation	0.39		0.43		0.38

to standard deviation of the portfolio. This ratio is known as the Sharpe ratio, and in terms of Figure 10-15, it measures the slope of the line from the risk-free return to the risk-return plot of the portfolio. Table 10-13 also shows the same risk-return statistics for market portfolio M and for a concentrated portfolio invested entirely in the most attractive group in terms of return-cyclical stocks. This concentrated portfolio might be construed as representative of portfolio C in Figure 10-15.

Note that the risk-return ratio of 0.43 for the optimum portfolio exceeds the ratio of 0.39 for the market portfolio. At the same time, the risk-return ratio of 0.38 for the concentrated portfolio is less than the ratios for both the optimum and market portfolio. These cases are depicted in Figure 10-15, in which portfolio G shows a more favorable plotting than portfolio M, whereas portfolio C shows a less favorable positioning than either M or G. The data thus illustrate both the problems in overemphasizing return and the usefulness of those techniques, which explicitly take into account risk as well as return when constructing a portfolio.

CONCLUSION

In devising a strategy for investing in the domestic equity market, major plan sponsors generally seek specialized managers whom they deem capable of adding value within a particular area of expertise. Furthermore, most sponsors think in terms of a breakdown of managers into broad groupings of growth and value, as well as a breakdown according to size. A typical line-up for a plan might include a growth stock manager that specializes in large-capitalization growth stocks and a value stock manager that specializes in large-capitalization value stocks. The line-up could also include a small-capitalization stock manager or a further breakdown into small-capitalization growth and value stock specialists.

In advising plan sponsors on the merits of an investment plan, investment management consultants also rely on style management classifications. Correspondingly, performance evaluators need style groupings and indexes of performance to properly evaluate the performance of specialized managers. At the same time, specialty managers need to describe their investment style properly to define their universe of stocks for selection and portray their capabilities to investors. Finally, those managers pursuing rotational strategies—group or style rotation—rely heavily on style groupings.

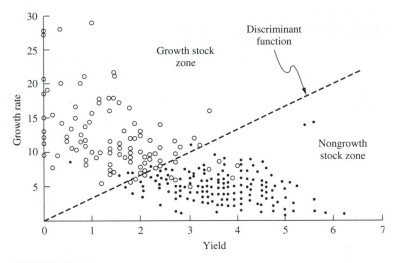

FIGURE 10-A1
Growth–yield characteristics (circles = growth; dots = nongrowth), 1971–1979.

In executing style-based strategies, we see that the critical underlying need is for stock groupings that are relevant, as well as for an appropriate classification of stocks into groupings. We have seen that conventionally based methods offer a workably useful way of classifying stocks into groupings. However, we have described and illustrated statistical methods that can help refine the classification of stocks, and better define relevant groupings of stocks. Furthermore, we described how groupings that are identified as homogeneous can be used in active/passive strategies of investment management. Correspondingly, we illustrated a framework based on the simplified portfolio selection techniques for balancing risk against the potential reward from an active strategy of group rotation.

APPENDIX A
DISCRIMINANT ANALYSIS AND FUNDAMENTAL VARIABLES

Though the diagrams in the body of the chapter show that growth stocks differ significantly from nongrowth stocks with respect to sustainable growth and dividend yield variables, we can use a statistical technique known as discriminant analysis to provide a more powerful test of the usefulness of these variables for classifying companies into the appropriate groupings. Discriminant analysis is a statistical technique that allows observations (firms, in this case) to be classified into appropriate priori groups on the basis of a set of independent or predictor variables. Discriminant analysis is similar to regression analysis, except that the dependent variable in discriminant analysis must be qualitative, such as growth or nongrowth. It has been employed in finance to distinguish bankrupt firms from nonbankrupt firms and to classify companies into different bond-rating groups.

For our purposes, discriminant analysis provides a way of partitioning the diagrams (Figures 10-1 and 10-2) into the two zones of growth and nongrowth stocks. Figure 10-A1 illustrates this partitioning by superimposing a dashed line on Figure 10-1. The line represents the graphing of the discriminant function that partitions the data into two zones. Those stocks falling into the zone to the right of the line would be classified in the nongrowth

TABLE 10-A1
Classification results for growth and nongrowth stocks

	Predicted based on fundamental variables			
	1971–1979		1980–1989	
Actual based on return behavior	**Growth**	**Nongrowth**	**Growth**	**Nongrowth**
Growth	89	23	114	10
	(79.46%)		(91.94%)	
Nongrowth	12	217	20	210
		(94.76%)		(91.30%)
	89.74% overall		91.53% overall	

Source: James L. Farrell, Jr., George Pinches, and James Scott, "Growth Stock Fundamentals: Implications for Portfolio Management," unpublished paper, 1991.

category by the discriminant function, and those to the left of the line would be classified in the growth category.

Table 10-A1 shows the classification results of discriminant analysis, using the fundamental variables of dividend yield and sustainable growth for the two periods of the test. It shows the number of actual growth or nongrowth firms over the 1971–1989 period based on return behavior, and it shows the predicted growth or nongrowth firms based on the fundamental variables of sustainable growth and dividend yield. Note that the discriminant analysis model classified 89.74 percent of the firms into their return-based growth and nongrowth groups in the 1971–1979 period, whereas 91.53 percent of the firms were correctly classified in the 1980–1989 period. The models seemed to have worked well in classifying growth and nongrowth stocks, except in the case of growth stocks in the 1971–1979 period.

APPENDIX B
A SIMPLIFIED TECHNIQUE FOR DETERMINING OPTIMUM GROUP WEIGHTS

This appendix illustrates in detail the application of the Elton and Gruber technique to developing optimum weightings of groups in a portfolio. The inputs necessary to apply the technique are the following: (1) expected return to the groups; (2) sensitivity of the group return to the market as measured by the beta coefficient; (3) the residual, or nonmarket, risk of the four groups; (4) expected return of the market and variance of market return; and (5) the risk-free rate. Table 10-B1 shows the input data for the market and for four stock groups.

Note that we are using a 12-percent return for the market along with a risk-free return of 5 percent. The return on the groups includes a market component of 12 percent and an additional increment or decrement, as the case may be, which was derived in the body of the chapter. The variance of the market, the beta coefficients of the groups with the market, and the residual risks of the groups were calculated with data from the more recent historical period.

This process first involves establishing a cut-off rate, so that we can determine which groups will be included in the portfolio. We can begin to determine the cut-off rate by calculating the excess return (return less risk-free rate) for each of the groups, dividing by the market risk, and then ranking the groups from the highest return-risk ratio to the lowest. Column 1 of Table 10-B2 indicates that the cyclical group ranks first and the stable group last on this basis.

Once we have ranked securities, we derive the ratios shown in column 2 of Table 10-B2 and cumulate the sum as shown in column 3. We also calculate the ratio shown in column 4 for each of the groups and again cumulate the sum as shown in column 5. We then use this data to calculate a C_k value for each of the groups shown in column 6.

The optimum C^* value is when the excess return-risk ratio of the group is less than the calculated C value. All groups with a return-risk ratio greater than this value would be included in the portfolio, but those with values less than the cut-off rate would be excluded. Note that, in this case, the excess return-risk ratios for the cyclical and energy groups are in excess of the cut-off value—that is, both exceed 6.48. As a result, these groups should be included in the optimum portfolio, but the growth and stable groups should be excluded.

Once the cut-off value has been calculated, and the groups to be included in the portfolio determined, the next step is to determine their weighting in the portfolio. Defining w_k as the group weight in the portfolio, Z_k as a value to be calculated, and Z as the sum of the Z_k values, we can use the following formula to determine the group weights:

$$W_k = \frac{Z_k}{Z}$$

In this formula, the Z_k values are calculated using information provided previously:

$$Z_k = \frac{b_k}{\text{Var}(e_k)} \left[\left(\frac{R_k - R_f}{b_k} \right) - C^* \right]$$

In this case, the Z_k values for each of the groups to be included in the portfolio are

$$Z \text{ cyclical} = 1.05/324(9.3 - 6.48) = 0.00914$$

$$Z \text{ energy} = 0.9/225(9.3 - 6.48) = 0.01128$$

Once these Z_k values are determined, we simply sum them to obtain a value of $Z = 0.02042$. We next divide each Z_k by Z to obtain the optimum weight for each group. The following are the calculated weights for each group:

$$W \text{ energy} = 0.55$$

$$W \text{ cyclical} = 0.45$$

Before concluding, we should note that Elton and Gruber have developed simplified portfolio optimization techniques, assuming differing underlying models of the correlation structure of stock returns, including the single-index and multi-index representations. For purposes of developing optimal group weights, the multi-index variation of the basic technique would be the most appropriate. Exposition of this variation is, however, more involved than warranted for our purposes, so we have illustrated the techniques assuming that the single-index model represents the underlying structure of returns. The reader should, however, be aware that the resulting weightings in the portfolio may be based away from optimality because of the use of a less than appropriate variation of the technique.

TABLE 10-B1
Risk-return data—market and stock groups

Stock group	Market return, % (1)	Incremental return, % (2)	Total return R_k, % (1) + (2) = (3)	Risk-free return R_f, % (4)	Excess return, % (3) − (4) = (5)	Beta (β) (6)	Nonmarket Var (e) (7)
Cyclical	12	+2.8	14.8	5	9.8	1.05	324
Energy	12	+1.4	13.4	5	8.4	0.9	225
Growth	12	−1.4	10.6	5	5.6	1.2	400
Stable	12	−2.8	9.2	5	4.2	0.9	225

Note: Variance of market = **324**; standard deviation of market = **18** percent.

TABLE 10-B2
Determining optimum group weights

Stock group	$\dfrac{R_k - R_f}{B_k}$ (1)	$\dfrac{(R_k - R_f)B_k}{\text{Var}(e)}$ (2)	$\displaystyle\sum_{k=1}^{k} \dfrac{(R_k - R_f)B_k}{\text{Var}(e)}$ (3)	$\dfrac{B_k^2}{\text{Var}(e)}$ (4)	$\displaystyle\sum_{k=1}^{k} \dfrac{B_k^2}{\text{Var}(e)}$ (5)	$C_k = \dfrac{\text{Var}_f[3]}{1 + [\text{Var}M(5)]}$ (6)
Cyclical	9.3	0.0318	0.0318	0.0034	0.0034	4.9
Energy	9.3	0.0336	0.0654	0.0036	0.007	6.48
Growth	4.7	0.0168	0.0822	0.0036	0.0106	6.01
Stable	4.7	0.0168	0.099	0.0036	0.0142	5.73

SELECTED REFERENCES

Arnott, R.: "Discussion of Cluster Analysis Project," paper presented at the Fall 1979 meeting of the Institute for Quantitative Research in Finance, Vail, CO.

——, J. Dorian, and R. Macedo: "Style Management: The Missing Element in Equity Portfolios," *The Journal of Investing,* Summer 1992, pp. 13–21.

Bailey, Jeffrey, and Robert Arnott: "Cluster Analysis and Manager Selection," *Financial Analysts Journal,* November–December 1986, pp. 20–28.

Banz, Rolf: "The Relationship Between Return and Market Value of Common Stocks," *Journal of Financial Economics* 9, 1981, pp. 3–18.

Barry, Christopher, and Stephen Brown: "Differential Approach and the Small Firm Effect," *Journal of Financial Economics,* June 1989, pp. 283–294.

Basu, S.: "Investment Performance of Common Stocks in Relation to Their Price-Earnings Ratio," *Journal of Finance* 32, 1977, pp. 663–682.

Boudoukh, J., M. Richardson, and R. Whitelaw: "Industry Returns and the Fisher Effect," *Journal of Finance,* December 1994, pp. 1595–1615.

Brown, P., A. Kleidon, and T. Marsh: "New Evidence on the Nature of Size-Related Anomalies in Stock Prices," *Journal of Financial Economics* 12, 1983, pp. 33–56.

Chan, K.C.: "On the Contrarian Investment Strategy," *Journal of Business,* April 1988, pp. 147–164.

Cohen, Kalman and Jerry Pogue: "An Empirical Evaluation of Alternative Portfolio Selection Models," *Journal of Business,* April 1967, pp. 166–193.

Collins, Bruce, and Frank Fabozzi: "Considerations in Selecting a Small Capitalization Benchmark," *Financial Analysts Journal,* January–February 1990, pp. 40–46.

Elton, Edwin J., and Martin J. Gruber: "Homogeneous Groups and the Testing of Economic Hypotheses," *Journal of Financial and Quantitative Analysis,* January 1970, pp. 581–602.

——: "Improved Forecasting through the Design of Homogeneous Groups," *Journal of Business,* October 1971, pp. 432–450.

——: "Estimating the Dependence Structure of Share Prices—Implications for Portfolio Selection," *Journal of Business,* December 1973, pp. 1203–1232.

Fama, Eugene, and Ken French: "Business Cycles and the Behavior of Metals Prices," *Journal of Finance,* December 1988, pp. 1075–1093.

——and ——: "The Cross-Section of Expected Stock Returns," *Journal of Finance* 47, 1992, pp. 427–466.

——and ——: "Commodity Futures Prices: Some Evidence on Forecast Power, Premiums, and the Theory of Storage," *Journal of Business,* January 1987, pp. 55–74.

Farrell, James L., Jr.: "Homogeneous Stock Groupings: Implications for Portfolio Management," *Financial Analysts Journal,* May–June 1975, pp. 50–62.

——: "Analyzing Covariation of Return to Determine Homogeneous Stock Groupings," *Journal of Business,* April 1974, pp. 186–207.

——: "The Multi-Index Model and Practical Portfolio Analysis," Financial Analysts Research Foundation, Occasional Paper no. 4, 1976.

——, George Pinches, and James Scott: "Homogeneous Stock Groupings: Fundamental Determinants," unpublished paper, 1991.

Flannery, Mark, and Christopher James: "The Effect of Interest Rate Changes on the Common Stock Returns of Financial Institutions," *Journal of Finance,* September 1984, pp. 1141–1153.

Fogler, Russell, K. John, and J. Tipton: "Three Factors, Interest Rate Differentials and Stock Groups," *Journal of Finance,* May 1981, pp. 323–335.

Good, Walter, Roy Hermansen, and T. Kirkham Barneby: "Opportunity: Actively Managed Investment Universes," *Financial Analysts Journal,* January–February 1986, pp. 49–57.

Hackel, Kenneth, Joshua Livrat, and Atul Roi: "The Free Cash Flow/Small-Cap Anomaly," *Financial Analysts Journal,* September–October 1994, pp. 33–42.

Harris, Robert, and Felicia Marston: "Value versus Growth Stocks: Book-to-Market, Growth and Return," *Financial Analysts Journal,* September–October 1994, pp. 18–24.

Harvey, Campbell: "Forecasts of Economic Growth from the Bond and Stock Markets," *Financial Analysts Journal,* September–October 1989, pp. 38–45.

Haugen, R., and D. Wichem: "The Elasticity of Financial Assets," *Journal of Finance,* September 1974, pp. 1229–1240.

Higgins, R.C.: "Growth, Dividend Policy and Capital Costs in the Electric Utility Industry," *Journal of Finance,* September 1974, pp. 1189–1201.

Huberman, G., and S. Kandel: "Value Line Rank and Firm Size," *Journal of Business,* October 1987, pp. 577–590.

Jaffe, Jeffrey, and Randolph Westerfield: "The Week-End Effect in Common Stock Returns: The International Evidence," *Journal of Finance,* June 1985, pp. 433– 454.

Jaffe, J., D.B. Keim, and R. Westerfield: "Earnings Yield, Market Value and Stock Returns," *Journal of Finance* 57, 1989, pp. 135–148.

Jones, Steven: "Another Look at Time-Varying Risk and Return in a Long-Horizon Contrarion Strategy," *Journal of Financial Economics,* February 1993, pp. 119– 144.

Keim, Donald: "The CAPM and Equity Return Regularities," *Financial Analysts Journal,* March–April 1986, pp. 19–34.

———: "A New Look at the Effects of Firm Size and E/P Ratio on Stock Returns," *Financial Analysts Journal,* March–April 1990, pp. 56–67.

King, Benjamin: "Market and Industry Factors in Stock Price Behavior," *Journal of Business,* January 1966, pp. 139–190.

Lakonishok, J., A. Shleiffer, and R. Vishny: "Contrarian Investment, Extrapolation, and Risk," *Journal of Finance,* December 1994, pp. 1541–1578.

Livingston, Miles: "Industry Movements of Common Stocks," *Journal of Finance,* June 1977, pp. 861–874.

Loeb, Thomas: "Is There a Gift from Small-Stock Investing?," *Financial Analysts Journal,* January–February 1991, pp. 39–44.

Martin, J.D., and R.C. Klemkosky: "The Effect of Homogeneous Stock Groupings on Portfolio Risk," *Journal of Business,* July 1976, pp. 339–349.

Meyers, S.L.: "A Reexamination of Market and Industry Factors in Stock Price Behavior," *Journal of Business,* July 1976, pp. 695–705.

Ng, V., and S. Pirrong: "Fundamentals and Volatility: Storage, Spreads, and the Dynamics of Metals Prices," *Journal of Business,* April 1994, pp. 203–230.

Roll, R.: "Orange Juice and Weather," *American Economic Review,* December 1987, pp. 861–880.

———: "On Computing Mean Returns and the Small Firm Premium," *Journal of Financial Economics,* November 1983, pp. 371–386.

Rozeff, Michael, and William Kinney: "Capital Market Seasonality: The Case of Stock Returns," *Journal of Financial Economics*, October 1976, pp. 379–402.

Schwert, William: "Size and Stock Returns and Other Regularities," *Journal of Financial Economics* 12, 1983, pp. 3–12.

Sharpe, William: "Asset Allocation: Management Style and Performance Measurement," *Journal of Portfolio Management,* Winter 1992, pp. 7–19.

Sinquefield, Rex: "Are Small-Stock Returns Achievable?," *Financial Analysts Journal,* January–February 1991, pp. 45–50.

Sorenson, Eric, and Terry Burke: "Portfolio Returns from Active Industry Group Rotation," *Financial Analysts Journal,* September–October 1986, pp. 43–50.

———and Clee Thum: "The Use and Misuse of Value Investing," *Financial Analysts Journal,* March–April 1992, pp. 51–58.

Sweeney, Richard, and Arthur Warga: "The Pricing of Interest-Rate Risk: Evidence from the Stock Market," *Journal of Finance,* June 1986, pp. 393–410.

Tierney, David, and Kenneth Winston: "Using Generic Benchmarks to Present Manager Styles," *Journal of Portfolio Management,* Summer 1991, pp. 33–36.

Tobin, J.: "A General Equilibrium Approach to Monetary Theory," *Journal of Money, Credit and Banking,* February 1969, pp. 15–29.

Treynor, Jack, and Fischer Black: "How to Use Security Analysis to Improve Performance," *Journal of Business,* January 1973, pp. 66–86.

QUESTIONS AND PROBLEMS

1. Describe in general the distinguishing characteristics of growth, cyclical, stable, and energy stocks. Also indicate how the market behavior of these groups qualifies them as homogeneous.

2. Describe the opportunities that are available from a strategy of underweighting and overweighting the major stock groups. Also explain the risks that are involved in such a strategy.

3. Indicate some variables that distinguish growth stocks from other groupings, as well as variables that distinguish the three categories of nongrowth stocks (cyclical, stable, and energy) from one another.

4. On average, stocks are expected to grow at a rate of 10.5 percent, and the current yield is 5.5 percent. A stock is growing at the rate of 30 percent per annum but currently pays no dividend. The P/E ratio for the average stock is 8, and for growth stock, it is 13. What is the expected duration of growth for the growth stock? Also, would the stock be undervalued or overvalued if your expectation for the period of superior growth is four years?

5. Assume a forecast of a period of accelerating real growth along with a decline in the general rate of inflation, as well as a decline in the rate of wholesale and energy prices. Which groups would be benefited, relatively, and which would be affected less favorably? Also indicate the strategy for such an environment.

6. Assume that the expected return for growth stocks is 18 percent, for cyclical stocks 16 percent, for stable stocks 17 percent, and for energy stocks 14 percent. Also assume the risk characteristics are the same as those given in Appendix B to this chapter. Determine the optimum weighting of the groups in a portfolio.

7. Determine the superior and inferior portfolios from the following three with risk and return characteristics:
   (*a*) excess return of 7 percent and standard deviation of 18 percent,
   (*b*) excess return of 9 percent and standard deviation of 28 percent, and
   (*c*) excess return of 5 percent and standard deviation of 11 percent.

8. Select your favorite growth stock and develop input data to calculate its payback period. Argue whether the stock is under-, over-, or fair-valued.

9. Calculate the standard deviation and correlation coefficient for growth and "value" stocks using the data in Table 10-6.

10. Assume bond yields increase from 7 percent to 8 percent. What is the likely impact on stocks in general and the P/E of stocks growing at 20 percent?

CHAPTER 11

International Investing

INTRODUCTION

This chapter is devoted to international equity investing and supplements the previous three chapters on domestic equity investing. Expanding the investment universe to include foreign equities should have a beneficial impact on portfolio performance because foreign equities provide an expanded set of assets that generally show a low degree of correlation with domestic (U.S.) assets. Augmenting the selection universe with these generally desirable (low correlation) assets expands the efficient frontier, thereby increasing the potential for constructing a portfolio that maximizes return at a given risk level.

Though foreign investing is likely to be beneficial to overall performance, it differs from domestic investing in one major respect: security holdings will be denominated in several different currencies rather than one currency (U.S. dollars). Because international investing means holding securities denominated in a variety of currencies whose relative values may fluctuate, it involves a foreign exchange risk: that is, exposure to gain or loss on assets or liabilities denominated in another currency. This additional risk should thus be considered in determining the degree of commitment to international investing and the sort of strategy to be employed in executing the investment plan.

This chapter begins by describing the size and characteristics of the international equity market and the potential benefits to be derived from an international investment program. We will then discuss the importance of the currency risk in international investing and establish a framework for analyzing the reasons for currency rate differentials and the fluctuations in these differentials over time. We will then describe a passive strategy for investing in international markets and conclude with an active counterpart to the passive investment strategy.

Size of Global Equity Market

Table 11-1 shows the market values for individual countries and their percentage weighting in a global equity portfolio. The countries shown here include most of the developed countries of the world in which the economies are generally more mature and the stocks have reasonably long trading histories. In comparison, emerging markets such as Thailand,

TABLE 11-1
World equity markets

	Capitalization, 3/31/94	
	In billions of U.S. dollars	As % of total
United Kingdom	$1096	10.20
Germany	449	4.00
France	453	4.00
Switzerland	277	3.00
Netherlands	172	2.00
Italy	184	1.60
Spain	118	1.20
Sweden	107	0.90
Belgium/Luxembourg	80	0.70
Denmark	44	0.40
Norway/Finland	57	0.50
Austria	27	0.30
Total Europe	3064	28.80
Japan	3346	27.60
Hong Kong	266	2.30
Singapore/Malaysia	279	2.10
Australia/New Zealand	219	1.90
Total Pacific	4110	33.90
United States	4396	35.00
Canada	285	2.30
Total North America	4681	37.30
Total	$11,855	100.00

Source: Morgan Stanley—Capital International.

Mexico, India, and Chile, though numerous, are much smaller in terms of market value individually and as a group. The potential for large returns is however greater than for the developed countries, but the risks are correspondingly considerable.

Though the United States is the most significant individual market, close to two-thirds (65 percent) of the global market value is outside the United States. Furthermore, the United States continues to decline in relative importance; at the beginning of the 1980s, the U.S. market was somewhat more than half the total (52 percent at 12/31/79). The United States will likely continue to lose its share of the world market value to more rapidly growing countries as the world market economy expands from new entrants, especially from the former Communist bloc. The logic for investing internationally for U.S. investors will then become even more compelling.

The countries are grouped according to three geographic regions that aggregate to approximately equivalent market weightings: (1) North America (37.3 percent), (2) Pacific Rim (33.9 percent), and (3) Europe (28.8 percent). Within the groupings, the economies and financial markets of individual countries tend to be more highly interrelated than with countries outside the groupings, hence, reinforcing the merits of such regional bloc groupings. Inclusion in a portfolio of the United States, Japan, and the United Kingdom, along with other significant European countries such as France, Germany, and Switzerland, would provide a high degree of global market representation because of their absolute size and dominance within regions. These six countries constitute more than 80 percent of the global market value, with three—the United States, Japan, and the United Kingdom—comprising over 70 percent. Correspondingly, omitting any of the three major markets from a portfolio would seriously degrade diversification.

Risk-Return Character of Global Equity Market

In illustrating the risk-return characteristics of international markets, we calculated realized returns and standard deviation of return for major international markets over the period from 1980 to 1993. During this period, there was a relatively large historical fluctuation in the U.S.-dollar exchange rate. Between January 1980 and December 1984, the U.S. dollar appreciated 83 percent relative to the Deutsche mark (and most other European currencies) and 5 percent relative to the yen. Between January 1985 and December 1993—especially after the Plaza Accord of September 1985, in which the G-5 (an earlier version of the G-7) nations agreed to bring down the value of the U.S. dollar—the dollar depreciated 45 percent against the Deutsche mark and 56 percent against the yen. We can gain further perspective on the way that currency changes impact the performance of international equity investing by subdividing the full period of analysis into (1) the 1980–1984 period of dollar strength and (2) the 1985–1993 period of dollar weakness.

Table 11-2 shows return in both local currencies and dollars for six major global equity markets, as well as an average of 12 majors over three periods: (1) 1980–1984 dollar strength, (2) 1985–1993 dollar weakness, and (3) 1980–1993 overall. Because foreign securities are denominated in local currency, returns are designated in local currency and must be converted to dollars at the prevailing exchange rate in order to be realized by the domestic (U.S.) investor. For example, returns earned on German securities need to be converted into dollars at the prevailing exchange rate of marks for dollars in order to be realized by the domestic (U.S.) investor.

Because exchange rates fluctuate, this conversion can result in an added gain or loss on returns earned in the foreign market. For example, if the rate of exchange for marks to dollars was $0.50 at the beginning of the year but changed to $0.525 by the end of the year, the mark would have appreciated (dollar depreciated) relative to the dollar over the year, resulting in a gain to a U.S. investor of 5 percent on currency over the year. This gain should be added to the return earned on the German market over the year; for example, if the return was 10 percent, the net return would be 15.5 percent.[1] Naturally, any currency loss should be subtracted from the return of 10 percent for the year.

The table shows that in the initial 1980–1984 period of dollar strength there was an average loss of 5.8 percent from the depreciation of foreign currencies, which in turn degraded the overall return to non-U.S. investments. Conversely, during the subsequent 1985–1993 period of dollar weakness in which foreign currencies appreciated, there was a gain on average of 6.5 percent, which enhanced the return to foreign investment. Over the full period, the losses on average tended to offset the gains, so that the net gain to currency over the 1980–1993 period was a modest 1.3 percent. Though currency can impact realized returns

---

[1]Denoting R_m as the market return and F_x as the currency change we derive the return as follows $(1 + R_m)(1 + F_x) - 1 = (1.10)(1.05) - 1 = 15.5\%$.

TABLE 11-2
Major international equity market returns

	Annualized return in local currency	Annualized currency return to U.S. $–based investor	Annualized total return in U.S. $
Panel (a)—Annualized return, January 1980–December 1984(%)			
United States	14.5		14.5
Japan	18.2	−0.9	17.1
United Kingdom	26.9	−12.3	11.4
Germany	13.7	−11.3	0.9
France	17.6	−16	−1.2
Switzerland	8.4	−9.4	−1.8
Average* Non-U.S.	19.2	−5.8	12.2
Panel (b)—Annualized return, January 1985–December 1993(%)			
United States	15.8		15.8
Japan	6.3	9.4	16.3
United Kingdom	16.9	2.7	20.1
Germany	12.7	6.8	20.3
France	17.5	5.6	24.1
Average* Non-U.S.	10.8	6.5	17.8
Panel (c)—Annualized return, January 1980–December 1993(%)			
United States	15.3		15.3
Japan	10.4	5.6	16.6
United Kingdom	20.4	−2.9	16.9
Germany	13	−0.03	13
France	17.5	−2.7	14.4
Switzerland	13.3	0.4	13.7
Average* Non-U.S.	13.7	1.9	15.7

Source: MSCI
*The average return was calculated using a weighted average of MSCI capitalization weights.

significantly over shorter intervals, it is unlikely to be a significant increment, or decrement for that matter, to international investing over extended periods.

However, variations in exchange rates will add to the risk of an international investment program, as illustrated in Table 11-3. This table shows the standard deviation of return measured in both local currency and dollars for the major international equity market over the same periods of analysis: 1980–1984, 1985–1993, and 1980–1993. The difference between the volatility measure in dollars and the volatility measure in local currency represents the currency risk component. Currency fluctuations added a small but significant component to overall volatility that averaged approximately 20 percent above local volatility over the three periods.

TABLE 11-3

	Annualized volatility in local currency	Annualized currency volatility to U.S. \$–based investor***	Annualized total volatility in U.S. \$
Panel (a)—Annualized volatility ** January 1980–December 1984 (%)			
United States	14.5		14.5
Japan	13.5	7.2	20.6
United Kingdom	17.1	4.1	21.2
Germany	13.4	5	18.4
France	19.1	3.7	22.8
Spain	17	1.9	18.9
Netherlands	19.5	2.2	21.6
Australia	24.3	2.8	27.1
Canada	22	2.8	24.7
Switzerland	10.2	7.5	17.7
Sweden	23	0.9	23.8
Italy	27.8	−1.1	26.7
Panel (b)—Annualized volatility ** January 1985–December 1993(%)			
United States	15.5		15.5
Japan	22.9	4.7	27.6
United Kingdom	18.9	3.1	22
Germany	22.4	2.1	24.5
France	21.9	1.7	23.7
Spain	24.8	2.1	26.9
Netherlands	16	−0.1	16
Australia	21.7	5.6	27.3
Canada	14.3	1.7	16
Switzerland	19	0.9	19.9
Sweden	25.9	−1.6	24.3
Italy	26.3	1.8	28.1
Panel (c)—Annualized volatility ** January 1980–1993(%)			
United States	15.2		15.2
Japan	20.1	5.3	25.4
United Kingdom	18.3	3.5	21.8
Germany	19.7	3	22.7
France	21	2.6	23.6
Spain	22.4	2.2	24.5
Netherlands	17.5	0.8	18.3
Australia	22.7	4.5	27.2
Canada	17.5	2.2	19.6
Switzerland	16.5	3	19.5
Sweden	25	−0.8	24.2
Italy	26.9	0.8	27.7

Source: MSCI

** Volatility was calculated based on monthly data annualized.

*** The annualized currency volatility to U.S. dollar-based investor component is the difference between the volatility measured in U.S. dollars and the volatility measured in local currency.

DIVERSIFICATION ADVANTAGES
OF INTERNATIONAL INVESTMENT

International investment would obviously have benefited domestic (U.S.) investors in a favorable currency period such as 1985 to 1993, but a more fundamental reason for considering it is the favorable effects on portfolio diversification. This benefit derives from the opportunity that foreign markets offer in providing a wider array of assets (securities) with relatively low correlation. These can, in turn, be combined with domestic securities to generate a lower overall portfolio risk (standard deviation) than would be possible when investing exclusively in domestic assets.

This principle is, of course, the same one from which the benefits of domestic diversification derive. Recall from Chapter 2 that the typical security in the U.S. equity market would have a correlation with a market index on the order of 0.5. This correlation means that some benefits can be derived from diversification because there is less than perfect correlation between securities; these benefits, however, are limited because the correlation is significantly positive. We have noted that empirical studies show that diversification can reduce the variance, or standard deviation, of a portfolio by 43 percent to something on the order of 57 percent of the risk of a nondiversified (single-security) portfolio.

Table 11-4 shows the correlation between the returns of several major equity markets over three periods—1960–1969, 1970–1979, and 1980–1989. Note that the U.S. and Canadian markets showed a high degree of correlation, as might be expected from the high level of economic integration between the two countries. There was a significantly lower degree of correlation between the United States and the other countries during both periods. On average, the correlation across countries was on the order of 0.31 in the initial period, 0.37 in the second period, and 0.40 in the latest, indicating opportunities for diversification.

Figure 11-1, which is similar to one used in Chapter 2 to illustrate the benefits of diversification, shows that it is possible to use this imperfect correlation among international markets to reduce the risk of a portfolio below the level that is possible when only dealing with domestic securities. Note that the lower line, which represents the possibility of international investing and hence diversification along with domestic investing, lies at a lower level over the full range of portfolio holdings than when diversification is limited exclusively to domestic investing. With international diversification the portfolio risk drops to 33

TABLE 11-4

Correlation of U.S. and key foreign markets, 1960–1969, 1970–1979, and 1980–1989

Return excluding dividends, dollar basis

	Coefficient of correlation with U.S.		
	1960–1969	**1970–1979**	**1980–1989**
Canada	0.81	0.71	0.77
France	0.27	0.40	0.45
Germany	0.36	0.31	0.37
Japan	0.08	0.31	0.27
Switzerland	0.49	0.47	0.52
United Kingdom	0.29	0.46	0.57
15 markets (average)	0.31	0.37	0.40

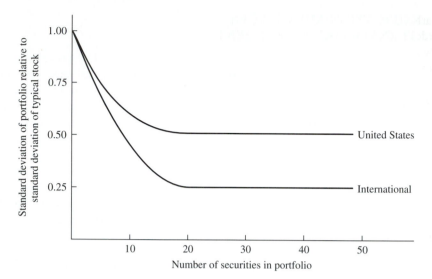

FIGURE 11-1
Risk reduction through national and international diversification. (*Source:* B.H. Solnik, "Why Not Diversify Internationally Rather than Domestically?" *Financial Analysts Journal,* July–August 1974, pp. 48–54.)

percent of the risk of a typical stock (undiversified portfolio), or about one-third less than the 57 percent that is possible with domestic diversification.

The potential of international diversification is likely to persist into the future because the degree of correlation across international markets should remain relatively low. To begin with, many of the factors that affect stock values—such as tax laws, monetary policy, and general political climate—are peculiar to the individual domestic economy. Furthermore, even factors that affect the world economy, such as the sudden increase in oil prices, can impact individual economies differently. These differences, which are the basic source of a lack of synchronization among markets, should persist into the future.

The data in Figure 11-2 further confirm that the degree of correlation among international markets is likely to remain low. The correlations across markets are broken down into several subperiods in the 1960–1989 period. The data show that correlations were high in the early 1960s, declined and remained low in the middle and late 1960s, but rose again to

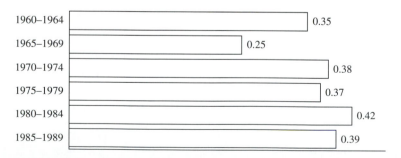

FIGURE 11-2
Correlation coefficients—U.S. market and average of fifteen foreign markets.

the earlier levels in the latter part of the period. Though correlations have varied over time, there does not appear to be any widespread trend toward greater correlation among the major equity markets. The most recent correlations appear to be a realistic, if not conservative, expectation for the future.[2]

Market Volatility and Cross-Correlation

Though correlations between markets have not trended up over time, an unpleasant characteristic has appeared: correlations seem to increase when markets are most volatile, particularly during market declines. In other words, correlations are larger when market movements are large. This fact is bad news for a portfolio manager because diversification (and low correlation) is most needed precisely in periods of large down movements.

The phenomenon was most evident during the market crash of October 1987, as illustrated by the equity market performance data in Table 11-5. As shown in the table, the performance results for each of the 23 countries were universally negative, whether stated in local currency or dollars. Furthermore, October 1987 is the only month over a long prior period of analysis in which all markets moved in the same direction. In October 1987, not only did every stock market fall, but most declined by more than 20 percent.

Given the generally low correlation between countries over time, the uniformity of performance results during October 1987 strongly implies that there was an international triggering variable that swamped the usual influences of country-specific events. As an underlying "trigger" for this event, some have pointed to the U.S. trade deficit, others to anticipations about the 1988 elections, some others to fears of a recession, and still others to the existence of a "speculative bubble." However, no one has been able to substantiate the underlying cause of the October market decline. Whatever the cause, the impact on the U.S. market as well as other markets around the world was universally negative and severe, as we have shown.

Minimum Return Required for International Investing

Because international investing provides added diversification that is unavailable from domestic sources alone, it would be useful to determine the minimum return required in order to invest internationally. Alternatively, we could consider how low returns would have to be in order to prevent us from investing internationally. Presumably, lower returns could be accepted more readily from international investments than from domestic investments because of the favorable impact these returns would have on reducing portfolio risk. The minimum return, or hurdle rate, in this context could be considered to be that which would give us the same risk-return trade-off as investing exclusively in domestic securities:

$$\text{Risk-return (international)} = \text{risk-return (domestic)}$$

Recall from our earlier analyses of the domestic equity market (Chapters 3 and 4) that the relevant risk of a security in a portfolio context is the contribution of that security to the portfolio risk. In effect, the systematic risk and not the total risk of the security is relevant

---

[2]We should note that a continued trend toward greater economic integration among major nations could lead to increased correlations across international markets. It is, however, unlikely that the increased correlations resulting from such a potential trend would be sufficient to eliminate all the benefits of international diversification.

TABLE 11-5
Stock price index percentage changes in major markets (October 1987)

	Local currency units	U.S. dollars
Australia	−41.8	−44.9
Austria	−11.4	−5.8
Belgium	−23.2	−18.9
Canada	−22.5	−22.9
Denmark	−12.5	−7.3
France	−22.9	−19.5
Germany	−22.3	−17.1
Hong Kong	−45.8	−45.8
Ireland	−29.1	−25.4
Italy	−16.3	−12.9
Japan	−12.8	−7.7
Malaysia	−39.8	−39.3
Mexico	−35	−37.6
Netherlands	−23.3	−18.1
New Zealand	−29.3	−36
Norway	−30.5	−28.8
Singapore	−42.2	−41.6
South Africa	−23.9	−29
Spain	−27.7	−23.1
Sweden	−21.8	−18.6
Switzerland	−26.1	−20.8
United Kingdom	−26.4	−22.1
United States	−21.6	−21.6

Source: Richard Roll: "The International Crash of October 1987," *Financial Analysts Journal,* Sept–Oct 1988.

in the portfolio context.[3] This analysis should, in turn, be applicable in an international context and hence, we can say that the systematic risk is the relevant component to consider when structuring an internationally diversified portfolio.

Table 11-6 shows risk-return data for several foreign equity markets along with data for the U.S. (domestic) market. The first three columns show risk data, including the standard deviation of return, the correlation with the U.S. market, and the beta of the foreign market with respect to the U.S. market. At any level of standard deviation or total risk, the beta will be high as the correlation between markets is high and, conversely, will be low as the correlation is low. For example, the U.K. market, with a total risk more than twice that of the U.S. market (33.3 percent versus 15.2 percent) but with a correlation of only 0.34 with the U.S. market, has a beta of 0.74. (Refer to Chapter 2 for the formula for calculating beta.) With respect to the standard deviation, note that all the foreign markets show higher risk than the U.S. market; however, the correlations with the U.S. market are relatively low, resulting in lower systematic risk as measured by beta values that are less than the beta of 1 for the U.S. market.

Because the beta values are all lower than 1, a lower return would be required for investing in foreign equities than for investing in U.S. equities. For example, with a beta of

---

[3] For active managers, who seek alpha returns and thus assume residual risk, this component also needs to be considered.

TABLE 11-6
Risk and required return measures for foreign market portfolios from U.S. perspective

Country	Annualized standard deviation of returns,%	Correlation with U.S. market (S&P 500)	Market-risk beta from U.S. perspective	Minimum risk premium from U.S. perspective, %*
France	22.3	0.32	0.47	3.6
Germany	16.7	0.38	0.42	3.2
Japan	18.8	0.36	0.45	3.4
Netherlands	24.2	0.5	0.8	5.8
Switzerland	22.6	0.45	0.67	5.1
United Kingdom	33	0.34	0.74	5.6
United States	15.2	1	1	7.2

* Risk premium = beta$_{U.S.}$ × U.S. risk premium.
Source: D.R. Lessard, "International Investment Strategies: Conceptual and Empirical Foundations," paper presented at the Eleventh Congress of the European Federation of Financial Analysts Societies, The Hague, The Netherlands, October 1990.

0.74, the required return for investing in the U.K. market is 5.3 percent (0.74 beta times 7.2 percent U.S. risk premium). The fourth column in the table shows these required returns under the assumption that the required risk premium (return less risk-free rate) for investing domestically (in the U.S. market) is 7.2 percent. These values are, as expected, lower than the required premium for investing in the U.S. market. It is thus possible to invest in international markets at the lower return derived in Table 11-6, and still maintain the same reward-risk ratio.

Based on the favorable foreign market returns for the 1985–1993 period and for the longer postwar period (not shown here), some might argue that these return targets would be easily exceeded. Extrapolating the historic return experience would, however, be unwise. To begin with, at least part of the long-term performance of foreign markets can be traced to circumstances that are unlikely to be repeated—the postwar economic recovery of Europe, its subsequent boom resulting from the Common Market, and the economic phenomenon of Japan aided in part by a major increase in the degree of world economic integration. In addition, some of the performance advantage of foreign markets in the 1970–1979 and 1985–1993 periods was due to currency gains that derived from the long downtrend in the value of the dollar. It is unlikely that such a trend would persist to provide continual gains on currency from foreign investing. The point of the previous analysis should be that foreign investing could be attractive even if historic experience does not repeat and that this investing could be justified even if the returns did not measure up to those available in the domestic market.

CURRENCY RISK

Though international investing appears to be generally beneficial to portfolio performance, it entails the additional risk of currency fluctuations. Given this, we then ask whether these exchange risks are so large as to offset the benefits of international diversification. A related question is what, if any, special strategy should be followed to reduce the impact of the foreign exchange risk. We primarily deal with assessing the source and degree of exchange risks in this section and discuss later how the exchange risk is incorporated into active and passive strategies.

TABLE 11-7
Spot and forward exchange rates, 12/31/89

| | Exchange rates | |
	$/£	$/DM
Spot	2.2320	0.5799
One month forward	2.2280	0.5831
Three months forward	2.2211	0.5886
Six months forward	2.2215	0.5973

The percent premium or discount is calculated as

$$P = \frac{F-S}{S} \times \frac{12}{n} \times 100$$

where S = spot rate
F = forward rate
n = number of months forward
p = forward premium or discount (percent per annum)

For example, the forward premium on the DM six months forward was

$$p = \frac{0.5973 - 0.5799}{0.5799} \times \frac{12}{6} \times 100 = 3\% \text{ per annum}$$

A similar calculation for the six-month forward £ would show that $P = -0.5\%$. Since the £ is selling at a discount, we would use the symbol D instead of the negative sign and indicate for the six-month forward £, $D = 0.5\%$.

In assessing the causes of currency fluctuations, we first need to differentiate between spot and forward exchange markets. In the spot market, currencies are exchanged immediately at the prevailing rate of exchange. In the forward market, traders buy and sell currency for delivery at a fixed future date but at a price that is set currently. Forward rates are typically quoted for delivery one month, three months, and six months forward; however, forward contracts can generally be arranged with most international banks for delivery at any specified date up to one year in the future. Contracts running beyond one year are also available but require special arrangements.

Table 11-7 shows the spot and forward rates of exchange for the U.S. dollar, the German mark (DM), and the British pound (£) as of December 31, 1989. Note that the forward DM was more expensive than the spot DM. In technical terms, the forward DM was selling at a premium relative to the spot DM, and the longer the contract is, the higher the premium will be. In contrast, the forward pound was selling at a discount relative to the spot pound. The bottom part of the table shows the formula for calculating the premium or discount on forward exchange. Note that the six-month forward premium on DM was 3 percent, but there was a discount of 0.5 percent on the six-month forward pound.

Fundamental Determinants of Exchange Rates

Figure 11-3 provides a graphic framework for evaluating fundamental determinants of changing exchange rates.[4] The figure shows that there is a four-way interrelationship among expected differences in inflation, differences in interest rates, expected changes in

---

[4]Ian Giddy, "An Integrated Theory of Exchange Rate Equilibrium," *Journal of Financial and Quantitative Analysis,* December 1976, pp. 883–892, offers an excellent exposition of this analytical framework.

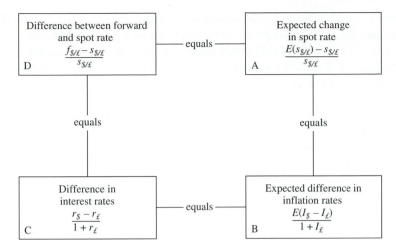

FIGURE 11-3

Inflation, interest rates, premiums, and exchange rates. (*Source:* R. Brealey and S.C. Myers, *Financial Planning and Strategy,* New York: McGraw-Hill, 1980.)

exchange rates, and forward exchange rates. These interrelationships are consistent, so that once any three are established, the fourth is then determined. Similarly, if any one of them is violated, at least one other must be violated.

In Figure 11-3, the corners A to B indicate that the expected change in spot rates should be related to the expected difference in inflation rates in the two countries. To begin with, identical goods should trade at the same price even if they are traded in different markets. If there is a difference, those goods that can be bought more cheaply abroad will be imported, forcing down the price of the domestic product. Similarly, those goods that can be bought more cheaply in the United States will be exported, forcing down the price of the foreign product. In particular, the price of foreign goods when converted to dollars should be roughly the same as the price in the United States. For example, for U.S. and U.K. goods, we would have sterling price of the goods times the exchange rate ($/£) equals dollar price of the goods. Equivalently, the exchange rate ($/£) should equal dollar price of the goods divided by sterling price of the goods. If the price of sterling is always equal to the ratio of domestic prices, then any change in the ratio of domestic prices must be matched by a change in the price of sterling. For example, if inflation is 5 percent in the United States and 10 percent in the United Kingdom, then, in order to equalize the dollar price of goods in the two countries, the price of sterling must fall by (0.05 − 0.10)/1.10 or about 5 percent.

This relationship is based on the purchasing power parity (PPP) theorem. The PPP has been tested empirically, and the evidence may be sensitive to the countries, time periods, and price indexes that are selected for testing. Despite these difficulties, it seems reasonably clear from the evidence that over long time periods and during periods of hyperinflation (when monetary factors swamp real changes), PPP offers a fairly good description of exchange rate behavior. However, over shorter time periods, say, three to twelve months, it has not been uncommon to observe substantial exchange rate changes, say, 10 to 20 percent, that are unrelated to commodity price changes.

Corners B to C in Figure 11-3 indicate that differences in interest rates should also be related to differences in inflation rates. This relationship derives from the Fisher Effect, which indicates that investors are interested in real rather than nominal returns. If this effect is so, then prices of securities or, alternatively, interest rates should adjust to provide the expected real return. We would in turn expect this to occur across different countries, so that there would be a tendency toward an equalization of real returns or real interest rates between countries. Differences in inflation rates would then account for the difference in nominal interest rates across countries. Empirical evidence on this relationship is limited, and though we might expect that the real rate of interest would be equilibrated across countries over the longer term, we are also aware that there are impediments, such as exchange controls, government intervention in exchange markets, and taxes, that can prevent this from occurring for extended periods.

The corners C to D in Figure 11-3 indicate that the difference in interest rates should be equal to the difference between forward and spot rates. This relationship is based on the interest rate parity theorem, and thus it is a very strong relationship because the theorem is based on arbitrage. If the exchange rate difference did not match the difference in interest rates, investors could profit without bearing any risk, by borrowing in the country with the relatively low interest rate (including the cost of forward cover), investing in the money market in the country with the high rate, and removing the exchange risk by covering in the forward market.

For example, if interest rates were 10 percent in the United States, investing $1 million would net $1.1 million at the end of the year. If the interest rate were 12 percent in the United Kingdom and the spot rate of exchange was $2/£, the investor could convert the $1 million to £500,000 and invest at the higher interest rate for a return of £560,000 at the end of the year. Because the future rate of exchange is uncertain, the investor can avoid risk (potential loss) by selling sterling forward at the prevailing forward rate, which in equilibrium should be $1.964/£. Converting the proceeds at this rate ($1.964 \times 560,000$) gives the same dollar proceeds of $1.1 million as investing directly in the United States. The gain on interest rates is offset by the loss on foreign exchange, as should be the case according to the analysis in Figure 11-2. Empirical tests in markets such as Eurocurrency markets, where exchange controls and tax considerations are not factors, indicate that this relationship holds almost exactly. In other markets, the relationship will diverge as tax factors and potential exchange controls are more significant considerations. (We describe interest rate parity more fully in Chapter 12.)

Finally, from corners D and A at the top of the quadrilateral in the figure, we expect the difference between forward and spot rates to be equal to the expected change in the spot rate. For example, a one-year-forward rate of $2/£ should mean that traders expect the spot rate in one year's time to be $2/£. If they expected it to be higher than this, no trader would be willing to sell pounds at the forward rate; if they expected it to be lower, no trader would be willing to buy at the forward rate. Alternatively, if forward rates differed from anticipated exchange rates, market participants would be induced to speculate on the difference between these rates, tending to move the forward rate toward the expected future spot rate. It appears generally that the forward rate is an unbiased estimate of future spot rates; that is, it consistently neither underestimates nor overestimates future spot rates and, in this respect, provides a good standard for assessing forecasting expertise.[5] We will,

[5]Though the forward premium is an unbiased predictor of future exchange rate changes, it is a poor predictor in the sense that it explains only about 10 percent of the fluctuations in the future spot rate. This lack of predictive ability

in fact, use it as such when we discuss active approaches to managing an internationally diversified portfolio. We should note, however, that empirical tests indicate violations of the forward/spot relationship for currencies of countries that have significant inflation problems and carry heavy debt loads. We describe this phenomenon in Chapter 12.

Managing Currency Risks

If the relationships just described held exactly, we would expect that interest rates and security prices would reflect expected changes in exchange rates and that currency would not represent a separate risk in international investing. We noted, however, that there is only a long-run tendency toward equilibrium and that real-world factors such as taxes, both actual and potential exchange controls, and transaction costs can further distort equilibrium. As a result, we would expect that exchange rates would diverge in the short run and would exhibit substantial unexpected fluctuations that investment managers need to consider in designing and implementing active and passive strategies of international investing.

In order to protect against currency risk, investors may hedge by borrowing or entering into forward currency contracts. These hedging strategies, of course, have a cost that may well outweigh the incremental risk reduction.[6] For bond investors to whom currency represents a high proportion of total risk and is more inter-related with interest rates, hedging currency risk is a natural component of the process despite the added cost. We will discuss this issue as it relates to bond investing later in Chapter 14.

However, for international equity investors, hedging is a less clear-cut decision because there are natural offsets to currency risk. One way that the investor might protect against currency risk is by simply investing across many foreign markets. In this way, losses on weak currencies would tend to be offset by gains on strong currencies. Presumably, passive strategies that entail holding a broadly diversified portfolio of international securities would benefit from this risk-reducing effect over the short term, but over the long term, as markets tend toward equilibrium, passive investors would find their exposure to currency risk to be minimal. Furthermore, those investors would avoid the high artificial transaction costs (perhaps 1 percent or more per year), as well as a heavy administration burden of constantly rebalancing the currency hedge that a systematic full hedging policy would require to track a benchmark.[7]

On the other hand, investors following an active strategy that involves overweighting in attractive countries or markets and underweighting in unattractive markets will, by virtue of this activity, become exposed to the currency risk because the investor is taking a bet on the currency in addition to the market. This strategy in effect cancels the balancing-out effect of a passive, or world, investing strategy. Therefore, such investors should carefully consider the direction and magnitude of currency movements and incorporate these explicit forecasts into their assessment of the relative attractiveness of the different markets. Doing

---

suggests that the bulk of the short-run exchange rate changes are dominated by unanticipated events and that the forward premium sits roughly in the middle of a wide distribution of exchange rate expectations. Alternatively, it implies that there is ample opportunity to apply forecasting techniques to attempt to explain this unaccounted-for exchange rate variation.

[6]Estimates are that the cost of such hedging for most major currencies is on the order of 0.5 to 0.7 percent per annum.

[7]Researchers have proposed other systematic hedging strategies that base the degree of currency hedging on assumptions about investor utility and wealth. Discussion of these strategies is beyond the scope of this book.

so would enable them to avoid undue penalties from possible currency risks and capitalize on potential opportunities from an especially well-positioned currency.

A PASSIVE STRATEGY

As is the case with domestic investing, investors in international markets can pursue active or passive strategies or combinations of these two alternative approaches. One way of investing passively is to create an international index fund, just as domestic investors following a totally passive strategy would attempt to replicate the market performance by investing in an index such as the S&P 500. When investing internationally, the investor would intend to replicate the performance of the world market rather than only a single domestic market. Ideally, the investor would want to obtain a representative index of the world market portfolio and invest in those companies according to their relative weights.

There are, however, several major impediments to direct application of the U.S. index approach in the international arena. First, there is no index that investors generally agree is representative of the world market portfolio, as is the case in the United States, where indexes like the S&P 500, Russell 3000, and Wilshire 5000, though perhaps flawed, are nevertheless deemed useful.[8] Furthermore, many foreign markets are dominated by only a handful of companies; many other companies, though sizable, might be quite closely held and not readily marketable. Finally, there is probably a greater degree of mispricing in foreign markets than in the U.S. market, with the attendant difficulties for passive strategies and indexing.

In order to overcome these difficulties, two complementary approaches can be used in constructing an index fund to proxy for a world equity market index. One direct way is to simply focus on major country markets that tend to dominate the market weighting of an index. For example, the ten countries shown in Table 11-8 represent 92 percent of the weighting of the MSCI global equity index and provide a balanced representation across the three major global regions: North America, Europe, and the Pacific. Naturally, this process will exclude the ten other countries constituting the MSCI index as well as emerging-type countries, but investors have an opportunity to participate in those through separate and identifiable strategies.

Within individual country markets, a second approach to reducing the number of companies and maintaining representatives is to use stratified sampling across industries and major companies. For example, using this approach we can reduce the number of companies in a country-component MSCI index, such as Australia, from a total of 80 to the more manageable (for indexing) 11 shown in Table 11-9. These companies are, by and large, the biggest in terms of market capitalization in the Australian market and also provide representation of six major Australian industries. Using the weighting of the company in the country

---

[8]We should note that use of market capitalization–weighted indexes like the MSCI are not universally acceptable by international investors as a benchmark for performance. Some investors prefer to use a GDP-weighted index, which better reflects the international distribution of productive economies. Because most Japanese companies are publicly listed and trade at high price/earnings ratios compared with the rest of the world, for example, the relative stock market capitalization of Japan is higher than its relative economic production. The effect is compounded by the cross-holdings of Japanese company shares, which artificially inflate reported market capitalization. Still other investors consider that currency risks should not be borne and use a currency-hedged EAFE benchmark. Unfortunately, international asset pricing theory does not provide clear guidance as to the choice of an appropriate benchmark.

TABLE 11-8
Morgan Stanley Capital International
Index Fund composition (12/31/93)

Region/country	Fund weighting
North America (MSCI)	
United States	35.00
Canada	2.30
	37.30
Europe	
United Kingdom	10.00
Germany	4.00
France	4.00
Switzerland	3.00
	21.00
Pacific (MSCI)	
Japan	27.60
Hong Kong	2.30
Singapore/Malaysia	2.10
Australia	1.70
	33.70
Other	8.00
Total	100.00%

Source: Morgan Stanley Capital Intl.

index along with the world index weight for the country, we derive, for an individual company such as CRA Limited, simply (12.94 percent of Australian index) times (1.7 percent Australian weighting) for a 0.2 percent weighting for CRA Limited in the world index.

Table 11-10 shows a listing for each of the 20 countries in the MSCI Index, the number of companies in each country index, and the number included from that country in the index fund. Note that the number included from the index is substantially less for each country

TABLE 11-9

Company name	Weighting	Industry
CRA Limited	12.94	Metals
Coles Myer Ltd	12.94	Retail
Westpac Bank Corp	12.94	Banking
Broken Hill Propty	12.90	Mining
Boral Limited	11.31	Mining
CSR Limited	10.38	Metals
General Prop Trust	8.50	Investment trust
Aberfoyle	7.16	Metals
Santos Limited	4.12	Mining
Brambles Inds Ltd	4.05	Retail
SA Brewing Hldgs	2.76	Beverage
Total	100.00	

TABLE 11-10

Index fund and global index countries and companies

Country	Region Pacific		Europe		EAFE*		North America		World
Australia	63	11			63	11			63
Hong Kong	32	10			32	10			32
Japan	265	64			265	64			265
New Zealand	11				11				11
Singapore	53	12			53	12			53
Austria			18		18				18
Belgium			24		24				24
Denmark			28		28				28
Finland			21		21				21
France			81	19	81	19			81
Germany			57	24	57	24			57
Italy			69		69				69
Netherlands			25		25				25
Norway			26		26				26
Spain			37		37				37
Sweden			38		38				38
Switzerland			52	12	52	12			52
United Kingdom			136	45	136	45			136
Canada							89	18	89
United States							330	79	330
MSCI countries	5		13		18		2		20
Index fund countries		4		4		8		2	10
MSCI stocks	424		612		1036		419		1455
Index fund stocks		97		100		197		97	294

* EAFE: Europe–Far East Index component that excludes North American region.
Source: A. Escolin and I. Matsuda, "Global Benchmark and an Approach to Indexing," *Japan Security Analysts Journal,* November 1991, pp. 30–43.

and aggregate to a total of 294 for the index fund compared to 1455 for the MSCI. The table also shows the breakdown of company representation by region: Pacific, Europe, and North America, as well as the non-U.S./Canadian region, also known as EAFE.

Figure 11-4 shows a simulation of the performance of this strategy over the 1986–1990 period compared to that of the MSCI World Index over the same period showed a close tracking of the performance of the world market index, with limited divergences for only a few periods. Correspondingly, the average annual return of 10.6 for the fund was close to that of the index of 11.0 percent. For a fund of this nature, the annualized tracking error of 1.47 percent was comparatively low. The strategy appears, as intended, to provide a reasonable proxy for the MSCI global index performance.

AN ACTIVE STRATEGY

An active strategy for investing internationally might be oriented to identifying relatively attractive and unattractive national markets. A market identified as attractive would be over-weighted in the portfolio, and one judged unattractive would be underweighted or perhaps even eliminated entirely from the portfolio. Of course, a decision to actively manage a port-

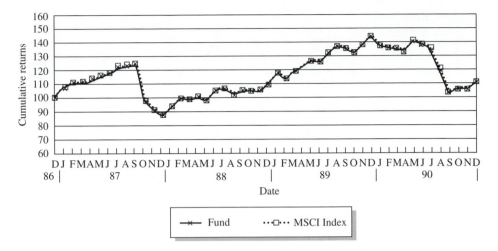

FIGURE 11-4
MSCI World Index Fund—December 1986 to December 1990.

folio in this fashion presupposes some predictive capability, just as the decision to operate actively in the domestic equity market did.

Figure 11-5 shows the steps that an organization should follow in executing an active strategy. The organization first needs to develop explicit forecasts of the market return for each of the international markets of interest. Because active management means that an organization is implicitly taking a position either "long" or "short" in currency, an explicit forecast of currency changes over the planning period needs to be developed. The second

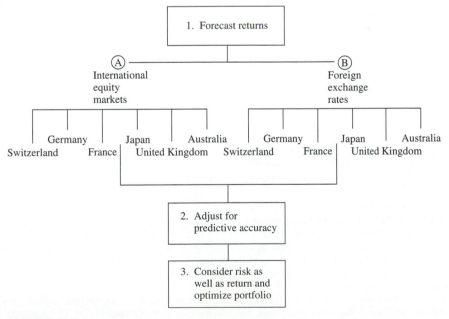
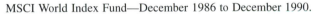

FIGURE 11-5
Executing an active international investment strategy.

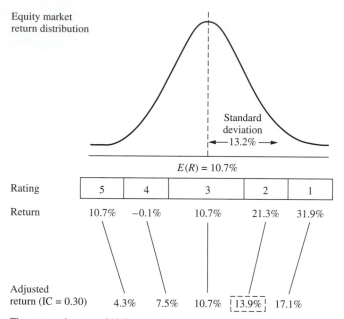

Equity market
return distribution

The expected return of 10.7 percent is an estimate of the consensus expectation
for the German market. (It was derived in a manner similar to the way we
estimated the expected return in previous chapters and with respect to U.S. equities.)

FIGURE 11-6
Equity return forecast—German market.

step is to adjust these forecasts for the organization's predictive capability. The final step is
to consider risk along with forecast return and generate an optimum portfolio.

In developing forecasts for the individual markets, we can again use an approach like
that used to generate forecasts of the domestic (U.S.) market. Recall from Chapter 9 that
this first involved assessing the likely variability of market return by using historical and/or
projected estimates of the standard deviation of return. We would then assess the relative
attractiveness of the market, using the five-way rating scheme we have been recommending throughout the book. The final step would be to adjust the implied return forecast for
predictive capability. Again, we have been recommending the information coefficient (IC)
method for making this adjustment.[9]

Figure 11-6 illustrates this procedure with a particular foreign market—the German
market. Note that the standard deviation of return is 13.2 percent, the same experienced

---

[9]This case is similar to the market timing illustration in Chapter 9, where we were attempting to assess divergences
of the market from its long-term expected return. The process first involves rating the relative attractiveness of the
market on a five-way scale—1 being the most attractive and 5 the least. We then need to convert these ratings into
units away from the mean by dividing the rating by the standard deviation of the rating distribution, which in this
case is 1.25. For example, we convert a rating of 2, which is 1 rating unit from the mean, into $1 \div 1.25 = 0.8$
standard deviations from the mean.

Once we have converted the ratings into standard deviations from the mean, we then multiply these by
the standard deviation of the return distribution, which in the case of the German market is 13.2 percent, and
thereby obtain an equivalent return for each rating category. For example, when we multiply a rating of 2, which
is 0.8 standard deviations from the mean, by the 13.2 standard deviation of the return distribution, we obtain a return

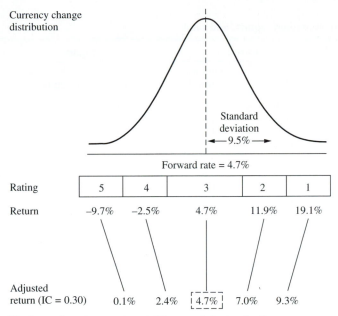

Currency change
distribution

Standard
deviation
←—9.5%—→

Forward rate = 4.7%

Rating	5	4	3	2	1
Return	–9.7%	–2.5%	4.7%	11.9%	19.1%

Adjusted
return (IC = 0.30)   0.1%   2.4%   4.7%   7.0%   9.3%

The forward rate is our estimate of the expected return for the currency over
the year. It is based on our theoretical analysis in an earlier section of the
fundamental determinants of differences in spot and forward exchange rates.

FIGURE 11-7
Currency change forecast—German market.

over a recent five-year period. For purposes of illustration, we have assessed the market
as attractive, indicated by a rating of 2 on the five-way rating scale. The implied return of
21.3 percent needs to be adjusted, however, and in this case we are assessing predictive
capability on the order of 0.30 for that purpose. The net result is a return forecast of 13.9
percent for the market.

As noted, it is also desirable to make an explicit forecast of the currency, in this case
German marks, when undertaking an active international investment strategy. The procedure here would again be to estimate the likely future variability of the currency rate of
exchange relative to the U.S. dollar. We could base this on historical and/or projected data
on the standard deviation of currency exchange rates. We would then rate the attractiveness of the currency relative to the domestic (U.S.) currency on the same five-way rating
scale. The final step would be to adjust the return forecast for the organization's predictive
capacity with respect to exchange rate changes.

Figure 11-7 illustrates the process using the exchange rate between U.S. dollars and
German marks.[10] Note that the exchange rate for marks has shown a standard deviation of

---

divergence of 10.6 percent. The final step is to adjust for predictive ability by multiplying the assessed IC of 0.30.
In this case, a 2 rating with a raw return divergence of 10.6 percent reduces to a divergence of 3.2, or an expected
return of 13.9 percent.

[10]Converting the rating distribution to a return distribution and adjusting for predictive capability is similar to the
procedure for the market forecast. First, we convert the ratings into standard deviations from the mean by dividing

TABLE 11-11

Return forecast—currency, equity, and total

	Currency		Equity		
	IC	Forecast return, %	IC	Forecast return, %	Total return, %
United Kingdom	0.10	1.1	0.15	18.2	19.3
France	0.15	1	0.15	13.6(−)	14.6
Germany	0.30	4.7	0.30	13.9(+)	18.6
Switzerland	0.30	10.2	0.30	7.2	17.4
Hong Kong	0.30	0	0.10	19.4(+)	19.4
Japan	0.15	6.1(+)	0.15	10.8	16.9
Netherlands	0.15	1.8(−)	0.15	11.6	13.4
Canada	0.15	1.3(+)	0.15	15.8	17.1

9.5 percent over the recent five-year period, which we will use as an estimate of the future variability. In addition, we are using the one-year forward rate as an estimate of the consensus expectation for the change in the spot rate over the period.[11] Because we have rated the currency as neutral, the consensus expectation becomes our forecast for the period. If we had rated the currency other than 3, we would have had to proceed as with the equity forecast by considering projected variability and adjusting for forecasting capability. Note that in this case we have assessed predictive capability on the order of 0.30, which is the same as for equities but could differ with regard to currency versus equities as well as across countries.

Table 11-11 shows the results of the same sort of forecasting process for several major international markets, including the German market. It shows the forecasts for both currency and the equity market for each country along with the organization's estimated level of predictive capability, as measured by the information coefficient. Note that the assessed level of predictive capability differs with respect to both the currency and equity forecasts, as well as across countries. The pluses and minuses next to the forecast return indicate where the organization has made an other-than-neutral forecast—that is, a rating of other than a 3. The final column combines the currency and equity forecast to give a total expected return in each of the markets over the next year.

Note that the Hong Kong, U.K., and German markets rank high in terms of total return forecast for the period. The German and Hong Kong equity markets were deemed to be of above-average attraction, and the German currency was forecast by consensus to be relatively strong over the period. On the other hand, the French and Dutch markets rank

---

them by the standard deviation of the rating distribution, which is 1.32. We can then multiply by the standard deviation of the currency, which is 9.5 percent, and obtain returns associated with the ratings. The final step is to adjust for the 0.30 predictive ability.

As an example, we will rate the currency 1 for the coming year. This is 2 rating points or 1.52 standard deviations from the mean. When we multiply 1.52 by the 9.5 standard deviation of the currency distribution, we obtain a return divergence of 14.4. Multiplying again by the 0.30 IC, we obtain a divergence of 4.6 from the "forecast" by the forward rate, or a forecast return of 9.3 percent.

[11] We noted before that the forward rate provides an unbiased benchmark for evaluating forecasting capability. Using this benchmark, studies show that some commercially available forecasting services have the capability to improve on the forward rate forecast. This evidence indicates that active strategies incorporating exchange rate forecasts have opportunities for improving portfolio performance.

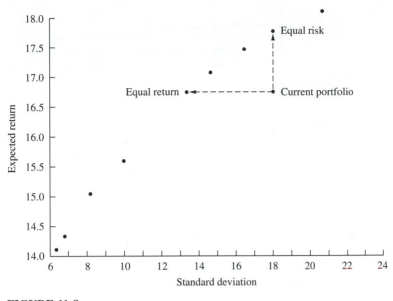

FIGURE 11-8
Efficient frontier and current portfolio.

at the bottom in terms of forecast return; the French equity market is rated as unattractive, and the Dutch currency outlook is rated below average. Other markets show mixed patterns with the equity market attractive but the currency unattractive, or vice versa. Hence, these markets tend to rank in the middle with respect to total return over the forthcoming year.

OPTIMUM INTERNATIONAL PORTFOLIO

In order to develop an optimum portfolio structure, we should consider risk as well as return, and the best way of doing this is within the framework of a portfolio optimization model such as was discussed in Chapter 2. We would, of course, use the estimates developed in Table 11-11 as our projected return inputs. For purposes of the illustration, we will use historical standard deviation and covariance relationships over the recent five-year period as risk inputs.

Figure 11-8 shows an efficient frontier of portfolios generated by the optimization routine, with the risk and return inputs already given.[12] It also shows the risk-return location of a currently held portfolio, designated CP, that was the object of the upgrading analysis. Note that the portfolio on the upper part of the efficient frontier offers a higher return at the same level of risk as the current alternative, but the portfolio on the lower part of the efficient frontier offers the same return at a lower level of risk. This dominance is the result of the presumed capability to forecast and, hence, generate not only a greater return than is available to a passive investor but also the more explicit consideration of risk (covariance relationships) than is possible without formal optimization procedures.

---

[12]Because the assets or, alternatively, countries to be considered for international diversification are unlikely to exceed fifteen (in this case, there are eight), return, variance, and covariance inputs can be readily developed. As in the case of asset allocation, the full-covariance Markowitz model can be and is generally employed in generating an efficient frontier of internationally diversified portolios.

TABLE 11-12
International portfolio composition, %

	Current portfolio	Optimum equal risk	Optimum equal return
United Kingdom	33	20	3
France	12	0	0
Germany	9	41	39
Switzerland	2	2	2
Hong Kong	5	5	5
Japan	19	23	19
Netherlands	5	0	0
Canada	2	2	2
	87	93	100
Cash equivalent	13	7	—
Total	100	100	100
Expected return	16.75	17.65	16.71
Standard deviation	16.44	16.72	13.00

Note: The optimum equal-risk portfolio is one that has the same risk (approximately) as the current portfolio but, as shown in Figure 13-8, a higher return. Correspondingly, the equal-return portfolio is one that has the same return as the current portfolio but, as also shown in Figure 13-8, a lower risk. Both dominate the current portfolio.

Table 11-12 shows the weightings of the individual countries in both portfolios (equal risk and equal return) from the efficient frontier compared with the weightings in the current portfolio. Note that the optimum portfolio carries relatively heavy weightings in the high-return countries—the United Kingdom, Germany, and Hong Kong—but no weightings in France and the Netherlands. The German market is, in a sense, acting as a substitute for the French and Dutch markets, which are highly correlated with the German market but have significantly lower forecast returns. In fact, the major divergence between the optimum and current portfolios is with respect to these three countries. A shift from the French and Dutch markets to the German market would improve prospective return and/or reduce risk, as indicated by the statistics on the expected return and standard deviation of the three portfolios.

Stock Selection Strategies: International Markets

In addition to an active strategy of global asset allocation, portfolio managers can also attempt to add value to portfolio performance through stock selection within individual country markets. The manager's objective in doing so would be to outperform a benchmark index for the stock market of interest. For example, an investor operating in the Japanese market might use the Nikkei 225 or Topix index as a standard of comparison, but an investor in Great Britain might use the FT-Times index as a benchmark. Furthermore, it is a natural extension to apply the same philosophy and sort of techniques for stock selection as described in Chapter 8, with regard to the U.S. market and to international markets as well.

Correspondingly, disciplined stock selection strategies also have potential to be effective in international markets. One market where this approach has been applied, and where it appears especially promising, is the Japanese stock market. This application is significant because the Japanese market is the largest outside the United States, representing almost 50

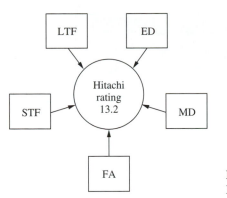

FIGURE 11-9
Multi-dimensional valuation.

percent of the non-U.S.-market equity market. For major investors, especially those domiciled in the United States, the decision to invest internationally is whether or not to invest in Japan. Having viable strategies such as disciplined stock selection available to investors has facilitated the growth of international investing.

In applying disciplined stock selection strategies to Japan, or other markets for that matter, we should recognize that there are similarities to the United States but also notable differences that need to be properly considered. As in the case of the United States, the essential components to these strategies are objective valuation and systematic portfolio construction. Actual experience shows that it is possible to implement these components, using many of the basic analytical and statistical techniques applied in developing these strategies for the U.S. equity market.

Valuation

With regard to valuation, we can also apply the same type of multidimensional valuation approach as used in the United States. The information coefficient (IC) technique again provides the method for both testing individual predictors and combining them into distinct dimensions of value. The development effort in Japan showed that the following valuation dimensions were effective: (1) long-term fundamental (LTF), including cash flow and asset valuation methods; (2) short-term fundamental (STF), including momentum-based and relative valuation methods; (3) fundamental analytical approaches (FA), provided by WRI[13]; (4) methods to assess market dynamics (MD); and (5) factors related to economic dynamics (ED).

Using this multidimensional valuation technique, we can value each company in an investment universe as illustrated in Figure 11-9. Note that the individual predictor dimensions of value can be combined into a composite valuation indicator or alpha rating that has the same meaning as for the U.S. application. We illustrate using Hitachi Corp., which had an alpha value at the time of 13.2 percent, indicating that we expect that stock to outperform by 13.2 percent over the next year, and which would represent an attractive opportunity.

Using the alpha value as the criterion for attractiveness, we rank the stocks in the universe from highest alpha to lowest alpha, that is, from most attractive to least attractive. This universe consists of 750 stocks and encompasses all the stocks in the Nikkei 225 and

---

[13] WRI: Wako Research Institute, Tokyo, Japan.

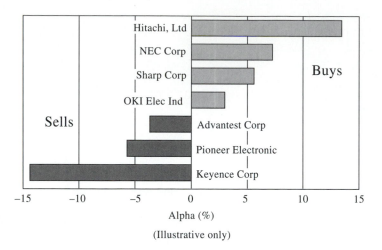

(Illustrative only)

FIGURE 11-10
Expected excess return—selected electrical companies.

Nikkei 500, plus some other significantly notable stocks. Figure 11-10 illustrates this relative ranking for some stocks from the universe classified into the electrical and electronics industry.

Note that the stocks are arrayed according to alpha value, with Hitachi, showing an alpha value of 13.2, ranked highest and Keyence, with an alpha value of −14.6, ranked lowest. Those stocks ranking highest would be candidates for inclusion in the portfolio, and low-ranked stocks would be candidates for sale, just as with selecting stocks for the U.S. strategies.

These alpha values also offer a basis for comparing the opportunities for stock selection in Japan to that available in the United States. We can do this by simply calculating the standard deviation of alpha values for both our universe of Japanese stocks and our universe of U.S. stocks, and we can use those calculated values as a measure of dispersion in each market. Figure 11-11 shows that the dispersion of alpha values for the market in Japan is over twice that of the U.S. market. This broader dispersion implies a greater opportunity to add value to a portfolio from stock selection in Japan than in the United States.

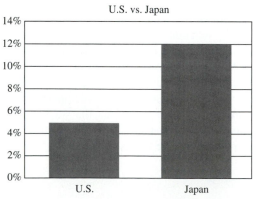

FIGURE 11-11
FWGI: alpha dispersion.

TABLE 11-13
Portfolio characteristics

	Japan		U.S.	
	DSS*	**Nikkei 225**	**DSS**	**S&P 500**
Stocks held	50–60	225	60–75	500
Industries represented	15–20	36	30–40	90
Beta	0.95–1.05	1.00	0.95–1.05	1.00
Cash percentage	Limit 5%	0%	Limit 5%	0%
Expected alpha	5%	0%	3%	0%

*Disciplined stock selection
Source: James L. Farrell, Jr: "Investing in Japan: Opportunities and Strategies," *Journal of Investing,* Summer, 1993, pp. 27–32.

Portfolio Construction

In building a portfolio, we focus on high-ranked (alpha) stocks but also give consideration to risk. We can do this through a multifactor model that considers four aspects of stock risk: (1) market risk, (2) macro risk, (3) industry risk, and (4) unique risk. By considering multifactor risk and the alpha valuation of individual stocks, we can, in turn, develop a portfolio combination that has a favorable return prospect and a controlled risk profile. Table 11-13 compares the resulting portfolio and Nikkei 225 benchmark to a portfolio constructed by a similar process for the U.S. market and its S&P 500 benchmark.

Note that the portfolio contains 50 to 60 stocks spread over 15 to 20 of the 36 industries in the Nikkei 225. The portfolio is fully invested, with only a small cash percentage to facilitate transactions and a beta in line with that of the Nikkei 225. Note that the U.S. DSS portfolio shows similar diversification and market risk characteristics relative to its S&P 500 benchmark.

Both portfolios show positive alphas in comparison to a 0 percent expectation for their respective benchmarks: the Nikkei 225 and the S&P 500. Based on the opportunity presented by the dispersion of alpha values for the U.S. stock universe and bolstered by past experience, we expect to realize a positive expected excess return in the United States of 3 percent over the S&P 500. Because of a greater opportunity presented by the wider dispersion of alpha values for the Japanese stock universe, we expect to realize a relatively greater portfolio alpha in Japan than in the United States. We estimate an alpha value of 5 percent that is less than the value implied by the relative alpha dispersions noted before, due to the lower liquidity and higher transaction costs in Japan.

CONCLUSION

International investing expands the set of opportunities available to the investor and thereby offers the potential for generating a portfolio with a higher return per unit of risk. We have indicated that investors could attempt to capitalize on this potential through active or passive strategies of investing. If an active country strategy of investing is chosen, the investor needs to consider explicitly the risk of fluctuating exchange rates and needs to deal with the problem of forecasting returns for the foreign markets of interest. We illustrated a framework of analysis for explicit consideration of forecasting both foreign exchange rates and market returns.

Though international investing appears to be generally beneficial, factors that represent potential obstacles should be considered in implementing strategies of international investing. These factors include formal barriers to international transactions such as exchange contacts, double taxation of portfolio income for certain investors in particular countries, and restrictions on ownership of securities according to the nationality of the investor. In addition, there are informal barriers such as the difficulty of obtaining information about a market, differences in reporting practices that make international comparisons difficult, transactions costs, and markets that are generally less liquid than the U.S. market. Finally, investors should be aware of the generally remote yet extreme risk (in terms of consequences) of governmental confiscation or expropriation of foreign assets.

SELECTED REFERENCES

Adler, Michael, and Bernard Dumas: "Exposure to Currency Risk: Definition and Measurement," *Financial Management,* Summer 1984, pp. 41–50.

—— and ——: "International Portfolio Choice and Corporation Finance: A Synthesis," *Journal of Finance* 38, June 1983, pp. 925–984.

—— and Bruce Lehmann: "Deviations from Purchasing Power Parity in the Long Run," *Journal of Finance,* December 1983, pp. 1471–1487.

Aggraval, R., and P. Rivoli: "Seasonal and Day-of-the-Week Effects in Four Emerging Stock Markets," *The Financial Review,* November 1989, pp. 541–550.

——, T. Kiraki, and R. Rao: "Price/Book Value Ratios and Equity Returns on the Tokyo Stock Exchange," *The Financial Review,* November 1992, pp. 589–605.

Agmon, Tamir: "Country Risk: The Significance of the Country Factor for Share Price Movements in the United Kingdom, Germany and Japan," *Journal of Business,* January 1973, pp. 24–32.

Arnott, Robert, and Roy Henrikson: "A Disciplined Approach to Global Asset Allocation," *Financial Analysts Journal,* March–April 1989, pp. 17–28.

Baillie, Richard, and Tim Bollerslev: "Common Stochastic Trends in a System of Exchange Rates," *Journal of Finance,* March 1989, pp. 167–187.

Bekaert, G., and Robert Hadrick: "Characterizing Predictable Components in Excess Returns on Equity and Foreign Exchange Markets," *Journal of Finance,* June 1992, pp. 467–511.

Bergstrom, Gary L.: "A New Route to Higher Returns and Lower Risks," *Journal of Portfolio Management,* Fall 1975, pp. 30–38.

Bierman, Harold: "Price/Earnings Ratios Restructured for Japan," *Financial Analysts Journal,* March–April 1991, pp. 91–92.

Black, Fischer: "Universal Hedging: Optimizing Currency Risk and Reward in International Equity Portfolios," *Financial Analysts Journal,* July–August 1989, pp. 16–21.

——: "International Capital Market Equilibrium with Investment Barriers," *Journal of Financial Economics,* December 1974, pp. 337–352.

—— and Robert Litterman: "Global Portfolio Optimization," *Financial Analysts Journal,* September–October 1992, pp. 28–43.

Bostock, Paul, and Paul Woolley: "A New Way to Analyze International Equity Market Performance," *Financial Analysts Journal,* January–February 1991, pp. 32–38.

Brenner, Menachem, Marti Subrahmanyam, and Jun Uno: "Arbitrage Opportunities in the Japanese Stock and Futures Markets," *Financial Analysts Journal,* March–April 1990, pp. 14–24.

Campbell, John, and Yasushi Hamao: "Predictable Stock Returns in the United States and Japan: Study of Long-Term Capital Market Integration," *Journal of Finance,* March 1992, pp. 43–69.

Chan, K., A. Karolyi, and R. Stulz: "Global Financial Markets and the Risk Premium on U.S. Equity," *Journal of Financial Economics,* October 1992, pp. 137–168.

Chan, K., Benton Gup, and M. Pan: "An Empirical Analysis of Stock Prices in Major Asian Markets and the United States," *The Financial Review,* May 1992, pp. 289–307.

Chan, Louis, Yasushi Hamao, and Josef Lakonishok: "Can Fundamentals Predict Japanese Stock Returns?" *Financial Analysts Journal,* July–August 1993, pp. 63–69.

Cochran, Steven, Robert DeFina, and Leonard Mills: "International Evidence on the Predictability of Stock Returns," *The Financial Review,* May 1993, pp. 159–180.

Corshay, Albert, Gabriel Hawawini, and Pierre Michel: "Seasonality in the Risk-Return Relationship: Some International Evidence," *Journal of Finance,* March 1987, pp. 49–68.

Divecha, A., J. Drach, and D. Stefek: "Emerging Markets: A Quantitative Perspective," *Journal of Portfolio Management,* Fall 1992, pp. 41–50.

Eim, Cheol, and Bruce Resnick: "Estimating the Correlation Structure of International Share Prices," *Journal of Finance,* December 1984, pp. 1311-1324.

——: "Estimating the Dependence Structure of Share Prices: A Comparative Study of the United States and Japan," *The Financial Review,* November 1988, pp. 387–402.

——: "Exchange Rate Uncertainty, Forward Contracts and International Portfolio Selection," *Journal of Finance,* March 1988, pp. 197–215.

Escolin, A., and I. Matsuda, "Global Benchmark and an Approach to Indexing," *Japan Security Analysts Journal,* November 1991, pp. 30–43.

Farrell, James L., Jr: "Investing in Japan: Opportunities and Strategies," *Journal of Investing,* Summer 1993, pp. 27–32.

Feinberg, Robert, and Seth Kaplan: "The Response of Domestic Prices to Expected Exchange Rates," *Journal of Business,* April 1992, pp. 269–280.

French, Kenneth, and James Poterba: "Were Japanese Stock Prices Too High?" *Journal of Financial Economics,* October 1991, pp. 337–364.

Froot, Kenneth: "Currency Hedging Over Long Horizons," Institute for Quantitative Research in Finance, Fall Seminar, 1993, Scottsdale, AZ.

——and J. A. Frankel: "Forward Discount Bias: Is It an Exchange Risk Premium?," *Quarterly Journal of Economics,* February 1989, pp. 139–161.

Fung, H., and W. Lo: "Deviations from Purchasing Power Parity," *The Financial Review,* November 1992, pp. 553–570.

Giddy, Ian: "Exchange Risk: Whose View?" *Financial Management,* Summer 1977, pp. 23–33.

——: "An Integrated Theory of Exchange Rate Equilibrium," *Journal of Financial and Quantitative Analysis,* December 1976, pp. 883–892.

Giovannini, Alberto, and Philippe Jorion: "The Time Variation of Risk and Return in the Foreign Exchange and Stock Markets," *Journal of Finance,* June 1989, pp. 307–325.

Grauer, Robert, and Nils Hakansson: "Gains from International Diversification: 1968–85 Returns on Portfolios of Stocks and Bonds," *Journal of Finance,* July 1987, pp. 721–741.

Grinold, R., Andrew Rudd, and Dan Stefek: "Global Factors: Fact or Fiction," *Journal of Portfolio Management,* Fall 1989, pp. 79–89.

Grubel, Herbert G.: "Internationally Diversified Portfolios: Welfare Gains and Capital Flows," *American Economic Review,* December 1968, pp. 1299–1314.

Hamao, Y.: "A Standard Data Base for the Analysis of Japanese Security Markets," *Journal of Business,* January 1991, pp. 87–102.

Harvey, Campbell: "The World Price of Covariance Risk," *Journal of Finance,* March 1991, pp. 111–157.

—— and G. Zhou: "International Asset Pricing with Alternative Distributional Specifications," *Journal of Empirical Finance,* June 1993, pp. 107–131.

Hazuka, Thomas, and Lex Huberts: "A Valuation Approach to Currency Hedging," March–April 1994, pp. 55–59.

Hodrick, Robert: "Understanding Foreign Exchange Risk," Institute for Quantitative Research in Finance, Fall Seminar, 1993, Scottsdale, AZ.

Huang, Roger: "Expectations of Exchange Rates and Differential Inflation Rates: Further Evidence in Purchasing Power Parity in Efficient Markets," *Journal of Finance,* March 1987, pp. 68–79.

Ibbotson, Roger, Richard Carr, and Anthony Robinson: "International Equity and Bond Returns," *Financial Analysts Journal,* July–August 1982, pp. 61–83.

Jorion, Philippe: "International Portfolio Diversification with Estimation Risk," *Journal of Business,* July 1985, pp. 259–278.

—— and Frederic Mishkin: "A Multicountry Comparison of Term-Structure Forecasts at Long Horizons," *Journal of Financial Economics,* March 1991, pp. 59–80.

Joy, Maurice, Don Panton, Frank Reilly, and Stanley Martin: "Co-Movements of International Equity Markets," *Financial Review,* Fall 1976, pp. 1–20.

Lessard, Donald F.: "World, Country and Industry Relationships in Equity Returns: Implications for Risk Reduction through International Diversification," *Financial Analysts Journal,* January–February 1976, pp. 31–38.

Levy, Haim, and Marshall Samat: "International Diversification of Investment Portfolios," *American Ecomomic Review,* September 1970, pp. 668–675.

Liu, C., and J. He: "Risk Premia in Foreign Currency Futures," *The Financial Review,* November 1992, pp. 571–587.

Logue, Dennis E., and Richard J. Rogolski: "Offshore Alphas: Should Diversification Begin at Home?" *Journal of Portfolio Management,* Winter 1979, pp. 5–10.

Makin, John: "Portfolio Theory and the Problem of Foreign Exchange Risk," *Journal of Finance,* May 1978, pp. 517–534.

Nesbitt, Stephen L.: "Currency Hedging Rules for Plan Sponsors," *Financial Analysts Journal,* March–April 1991, pp. 73–80.

Odier, Patrick, and Bruno Solonik: "Lessons for International Asset Allocation," *Financial Analysts Journal,* March–April 1993, pp. 63-77.

Officer, R.R.: "Seasonality in Australian Capital Markets," *Journal of Financial Economics,* March 1975, pp. 29–52.

Perold, Andre, and Eric Sirri: "The Cost of International Equity Trading," Institute for Quantitative Research in Finance, Spring Seminar 1994, Palm Beach, FL.

Praivie, Stephen: "The Structure of Corporate Ownership in Japan," *Journal of Finance,* July 1992, pp. 1121–1140.

Ripley, Duncan: "Systematic Elements in the Linkage of National Stock Market Indices," *Review of Economics and Statistics,* August 1973, pp. 356–361.

Roll, Richard: "The International Crash of October 1987," *Financial Analysts Journal,* September–October 1988, pp. 19–35.

——: "International Structure and the Comparative Behavior of International Stock Market Indices," *Journal of Finance,* March 1992, pp. 3–41.

Solnik, B.: "The Performance of International Asset Allocation Strategies Using Conditioning Information," *Journal of Empirical Finance,* June 1993, pp. 33–56.

——: "Why Not Diversify Internationally Rather than Domestically?," *Financial Analysts Journal,* July–August 1974, pp. 48–54.

Speidell, L., and V. Bavishi: "GAAP Arbitrage: Valuation Oppportunities in International Accounting Standards," *Financial Analysts Journal,* November–December 1992, pp. 58–66.

Stein, J., Mark Rzepezynski, and Robert Selvaggio: "A Theoretical Explanation of the Empirical Studies of Futures Markets in Foreign Exchange and Financial Instruments," *The Financial Review,* February 1983, pp. 1–32.

Stulz, Rene: "A Model of International Asset Pricing," *Journal of Financial Economics,* December 1981, pp. 383–406.

Subrahmanyam, Marti: "On the Optimality of International Capital Market Integration," *Journal of Financial Economics,* March 1975, pp. 3–28.

Swanson, Joel R.: "Investing Internationally to Reduce Risk and Enhance Return," Morgan Guaranty Trust Co., 1980.

Thomas, Lee R.: "Currency Risks in International Equity Portfolios," *Financial Analysts Journal,* March–April 1988, pp. 68–71.

Wahab, M., and M. Lashgari: "Covariance Stationarity of International Equity Market Returns: Recent Evidence," *The Financial Review,* May 1993, pp. 239–260.

QUESTIONS AND PROBLEMS

1. Identify the major international equity markets and compare the relative sizes of these markets.
2. Why might the return generated in local currency differ from the return earned in dollars for a U.S. investor investing internationally?
3. Why were returns stated in local currency and dollars virtually identical in the 1960–1969 period but significantly different in the 1970–1979 period?
4. Explain why international investing can be beneficial to portfolio diversification.
5. Why might the correlation across international equities continue to be low into the future?
6. Discuss why inclusion of foreign securities in a portfolio might be beneficial even if the expected return was less than that expected from domestic securities.
7. Differentiate between the spot and forward foreign exchange markets.
8. Define premium and discount on forward foreign exchange markets.
9. Explain why the difference between forward and spot rate should be equal to the expected change in the spot rate.
10. Explain how the expected change in spot rates for two countries should be related to the expected difference in inflation rates in those two countries.
11. Explain why differences in inflation rates between countries should be related to differences in interest rates.
12. Explain how the difference in interest rates between countries should be equal to the difference between forward and spot rates.
13. Explain how exchange rate variation creates an additional uncertainty (risk) in international investing.
14. Explain how we might go about executing a passive strategy of international investing.
15. Indicate the problems of conducting a totally passive international investment strategy, and suggest a workable way around these problems.
16. Indicate the essential elements of an active strategy of investing in international markets, and briefly describe the importance of each.
17. How might we use the forward rate as a benchmark in the forecasting of exchange rates?
18. Compare and contrast active and passive strategies of international investing.
19. In general, are foreign securities markets as efficient as U.S. markets? Explain why or why not, citing evidence.
20. Using the data in Tables 11-2 and 11-3, rank the countries according to return per unit of risk (standard deviation) for both the 1980–1984 and 1985–1993 periods.

21. Assume that the exchange rate of marks to dollars was $0.50 at the beginning of the year and $0.48 at the end of the year. Over the same period the return on German stocks has been 18 percent. What was the net return to the U.S. investor over the year?

22. Assume that the exchange rate of Swiss francs to dollars was $0.20 at the beginning of the year and $0.25 at the end of the year, and the Swiss market showed a return of −5 percent. What was the net return to the U.S. investor after the year?

23. The spot rate for the German mark is currently 0.4055 per dollar, and the 6-month forward rate is 0.4178 per dollar. Is the forward rate at a premium or a discount? Calculate it.

24. The spot rate for the British pound is 2.230 per dollar, and the 6-month forward rate is 2.2215 per dollar. Calculate and indicate whether the pound is at a premium or a discount.

25. Assume that the inflation rate in the United States is expected to be 8 percent over the next year, while in Britain it is expected to be 3 percent. What is the expected change in the currency spot rate over the next year?

26. The rate of inflation in the United States is expected to be 5 percent over the next year, while in Britain it is expected to be 9 percent. The rate on one-year bills in Britain is 12 percent. In equilibrium, what should be the rate on one-year U.S. Treasury bills?

27. Assume that the rate of interest is 9 percent in the United States and 12 percent in the United Kingdom, and that the spot rate of exchange is $2 per pound. Determine what the forward rate of exchange should be to ensure equilibrium.

28. Assume that the spot rate of exchange is $2.00 per pound, and the forward rate is $2.10 per pound. Determine the interest rate in the United States if the U.K. rate of interest is 7 percent.

29. Correlations across international markets have tended to increase significantly at times of market stress. What is the impact of this phenomenon on an international investment program?

30. Refer to Figure 11-7. Assume that the standard deviation of currency was 8 percent and that the organization deemed its IC to be 0.15. Determine the expected return on the currency when it is rated 1.

31. An investor bought a Japanese stock one year ago when it sold for 500 yen per share and the exchange rate was $0.008 per yen. The stock now sells for 650 yen and the exchange rate is $0.010 per yen. The stock paid no dividends over the year. What was the rate of return on this stock? What would be the rate of return on the stock to a Japanese investor?

The following international security market returns are to be used with Problems 32 through 34.

Year	United Kingdom	Japan	Hong Kong	Australia	United States
1986	18.9%	42.6%	46.5%	46.8%	14.6%
1987	2.0	15.3	−10.3	−10.5	2.0
1988	4.7	39.9	16.7	12.8	12.4
1989	35.1	29.0	5.5	10.9	27.2
1990	−11.5	−38.7	6.6	−22.4	−6.6
1991	16.3	−3.6	42.1	29.0	26.3
1992	17.2	−26.4	28.3	−6.1	4.5
1993	20.1	2.9	115.7	40.2	7.1
1994	−10.3	13.2	−31.1	−12.0	−1.5
1995	20.3	.7	23.0	15.2	34.1

32. Determine the correlation of returns for the United States, United Kingdom, and Japan over the 10-year period. In addition, determine the standard deviation of returns for the three countries over the same period of time.

33. Determine the correlation between the returns from Japan, Australia, and Hong Kong over the 10-year period. Also, determine the standard deviation of returns over the same period.

34. With the information generated in Problem 31, determine the expected return and risk (as measured by the standard deviation) for a portfolio of 25 percent U.K. stocks, 25 percent Japanese stocks, and 50 percent U.S. stocks. Assume that the historical means, standard deviations, and correlation coefficients are the expected values.

35. For the following returns:

Period	U.S.	Japan	Exchange rate*
1	12%	18%	120
2	15%	12%	105
3	5%	10%	110
4	10%	12%	90
5	6%	7%	95
6			100

* Beginning of period value of yen for dollars.

(a) What is the average return in each market from the point of view of a U.S. investor? A Japanese investor?

(b) What is the standard deviation of return from the point of view of a U.S. investor? A Japanese investor?

(c) What is the correlation of return between markets from the point of view of each investor?

PART FIVE

Derivatives: Valuation and Strategy Applications

Financial futures and options are derivative instruments that offer portfolio managers more flexibility and efficiency in developing and applying strategies than when restricted to basic underlying asset classes such as stocks, bonds, and money market instruments. These derivative instruments are now in widespread use, and the volume of trading in these is substantial; but this has been a relatively recent phenomenon. The growth in derivatives has been propelled by (1) the development of models for better valuation of these instruments, (2) the emergence of central organized exchanges for trading these securities, and (3) the accumulated body of procedures for applying them.

Security options have had a long history but have experienced only a limited scope of application until the development of rigorous methods of valuation in the early 1970s, most notably the model of Black and Scholes. The institution of the Chicago Board Options Exchange (CBOE) shortly thereafter provided a central clearinghouse and standardized options contract that facilitated trading of options. Options on individual securities and on broader indexes are unique in allowing portfolio managers to generate tailor-made patterns of returns for their portfolios that have the potential for enhancing return and controlling portfolio risk.

Financial futures allow portfolio managers to hedge risk effectively as well as change the underlying risk-return characteristics of a portfolio rapidly and with minimal cost. Plan sponsors utilizing a multiple-manager program find futures to be especially useful in that they allow changes in the plan asset allocation without disturbing the activities of individual managers in the program. Use of futures has increased as these instruments are applied to an expanding variety of market indexes.

Though there are notable applications of futures to equities, the greatest volume of activity takes place with regard to interest rates, where the futures on Treasury bonds and Eurodollars are clearly the most actively traded of all futures instruments. In addition, a strategy of investing in international bonds is most productively conducted in concert with a program of hedging the foreign currency risk through the use of futures. Finally, many, if not most, bonds are issued with call provisions and other optionlike features. To value these embedded options, we need to rely on techniques based on option valuation theory.

Because of the pervasive use of derivatives and related analysis to bond market strategy, extensive trading of bond-related derivatives, and insights into valuation, we include bond management as a naturally related component of this fifth part of the book. We begin this series of chapters by describing the valuation and application of futures in Chapter 12, and then describe option valuation models and the ways that these derivatives can be used to generate differing patterns of returns. Chapter 14 on bond management concludes the series and offers examples of important applications of derivatives to fixed-income securities along with other approaches to managing this major asset class.

Financial Futures: Theory and Portfolio Strategy Applications

INTRODUCTION

Financial futures offer significant benefits in the portfolio management process. The major types of financial futures that are in wide use and relate to our purposes include (1) futures on stock market indexes, (2) futures on interest rates, and (3) foreign currency futures. These instruments offer efficient means of executing strategies quickly and at relatively low cost. The major uses of futures are with regard to hedging as well as to facilitate the application of strategies, but other uses include price discovery and speculation on price moves.

Because of the intimate relationship between spot prices, forward rates, and future rates, we begin the chapter by defining these terms more explicitly and showing their relationship. We then go on to describe the mechanics of futures trading and settlement and briefly describe the institutional structure that characterizes the organized financial futures markets. In addition, we discuss the principles of valuation of financial futures and illustrate them with respect to each of three main types: foreign currency, interest rate, and stock market index. In the final segment of the chapter, we focus on the major applications of financial futures in the portfolio management process: hedging and strategy application.

SPOT AND FORWARD TRANSACTIONS

Spot transactions are the same as cash transactions, and they take place at current (spot) prices, current (spot) interest rates, or current (spot) exchange rates, depending on the financial instrument of interest. Forward transactions are somewhat more complex but relate easily to spot transactions in a rather straightforward fashion. Specifically, forward transactions take place at a later (forward) date and in the same fashion as spot or cash transactions when executed. Alternatively, these are transactions that are agreed upon currently by transacting parties with respect to the specific financial instrument to be traded and at a specified price or rate, but they are deferred for execution to a later but fixed date.

The forward prices or forward rates that are negotiated and agreed upon by the parties to the agreement are firmly established. The parties in essence enter a contract so that the future prices and future rates do not change from the beginning to the forward date of transaction. It is quite likely that the actual market prices of stocks, interest rates, or exchange rates will vary over the time of the contract. One of the major purposes of the forward contract is to ensure a set price or rate for a transaction that is desired or contemplated at a future date.

Actual *or realized spot* prices, interest rates, or exchange rates at the termination date may differ from the forward prices or rates established at the beginning of the period. However, over time, we would expect that the forward price or forward rate on average would correspond to the realized spot prices or spot rates. Alternatively, we might reasonably propose forward prices and rates as unbiased estimates of expected spot rates. This supposition is both a theoretical and empirical question that we cover in more detail in a later section of this chapter. For now, it is useful to summarize and compare the four kinds of prices and rates discussed so far:

Prices and Rates
(1) Spot prices and rates are those prevailing currently and at which investors make current cash transactions.
(2) Expected spot prices and rates are those that investors expect to prevail at the end of an investment time horizon.
(3) Forward prices and rates are those established currently to be used to transact at an agreed time period in the future.
(4) Realized spot prices or rates are those that actually prevail at the end of the investment time horizon and used by investors at that time to transact.

FUTURES

Though virtually identical in concept and intended use, futures and forwards have important differences that condition the type and extent of application of each in portfolio management. In broad terms, forward contracts might be viewed as special-purpose financial instruments that have terms set to meet the specific needs of two parties to the agreement. As such, the forward market is a dealer market where transactions are negotiated. Correspondingly, buyers of a forward contract need to find a trader or seller willing to sell a contract suitable to the buyer's needs. Because there is generally not a secondary market for forward contracts, both parties are locked into the contract and subject to the risk of failure to perform on the contract by either party as well as the uncertainty of subsequent price fluctuations or rate changes.

A futures contract overcomes some of the shortcomings of forward contracts. First, futures contracts are standardized with respect to such terms as (1) the amount and type of asset to be delivered, (2) the delivery date or maturity date, and (3) the exact place and process of delivery. In addition, futures contracts are traded in auction markets organized by futures exchanges, which means that buyers and sellers do not have to rely on fortuitous matching of interests. Because there is a fairly active secondary market for many futures contracts, it is possible for traders to close their position prior to the predetermined delivery date by executing a reverse transaction. Finally, the clearinghouse of the futures exchange guarantees the performance of each party to the contract.

In futures we need to recognize two distinct types of investors: (1) end users, or covered positions, and (2) speculators. End users or covered positions are investors who have the underlying security or need it to hedge an investment position. Speculators are investors who do not have or do not need the underlying instrument. Rather, speculators anticipate price movements that will generate a profit, which they will realize by closing their position. It should be noted that losses are also possible, and typically speculation in futures is considered a highly risky activity.

To help ensure the guarantee of final payment on a futures contract, the clearinghouse of the futures exchange establishes several requirements for trading on the exchange. First, at execution of a futures contract, both the buyer and seller are required to post *initial margin.* That is, both the buyer and the seller are required to make security deposits that are intended to guarantee that they will in fact be able to fulfill their obligations. This initial margin may also be referred to as *performance margin.* The amount of margin is a fixed dollar amount based on the type of contract and typically ranges from 5 percent to 15 percent of the total base price of the futures contract.

As a further assurance, the exchange also revalues the futures contract on a daily basis to reflect changes in the price. As the value of the futures changes, so also does the amount of margin required by the buyer and seller of the contract. When the price rises, the value of the future for the buyer is greater and the required margin is less, but for the seller the obligation is greater and hence the margin requirement is greater. Conversely, with a decline in price, the value of future to the buyer is less and the need for margin greater, but the required margin for the seller is less. This process is known commonly as marking to market (mark-to-market), and it effectively keeps the margin amount in line with current market conditions. The dollar amounts of increase and decrease in the margin accounts are exactly equal because they represent a transfer of funds from one account to another.

A third margin requirement that helps ensure performance by buyer or seller is known as *maintenance margin.* According to this requirement, the investor must keep the account's equity equal to or greater than a certain percentage of the amount deposited as initial margin. Because this percentage is conventionally 75 percent to 80 percent, the investor must have equity equal to or greater than 75 percent to 80 percent of the initial margin. If margin drops below the maintenance level because of mark-to-market, the investor receives a *margin call* and must come up with additional funds to bring the account back to the original margin level. If the investor does not deposit the added margin, the exchange will close out the investor's position by entering a reversing trade in the investor's account. The strong possibility of a margin call during mark-to-market on a daily basis is one reason why investors are required to have an additional $5,000 to $20,000 in liquid assets in their brokerage account.

Cash Flows and Futures Settlement

Because of mark-to-market, the cash flows and ways that futures are settled differ significantly from forward contracts. Futures follow a pay (or receive)-as-you-go method, in which profits are credited to the account and losses debited as the prices of the future varies over time. The profits and losses are in turn cumulated over time, so that at any point in time, there is a net profit or loss in each futures margin account. On the other hand, forward contracts are simply held until maturity, and no funds are transferred until that date, although contracts may be traded.

The data in Table 12-1 illustrate how the cash flows and final settlement process differ between futures and forwards. For this purpose, we assume a single contract on government bonds that are due in seven days. Government bonds trade in $100,000 units with a price per 1000 of principal value. The table shows the beginning price of 80, which represents

TABLE 12-1
Profits and losses/forwards and futures

Day	Price	Long future	Short future	Long forward	Short forward
0	80	—	—	—	—
1	81	+1000	−1000	0	0
2	79	−2000	+2000	0	0
3	78	−1000	+1000	0	0
4	79	+1000	−1000	0	0
5	81	+2000	−2000	0	0
6	82	+1000	−1000	+2000	−2000
Total profit/loss		+2000	−2000	+2000	−2000

80,000, and the series of prices for the other days. Note that prices fluctuate over the period but end at a higher level of 82 at day 6.

Because of the requirement to mark-to-market, there is a cash flow to or from the futures contract each day, whereas in the case of the forward contracts there is a single cash flow at the end of period. Note that in the case of both forwards and futures, positive returns to the purchaser of the contract are losses (negative returns) to the seller of the contract, and vice versa. These profits and losses are equal, so that the net returns to futures and forwards are zero. Finally, the end-of-period summed return to the futures contracts is the same as that of the forward contracts.

Though the end-of-period profits and losses for futures and forwards are the same, the existence of interim cash flows makes the futures pattern different and more complex than in the case of forward contracts. Because of the opportunity to invest these interim cash flows, or the need to supply funds, futures and forwards have a potential difference. Some empirical evidence, however, suggests that interest earnings on daily settlements have only a small effect on the determination of futures and forwards prices. For this reason and for simplicity of analysis, we will assume that the profits and losses on a futures contract held to maturity are simply the summation of daily settlement and thereby equivalent to the returns to the forward contract. Another way of looking at this is to assume that the interest earnings are offset by the interest paid (or lost) when funds are supplied for daily settlements.

Liquidity Reserve

As described in the prior section, futures users must recognize gains or losses on a daily basis, directing cash flows to, or from, their clearing member of the futures exchange. Because of the marking to market and daily resettlements, there is the risk of sizable negative cash flows for futures positions when underlying assets show strong moves. Even in a relatively stable market environment, changes in the value of spot market positions typically do not generate immediate offsetting flows because changes in the value of underlying debt or equity positions are likely to be merely "paper" gains or losses. As a result, the futures user needs to estimate the funds that will be needed potentially to meet the conditions of daily resettlement and establish a liquidity reserve for this purpose over the life of the investment.

Determining the size of the liquidity reserve is analogous to inventory management, in which we try to develop an "optimal" reserve or level of inventory that best meets our needs. In this case, the variables to be considered in setting a liquidity reserve are (1) the length of time the position will be held, (2) the number of contracts to be traded, (3) the volatility of the futures contract being traded, and (4) the acceptable probability of a zero balance in the liquidity pool. Using these variables and assuming that futures price changes are normally distributed and have a constant variance and that prices follow a continuous process, researchers have developed a model that provides the probability that a liquidity reserve will be exhausted within a given time frame T. The model giving the probability of a cash deficit is expressed as follows:

$$\text{Probability of cash deficit} = 2[1 - \Phi \lambda / \sigma \sqrt{T}]$$

In the expression, Φ is the cumulative distribution function for a standardized normal variate, and σ is the standard deviation of the futures price change. Intuitively, the model determines the probability of an investment in one futures contract losing λ dollars within T trading days. Despite a lack of conformance of some of the underlying assumptions with reality, the model is practical and usable because of its relative simplicity and the fact that the input variables can be estimated with sufficient accuracy.

To illustrate an application, we assume a hedged S&P 500 index fund that requires a liquidity reserve where there is only a 5 percent probability that the funds will be depleted in a given month. For this purpose, we would naturally use the S&P 500 futures contract. We further assume that the standard deviation of the futures will be in line with that of the underlying S&P 500 index. Over the postwar period, the standard deviation of the S&P 500 has averaged between 15 percent to 20 percent per annum. Using the midpoint and converting to a monthly basis we obtain a standard deviation estimate of 5.05 percent ($17.5\%/\sqrt{12}$). With the March 1995 futures selling at 460, the value of a contract is $230,000 ($460 \times 500$). Applying our estimated standard deviation of 5.05 percent to this value, we obtain a standard deviation $11,615 for the futures contract. Using these data as input, we derive a value for the liquidity reserve using the formulation as follows:

$$\text{Probability of cash deficit} : 2[1 - \Phi(\lambda / \sigma \sqrt{T}] = 0.05$$

$$2[1 - \Phi(\lambda/11615 \sqrt{1}] = 2[1 - \Phi(1.96)] = 0.05$$

$$\lambda/11615 \sqrt{1} = 1.96$$

$$\lambda = \$22,765$$

Assuming the aggregate market value of the index fund is $10 million, we need to sell 43 S&P 500 contracts to hedge the portfolio. Using the calculated liquidity reserve per contract of $22,765, we obtain a total revenue for the hedged portfolio of $978,895 or approximately 10 percent of the total value of the program. It is reassuring to note that futures practitioners and advisors often use a 10 percent level as a rule of thumb for liquidity reserves for a hedged equity program.

Futures Settlement

As a final note, for the futures trading process the obligation to deliver the financial instrument of interest can be fulfilled in several ways. First, the delivery can be the underlying instrument exactly in form and quantity as designated in the contract, for example an exact amount of a foreign currency. Alternatively, some contracts are settled with a cash delivery that is equivalent in value to the security of interest. Cash delivery is especially suitable in cases such as stock indexes, in which settlement with each of the underlying stock issues would present logistical problems. Finally, settlement can be satisfied by the delivery of an equivalent security. Ability to deliver comparables broadens the supply of instruments that can be delivered but may set up other problems that we will describe as follows.

For example, the Treasury bond future is one that facilitates settlement by relating the contract to a standardized underlying instrument. For this purpose, a Treasury bond with at least 15 years maturity and an 8 percent coupon becomes the underlying instrument that meets the standard. Conversion factors have been established for equalizing those other bonds with differing coupons to the standard. This conversion process broadens the list of potential government bonds suitable for delivery at expiration. Typically, one of the eligible bonds will be "cheapest" to deliver.

Table 12-2 illustrates the conversion process for the December 1995 T-bond future that was selling at 117-20 as of 11/10/95. It shows a listing of 26 bonds that would be eligible to settle the December 1995 T-bond future. All the bonds have maturities greater than 15 years, with coupon rates varying from $6\frac{1}{4}$ to $11\frac{1}{4}$, and market prices ranging from 98-09 to 115-04. The column labeled "C. factor" gives conversion factors to equalize each bond to the standard. Note how the conversion factors vary directly with the level of the coupon. The column labeled "Gross basis" is the difference between the bond price and delivery price, which in turn equals futures price times the conversion factor. Using the net basis, the bonds are arranged from the cheapest to the most expensive to deliver. The $10\frac{5}{8}$ bond of 8/15/95 was assessed as the cheapest to deliver.

Futures Markets

Because of standardization, assurance of contract execution, and the availability of central trading exchanges, futures contracts and futures exchanges offer greater flexibility in providing liquidity and efficiency of implementation. As a result, there has been a growing use of financial futures as a component of portfolio management strategies and other investment applications. Correspondingly, there has been a growing proliferation of futures contracts applicable to debt instruments, stock indexes, and foreign currencies of many types. Also many of these futures are actively traded, thereby providing the level of liquidity needed to implement various kinds of portfolio strategies.

Table 12-3 shows the five most actively traded financial futures ranked by the daily average volume of contracts over the most recent twelve months. It is conventional to count the long and short futures positions as a single contract and in turn refer to the aggregation of these contracts as *open interest.* Note that Treasury bond and Eurodollar futures are the most actively traded, with open interest positions at about the same level. The five- and ten-year Treasury note futures that are also interest rate–related rank among the most actively traded, implying that fixed-income investors have exploited the futures market to a relatively greater degree than equity investors. The S&P 500 future is the only equity-related future that ranks among the most actively traded financial futures.

In the United States, financial futures are traded on 12 different exchanges. Short-term interest-related futures such as that on Eurodollars are traded on the International Monetary Market (IMM) of the Chicago Mercantile Exchange (CME). Longer-term bonds such as Treasury bonds and notes are mainly traded on the Chicago Board of Trade (CBOT). The S&P 500 future is traded on the Index and Option Market (IOM) of the CME, but other

TABLE 12-2
Cheapest-to-deliver U.S. long bond (CBT) December 1995 selling at 117-20 as of 11/10/95 to deliver 12/29/95

Coupon	Maturity	(Mid) price	Source	Conv. yield	C. factor	Gross basis (32nds)	Implied repo%	Actual repo%	Net basis (32nds)
$10\frac{5}{8}$	08/15/15	148-09	BGN	6.313	1.2570	13.7	4.81	5.64	5.4
$11\frac{1}{4}$	02/15/15	155-04	BGN	6.276	1.3147	15.5	4.72	5.64	6.3
$9\frac{7}{8}$	11/15/15	139-25	BGN	6.339	1.1843	15.3	4.46	5.64	7.2
$9\frac{1}{4}$	02/15/16	132-26+	BGN	6.347	1.1237	20.9	3.15	5.64	14.6
$8\frac{3}{4}$	05/15/17	127-20	BGN	6.373	1.0758	34.7	.53	5.64	28.5
$8\frac{7}{8}$	08/15/17	129-07+	BGN	6.372	1.0891	36.1	.30	5.64	30.6
$9\frac{1}{8}$	05/15/18	132-17+	BGN	6.381	1.1158	41.6	−.41	5.64	35.0
9	11/15/18	131-10	BGN	6.385	1.1038	47.3	−1.49	5.64	40.9
$8\frac{7}{8}$	02/15/19	129-29	BGN	6.388	1.0914	49.0	−1.94	5.64	43.6
$7\frac{1}{4}$	05/15/16	110-06	BGN	6.354	0.9252	43.5	−2.57	5.64	39.5
$7\frac{1}{2}$	11/15/16	113-05+	BGN	6.355	0.9496	47.2	−3.02	5.64	42.8
$8\frac{1}{2}$	02/15/20	125-23+	BGN	6.396	1.0530	60.0	−4.28	5.64	55.2
$8\frac{3}{4}$	05/15/20	128-30	BGN	6.396	1.0795	62.8	−4.46	5.64	56.9
$8\frac{1}{8}$	08/15/19	121-01+	BGN	6.390	1.0132	59.8	−4.70	5.64	55.4
$8\frac{3}{4}$	08/15/20	129-01+	BGN	6.396	1.0800	64.4	−4.74	5.64	59.3
$7\frac{7}{8}$	02/15/21	118-11+	BGN	6.399	0.9866	73.9	−7.71	5.64	69.9
$8\frac{1}{8}$	05/15/21	121-18	BGN	6.399	1.0133	75.9	−7.72	5.64	70.9
$8\frac{1}{8}$	08/15/21	121-23	BGN	6.393	1.0135	80.2	−8.46	5.64	75.9
8	11/15/21	120-07+	BGN	6.394	0.9998	84.3	−9.49	5.64	79.4
$7\frac{1}{4}$	08/15/22	110-31+	BGN	6.387	0.9180	96.1	−13.29	5.64	92.9
$7\frac{5}{8}$	11/15/22	115-29+	BGN	6.381	0.9587	101.0	−13.46	5.64	96.7
$7\frac{1}{8}$	02/15/23	109-16+	BGN	6.383	0.9038	102.6	−14.91	5.64	99.5
$7\frac{1}{2}$	11/15/24	114-29+	BGN	6.366	0.9439	124.7	−18.41	5.64	120.7
$7\frac{5}{8}$	02/15/25	116-23	BGN	6.358	0.9579	129.5	−18.79	5.64	126.1
$6\frac{1}{4}$	08/15/23	98-09	BGN	6.382	0.8065	109.3	−19.03	5.64	107.2
$6\frac{7}{8}$	08/15/25	107-28	BGN	6.286	0.8733	164.9	−28.43	5.64	162.5

Source: Bloomberg.

equity-related futures trade on a variety of other exchanges. Outside the United States, there have developed active markets for futures, including most notably those exchanges located in Tokyo, Osaka, Hong Kong, Singapore, London, Paris, Toronto, and Sydney.

FUTURES VALUATION OF THE SPOT/ EXPECTED SPOT PRICING RELATIONSHIP

There are economic interrelationships between spot prices, futures/forwards, and expected spot prices that are important to understand as background for the application of these

TABLE 12-3
Most active futures contracts (12/94 to 12/95)

Futures contract	Exchange	Open interest (contract volume)
Treasury bonds	CBOT[(1)]	392,186
Eurodollars	IMM[(2)]	383,629
Treasure notes, 10 years	CBOT	241,274
S&P 500	IOM[(3)]	197,732
Treasury notes, 5 years	CBOT	163,821

(1) Chicago Board of Trade
(2) International Monetary Market
(3) Index and Option Market

instruments in portfolio management. For example, the relationship between spot prices and futures/forwards provides the basis for establishing a fair value for futures/forwards. The relationship between futures/forwards and expected spot prices, in turn, has potential for use in price discovery and for setting standards of comparison for appraising the success of investment strategies.

Because the pricing of futures, spot, and expected spot is a simultaneous one, there is a three-way relationship between spot prices, forward/futures prices, and expected spot prices, as shown in Figure 12-1. The diagram shows that forward prices are related to expected spot prices, which in turn are related to current spot prices. The relationship of forward prices and expected spot prices is a plausible one that has economic rationale underlying it, but it is less defined with respect to precise linkage. However, the interplay between futures prices and expected spot prices has significant potential with regard to issues of price discovery and the setting of standards of comparison.

As shown in this diagram, forward prices are also related back to spot prices, but in this case the two are more directly and precisely related. To show this, we can simply express the forward price in terms of the current (spot) price of the security and the risk-free rate of interest across the time period to expiration. For example, if investors sell a forward contract, they are assuring themselves of a payment equal to the forward price at the expiration date. They can at the same time buy the underlying security at its present value and receive the forward price for the security when sold at expiration. Because this transaction is riskless, the following relationship holds in the absence of interim cash flows:

$$\text{Current security price} = \text{Forward price}/(1 + i)^T$$

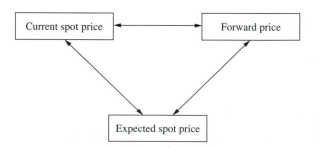

FIGURE 12-1
Spot-futures pricing relationships.

where i is the yield to maturity for a risk-free bond with a maturity equal to the term of the forward contract. Alternatively, the forward price is also equal to the future value (price) of the current security price invested at the risk-free interest rate for the term of the contract:

$$\text{Forward price} = \text{Current security price} \times (1 + i)^T$$

This relationship is a strong one because forces of arbitrage can be easily set in motion to keep the pricing in line. The investor thus has two equivalent alternatives to obtain the security: (1) buy the security now at price P_T and hold it until time T when its price will be P_T, or (2) purchase a forward contract F and invest sufficient funds (P at i) now to pay the forward price when the contract matures. The second strategy will require an immediate investment of the present value of the forward price in a risk-free security—specifically, an investment $F/(1 + i)^T$ funds at the rate i over the maturity period. Table 12-4 shows the cash flows for each of these alternative investment strategies.

Note that the initial cash flow for the first alternative strategy is negative, reflecting the cash outflow necessary to purchase the stock at the current price P. At the maturity time T, the stock will be worth P_T. Correspondingly, the second alternative involves an initial investment equal to the present value of the futures price that will be paid at maturity of the futures contract. By maturity, that investment grows to the value F of the contract. The summation of the two components of alternative 2 will be P, the exact amount needed to purchase the stock at maturity regardless of its actual price at the time. Thus, each alternative results in an identical value of P; so the initial cash outlay for the two strategies must be equal. Divergences in value between the two will be corrected by swap/arbitrage—selling or shorting the more expensive and buying the cheaper.

Viewed in another way, purchase of a security currently incurs the opportunity cost of earning a return on funds that are used for the purchase. Deferring the purchase with a forward allows the investor to earn a return, in this case the risk-free rate, until the later date of purchase. Because of this opportunity to use funds in the interim, futures should sell at a higher price than the underlying security. The interest rate should provide the standard, and arbitrage should ensure the consistencies of the relationship. This generalized process for ensuring equilibrium pricing between future and current (spot) is sometimes referred to as the *spot-futures parity theorem.*

As noted at the beginning of this section, there is also a relationship between forward prices and expected spot prices, which are in turn related back to spot prices. We show this by indicating that there is a need first to account explicitly for the relationship between the spot (current) price of the security and its expected spot price. Accordingly, we can define the current price of the security as its expected price or value discounted back to present

TABLE 12-4
Spot-forward investment alternatives

Alternative	Action	Cash flow	
		Beginning	**Ending**
(1) Immediate	Buy security	$-P$	P_T
(2) Deferred	Buy forward/take delivery	0	$P_T - F$
	Invest $F/(1 + i)^T$	$-F/(1 + i)^T$	F
	Total	$-F/(1 + i)^T$	P_T

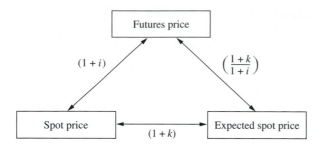

FIGURE 12-2
Spot, futures, expected spot price relationships.

value (spot price) by the appropriate discount rate. For risky securities, we can define this rate k, which will be higher than the risk-free rate i and will be higher or lower in line with the risk of the security. Using a simple valuation model, we then show the relationship between the spot price S and expected spot $E(S)$ as:

$$S = \frac{E(S)}{(1 + k)} \quad \text{or alternatively,} \quad E(S) = (1 + k)S$$

Once we establish the link between the spot price and expected spot price, we can then logically define the appropriate relation between the forward price and expected spot price because we can analytically define two sides of the three-way pricing relationship and thereby deduce what should be the third side of the relationship. With the risk-free interest rate i as the link between the spot price and futures price and the discount rate k as the link between the spot rate and expected spot rate, the ratio of the discount rate to the risk-free rate $(1 + k)/(1 + i)$ should be the connection between the futures price and expected spot price.

Figure 12-2 reproduces the three-way relationship between spot, futures, and expected spot prices similar to the prior diagram (Figure 12-1), only in this case, the diagram shows the three rates connecting these prices: (1) risk-free rate (i), (2) discount rate (k), and (3) ratio of the two basic rates $(1 + k)/(1 + i)$. According to this three-way relationship, futures prices should be higher than spot prices, which should in turn be lower than expected spot prices. Futures prices will correspondingly be lower than the expected spot price to the extent that the underlying security bears risk. The higher the risk premium $(k - i)$ of the security is, then the lower the future price will be, and vice versa. Because of the difficulty in assessing the size or stability of a risk premium, the forward/expected spot relationship has been less successfully verified empirically or used with less successful practice.

VALUING FUTURES

We saw in a prior section that there is a generalized process based on the interest rate and arbitrage that ensures an equilibrium pricing between future and current (spot) prices. This process, which is sometimes referred to as the spot-futures parity theorem, underlies the pricing of futures/forwards across differing categories of financial instruments. It, however, needs some amending for individual idiosyncrasies in cash flows and other institutional peculiarities, depending on the financial future of interest. In the following sections, we illustrate valuation and general characteristics for three categories of financial futures: interest rate, stock index, and foreign currencies.

Interest Rate Futures

Futures on interest rates have been highly successful. Their popularity is due to the increased volatility of interest rates over the last fifteen years. Interest rate futures volume has also increased because individuals and firms that formerly traded only in the spot bond market have begun trading futures contracts as well. Though futures on Treasury bonds and notes have been highly successful and continue to grow in volume, other futures contracts such as those on corporate bonds or GNMA-backed mortgages have failed totally or faltered after some initial success. In the short-term interest rate arena, the Eurodollar contract has far surpassed the Treasury bill contract in usage. The Eurodollar interest rate, called LIBOR for London Interbank Offer Rate, is considered one of the best indicators of the cost of short-term borrowing. The Eurodollar contract's success is at least partly due to its cash settlement feature.

Table 12-5 shows contract specifications for interest rate futures for T-bonds and notes, Eurodollars, and U.S. Treasury bills. Note that the contract size for the T-bonds and notes is the same at $100,000, while the Eurodollar and T-bill contract size is $1 million. All five contracts settle four times a year in the same months: March, June, September, and December. The first delivery day is the same for the T-bonds and notes, but it differs for Eurodollars and T-bills. As noted before, the long-term interest rate futures are listed on the CBOT, and the short-rate futures are listed on the IMM.

Determining the fair value of an interest rate futures contract is based on the notion of arbitrage that we described in an earlier section with regard to the spot-forward parity relationship. To illustrate by way of the Treasury bond futures, consider that such a bond has two alternatives: (1) purchase directly, or (2) deferred purchase by entering the futures market. For the direct purchase, the investor would buy the bond at the current spot rate P, whereas for the deferred purchase the investor would buy a Treasury bond future with a delivery price of F. In executing the futures transaction, we assume that the investor simultaneously invests in a Treasury bill with a face value of F that matures at the delivery date of the futures contract. To ensure adequate funds at maturity, the investor should purchase Treasury bills amounting to the present value of the future or $F/(1 + i)$, where i is the current interest rate. When there are no interest payments on the bond before maturity, then the pricing expression for the future is the same in form as we previously illustrated for the general case for valuing futures:

$$F/(1 + i) = P$$

TABLE 12-5
Interest rate futures contract specifications

Contract	Exchange	Delivery months	Contract size	First delivery day
U.S. Treasury bonds	CBOT	M,J,S,D	$100,000	First business day of month
U.S. Treasury notes (6 1/2–10 yr.)	CBOT	M,J,S,D	$100,000	First business day of month
U.S. Treasury notes (5 yr.)	CBOT	M,J,S,D	$100,000	First business day of month
Eurodollars	IMM	M,J,S,D	$1,000,000	Cash settled on last trading day
U.S. Treasury bills	IMM	M,J,S,D	$1,000,000	Business day after last trading day

Because the Treasury bonds and other long-term fixed-income securities pay out regular cash flows in the form of coupons and other cash payments, it is likely that there will be many instances of interest payment before maturity. We can account for these interim payments by simply adjusting the purchase price of the security for the cash distributions (C). We then amend the general futures valuation expression to one that is more appropriate for long-term fixed-income securities with interim flows:

$$F/(1 + i) = P - (C)$$

Though this expression is of general use in valuing interest rate futures, we should note that it will not be exact. First, the expression was derived ignoring cash flows attributable to marking to market but is technically appropriate for forward pricing. There will be some divergence between this pricing and that appropriate to the future. In addition, the type of bond actually delivered at the time of settlement will have an impact on the futures value. Though many bonds may be deemed equivalent for delivery at settlement, there is usually one that is the cheapest to deliver, which will have an impact on valuation. Despite these potential discrepancies, the valuation expression has provided a reasonably accurate appraisal of the value of the futures in practice.

As an example of interest rate future valuation, assume that a Treasury bond is currently valued at par (100), the three-month riskless interest rate is 1.50 percent, and the coupon return on the Treasury bond for the next three months equals 1.25 percent. The price of a futures contract on the Treasury bond that expires three months from now should equal 100,250. At this price, we are indifferent between purchasing the Treasury bond on margin or purchasing a futures contract on the Treasury bond.

To demonstrate that this is the fair value of the future, assume that we purchase a unit of the Treasury bond futures contract for $100,000 with borrowed funds. Assume also that after three months, the Treasury bond's price rises to 102, at which time we sell our unit. We receive $103,250—the price for which we sell our contract ($102,000) plus coupon payment equal to $1,250. At the same time, we must pay $101,500—the principal of our loan ($100,000), plus interest of $1,500, for a net gain of $1,750. If instead we purchase a futures contract on the Treasury bond priced at $100,250 and sell it at expiration, when its price equals $102,000, we earn the same profit—$1,750.

What happens if the Treasury bond declines to $98 after three months? In this case, the strategy of purchasing the Treasury bond on margin loses $2,250. We experience a capital loss of $2,000, receive coupon income of $1,250, and incur an interest expense of $1,500.

TABLE 12-6
Treasure bond futures and equivalence of leveraged exposure

	Treasury bond leveraged	Treasury bond futures
Purchase price	100,000	100,250
Interest cost	1500	0
Coupon income	1250	0
Sale price	102,000	102,000
Profit/loss	1750	1750
Sale price	98,000	98,000
Profit/loss	−2250	−2250

If we purchase a futures contract on the Treasury bond for $100,250 and sell it for $98,000, we experience the same loss of $2,250.

Table 12-6 summarizes the Treasury bond example and illustrates the equivalence of a futures contract and a leveraged exposure to the underlying asset. In general, the value of a futures or forward contract equals the price of the underlying asset plus the cost of the carry. For financial securities, the cost of carry is defined as the interest cost associated with purchasing the security on margin, less any income the security generates during the term of the contract. The model for valuing futures is also known as the *cost of carry model*.

Stock Index Futures

Stock market index futures are also useful for hedging and for applying stock market strategies. These futures, in turn, are efficient for these purposes depending on the degree to which the underlying index is representative of the investor's portfolio. Again, differences between the index and portfolio to the extent that these differences are significant can lead to divergences and potential disappointments in results. Fortunately, there are a variety of futures available on indexes that cover a spectrum representative of a diversity of investor portfolios.

Table 12-7 shows a list of eight futures contracts representative of the types available for investors. It describes the indexes underlying each of the futures and the exchange where the future is traded. In addition, it shows under the heading "Contract Size" the multiplier used to calculate contract settlements. An S&P 500 contract, for example, with a futures price of 430 and final index value of 440 would result in a profit for the long position of $500 \times (440 - 430) = \$5000$. The short position in the same contract would incur a corresponding loss of $5000. These profits and losses would be settled in cash through the clearinghouse to avoid the costs associated with actual delivery of the individual stocks in the index. As noted before, cash settlement is common practice with stock index futures, including all those listed in Table 12-7.

Because of the value weighting as well as large numbers of companies in the S&P 500 and NYSE indexes, the futures based on these indexes are most relevant for portfolios that are positioned in large companies covering a diversity of industries and economic sectors. The major market index is composed of a small number of very large companies most representative of the DJIA and thus most relevant to portfolio strategies emphasizing major companies and high liquidity. The S&P 400 Mid-Cap Index is representative of the intermediate-sized companies and its future is most useful for those portfolios addressing this segment of the market. The NASDAQ OTC future would be most representative of portfolios stressing smaller, more rapidly growing companies that are characteristic of that index. Correspondingly, the Russell 2000- and Value Line–based futures would be representative of smaller capitalization issues due to the index weighting method as well as its broad and diverse company coverage. The Nikkei 225 Index is representative of Japanese companies and would be most useful for investors pursuing international strategies that encompass participation in the Japanese market.

Though there are a multitude of indexes with futures available, the S&P 500 future appears to be the most popular as evidenced by open interest positions that are far in excess of that of any other index future. This high degree of acceptance and liquidity derives from the representatives of the index and its widespread use as the market proxy for index funds.

TABLE 12-7
Representative stock index futures

Contract	Underlying market index	Contract size
S&P 500	Standard & Poor's 500 Index. It's a value-weighted index of 500 stocks, averaged arithmetically.	$500 times the S&P 500 Index.
S&P Mid-Cap 400	Standard & Poor's Mid-Cap 400 Index. It's a value-weighted index of approximately 400 medium-sized actively traded U.S. stocks, averaged arithmetically.	$500 times the S&P Mid-Cap 400 Index.
NYSE	NYSE composite Index composed of all stocks listed in the NYSE. These are value-weighted and averaged arithmetically.	$500 times the NYSE Index.
Major Market	Price-weighted arithmetic average of 20 large representative stocks. Index is most representative of the Dow Jones Industrial Average.	$250 times the Major Market Index.
NASDAQ	The NASDAQ-100 Index. This capitalization-weighted index is composed of 100 of the largest nonfinancial stocks in the NASDAQ National Market System	$250 times the value of the NASDAQ-100 Index.
Value Line	Value Line Composite Average. It's an equally weighted index of approximately 1,700 stocks. The geometric average is used.	$500 times the Value Line Index.
Russell 2000	Russell 2000 Index. It's a value-weighted index of the smallest 2000 companies in the Russell 3000 composite index.	$500 times the Russell 2000 Index.
Nikkei 225	Nikkei 225 Index. It's a price-weighted index of 225 representative Japanese stocks.	$5 times the Nikkei 225 Index.

Though introduced only recently in May 1991, the S&P 400 Mid-Cap Index has grown in popularity and now shows open interest positions considerably in excess of those for the other smaller capitalization–oriented futures of the Russell 2000 and Value Line Indexes. Finally, the Nikkei 225 generates a sufficient amount of short interest and liquidity to be useful for executing some internationally oriented investment strategies.

In valuing stock market indexes, we can again begin as before by indicating that an investor has two alternatives in investing in a market index, and for purposes of illustration, we will assume that the S&P 500 Index is the future of interest. The investor could purchase the index directly for the current price P. Because of dividend payments over the period, the net payment for the index can be adjusted downward by the present value of the dividends $PV(D)$. The second alternative is a deferred purchase by executing a forward contract F and simultaneously investing the present value of face amount of the future $F/(1 + i)^T$ in a T-bill. These equivalent transactions are virtually the same in form as those with respect to interest rate futures, except for a dividend payment rather than a coupon adjustment to the purchase price. The following shows the futures pricing expressions:

$$F/(1 + i) = P - (D)$$

In contrast to interest rate futures and other types, stock index futures are settled in cash rather than the underlying security or comparable instruments. Cash settlement is reasonable and practical and has facilitated the use of stock index futures. The alternative would be delivery of the component stocks in the appropriate proportions in the index. For an index such as the S&P 500 or most other indexes, this alternative would be virtually impossible to satisfy for small investors and highly difficult for large investors.

Just as in the case of interest rate futures, the stock futures pricing expression is not exact. Again, the fact that we ignore the cash flows due to mark-to-market of the future as opposed to a forward creates potential for some discrepancy in the pricing relationship. In addition, we need to adjust for dividends, which necessitates a forecast that may be inaccurate, although less so with an index than with respect to an individual stock. Even with these discrepancies, the pricing relationship offers a useful benchmark comparing futures to current prices.

Index Arbitrage

Traders at major brokerage firms—known as program traders—constantly monitor the relationship between the future and the underlying index to detect any pricing discrepancies. Index fund managers also monitor this relationship, as they are in an ideal position to capitalize on pricing discrepancies. For example, the manager of an S&P 500–based index fund would have the alternative of directly purchasing the individual issues in the S&P 500 in proportion to their weighting or of purchasing an S&P 500 future. In making the choice, the manager would evaluate which alternative offered the less expensive way of establishing the portfolio position.

As a direct way of monitoring for discrepancies in the futures/index pricing relationship, we can convert the generalized valuation technique for index futures into an expression more specific for this purpose. In adapting this general expression, we can use the fact that an investor who purchases the S&P 500 and sells an equivalent amount of S&P 500 futures contracts against his position has created an essentially riskless portfolio if his time horizon coincides with the life of the futures contract. Any gain or loss on his long position will be offset by a loss or gain on the futures date to the convergence of the instruments at settlement. Let I_0 and F_0 be the current prices of the S&P 500 and the futures contract, respectively; and let I and F be the prices of each at expiration of the futures. The dollar return to the hedged investor is

$$R = (I - I_0) + D - (F - F_0)$$

where D is the dollar amount of dividends with ex-dates between today and settlement. At settlement, the futures contract is marked to the index, so that $F = I$. Therefore,

$$R = (I - I_0) + D - (I - F_0)$$
$$= (F_0 - I_0) + D$$

independent of I, the price of the index at settlement. If we divide R by the initial investment

I_0, we obtain the RHP or Return to the Hedged Portfolio. That is,

$$\text{RHP} = \frac{F_0 - I_0}{I_0} + \frac{D}{I_0}$$

The first term on the right-hand side of the equation is called the basis. It is simply the current futures price minus the current index price divided by the current index price. The second term is the dividend yield on the S&P 500. Thus:

$$\text{RHP} = \text{Basis} + \text{Yield}$$

Because the RHP is the return on an essentially riskless portfolio, we would expect it to be approximately equal to the return on a risk-free instrument, such as the Treasury bill. Notice, however, that the determination of the RHP does not require as an input the risk-free rate. Rather, it is the risk-free rate implied by the current future price, which may then be compared with a particular investor's "risk-free" alternative and may help to determine the subsequent investment action. If the RHP is less than an investor's risk-free rate, then relative to the cost of money, the futures are undervalued. This undervaluation is readily seen from the equation because the current future price F_0 must be increased to increase the RHP, everything else being equal. Likewise, if the RHP is greater than the investor's risk-free rate, the futures are overvalued. The purchase of undervalued futures and money market instruments makes outperformance of the S&P 500 a virtual certainty, if the position is held until expiration of the futures. Similarly, the sale of overvalued futures contracts against an index fund creates a short-term fixed-income portfolio with a return that exceeds that available in the money market.

Table 12-8 illustrates this *fair value comparison* with the June 1995 S&P 500 future. At the beginning of 1995, the S&P 500 future was trading at 472.75 compared to 465.97 for the S&P 500 Index, or at a premium of 1.45 percent over the index. With the expected dividend yield on the S&P 500 of 2.91 percent and the current T-bill rate (risk-free) of 6.19 percent,

TABLE 12-8
Fair value comparison

	SPM5 vs. SPX
Cash	465.97
Risk-free	6.19%
Implied rate	6.31%
Future	472.75
Theoretical future	472.51
Expire	6/16/95
Days	154
Fair value	6.54
Spread (basis)	6.78
Upper Bound	7.72
Lower Bound	5.35
Dividend	5.79
Dividend Yield	2.91%
Percent of gross dividend	100.0%

Source: Bloomberg

the fair value premium (basis) should be 3.28 percent (6.19 percent minus 2.91 percent). In points, the basis should be 6.54, which compares to an actual spread of 6.78. At the current spread, the implied risk-free rate is 6.31 percent and is only slightly greater than the actual risk-free rate of 6.19 percent. For all intents, the future could be considered fairly valued. When transaction costs for an arbitrage are considered, fair value for the future should be considered as a range rather than a point estimate. Using 0.25 percent as an estimate for this cost, we derive a range of plus or minus 1.16 points around the 6.54 value as an estimated fair value range.

Because many traders and large institutional investors monitor this pricing relationship, futures now tend to trade within a "fair value" range, unlike the period after the introduction of these instruments when there were extended intervals of mispricing. Even in recent times, there have been occasions when mispricing of the futures is evidenced, which is especially likely during periods of market stress. For example, in a surging bull market, the future can tend toward overpricing because of excess demand from optimistic buyers. Conversely, the future can become underpriced during bear market periods, when there is excess selling pressure in the market from panicky investors. This underpricing was especially notable during the crash of October 1987 when the arbitrage process was largely short-circuited. These cyclically related periods of mispricing can present opportunities for those pursuing tactical asset strategies.

Foreign Currency Futures

Historically there has been an active use of forward contracts in the foreign currency markets. Use of foreign currency forwards continues but mainly with large buyers and sellers where direct negotiation is appropriate and the cost can be lower because of the large volumes involved. The primary currency futures market is the International Monetary Market (IMM), a subsidiary of the Chicago Mercantile Exchange. It offers the same advantages of standardization, liquidity, central trading, and assured settlement as in the interest rate futures and stock index futures markets. Futures are available in the major foreign currencies such as the yen, pound, mark, Swiss franc, Australian dollar, and franc, along with futures on such composites as the U.S. Dollar Index.

To illustrate the development and meaning of this, Table 12-9 shows some relevant characteristics of some of the currency futures traded on the IMM. Note that the minimum

TABLE 12-9
Futures contract characteristics international monetary market

Currency	Contract size		Initial margin for hedge	Daily open interest
Japanese yen	12,500,000	JY	2025	62427
Pounds sterling	62,500	BP	2025	44489
German marks	125,000	DM	2025	50977
Swiss francs	125,000	SF	2025	35124
Canadian dollars	100,000	CD	810	33416
Australian dollars	100,000	AD	1350	116600

Settlement: third Wednesday of the months of March, June, September, December.

contract size for each of the currencies is significant. For example, dealing in the British pound requires a minimum contract of 62,500. These contracts settle on the third Wednesday of the month in March, June, September, and December. As with other types of futures, there is an initial margin that varies from $900 for the Canadian dollar to $2000 for the Swiss franc. The open interest shown in the last column indicates that the yen contract is the most active, followed by the British pound and German mark with closely equivalent volume.

As is illustrated in Chapter 14, hedging currency when engaging in an international bond management program can be helpful in improving the risk-return relationship of the portfolio. A foreign currency hedge is usually carried out by buying (selling) a contract to initiate a futures position and closing out the position at a later date by selling (buying) the contract in the futures market, rather than by taking delivery. The hedger benefits to the extent that a gain in the futures position offsets a loss in the spot position.

For example, assume that a portfolio manager investing in German bonds desires to protect against unanticipated currency price changes between March 1 and June 1. Table 12-10 shows how the portfolio manager could sell a June mark futures contract to offset interim movements in the mark. If the value of the mark falls, the loss in the spot market will be balanced by a gain in the futures; if the market appreciates, of course, the gain will be offset by a loss in the futures market. In our example, the mark depreciation is compensated by the gain in the futures.

Interest Rate Parity

Similar to the cases of interest rate and stock index futures, there is an explicit relationship between spot and future currency rates that is defined by interest rates. For foreign currency, the interest rate connecting the spot and forward rate is a relative one, where the domestic interest rate is related to the foreign interest rate as a comparative ratio. In addition, spot and future currency rates represent rates of exchange between domestic and foreign currency, with the spot rate representing the current rate of exchange and the future or forward rate representing the future rate. The resulting spot-futures currency exchange rate is known

TABLE 12-10
Currency futures hedge

Cash	Futures
March 1	
Have commitment to receive in June $5 million in marks at exchange rate 0.3785 (13.21 million marks)	Sell 105 June mark futures (contract size 125,000 marks) at price 0.3795 Total value: $4,980,937
June 1	
Receive marks Able to convert to $ at exchange rate 0.3740 Total receipts: $4,940,000	Buy 105 June mark futures at price 0.3745 Total value: $4,915,312
Currency loss: $60,000	Gain: $65,625
Net gain: $5,625	

as the *interest rate parity* relationship and is similar in form to those described before for interest rates and stock indexes.

To illustrate the development and meaning of this relationship, we assume that an investor compares a foreign rate of interest I_f to the domestic rate I_d and decides to invest at the higher interest rate assumed to be offered in the foreign market. In order to execute this transaction, the investor first needs to obtain foreign currency by converting domestic currency at the prevailing spot rate of exchange S, and using those proceeds to purchase the foreign bond. To eliminate the risk of adverse exchange rate changes, the investor would purchase currency futures with a term to maturity in line with the foreign bond. The proceeds from the maturing bond could then be converted back to domestic currency at the exchange rate assured by the futures contract.

Assuming that the interest rates—domestic and foreign—are riskless (government rates) and that the exchange markets are functioning without impediment, the set of transactions just described sets up the possibility of earning risk-free profits without net investment unless the rate of exchange in the forward market is such as to offset it. In particular, we would expect the futures rate to result in an exchange of a lesser amount of domestic currency for foreign currency and that this "depreciation" of foreign currency would be in an amount to offset the excess return from the foreign interest rate versus the domestic rate. The following expression shows specifically how foreign currency should be priced in the futures market in order to offset the excess return to be earned from the differential in interest rates:

$$F = S\frac{(1 + I_f)^T}{(1 + I_d)}$$

In this expression, F represents the future rate at which domestic currency is exchanged for foreign currency, and S represents the rate at which this exchange takes place in the spot market. The rate of interest in the domestic market is represented as I_d, and the foreign rate is represented as I_f, with the two shown in ratio form to represent a relative interest rate. This expression shows that the forward rate is a function of the current spot rate of exchange, adjusted by the relation between foreign and domestic interest rates—relative interest rates.

In our illustration, we assume that foreign interest rates are higher than domestic rates, which in turn means that the rate of exchange of domestic for foreign currency should be lower in the futures market than in the spot market. The depreciation in the foreign currency—less domestic currency to be exchanged per unit of foreign currency—is necessary to offset the advantage of a higher foreign interest rate. In effect, the investor loses an amount on the change in exchange rates that offsets the profit on relative interest rates, and the future rate of exchange adjusts to make this countervailing effect equal in magnitude.

To illustrate by way of example, we assume that the rate on short-term government securities in Japan is 5 percent, whereas the rate on three-month Treasury bills is 4.5 percent in the United States. To take advantage, the U.S. investor would exchange dollars for yen at the current spot rate, which in this case is assumed to be 130 yen for each dollar. At the same time, the investor would buy futures on the yen, to result in a "covered interest arbitrage" transaction. The futures exchange rate of U.S. dollars for yen that would equilibrate the market would be

$$F = 130\frac{(1 + 0.050)}{(1 + 0.045)} = 130.6$$

TABLE 12-11
Profit from undervalued future

Action	Beginning cash flow ($)	Ending cash flow ($)
(1) Borrow in U.S. and convert to yen	130	$-S(1.045)$
(2) Lend 130 yen in Japan	-130	$130(1.05)$
(3) Contract to purchase 1.05 yen at a future price of $F = 129$	0	$1.045(S - 129)$
Total	0	1.70

When the future rate of exchange is out of line with this equilibrium relation, there will be incentive for arbitrageurs to take profitable action. If the futures rate is too high—does not depreciate sufficiently to offset—the strategy would be to continue to invest in foreign debt and "cover" by buying currency futures. For example, if the future rate F was 129 yen per dollar, the investor could take advantage by borrowing at the rate of 4.5 percent in the U.S. market, converting to yen at the spot rate of 130 yen per dollar and investing in Japan at the 5 percent interest rate. The investor would cover this transaction by buying futures at the rate of 129 yen per dollar. Table 12-11 shows the cash flows necessitated by these transactions and illustrates that the total impact is a positive profit (1.70) with no net investment to the arbitrage.

Should the futures rate overadjust—the yen depreciate by too much—then another set of transactions could be set in motion to reverse the overadjustment. In this instance, the investor or arbitrageur would borrow in the foreign market at the rate I_f and convert from foreign currency to domestic currency at the spot rate S and invest the proceeds in the domestic market at the rate I_d. In contrast to the previous arbitrage, there would be need to sell futures to cover the need to repay the loan in foreign currency. These transactions and resulting cash flows, shown in Table 12-12, would continue as long as the difference between the investing at the domestic rate $S(1 + I_d)$ and the repayment of the loan at the forward rate F is positive.

Empirically, interest rate parity seems to hold rather well. For example, using the U.S. dollar and the Swiss franc we can test the relationship. In May 1996, the rate on three-month U.S. Treasury bills was 5.0 percent, while the rate on comparable Swiss instruments with the same maturity was 4.2 percent. The dollar could then be converted into 1.25 Swiss francs. Using the interest rate parity equation and these determining values, we obtain $F = 1.25(1.050/1.042) = 1.24$. The actual forward exchange rate at

TABLE 12-12
Futures rates and arbitrage actions

Action	Initial cash flow	Cash flow at maturity
(1) Borrow in foreign market and convert to domestic currency at S rate.	D.C. (domestic currency)S	$-(D.C.)S_1(1 + I_f)$
(2) Use proceeds to invest in domestic bond.	D.C. $-$(domestic currency)S	$(D.C.)S(1 + I_D)$
(3) Enter $(1 + I_f)$ futures position to sell domestic for foreign currency.	0	$(1 + I_f)(S_1 - F_0)$
Total	0	$S(1 + I_D) - F(1 + I_F)$

that time for a three-month maturity was 1.2399 per Swiss franc and virtually identical to the theoretical value, which is not surprising given the strong theoretical relationship and the significantly large extent of activity in foreign exchange markets.

Though the relationship is strong and actual rates tend to be priced closely in line with it, there are some circumstances that can create divergences. First, there is the risk of exchange controls, as governments can and do restrict conversion from one currency to another. When the risk is material and immediate, divergences can be significant. In addition, governments can tax the returns to foreign investors and thereby affect the relative return. Correspondingly, there can be a change in tax regime during the period of using a hedge to currency risk. Finally, there is again the divergence of futures, due to mark-to-market, that is a potential factor common to interest rate and stock index futures.

Uncovered Interest Rate Parity

Uncovered interest rate parity is a second version of how interest rates and exchange rates are related. Though the previously described covered version of interest rate parity is an arbitrage condition, the uncovered version explains how we expect investors to behave. Uncovered interest rate parity states that the expected change in the exchange rate over time will equal the domestic-foreign interest rate differential.

Figure 12-3 shows how uncovered interest rate parity works. If the U.S. yield curve is higher than the foreign yield curve (U.S. interest rates are higher), the value of the foreign currency would be expected to appreciate against the U.S. dollar over time. Furthermore, the expectation would be for the dollar to decline at a rate equal to the interest rate differential; otherwise, investors would earn an extra return by owning U.S. fixed-income instruments.

This theory of investor behavior in turn has implications for the use of the forward rate as a forecast of expected exchange rates as well as the potential for excess profit or loss opportunities in the foreign exchange markets. Recall from the prior section that according to interest rate parity, the differential between domestic and foreign interest rates will be equal to the forward premium or discount. Furthermore, the interest rate differential will be equal to the expected change in spot rates, when inflation adjusted (real) rates are equalized across countries. This relationship is sometimes termed the *international Fisher effect* and assumes that currency markets and their respective domestic markets are closely linked; interest rate adjustments that occur in international markets also occur in domestic markets.

If the international Fisher effect and interest rate parity hold, there is a three-way relationship between interest rates, expected spot rates, and forward rates, where the expected

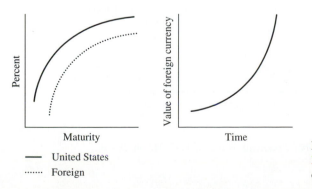

FIGURE 12-3
Interest rates and exchange rate changes.

rate of change of the exchange rate equals the forward premium or discount, as Figure
12-4 illustrates. Correspondingly, the forward rate is said to be an "unbiased" estimate of
the future spot rate. It does not suggest that the forward rate is a particularly accurate forecast
of the future spot rate; it merely holds that it does not systematically over- or underforecast
subsequent changes in the spot rate, which empirically implies that errors (e) in a forecasting
relationship of forward (F) and expected spot $E(S)$ should average to zero over time.

Though there are logical and theoretical reasons for uncovered interest rate parity to
hold, there have been significant instances in which interest rate differentials have not been
offset by changes in exchange rates. In particular, although high-yield currencies are expected to decline, they do not decline as much as theory would suggest. Therefore, high-
yielding markets have tended to outperform low-yielding markets, and some analysts argue
that investors would do better if they consistently overweighted the high-yielding markets
in their portfolios.

It is likely, however, that an added return to investing in high-yielding currencies is
evidence of a risk premium to such investing. When there is a risk premium, the forward
rate will differ from the expected spot rate. The relationship between spot, forward, and
expected spot rates becomes like that described in a prior section and illustrated in Figure
12-2. The forward rate and expected spot rate are then related in equation form as follows
when a risk premium RP is included:

$$F = E(S) + RP + e$$

Though empirical tests of this equation show some evidence of a risk premium, it is unstable over time and differs across countries. Inflation risk, as proxied by the net debt position
of a country, appears to be the best explanation for the presence of a risk premium. Countries with relatively large excess debt and poor records for controlling inflation showed the
strongest evidence of a risk premium in tests. Because net indebtedness changes over time,
it is not surprising that the risk premium would also be unstable. With varying degrees of
inflation risk, the ability to earn equivalent real returns across countries becomes less attainable, thereby short-circuiting the international Fisher effect. In turn, the forward rate
becomes a less effective forecast of future spot rates in the presence of a risk premium.

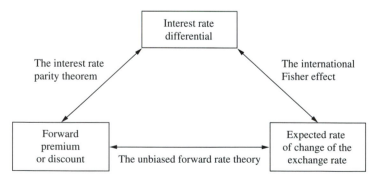

FIGURE 12-4
(*Source:* Ian Giddy, *Global Financial Markets,* D.C. Heath & Co.,
Lexington, Mass., 1994.)

USES OF FUTURES

The primary uses of financial futures in portfolio management are (1) to facilitate the application of strategies, and (2) as a way of hedging risk exposure. Purchase or sales of a future without an underlying asset position or in conjunction with a broader strategy is generally a highly risky activity because the future represents a highly leveraged position in the underlying security and, as such, price changes as well as profits and losses are compounded. This activity is referred to as speculation and is often listed as a third investment application of futures. In the remainder of this chapter, we focus on futures as hedging devices and strategy implementors. We first describe the use of futures as implementors of broad asset class shifts in a tactical asset allocation program and then go on to describe how futures can be useful within the broad asset class categories of bonds and stocks.

TACTICAL ASSET ALLOCATION

In executing an investment program, major plan sponsors generally employ a multitude of managers who specialize at investing within major asset categories. The objective for such managers is to add value from selecting undervalued securities within the asset class—that is, security selection. Over time, valuation discrepancies arise across asset classes that present opportunities to add value by tactically molding shifts in the weighting of the major asset classes—tactical asset allocation. Recognizing and capitalizing on these opportunities in turn is the responsibility of the plan sponsor rather than the specialist managers. Alternatively, some plan sponsors retain managers known as tactical asset allocators (TAA) to monitor and act on these opportunities.

Though plan sponsors or TAA managers can either buy and sell the underlying assets in the portfolio or buy and sell futures contracts, the preference is to use futures in making tactical reallocations. A major advantage is that a shift in mix implemented by futures is not disruptive to the management of the underlying assets. If investors want to sell $100 million in stocks and buy $100 million in bonds, they will have to carefully design a sell program that will not alter the characteristics of the equity portfolio in unintended ways—a task that can take some time. They then have to execute the trade, carefully working the order in conformity with available liquidity. Then they have to do the same thing on the bond side. The whole process could take several days. With futures, the underlying stock and bond portfolios are not disrupted. Indeed, the futures strategy can be implemented without concerning the underlying asset manager.

This separation of the futures positions from the asset managers has another advantage. If the active asset managers are outperforming the index, the use of futures will permit the investor to fully capture the value added within the asset classes. The futures only reflect the index return, but the assets are earning the index return plus something extra. Thus, any excess returns stay with the portfolio. However, the reverse is also true: any underperformance within the asset classes relative to the index also stays with the portfolio.

Finally, TAA managers may be able to take advantage of the occasional mispricing of futures that occurs around cyclical peaks and troughs in the market. TAA shifts in allocation weightings are designed to purchase when there is pressure on stocks and prices are down. As noted before, there is a tendency for the futures to be undervalued at such times. Conversely, TAA programs are designed to sell when there is buying pressure and stocks have risen. Again these are periods when the future tends to be underpriced. Assuming that the TAA manager can in fact identify such cyclical turning points, there is potential to augment return by selling an overvalued future at market peaks and buying an undervalued future at market troughs.

To illustrate, we compare the process of shifting an asset allocation by means of transactions in the underlying assets to the use of futures. Assume that the manager of a $100 million fund consisting of $50 million in equity and $50 million in bonds wishes to shift the stock/bond asset mix from 50/50 to a 60/40 stock/bond mix. Using the cash market, we would sell $10 million of bonds and buy $10 million of stocks. The resulting portfolio would be shifted to $60 million in equity exposure and $40 million in bonds.

In comparison, Figure 12-5 illustrates the asset reallocation using futures, again using a $100 million portfolio. Note that the use of futures requires a liquidity reserve in order to fund the margin requirements for the futures positions. As a result, we begin with a portfolio totaling $100 million, composed of $45 million worth of equity, $45 million worth of bonds, and $10 million in cash equivalents. The cash reserve is used as collateral for the futures positions. In order to accomplish the asset allocation shift, we must buy $15 million worth of equity exposure and sell $5 million worth of bond exposure. With these futures transactions, equity exposure in the portfolio would total $60 million, which is achieved by having $45 million of equity exposure in the underlying stocks and $15 million of equity exposure through the futures market. The bond exposure in the portfolio would be reduced to $40 million from the initial $45 million by the short position of $5 million worth of bond futures. As a result of the futures transactions, the total portfolio exposure has been changed to 60 percent equities and 40 percent bonds, and underlying assets have been left in place.

It is important to understand how the cash reserve is accounted for. Futures are priced such that when the futures contract is combined with an equivalent amount in cash reserves, the combination behaves as if it were invested in the equity or bond index. Consequently, the $10 million in cash plus $10 million in equity futures will behave as if they were invested in the equity index. The short position of $5 million in bond futures creates an additional

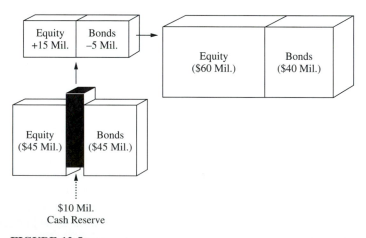

FIGURE 12-5
Asset allocation shift using futures. (*Source:* Rob Arnott and Frank Fabozzi, *Active Asset Allocation,* Probus, Chicago, Ill., 1992.)

$5 million in synthetic cash (the combination of the $5 million short futures position and $5 million of the long bond position will behave as if it were cash). This additional $5 million cash created synthetically supplies the cash base needed for the rest of the $15 million equity futures position. In short, the combined investment in cash reserves plus the futures contracts behave like the underlying assets. To count the cash again in the portfolio would double count the investment exposure.

BOND APPLICATIONS

Financial futures also have useful applications within broad asset classes. For bonds, futures can be highly effective means of hedging interest rate risk as well as efficient instruments for changing the duration of a bond portfolio. However, in implementing these techniques, it is important that the bond future used for either purpose correlate well with the underlying portfolio or security. Some major brokerage funds incurred major losses several years ago in a volatile interest rate environment when attempting to hedge short-duration mortgage-backed securities using Treasury bond futures having an underlying long duration.

Interest Rate Hedging

Interest rate futures can provide an effective means of hedging risk exposure for fixed-income investors. For example, a bond portfolio manager disposing of a relatively illiquid bond position that would likely require an extended period for disposal could sell futures against the bond position to avoid possible loss in the interim. If interest rates rise, the loss on the bond position would be offset by the increase in value of the futures position. Naturally, if interest rates declined, the bond position would be more valuable but the gain would be offset by the loss on the short futures position. This sort of positioning is known as a short hedge and should create a situation of no net loss but no net gain as well.

To illustrate, we assume that a bond manager holding $5 million face value of the current cheapest-to-deliver Treasury bond is concerned about a potential rise in interest rates and the effect this would have on the value of the bonds. In order to protect the bonds from a decline in value, the bond manager decides to fully hedge by selling Treasury bond futures. Again, for illustration we assume that the period for protection is 30 days and that the short-term financing rate is 8 percent. The upper panel in Table 12-13 shows current period T input data as well as bonds and futures pricing outcomes at the end of the 30-day holding period $(T + 1)$.

As shown in the middle panel of Table 12-13, the bond manager needs to sell 69 Treasury bond futures contracts in order to hedge the portfolio. In determining the number of contracts, we need to apply a conversion factor that will equate bonds with differing coupons to the equivalent of an 8-percent coupon Treasury bond. The conversion factors for different "deliverable" bonds will vary, depending on the bonds' maturities and coupons. For long-term bonds with coupons higher than 8 percent, the conversion factor will be a ratio greater than 1.00, but for lower-coupon bonds, the conversion factor will be less than 1.00. In this example, the bonds have a 12-percent coupon so that the conversion factor is well above 1.00.

The bottom panel of Table 12-13 compares the results of the hedged portfolio over the period against an unhedged portfolio. With an assumed decline in bond prices over the period, the unhedged portfolio shows a capital loss that is offset by accrued interest that

TABLE 12-13

A. Input data		
	T	*T* + 30
Treasury bond (CTD)		
Price	131-02	130-05
Coupon rate	12%	
Conversion factor	1.3782	
T-bond futures price	94-22	94-03
Short-term financing rate	8%	

B. Determining contracts

Using conversion factors, we determine the number of futures contracts required as follows.

$$\frac{\text{Face value of Treasury bonds}}{\text{Face value of futures contract}} \times \frac{\text{Conversion}}{\text{factor}} = \frac{\text{Number of}}{\text{futures contracts}}$$

$$\frac{\$5,000,000}{\$100,000} \times 1.3782 = 69 \text{ contracts}$$

C. Comparative results		
	T	*T* + 30
Without futures:		
Portfolio value	$6,553,12.50	$6,507,812.50
Accrued interest		+ 50,000.00
Net value		$6,557,812.50
Annualized return		0.87%
With futures:		
Portfolio value	$6,553,125	$6,507,812.50
Futures gain		40,968.75
Accrued interest		50,000.00
Net value		$6,598,781.25
Annualized return		8.48%

results in a slightly positive return of 0.87 percent. For the hedged portfolio, the bond price decline is compensated by a gain on the futures; the return on the portfolio is 8.48 percent. Note that the annualized return on the portfolio, when protected by the short futures hedge, approaches a short-term financing rate. If the manager had sold the bonds and invested short-term instead of hedging, the return would have equaled the short-term rate of 8 percent.

Correspondingly, we characterize a long hedge as one involving the purchase of interest rate futures contracts to offset adverse price movements related to the future purchase of bonds. An example of appropriate use of a long hedge would involve a portfolio manager who expected a future cash flow that would be used to buy bonds. In order to lock in current yields that are deemed to be attractive and avoid positioning at a lower yield, the manager could buy futures contracts on the bonds. If rates declined in the interim, the manager could simply use the gain on the futures to offset the lower yield available on bonds purchased at the later date. Naturally, if yields rose, the long futures position would show a loss, but the investor would be able to purchase higher-yielding bonds at that time.

Changing Duration

As noted before, futures can be useful in facilitating the implementation of active invest-ment strategies. In striving to generate above-average returns, bond portfolio managers will attempt to anticipate interest rate movements and change the duration of the portfolio in line with the projected change. If the manager expected a decline in interest rates, he or she would increase the duration of the portfolio, and expectation of an increase in rates should be accompanied by a decrease in duration to reduce the volatility of the portfolio. Futures provide a way of implementing these portfolio changes quickly and at a relatively low cost. Accordingly, a manager may wish to maintain the portfolio duration at a target level over time and could use futures to adjust the portfolio when it drifted away from the target. The more frequently these adjustments are required, the more useful the futures become because of lower transaction costs and greater liquidity and speed of implementation.

To illustrate the use of futures for changing the duration of a portfolio, we assume a portfolio manager has strong conviction that a deep decline in bond yields is imminent. The portfolio is tied to a broad-based bond index, and the portfolio manager would prefer to avoid disrupting this externally managed portfolio. Because of these factors and in order to take the greatest advantage of this opportunity to improve the performance of the portfolio, a decision is made to more than double the duration by buying Treasury bond futures.

The upper panel of Table 12-14 shows the current yield to maturity and duration of the portfolio along with current (T) and future ($T + 60$) portfolio values, bond index levels, and Treasury bond futures prices. The middle panel of the table shows that it is a three-step procedure to derive the number of futures contracts needed to change the portfolio duration. For this example, we need to purchase 603 Treasury bond futures contracts to increase the duration of this $100 million portfolio from 4.6 to 10.0. The bottom panel of the table compares the return of the portfolio with futures to one without Treasury bond futures.

With an assumed increase in bond prices, both portfolios show an increase in value over the 60-day holding period. The portfolio with futures, however, derives an additional increment of value to the underlying portfolio from the gain on futures in the rising bond market. The annualized return of 54 percent for the portfolio with futures is about twice as great as the return of 27 percent for the underlying portfolio without futures.

In addition, note that because futures were used to achieve the duration adjustment in this portfolio, the desired results were obtained while keeping the portfolio intact—no dis-ruption of the assets was necessary. It can also be assumed that the costs of implementing this strategy were much lower in the futures markets than in the cash markets because the duration adjustment occurred in one transaction (purchasing futures) instead of the several transactions that may be required to sell and buy the appropriate cash securities. By using futures to make a duration adjustment, it is possible to achieve a longer duration more effi-ciently than through the use of cash instruments. Futures also allow a target duration to be achieved with a much smaller capital outlay than with cash instruments.

Though interest rate futures have significant advantages in hedging and portfolio ap-plication, there can be distortions in expected results. One of these distortions arises when the bond portfolio and the underlying security or index on which the future is based differ significantly. For example, a portfolio of high-yield "junk" bonds is likely to react quite differently from long-term government bonds, on which T-bond futures are based. Using such futures for hedging or market timing could prove to be disappointing if not counter-

TABLE 12-14
Changing the duration of a portfolio

A. Input data

	T	T + 60
Portfolio duration (Macauley)	4.6	
Target duration	10.0	
Broad-based index	219.40	229.35
Bond futures price	84-20	92-01
Portfolio value	$100,000,000	$104,535,095
BPV of futures	$85.59	
Portfolio yield to maturity	9.27%	

B. Determining futures contracts

1. Convert portfolio duration to a BPV:

$$\frac{\text{Duration}}{(1 + \text{Yield}/2)} \times \text{Portfolio Market Value} \times 0.0001 = \text{BPV}$$

$$\frac{4.6}{(1 + 0.0927/2)} \times \$100,000,000 \times 0.0001 = \$43,962.34$$

2. Convert target portfolio duration to a BPV:

$$\frac{10.0}{(1 + 0.0927/2)} \times \$100,000,000 \times 0.0001 = \$95,570.32$$

3. Determine the number of contracts required to achieve the desired portfolio duration:

$$\frac{(\$95,570.32 - \$43,962.34)}{\$85.59} = 603 \text{ contracts}$$

C. Comparative results

	T	T + 60
Without futures:		
Portfolio value	$100,000,000	$104,535,095
Annualized return		27.21%
With futures:		
Portfolio value	$100,000,000	$104,535,095.00
Futures gain		+ 4,465,968.75
Net value		$109,001,063.75
Annualized return		54.01%

productive. Naturally, the most predictable results derive when a future is available with an underlying security most like the portfolio. Even in such cases, there can be divergences arising from differential movement in the price of the future and the price of the underlying security. This change in the differential between the two instruments is known as basis risk.

STOCK APPLICATIONS

Stock index futures can be useful for hedging or changing the exposure of an equity portfolio with respect to its three major risk-return components: (1) market, (2) sector, and (3) specific stock. Futures can be an efficient way of changing the beta of a portfolio and thereby facilitate the implementation of market timing decisions. In addition, futures can facilitate the implementation of strategies of group rotation by providing a way of altering the exposure of the portfolio to major sectors within the equity market. Finally, by providing a way for hedging out the market risk component of a portfolio, futures allow the manager to strip out the stock selection or alpha component of a portfolio. As described in a prior section, there is an array of types of equity futures that allow a latitude in finding futures that correlate with the underlying portfolio or its components.

Changing Portfolio Beta

Stock market index futures can be highly useful to managers employing stock market timing strategies. Given a forecast of the direction of the market, the manager needs to change the risk exposure of the equity portfolio according to the assessed market condition. For example, prediction of a declining market would entail a reduction in portfolio risk exposure, but forecast of a rising market would entail an increase in risk exposure.

In implementing the market forecast, the manager has three alternatives. First, the manager could increase the cash position in the portfolio and reduce the risk exposure if the forecast was for declining market, or alternatively, for a more optimistic forecast, the cash position would be reduced. Correspondingly, the manager could change the beta level of the equity component of the portfolio by selling and purchasing stocks with differing beta characteristics, with sale of high-beta stocks and purchase of low-beta stocks to decrease exposure and the converse to increase exposure. A third alternative, which perhaps would be the best for a portfolio that was highly correlated with an underlying stock market index, would be to use futures—buy or sell futures on the market index against the underlying portfolio. As a matter of interest, an index fund such as the S&P 500 would be ideal for future applications, and many specialist market timing managers, in fact, structure their operation using an S&P 500 index fund as the representative equity portfolio.

Use of futures in changing the risk exposure to the equity portfolio offers significant advantages of speed in implementation and lower transaction costs because of the generally greater liquidity of the futures market. In addition, futures can be used to implement the strategy without interfering with the underlying portfolio. As a result, the market timing component of the manager's investment program can be isolated from other strategic goals. For example, managers attempting to add value through stock selection can obtain the incremental results from this activity and yet change risk exposure over time, as we describe in Chapter 8. Correspondingly, large plan sponsors who employ many managers to accomplish plan goals can change the overall risk exposure with less disruption to individual managers through use of futures. We will describe this process as well in the next section of this chapter.

In utilizing futures for this purpose, the manager needs to first determine the desired level of risk exposure for the portfolio. If the intent is to decrease risk exposure, the action would be to sell futures, but a desire to increase exposure would necessitate purchase of futures. The manager would also need to assess the number of futures to be bought or sold to reach the target exposure level. In doing this, we might proceed by first assessing the beta of the underlying portfolio (β_p) and then designate (β_T) as the target level beta. For an S&P 500 index fund, the portfolio beta would by definition be 1.00 and when the manager has a neutral market forecast, the target beta would be in line with that or a 1.00 beta as well.

To achieve a beta target different from the neutral position, the manager would need to purchase or sell sufficient units of futures to reach the target. If, for example, the objective is to reduce the portfolio risk exposure by one half, the target beta becomes 0.5. In this case, the manager needs to sell sufficient futures to reduce the exposure. Analytically, we can express the target beta (β_T) for a market timing portfolio (p) that is composed of a long position in the cash market and a position in the futures market as follows:

$$\beta_T = \beta_p - H\beta_f$$

With a target of $\beta_T = 0.5$, we need to reduce the portfolio beta β_p by one half as well so that the term H or the reduction term is one half as well. The reduction term H is simply the ratio of the units of futures purchased or sold to the total value of the underlying portfolio expressed in units comparable to the futures. The value H represents the proportion hedged. Because a stock market index futures contract will have a beta equal to one, β_T will equal $\beta_p - H$. Also, we assume that the underlying portfolio is an index fund. With a unit of the S&P 500 futures equal to 500 and a value of the index, say 300, then an index unit would be $150,000. Assuming a total portfolio value of $15 million, the underlying portfolio would then be worth 100 units. To achieve the desired ratio H, the manager would need to sell 50 units of the S&P 500 future:

$$H = \frac{\text{Number of index units sold}}{\text{Value of underlying portfolio in index units}} = \frac{50}{100} = 0.5$$

Based on this analytical relationship, the manager could alter the beta of the portfolio in line with the desired level, reducing risk exposure to a greater or lesser degree by selling a greater or lesser number of S&P 500 index units. Alternatively, the manager could increase the risk exposure of the portfolio by purchasing S&P 500 index units. To achieve a highly aggressive risk exposure or beta of 1.5, the manager would purchase 50 units of the S&P 500. Again, using the analytical expression with a target of 1.5,

$$\beta_T = \beta_p + H = 1.5 = 1.0 + 0.5$$

Sector Allocation

Futures markets provide expanded opportunities for altering the exposure of the portfolio to major sectors within the equity market. For example, a manager may determine that the general level of stock market prices is appropriate but that the sector represented by intermediate-to smaller-capitalization stocks is underpriced—medium and small stocks are underpriced relative to large stocks. This manager could take advantage of this presumed disparity in valuation by selling a future on a broad-based index and buying the future on an index that is structured more in line with smaller-capitalization issues. Presumably the compound future purchase and sale would allow the manager to capture the differential performance of small-versus large-capitalization stocks through the differential in performance exhibited by the broad-based large-capitalization index versus a smaller issue-oriented index.

This investment technique is known as spreading. For this purpose, the manager could buy a future on the S&P 400 Mid-Cap index while selling the S&P 500 index future to take advantage of the presumed relative attractiveness of smaller versus large-capitalization stocks. In implementing the trade, the manager must balance the trade by equating the dollar values of the two positions. Finding the appropriate spread proportions simply requires solving the following equation:

$$\frac{\#MD}{\#SP} = \frac{SPX}{SPMX}$$

where $\#SP$ = number of S&P 500 futures
   SPX = S&P 500 index price
   $\#MD$ = number of S&P Mid-Cap 400 futures
   $SPMX$ = S&P Mid-Cap 400 index price

At June 30, 1996, the price of the S&P 500 was 670.63, while the S&P Mid-Cap index price was 236.00. Using the formulation would indicate need for 2.84 times as many Mid-Cap futures as S&P 500 futures. For example, a spread for a $10 million position would involve purchase of 85 Mid-Cap futures and sale of 30 S&P 500 futures. Over the subsequent quarter, the Mid-Cap index outperformed the S&P 500 index by 2.4 percent. The Mid-Cap futures showed a gain, while the S&P 500 short future position showed a loss. The relatively better performance of smaller stocks resulted in a net gain to the spread.

ALPHA CAPTURE

Hedging strategies are employed when the investor wishes to retain an existing position but offset the market risk created by this position. For example, the investor may sell (or "short") futures contracts to offset a "long" position in the cash (stock) market. A hedging strategy may be used for many purposes, but one that is particularly appropriate is known as *alpha capture.*

Recall that total return to a portfolio may be simply broken down into two components: that attributable to market movement and that attributable to stock selection. Stock index futures may be used in conjunction with an existing stock portfolio to hedge the market risk without selling current holdings. As a result, returns will reflect the risk-free rate plus stock selection capabilities, or alpha. Alpha capture strategies, however, will most likely be imperfect due to the improbability of an exact correlation of price movement between the underlying portfolio of stocks (with alpha removed) and any index.

As an example, assume the investor has a fully invested portfolio. Though the individual securities held are viewed as extremely attractive, the investor's outlook on the market for the next year is negative. Thus, the investor would like to completely hedge the market risk of the portfolio using stock index futures but without selling any current holdings.

Assumptions:	S&P 500 Index: 450
	Risk-free rate: 4%
	Annual dividend yield S&P 500: 3%
	Invested position: $10,000,000
	Average variation margin: zero
	Portfolio beta: 1.00
Trading action:	Sell 44 futures contracts
Futures price:	454.50

Index price: 450.00
Fair value: 450.00
Undervaluation: 0

As before, the fair annual premium is 1.0 percent or 4.5 points. Thus, the fair price is 454.5 (450 plus 4.5). Assume that over the year the market drops 10 percent and the investor's stock portfolio drops 8 percent. The index price is then 405 at settlement (450 minus 45) as is the futures price. The investor has earned the following:

$1,089,000   on futures position
$+300,000$ in dividends
_____
$1,396,500   total

The investor has also lost $800,000 on the invested portfolio, however, which brings the net return to $589,000, or approximately 6 percent ($589,000/$10 million). This 11.9 percent may be broken down as follows:

$$1.0\% \text{ (basis)} + 3.0\% \text{ (yield)} + 2\% \; (\alpha)$$

The "basis" is simply the current future price minus the current index price divided by current price, or in this example (454.50 minus 450/450), or 1 percent. The basis is a component of return unique to the hedged (or essentially riskless) portfolio. The basis plus the yield approximates the risk-free rate when the futures are fairly priced. Thus, total return to the hedged portfolio is the risk-free rate plus alpha.

In this example, the beta of the portfolio was assumed to be 1.00. If the portfolio beta had deviated from 1.00, then the number of contracts sold would differ. For example, if the beta of the portfolio has been 1.15, the short position would require an additional 15 percent to hedge all of the market risk. If the portfolio beta had been 0.85, 15 percent less would be required of the short position.

Alpha Capture Applied

We can illustrate alpha capture strategy as applied to a small- to medium-capitalization portfolio strategy that was described in Chapter 10. Recall that the goal of the strategy is to provide exposure to a universe of small- to medium-capitalization stocks, while also generating a premium return (alpha) over a benchmark index for that section of the market. The manager attempts to achieve these goals by using a disciplined approach to valuing individual stocks and then assembling a grouping of stocks into a portfolio that is broadly diversified with respect to numbers of securities and industry type.

Table 12-15 shows the general characteristics of the portfolio strategy with respect to things such as selection universe, average size of stock, goals, and other descriptors. Note that the strategy excludes the largest 600 stocks that would be most representative of the S&P 500 large-cap universe. Also, the average cap size of $800 million for portfolio companies is much smaller than the average for the S&P Index and more in line with that of the S&P Mid-Cap Index or Russell 2000 Index, which is representative of small-cap investing. Over time, the return of the mid- to small-cap portfolio has shown correlation in excess of 0.90 with both indexes. Though the futures related to either index could be useful for hedging out the market risk of small- and medium-capitalization stocks, the S&P Mid-Cap was chosen because of its greater liquidity; open interest for the mid-cap future averages about ten times that of the Russell 2000 future.

TABLE 12-15
Summary of the characteristics of the small/mid-cap strategy

Number of stocks	Approximately 50–70 stocks
Universe of stocks	2400 stocks below 600 largest capitalized stocks
Portfolio holdings	Maximum 2 percent position with industry diversifications
Stock selection process	Select stocks with high forecast alpha values
Re-balancing method	Every month, with adjustments every quarter on level of share holdings

The number of index futures contracts will be further adjusted so that the value of the fund approximates that of the futures position.

Table 12-16 shows quarter-by-quarter results of applying the alpha capture strategy to small- to mid-cap stocks over the 1992-1995 period. The returns for the small- to mid-cap strategy are matched against the returns of the S&P 400 Mid-Cap future over comparable quarters over the three-year period. Because neutralizing the market effect calls for selling the future, the futures return will be opposite in sign to the actual return experienced over the quarter and is shown as such in the second column of the table. The final column shows the difference between the returns to the small- to mid-cap strategy and the returns to the short future, and is designated alpha capture.

Note that over the period, the differential return between the small- to mid-cap strategy was generally positive, with returns in excess of short futures in 10 of the 11 quarters. On average the differential quarterly excess return (alpha) was 3.2 percent, and the standard deviation of the excess return was 2.5 percent. The resulting return-risk ratio of 1.28 for the alpha capture strategy was quite high, as was the ratio of 1.06 for the small- to mid-cap strategy. Both ratios were well in excess of the ratio for the S&P 400 Mid-Cap Index over the same period. We explain the significance of these ratios in Chapter 15.

Figure 12-6 shows the cumulative results of the small/mid-cap and alpha capture strategies as well as the mid-cap futures over the three-year period, assuming an initial $10,000 investment in each. Note that the mid- to small-cap strategy showed the higher cumulative growth in value, reflecting the fact that the trend in the market over the period was positive.

TABLE 12-16
Simulated returns

QTR	Small/mid-cap strategy	S&P mid-cap futures	Small/mid-cap alpha capture
Sep. '92	4.21%	−2.56%	1.65%
Dec. '92	19.59%	−10.80%	8.79%
Mar. '93	7.75%	−2.07%	5.68%
Jun. '93	1.66%	−1.85%	−0.19%
Sep. '93	8.08%	−3.46%	4.62%
Dec. '93	6.39%	−1.66%	4.73%
Mar. '94	−1.50%	4.41%	2.91%
Jun. '94	3.50%	−4.79%	1.29%
Sep. '94	5.78%	5.40%	0.38%
Dec. '94	−0.43%	−3.62%	3.19%
Mar. '95	8.27%	6.28%	1.99%

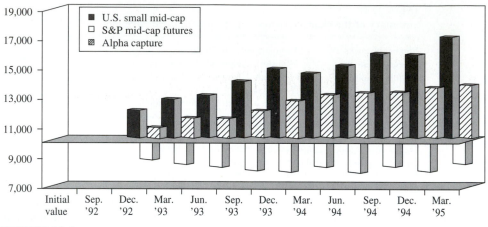

FIGURE 12-6
Simulated growth of $10,000.

The alpha capture strategy showed lower cumulative results because the futures that neutralized the market effect and slowed cumulative losses from shorting removed that source of return. For longer-term investors, loss of the market-related return over long periods is a significant disadvantage of this type of strategy. However, during periods of market uncertainty or for specialized investment programs, the alpha capture strategy can be an attractive alternative.

Transporting Alpha

Once the alpha has been captured through the use of futures, it can then be "transported" to be combined with other strategies. The combining of the alpha could be with a passive strategy, or alternatively, it could be combined with another active investment strategy. In either case, the intent would be to enhance the risk-return characteristics of the basic strategy with the augmented alpha. The risk of course is that the expected alpha is not realized or that it is highly variable over time, so that the resulting risk-return characteristic of the combination is less favorable than that of the stand-alone strategy.

For example, a U.S. investor may consider that the market for large institutional stocks is highly efficient and employs an index fund as a basic means of obtaining exposure to U.S. equities. At the same time, the investor may consider that certain sections of the market, such as small-capitalization stocks, offer opportunity to add value to a passive strategy because of presumably less efficient pricing of these securities.

Table 12-17 illustrates the process of transporting an alpha captured from the small- to mid-cap strategy to a passive strategy. As representative returns for the passive strategy, we use quarterly returns for the S&P 500 over the three-year period from 1992 to 1995. Column three in the table shows the series of combined quarterly S&P 500 and small- to mid-cap excess returns, and the fourth and fifth columns show the cumulative and average annual returns by the two strategies. The bottom part of the table shows risk and return characteristics of the stand-alone and combined strategies along with correlations across the three strategies.

TABLE 12-17

	Alpha from small/mid-cap and S&P mid-cap futures	S&P 500	Alpha and S&P 500	Alpha and S&P 500	S&P 500
	(1)	(2)	(3)	(4)	(5)
				1.000	1.000
9209	1.65	3.15	4.80	1.048	1.032
9212	8.79	5.04	13.83	1.193	1.083
9303	5.67	4.37	10.04	1.313	1.131
9306	−0.19	0.49	0.30	1.317	1.136
9309	4.62	2.58	7.20	1.411	1.166
9312	4.73	2.32	7.05	1.511	1.193
9403	2.91	−3.79	−0.88	1.498	1.148
9406	1.29	1.18	2.47	1.535	1.161
9409	0.38	4.11	4.49	1.604	1.209
9412	3.19	−0.02	3.17	1.654	1.209
9503	1.99	9.74	11.73	1.848	1.326
9506	3.84	9.55	13.39	2.096	1.453
9509	3.31	7.95	11.26	2.332	1.568
9512	1.64	6.02	7.66	2.511	1.663
Mean	3.13	3.76	6.89	30.09	15.64
Std	2.35	3.79	4.73		
M. std	1.33	0.99	1.46		

	Column 1	Column 2	Column 3
Column 1	1.00	—	—
Column 2	0.14	1.00	—
Column 3	0.61	0.87	1.00

Note that the captured alpha combined with the S&P 500 index returns produced a more favorable return to risk ratio (1.46 to 0.99) as well as a higher average annual return than the passive strategy alone (30.09 versus 15.64). The combination results were more favorable than the stand-alone S&P 500 passive index, because the captured alpha premium was large and relatively stable over the three-year period. In addition, the favorable combined result was enhanced by the low correlation between the S&P 500 and alpha returns of 0.14, which provided a diversifying effect in dampening the volatility of returns of the combined series.

In addition to enhancing a basic strategy—either active or passive—with an alpha from a strategy like the small- to mid-cap, there are opportunities to use futures to strip out the alpha components from other market segments. Individual countries in the international marketplace offer a wide variety of natural opportunities to capture foreign market alphas through the use of foreign consultant index futures. For example, the Nikkei 225 futures contract could be used to isolate the alpha component from the Japanese stock selection strategy—as we described in Chapter 11—and transport that alpha into the domestic market. These and others that were captured could, in turn, be added as a portfolio of captured alphas to a basic underlying strategy. The risk-return characteristic of such a portfolio would be further enhanced to the extent that the captured alphas showed low cross-correlation between individual countries.

CONCLUSION

As we have seen, futures markets offer investors increased latitude to hedge risk in three major areas: (1) stock market indexes, (2) fixed-income securities, and (3) foreign currencies. In addition, futures provide opportunity to create new strategies or variations on existing strategies and thereby expand the range of choice for investors. Finally, availability of futures increases the flexibility in applying strategies and expands the opportunity for adding value in the investment process, albeit not necessarily without added risk.

SELECTED REFERENCES

Arnott, Robert, and Tom Pham: "Tactical Currency Allocation," *Finanicial Analysts Journal,* September–October 1993, pp. 47–52.

Brennan, Michael, and Eduardo Schwartz: "Arbitrage in Stock Index Futures," *Journal of Business,* January 1990, pp. 7–31.

Celebruski, Mathew, Joanne Hill, and John Kilgannon: "Managing Currency Exposures in International Portfolios," *Financial Analysts Journal,* January–February 1990, pp. 16–23.

Chance, Don: *Futures and Options,* New York: Addison-Wesley, 1991.

Chiang, T.: "On the Predictors of the Future Spot Rates—A Multi-Currency Analysis," *The Financial Review,* Fall 1986, pp. 69–83.

Cornell, Bradford: "Spot Rates, Forward Rates, and Exchange Market Efficiency," *Journal of Financial Ecomomics,* August 1977, pp. 55–67.

Cox, J., J. Ingersoll, and S. Ross: "The Relation between Forward Prices and Futures Prices," *Journal of Financial Economics,* December 1981, pp. 321–346.

Fama, E.: "Forward Rates as Predictors of Future Spot Rates," *Journal of Financial Economics,* October 1976, pp. 361–377.

Figlewski, Stephen, and Stanley Kon: "Portfolio Management with Stock Index Futures," *Financial Analysts Journal,* January–February 1982, pp. 52–60.

Gastineau, Gary, and Albert Madansky: "S&P 500 Stock Index Futures Evaluation Tables," *Financial Analysts Journal,* November–December 1993, pp. 68–75.

Grammatikos, T.: "Intervaling Effects and the Hedging Performance of Foreign Currency Futures," *The Financial Review,* February 1986, pp. 21–36.

Hill, Jerome, and Thomas Schnelweis: "Reducing Volatility with Financial Futures," *Financial Analysts Journal,* November–December 1984, pp. 34–70.

Jorion, Phillipe: "Mean/Variance Analysis of Currency Outlays," *Financial Analysts Journal,* May–June 1994, pp. 48–56.

Kawaller, Ira: "Foreign Exchange Hedge Management Tools: A Way to Enhance Performance," *Financial Analysts Journal,* September–October 1993, pp. 79–80.

Kolb, Robert, Gerald Gay, and William Hunter: "Liquidity Requirements for Financial Future Investments," *Financial Analysts Journal,* May–June 1985, pp. 61–68.

Kritzman, Mark: "A Simple Solution for Optimal Currency Hedging," *Financial Analysts Journal,* November–December 1989, pp. 47–50.

———: "The Minimum Risk Currency Hedge Ratio and Foreign Asset Exposure," *Financial Analysts Journal,* September–October 1993, pp. 77–78.

Levich, Richard, and Lee Thomas: "The Merits of Active Currency Risk Management: Evidence from International Bond Portfolios," *Financial Analysts Journal,* September–October 1993, pp. 63–77.

Moriarty, Eugene, Susan Phillips, and Paula Tosini: "A Comparison of Options and Futures in the Management of Portfolio Risk," *Financial Analysts Journal,* January–February 1981, pp. 61–67.

Nesbitt, Stephen: "Currency Hedging Rules for Plan Sponsors," *Financial Analysts Journal,* March–April 1991, pp. 73–81.

Samorajski, Gregory, and Bruce Phelps: "Using Treasury Bond Futures to Enhance Total Return," *Financial Analysts Journal,* January–February 1990, pp. 58–65.

Trainer, Francis: "The Uses of Treasury Bond Futures in Fixed-Income Portfolio Management," *Financial Analysts Journal,* January–February 1983, pp. 27–37.

Wolf, Jesse: "Calendar Spreads for Enhanced Index Fund Returns," *Financial Analysts Journal,* January–February 1990, pp. 66–79.

QUESTIONS AND PROBLEMS

1. What factors distinguish a forward contract from a futures contract? What do forward and futures contracts have in common?
2. What is open interest, and what financial futures and currency futures generally show the greatest open interest?
3. List and briefly explain the important contributions provided by futures exchanges.
4. What factors would determine whether a particular strategy is a hedge or a speculative strategy?
5. Explain the differences between the three means of terminating a futures contract: an offsetting trade, cash settlement, and delivery.
6. Suppose you sell an S&P 500 futures contract on March 1 at the opening price of 460. The multiplier on the contract is 500, so that the price is $500(460) = $230,000$. You hold it until buying it back at the closing price of 475 on March 5. The initial margin is 5%. Construct a table showing the changes and credits to the margin account. The daily settlement prices over the interval are $3/1 = 463$; $3/2 = 467$; $3/3 = 470$; $3/4 = 474$; and $3/5 = 475$.
7. On July 20, the September S&P 500 stock index futures were priced at 475. The contract expires on September 21. The S&P 500 index was at 465. The risk-free rate is 6 percent, and the dividend yield on the index is 3 percent. Is the futures overpriced or underpriced?
8. Explain the difference between a short hedge and a long hedge. Give an example of each.
9. What is the basis? How is the basis expected to change over the life of a futures contract?
10. Explain why a strengthening basis benefits a short hedge and hurts a long hedge.
11. Your are the manager of a bond portfolio of $10 million face value of bonds worth $9,448,456. The portfolio has a yield of 12.25 percent and a duration of 8.33. You plan to liquidate the portfolio in six months and are concerned about an increase in interest rates that would produce a loss on the portfolio. You would like to lower its duration to five years. A T-bond futures contract with the appropriate expiration is priced at 72 3/32 with a face value of $100,000, an implied yield of 12 percent, and a duration of 8.43 years.
    (a) Should you buy or sell futures? How many contracts should you use?
    (b) In six months, the portfolio has fallen in value to $8,952,597. The futures price is 68 16/32. Determine the profit from the transaction.
12. You are the manager of a stock portfolio worth $10,500,000. It has a beta of 1.15. During the next three months, you expect a correction in the market of about 5 percent. With a beta of 1.15 you expect the portfolio to fall 5.75 percent (5 times a beta of 1.15). You wish to lower the beta to 1.00. An S&P 500 futures contract with the appropriate expiration priced at 325.75 with a multiplier of $500.
    (a) Should you buy or sell futures? How many contracts do you use?
    (b) In three months, the portfolio has fallen in value to $9,870,000. The futures has fallen to 307.85. Determine the profit and portfolio return over the quarter. How close did you come to the desired result?
13. Explain the difference between spot prices and forward prices. Also, how are these related analytically?

14. Assume that the S&P 500 three-month future is selling at 475, and that the portfolio value is $5 million. The manager desires to maintain a liquidity reserve such that there is only a 10 percent probability of exhausting it over a three-month period. Determine the size of a reserve that meets this requirement.

15. Describe the settlement process for bond futures. What is the role of conversion factors?

16. Assume as in the body of the chapter that the S&P 500 is trading at 465.97 with an estimated dividend yield of 2.91 percent and a current risk-free rate of 6.19 percent. Calculate the implied risk-free rate when the future is selling at 480. What action should be taken?

17. How does the relationship linking spot and future rates differ for foreign exchange, and what is this relationship known as?

18. Assume that the short-term interest rate is 6 percent in the United States and 4 percent in Japan. With the spot rate of exchange for dollars and yen at 100 yen per dollar, what should be the three-month futures rate of exchange?

19. Describe and compare various explainations for the relationship between futures prices and expected spot prices.

20. Compare the strategies of full hedging and tactical hedging. Also, what action would a tactical hedger take when the currency is forecast to appreciate and then when it is forecast to depreciate?

21. What are the advantages of implementing a tactical asset allocation (TAA) program with futures?

22. Assume that the manager assesses that smaller-capitalization stocks are overpriced relative to large-capitalization stocks. Describe a course of action to take advantage of this pricing divergence.

23. Refer to the analysis in the chapter on alpha capture and assume that the market increases by 5 percent over the year rather than declines. Calculate the return to the portfolio under this circumstance.

CHAPTER 13

Options: Valuation and Strategies

INTRODUCTION

Options offer an opportunity to generate patterns of return for a portfolio not available with other financial instruments. Some of the most commonly used option-related strategies are (1) spreads, (2) straddles, (3) covered-call writing, and (4) the protective put. These strategies have the potential for enhancing portfolio return or for providing a way of controlling portfolio risk. In utilizing options, it is also important to assess a fair value for these instruments. Proper use of valuation models can help the investor to avoid excessive cost of implementation of strategy and can present opportunities for return enhancement.

The chapter begins by defining an option and describing the two basic types of options: *calls* and *puts*. We then describe the differing patterns of returns provided by options and compare these with the patterns that are achievable when dealing with conventional securities: stocks and fixed-income securities. We then discuss the binomial method of option valuation in the next chapter. The Black-Scholes model is an alternative method of option valuation that is widely used, and we describe its application in valuing listed options and its relevance to such strategies as spreads and straddles. We conclude by describing how options analysis can be used to implement two popular portfolio strategies: protective puts and covered-call writing.

SECURITY OPTIONS

It is useful to begin this discussion of options by defining some terms. In general, a stock option is an agreement conveying the right to buy or sell common stock at a later date for a specified price. This price is called the *exercise price,* more commonly referred to as the "striking" or "strike" price. For the right to buy or sell common stock, the buyer of the option pays the writer (seller or maker) a price or premium for selling the option. The premium is a dollar amount that generally ranges between 5 percent and 15 percent of the market value of the underlying stock. We will discuss the methods of valuation for establishing this price or premium in a later section of the chapter.

The most common forms of security options are puts and calls. A put gives the buyer the right to deliver (sell) to the writer a specified number of shares, generally 100, of a certain stock at any time on or before the expiration date of the option.[1] The buyer of a put profits and the writer loses if the market value of the stock falls below the striking price by an amount exceeding the premium. For example, if the premium paid for the put is $5 and the exercise price is $60, the buyer would gain if the price of the stock were below $55 at expiration. A call provides the buyer with the opposite opportunity, the right to receive delivery of shares at any time within the option period at the striking price. The buyer of a call profits if the market value of the stock when the call is exercised exceeds the striking price by more than the premium. For example, if the price of the call is $5 and the exercise price is $60, the buyer would gain if the price of the stock were above $65 at exercise.

Option terminology:

Premium	Price paid for the option
Striking price	Exercise price
Writer	Seller of option
Call option	Gives the right to buy stock
Put option	Gives the right to sell stock
Buyer	Buyer of the option

Table 13-1 illustrates how the option process works for a buyer with a put and a call for hypothetical stocks J and K. The table shows the current price of each stock, $60 per share, as well as the exercise price of the put and call, also $60 for both options. The expiration date for the two options is January 1994, and the current date is July 1993, so that each has a term to expiration of six months. This means that in the case of the call, the holder can buy stock J at $60 per share at any time over the six-month term to expiration, but in the case of the put, the holder can sell stock K for $60 per share at any time between July 1993 and January 1994.

For example, if the call is held to expiration, at which time the price of stock J was $70 per share, we could exercise the option at that time, buy the stock for $60 per share, and then sell it for a market price of $70. Doing so would yield a $10 gain per share, as shown in the first column of Table 13-1 in the row labeled "value at expiration or gross return on option." On the other hand, for a put, the option is of value as long as there is some chance that the stock price will move below the exercise price. For example, if we held the put to expiration, at which time the price of the stock was $53 per share, we could buy the stock at $53 per share and then exercise the option to realize a sale price of $60. Doing so creates a $7 per share gain, which is shown in the second column of the table, again in the row labeled "value at expiration or gross return on the option." In practice, it is unlikely that the buyer of the options would exercise the options due to higher transaction costs associated

---

[1]Options can be written to provide for exercise at any time prior to expiration or only at expiration. Those options that allow exercise at any time over the life of the option are known as American calls or puts. Options that allow exercise only at the date of expiration are known as European calls or puts. The added flexibility of American options gives them more value than European options. The American option, as the name would imply, is the predominant type traded on the U.S. market.

TABLE 13-1
Options valuation: successful buyer for a call and a put

	Stock J call option	Stock K put option
Current price of stock	$60	$60
Exercise price of option	$60	$60
Current date	July 1993	July 1993
Expiration date	January 1994	January 1994
Term to expiration	6 months	6 months
Price of stock at expiration	$70	$53
Value at expiration or gross return on option*	$10	$7
Price of option	$5	$4
Net return on option*	$5	$3

*These returns disregard commissions and the costs of tying up the dollar cost of the options. Adjustment for those costs would lower the return from option strategies.

with buying and selling stock. Rather, the buyer would create a net-zero position by selling an option to offset the prior purchase. The buying and the selling of an option are commonly called a round-trip.

To determine the value of a call at expiration, first let

$$C = \text{value of call}$$

$$S = \text{price of stock}$$

$$E = \text{exercise price}$$

Thus, on the expiration date,

$$C = S - E \text{ for } S > E$$

$$= 0 \text{ for } S \leq E$$

Figure 13-1 graphs the formulation and indicates that the higher the stock price is above the strike price ($60), the higher the profitability to the call buyer will be. At the same time, when the stock price is below the strike price ($60), there is a constant zero value at all stock price levels; in particular, the risk for the buyer of the call is limited to the premium paid.

The general formula at expiration for computing the value of a put (P) is

$$P = E - S \text{ for } S < E$$

$$= 0 \text{ for } S \geq E$$

This formula again says that the value of the put is simply the difference between the price of the stock at expiration and the striking price, which for purposes of illustration is $60 per share. Figure 13-2 graphs the formulation and indicates that the lower the price is below the strike price of $60, the higher the value of the put will be. At the same time, when the stock price is above the strike price ($60), there is a constant zero value at all stock price levels. As in the case of calls, the risk for the buyer of puts is limited to the premium paid, the difference being that the risk protection is in the opposite direction.

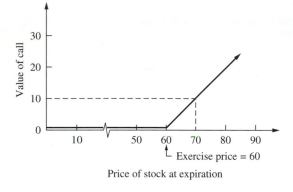

FIGURE 13-1
Value of a call at expiration (stock J).

Price of stock at expiration

The previous calculations and graphs illustrate gross value to puts and calls at expiration. To compute the net return on the option, we simply subtract the price, or premium, of the option from the option value.[2] If a call option expires when the stock is below the striking price, the result is a net loss of 100 percent. If a put option expires when the stock price is above the strike price, the result is also a net loss of 100 percent. Adjustments for the cost of the option lowers profitability at all levels of return, which effectively raises the break-even price for the buyer of the call; break-even price = strike price + premium. The break-even price for the buyer of the put is lowered; break-even price = strike price − premium. Commissions and the cost of tying up the dollar cost of the options would have a similar effect.

THE LISTED OPTIONS MARKET

We should note that the previous discussion provides an overly simplified example of the mechanics of option trading. In practice, trading in options generally takes place through one

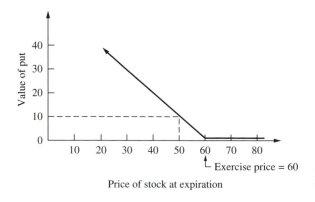

Price of stock at expiration

FIGURE 13-2
Value of a put at expiration (stock K).

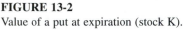

[2]To calculate the relative return on the option, we divide the net return by the investment base, which in this case is the price, or premium, of the option. As noted before, we will discuss the factors giving value to options and describe a model for determining their value in the final part of this chapter.

of the organized exchanges: the Chicago Board Options Exchange (CBOE); the American Stock Exchange; the Philadelphia, Baltimore, Washington Exchange; or the Pacific Stock Exchange. Options for a stock listed on an exchange come due at specific times throughout the year, and each option has fixed strike prices. The expiration date is the Saturday following the third Friday of the month in which the option expires. Actively traded options may have monthly expiration dates, and others have quarterly (three months apart) expiration dates.[3] Variation in the value of a listed option as the price of the underlying stock changes is reflected in the level of the quoted premium.

Organized options exchanges offer several significant advantages to investors. First, options contracts on these exchanges are standardized and simple. In addition, the exchange acts as an intermediary so that the contracts are not between specific buyers and sellers but are the obligations of the exchange. Finally, the exchange promotes a more efficient market by quickly providing information on prices, volume, and other attributes of an option and by making this information widely available. As a result of these factors, the listed options market has a liquidity that an unlisted or over-the-counter market would not, and trading in options can generally take place continuously over the life of most listed options.

The availability of an actively traded options market thus allows an option holder the choice of either exercising his or her option at expiration or selling it in the market prior to expiration. Correspondingly, the writer of an option on a stock that is now selling above its exercise price may wish to close out this position by going into the open market and purchasing the same option contract. The purchase of the option then cancels out the position. Again, as in the case of the buyer, this purchase is considered a round trip, and the investor has a net zero position.

Patterns of Returns

As indicated before, the primary attraction of options is that they allow investors to obtain a pattern of returns that would be unattainable when dealing exclusively with the more conventional sort of securities.[4] To illustrate this, we compare the returns on options—calls and puts—with those attainable from investing in stocks and bonds. We show these patterns for both long and short positions in the different securities, relying heavily on the same sort of graphs used in Figures 13-1 and 13-2 to compare the patterns of return. These graphs are useful both for illustrating an individual strategy and for comparing strategies.[5]

---

[3]For exact details the reader is referred to a more specialized book or to publications of the organized exchanges.

[4]There are other securities that are options or have optionlike features. For example, a warrant is a longer-term call option issued by the firm whose stock serves as the underlying security. A major difference between warrants and options is the limitation on the number of warrants outstanding. A specific number of warrants of a particular type will be issued; the total cannot easily be increased and typically will be reduced as the warrants are exercised. An option, however, can be created whenever two parties wish to create one; therefore, the number of outstanding options is not fixed. Options are thus more suitable for providing the function of risk transfer or insurance with which we are primarily concerned in this book. For this reason, we will not devote much space to discussing warrants and other optionlike securities.

[5]Their advantage lies in the fact that they describe position values (or net values) only at expiration and not at intermediate times prior to expiration.

TABLE 13-2
Stock, bond, and option data

	Stock	Bond	Call	Put
Current price	60	95	5	5
Exercise price	—	—	60	60
Term to expiration	—	6 months	6 months	6 months
Price at termination	Variable	100	Variable	Variable

To facilitate the illustration, we will make the same assumptions about the analyzed securities shown in Table 13-2. The table shows four securities: a short-term bond, a common stock, a put option, and a call option. The characteristics of the put and call that are written against the stock are the same with respect to the striking price and term to expiration. In addition, we have initially assumed that the price of the put and the call is $5 each.

In the analysis, we have ignored other factors, such as dividends, commission costs, taxes, interest, or opportunity costs, that can affect the profit and loss to the different strategies. These factors can be important in the actual execution of an option strategy and should be understood and evaluated accordingly. However, for our purposes, fully considering those factors would unnecessarily complicate the analysis. (Several excellent books and articles listed in the reference section of this chapter provide perspective on the impact of those factors in managing options programs.)

Figure 13-3 shows the profit and loss associated with different strategies—both conventional and option-related. The data indicate the return that would be earned on the particular security at differing price levels of the hypothetical stock at the end of the assumed six-month holding period for the security. The lines showing the pattern of returns essentially give a notion of how the return of the security responds to changes in the price of the hypothetical stock.

Figure 13-3a shows the profits associated with investing in the short-term fixed income instrument. Note that the return pattern is a horizontal straight line. Variations in the price of the stock have no effect on the return of this security because the return of $5 is certain, at least nominally, over the six-month holding period. Figure 13-3b illustrates a short position in the bond, which would correspond to borrowing. Note that the returns are opposite those of the long position; that is, there is a net loss of $5 at all levels of the stock price.

Figure 13-3c shows the pattern of returns associated with purchasing and holding the stock long, and Figure 13-3d shows the pattern associated with selling the stock short.[6] When the stock is held long, the profits increase directly in line with increases in the stock price, but losses increase directly with decreases in the stock price. For example, the buyer of a stock at $60 would realize a $10 profit if the stock went to $70 and a $10 loss if it dropped to $50. Conversely, when the stock is sold short, profit increases with decreases in the stock price, and losses accrue when the price increases. For example, a short seller of

---

[6] A short sale occurs when an investor sells a security he or she does not own. In essence the investor borrows the security from the brokerage firm to sell it. Short sellers sell a security short because they expect its price to fall and want to profit from that price fall. The short seller will sooner or later buy the security to cover (or close out) the short position. If prices fall, the short seller makes a profit, but if they rise, the short seller has a loss.

stock at $60 would realize a profit of $10 if the stock dropped to $50 and a loss of $10 if it increased to $70. The diagonal lines in the two charts show similar patterns, except that the long position for the stock is upward-sloping while the short position is downward-sloping. The long buyer's gain is the short seller's loss, and vice versa.

Figure 13-3e, which shows the pattern associated with purchasing a call, is similar to Figure 13-1, and it includes the cost of the premium. The position here can be most usefully compared with the position of a long holder of the stock. Note first that the buyer of the call derives a greater percentage gain on his investment when the stock price rises than would the long holder of the stock. For example, when the stock rises to $70, the buyer derives a net profit of $5 for a 100 percent gain ($10 gross gain less the $5 premium for the call) versus a 17 percent gain for the long holder of the stock [(70 − 60)/60]. The call buyer has greater leverage than the long holder of the stock. At the same time, the loss to the call buyer is limited to the $5 price of the call, whereas the loss to the long holder is the $60 price of the stock, which is higher than the call price. The call buyer will, however, suffer a total loss if the stock price remains even (at $60) over the period, whereas the stockholder will break even.

Figure 13-3f, which shows the pattern associated with purchasing a put, is similar to Figure 13-1, and it includes the cost of the premium. The position here can be most usefully compared with the position of a short seller of the stock. Note first that the buyer of the put derives a greater percentage gain on his or her investment when the stock price declines than would the short seller of the stock. For example, when the stock declines to $50, the buyer of the put derives a net profit of $5 for a 100 percent gain ($10 gross gain less the $5 cost of the put) versus a 17 percent gain for the short seller of the stock. Again, the buyer of the option, in this case a put, has greater leverage than the short seller of the stock. At the same time, the loss to the buyer of the put is limited to the price of the put, whereas the loss to the short seller is unlimited because stock prices are theoretically unlimited on the upside. As in the case of the call buyer, the put buyer will suffer a total loss if the stock price remains even (at $60) over the period, whereas the short seller will essentially break even.

Figure 13-3g shows the pattern associated with selling a call, and Figure 13-3h shows the pattern associated with selling a put. Note that the seller of the call derives a fixed profit—the call premium—as long as the stock price remains below the exercise price but can suffer unlimited losses when the price rises above the exercise price. In this case, the profit is the $5 premium for the call, so that a loss accrues when the price rises above $65. Conversely, the seller of the put earns a fixed profit as long as the stock price remains above the striking price but can suffer losses to the extent that the price of the stock declines below the exercise price. In this case, the profit is the $5 premium for the put, so that a loss accrues when the price declines below $55. In the case of the call seller, note that the risk position is similar to that of a short seller of stock, but for the seller of the put, the risk position is similar to that of a purchaser of stock. In both cases, the reward is the option premium, or the price of the call or put, as the case may be.

As noted before, options allow the investor to attain patterns of return that are unavailable from the more conventional ways of investing. The return patterns attainable from the conventional stock and bond strategies shown in panels a, b, c, and d contrast sharply with those attainable from the option strategies shown in panels e, f, g, and h. The differing patterns associated with option strategies can in turn be combined with conventional strategies to obtain more desirable risk-return combinations for the portfolio than would be available

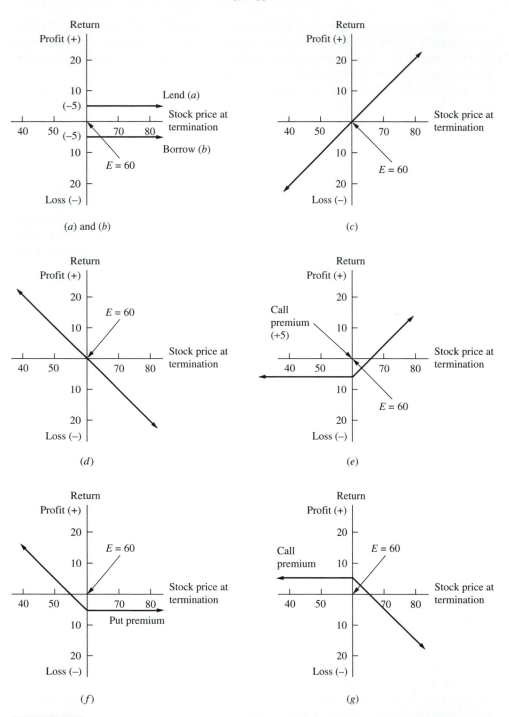

FIGURE 13-3

Profit and loss from various strategies. (*a*) Buy a short-term bond; (*b*) Sell the bond short (borrow); (*c*) Purchase the stock; (*d*) Sell the stock short; (*e*) Buy a call; (*f*) Purchase a put; (*g*) Sell a call.

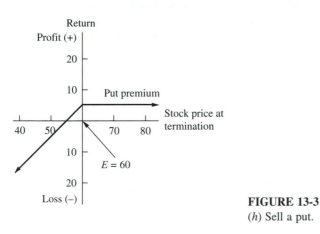

FIGURE 13-3
(*h*) Sell a put.

when only conventional approaches are used. Furthermore, strategies such as selling puts or calls, which would seemingly appear unattractive when used alone, become attractive for certain purposes when used in combination.

Index Options

In addition to the availability of listed options on a multitude of individual stocks, options on indexes of securities have been increasingly available. This availability has been a favorable development in that index options offer benefits of lower cost and efficiency in many applications. Specifically, an option on an index will have a lower cost (premium) than a package of options on the individual component securities in the index simply due to the diversifying effects of operating with a quasi-portfolio, which an index represents, rather than individual securities. A reasonable benchmark is that an option on an index will cost 40 percent less than a bundle of options on individual stocks composing the index. Correspondingly, the transaction costs will be lower and the speed of implementation will be greater with an index than with individual components.

Table 13-3 lists four of the most prominent market indexes, along with a brief description of the index and its related options. The S&P 500 index is a widely used index for

TABLE 13-3
Options on market indexes

Standard & Poor's 500 Index: These options are for the 500 stocks in the S&P 500 Composite Index. It is a value-weighted index, and the options are traded on the Chicago Board Options Exchange (CBOE) with strike prices at five-point intervals.

Standard & Poor's 100 Index: These options, traded on the CBOE, are for a portfolio of 100 stocks included in the S&P 500 Index. Similar to the other S&P indexes, it is a value-weighted series.

New York Stock Exchange Composite Index: These options, traded on the NYSE, are based on the 1500-plus stocks traded on the NYSE. Striking prices are at 5-point intervals.

National OTC Index: These options, traded on the Philadelphia Stock Exchange, are based on the National OTC Index, which includes the largest 100 stocks (based on market value) traded on the national OTC list. Similar to the NASDAQ series, the index is value-weighted.

performance comparison purposes and as a standard for development of index fund strategies, and, as such, the option can have significant application in investment strategies. The
S&P 100 index is composed of 100 of the largest companies from the S&P 500, and its
related option tends to be actively traded because it relates well to many investment strategies. The NYSE-index option provides a way of relating an option to strategies that are tied
to broad-based universes of stocks—those including large as well as small companies. The
NASDAQ option allows the portfolio manager to relate his or her strategy to smaller and
more rapidly growing companies that are reflective of the O.T.C. market. Finally, there are
options on subindexes (not shown on the table) that reflect the market behavior of subcomponents of the broad markets, such as, for example, the Oil Index. Investors concerned with
executing strategies related to the oil group could find an oil index option useful.

   Contracts for index options differ from those on individual stocks in that these are not
stated in terms of numbers of shares. Instead, the size of a contract is determined by multiplying the level of the index by a multiplier specified by the exchange on which the option
is traded. The premium (price) of an index option times the applicable multiplier indicates
the total amount to be paid. For example, the multiplier for the S&P 100 index option traded
on the Chicago Board Options Exchange is 100, meaning an investor would have to pay 100
times the current premium (price) for an option. On February 11, 1993, a call option on the
S&P 100 with an exercise price of $430 and expiring in April was selling at $$1\frac{1}{8}$$, meaning
that the investor would have to pay $$\$112.50(1\frac{1}{8} \cdot 100)$$ for this contract (ignoring transaction
costs).

   In all other major respects, index options are the same as options on a single stock,
except that index options are related to a market aggregate or subcomponent. As a result,
we can implement the same techniques discussed in subsequent sections of this chapter to
index options just as for single stocks. In particular, we can use the Black-Scholes formula
to value index options just as we do for single stocks. In addition, we can engineer many
of the same sort of option-related strategies using index options as we do for single stocks.
In many cases, the application can be more suitable and rewarding because it relates more
directly to broader portfolio management activities.

OPTION VALUATION

In the analysis so far, we have assumed that the current price of the stock was the same as
the exercise price of the stock and that any valuation of the option was with respect to the
expiration date. We now discuss valuation in a more general context, which will enable us
to consider the appropriate value of the option at any time before expiration as well as at
expiration. In our discussion, we use a call option and view events from a buyer's point of
view. This perspective is typically assumed in academic writings and pragmatic settings.
Thus, many times the word "option" is used by itself with an implied "call" in front of it,
and the discussion is from the purchaser's perspective. We consider how the value of the
option varies as the price of the stock varies, both above and below the exercise price prior
to expiration. Analyzing these variations in a more general context means in turn that we
need a different, yet essentially similar, option valuation diagram than the one we have been
discussing so far.

   Figure 13-4 shows a diagram that is more suitable for appraising the value of a call
option both before and at expiration. The horizontal axis is much the same as in the previous

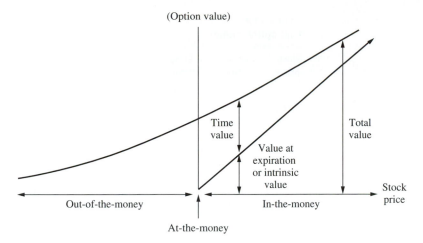

FIGURE 13-4
Value of the call option, buyer's perspective.

diagrams, except that the stock prices are broken into three separate zones: (1) out-of-the-money, where the stock price is below the exercise price; (2) at-the-money, or close to the exercise price; and (3) in-the-money, where the stock price is above the exercise price. The vertical axis refers to the value of the call rather than the profit and loss associated with the strategy, as was the case in the previous diagrams.

Note that the solid line running along the horizontal axis—below the exercise price and bisecting the angle above the exercise price—is identical to the line used in the previous diagrams to depict the profits and losses at expiration associated with the strategy of purchasing a call. This line might alternatively be thought of as a lower bound—a minimum economic value for a call option. At prices of the stock above the exercise price, the option would have value as depicted by the diagrams and calculated in the usual fashion; it is the area under the 45 degree line between the exercise price and the ending stock price. Below the exercise price, the option would have zero value at termination.

Prior to expiration, however, the option will have value in excess of this baseline intrinsic value, which we will refer to as the time value of the option. The way this value varies around the exercise price of the option is illustrated by the curved line in Figure 13-4. Note that the time value of the option is at the maximum when the price of the stock is at the exercise price. This excess or time value decreases when the price of the stock moves away from the exercise price in either direction.

Table 13-4 illustrates this notion of the time value of options by showing the intrinsic value of the option, the time value of the option, and the total value of the option, which is the sum of the time value and intrinsic value of the option. It shows these values again for a six-month option on a hypothetical stock with an exercise price and current price of $60. These values were calculated at prices above, below, and at the exercise price using the Black-Scholes option valuation formula, which will be described later in this chapter.

In Table 13-4, note that the value of the option increases as the price of the stock is higher, reaching its highest value of $23.80 at the high stock price of $80. When the stock price is at or below the exercise of $60, the option has no intrinsic value; however, it has some value—time value—reflecting the probability of the stock moving above the exercise

TABLE 13-4
Call option values

Stock price	Intrinsic value	Time value	Total value
40	0	0.22	0.22
50	0	1.97	1.97
60	0	6.86	6.86
70	10	4.58	14.58
80	20	3.80	23.80

price before expiration. For example, when the stock is at $50, the option has a time value of $1.97, which represents its total value. In essence, the call option has no intrinsic value. When the stock is above the exercise price of $60, the option has both intrinsic value and time value. As the stock price increases, intrinsic value becomes the predominant component of total value. For example, at the high price of $80 the intrinsic value is $20 ($80 current price less $60 exercise price) and the time value is $3.80.

Table 13-4 also indicates, as we have noted before, that the time value of the option is at a maximum when the stock is at the exercise price, and it is lower when the stock is above or below the exercise price. For example, at the $80 high price the time value of $3.80 is only slightly more than one-half the value at the exercise price of $60, but at a price of $50 the time value of $1.97 is less than one-third the value at the exercise price. The time value is smaller at lower prices because there is less chance of a profit on the call and, correspondingly, a greater chance of total loss. At higher prices the option becomes more like the stock in terms of variance, beta, and capital investment; thus, there is less reason to pay a premium over its intrinsic value.[7] Also, at higher prices the probability of even higher prices decreases.

FACTORS AFFECTING VALUE OF OPTIONS

Three primary factors influence the value of an option—that is, the level of the time-value curve on the diagram. These are (1) the expected variance in return of the underlying stock, (2) the time remaining to expiration of the option contract, and (3) the level of interest rates. In addition, the relationship between the market price and exercise price of the stock is important because it determines whether the option is in-the-money, and therefore has economic value, or it is out-of-the-money and has only time value. Finally, dividends on the underlying stock can also influence the value of the option, but because this factor is generally of only secondary importance, we focus mainly on the influence of the three primary factors of valuation.[8]

---

[7]It should be noted that stock itself might be considered an option on the stock value; the exercise price is zero and the expiration date is infinite. Of course, this option would not maintain any premium over the stock itself, which might be attributed to the fact that the option is "deep in the money."

[8]Listed options do not receive the dividends accruing to the stock over the holding period, which makes the stock more attractive relative to the options, at least in this sense. To take advantage of this situation, the investor may want to execute or sell the option prior to the ex dividend date.

We can begin analyzing how the variance in return of the underlying stock influences the value of the option by referring to the two diagrams in Figure 13-5. The diagrams compare the payoffs at expiration of two options with the same exercise price and the same stock price. The only difference is that the price of stock B at its option's expiration date is harder to predict than the price of stock A at its option's expiration date. The probability distributions superimposed on the diagrams illustrate the greater uncertainty associated with stock B than with stock A because stock B is seen to have a wider distribution, or variance, than stock A.[9]

Note that in both cases there is a 50 percent probability that the stock price will decline below the exercise price, thereby making the option worthless; however, when the stock price rises above the exercise price, there is a greater probability that stock B will have a greater value than stock A. The option on stock B, correspondingly, has greater probability

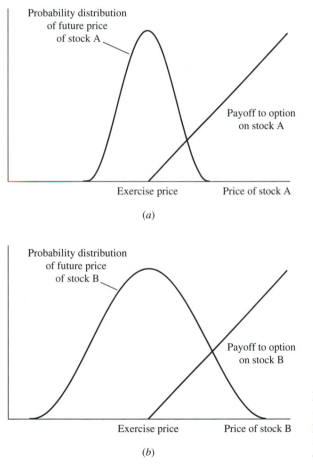

(a)

(b)

FIGURE 13-5
Stock price distribution and option payoff. (a) Payoff to call option on stock A; (b) payoff to call option on stock B.

---

[9] Actually, the log normal distribution is more commonly used to portray the distribution of stock price changes. For clarity of exposition we have simply used the normal distribution because the one reason for using a logarithmic function is that it converts the actual underlying distribution of returns into a more normal bell-shaped curve.

of a higher final payoff than the option on stock A. Since the probability of a zero payoff is the same for the two stocks, the option on stock B should be worth more than that on stock A.

Figure 13-6a shows how the greater underlying variability of the stock affects the time value of the option. Note that the value line of an option on a stock with greater variability will be at a higher level than that of an option on a stock with lower variability. The upper line might be considered the value of the option on stock B, and the lower line is the value of the option on stock A. Note that when the variance of the stock is zero, as it would be at expiration, the value of the option should correspond to the baseline economics value—that is, the time value will be zero.

The principle illustrated in Figure 13-6 is that the greater the expected variance of price changes for a stock, the higher the option value from that stock should be. For example, a

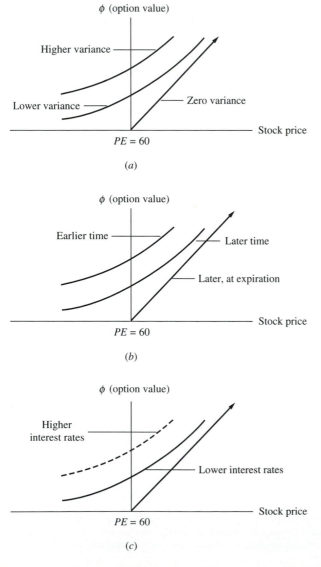

(a)

(b)

(c)

FIGURE 13-6
Factors affecting time value of an option. (a) Variance; (b) time; (c) interest rates.

comparison of two companies with approximately the same current stock prices and with six-month options at the same exercise price showed that the option of the more risky oil and gas exploration company—Mesa Petroleum—sold at $3.75, whereas the option on the more stable company—Bankamerica—sold at $2. This difference in selling price is because investors would expect Mesa Petroleum to trade over a wider range (have higher variance) over any period of time than Bankamerica. Observation of the values of options over time bears out that options on higher-risk stocks persistently tend to have greater value than those on lower-risk stocks. This difference in value again derives from the fact that the variance of return of the stock is a prime determinant of the value of the option.[10]

The second important factor in determining the value of an option is the time remaining to expiration of the option. It seems reasonable that the longer the life of the call option is, the greater should be the opportunity for the price of the stock to move into the area above the exercise price. Analytically, we know that the variance of the distribution of returns, or price changes, will increase with time. In fact, the standard deviation increases with the square root of time, so that a stock with a standard deviation of return of 5 percent over a three-month period would be expected to have a standard deviation of 10 percent over the full year, or four-quarter period (standard deviation of 5 percent times the square root of four quarters). In effect, this increased variance due to the lengthening of the time horizon gives added value to the option. Conversely, the maturing of the option automatically reduces the value of the option. Figure 13-6b shows that over time the curve shifts down as the variance becomes smaller, until at expiration it lies on the baseline, as we previously noted it should.

The third major factor determining the value of an option is the level of interest rates. Higher interest rates would lead to greater values for the options, but lower interest rates would lead to lower values. We can justify this fact in two ways. First, investors can obtain leverage in stock investment by borrowing (establishing a margin account) or by purchasing calls, and in this sense, the two techniques can be considered competitive investment strategies. When interest rates rise, the cost of the margin account increases, making this technique relatively less attractive than the call strategy. Investors would presumably be attracted to the use of calls, thereby driving their prices up. Second, we noted that a strategy of buying fixed-income securities (Treasury bills) and calls is equivalent to creating an artificial convertible security. This quasi-equity security can be considered an alternative, or competitive instrument, to the stock. At higher interest rates more can be earned on the Treasury-bill portion of the "convertible" package, which makes the overall approach relatively more attractive and should lead to greater demand for calls with the attendant upward pressure on call prices. Figure 13-6c shows the effect on the option-value curve; the curve will be at a higher level at higher interest rates and a lower level at lower interest rates.

OPTION VALUATION MODELS

Two complementary approaches to value an option are the binomial model and the Black-Scholes option-valuation model. The binomial model is simpler in derivation and is usually more suitable for illustrating the underlying concepts of option valuation. It is also useful as

---

[10]Later in the chapter we will see that estimating the variability of the underlying security is perhaps the most critical input to determining the appropriate value of an option. Assume for the moment that the standard deviation estimate is a "given." We will discuss ways of developing this estimate in a later section of this chapter.

a model for valuing more complex options such as those embedded in bonds and mortgage-backed instruments, but this model requires considerable computer power and programming to generate the valuation. For organizations heavily involved in such securities, it has proven to be worth the effort to develop elaborate models for purposes of valuation; we describe some of the salient elements of these kinds of models in Chapter 14. The Black-Scholes model, though more complex to derive, provides a more compact expression that can be relatively easily manipulated to derive option values. As such, it has found widespread use in valuing listed options.

In describing the basic elements of option valuation, we use the concepts of replication of securities and arbitrage. For purposes of replication, we can consider the call option as the equivalent of a leveraged position in the underlying stock. In developing this relationship, however, we need to ensure that there is a proper ratio of call holdings relative to stock holdings. When this ratio—known as the hedge ratio—is correct, price movements in the call position will counterbalance price movements in the stock position. Furthermore, forces of arbitrage will ensure that the call is properly priced, so that riskless profit opportunities are not available to this risk-free hedge.

Since the binomial model is simpler to illustrate, we begin by describing this model and how it is used in option valuation. Underlying the binomial model is a basic assumption that security prices can move in two directions, either up or down, over any given time interval. Though this assumption is remarkably simple, the binomial model can be used to represent more complex processes, as we subdivide a given interval into smaller units or extend the analysis over a greater number of intervals. For example, we could subdivide a yearly price-change interval into 365 daily price-change intervals. Furthermore, it is well known that as the number of price changes considered increases, the binomial-model distribution begins to resemble the more familiar and analytically tractable normal distribution. As a matter of interest, Black and Scholes also assumed that price changes are log-normally distributed in deriving that model. We will illustrate the connection between the binomial and Black-Scholes model in later sections.

BINOMIAL OPTION PRICING

To determine the value of an option over a single period using the binomial option pricing model, we proceed as follows. First, we determine the portfolio action that matches the option with a security that replicates the price action of the option but that moves in a contrary direction. Second, we determine the number of options needed to establish an appropriate hedge, so that the returns from the portfolio are the same (riskless) no matter the subsequent outcome. Finally, we derive the price of the call based on the risk-free hedge and the composition of the replicating portfolio.

As a specific example of this binomial option-pricing process, we can consider a hypothetical stock (S) currently selling for $60 per share. We further assume that in the next year, the stock will either decrease to $30 or sell at the higher price of $120. This two-stage price change is, as indicated, the basic form of the binomial model. Also, we assume that there is a call option (C) available on each share with an exercise price (E) of $60 and time to expiration of one year. Furthermore, the risk-free rate (r) for borrowing (B) to finance the stock is assumed, for illustrative purposes, to be 25 percent, so that at the end of the period the amount owed on any borrowing to finance a stock purchase would be $(1 + 0.25)B$. At year end, the payoff to the holder of the call option will be either zero if the stock falls to 30 or $(S - E) = \$60$ if the stock price goes to \$120.

In Figure 13-7, panel A illustrates this binomial-based pricing pattern for this hypothetical stock and its associated option. Note that the diagram illustrates the rudiments of an event tree in which the root (or node) shows the current stock price and the branches show the price of the stock along with the call value. With an upward move in the stock price, the call has an ending value of 60, whereas a down move in the stock to 30 results in a call value of zero. Correspondingly, the stock and call price action are perfectly correlated, as illustrated by the straight line connecting the two price plots in panel B of Figure 13-7. Finally, note that there are two unknowns to determine in the analysis: (1) the beginning value for the call $= X$, and (2) the amount to be borrowed $= Y$.

Because the stock and call prices are perfectly positively correlated, we can set up a hedge by buying one and selling the other. Thus, we can hedge by buying the stock and selling some options or by selling short the stock and buying some options. If we decided to hedge by selling the option and purchasing the stock, we would need to determine the number of options to sell for each share purchased. To do so, we would compare the high–low range of prices for the stock to the high–low spread of prices for the option. Designating $S+$ as the up price of the stock, $S-$ as the down price, $C+$ as the call value when the stock is up, and $C-$ as the call value in a stock-price decline, we derive this appropriate hedge ratio (h) as follows:

$$h = \frac{S^+ - S^-}{C^+ - C^-}$$

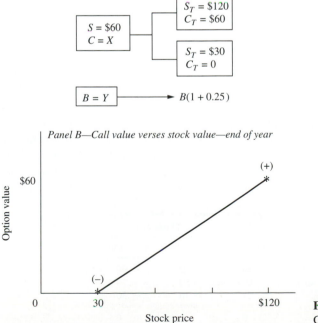

Panel A—General pattern—One-period valuation

$S = \$60$
$C = X$

$S_T = \$120$
$C_T = \$60$

$S_T = \$30$
$C_T = 0$

$B = Y$ $\longrightarrow$ $B(1 + 0.25)$

Panel B—Call value verses stock value—end of year

Option value

\$60

(+)

(−)

0   30   \$120

Stock price

FIGURE 13-7
Call option valuation.

Using input for hypothetical stock and call option, we derive a hedge ratio:

$$h = \frac{120 - 30}{60 - 0} = \frac{90}{60} = 1.5 \text{ call options per share of stock}$$

At the end of the year, a portfolio of 1.5 call options sold short and one share held long should have an equal payoff under either stock price scenario. When the stock decreases to $30, the call option becomes worthless because the stock price is below the $60 exercise price. The terminal value of this position is then $30, or the value of the stock. Correspondingly, when the stock increases to $120, the option is worth $60 ($120 − $60 exercise price) and has a total value for the 1.5 options of $90 (1.5 × $60). Offsetting this value is the current value of the stock of $120. The net value of the holdings is again $30 ($120 stock values −$90 short-option loss).

Thus, the portfolio is worth $30 irrespective of whether the stock moves up or down. Because the binomial model assumes that these states are the only that can occur, the payoff is a riskless investment; it has the same terminal value in either state. Because the payoff to the hedged strategy is risk-free, we can borrow this amount at the risk-free rate to finance the stock purchase. Discounting the payoff value of $30 at the 25 percent rate, we obtain a present value of 30/1.25 = 24. To equate the flows, the option value needs to be equal to the initial stock value less the amount borrowed to finance the purchase; $1.5C = S - B$. With a stock value of $60 and borrowings of $24, the 1.5 calls have the same value; $S - B = (60 - 24) = \$36$, or an individual call should sell at 24 ($C = 36/1.5$).

Using the data for our example option, Table 13-5 summarizes the cash flows for the initial and terminal period one year later for the replicating portfolio. The table shows that the sale of the call options resulted in a positive cash flow in the initial period. Because a call option is equivalent to a leveraged position in the stock, we can offset the sale of the calls by purchasing the stock and borrowing to finance the purchase. The table shows that the amount borrowed is $24, which is the present value at the risk-free rate: [$30/(1 + 0.25) = 24$] of the payoff. Because the cash flows in the initial period net to zero, the return to the hedged portfolio should be zero. The table shows that the net flows to the strategy under either stock price scenario net to zero.

The cash flows net to zero on Table 13-5 because the call option is properly valued at $24. If the option is mispriced, there is potential to earn riskless profit. For example, if the option in our example was selling at $30 instead of its fair value of $24, the investor would simply sell the call option, borrow, and buy stock as before. The flows to these transactions would be the same as illustrated in Table 13-5, except that the investor would generate an extra cash flow of $12 from selling the same 1.5 options in the initial period, again with no risk to the payoff in the terminal period. Conversely, if the option were undervalued, selling

TABLE 13-5

	Flows at 0	Flows at 1	
		$S_t = 30$	$S_i = 120$
Write 1.5 at $24	+36	0	− 90
Buy 1 share stock	−60	+30	+120
Borrow $24	+24	−30	− 30
	0	0	0

for less than $24, investors could reverse this process by selling the stock short, borrowing, and buying the call option to also generate riskless profit. The ability to replicate securities and set up a riskless arbitrage for investors is a powerful force to drive an option to fair value and maintain it at that value.

In the preceding analysis, we saw that the call option can be considered as equivalent to a leveraged position in the stock, and we also showed how the positions could be replicated. We also showed how we could hedge with these two equivalent securities, and thereby create a riskless cash-flow payoff. With hedging and riskless cash flows, we see that the option needs to sell in line with the following relationship in order to maintain an equilibrium price:

$$C(h) = S - B \tag{1}$$

This expression illustrates that writing an appropriate number of calls (C) is equivalent to a leveraged purchase of stock $(S - B)$. The appropriate number of calls to write is, in turn, given by the hedge ratio (h). The amount to be borrowed B is, as we have seen, equivalent to the present value of the riskless payoff. Though this expression for one-period call valuation is simple, we will see in a later section that it is equivalent in form to the Black-Scholes valuation model for call options.

For valuing a one-period option, we need as basic inputs the current stock price, the exercise price, the volatility of the stock price, and the interest rate. The volatility of the stock price and the exercise price condition the value of the hedge ratio (h). The value of the call option increases with greater volatility of the stock but decreases with a lower volatility. Again, there is greater opportunity for the option to have value with higher volatility than with lower volatility. Correspondingly, the favorable impact of higher volatility is compounded as the exercise price is lower and reduced as it is higher. Finally, interest rates have a direct relationship to call values. At higher interest rates, the amount that can be borrowed against the payoff is lower, and thus the value of the option becomes greater as the spread between the stock price and the borrowing amount is larger. Conversely, lower interest rates increase borrowing capacity, reduce the spread, and thereby lower the value of the option.

Pricing Over Multiple Periods

Given the principles described in the prior section for valuing the one-period option, we can easily extend the process over multiple time periods. This extension simply becomes a matter of repeating the same steps as before in an iterative fashion over time. As the periods increase, the process becomes complex only to the extent that the volume of data and calculations multiply enormously. As mentioned before, the application of the technique to practical problems of option valuation requires extensive programming and computer power.

Figure 13-8 illustrates this extension for a two-period analysis, assuming that we are valuing the same option over two individual years for a total period of two years. Note that this figure merely portrays an extension of the same tree pattern as shown in the prior Figure 13-7 for a second (additional) period. It again makes the assumption that price moves are in only two directions from a node and that the stock can move up by the same 100 percent and down by the same 50 percent as before. For example, the stock can move from the high first-period value of $120, either up by 100 percent to $240 or down by 50 percent to $60. The mid-range value of $60 can also be obtained by an up-move of 100 percent from the low

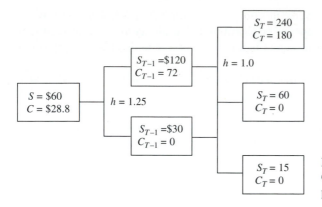

FIGURE 13-8
Call option valuation over two periods.

first-period value of $30. There are now three possible end-of-period values for the stock and three for the option.

In valuing these options, we proceed from right to left on the diagrammed tree, beginning with one period prior to expiration. There is good reason for starting with the period prior to expiration because at that time the option value associated with every possible stock price is known. It is simply $(S_T - E)$ or zero, whichever is larger. For the three ending stock prices shown in the figure, the related option price at the high stock value of $240 will be $180. At the two other ending stock prices, the option will have zero value, because the stock ended up at or below the $60 exercise price.

In valuing options in the prior period, or after one year in this case, note that if a situation will lead to a worthless option no matter what, the option is already worthless. We see from the diagram that when the stock price moves down in the first year, the option will take on zero value at that point. This is so because the price can only recover to the $60 exercise price at best in the second year. On the other hand, the option has value after the first year at the high stock price because of the chance that the stock can move to an even higher price of $240 at the end of the second year. We value this option for the end of the first year, using the same procedures as described in the prior selection and based on inputs for the second year.

Similarly, we use the one-period valuation procedures to value the option for the beginning of the period based on the input from the first year rather than the second year, as in the prior illustration. Note that the resulting value for the option at the beginning of the two-year period has a value of $28.80, which is greater than the value of $24 determined for the one-year option using the same basic input and which illustrates that extending the time horizon has a positive impact on option values. We can see from the diagram that the stock has a possibility of reaching a higher value over a two-year period than over a one-year period—hence, giving the two-year option greater value than the one-year option.

We can extend this analysis over multiple periods by either subdividing a given interval or adding more periods and by applying the same one-period valuation process recursively over many periods. In addition to compounding the number of calculations greatly, extending the analysis considerably increases the burden of developing inputs, particularly with regard to setting the up and down movements of the security price. To avoid estimating these movements individually for each time period, users typically set values for these price movements such that the return distribution resulting from these is considered reasonable. Standard practice has evolved such that the user first specifies the standard deviation of the security price and the number of intervals until expiration, over which a movement up or down takes place. We then calculate a value of the up and down movement that would result in the return process having the standard deviation that was specified. The specific formulas are

$$u = e^{+\sigma \sqrt{t/n}}$$
$$d = e^{-\sigma \sqrt{t/n}}$$

where n = the number of intervals until expiration
$\quad\quad \sigma$ = the annual continuous-time standard deviation of the return on the stock (the standard deviation of the log of returns)
$\quad\quad t$ = the time to expiration in years
$\quad\quad e^x$ = the exponential function

We illustrate application of this method for generating inputs for a multiperiod version of the binomial model as part of a general discussion of methods of valuing options embedded in bonds in Chapter 14.

Finally, we again point out that, when the intervals used to evaluate the option are extended to a great number, the valuation provided by the binomial model approaches the valuation derived by the Black-Scholes model. Figure 13-9 illustrates by showing a plotting of option values against stock prices at specific times prior to expiration and developed from the recursive valuation process of the binomial model. Note that at expiration, the curve is the same form as we used before to value options. As the time prior to expiration extends further from $T - 1$ to $T - 4$ in the illustration, it begins to take the shape of a curve. When the time period lengthens or, alternatively, the number of intervals increases to a very large number, the curve will take the smooth shape of the one we developed using the Black-Scholes model and shown previously in Figure 13-4. Use of this curve to evaluate the hedge ratio and other aspects of option valuation thus has relevance to both the binomial and Black-Scholes models.

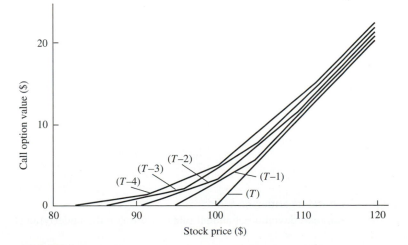

FIGURE 13-9
Option values at various times prior to expiration. (*Source:* William Sharpe and Gordon Alexander: *Investments,* 4th ed. Prentice Hall, Englewood Cliffs, New Jersey, 1990.)

THE BLACK-SCHOLES OPTION VALUATION MODEL

As with the binomial model, the operation of hedging and the hedge ratio are critical notions of the Black-Scholes option valuation model. The model is based on the fact that it is possible, given a number of assumptions, to set up a perfectly hedged position consisting of either a long position in an underlying stock and a short position in options on that stock or a long position in the option and a short position in the stock. By "perfectly hedged," Black and Scholes mean that over a stock price interval close to the current price, any profit resulting from an instantaneous increase in the price of the stock would be exactly offset by an instantaneous loss on the option position, or vice versa.[11]

The Black-Scholes formula is developed from the principle that options can completely eliminate market risk from a stock portfolio. Black and Scholes postulate that the ratio of options to stock in this hedged position is constantly modified at no commission cost in order to offset gains or losses on the stock by losses or gains on the options. Because the position is theoretically riskless, we would expect the hedge to earn the risk-free rate, somewhat analogous to the assumption invoked in deriving the capital-asset pricing model (CAPM). Given that the risk-free hedge should earn the risk-free rate, we infer that the option premium at which the hedge yields a return equal to the risk-free short-term interest rate is the fair value of the option. If the price of the option is greater or less than fair value, the return from a risk-free hedged position could be different from the risk-free interest rate. Because this is inconsistent with equilibrium, we would expect the option price to adjust toward fair value.

Using this notion, Black-Scholes derived an explicit formula for determining the price of the option. The formula is

$$C = S[N(d_1)] - E[e^{-rt}][N(d_2)] \qquad (2)$$

where
$$C = \text{market value of option}$$
$$S = \text{current market price of underlying stock}$$
$$N(d_1) = \text{cumulative density function of } d_1, \text{ as defined below}$$
$$E = \text{exercise price of call option}$$
$$r = \text{"risk-free" interest rate}$$
$$t = \text{time remaining before expiration, in years (e.g., 180 days} = 0.5)$$
$$N(d_2) = \text{cumulative density function of } d_2, \text{ as defined below:}$$

$$d_1 = \left[\frac{\ln(P/E) + (r + 0.5\sigma^2)t}{\sigma \sqrt{t}} \right]$$

$$d_2 = \left[\frac{\ln(P/E) + (r - 0.5\sigma^2)t}{\sigma \sqrt{t}} \right]$$

$$\ln(P/E) = \text{natural logarithm of } P/E$$
$$\sigma = \text{standard deviation of annual rate of return on the underlying stock}$$

---

[11] The Black-Scholes assumption that one can instantly and continuously rebalance means that the relationship between the stock price and option value is effectively linear, so that gains and losses are exactly offsetting.

As mentioned before, the simple binomial model we have previously described also becomes comparable to the Black-Scholes model by allowing the time interval to approach zero and by continuously rebalancing the hedge. We can now see the relationship between the two option pricing approaches more clearly by first expressing the basic one-period hedging equation (1), so that the hedge ratio h is with respect to the stock rather than the call.

$$C = Sh - B$$

Comparing this equation with the Black-Scholes option pricing formula, we see that the arithmetic form of each equation is the same. The first term $S[N(d_1)]$ is the amount of money invested in stock, with the hedge ratio $N(d_1)$ being the fraction of share that must be purchased. The second term, $-E(e^{-rt})[N(d_2)]$, is the amount invested in risk-free asset. The negative sign means that the amount is borrowed. We might thus interpret the Black-Scholes formula as the instantaneous value of the hedge equation used for the one-period binomial model.

Although the formula appears quite forbidding, using it is fairly direct. The major inputs are (1) current stock price S, (2) exercise price E, (3) time to maturity t, (4) market interest rate r, and (5) standard deviation of annual price changes σ. The first three inputs are readily observable from current market quotations or are known items of data. The market interest rate must be estimated, but it can be established fairly easily. Possible sources are the T-bill rate or the rate on prime commercial paper quoted daily in *The Wall Street Journal* for different maturities ranging from 30, 60, and 90 to 240 days. The rate for the maturity that corresponds to the term of the option should be used. The other estimated input—the standard deviation of the stock price change—is more difficult to estimate, and errors can have a significant impact on the established option value.

There are several techniques for estimating the variability of the stock price. One technique uses historically derived values of the standard deviation of price changes of the stock as an estimate of the standard deviation to be generated in the future. The time period of the measurements becomes important in this regard: too long a period may result in the inclusion of irrelevant observations, and too short a period may exclude valuable information and not be representative. Some recommend the most recent six months' or year's trading data as the best measurement interval with the use of historical data.

An alternative way to estimate the variability of a stock is the option valuation formula. Rather than using the formula to assess the proper price of an option, we can observe the current price of an option and deduce the standard deviation of the stock price as implied by the formula. Calculating and averaging the implied deviation over a series of past periods may provide a more accurate assessment of the expected variability of the stock than a straightforward averaging of past values. In either case, it may be necessary to adjust these derived values for possible future changes in the variability of the stock price. Here, we would want to examine those underlying factors that are basic determinants of the riskiness of securities: (1) interest rate risk, (2) purchasing power risk, (3) business risk, and (4) financial risk. If the exposure of the stock to these factors is changing, the historically derived variability estimate should be adjusted to reflect this change. For example, if the company is now financing more heavily with debt, its exposure to financial risk and expected future variability would be greater than in the past.

Valuing an Option

To illustrate use of the Black-Scholes option valuation, or pricing, formula,[12] we can use the following inputs for a hypothetical option: $S = 60$, $E = 60$, $r = 0.12$ (the rate on 180-day prime commercial paper), $t = 6$ months or 0.5 years, and $\sigma = 0.3$. Given these inputs, we can begin by calculating values for d_1, and d_2.

$$d_1 = \frac{\ln(60/60) + [0.12 + 1/2(0.09)](0.5)}{0.3\sqrt{0.5}} = 0.389$$

$$d_2 = \frac{\ln(60/60) + [0.12 + 1/2(0.09)](0.5)}{0.3\sqrt{0.5}} = 0.177$$

Using a table for the cumulative normal distribution, we then compute

$$N(d_1) = N(0.389) = 0.651$$

$$N(d_2) = N(0.177) = 0.563$$

The value of the call is then computed as

$$= 60(0.651) - 60[e^{-0.12(0.5)}](0.563) = 6.86$$

To assess whether the call option was undervalued or overvalued, we could compare this calculated value to the market price of the call. For example, an actual market price of, say, $5 for the call would indicate that the call is undervalued, and an investor might take advantage of this undervaluing by directly buying the call. Alternatively, the investor could be protected against adverse stock price changes by buying the call and selling the stock short in the appropriate ratio and by constructing a riskless hedge. According to the Black-Scholes valuation model, the appropriate hedge ratio to use for this purpose is given by $N(d_1)$, or in this case 0.651, which means that for every call option purchased, 0.651 shares of stock should be sold short or, alternatively, for every share of stock sold short, 1.54 calls should be purchased.

Though the Black-Scholes model is theoretically elegant, we should note before concluding that there are some concerns regarding practical application of the model. To begin with, we should be concerned with the realism of the basic assumption of being able to set up a riskless hedge by rebalancing continuously and instantaneously. In actual practice, transaction costs would impede the continuous process of buying and selling securities; these costs could eventually dissipate any investment return. In addition, though price changes are generally small over a short interval, the price change can be quite sizable on some occasions. Finally, the assumption of a risk-free rate is unrealistic.

With respect to the actual estimate of option values, we should emphasize the importance of developing appropriate inputs to the model because differences in the estimates—

---

[12]Mark Rubinstein, "How to Use the Option Pricing Formula," Salomon Brothers Center, New York University, Working Paper 115, May 1977. In this paper Rubinstein outlined the programming steps for mounting the formula on a hand calculator such as the HP-65. He also gave a listing of a computer program written in APL that would be suitable for use on a minicomputer. Some calculators, such as the T1-59, have prepackaged programs for calculating option values. Naturally, availability of these programs speeds up the calculation of option values considerably.

TABLE 13-6
**Black-Scholes option values as a function
of interest rates and standard deviation**

Interest rate	Standard deviation		
	0.20	0.30	0.40
0.10	4.97	6.54	8.15
0.12	5.32	6.86	8.44
0.14	5.69	7.19	8.45

interest rate and standard deviation—can affect the calculated value of the option significantly. Table 13-6 illustrates this effect by showing calculated values for options with different interest rate and standard-deviation inputs to the Black-Scholes formulation.

Note, for example, that using a 10 percent interest rate rather than a 12 percent interest rate, as in our previous example, provides an option value of $6.54, or 5 percent lower than in the prior calculation. Alternatively, using an estimated standard deviation of 0.40, which is 33 percent greater than the original estimate of 0.30, provides an option value of $8.44, or 23 percent greater than in our previous example. The sensitivity of option values to variations in these inputs, especially the standard deviation, emphasizes that the avoidance of input errors should be a prime consideration in using the model.

Put Option Valuation

We focused on the use of the Black-Scholes model for valuing call options in the prior section. The Black-Scholes model can also be used to value put options but only indirectly by relating the derived value of a call to that of a put. The put–call parity relationship provides a theoretically strong linkage between the two option values. It has also been shown to be an empirically consistent relationship between call and put values. As a result, in discussing put option valuation, we first describe the parity relationship between puts and calls and then illustrate the valuation of puts using the Black-Scholes formulation.

We begin to illustrate the relationship between put and call values by first assuming that we purchase a call (C) on a stock (S) with an exercise price (E). At the same time, we assume that we can sell a put (P) on that same stock (S) with the same exercise price (E) and expiration date (T). Figure 13-10 is a three-panel chart showing (A) purchase of a call (C) on stock (S), (B) sale of a put (P) on stock (S), and (C) the return pattern resulting from the combination of the two strategies at exercise price (E) and expiration date (T).

Note that the combined option pattern (Panel C) shows investors accruing increasing profits as stock prices reach and exceed the exercise price but incurring increasing losses as the stock price is below the exercise price. This option-based strategy can be compared to a leveraged-equity position in which we invest in the stock at its current price S_0 and borrow an amount today that is equal to the present value or the exercise price, PV(E). The amount PV$(E) = E/(1 + R_f)^T$ when invested at the rate R_f over the life of the option represents the amount to be repaid at the maturity or terminal (T) date of the option.

Table 13-7 compares the regular payoffs for the option-based strategy (buy call, sell put) and the leveraged-equity strategy (buy stock and borrow). As the table shows, when the stock is selling for more than the exercise price on the expiration date, both strategies result in a profit that is the difference between the stock price and exercise price. Alternatively,

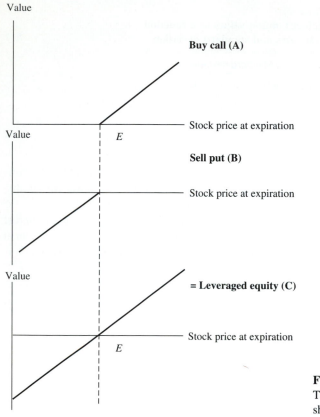

Value

Buy call (A)

Stock price at expiration

Value

E

Sell put (B)

Stock price at expiration

Value

= Leveraged equity (C)

Stock price at expiration

E

FIGURE 13-10
The value pattern of a long call–
short put position.

when the stock is selling for less than the exercise price on the expiration date, both strategies result in a loss that is the difference between the exercise price and the stock price. Thus, regardless of the ending stock price, the investor will end up being exactly as well off with the option-based strategy as with the leveraged-equity strategy.

Because the two strategies have identical payoffs, the costs of establishing both must be equal. The net cost of establishing the option position is $C - P$; the call is purchased for C,

TABLE 13-7
Payoff of two strategies

Strategy	Value at expiration	
	Stock price $> E$	Stock price $< E$
Option-based (1)		
Buy call	$S_T - E$	0
Sell put	0	$-(E - S_T)$
Total	$S_T - E$	$S_T - E$
Leveraged-equity (2)		
Buy stock	S_T	S_T
Borrow $PV(E)$	$-E$	$-E$
Total	$S_T - E$	$S_T - E$

and the written put generates premium income of P. Correspondingly, the leveraged-equity position requires a net outlay of $S_0 - \text{PV}(E)$—the cost of the stock less the funds borrowed. We can then equate the costs of these two equivalent strategies as follows:

$$C - P = S_0 - \text{PV}(E)$$

This equation is known as the put–call parity theorem because it represents the proper relationship between put and call prices. If the parity relationship is violated, an arbitrage opportunity arises for risklessly making abnormal profits. We have seen from the prior discussion of the Arbitrage Pricing Theory that the mechanism for correcting mispricing is to sell the overpriced security or portfolio, and purchase the underpriced security or portfolio. Similarly, option mispricing, in this case puts and calls, can be corrected by such a process. For example, if the difference between the call and put was greater than the leveraged equity, investors would be certain of making more than the risk-free rate by buying a call, writing a put, selling the stock short, and investing at the interest rate R_f for the maturity period.

We can, in turn, rearrange the put–call parity relationship so that it can be used to estimate the value of a put option.

$$P = C + \text{PV}(E) - S \tag{3}$$

Thus, the value of a put can be estimated by first using the Black-Scholes formula to estimate the value of a matching call option. We then add an amount equal to the present value of the exercise price to this estimate. Finally, we subtract from this sum an amount that is equal to the current market price of the underlying common stock.

We can use the same values from the numerical example of the prior section, applying the Black-Scholes call valuation model to illustrate determining the value of a put option on the same stock. We assume that the put option has the same maturity of six months and exercise price of $60 as the call option from the previous example. Recall that the current market price of the underlying stock was $60 with a volatility of 30 percent. Assuming that the rate on a six-month commercial was 12-percent, we showed before that the Black-Scholes estimate of the value for a matching call option was $6.86. Since the 12-percent interest rate is a continuously compounded rate, the present value of the exercise price is equal to $60/(e^{0.12 \times 0.5}) = 56.6$. Having determined that $C = \$6.86$, $\text{PV}(E) = 56.6$, and $S = 60$, we simply substitute in the pricing equation above to estimate the value of the put option as being equal to $3.28 = \$6.86 + \$56.6 - \$60$.

We should note, however, that the preceding pricing equation is valid only for European puts on non-dividend-paying stocks. Because an American option allows its owner to exercise at any time before the expiration date, it must be worth at least as much as the corresponding European option. Therefore, the put-pricing equation describes only the lower bound on the true value of the American put.

Hedge Ratio

Because the value of $N(d_1)$ is a probability, it must lie between 0 and 1. Therefore, the number of shares owned for each call written is between 0 and 1, which means that to construct a hedge, the number of shares must be less than the number of calls. Since $N(d_1)$ is less than 1, the change in the call price is never greater, and usually is less, than the change in the stock price. Thus, for the hedge to work, the number of calls must exceed the number of shares of stock.

TABLE 13-8
Option curve data

Stock price (1)	Option value (2)	Slope, or hedge ratio (3)	Calls to neutralize stock (4)
$40	$0.22	0.06	16.67
50	1.97	0.32	3.12
60	6.86	0.65	1.54
70	14.58	0.87	1.15
80	23.80	0.96	1.04

The data in Table 13-8 help illustrate the significance of the shape of the option-value curve, depicted in Figure 13-11 and using our hypothetical stock as it ranges in price from $40 to $80 per share. Column 1 shows the stock price, and Column 2 the values of the option at that price, which are the same as those given in Table 13-4. Column 3 shows the slope of the option-value curve at the particular price level; this slope is also known as the *hedge ratio*. The slope will change with the price level. As the price of the stock increases more and more above the exercise price, the slope will approach 1 (a 45-degree angle). As the price of the stock declines below the exercise price, the slope of the curve approaches zero (a horizontal line). Note that in this case the slope is 0.65 at the exercise price of $60 and 0.96 at the highest price of $80.

For ease of interpretation Column 4 shows the reciprocal of the slope. It gives the number of short-call options needed to neutralize a long position in the stock. Correspondingly, it represents the number of long-call options that will neutralize a short position in the stock.

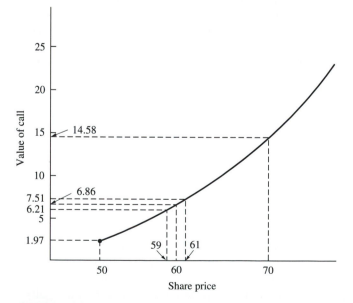

FIGURE 13-11
Stock price and value of call option.

Note that when the stock price is $50, 3.12 short calls are needed to neutralize a position in the stock. Also, note that the ratio decreases as the stock price increases, so that at $80 per share only 1.04 calls will be needed to neutralize a position in the stock.

Using these hedge ratios can then ensure that gains (losses) on long positions are offset exactly by losses (gains) on short positions, so that the investor's beginning and ending positions are identical. Figure 13-11 more specifically illustrates how this process of hedging eliminates investment risk. The diagram is a plotting of the option values against the stock price as it ranges from $40 to $80. It shows the value of the option at the exercise price of $60 and allows us to assess how the value of the option changes as the stock price varies around the exercise price.

Note that the value of the call option rises or falls by $0.65 when the stock price changes by $1. Recall from Table 13-8 that the reciprocal of the hedge ratio at the exercise price of $60 is 1.54 to 1, indicating that investors can protect themselves against the stock price change by selling 1.54 call options for $6.86 each. In this instance, when the stock price declines by $1 to $59, the investor gains $1 on the short position in the options; it is now possible for the investor to repurchase the 1.54 call options for $1 less than the price at which they were sold because each option has declined by $0.65 with the fall in the stock price. Correspondingly, when the stock rises by $1 to $61, the investor gains $1 on the stock position but loses $1 on the short position in the options. In this case, the cost of repurchasing the 1.54 options is $1 more than the price at which they were sold because each has risen by $0.65.

For any sufficiently small change in the stock price, the relationship between the stock and option price changes is effectively linear; however, for larger changes the relationship is curved, so that gains and losses will not be perfectly offsetting. For example, as shown in Figure 13-11, when the stock price rises to $70, there will be a gain of $10 on the long position in the stock but a loss of $11.89 on the short position in the options. Similarly, if the price falls to $50, there will be a loss of $10 on the long position in the stock but a gain of only $7.53 on the short position in the options. The hedge ratio is thus a valid indicator only for small changes in price and for short intervals of time.[13]

Changing Option Values

In the parlance of option trading, the hedge ratio as given by the value of $N(d_1)$ from the Black-Scholes model is also known as the option's *delta*. As illustrated graphically in Figure 13-11, it is the slope of the option curve at the price level of the stock. For example, at the price of $60, the slope of the curve and hence its delta is 0.651. Mathematically, it is the first partial derivative of the call premium (C) with respect to the stock price (S). In turn, the hedge ratio, or delta, will change when the stock price changes. As the call price increases, the delta increases; as the call price decreases, the delta decreases.

The change in the delta when the stock price changes is referred to as *gamma*. Mathematically, the gamma is the second partial derivative of the call premium with respect to the stock price, and as such measures the rate of change of the delta value. Gamma measures the approximate change in the delta for a $1 change in the stock price. Gamma is always

---

[13]We should note that it would be difficult to maintain a neutral position over time because all factors, including time, are changing.

positive, meaning that the delta increases as the stock price increases. The magnitude of the gamma can be useful in determining how often the hedge ratio needs to be revised. The gamma is positive but fairly small when the call is deep-in- or deep-out-of-the-money, and it is fairly large when the call is at-the-money.

The delta will also change with the passage of time. Again, in the parlance of option trading, the measure of the effect on the call price as it moves toward expiration is known as *theta* and it is negative. Though the call price declines as it moves toward expiration, the rate of decline will vary. As expiration approaches, the delta of an in-the-money call will approach one, and the delta of an out-of-the-money call will approach zero.

As with other variables, there is also option trading terminology commonly used to characterize the change in call prices from small changes in underlying interest rates and standard deviation variables. The measure for the impact of changes in volatility on the call price is known as *vega*. As was illustrated in Table 5-6, the call price is rather sensitive to changes in the volatility, and this measure can be used to compare the sensitivities of different calls. *Rho* measures the effect of a change in the interest rate on the value of the call option. The calculated measures illustrate that the interest rate has a relatively lesser impact on the call price.

As the analysis in this section illustrates, there are many factors that will result in changes in the option price over time; maintaining a riskless hedge becomes a dynamic process. In theory this riskless hedge should be rebalanced instantaneously. In actual practice transactions costs impede the continuous process of buying and selling securities; these costs could eventually dissipate any investment return. In addition, though price changes are generally small over a short interval, on some occasions the price change can be quite sizable. Options traders need to adjust for these frictions and be alert to these idiosyncratic price moves.

Option hedging terminology

Delta	Δ	Change in hedge ratio when stock price changes. Mathematically, the first derivative with respect to the price change.
Gamma	Γ	Rate of change of the delta when stock price changes. Mathematically, the second derivative with respect to the price change.
Theta	Θ	Impact on the call price from the passage of time.
Vega	Y	Impact on the call price from change in volatility.
Rho	ρ	Impact on the call price from changes in interest rates.

OPTIONS-RELATED PORTFOLIO STRATEGIES

Options offer portfolio managers the opportunity—not easily available through other instruments—to efficiently tailor strategies for enhancing returns or controlling risk. Some of the most widely used strategies include (1) spreads, (2) straddles, (3) covered-call writing, and (4) the protective put. Spreads and straddles offer ways of enhancing return for a portfolio, whereas covered-call writing can provide some risk protection and the potential for return enhancement under certain market conditions. The protective put offers the means of insuring a portfolio from major losses and is the most notable example of the application of options for risk control. In the following sections, we describe these strategies and illustrate their application.

TABLE 13-9

Option spread data—Compaq Computer (11/30/94)

	1	2
Days to exercise	120	120
Risk-free rate	6.05	6.05
Current stock price	$38.25	$38.25
Exercise price	40	45
Call premium	3.5	1.5
Expected cost dividend	$0.00	$0.00
Delta	0.517	0.312

Spreads

One way to take advantage of the dynamics of changing option values is through the use of spreads. A spread involves buying an option and selling an equivalent option that differs in only one respect. The two major types of spreads are (1) money spread and (2) time spread. A money spread consists of buying an option at one striking price and selling an option at a different striking price. Both options would be on the same stock and have identical maturities.[14] A time spread involves buying and selling options similar in all respects except for expiration dates.

To illustrate spreading strategies, Table 13-9 shows some relevant data for options, using Compaq Computer for illustration. Note that options (1) and (2) are identical except for differing exercise prices. Option (1) is exercisable at $40 and option (2) at $45. Correspondingly, the deltas for these two options differ. Option (1) with a lower exercise price shows a higher delta of 0.517 and will be more responsive to stock-price moves than option (2) with a higher exercise price and lower delta of 0.312.

By purchasing option (1) with the lower exercise price and selling option (2) with the higher exercise price, we can create a *bull spread*. With the difference between the delta values of the two options a positive 0.205 (0.517 − 0.312), we expect the combined option position to react positively in a rising (bull) market and negatively in a declining (bear) market. The net cost for the spread will be the difference between the proceeds from the sale of one option and the price for purchasing the other. In this example, the net cost is $2.00, resulting from the purchase of option (1) at $3.50 and the sale of option (2) at $1.50.

Figure 13-12 diagrams the pattern of profits and losses to the bull-spread position over a range of prices for the underlying Compaq Corporation stock. At prices above the higher exercise price of $45 and when both calls are in-the-money, the short call is exercised on the spreader, who exercises the long call and then delivers the stock. The gain is the difference in stock prices minus the difference in premium or 100($45 − $40 − $2) = $300, and it is constant over the upper price range. Similarly, there is a constant loss to the spread at prices below $40, when the options expire out-of-the-money. The maximum loss is simply the net premium and in this example is 100($3.50 − $1.50), or $200.

There is a variation in profit and loss to the spread position only between the lower and upper exercise prices, or within a stock price range of $40 to $45. The spreader will exercise the call when the stock price exceeds the lower exercise price (E_1) and will gain

---

[14]Furthermore, money spreads can be designed to profit in either a bull market—a *bull spread*—or a bear market—a *bear spread*.

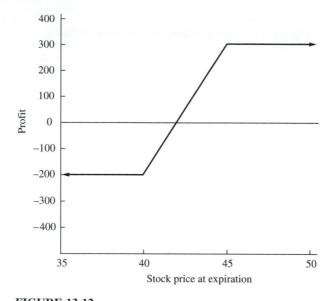

FIGURE 13-12
The bull spread. Compaq Computer—April expiration;
exercise prices: $40 and $45.

a greater amount from the exercise as the stock price is higher. To break even, the spreader
must receive enough to recover the difference between premiums on the long call (C_1) and
the short call (C_2). The break-even stock price (S_{T^*}) can be obtained from the following
formulation:

$$S_{T^*} = F_1 + C_1 - C_2$$

For the bull spread on the Compaq options, the break-even stock price at expiration is $40 +
$3.50 - $1.50 = $42. If the portfolio manager expected the stock price to exceed $42 over
the time horizon of interest, then the bull spread strategy would make sense. On the other
hand, if the expectation were for a stock price below $42, the portfolio manager would take
advantage by constructing a bear spread, which is the mirror image of a bull spread. A
bear spread can be constructed by simply reversing the call transactions, selling the low
exercise call, and buying the high exercise call. This action then reverses the sign of the
delta difference between the two options to a negative, so that we expect the combined
option position to increase in value in a bear market but decrease in value in a bull market.

Straddles

A straddle is the purchase of a call and a put that have the same exercise price and expiration
date. By holding both a call and a put, the trader can capitalize on stock price movements
in either direction. With only one exercise price involved, there are only two ranges of the
stock price at expiration. For the case in which the stock price S_T equals or exceeds the
exercise price E, the call expires in-the-money.[15] It is exercised for a gain of $S_T - E$, but

---

[15]The case in which $S_T = E$ is included in this range. Even though $S_T = E$ means that the call is at-the-money,
it can still be exercised for a gain of $S_T - E = 0$.

the put expires out-of-the-money. The profit is the gain on the call minus the premiums paid on the call and on the put. For the second case, in which the stock price is less than the exercise price, the put expires in-the-money and is exercised for a gain of $E - S_T$. The profit is the gain on the put minus the premiums paid for the put and the call.

For the range of stock prices above the exercise price, the profit increases dollar-for-dollar with the stock price at expiration. For the range of stock prices below the exercise price, the profit also increases dollar-for-dollar with the stock price at expiration. When the options expire with the stock price at the exercise price, both options are at-the-money and essentially expire worthless. The profit then equals the premiums paid, which, of course, makes it a loss.

The straddle strategy is designed to capitalize on high stock price volatility. To create a profit, the stock price must move substantially in either direction. It is not necessary to know which way the stock will go; it is necessary only that it make a significant move. The upside break-even is simply the exercise price plus the premiums paid for the options. Correspondingly, the downside break-even is the exercise price minus the premiums paid on the options.

Thus, the break-even stock prices are simply the exercise price plus or minus the premiums paid for the call and the put. On the upside, the call is exercised for a gain equal to the difference between the stock price and the exercise price. For the investor to profit, the stock price must exceed the exercise price by enough that the gain from exercising the call will cover the premiums paid for the call and the put. On the downside, the put is exercised for a gain equal to the difference between the exercise price and the stock price. To create a profit, the stock price must be sufficiently below the exercise price that the gain on the put will cover the premiums on the call and the put.

To illustrate, we consider the Columbia Gas February 1995 put and call options. The exercise price for both options is $25, and the premiums are $1.00 for the call and $1.81 for the put, for a total of $2.81. Thus, the break-even stock prices at expiration are $25 plus or minus $2.81, or $22.19 and $27.81. The stock price currently is at $23.88. To create a profit, the stock price must increase by $3.93 or decrease by $1.69 in the remaining 61 days until the options expire.

The worst-case outcome for a straddle is for the stock price to end up equal to the exercise price, in which case neither the call nor the put can be exercised for a gain.[16] The option trader will lose the premiums on the call and the put, which in this example total $100(1.00 + 1.81) = \$281$. Figure 13-13 graphs the profits and losses for the Columbia Gas February 1995 options over a range of stock prices and illustrates the V-shaped return pattern for a straddle.

For stocks such as Columbia Gas, in which the expectation is for significant volatility, straddles may be appropriate. Columbia Gas is a major gas pipeline company that had to default on payments to supplier gas producers because of adverse changes in the price of natural gas. The company is currently in Chapter 11 bankruptcy and negotiating with its creditors on terms of payment settlement. The courts will rule on the terms, which range from highly onerous settlements for the company to ones that leave the company in an economically viable and relatively profitable position. Depending on the outcome of the proceedings and subsequent reorganization, the stock could potentially show strong appreciation or suffer a sharp decline.

---

[16]Either the put, the call, or both could be exercised, but the gain on either would be zero. Transaction costs associated with exercise would suggest that neither the call nor the put would be exercised when $S_T = E$.

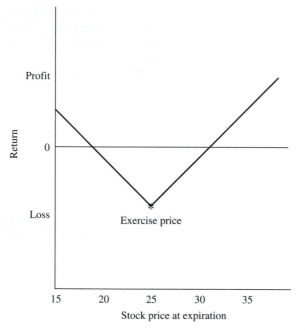

Profit

Return

0

Loss

Exercise price

15   20   25   30   35

Stock price at expiration

FIGURE 13-13
Options straddle—return pattern.

Table 13-10 shows prices for the March 1995 calls and puts for Columbia Gas, along with the underlying volatility estimates for these options. Note that the implied volatility for the option is significantly higher than the historic volatility as measured by the experienced volatility over recent intervals of 30, 50, and 100 days. Apparently, the market has anticipated the likely high level of volatility for the stock from an anticipated resolution of the reorganization proceedings. The options appear to be fairly priced given volatility implied and using the Black-Scholes option model.

To break even, the purchasers of a straddle need to have the stocks move either up by 16.5 percent or down by 7.1 percent from the current price of $23.88. The manager who thinks that the volatility over the period will be in line with or greater than that currently implied might consider the purchase of a straddle (by the put and call). On the other hand, the manager who assessed that the volatility over the period is likely to be less than that implied might consider selling a straddle on the Columbia Gas options (sell the put and call at the same exercise price). The seller of the straddle (short) should be aware that selling can be a high-risk strategy because of the potential for almost unlimited losses, if in fact the stock moved substantially.

TABLE 13-10
Put and call options—Columbia Gas

February 1995 options	Stock price	Stock price	Premium	Implied volatility	Historic volatility		
					30 days	50 days	100 days
Call	23 7/8	25	1	35.70%	29.12%	31.63%	25.62%
Put	23 7/8	25	1 13/16	32.25%			

Trading Volatility

One of the necessary inputs to the Black-Scholes model in determining an option value is an estimate of the volatility of the stock. We illustrated in a prior section that variations in volatility impact the value of options more significantly than other model inputs. Correspondingly, volatility changes over time and often in ways that are hard to predict, thus introducing a major source of option misvaluation. Though errors in the volatility present risk in the use of a valuation model, the instability of this input variable also offers an opportunity to capitalize on the mispricing of options for those who can anticipate or adjust for changes in the volatility.

Financial traders have observed that when volatility changes, certain patterns occur. First, there are clusters of volatility; high volatility is often followed by high volatility, and low volatility is often followed by low volatility—until it gets to a high again. Second, volatility tends to "mean revert," or trend back to some long-term norm. Third, the type of mean reversion tends to be an abrupt "spike" and subsequent "slow decay." News of unexpected events sends volatility quickly higher; volatility then takes a period of time to slowly revert back to a normal level. Fourth, there tends to be a "negative correlation" between volatility and the trend in return—that is, average returns are higher (lower) when volatility decreases (increases).

Observing this pattern of volatility, researchers at Salomon Brothers have applied advanced statistical techniques to develop a model that has some power for forecasting changes in underlying volatility. These researchers have, in turn, developed a strategy to take advantage of this capability to anticipate changes in implied volatility. The strategy entails buying a straddle when the estimated volatility from the model rises above the implied volatility. With the presumed subsequent increase in implied volatility, the purchase options should experience an increase in value above the purchase price, thereby leading to a gain over the cost of the options. Correspondingly, when the estimated volatility from the model is below the implied volatility, the strategy would call for sale of the straddle. If implied volatility subsequently declines, the options should lose value, and the seller could close out the option positions at a lower value and lock in a profit.

Table 13-11 describes straddle trade using S&P 500 puts and calls and using the Salomon Brothers model forecasts of volatility. Over the period, there were five straddle transactions—three trades involving sale of the straddle when the model volatility was above implied volatility and two purchases of the straddle when model volatility was below implied volatility. Note that implied volatility moved in the direction that the model measure was indicating in all five cases. In addition, four of the five trades were profitable, with only the April 26 trade showing a loss. Note that these are all short-term trades and that other factors such as interest rate changes can impact the pricing of the options.

Writing Covered Calls

Call options are often written against stock that is already owned by the call writer. When this is the case, the call is said to be a covered call. Writing covered calls is a conservative strategy that is commonly used by both individual and institutional investors. In comparison, a call written without owning the underlying stock is known as a naked call; writing these is a highly risky strategy. Naked calls expose the writer to large potential losses if the underlying stock shows strong appreciation.

TABLE 13-11
S&P 500 trades using GARCH forecasts

Trade date	G vol	I vol	Option expiration	Strike price	Put price	Call price	Unwind date	G vol	I vol	Put price	Call price	Profit/ loss
9-Oct-92	13.80%	17.10%	21-Oct-92	405	$10.50	$8.50	10-Oct-92	13.72%	16.40%	$7.88	$10.13	$1.00
6-Oct-92	13.75%	16.10%	21-Oct-92	410	$10.19	$8.75	16-Oct-92	13.31%	14.10%	$5.13	$10.50	$3.31
21-Oct-92	13.16%	14.70%	21-Nov-92	415	$6.63	$7.25	23-Oct-92	13.08%	12.90%	$4.75	$5.71	$3.41
26-Apr-94	11.70%	10.50%	21-May-94	450	$6.38	$3.63	5-May-94	11.21%	11.60%	$6.00	$2.38	($1.63)
2-Nov-93	11.17%	9.10%	20-Nov-93	470	$4.75	$3.00	3-Nov-93	11.24%	11.80%	$9.50	$1.06	$2.81

Source: Eric Sorensen, Salomon Bros.

Figure 13-14 illustrates the strategy of covered-call writing. It shows that the investor in this case holds the stock long and at the same time sells (or writes) a call on the stock. The resulting graph is, in effect, a combination of Figure 13-3c, showing the results of purchasing a stock, and Figure 13-3g, showing the results of selling a call. The use of the call truncates the return distribution but in this case puts a ceiling on the upside potential of the stock. The seller of the call in this instance is exposed to the downside movements of the stock but not to the unlimited risk associated with selling the call outright when the stock position is similar to that of a short seller of the stock. The premium received helps offset any loss from downside movements of the stock price.

In determining to undertake a program of writing covered calls, the portfolio manager needs to consider the opportunity cost of having underlying stocks called away against the benefit of premium income received from the calls written. In a bull market, the risk is substantial for the call writer when it is likely that many stocks will move above the striking price and will be called away from the writer. The incremental return above the call premium would go to the buyer of the call. Overwriters suffered this experience repeatedly in the 1980s when the stock market showed a steady secular uptrend and again in 1991 when the market rebounded strongly from the 1990 downturn.

On the other hand, writing covered calls can provide some protection in a bear market, with the premium income from call writing helping to buffer the downturn. During such a period, the writer continues to earn premium income from selling the option, which might be 5 to 10 percent of the value of the portfolio on average. This incremental return provides some offset against downside risk. In a severe and sustained downtrend such as occurred in the 1973–1974 period when the market loss was 40 percent, the added premium would be small solace to the investor.

The ideal environment for writing covered calls would be one in which the market shows little direction—up or down—and trades in a range. During such time, there is less risk of stock being called away and losing potential appreciation. Correspondingly, the underlying stock portfolio would not be subject to extraordinary depreciation attendant on a bear market. As a result, the premium income earned in such a flat market can represent

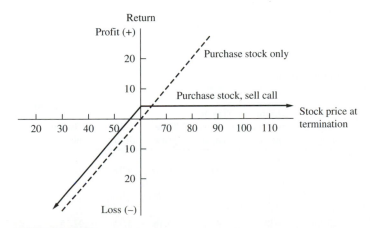

FIGURE 13-14
Covered-call writing strategy.

a significant increment to performance. The market action from late 1993 and throughout 1994 showed a trendless trading pattern, and those that anticipated such an environment had the potential for profitable option overwriting.

Overwriting Opportunities

At the same time, returns could be further enhanced by opportunistically timing the sale of options with especially desirable characteristics. Prime candidates for overwriting are those options with the potential for the highest rate of premium erosion—that is, the maximum decay over a given time period—that provides the overwriter the opportunity to lock in profits on the transaction. Assuming the stock price is unchanged, we can approximate the expected decay as follows:

$$\text{Expected premium decay over } n \text{ days} = (\Theta \cdot n) + (Y \cdot \Delta\sigma)$$

Θ = Option Theta: price impact of one day

Y = Option Vega − price impact of a 1% change in volatility

$\Delta\sigma$ = expected change in volatility over the next n days

The premium decay reflects a time effect and a volatility effect. The time effect is highest for near-term options, but the volatility effect is highest for long-dated options. To determine the appropriate maturity, the overwriter must decide whether calls are expensive or cheap or, in other words, whether $\Delta\sigma$ will be positive or negative. If he or she expects volatility to fall, the overwriter would sell longer-term calls to maximize the volatility effect. Note that even if the overwriter has no view on volatility ($\Delta\sigma = 0$), the fast-decaying nearby calls are preferable to the longer-term calls that top the rankings when options are sorted by time premium.

Table 13-12 illustrates by showing option-related data on four stocks. Note that the options on all four stocks are approximately "at-the-money," with current stock prices close to option exercise prices. Also, the time to exercise of 47 days is identical for all four options, with an expiration date of January 1995. The table also shows the time value for the options along with the 7-day decay as a measure of the rate of decay in time value for the options. The last three columns of the table show the volatility characteristics of the options. The table

TABLE 13-12
Option values and sensitivities

Stock	Current stock price	Option exercise price	Time to exercise (days)	Time value	7-day decay	Volatility		Vega
						Historic (100 days)	Implied	
Columbia Gas (CG)	24	25	47	9/16	1/16	24.80%	27.60%	1/32
Cabletron (CS)	48	50	47	1 5/8	3/16	32.5	30.50%	1/16
Kroger (KR)	23 3/8	25	47	5/16	1/16	27.75	24.50%	0.028
Safeway (SWY)	30 1/4	30	47	1 1/16	3/32	23.2	24.70%	1/32

shows both historic volatility as measured over the last 100 days and implied volatility. The vega value measures the sensitivity of the option value to changes in volatility.

Note that Cabletron has a high time value along with a high rate of time decay, but the Kroger option has a relatively low time value and decay rate. For all four options, the historic and implied volatility measures are approximately equivalent. Cabletron shows significantly greater volatility than the other four stocks with volatility values that are at an equivalently lower level. Correspondingly, Cabletron shows the greatest sensitivity to volatility changes as illustrated by a significantly higher vega value than the other options, but the Kroger option shows the least sensitivity. Cabletron combines high time-value decay with high volatility sensitivity and might warrant consideration for an options overwrite. The Kroger option would seem relatively less attractive for overwriting based on a relatively lesser volatility sensitivity and time decay rating.

The Protective Put

As discussed in the previous section, a stockholder who wants protection against falling stock prices may elect to write a call. In a strong bull market, the stock is likely to be called away by exercise. One way to obtain protection against a bear market and to still be able to participate in a bull market is to buy a *protective put;* that is, the investor simply buys stock and buys a put. The put provides a guaranteed selling price for the stock.

The protective put works like an insurance policy. When you buy insurance for an asset such as a house, you pay a premium that assures you that in the event of a loss, the insurance policy will cover at least some of the loss. If the loss does not occur during the policy's life, you simply lose the premium. Similarly, the protective put is insurance for a stock. In a bear market, a loss on the stock is somewhat offset by the put's exercise. This loss is like a claim filed on the insurance policy. In a bull market, the insurance is not needed and the gain on the upside is reduced by the premium paid.

The amount of coverage the protective put provides is affected by the chosen exercise price, which is equivalent to the insurance problem of deciding on the deductible. A higher deductible means that the insured bears more of the risk and thus pays a lower premium. With a lower deductible, the insurer bears more of the risk and charges a higher premium. With a protective put, a higher exercise price is equivalent to a lower deductible.

Figure 13-15 illustrates the protective-put strategy, in which the investor holds the stock long and at the same time purchases a put on the stock. The resulting graph is, in effect, a combination of Figure 13-3c, showing the results of purchasing a stock, and Figure 13-3f, showing the results of purchasing a put. The graph shows that the long holder of the stock participates fully in the upward movement of the stock. For example, the investor earns a $5 net profit when the stock goes to $70 (gross gain less cost of the put), a $15 net profit when it moves to $80, and so on. The investor's return opportunity is unaltered, but the investor has limited the downside risk on the stock to the exercise price of the put, in this case $60. The net loss even in the event of a decline below $60, would be the $5 cost of the put. The use of the put has, in effect, truncated the return distribution.

Portfolio Insurance

Though investors can buy puts to protect against downside moves from individual stocks, a more common practice is to insure the total portfolio from adverse market moves. For this purpose, portfolio managers utilize index options. To illustrate, we assume a well diversified

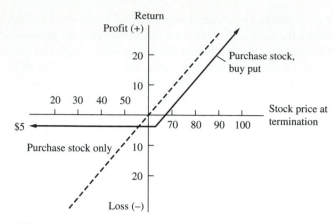

FIGURE 13-15
Protective-put strategy.

portfolio. For simplicity we assume it is an index fund portfolio consisting of N_s shares of stock and N_P puts. The stock price is S, and the put price is P. The value of the portfolio V is

$$V = N_s S + N_P P$$

Letting $N_s = N_P$ and calling this N, we have

$$N = \frac{V}{S + P}$$

This equation tells how many shares of stock and how many puts we can buy. At expiration the portfolio's value is

$$V_T = NS_T \qquad\qquad \text{if } S_T > E$$
$$V_T = NS_T + N(E - S_T) = NE \qquad \text{if } S_T \leq E,$$

where S_T is the stock price when the put expires.

The worst possible outcome is that in which $S_T = 0$. Suppose we define V_{min} as the minimum value of V_T, which occurs when $S_T = 0$. Then $V_{min} = NE$ and, because N must also equal $V/(S + P)$,

$$V_{min} = \frac{EV}{S + P}$$

This equation establishes the minimum insured value of the portfolio at expiration.

To illustrate use of puts to protect a portfolio, we assume application to an S&P 500 index fund portfolio with a market value of $10 million. At December 31, 1994, the S&P 500 was trading at 460; so the portfolio was worth 21,739 times the S&P 500 or equivalent of 21,739 units of the index. Correspondingly, the March 1995 put option on the S&P 500 index with an exercise price of 460 was priced at 8.75. Using these data as input, we determine the minimum insured level of the portfolio as

$$V_{min} = \frac{EV}{S + P} = \frac{(460)(10,000,000)}{460 + 8.75} = 9,813,333$$

Because we need to pay for the put protection at the beginning of the period, the amount to be insured will be less than the initial $10 million portfolio by the cost of the puts. We obtain the number of index units to be owned as well as puts needed to insure this amount as

$$N = \frac{V}{S + P} = \frac{\$10,000,000}{460 + 8.75} = 21,333$$

As a result, we will hold 21,333 "index units" and 21,333 S&P 500 put options. The cost of this protection is simply the put price times the number of puts $(N) = (8.75$ times 21,333) $= \$186,664$. Note that this calculated put cost represents the difference between the initial and insured portfolio value.

If at expiration, the S&P 500 is below the strike price of 460 (same as current price), we exercise the 21,333 puts at the strike price of $460 to ensure the minimum value of $9,813,333 $= (21,333$ puts ·460 strike price). On the other hand, if the S&P 500 is above the strike price at expiration, the puts expire worthless, and the value of the portfolio is a function of the number of index units held and the index price; for example, if the S&P 500 index ends up at a 475 level, the portfolio value would be $10,133,175 (21,333 index units times 475 market level).

Correspondingly, if the portfolio had not been insured, the ending portfolio value would be higher at a market level of 475 because more units would be invested in the market index, 21,739 versus 21,333; so that there would be a resulting ending value of $10,326,025 = (21,739 index units times 475 market level). The difference between the return of the insured portfolio and the uninsured portfolio, which is 192,850 in this example, is the cost of the portfolio insurance. Alternatively, it is the percentage of the uninsured return in a bull market that is earned by the insured portfolio, often referred to as upside capture. In this example, the insured portfolio earned 98.1 percent of the return of the uninsured portfolio in the up-market.

For long-term investors, the less-than-complete capture of upside gains over intervals that might range from 10 to 20 years or more is likely to preclude the persistent use of protective put strategies over time. However, for investors with short-term horizons—and especially where there is a defined need for the investment funds—use of a put to protect the equity component against a severe bear market in the interim might well be warranted. Correspondingly, the protective put strategy could be useful for investors who need to avoid losses on the equity account because of policy or regulatory requirements. An example would be a fire and casualty insurance company that needs to maintain a certain level of policyholder surplus to sustain its underwriting. Reductions in the value of an investment portfolio—particularly the stock portion—would directly translate into a reduction in the surplus account and would lead to an impairment of the ability of the company to operate effectively.

CONCLUSION

Most options are actively linked to other investment decisions or positions because the use of options allows the investor to alter the return distribution of the underlying position(s); different strategies may be used to reduce risk or boost leverage and returns. Of particular interest are those strategies which provide the portfolio manager with the insurance capability mentioned in the introduction to this chapter. The purest insurance play is the protective put, in which the minimum value of the underlying stock is guaranteed over the life of the option. By comparison, covered-call writing provides limited insurance through the proceeds of selling the upside potential of the underlying stock. Spreads and straddles offer the opportunity to enhance portfolio returns.

Given the right market price for the option, any investor would find these strategies desirable; free puts would be coveted by all investors. Thus, the big question always is: does the option price warrant the use of these or other strategies? Some insight is provided by theoretical valuation models, such as the Black-Scholes formula. The investor must be wary, however, of the limitations of the model as well as of the need to provide suitable inputs, particularly variance estimates for the underlying stock. In the final analysis, the investor must decide whether the market price of the option justifies a strategy, given the preference of the portfolio manager.

SELECTED REFERENCES

Akgeray, V.: "Conditional Heteroscedasticity in Time Series of Stock Returns: Evidence and Forecasts," *Journal of Business,* January 1989, pp. 55–70.

Ball, Clifford, and Walter Tarous: "The Maximum Likelihood Estimation of Security Price Volatility: Theory, Evidence, and Application to Option Pricing," *Journal of Business,* January 1984, pp. 97–112.

Black, Fischer: "Fact and Fantasy in the Use of Options," *Financial Analysts Journal,* July–August 1975, pp. 36–72.

——and Myron Scholes: "The Pricing of Options and Corporate Liabilities," *Journal of Political Economy,* May–June 1973, pp. 637–654.

Bollerslev, T.: "Generalized Autoregressive Conditional Heteroscedasticity," *Journal of Econometrics* 31, 1986, pp. 307–327.

Bookstaber, Richard, and Roger Clarke: "Problems in Evaluating the Performance of Portfolios with Options," *Financial Analysts Journal,* January–February 1985, pp. 48–62.

Boness, A. James: "Elements of a Theory of Stock-Option Value," *Journal of Political Economy,* April 1964, pp. 163–175.

Boyle, Phelin, and David Emanuel: "Discretely Adjusted Option Hedges," *Journal of Financial Economics,* September 1980, pp. 259–282.

Brenner, Menachem, and Marti Subrahmanyam: "A Simple Approach to Option Valuation and Hedging in the Black-Scholes Model," *Financial Analysts Journal,* March–April 1994, pp. 25–28.

Brigham, Eugene F.: "An Analysis of Convertible Debentures: Theory and Some Empirical Evidence," *Journal of Finance,* March 1966, pp. 35–54.

Brooks, Robert: "Investment Decision Making with Derivative Securities," *The Financial Review,* November 1989, pp. 511–528.

Chance, Don M.: "Translating the Greek: The Real Meaning of Call Option Derivatives," *Financial Analysts Journal,* July–August 1994, pp. 43–49.

Clarke, Roger, and Robert Arnott: "The Cost of Portfolio Insurance: Tradeoffs and Choices," *Financial Analysts Journal,* November–December 1987, pp. 35–47.

Chiras, D.P., and Steven Maraster: "The Information Content of Options Prices and a Test of Market Efficiency," *Journal of Financial Economics,* January 1978, pp. 213–244.

Choi, S., and Mark Wahar: "Implied Volatility in Options Markets and Conditional Heteroscedasticity in Stock Markets," *The Financial Review,* November 1992, pp. 503–530.

Christie, Andrew: "The Stochastic Behavior of Common Stock Variances: Value, Leverage and Interest Rate Effects," *Journal of Financial Economics,* December 1982, pp. 407–432.

Conrad, Jennifer, and Gautam Kaul: "Time-Variation in Expected Returns," *Journal of Business,* October 1988, pp. 409–426.

Cootner, Paul (ed.): *The Random Character of Stock Market Prices,* M.I.T. Press, Cambridge, MA, 1964.

Cox, John C., Stephen Ross, and Mark Rubinstein: "Option Pricing: A Simplified Approach," *Journal of Financial Economics,* September 1979, pp. 229–263.

Engle, Robert, "Statistical Models for Financial Volatility," *Financial Analysts Journal,* January–February 1993, pp. 72–78.

Figlewski, Stephen: "Options Arbitrage in Imperfect Markets," *Journal of Finance,* December 1989, pp. 1289–1314.

Figlewski, Stephen, N.K. Chidamburan, and Scott Kaplan: "Evaluating the Performance of the Protective Put Strategy," *Financial Analysts Journal,* July–August 1993, pp. 46–56.

Fong, Gifford, and Oldrich Vasicak: "Forecast-Free International Asset Allocation," *Financial Analysts Journal,* March–April 1989, pp. 29–33.

Galai, D.: "The Component of the Return from Hedging Options Against Stocks," *Journal of Business,* January 1983, pp. 45–57.

Garcia, C.B., and F.J. Gould: "Empirical Study of Portfolio Insurance," *Financial Analysts Journal,* July–August 1987, pp. 44–54.

Gastineau, Gary: *The Stock Options Manual,* McGraw-Hill, New York, 1990.

Harvey, Campbell, and Robert Whaley: "Market Volatility Prediction and the Efficiency of the S&P 500 Index Option Market," *Journal of Financial Economics,* February 1992, pp. 43–74.

Hill, Joanne, and Hardy Hodges: "S&P 500 Hedging Costs: A Look Over Time and Market Environments," *Financial Analysts Journal,* July–August 1994, pp. 69–75.

Leland, Hayne, and Mark Rubinstein: "Replicating Options with Positions in Stock and Cash," *Financial Analysts Journal,* July–August 1981, pp. 63–72.

Malkiel, Burton G., and Richard E. Quandt: *Strategies and Rational Decisions in the Securities Options Market,* M.I.T. Press, Cambridge, MA, 1969.

Margrabe, William: "The Value of an Option to Exchange One Asset for Another," *Journal of Finance* 33, 1978, pp. 177–86.

Merton, Robert C.: "Theory of Rational Option Pricing," *Bell Journal of Economics and Management Science,* Spring 1973, pp. 141–183.

———Myron S. Scholes, and Matthew L. Gladstein: "A Simulation of the Returns and Risk of Alternative Option Portfolio Investment Strategies," *Journal of Business,* April 1978, pp. 183–242.

O'Brien, Thomas, and Michael Selby: "Option Pricing Theory and Asset Expectations: A Review and Discussion in Tribute to James Boness," *The Financial Review,* November 1986, pp. 399–418.

Pettit, Richardson, and Ronald Singer: "Instant Option Betas," *Financial Analysts Journal,* September–October 1986, pp. 51–62.

Pozen, Robert C.: "The Purchase of Protective Puts by Financial Institutions," *Financial Analysts Journal,* July–August 1978, pp. 47–60.

Rubinstein, Mark: "Alternative Paths to Portfolio Insurance," *Financial Analysts Journal,* July 1985, pp. 42–52.

———and Hayne Leland: "Replicating Options with Positions in Stock and Cash," *Financial Analysts Journal,* July–August 1981, pp. 63–72.

Sharpe, William F.: *Investments,* Prentice-Hall, Englewood Cliffs, NJ, 1978.

Shelton, John P.: "The Relation of the Price of a Warrant to the Price of Its Associated Stock," *Financial Analysts Journal,* May–June 1967, pp. 143–151, July–August 1967, pp. 88–99.

Smith, Clifford W.: "Option Pricing," *Journal of Financial Economics,* January–March 1976, pp. 3–51.

Stoll, Hans R.: "The Relationship between Put and Call Option Prices," *Journal of Finance,* December 1969, pp. 801–824.

Stulz, R.: "Options on the Minimum or the Maximum of Two Risky Assets," *Journal Of Financial Economies* 10, 1982, pp. 161–185.

QUESTIONS AND PROBLEMS

1. How does the return to bond, stock, call, and put change as the price of the underlying stock declines in price?
2. How is the position of a call buyer analogous to a holder of common stock, and how do their positions differ?
3. How is the position of a put buyer analogous to a short seller of a common stock, and how do their positions differ?
4. How is the position of a call seller analogous to a short seller of a common stock?
5. How is the position of a put seller analogous to the holder of a common stock?
6. What is meant by an option being (*a*) in-the-money, (*b*) out-of-the-money, and (*c*) at-the-money?
7. What is meant by the time value of an option? Compare that value with the economic value of the option.
8. How does the time value of an option change as the price of stock varies, and when is this value at a maximum?
9. Why does an option have value even when the stock is selling well below the exercise price?
10. Explain why the term value of an option decreases both when the stock price declines below the exercise price, as well as when it increases above the exercise price.
11. Explain why lengthening the time to expiration will increase the value of an option.
12. Discuss how interest rates impact the value of an option.
13. Discuss why valuation of an option at expiration differs from valuation prior to expiration.
14. Explain what the hedge ratio is, and discuss how it is relevant to the valuation of options.
15. Explain why the hedge ratio is relevant for option evaluation only over relatively small price changes and time intervals.
16. Discuss the notion underlying the Black-Scholes option valuation model.
17. Discuss techniques used to estimate the price variability of the underlying common stock.
18. Why might observed option values differ from those calculated according to the Black-Scholes option valuation model?
19. A call option has a striking price of $40. Calculate the expiration value on the option when the stock price is $50 at expiration and when it is $40 at expiration.
20. Calculate the net return to the option at expiration if the premium has been $3.
21. A put option has a striking price of $40 and sells at a premium of $3. Calculate the expiration value on the option when the stock price is $50 at expiration and when it is $30 at expiration.
22. Assume that an investor has purchased a call option and a put option each at a price of $3 and with an exercise price of $27. Determine the value and net profit of each assuming that the stock sells at (*a*) $35, (*b*) $27, and (*c*) $22 at expiration. Also, determine the net profit on the combined position under each terminal stock price assumption.
23. Assume that a bond yields 10 percent, a stock sells at $20, and a call and put on the stock each sell at $3 and have an exercise price of $20. Graph the profit and loss from the following categories:
   (*a*) buy the bond
   (*b*) sell the bond, i.e., borrow
   (*c*) buy the stock
   (*d*) sell the stock short
   (*e*) buy the call
   (*f*) sell the call

(g) buy the put

(h) sell the put

24. An investor holding 100 shares of stock sells a call for $5 with a striking price of $50. What is the return to the seller if the stock goes to $70?

25. What would be the return of the call seller if the stock price declined to $40?

26. An investor holds 100 shares of a stock and buys a put for $5 with a striking price of $50. What is the return to the put buyer if the stock goes to $70?

27. What would be the return to the put buyer if the stock price declined to $40?

28. Discuss and show graphically how to undertake a protective put strategy.

29. Show graphically the effect on the value of an option of
(a) an increase in the variability of the underlying
(b) a reduction in the maturity of the option from six months to three months
(c) an increase in interest rates from 10 percent to 12 percent

30. The hedge ratio for a particular stock is 0.333. Evaluation shows that the option is overvalued. Indicate what action should be taken to earn a "risk-free" profit.

31. Assume that a stock is selling at $30, has an exercise price of $40, has a maturity of three months, and has a standard deviation of 0.50 for the underlying stock; also, the current interest rate is 15 percent. Calculate the value of the option using the Black-Scholes model, and indicate the hedge ratio.

32. Describe the advantages of index options as compared to options on individual stocks. Also describe how payments for options on indexes are determined.

33. The S&P 500 is selling at 460 and the premium for a three-month call is $12.00. Determine the amount to be paid for the call option.

34. Assume that the S&P 500 is selling at 480 and that a three-month put option with a strike price of 480 is selling at $11.00. How many put options would we need to buy to insure an index-like portfolio with a market value of $25,000,000, and what would be the cost of this protection?

35. If the S&P 500 declines to 460 at the end of the period, what would be the amount realized? Correspondingly, what would be the value of the portfolio when the S&P 500 sells at 510 at the end of the three-month period?

36. What is the percentage of upside capture for this protected portfolio when the S&P 500 sells at 510?

37. For what kinds of investors would a protective put be inappropriate, and what investors would find such a put useful?

38. Assume that a stock is selling at $40 with an equal probability of selling at $20 and $80 in the next period. Derive the premium for a call that has an exercise price of $40 and where the borrowing rate is 10 percent.

39. If the call is selling at $35, what action should be taken to generate a risk-free profit?

40. Compare the form of the one-period binomial model to the Black-Scholes option valuation model, and indicate how these models are similar and how they differ.

41. Describe the problems in maintaining a riskless hedge over time. Indicate the impact on the hedge ratio from changes in (a) stock price, (b) standard deviation of stock price volatility, (c) interest rates, and (d) the passage of time.

42. Assuming the same data for the Compaq option shown in Table 13-9, calculate the break-even price for a bear spread, and graph the profit and loss pattern for the spread.

43. The S&P 500 is currently at 460 with the three-month call selling at $9.00 and the risk-free rate at 6 percent. Calculate the put price.

44. If the put price is above or below the calculated fair value, what action should be taken to generate a risk-free profit?

45. Assume the same data for the Columbia Gas options shown in Table 13-10, and graph the profit and loss pattern for the sale of a straddle.

46. Describe how options traders can take advantage of changes in volatility of underlying stocks.

47. Describe the advantages and disadvantages of writing covered calls. What types of market environment would be most favorable to such a strategy? Describe the characteristics of stock options most favorable for option overwriting.

48. Why do higher interest rates lead to higher call option prices but lower put option prices?

49. Discuss each assumption of the Black-Scholes model, and comment on the extent to which it is violated in the real world.

50. Explain how a protective put is like purchasing insurance on a stock.

51. Why is the choice of exercise price on a protective put like the decision on which deductible to take on an insurance policy?

52. Construct a bear spread using the same Compaq options shown in Table 13-9. Determine the profits and graph the results. Identify the break-even stock price at expiration and the maximum and minimum profits.

CHAPTER 14

Managing the Bond Portfolio

INTRODUCTION

Managers can endeavor to increase returns in the bond portfolio in several ways. One strategy is to attempt to forecast changes in interest rates across the spectrum. In doing so, the manager assumes interest-rate risk. In addition, many bonds contain call provisions and other optionlike features. Valuing these embedded options can offer opportunity to enhance return but also entails risk if the forthcoming volatility of interest rates is misassessed. Another approach is to seek added return from bonds of lesser-than-prime-grade quality, but in doing so, the manager assumes credit risk. A fourth strategy is to search for mispricing of bonds within a peer grouping or across different sections of the bond market. Return prospects can be improved by switching—also known as swaps—from, say, an overpriced bond to an underpriced bond. However, with this strategy there is a corresponding risk of misappraisal of value. Finally, portfolio managers can seek to improve the risk-return trade-off by investing in foreign bonds. In doing so, however, the investor becomes exposed to currency risk.

The purpose of this chapter is to describe methods of bond portfolio management along those dimensions. One of the basic analytical structures managers use in these endeavors is the yield curve; we begin by describing models that explain the structure of the yield curve and illustrate how these models can be used to analyze the positioning of a portfolio with respect to a standard of comparison. The yield curve also provides a convenient framework for developing and implementing active bond strategies, and we illustrate these as well. We then describe how the binomial option valuation model can be applied to value the bond call provision, and we illustrate the way that changes in the volatility of interest rates can impact the value of this embedded option. After that, we describe a framework for monitoring trends in the credit risk exposure of a portfolio over time. We continue by describing an analytical approach to evaluating bond swaps, and we illustrate its application to three major types of swaps. Finally, we describe the benefits of investing in international bond markets, as well as ways of coping with exchange rate variation that is an added risk when investing in non-U.S. bonds.

THE TERM STRUCTURE OF INTEREST RATES

The term structure of interest rates refers to the relationship, at a given point in time, between yield to maturity and time to maturity. Ideally, to discern this relationship, it would be necessary to find a sample of publicly traded bonds that are virtually identical in quality, coupon, sinking-fund pattern, callability, and tax status, differing only in maturity. In practice, it is not possible to find so homogeneous a sample. The closest approximation is the universe of U.S. Treasury obligations.

U.S. Treasury obligations are, by definition, identical in quality, have no default risk, have no sinking funds, are for the most part noncallable, and are subject to federal income tax. From this universe, an even more homogeneous sample can be created by omitting those that are callable and those that have special tax consequences. A scatter diagram can then be constructed based on the prices and yields of this sample at any given point in time, as illustrated by Figure 14-1.

The horizontal axis of a term-structure scatter diagram represents time to maturity, and the vertical axis represents yield to maturity. Through the scatter of points on the diagram, we can draw a smooth curve that reflects the shape of the scatter. This curve is referred to as a yield curve. It is a visual image of the relationship between yield and maturity of U.S. Treasury obligations at the chosen point in time.

The level of the curve is determined by the general level of interest rates and will be high when rates of interest are high and low when rates of interest are low. The shape of the curve is largely determined by what investors expect interest rates to be in the future, and

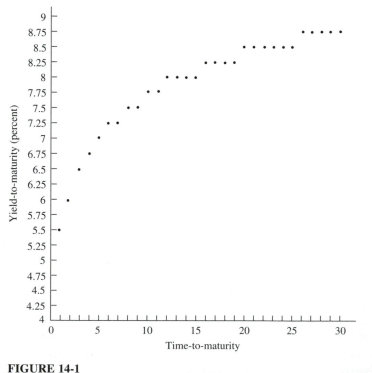

FIGURE 14-1
Yield curve.

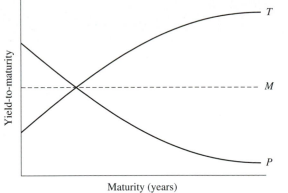

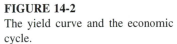

FIGURE 14-2
The yield curve and the economic cycle.

it will vary as investor expectations about rates change. These expectations tend to change in line with the economy as it progresses through the economic cycle from recession to economic peak and back again to recession. Expectations are also affected by money supply and inflation levels, which, in turn, relate to the economy.

Figure 14-2 shows several typical curve shapes that are encountered over the course of the economic cycle. Curve *T* is upward-sloping, indicating that investors expect rates to be higher in the future than currently, and it is typically the shape of the curve in the trough of the cycle. On the other hand, curve *P* is downward-sloping, indicating that investors expect rates to decline in the future, and it is typical of the state of affairs at the peak of the cycle. The third case, labeled *M*, indicates that investors expect rates to be the same in the future as they are currently, and it might be typical of the state of affairs at the midpoint of the economic cycle.

Though the curve varies in shape over time, generally in line with the economic cycle, it has over most periods been typically upward-sloping, as illustrated by curve *T* in Figure 14-2. This slope is generally attributed to the risk aversion of investors and their expectations about rates. In particular, it is generally assumed that investors require a premium return to invest in long-term rather than short-term bonds to compensate for the sacrifice in liquidity. Long-term bonds have greater capital risk—their prices vary the most with interest-rate changes—than short-term bonds, which leads to lesser liquidity and the assumed need for a higher return. Recall that the Ibbotson and Sinquefeld data showed that long-term bonds provided an added return of approximately 1 percent (presumably a liquidity premium) over short-term bonds in the 1926–1978 period of analysis.[1]

Yield Curve and Forward Rates

Though there are at least three theoretical explanations for the changing shape of a yield curve, the theory that best explains the shape and most of the changes in shape is the *expectations hypothesis*. The curve in Figure 14-3 is an upward-sloping curve, with longer-term bonds offering higher yields than shorter-term bonds—the implication being that investors expect interest rates to rise. If rates rise, prices will fall because prices of long-term bonds will probably fall more than prices of short-term bonds, other things being equal. But other

---

[1]Ibbotson, Roger G., and Rex A. Sinquefeld, *Stocks, Bonds, Bills, and Inflation: The Historical Record (1926–1978)*, Financial Analysts Research Foundation, Charlottesville, VA, 1979.

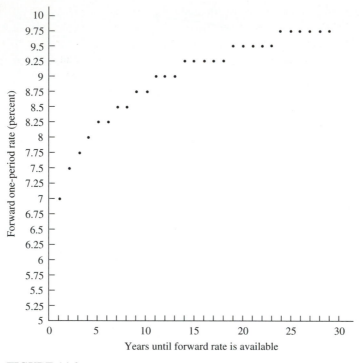

FIGURE 14-3
Forward rate curve.

things are not equal; long-term bonds are offering higher yields than short-term bonds, with those yields just high enough to offset the preference for short-term bonds.

This yield difference between long-term bonds and short-term bonds can thus be used as a measure of what investors apparently think is going to happen to interest rates. If a four-year bond, for example, is yielding 6.8 percent to maturity (as shown in Figure 14-1) and a five-year bond is yielding 7 percent, an investor with a five-year horizon can buy the five-year bond and hold it to maturity. In the first case, $100 will grow to $100(1 + 0.07/2)^{10}$ because interest is paid semiannually and there are ten half-years to maturity. In the second case, $100 will grow to $100(1 + 0.068/2)^8$ by the end of four years. To make the two investments equivalent at the end of five years, the one-year bond will have to yield F, where

$$100(1 + 0.068/2)^8(1 + F) = 100(1 + 0.072/2)^{10}$$

$$F = 0.080 = 8.0 \text{ percent}$$

F is the forward one-year rate for four years in the future. It is the one-year rate that investors apparently expect will be available at the end of four years—"apparently" because that is what the four- and five-year bond yields imply. An investor who believes F will be less than 8 percent will buy five-year bonds rather than four-year bonds. If other investors agree, they will do the same, until four- and five-year yields have adjusted to a value of F that investors do expect.

Because the current yield curve represents equilibrium, in which there are buyers and sellers at all maturities but no stampede from one maturity to another, the yields on four-year bonds and five-year bonds can be used to deduce the expected forward rate F as shown above. Similarly, yields on three- and four-year bonds can be used to deduce the one-year forward rate expected to be available three years in the future. We can go right across the yield curve, computing the forward rates for one year, two years, or any number of years, for that matter. For the yield curve in Figure 14-1 we get a set of forward rates that looks like those shown in Figure 14-3. In Figure 14-3 each point on the curve represents a one-year forward rate plotted at the particular point in time when that rate is expected to be available on a one-year instrument.

We should note, however, that the equation shown above for calculating F assumes that the bonds being analyzed are discount instruments, or zero-coupon for longer-maturity bonds, which presented a significant practical problem of estimation. The bulk of the universe of bonds, at least the long-term variety, were coupon instruments until early 1985, when the Treasury Department introduced STRIPS (Separate Trading of Registered Interest and Principal Securities). The STRIPS program greatly facilitated the process of creating zero-coupon bonds in a broad spectrum of maturities by separating each of the periodic interest payments from the principal repayment components of Treasury coupon bonds. This process of "stripping" coupon bonds began in 1982 under the sponsorship of several leading broker/dealers, who produced zero-coupon bonds under the trade names CATS, TIGRs, and the like. With the Treasury action in 1985, bond holders became able to strip their own bonds, keeping the maturities they desired and selling the undesired maturities to others. A great expansion in the secondary market for zero-coupon Treasuries took place as a result. Billions of dollars of par value of zero-coupon Treasuries are now available in maturities ranging from very short to 25 or more years, and the "true" risk-free yield curve is now more directly observable than before.

Though the development of a large-scale zero-coupon bond market has reduced the estimation problem, measurement errors can still arise from such factors as income taxes, embedded options, and market imperfections such as transaction costs. Furthermore, the equation ignores the fact that there may be a liquidity premium in the forward rate to compensate investors for the added risk of holding long-term bonds rather than short-term bonds. Finally, we should indicate that forward rates are a theoretical construct and can only be inferred but not measured.

Though some of the underlying assumptions may seem unrealistic and there are undoubtedly errors of estimation, forward rates so derived have found widespread use as discounters of the cash flows of various types of bonds, as well as other securities for that matter. This method of bond valuation by first assessing a discount rate and then deriving a present value for cash flows is complementary to the previously described yield-to-maturity method, which takes a known price and then determines a discount rate (YTM) through an internal (IRR) calculation. Use of forward rates and the present-value approach to valuation is necessary and appropriate for valuing options embedded in bonds, as we will illustrate in a later section.

Term-Structure Models

Determining the way in which a portfolio will respond to a change in the yield curve (level and structure of interest rates) is a critical task in the management of bonds. First, the portfolio manager assesses those systematic factors that are most important in the responsiveness of the bond portfolio holdings to changes in the level and structure of interest rates. Then the portfolio manager measures the exposure (sensitivity) of the bond portfolio to these factors. The process is directly analogous to analyzing the risk characteristics of an equity portfolio, which was descirbed in chapters 3, 4, and 10.

Wilshire Associates, a leading quantitative consultant, has utilized factor analytics to develop a model that measures the responsiveness of bonds to three factors. Their research verifies that this three-factor model explains a large proportion of return variability for high-quality bonds or those without credit risk—government bonds characterize this class. This term structure model is based on the idea that yield curves have three major attributes, as shown in Figure 14-4: (1) level, as represented by the short rate in the graph; (2) slope, as represented by the spread between the short rate and the long rate; and (3) curvature, represented by the convexity in the curve.

In turn, these principal aspects conform to the three risk factors as follows. As expected, the first factor in the model is duration (d_1), and it measures the bond's exposure to uniform (parallel) shifts, in which yields change by the same amount across the yield curve. The second factor (d_2) measures exposure to twists, where the yield curve steepens or flattens.[2] Because it is defined at the long end of the curve, d_2 is also a straightforward measure of how barbelled the portfolio is: The higher d_2, the more barbelled is the portfolio. The third factor d_3 measures the intermediate risk and has its greatest value for bonds with cash flows concentrated in the intermediate part of the curve. With this model, yield curve movements can be described as some composite of these basic types of shifts.

To illustrate use of the three-factor model to analyze bond returns, Figure 14-4 shows the case of an upward flattening of the yield curve. Note that the level of the curve shifts upward by 100 basis points, while the slope declines by 50 basis points. The bottom part of the figure shows, for a hypothetical bond, the change in return deriving from exposure to each of the return factors: duration, d_2, and d_3. Note that there is a loss of 4 percent due to duration exposure as interest rates rise by 1 percent. On the other hand, the bond benefits

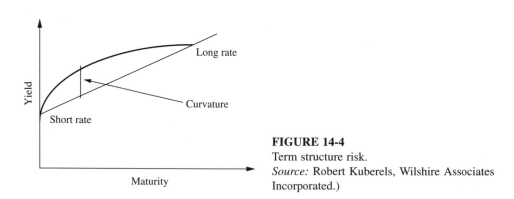

FIGURE 14-4
Term structure risk.
Source: Robert Kuberels, Wilshire Associates Incorporated.)

---

[2]Fong, Gifford, and Oldrich Vasicek: "Fixed Income Volatility Management," *Journal of Portfolio Management,* Spring 1991, argue that changes in the slope and shape of the yield curve are driven by changes in the volatility of interest rates.

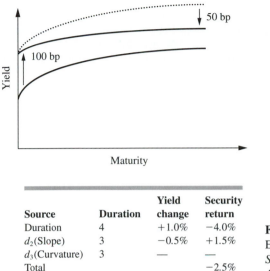

Source	Duration	Yield change	Security return
Duration	4	+1.0%	−4.0%
d_2(Slope)	3	−0.5%	+1.5%
d_3(Curvature)	3	—	—
Total			−2.5%

FIGURE 14-5
Example: upward flattening.
Source: Robert Kuberels, Wilshire Associates Incorporated.)

from exposure to the second factor, as the slope declines to provide a 1.5 percent increase in return. The net return to the bond is a loss of 2.5 percent, as there is no return from curvature because of no change in that third factor.

BOND PORTFOLIO ANALYSIS

Determining these exposures for a portfolio is a straightforward process because the portfolio will simply be a weighted average of the individual bonds composing the portfolio. In particular, the duration of the individual bond components can be combined as a simple weighted average to determine the portfolio duration; this process is directly analogous to computing a cross-sectional beta from individual stock components as an estimate of the market risk of an equity portfolio. Similarly, we can combine the slope and curvature exposures of individual bonds as a simple weighted average to determine the portfolio factor exposures.

Table 14-1 illustrates the calculation of these duration, d_2 and d_3 exposures for a portfolio of seven Treasury bonds ranging in maturity from two to 30 years and having equal weighting in the portfolio. Note that the duration of individual bonds ranges from 1.86 to 12.66, whereas the weighted-average portfolio duration exposure is 6.22. A one-percentage-point increase in interest rates should result in a 0.6 percent decrease in price. Note that the d_2 sensitivity of individual bonds ranges from .45 to 11.15, with a portfolio exposure of 4.38. A one-percent increase in either the d_2 or d_3 factor would result in a −0.44 percent change in the value (price) of the portfolio.

We can, in turn, compare these duration and sensitivity exposures for the portfolio to those of an index that is considered representative of the market or the bond universe of interest to the investor. A bond index that investors commonly refer to for benchmark purposes is the Shearson Lehman Bond (SHLB) Index. It is composed of the major types of

TABLE 14-1
Bond portfolio factor exposure

Holding		Cash Flow Yield	Maturity	Sect	Effective Duration	Effective d_2	Effective d_3	Effective Convexity	% of Part
Government									
	1	6.03	04−30−98	TREA	1.86	0.45	1.07	0.04	14.54
	1	6.17	02−15−99	TREA	2.53	0.82	1.81	0.08	14.29
	1	6.40	04−30−01	TREA	4.23	2.07	3.90	0.21	14.49
	1	6.57	02−15−03	TREA	5.37	3.15	5.21	0.35	14.51
	1	6.65	02−15−06	TREA	7.21	5.07	6.71	0.65	13.68
	1	7.06	05−15−16	TREA	10.07	8.41	6.33	1.54	15.35
	1	6.89	02−15−26	TREA	12.66	11.16	5.74	2.61	13.13
		6.54			6.22	4.39	4.38	0.77	100.00
Index Benchmark		6.70			5.00	3.30	3.59	.47	
Difference		−0.16			1.22	1.09	.79	.30	

Source: Robert Kuberele, Wilshire Associates Incorporated.

bonds—government, agency issues, corporate—ranging over a wide spectrum of maturities. As of April 30, 1996, this index had a duration of 5.0, and sensitivity to d_2 of 3.30 and d_3 of 3.59. Each of these factors for the index were calculated in the same way as for the portfolio and are shown at the bottom of Table 14-1 for comparison. Note that the portfolio factor exposures exceed those of the index.

Investors can use this comparative information to position a portfolio to conform with longer-range goals or to make changes to take advantage of perceived trends in interest rates or volatility of those rates. For example, an investor desiring to obtain a return in line with that of a broad market index like the SHLB would position the portfolio duration and d_2 and d_3 sensitivity in line with those of the index to ensure that the portfolio generated an index return with a minimum of divergence. On the other hand, investors intent on outperforming the index might endeavor to forecast the direction of interest rate changes or other yield curve changes and position the portfolio sensitivities accordingly. For example, forecast of a decline in interest rates would imply an increase in exposure to duration above that of the index, whereas forecast of a steepening in slope of the curve would imply a decrease in portfolio exposure below that of the index.

An Active Bond Strategy

In executing an active management strategy, investors can attempt to forecast the level and shape of the yield curve at the end of a particular forecasting horizon. This forecast yield curve provides the structure of yields for short-term, intermediate-term, and long-term government bonds in the investor's bond portfolio at the horizon. Given the forecast structure of yields to maturity and the current yield structure, the investor can calculate the returns attributable to the bonds in the portfolio owing to the yield curve change because we know current prices and can derive future prices from the projected yield curve. We can thus determine any capital gain or loss. Total return is derived by including the known coupon payments along with the executed price change.

For example, Figure 14-6 shows yield curve at the beginning of the period—that is, current yield curve and the forecast yield curve at the end of the year. Note that the one-

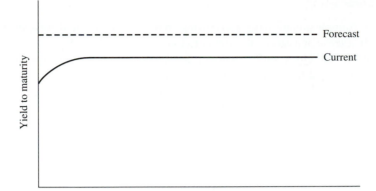

Maturity	Current yield to maturity	Yield shift (basis points)	Total return (percent)
1	6.00	132	2.95
2	7.10	119	2.05
3	7.10	107	1.37
4	7.10	99	0.34
5	7.00	94	−0.12
10	7.65	72	−0.73
20	8.00	84	−4.02
39	7.90	82	−4.53

FIGURE 14-6
Current and forecast yield curve.

year forecast in this case calls for an upward shift in the curve, with the short end of the yield spectrum up by more than the long end of the bond spectrum, which means, of course, that yields across the whole spectrum of the bond universe would increase, and a decline in prices of bonds would accompany the upward shift in yields.

The table below the graph in Figure 14-6 shows specific data for the eight individual bonds in a hypothetical portfolio, ranging from a one-year Treasury issue to a thirty-year government bond. The second column shows the yield on each of the bonds at the beginning of the period, and the third column shows the basis-point shift in yields on each at the end of the period.[3] These yields are uniformly higher, as is indicated by the upward shift in the yield curve. Prices of the bonds, of course, would all be lower at the end of the period than at the beginning. The resulting capital loss on the bonds, shown in the last column, is greater than the coupon rate in some cases, so that there would be a net loss on some bonds in the portfolio over the year.

---

[3] A basis point is the same as 0.01 percent, so that 100 basis points equal 1 percent. Many investment professionals, especially in the bond area, commonly refer to basis-point changes rather than percentage changes. For small percentage changes it is probably clearer to refer to basis points.

Scenario Forecasting

The previous example illustrated the forecasting ability of a single yield curve over a horizon of one year. In a sense, it assumes the ability to forecast precisely and ignores the possibility of other sorts of yield curve shifts. In effect, forecasting a single yield curve focuses only on return and ignores different risk possibilities. Below, we describe the scenario approach with regard to asset allocation, which can also be applied in this circumstance to provide a way of explicitly taking into account interest rate risk in active bond management.

In applying the scenario approach to bond analysis, we can proceed similarly to the way described in Chapter 9. The investor would first develop mutually exclusive scenarios describing possible shifts in the yield curve over the forecasting horizon. The scenarios could vary between, say, three and seven, again depending on the preference of the forecaster. The investor then assigns probabilities to the occurrences of the scenarios, with the total probabilities assigned adding to 100 percent to ensure consistency in the forecast. The final step would be to weight the scenarios on the basis of these assigned probabilities and develop an expected return and standard deviation for each of the bonds in the portfolio.

Figure 14-7 shows a current yield curve along with yield curves associated with three hypothetical scenarios that are presumed to be possible at the end of a forecast horizon, which in this case is one year. Curve A reflects an upward shift in the yield curve as credit demand and economic activity continue at a high level. This scenario is considered pessimistic because bond prices would be expected to fall. Curve C is the most optimistic scenario because it projects a decline in yield across the whole spectrum, especially in the short end, with the attendant rising prices. This scenario would be associated with the entry into a recession and the consequent softening in credit demands. The third curve, B, is a more neutral scenario, with yields expected to rise somewhat but not excessively as bond prices decline over the forthcoming year.

The table below the curves in Figure 14-7 shows the yield shift in basis points for each of the bonds in the portfolio associated with each of these forecasted yield curves. Also shown are returns over the one-year holding period for each of the bonds in the portfolio that is attributable to each of the forecast scenarios. For purposes of illustration we are assuming that each scenario has an equal probability of occurring, so that we can simply average the returns associated with each scenario to derive an expected or composite return for each of the bonds in the portfolio, as shown in the next-to-last column of the table. The last column of the table shows the standard deviation as a measure of the uncertainty of the expected return for each of the bonds.

Portfolio managers next evaluate the uncertainty of the expected return. Figure 14-8 provides a way of evaluating the trade-off between risk and return for bonds in the portfolio. The horizontal axis refers to the return associated with the pessimistic scenario, whereas the vertical axis refers to the more favorable return experience associated with the composite or average scenario. This is a two-dimensional return diagram on which we can plot the bonds in a portfolio and the return associated with each of two scenarios on the diagram.

As a matter of perspective, those securities plotting in the upper-left-hand area will do well in the composite scenario but will perform poorly in the worst case—the pessimistic scenario. Conversely, those securities in the lower-right-hand area will do well in the pessimistic scenario but poorly in the case of the composite scenario. Those securities plotting in the upper-right-hand area will do well in either case. As a general rule,

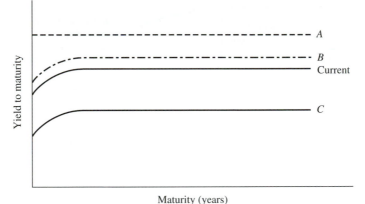

Maturity	Current yield to maturity	Yield shift-basis points scenario			Total return scenario			Composite return	Standard deviation
		A	B	C	A	B	C		
1	6.00	132	23	−146	2.95	3.32	3.96	3.41	0.4
2	7.10	119	19	−119	2.05	3.33	5.18	3.52	1.3
3	7.10	107	18	−107	1.37	3.27	6.03	3.56	1.9
4	7.10	99	18	−97	0.34	3.13	7.10	3.52	2.8
5	7.00	94	17	−87	−0.12	3.01	7.41	3.57	3.3
10	7.65	72	15	−54	−0.73	2.55	7.55	3.23	3.4
20	8.00	84	6	−48	−4.02	3.45	9.04	2.82	5.4
30	7.90	82	6	−41	−4.53	3.34	8.53	2.55	5.5

FIGURE 14-7
Current and forecast yield curves. (*Source:* Gifford Fong Associates, Santa Monica, Calif.)

moving the portfolio holdings and weighting toward those holdings that are in the middle-right region would appear to provide the best balance between risk and return for the portfolio.

To illustrate this, in Figure 14-8 we have plotted the data for the eight bonds, designating each according to its maturity. We have also constructed a hypothetical portfolio giving equal weight to each of the eight bonds in the portfolio and plotted this as P_a. As indicated, we can upgrade a portfolio by emphasizing those bonds that will perform relatively well in either scenario, while de-emphasizing those that will do poorly in one or the other scenario—that is, emphasizing those bonds in the middle-right and de-emphasizing those at the extremes.

Note that bonds 1, 2, and 3 will do well in either scenario, but bonds 20 and 30 will do poorly in the pessimistic scenario, as they plot on the extreme left of the diagram. We might well consider eliminating bonds 20 and 30 to upgrade the portfolio. For purposes of illustration, we have eliminated these two bonds and constructed a portfolio of the six remaining bonds, again weighted equally. Note that this portfolio, designated P_b, plots farther to the right and higher on the diagram, indicating a more desirable portfolio than portfolio P_a.

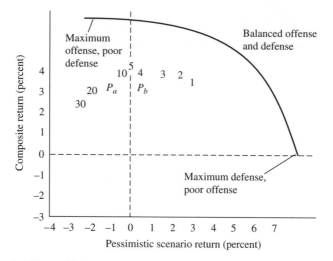

FIGURE 14-8
Risk-reward analysis. (*Source:* Gifford Fong Associates, Santa
Monica, Calif.)

BOND CALL PROVISION

Many, if not most, corporate bonds are issued with a call provision that allows the company
to redeem the bond in the future at a specified sequence of prices prior to maturity. It is
usual to preclude the possibility of call for an initial period, with the period of call protection
ranging from five years for telephone and finance issues to ten years for typical industrial
issues. The first call price is customarily set at the offering price plus a large fraction of the
annual interest rate. As the bond matures the call price declines, usually reaching par a few
years prior to maturity. The difference between the call price and par is referred to as the
call premium.

The call provision is useful for the corporation in providing added flexibility if interest
rates change in a favorable direction. For example, a bond issued during a period of high
interest rates at a high coupon could be called by the corporation and replaced with a lower-
coupon issue, thereby reducing interest payments. With a call provision, the corporation
redeems at a lower cost than if a noncallable bond was repurchased at current lower market
rates or alternatively at prices that would be higher than the call provision price.

Though a call provision is an obvious benefit to the corporation, it is a disadvantage to
the investor who does not fully benefit from the capital gain attendant on a decline in interest
rates and who would need to invest at a lower coupon rate. Because the call provision is of
value to the corporation but a disadvantage to the investor, callable bonds must offer a higher
coupon rate or alternatively sell at a lower price than noncallable bonds. Depending upon
the terms of the issue and the prevailing market conditions, this coupon premium might be
either substantial or negligible.

The price discount on callable bonds then equals the premium for a call option that is
embedded or implicit in the bond. In a sense, the callable-bond investor buys a bond and
simultaneously sells back to the issuer of the bond a call option in which the exercise price

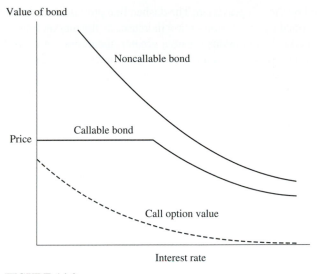

FIGURE 14-9
Callable bond chart.

is equal to the price at which the bond can be repurchased. Consistent with general option pricing theory, the coupon premium increases with the maturity of the bond and decreases as the call price increases.

Figure 14-9 illustrates the optionlike property and typical price pattern of a callable bond. The figure compares the price line of a callable bond to that of a noncallable bond, along with the value of the embedded call option over a range of interest rates. Note that the call price imposes a ceiling on the callable bond's price and that the callable bond's price is lower at all levels of market interest rates than an identical bond that is not callable. This pattern reflects both the call premium and hence lower value of the callable bond, as well as the limit on cap-

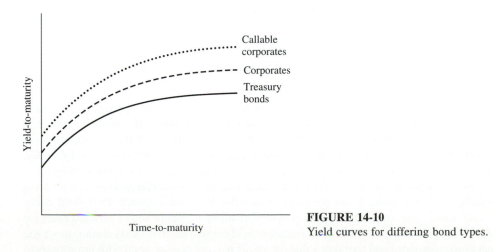

FIGURE 14-10
Yield curves for differing bond types.

ital gains imposed by the call provision. The dashed line provides a notional view of how the value of the embedded call-provision option increases as the market interest rate decreases.

Because embedded call options create a greater uncertainty of cash flows and reduce the potential for return, these bonds must offer a premium return over those without options to compensate for this risk. To illustrate this effect within the context of the term structure, Figure 14-10 shows hypothetical yield curves constructed for corporate bonds without call features and for corporates with embedded options; these yield curves are also superimposed on the yield curve for Treasuries. Note that the yield curve for straight corporates plots at a higher level than the Treasuries curve to reflect the added premium return for credit risk. Corporates with embedded options plot at an even higher level that reflects a premium return to compensate for the risk of call, as well as for the added return for credit risk. The figure thus illustrates the tiering of return premia for differing aspects of bond risk.

VALUING EMBEDDED OPTIONS

For listed options, the Black-Scholes model can be directly applied for valuation, and it is commonly used by practitioners for such a purpose. However, for options that are not explicitly stated but embedded as part of the condition of another instrument and thus implicit, a less direct method incorporating the binomial model is commonly used by practitioners. In this section, we illustrate this mode of option valuation with respect to valuing the call provision for a bond.

For purposes of assessing embedded options, it is usual to view the option-bearing bond as a package of cash flows and a package of options on those cash flows. As an example, a callable bond, or one that allows an issuer to redeem the bond at a specified price prior to maturity, can be viewed as a package of cash flows (coupons and principal payments) and a package of call options on those cash flows. As such, the position of an investor in a callable bond can be viewed as

Long a callable bond = Long an option-free bond

+ Short a call option on the bond

Developing a value for an embedded option entails a valuation of both the bond with an embedded option and a comparable bond without an option. The difference between these two becomes the estimated value of the embedded option.

Value of call option = Value of option-free bond

− Value of callable bond

To generate comparative values for option-free and option-embedded bonds, the generalized procedure is to (1) project cash flows for each bond and (2) discount these back to present value at an appropriate interest rate. For discounting these cash flows, standard practice is to use a risk-free rate as estimated from the term structure of interest rates. Typically, the current term structure is used as the market's forecast of where future rates will go.

We can illustrate this mode of bond valuation with the interest rate and bond data shown in Table 14-2. The table shows the yield to maturity from the Treasury bond yield curve for individual years over a three-year period. The middle column shows forward rates for individual years, which were derived from the yield curve data. The final column shows the cash flows—coupons and terminal value for a 5.25 percent coupon bond with three years to maturity as an example for the analysis.

As noted, the forward rates can be used as discounters for the cash flows of the bond. For this example, we use the forward rate for year one to discount the cash flow in year one, in year two we use the compounding of the year-one and year-two forward rates to discount the year-two cash flow, and finally we use the compounding of all three forward rates to discount the year-three flow.

$$\frac{\$5.25}{(1.035)} + \frac{\$5.25}{(1.035)(1.04523)} + \frac{\$100 + \$5.25}{(1.03500)(1.04523)(1.03580)} = 102.075$$

The resulting value of 102.075 provided by this procedure is appropriate as a valuation for a bond that is free of call provisions or other embedded options.

Valuing the Callable Bond

However, for a bond with an embedded option, we also need to consider the likely volatility of interest rates over the maturity of the bond because the cash flows to a bond with an embedded option will depend on the path that bond prices follow over the life of the bond and because the differing bond prices will depend on the volatility of interest rates.

To properly value a bond with a call provision, we need to consider the differing interest rate scenarios that might transpire over the period to maturity of the bond. The binomial model that we described previously in Chapter 13 with respect to option valuation provides a way of analytically portraying these different interest rate paths, given an assumed level of interest rate volatility. Furthermore, we can derive the implied price of the bond given the interest rate event that occurs by means of this model. Obviously, this process requires considerable programming and computer power, especially for bonds with long maturities.

To illustrate valuation of the call option provision most simply, we can again use the example of a three-year bond with the same coupon as before but providing a right to redeem (call) at the end of year one and also at the end of year two at $100 or par. Given this right to call, we assume that the bond will be redeemed when interest rates decline and the resulting bond price exceeds the call price of $100. As a consequence of such a call, cash flow to the bondholder will be impacted (adversely). Furthermore, increased interest rate volatility will increase the probability of redemption and the resultant cash flows for such bonds.

In deriving a value for our hypothetical bonds, we assume a simplified binomial process with valuations at one-year intervals over the three-year period and assume the same set of forward rates over the period shown in Table 14-2. In keeping with the binomial model, we also assume that the one-year rate can take on with equal probability either of two values: the higher value resulting from a rise in rates or the lower value resulting from a fall in rates.

TABLE 14-2
Yields and forward rates

Maturity	Yield to maturity	One-year forward rate
1 year	3.50%	3.500%
2 years	4.00%	4.010%
3 years	4.50%	4.531%

Source: Andrew Kalotay, George Williams, and Frank Fabozzi, "A Model for Valuing Bonds and Embedded Options," *Financial Analysts Journal,* May–June 1993, pp. 35–46.

Finally, we assume that the volatility (σ) of one-year forward rates is 10 percent and that the level of volatility of rates remains constant over the three-year period.

Though the one-year later interest rate is unknown, the 10 percent volatility assumption and equal likelihood indicates that it will be either 4.976 percent or 4.074 percent. We illustrate by using the assumed 10 percent interest rate volatility (σ) and the one-year forward rate (r) of 4.523 percent to derive the standard deviation of the forward rate as $r\sigma$ = (4.523 percent) times (10 percent), which equals 0.45 percent or 4523 basis points. With an equal probability of upward and downward movements in interest rates, we can derive the high and low rates for the first period by simply adding or subtracting the standard deviation ($r\sigma$) to the expected forward rate.

Similarly, interest rates were generated for periods farther in the future and extending over the full three-year maturity of the security. Note that there are no views built into the model about where interest rates are going, other than those that are implicit in the market's current term structure. The market term structure forecast plus the volatility assumption thus determine the future paths of interest rates. The volatility assumption is, of course, highly important because callable bonds have an option embedded in them, as we have seen, and the value of the option is related to volatility.

Figure 14-11 illustrates the interest rates and related bond values from this process by showing one period—the first year—from the three-period interest rate tree. Note that the root of the tree is denoted N and represents the current one-year rate of 3.5 percent as before. The branches show the two states for interest rates over the first year; the upper branch reflects an above-average rate and the lower reflects a below-average rate for the period.

Note that when the interest rate is at the upper level, the value of both bonds—callable as well as noncallable—is the same and below par at 99.461. Correspondingly, at the lower interest rate, the value of the noncallable bond is above par at 101.002. The value of the callable bond is however lower at 100 because we assume that the bond will be called at that price as interest rates decline, which illustrates that holders of callable bonds forgo potential capital gains and suffer a reduction in cash flow as interest rates decline.

Appendix A describes the derivation of bond values resulting from the evolution of interest rates over each of the three periods, and it illustrates the full-blown binomial tree over the three-year period. Using this process results in a value of \$101.432 for the callable bond, which is lower than the value for the option-free bond. As a matter of interest, the binomial process generates the same value of \$102.075 for the option-free bond as before because volatility does not impact such bonds' valuation. The lesser value for the callable bond derives simply from the fact that expected cash flows for the bond will be reduced by

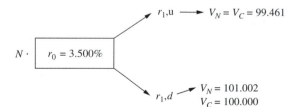

Note: r = Interest rate
V_N = Value of non-callable bond
V_C = Value of callable bond

FIGURE 14-11
Interest rate tree—one-period valuation.

the possibilities of call. The binomial process provides an objective method for estimating the likely reduction in cash flows and the resulting impact on bond value.

Because the value thus obtained for the bond with the embedded option—as well as that for the option-free bond—are obtained from the same procedure, we can compare the two bond valuations to derive the value of the embedded option.

$$\text{Value of call option} = \text{Value of option-free bond} - \text{Value of callable bond}$$

In our example, the value of the noncallable bond is $102.075 and the value of the callable bond is $101.432; so that the value of the call option is $0.643.

CHANGING VOLATILITY AND BOND VALUE

In this section, we illustrate how changing volatility impacts the value of callable bonds. For this purpose, we compare a 10-year Treasury bond to a 25-year corporate bond that is callable in five years. Though the two bonds differ in maturity, both have the same duration, and thus each has equivalent exposure to interest rate risk. Assuming that at the end of 1989, 10-year Treasuries were yielding 8.25 percent, while the long-term corporates were yielding 9.50 percent, there would be a 125-basis-point premium currently offered by the corporate.

If interest rates did not change, the realized return on both bonds would be the same as the current yield, and the investor in the corporate would earn the 125-basis-point premium. However, if interest rates vary over time—there is volatility—the return premium for the corporate will be lower.

To demonstrate the impact of volatility on the return, we developed a series of returns for each of the bonds over a range of interest rates and plotted the price lines for both bonds in Figure 14-12, assuming two levels of volatility—panels *a* and *b*. Note that the Treasury bond line shows the standard pattern of upward-sloping curvature over the interest rate range, whereas the corporate bond shows an opposite pattern of curvature. Because of the call provision, the corporate behaves like a short-term bond as interest rates decline but like a long-term bond as interest rates rise, due to its long maturity. On average, the slope of the price line for the corporate is the same as for the Treasury, indicating that each has the same amount of interest rate risk.

To focus on the way volatility reduces return, we also divided the bond price line chart into three segments in both panels *a* and *b* of Figure 14-12. Note that corporates earn the maximum premium of 125 basis points when interest rates are stable (zero change) but do worse when rates move in either direction. As long as the change in rates is moderate—as in the middle segments of the charts—the corporate still outperforms the Treasury, albeit by less than 125 basis points. But if interest rate volatility is high—if rates move by quite a bit to the range in the outside segments—the corporate actually underperforms the Treasury.

Panel *a* of Figure 14-12 shows what happens at a 10 percent volatility rate. In this case, there is an 88 percent chance that rates will stay in the range favorable to corporates, and the net relative return we should expect from corporates is 58 basis points. But when we assume a 16 percent volatility rate, as in panel *b* of Figure 14-12, the probability of corporates outperforming drops to 64 percent and the corresponding probability of a negative return of 36 percent. Because the probability of outperforming is lower and the probability of underperforming higher, the expected premium on the corporate must be lower. In fact, it is now only 14 basis points.

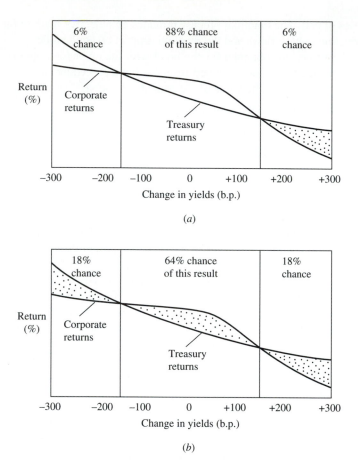

FIGURE 14-12
Interest rate volatility. The higher the interest rate volatility, the
lower the return on callable bonds. (*a*) 10% volatility: expected
premium for corporates is 58 basis points. (*b*) 16% volatility:
expected premium for corporates is 14 basis points. (*Source:*
Francis Trainer, Sanford Bernstein & Co.)

During the decade of the 1980s, corporates were, in fact, priced to provide a return
premium that averaged 125 basis points over Treasuries, which implied a volatility in line
with our 10 percent assumption for the panel *a* illustration. Actual volatility over the period
was, however, more in line with the 6 percent volatility assumed for the illustration in panel
b of Figure 14-12. The return premium offered by corporates over that period was inadequate to compensate for the risks of corporates. It is thus not surprising that the resulting
performance of corporates turned out to be inferior over the period of the 1980s.

CHANGING CREDIT QUALITY

As mentioned before, portfolio managers can seek higher returns by investing in bonds
of lesser quality, but in so doing they will assume credit risk. As a result, monitoring the

TABLE 14-3
Bond quality rating trends—percent of original issues by rating (1970–1989)

Rating	Time since issuance			
	One year	Three years	Five years	Ten years
AAA	94.6	81.0	69.8	52.1
AA	92.6	77.8	67.9	46.7
A	92.1	78.9	72.5	61.5
BBB	90.1	73.4	65.7	43.3
BB	86.1	62.9	40.8	21.6
B	94.0	75.4	59.9	53.9
CCC and lower	Results for these catagories not meaningful due to small number of bonds.			

Source: Edward Altman and Duen Li Kao, "The Implications of Corporate Bond Rating Profit," *Financial Analysts Journal,* May–June 1992, pp. 64–75.

credit quality of bonds becomes important because the level of credit quality of individual bonds changes over time. These changes present both opportunities and risk. Increases in the quality of credit enhances the probability of meeting the terms of the bond indenture and should also result in an increase in the price of the bond as the required risk premium (k) should decline accordingly. Conversely, decreases in credit quality degrade the likelihood of meeting the debt obligations and should also lead to a decrease in the price of the bond as the required risk premium (k) should increase. The most severe outcome would be, of course, a decline in credit quality such that bankruptcy and an attendant severe loss in bond value result.

Table 14-3 shows partial results of a study that monitored trends in the quality ratings of bonds over the 1970–1989 period and provides some perspective on the degree of stability, or alternatively, instability of bond ratings. This study[4] evaluated the total population of over 7000 bonds issued over that period and classified them into the standard rating categories of AAA to C, as used by the Standard & Poor Bond Service. It assessed the proportion of bonds that remained in the same rating category over subsequent time periods of 1, 3, 5, and 10 years. Alternatively, the study assessed the degree of migration of bonds out of the original rating category into other rating classifications over the subsequent 1-, 3-, 5-, and 10-year periods.

On balance, the table shows that there was considerable migration from the original rating category over time. In particular, note that all rating categories showed a continuously declining proportion of bonds retaining their initial ratings as the investment horizon lengthened. Correspondingly, some 40 percent to 80 percent of bonds initially rated BB and above experienced at least one rating change in the 10 years following issuance. In addition, note that A-rated bonds appeared to be more stable than AAA-rated bonds, whereas BB-rated bonds (the highest "junk bond" category) showed the least stability.

Though not shown in the table, another conclusion from the study data is that bonds initially rated A and above had a greater tendency to be downgraded than to be upgraded. Also, among the investment grades, only bonds initially rated BBB tended to be upgraded more

---

[4]Altman, Edward I., and Duen Li Kao, "The Implications of Corporate Bond Rating Profit," *Financial Analysts Journal,* May–June 1992, pp. 64–75.

than they were downgraded. For those bonds originally rated non-investment-grade (junk), there did not appear to be a tendency toward either upgrades or downgrades in the sample period. Finally, there was a tendency for a downgrade in rating to be followed by another subsequent downgrading. Alternatively, there was some degree of positive autocorrelation for downgrading but not for upgrades in rating categories.

Ratings Change and Performance

Because bond ratings change over time, the bond manager should attempt to assess the impact of such changes on the performance of the bond portfolio over time. We can again use a framework of analysis similar to that illustrated in a prior section of this chapter and used to assess the impact of term structure changes on bond performance. For purpose of assessing the impact of rating changes on bond performance, we can first categorize bonds in the portfolio into standard rating classifications (AAA, AA, etc.) and forecast the likely change in ratings and these bonds over a holding period. Given the projected rating change and any forecast change in the general structure of interest rates, we can then calculate the return on the individual bonds and the portfolio over the period.

Table 14-4 illustrates this process for a hypothetical portfolio of bonds, with a 3-year holding period. It assumes that all bonds in the portfolio were originally issued with a 10-year maturity and are purchased at par at various ages at the beginning of the expected three-year investment horizon. Furthermore, yields on bonds of credit quality (excluding non-investment-grade issues) are assumed to decrease by 100 basis points by the end of the holding period, and the yield spread between adjacent investment-grade categories is assumed to remain constant at 25 basis points. The first column of the table shows the expected total return of individual bonds and a portfolio return of 38 percent, assuming no change in ratings of bonds and using the portfolio weights as shown.

The final column of the table shows the expected total return of the bonds, assuming that ratings change over the three-year holding period. For purposes of illustration, it is assumed that bond ratings change in line with the experience of the aforementioned study of the 1970–1989 period. Because of ratings changes (some downgrades as well as upgrades), the returns by individual category differ from the no-change assumption, and the total portfolio return differs as well. Naturally, these differences would become larger as the holding period

TABLE 14-4
Bond-rating changes—impact on portfolio changes

			Expected returns	
Bond age	Portfolio weights	Bond rating	Rating unchanged	Historic transition
0	25%	AAA	38.21%	37.09%
2	40%	AA	37.97%	37.67%
5	20%	A	36.76%	36.65%
3	10%	BBB	39.20%	38.14%
1	5%	BB	44.91%	46.21%
Portfolio	100%		38.26%	38.00%

Source: Edward Altman and Duen Li Kao, "The Implications of Corporate Bond Rating Profit," *Financial Analysts Journal,* May–June 1992, pp. 64–75.

lengthens and the ratings drift becomes more pronounced. Correspondingly, the differences could be more significant as forecast of change is greater, perhaps because of the state of the general economic environment.

Monitoring Bond Quality

We have seen that ratings of bonds change over time as the level of bond quality improves or deteriorates. To the extent that these changes can be anticipated, bond investors can improve performance by investing in bonds expected to experience an upgrade in rating and avoid or sell those that are anticipated to show a deterioration. Naturally, the investor would be most keenly interested in monitoring bond quality trends to avoid the ultimate in deterioration, which is bankruptcy and its attendant severe consequences. It is estimated that bond investors on average lose 60 percent of the value of an investment consequent to a bankruptcy.

Investors can monitor bond credit quality by assessing trends in such fundamental determinants as, for example, interest coverage and the debt/equity ratio that we described in an earlier section. A technique based on discriminate analysis provides a systematic and objective way of monitoring these basic variables simultaneously, while taking into account the interaction between these variables. The method of discriminate analysis is described in detail in the appendix to Chapter 10, and illustrated as an application in that chapter. Briefly, discriminate analysis is a statistical technique that allows us to classify securities into groups based on a variable of interest (simple discriminate analysis) or multiple variables (multiple discriminate analysis).

Multiple discriminate analysis (MDA) is well suited to classifying securities with respect to credit risk, and researchers have demonstrated the efficacy of this approach for classifying firms into those most vulnerable to bankruptcy risks and those that have a high degree of safety from risk.[5] More recently, commercial services are providing a measure of MDA known as the z-statistic. One of these services generates a z-statistic for companies in a universe using multiple discriminate analysis of seven fundamental variables in an equation of the following form:

$$z = a_0 + a_1 x_1 + a_2 x_2 + a_3 x_3 + \cdots + a_7 x_7$$

where
z = overall credit score
$a_0, \ldots, a_7$ = weightings or coefficients of fundamental variables $x_1, \ldots, x_7$, respectively
x_1 = profitability: earnings before interest and taxes (EBIT)/total assets (TA)
x_2 = stability of earnings measure: the standard error of estimate of EBIT/TA (normalized for ten years)
x_3 = debt service capabilities: EBIT/interest charges
x_4 = cumulative profitability: retained earnings/total assets
x_5 = liquidity: current assets/current liabilities

[5]Edward Altman, "Financial Ratios, Discriminant Analysis and the Prediction of Corporate Bankruptcy," *Journal of Finance,* Sept. 1968, pp. 589–609.

x_6 = capitalization levels: market value of equity/total capital (five-year average)

x_7 = size: total tangible assets (normalized)

Given data on fundamental variables, we can calculate a z-statistic for each firm in a universe of interest as a measure of credit risk. The higher the value of the calculated z-statistic for a firm is, the greater the degree of assurance of credit quality will be, whereas the lower the z-value is, the greater the vulnerability to credit risk will be. Naturally, very low values of the z-statistic are indicative of high risk of bankruptcy for the firm.

Figure 14-13 is a plotting of z-statistics for a universe of the largest 1000 firms as of September 1, 1992. Note that the mean value of the z-statistic was 2.57, implying that a z-statistic above this value was representative of above-average credit quality, whereas those below that value are of below-average quality. Negative values of the z-statistic, or those in the lower 5 percent of the distribution (the left two columns of Figure 14-13), would be representative of firms with quite high levels of credit risk and potential bankruptcy. At a minimum, those firms should require further intensive analysis.

BOND SWAPS

A bond swap is the simultaneous purchase and sale of two or more bonds with similar characteristics in order to earn a yield differential. Differences among bonds in coupons, default

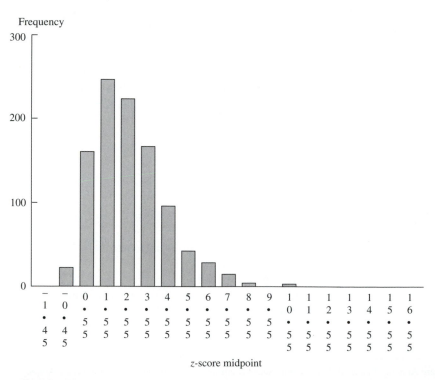

FIGURE 14-13

z-score distribution. Mean = 2.565; standard deviation = 1.781.

risk, interest rates, maturity (duration), marketability, tax treatment, call provisions, sinking funds, and other factors determine the potential profitability of the swap. For example, suppose an investor monitors the yield on AAA- and AA-rated bonds and finds that this spread has widened to 75 basis points from its historic average of 50 basis points. Believing this wider-than-normal yield spread is a temporary aberration, the investor will buy AA-rated bonds and sell AAA-rated bonds until, hopefully, the yield spread returns to the historic average of 50 basis points. Portfolio managers utilize the swap for a variety of purposes, but the overriding objective is to generate incremental capital gains and/or increased income from switching bonds.

When evaluating bonds, investors who engage in bond swaps search for two factors: large yield differentials and short workout periods. The workout period is the time in which a realignment of bond values takes place. In general, the larger the yield differential between bonds and the shorter the workout period is, the greater the return from the bond swap will be. Investors face the risks that the yield differentials may not change as anticipated and that the workout period will be longer than expected. Because of these risks, some portfolio managers close out their swap positions quickly if the market moves in an unexpected direction.

The evaluation of swaps is a difficult task even with computer programs. A simple approach to this evaluation is horizon analysis.[6] Horizon analysis is a logical framework that decomposes the various aspects of swap returns into four components with different levels of risk—two certain and two uncertain. The certain-return components are those aspects of yield changes that are attributable to (1) the passage of time (time component) and (2) the coupon interest. Uncertainty surrounds (3) the realization of any capital gains or loss due to changes in the yield to maturity (Δ yield component) and (4) the interest on invested coupons, a return component of increasing importance as the holding period increases. Thus:

$$
\begin{array}{ccccccc}
& \text{time} & & \text{coupon} & \Delta\text{ yield} & & \text{interest on} \\
\text{Total return} = & \text{component} + & \text{interest} & + & \text{component} + & \text{reinvested coupons} \\
& \text{(certain)} & \text{(certain)} & \text{(uncertain)} & & \text{(uncertain)}
\end{array}
$$

To illustrate horizon analysis, we consider Table 14-5, which lists various prices for a $14\frac{1}{2}$ percent coupon bond. Let us examine the bondholder's total return, assuming the bond is purchased with 10 years to maturity and a 13-percent yield to maturity and sold one year later at an 11 percent yield to maturity. The initial purchase price would be $1081.22, which can be found in the 10-year column and the 13-percent row in Table 14-5. One year later, and with a yield to maturity of 11 percent, the bond would be priced at $1195.90, resulting in a capital gain of $114.68. This capital gain can be broken down into two components—the certain time component, which assumes no change in yield to maturity, and the uncertain component due to changes in yield to maturity. Notice that if the yield has not changed, the bond price with nine years to maturity would be $1077.17, resulting in a decrease of $4.05 in price due simply to the passage of time (the time component).[7] However, because of the change in yield to maturity from 13 percent to 11 percent, the bond price would increase from $1077.17 to $1195.90; thus, the uncertain gain due to the change in yield would be $118.73. To complete the example, we must recognize the coupon interest and the interest on

[6]M. Leibowitz, "Horizon Analysis for Managed Portfolios," *Journal of Portfolio Management,* Spring 1975.

[7]This systematic decrease in price over time for a premium bond (increase in price for a discount bond) is obvious once we note that the bond will be redeemed at par on the maturity date.

TABLE 14-5
An illustration of horizon analysis

	Prices for a 14½ percent coupon bond, for various yields to maturity and time to maturity		
Yield to maturity, %	**Time to maturity**		
	10 years	**9½ years**	**9 years**
10	1280.35	1272.52	1262.52
11	1209.37	1203.72	1195.90 ↑
12	1141.85	1139.10	1135.17 ↑
13	1081.22 →	1079.82 →	1077.17
14	1026.06	1025.78	1025.07

Example of horizon analysis: Purchase bond at 13% YTM with 10 years to maturity and sell 1 year later, at which time YTM changes to 11%.

Certain components
- price change due to passage of time: $\dfrac{1077.17 - 1081.22}{1081.22} = -0.4\%$
- coupon interest: $\dfrac{145.00}{1081.22} = 13.4\%$

Uncertain components
- price change due to Δ yield: $\dfrac{1195.90 - 1077.17}{1081.22} = 11.0\%$
- interest on invested coupons: $\dfrac{(72.50)(.13)(1/2)}{1081.22} = \underline{0.5\%}$

Total return: $\dfrac{-4.05 + 145.00 + 118.73 + 4.71}{1081.22} = \underline{\underline{24.5\%}}$

Source: Adapted from M. Leibowitz, "Horizon Analysis for Managed Portfolios," *Journal of Portfolio Management,* Spring 1975, pp. 23–34.

the invested coupon interest. The total coupon interest for one year is $145, and interest on the first coupon invested at 13 percent for the final six months is $4.71 ($145/2 × 13% × $\frac{1}{2}$). By placing these return components over the purchase price of $1081.22, we compute the total return of 24.5 percent:

$$\text{Total return} = \frac{-4.05 + 118.73 + 145.00 + 4.71}{1081.22} = \frac{264.39}{1081.22} = 24.5\%$$

If the workout period is shorter, say six months, the yield and coupon components will constitute a greater and lesser portion, respectively, of total return. If interest rates were to fall from 13 percent to 11 percent in six months, the total return is 18.0 percent for the six-month period (39.2 percent on an annualized basis).

$$\text{Total return} = \frac{1079.82 - 1081.22}{1081.22} + \frac{1203.73 - 1079.82}{1081.22} + \frac{72.50}{1081.22}$$

$$= -0.00129 + 0.11459 + 0.06705 = 0.180 = 18.0\%$$

Horizon analysis thus provides a mechanism for evaluating the returns generated by bonds, and we illustrate for categories of bond swap: substitution swaps, intermarket spread swaps, and tax-motivated swaps.

Substitution Swap

A substitution swap is an exchange of one bond for a perfect-substitute bond to earn several additional basis points due to a transitory mispricing.[8] For example, an investor might hold a 30-year, 7 percent government bond yielding 7 percent but he or she might be offered an identical bond yielding 7.10 percent. The expectation is that the 7.10 percent yield on the offered bond will fall to the level of the bond currently held. The investor makes a substitution swap by selling the bond yielding 7 percent and purchasing the bond yielding 7.10 percent.

Table 14-6 describes this swap. The realized yield for the bond with the promised yield of 7.10 percent will be 8.29 percent, assuming the bond is priced to yield 7.00 percent at the end of one year. For the bond currently held, 7.00 percent is both the promised and the realized yield. Thus, the investor will earn an additional 129 basis points in one year by selling the bond currently held and buying the bond offered. Of course, this swap is not riskless. There is risk from (1) a slower workout period than anticipated, (2) adverse interim yield differentials, (3) adverse changes in overall interest rates, and (4) the possibility that the bond offered is not a perfect substitute for the bond held. For example, if the workout time is the total 30 years to maturity, the investor will earn only a slight improvement in yield (less than 10 basis points per year if the coupons are reinvented at only 7%).

TABLE 14-6
Substitution swap

Bond currently held: 30-year, 7% government bond priced at $1000 to yield 7%
Bond offered for swap: 30-year, 7% government bond priced at $987.70 to yield 7.10%
Assumed workout period: 1 year
Reinvestment rate: 7%

	Current bond	New bond
Dollar investment per bond	$1000.00	$987.70
Total coupons received	70.00	70.00
Interest on one coupon @ 7% for 6 months	1.23	1.23
Principal value at year-end @ 7% YTM	1000.00	1000.00
Total dollars accrued	$1071.23	$1071.23
Total dollar gain	71.23	83.53
Gain per invested dollar	.07123	.08458
Realized semiannual compound yield	7.00%	8.29%
Value of swap	129 basis points in 1 year	

Source: Sidney Homes and Martin Leibowitz, *Inside the Yield Book,* Prentice-Hall, Englewood Cliffs, N.J., 1972, p. 84.

[8]The classification of various swaps into substitution swaps and other categories was first described in S. Homer and M. Liebowitz, *Inside the Yield Book,* Prentice-Hall, Englewood Cliffs, N.J., 1972.

Intermarket Spread Swap

The intermarket spread swap refers to the switching of bonds from different market sectors. The motive behind this swap is the investor's belief that yield differentials, or yield spreads, between two market sectors are out of their proper alignment. In contrast with the substitution swap, the two bonds in the intermarket spread swap are entirely different bonds; for example, an industrial bond is swapped for a utility bond.

Investors execute intermarket spread swaps in two directions. One direction is to buy a new bond offered at a higher yield and sell the bond currently held. The expectation is that the intermarket spread will narrow with the yield of the newly acquired bond decreasing (relative to the bond sold) and its price rising. The higher price will produce a capital gain. In the second direction, in which the newly acquired bond has a lower yield than the bond currently held, the investor expects the yield spread to widen, which would lower the yield of the newly acquired bond (relative to the bond sold) and raise its price sufficiently to offset the yield decline.

An example of an intermarket spread swap in the direction of narrowing yield spreads is shown in Table 14-7. The rationale of the swap is that the current spread of the 50 basis points will narrow to 40 basis points. By switching to the corporate bond yielding 7.00 percent with the expectation that its yield will fall to 6.90 percent, the bond's price will rise from $1000 to $1012.46 if the swap works out as expected. This price plus the coupon interest and the interest on the invested coupon result in total value of $1083.69 at the end of the year. Thus, the investor will earn 8.20 percent for the year, which represents a gain of 170 basis points in one year over the alternative of continuing to hold the government bond.

TABLE 14-7
Intermarket spread swap in the direction of narrowing spreads

Bond currently held: 30-year, 4 percent government bond priced at $671.82 to yield 6.50 percent
New bond offered for swap: 30-year, 7 percent AAA corporate bond priced at $1000 to yield 7 percent
Assumed workout period: one year
Investment rate: 7 percent
Swap rationale: Spread of 50 basis points will narrow to 40 basis points with corporate bond yielding
6.90 percent and government bond continuing to yield 6.50 percent

	Current bond	**New bond**
Dollar investment per bond	$671.82	$1000.00
Coupons	40.00	70.00
Interest on one coupon @ 7% for six months	0.70	1.23
Principal value at year-end	675.55	1012.46
Total dollars accrued	$716.25	$1083.69
Total dollar gain	44.23	83.69
Gain per invested dollar	0.0661	0.0837
Realized semiannual compound yield	6.50%	8.20%
Value of swap	basis points in one year	

Source: Sidney Homer and Martin Leibowitz, *Inside the Yield Book,* Prentice-Hall, Englewood Cliffs, N.J., 1972, p. 90.

An investor who makes intermarket spread swaps faces several risks. The market may move in an adverse direction, the workout period may elongate, and adverse interim price movements may occur. Or, the rationale for the swap may be swamped by other differences between the two bonds. Clearly, swaps of this type are not for the faint-hearted and involve a considerable amount of market knowledge.

Tax-Motivated Swap

As discussed previously, taxes influence the type of investments we make, from the taxability of the flow (municipal versus corporate bonds), the form of the flow (capital gain or loss versus income), and the timing of the flow (generally, paying taxes later is preferred). An example of a tax-motivated swap is presented in Table 14-8. The primary rationale of this swap is to recognize a capital loss that can be used to offset a capital gain, which in turn reduces the tax liability due this year. Other benefits include increasing income, returning capital, and maintaining the face value of the bonds. Obviously, this type of swap occurs during periods of rising interest rates.[9]

Recognizing the tax loss of approximately $59,500.00 provides a tax shield to reduce taxes due on capital gains, for a tax savings of around $16,660 (capital-gain tax rate of 28 percent). In the future, we need to recognize that a capital gain of approximately $66,900 will occur if the bonds are held to maturity, for a tax bill of around $18,732. However, in present-value terms the tax bill in the future (assuming 14 years, discounted at the current yield of 8.75 percent) is $5,648 for a net benefit of $11,012. This benefit alone represents a one-time gain of over 310 basis points. The notes in Table 14-8 indicate additional benefits that were generated by the swap. This partial analysis shows the power of tax-motivated swaps, and during the correct economic times, these types of swaps are common.

There are many other types of tax swaps we could discuss. Another type of tax swap involves substituting nontaxable municipal bonds for taxable corporate bonds of the same risk to increase the investor's after-tax return. Similarly, high-coupon bonds selling near par might be swapped for low-coupon bonds selling at a large discount in order to increase the after-tax return and because of the differential tax rate on capital gains versus interest income. Other types of swaps exist, but they are beyond the scope of our discussion. The serious bond investor will want to examine bond swaps in more detail, and the starting point is *Inside the Yield Book* by Homer and Leibowitz, one of the references at the end of this chapter.

FOREIGN BONDS

One of the critical concepts that we have described and emphasized in this book is reducing risk by diversification. Within the bond market, investors can diversify credit risks by spreading funds among corporate, agency, and government issues. Investors can also reduce interest rate risk to some extent by investing in different segments of the domestic yield curve. Unfortunately, the opportunity to diversify in this way within the U.S. bond market

---

[9]The date of the swap in Table 14-8 is May 12, 1981 and is indicative of a period of rising interest rates. From the early to mid-1980s to 1993, interest rates have been flat or decreasing.

TABLE 14-8
Tax-motivated swap

Bonds sold
Date: May 12, 1981

Rating	Yearly income	Amt (m)	Description	Coupon	Maturity	Market value	Proceeds	Accrued interest	Book cost	Loss	Profit
BBB	$3200	50	Boston, Ma.	6.4%	6-1-86	73.0	$36,500.00	1448.89	$50,000	$13,500.00	
AA	2750	50	Florida State Board of Higher Education	5.5	1-1-89	73.125	36,562.50	1015.97	50,000	13,437.50	
A	2625	50	Ohio State Public Facility	5.25	5-1-88	70.087	35,043.50	94.79	50,000	14,956.65	
AAA	3100	50	State of Maryland	6.2	5-1-93	70.50	35,250.00	766.39	50,000	14,750.00	
AAA	3,200	50	State of Maryland Department of Transportation	6.4	7-15-87	94.355	47,127.50	1057.78	50,000	2822.50	
	$14,875	250					$190,533.50	$4383.82		59,466.65	

Bonds purchased

Rating	Yearly income	Amt (m)	Description	Coupon	Maturity	Market price	Net cost	Accrued interest	Total cost
AA	$3125	50	State of Connecticut	6.25%	3-1-96	$70.72	$35,360.00	$633.68	$35,993.68
AA	3300	50	State of W. Virginia	6.60	11-1-93	78.00	29,000.00	119.17	39,119.17
AA	3100	50	State of Massachusetts	6.20	8-1-93	69.89	34,945.00	886.94	35,831.94
AA	6500	100	State of Oregon	6.50	11-1-95	73.83	73,830.00	234.72	74,064.22
	$16,025	250					$183,135.00	$1874.51	$185,009.51

Notes
(1) Recognize tax of $59,466.65
(2) Increase income $1150
(4) Overall risk about the same, but no longer has BBB rating
(5) Face value the same $250,000

is limited because all interest rates often move in the same direction when the yield curve shifts.

Foreign bond markets, however, are large and offer the potential for diversification of interest rate risk not available when investing only in domestic bonds. Though foreign bonds carry their own interest rate risks, they are not directly exposed to U.S. interest rate changes. As long as foreign and U.S. interest rates are not perfectly correlated, some of the interest rate risk will be self-canceling. In general, correlations between the returns on debt instruments in different national markets are much lower than the return correlations between instruments within the U.S. market.

However, diversifying into foreign bond markets to reduce domestic interest rate risk entails accepting exchange rate risk. Because U.S.-dollar exchange rate changes are highly correlated, exchange rate risk cannot be eliminated by spreading foreign-bond holdings across many countries. As a result, devising ways of coping with exchange rate risk becomes a prime consideration when developing strategies for investing in foreign bonds. After describing the size and characteristics of foreign bond markets, we discuss strategies for investing in these markets and ways of coping with exchange rate risk.

Market Size and Characteristics

Foreign (non-U.S.) bonds are a major asset category. Figure 14-14 indicates that nondollar bonds constitute more than a quarter of the world wealth. Figure 14-15 breaks down the individual country composition of the world bond market. Note that the U.S. bond market is substantial, but represents less than half the total market value. Correspondingly, nondollar bonds represent better than half the total, with the Japanese and German bond markets representing significant proportions of the foreign bond component.

Table 14-9 shows average annual returns and standard deviation of return for U.S. domestic bonds and foreign bonds over the 15-year period from 1975 to 1989. Note that foreign bonds provided a return of 11.3 percent, which was higher than the 10.2 percent return provided by U.S. domestic bonds. At the same time, the standard deviation of return of 11.7 percent for foreign bonds was significantly higher that the 8.9 percent standard deviation of domestic U.S. bonds.

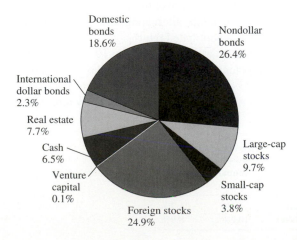

FIGURE 14-14
Aggregate value of investment opportunities, worldwide market—$19.8 trillion as of December 31, 1987. (*Source:* Brinson Partners.)

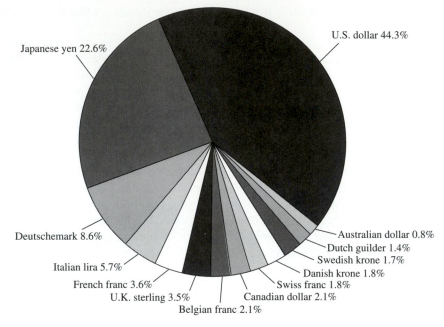

U.S. dollar 44.3%

Japanese yen 22.6%

Deutschemark 8.6%

Italian lira 5.7%

French franc 3.6%

U.K. sterling 3.5%

Belgian franc 2.1%

Canadian dollar 2.1%

Swiss franc 1.8%

Danish krone 1.8%

Swedish krone 1.7%

Dutch guilder 1.4%

Australian dollar 0.8%

FIGURE 14-15
Aggregate value of major global bond markets, totaling $9.4 trillion as of December
31, 1987. (*Source:* Salomon Brothers. Government and corporate issues are included,
as are international bonds.)

Figure 14-16 illustrates, however, that the relative returns and volatilities of U.S. and
foreign bonds varied significantly over three subperiods within the overall 15-year period:
1975–1979; 1980–1984; and 1985–1989.

The dollar was quite strong during the 1979–1984 period; it showed significant appreciation relative to other currencies over an extended period. However, the earlier 1975–1979
and the later 1985–1989 periods were characterized by dollar weakness; the dollar depreciated relative to other currencies persistently and extensively over these two periods. For the
full period, the dollar ended up about where it began, but the alternating periods of weakness
and strength led to substantial volatility in dollar-denominated returns.

Finally, Figure 14-17 shows the correlation of quarterly returns from 1975 to 1990 and
provides some insight into the diversification potential of different bond classes. It shows
rolling 20-quarter correlations between the U.S.-bond and foreign-bond markets. For example, the first plot point in 1975, about 0.25, describes the correlation of quarterly returns for

TABLE 14-9
Historical performance (1975–1989)

	Annual returns	Standard deviation
Non-dollar bonds	11.3%	11.7%
U.S. domestic bonds	10.2%	8.9%

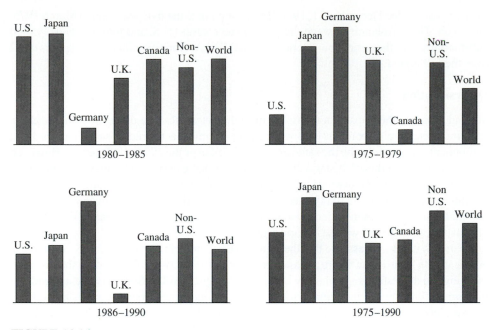

FIGURE 14-16
International bond market returns in U.S. dollars. (*Source:* Adrian Lee: "A Practitioner's View: The Importance of Separating Bonds and Currencies," *International Bonds and Currencies,* CFA Institute, November 1985, pp. 79–84.)

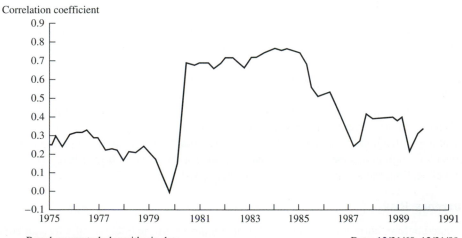

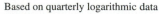

FIGURE 14-17
U.S. and non-U.S. bond markets—5-year trailing correlation. (*Source:* Brinson Partners, Inc.)

the five years ended December 31, 1974. The next point is the five years ended March 1975, and so on. The correlation between these two asset classes (U.S. and foreign bonds) varied substantially over the period, but averaged a usefully low (for diversification purposes) 0.42 over the full period.

Diversification

We can illustrate the impact on the risk-return characteristics of a domestic-bond portfolio from including foreign bonds as follows. First, we assume that the return on the foreign-bond component is expected to be the same as experienced over the 1975–1990 period. However, we should note that though historically foreign bonds have performed somewhat better than domestic bonds, it is not obvious why there should be any significant return advantage in the future; bond returns are likely to equilibrate across national markets. In contrast to international equities, we cannot identify a growth-driven excess-return rationale. For purposes of illustration, however, we use historic returns.

For risk inputs, we assume that the standard deviation of return for the U.S. and foreign bonds are the same in the future as experienced over the 1975–1990 period, so that the ratio of foreign to domestic bond volatility is approximately 1.3 to 1.0. Similarly, we assume that the correlation between the returns of the domestic- and foreign-bond markets is the same as experienced over the same 15-year period, or a 0.42 correlation. Using these return and risk inputs, we generated a series of portfolios with differing proportions of foreign bonds ranging in increments of 10 percent from no foreign bonds to a 100-percent proportion of the total portfolio.

Figure 14-18 is a risk-return diagram showing an efficient frontier of bond portfolios, differing only with regard to the proportion of foreign versus domestic bonds in the total portfolio. Note that the portfolio at point D is composed entirely of domestic bonds, while the portfolio at point F is composed entirely of foreign bonds. The other points along the frontier beginning at point D represent portfolios with additional increments of 10 percent in foreign-bond holdings.

The figure shows that all the portfolios with a foreign-bond component offer higher expected returns than the domestic-bond portfolio D and that the all-foreign-bond portfolio F shows the highest return. Such a result, of course, would be expected given our basic input assumption of a higher projected return for foreign bonds than for domestic bonds. In addition, at lower increments of additional foreign bonds, the overall portfolio shows not only a higher level of return, but also a reduced level of risk. Note that this result takes place up to a mix of 30-percent foreign bonds, with the 20-percent allocation showing the lowest risk along with a higher return than the all-domestic bonds. The relatively lower correlation between foreign and domestic bonds drives this favorable result; at higher levels of foreign bond allocation, the low correlation effect is dampened.

Currency Risk

As noted before, currency risk is a significant component of the total risk of a foreign bond. Its impact can be estimated by comparing the standard deviation of the bond return measured in a foreign currency with its standard deviation measured in its domestic currency; the difference represents the contribution of currency risk. The total risk of a foreign bond can, therefore, be broken down into its volatility in local-currency terms and its currency-risk

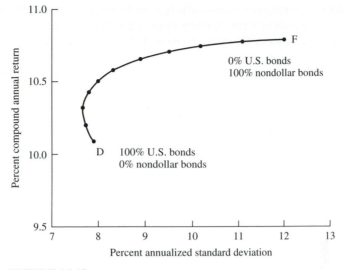

FIGURE 14-18
Portfolios of risk and return—U.S. and non-U.S. bonds. (*Source:*
Richard Carr: "The Rationale for Investing in International Bonds
and Currencies—Historical Returns, Risk, and Diversification,"
International Bonds and Currencies, CPA Institute, 1986, pp.
11–21.)

component. Exchange rate risk is generally a much larger component of the total risk of
a bond investment than that of an equity investment. Currency risk has a stronger effect
on foreign bonds than on foreign stocks because bond markets are less volatile than stock
markets.

Table 14-10 analyzes the returns and standard deviations of returns of nondollar bonds
in dollar terms, as compared with the same measures in local currency terms before converting into dollars, again using the 1975–1990 period. As a point of comparison, the table also
shows the returns and standard deviation of U.S. domestic bonds. In local-currency terms,
nondollar bonds provided a 10.1 percent annualized return. Converting into dollars over
this time period actually increases returns slightly and leaves them in excess of returns on

TABLE 14-10
Historical Performance Monthly Returns 12/31/74–12/31/89

	Annualized returns	Standard deviations	Correlations		
			1.	2.	3.
1. Nondollar bonds in U.S. dollar terms	11.3%	11.7%	1.000		
2. Nondollar bonds in local currency terms	10.1%	3.9%	0.680	1.000	
3. U.S. domestic bonds	10.2%	8.9%	0.422	0.613	1.000

Source: Richard Carr: "The Rationale for Investing in International Bonds and Currencies—Historical Returns, Risk, and Diversification," *International Bonds and Currencies,* CFA Institute, 1986, pp. 11–21.

U.S. bonds. More interesting are the relationships in the standard deviation column, which show that nondollar bonds in local-currency terms were surprisingly stable, much more in line with U.S. domestic bonds. The conversion into U.S. dollars and the associated exchange risk are what push up the standard deviation in dollar terms.

At the same time, the currency dimension reduces the correlations. In other words, if exchange rate fluctuations are removed, the cost of the reduced return volatility would be a greater correlation of nondollar bond returns with the U.S. bond market. The last three columns of Table 14-10 show a simple correlation matrix for the same time period between nondollar bonds in dollar terms, nondollar bonds in local-currency terms, and U.S. bonds. In dollar terms international bonds had a 0.42 correlation with the U.S. bond market, but in local currency terms, the correlation with U.S. bonds rises to 0.61.

Currency Hedging

As the prior analysis demonstrates, the risk of fluctuating exchange rates is a prime factor causing volatility of returns for foreign bonds. In dealing with currency risk, investors can determine to either accept full exposure to it or hedge this risk component. For bond portfolios in which the proportion of foreign bonds is minimal, usually considered as 25 percent or less, the generally accepted course of action is to consider this risk as a negligible incremental part of the total portfolio. As we have illustrated, at that level of participation in foreign bonds, the low correlation between these bond classes has the most powerful impact on diversification. Furthermore, research has shown that exposure to currency risk at these low levels may, in fact, provide good diversification for domestic budget-deficit/monetary-policy risk.

However, for portfolios with high weightings in foreign bonds and a consequent greater exposure to exchange rate fluctuations, one of the recommended courses of action is to undertake a program of hedging. Currency hedging consists of transactions that reduce the impact of exchange rate fluctuations on the dollar value of foreign security. By hedging currency risk, a U.S. investor locks in a dollar exchange rate on a specified amount of foreign currency for a specified period of time. The investor can do this by selling foreign currency "forward" for dollars or by selling foreign currency futures contracts. These transactions allow a U.S. investor to lock in an exchange rate for a relatively short period of time— typically three months and rarely more that two years.

For example, a bond investor desiring to hedge exchange rate risk over a three-month period would sell the bond's current foreign-currency value, plus future coupon payments or accrued interest, for three-month delivery against U.S. dollars. The forward exchange rate for this hedging transaction will reflect the foreign currency's discount or premium. At quarter-end, the investor sells the foreign bond and delivers this foreign currency realized from its sale to satisfy his forward-exchange contract.

At the same time, hedging a nondollar bond portfolio also entails three types of direct costs: (1) execution costs associated with buying and selling hedging instruments (establishing hedges), (2) execution and opportunity costs associated with settling hedging transactions, and (3) management fees. For execution costs, most estimates average around 25 basis points, whereas the additional cost occasioned by the settlement of hedging transactions is estimated at approximately 10 basis points. Finally, the management fees for hedging services are at least 5 basis points on an unbounded basis. As an aggregate, the total cost of hedging a foreign-bond portfolio is likely to approximate at least 50 basis points per year, depending upon portfolio size and the nature of the hedging program.

Risk-Return Characteristics of Hedged Bonds

The data in Figure 14-19 allows a comparison of the risk-return characteristics of hedged foreign bonds to domestic (U.S.) bonds and foreign (nonhedged) bonds. The returns and standard deviations for U.S. bonds, as well as foreign (unhedged) bonds, were those generated using data over the 1975–1990 period. Results for hedged foreign bonds represent those for a hypothetical portfolio invested in the non-U.S. markets, and continuously hedged back into the dollar. In other words, whenever there was a foreign currency exposure owing to assets held in a foreign currency, the exact amount of that currency was sold forward into the dollar.

Note that the standard deviation of annual returns in the U.S. bond market over the 15-year period was 8.9 percent, while the volatility of unhedged foreign bonds was greater at 11.7 percent. At the same time, the volatility of the hedged portfolio was 5.7 percent, or substantially less than the 11.7 percent associated with the unhedged portfolio. The currency risk, which was eliminated, was about 400 basis points. As a percentage of total risk, the 4-percent currency risk was 34 percent over the period. Note also that the return from the hedged portfolio was not significantly different from the unhedged foreign-bond portfolio, which is consistent with the observation that over a long period of time, currencies have not added or detracted from return.

Figure 14-20 compares an efficient frontier of bonds, domestic and foreign, to one in which the foreign bond component is hedged. The efficient frontier of unhedged bonds is the same as the one shown previously in Figure 14-18, using historic data over the 1975–1990

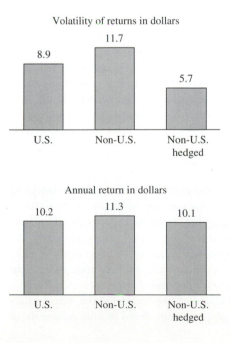

FIGURE 14-19
International bond market returns 1975–1990.
(*Source:* J.P. Morgan Investment.)

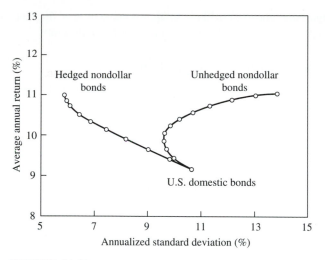

FIGURE 14-20
Efficient frontier—hedged and unhedged bonds. (*Source:* Merrill Lynch & Co.)

period as inputs. The frontier generated for the hedged bonds also evaluates over the same 1975–1990 period but adjusts the input data in the following way. First, the standard deviations of return are adjusted downward to reflect a policy of fully hedging the foreign-bond component over the 1975–1990 period. Correspondingly, we assume that the correlation between domestic and foreign bonds increases with the hedging, and we use a 0.61 correlation versus 0.42 that reflects correlation over the period when currency effects are included. Finally, we adjust the return input down by 0.5 percent to reflect the cost of hedging.

Note that the efficient frontier for the hedged bond portfolios dominates the unhedged ones, except at low levels of foreign-bond participation. We mentioned previously that at low levels of foreign-bond participation unhedged diversification was the generally recommended course of action, and this comparison tends to affirm that course. At higher levels of participation, hedging is productive due to the reduction in volatility that more than offsets the cost of hedging and to the increased correlation consequent to that activity. In the case of bonds, hedging appears to be a clearer course of action for long-term investors than for equities.

CONCLUSION

Bond managers monitor the maturity positioning of the portfolio by reference to the yield curve. Correspondingly, the yield curve provides a structure for developing active strategies for adding value to the bond portfolio. Furthermore, bond managers can add potential return by accepting credit risk and the premium that the market offers. However, we need to monitor trends in credit risk of the portfolio over time and assess trends of individual issues to avoid an undue penalty from adverse changes. Furthermore, swaps can add value if appraised within a disciplined framework and executed judiciously. Finally, investing in international bond markets has the potential of improving the risk-return character of a portfolio, but currency risk needs to be properly considered to fully realize these benefits.

APPENDIX A

For bonds with embedded options, consideration can be given to interest rate volatility by introducing a binomial interest rate tree. This tree is nothing more than a discrete representation of the possible evolution over time of the one-period rate, based on some assumptions about interest rate volatility. It is also a specific application of the concept of the binomial option valuation that we described in Chapter 13. The reader may wish to refer back to that chapter for a description of how to construct such a tree.

Figure 14A-1 shows a binomial interest rate tree representing the way that interest rates evolve, as well as the resulting bond values at each interval over a three-year horizon. In this tree, the nodes are spaced one year apart in time (left to right). Each node N is labeled with one or more subscripts indicating the path the one-year rate followed in reaching that node. The one-year rate may move to one of two values in the following year; U represents the higher of these two values, and D represents the lower. For example, the rotation N_{UU} means that the one-year rate followed the upper path in both the first and second years.

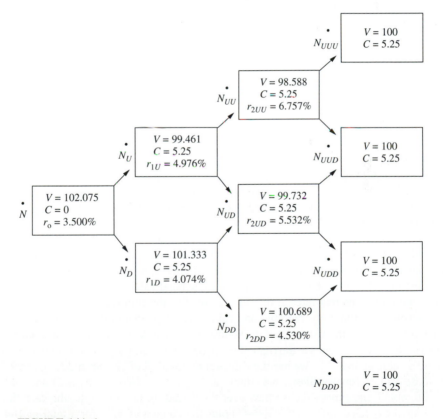

FIGURE 14A-1

Valuing an option-free bond with three years to maturity and a coupon of 5.25 percent. (*Source:* Andrew Kalotay, George Williams, and Frank Fabozzi, "A Model for Valuing Bonds and Embedded Options," *Financial Analysts Journal,* May–June 1993, pp. 35–46.)

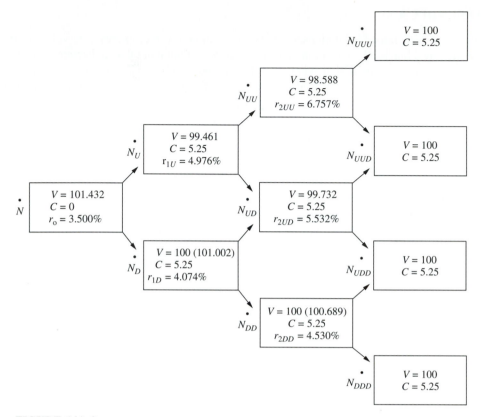

FIGURE 14A-2
Valuing a callable bond with three years to maturity and a coupon of 5.25 percent, callable in
years one and two at 100. (*Source:* Andrew Kalotay, George Williams, and Frank Fabozzi, "A
Model for Valuing Bonds and Embedded Options," *Financial Analysts Journal,* May–June
1993, pp. 35–46.)

In addition to interest rates being used as discounters, the tree also shows coupons and
bond values at each period. Bond coupons are, of course, a cash flow component that is
certain and thus the same at 5.25 in each period. The bond value is, however, a variable that
will depend on the interest rates at the time, as well as the future bond values in the time
period beyond. Alternatively, current bond values will depend on future cash flows.

Therefore, to find the value (V) of the bond at a given node, we need to first calculate the
bond's value at the two nodes to the right of the node of interest. For example, in determining
the bond's value at node N_U, we use the values at nodes N_{UU} of 98.588 and N_{UD} of 99.732.
With these values equally likely, we simply average these $(N_{UU} + N_{UD}/2)$ and add the
coupon to obtain the expected cash flow over the period. In this example, the cash flow is
the averaged expected values $\left(\frac{98.588 + 99.732}{2}\right)$ plus the coupon of 5.25 for a total of 104.41.
To determine the present value of this cash flow, we discount at one-year rate at the node
where we seek the value. Discounting the cash flow at the rate of 4.976 percent, we derive
the bond value $(V) = 99.461$ shown in the box. Other values shown in the tree were derived
similarly.

Using the values and interest rates shown in Figure 14A-1, we obtain a value for the bond of $102.75. Note that this value is identical to the bond value found earlier by discounting at the forward one-year rates shown in Table 14-1. We should expect to find this result because the bond used in this example is option-free, which, in turn, demonstrates that, for an option-free bond, the tree-based valuation model is consistent with the standard valuation approach illustrated in a prior section. Alternatively, interest rate volatility has no effect on the valuation when appraising option-free bonds.

The binomial interest rate tree can also be applied to callable bonds. The valuation process proceeds in the same fashion as in the case of an option-free bond, with one exception. When the call option can be exercised by the issuer, the bond's value at a node must be changed to reflect the lesser of its value if it is not called at the call price. Again, we use the value at each node as that determined by the procedure described before.

Figure 14A-2 shows the value at each node of the binomial interest rate tree, again using the 5.25 percent bond with three years remaining to maturity but assuming that it has an embedded call option exerciseable in years one and two at $100. The discounting process is identical to that shown in Figure 14A-1, except that at two nodes, ND and NDD, the derived values ($101.002 at ND and $100.689 at NDD) exceed the call price ($100). Note that the values have been struck out and replaced with $100 because we assume they will be called. The value for this callable bond is $101.432, lower than that for the option-free bond, which illustrates that interest rate volatility matters when valuing bonds with embedded options.

SELECTED REFERENCES

Ahu, C., and Howard Thompson: "Jump Diffusion and the Term Structure of Interest Rates," *Journal of Finance* 73, March 1988, pp. 155–74.

Altman, Edward, and Duen Kao: "The Implications of Corporate Bond Rating Profit," *Financial Analysts Journal*, May–June 1992, pp. 64–75.

Ayres, H.F., and John Barry: "Dynamics of the Government Yield Curve," *Financial Analysts Journal*, May–June 1979, pp. 31–39.

Benari, Yoav: "Linking the International Bond Investment Decision to Hedging," *Financial Analysts Journal*, September–October 1992, pp. 55–62.

Bernstein, Peter: "The Gibson Paradox Revisited," *The Financial Review*, September 1982, pp. 153–164.

Brennan, Michael, and Eduardo Schwartz: "Bond Pricing and Market Efficiency," *Financial Analysts Journal*, September–October 1982, pp. 49–56.

Brown, Roger, and Stephen Schaefer: "The Term Structure of Real Interest Rates and the Cox, Ingersoll, and Ross Model," *Journal of Financial Economics*, February 1994, pp. 3–42.

Brown, Stephen, and Philip Dybrig: "The Empirical Implications of the Cox, Ingersoll, Ross Theory of the Term Structure of Interest Rates," *Journal of Finance* 41, July 1986, pp. 617–30.

Burik, Paul, and Richard Ennis: "Foreign Bonds in Diversified Portfolios: A Limited Advantage," *Financial Analysts Journal*, March–April 1990, pp. 31–40.

Campbell, John: "A Defense of Traditional Hypotheses about the Term Structure of Interest Rates," *Journal of Finance* 41, March 1986, pp. 183–193.

Carlton, Willard T., and Ian A. Cooper: "Estimation and Uses of the Term Structure of Interest Rates," *Journal of Finance*, September 1976, pp. 1076–1083.

Carr, Richard: "The Rationale for Investing in International Bonds and Currencies—Historical Returns, Risk, and Diversification," *International Bonds and Currencies*, CFA Institute, 1986. pp. 11–21.

Evans, Martin, and Paul Wachtel: "Interpreting the Moments in Short-Term Interest Rates," *Journal of Business,* July 1992, pp. 395–423.

Fama, Eugene: "The Information in the Term Structure," *Journal of Financial Economics* 13, December 1984, pp. 509–546.

———: "Short-Term Interest Rates as Predictors of Inflation," *American Economic Review,* June 1975, pp. 269–282.

———: "Term Premiums in Bond Returns," *Journal of Financial Economics,* December 1984, pp. 529–46.

Filatov, Victor, and Peter Rappaport: "Is Complete Hedging Optimal for International Bond Portfolios?," *Financial Analysts Journal,* July–August 1992, pp. 37–47.

Fong, Gifford: "Bond Portfolio Analysis," Monograph 11, *Financial Analysts Research Foundation,* Charlottesville, VA, 1980.

———and Oldrich Vasicek: "Fixed-Income Volatility Management," *Journal of Portfolio Management,* Summer 1991, pp. 41–46.

Froot, Kenneth: "New Hope for the Expectations Hypothesis of the Term Structure of Interest Rates," *Journal of Finance,* June 1989, pp. 283–305.

Homer, Sidney, and M.L. Liebowitz: *Inside the Yield Book,* Prentice-Hall, Englewood Cliffs, N.J., 1972.

Johnson, Brian and Kenneth Meyer: "Managing Yield Curve Risk in an Index Environment," *Financial Analysts Journal,* November–December 1989, pp. 51–59.

Kessel, Reuben: "The Cyclical Behavior of the Term Structure of Interest Rates," Occasional Paper 91, *National Bureau of Economic Research,* New York, 1965.

Lee, Adrian: "A Practitioner's View: The Importance of Separating Bonds and Currencies," *International Bonds and Currencies,* CFA Institute, November 1985, pp. 79–84.

Leibowitz, Martin: "Horizon Analysis for Managed Portfolios," *Journal of Portfolio Management,* Spring 1975, pp. 23–34.

———: "The Horizon Annuity," *Financial Analysts Journal,* May–June 1979, pp. 68-74.

Levich, Richard and Lee Thomas: "The Merits of Active Currency Risk Management: Evidence from International Bond Portfolios," *Financial Analysts Journal,* September–October 1993, pp. 63–70.

Levy, Haim, and Zvi Leman: "The Benefits of International Diversification in Bonds," *Financial Analysts Journal,* September–October 1988, pp. 56–67.

Longstaff, Francis, and Eduardo Schwartz: "Interest Rate Volatility and Bond Prices," *Financial Analysts Journal,* July–August 1993, pp. 70–74.

———and ———: "Interest Rate Volatility and the Term Structure: A Two-Factor General Equilibrium Model," *Journal of Finance,* September 1992, pp. 1259–1282.

McAdams, Lloyd, and Evangelos Karagiannis: "Using Yield Curve Shapes to Manage Bond Portfolios," *Financial Analysts Journal,* May–June 1994, pp. 57–60.

McCulloch, J. Huston: "Measuring the Term Structure of Interest Rates," *Journal of Business,* January 1971, pp. 19–31.

McMillan, T.E., Louis Buck, and James Deegan: "The Fisher Theorem - An Illusion, But Whose?," *Financial Analysts Journal,* November–December 1984, pp. 63–71.

Meiselman, D.: *The Term Structure of Interest Rates,* Prentice-Hall, Englewood Cliffs, N.J., 1962.

Meyer, Kenneth: "Yield Spreads and Interest Rate Levels," *Financial Analysts Journal,* November–December 1978, pp. 58–63.

Modigliani, Franco, and Richard Sutch: "Debt Management and the Term Structure of Interest Rates: An Empirical Analysis of Recent Experience," *Journal of Political Economy,* August 1967 Supplement, pp. 569–589.

Nelson, Charles, and Andrew Siegel: "Parsimonious Modeling of Yield Curves," *Journal of Business,* October 1987, pp. 473–490.

Perold, Andre, and Evan Schulman: "The Free Lunch in Currency Hedging: Implications for Investment Policy and Performance Standards," *Financial Analysts Journal,* May–June 1988, pp. 45–52.

Schaefer, Stephen and Eduardo Schwartz: "A Two-Factor Model of the Term Structure: An Approximate Analytical Solution," *Journal of Financial and Quantitative Analysis* 19, December 1984, pp. 413–421.

Sharpe, William F.: *Investments,* Prentice-Hall, Englewood Cliffs, N.J., 1978, pp. 58–72.

Thomas, Lee: "The Performance of Currency-Hedged Foreign Bonds," *Financial Analysts Journal,* May–June 1989, pp. 25–31.

QUESTIONS AND PROBLEMS

1. Using the most recent *Federal Reserve Bulletin,* construct a yield curve.
2. What is the expectations theory of term structure, and how is it related to market efficiency?
3. According to the liquidity premium theory, implicit forward rates are biased upward. Why?
4. In general, why might a liquidity premium exist for longer bonds?
5. What is meant by the term structure of interest rates? Who would be more interested in it: the investor who buys 10-year bonds at 10 percent in order to later make a balloon payment of $5000 at the end of 10 years or a pension fund manager who has a series of pensioners retiring within the next 10 years?
6. Discuss the role of the yield curve in active bond management and the reasons for its shape and change in shape over time.
7. Discuss why the realized return on a bond may differ from the anticipated return, as indicated by the yield to maturity.
8. Assume that the average yield spread between AAA and BAA corporate bonds is currently below the historical spread. Describe the sort of bond swap that might be undertaken and the risks that would be associated with that action.
9. Assume that a bond is now rated A and your credit evaluation indicates that it should be rated AA. What opportunity does this present?
10. A new 20-year bond with an 8 percent nominal yield is priced to yield 10 percent. An investor purchasing the bond expects that two years from now, yields on comparable bonds will have declined to 9 percent. Calculate the realized yield if the investor expects to sell the bond in two years.
11. You have forecasted the year-end term structure of interest rates to be flat at 12 percent, and you have estimated the yield differentials for your three-bond portfolio to be 1.10, 1.01, and 1.05. All your bonds are three-year bonds and carry a $100 annual interest payment and a face value of $1000.
    (*a*) What is the expected year-end yield to maturity for each of your bonds?
    (*b*) What is the expected market price for each of the bonds at the end of the first year?
12. What role do factor models play in analyzing bond portfolios? Describe what factors might be important to this analysis.
13. How would bond portfolios respond to a change in interest rates across the yield curve, and what would distinguish the differing performance of these portfolios?
14. How would an increase in the volatility of interest rates impact the performance of long-, short-, and intermediate-term bond portfolios?
15. Why is it important to monitor the quality of bonds over time? Describe a framework for monitoring bond quality.
16. What is horizon analysis, and why is it useful?
17. How are the substitution and intermarket spread swaps similar?

18. How do nondollar bonds fit into a bond portfolio management program?

19. What special risks do foreign bonds present, and how do managers deal with these risks?

20. How do return volatilities for foreign bonds compare in local currency and in dollar terms?

21. What are the advantages and disadvantages of hedging currency risk when investing in nondollar bonds?

22. Describe the costs of hedging.

23. How did the emergence of programs such as the STRIPS program facilitate estimation of forward rates?

24. Describe practical problems of measuring forward rates from the term structure of interest rates.

25. Compare the IRR and PV methods of bond valuation.

26. The current yield curve for default-free pure discount (zero-coupon) bonds is as follows:

Maturity (years)	YTM
1	10%
2	11%
3	12%

(a) What are the implied one-year forward rates?

(b) Assume that the pure expectations hypothesis of the term structure is correct. If market expectations are accurate, what will the pure yield curve, that is, the yields to maturity on one- and two-year pure discount bonds, be next year?

(c) If you purchased a two-year pure discount bond now, what is the expected total rate of return over the next year? If it were a three-year pure discount bond? (*Hint:* Compute the current and expected future prices.) Ignore taxes.

(d) What should be the current price of the three-year maturity bond with a 12 percent coupon rate paid annually? If you purchased it at that price, what would your total expected rate of return be over the next year (coupon plus price change)? Ignore taxes.

27. Assume the following average yields on U.S. Treasury bonds at the present time:

Term to maturity	Yield
1 year	8.50%
2 years	8.90%
5 years	9.25%
9 years	9.75%
10 years	10.00%
15 years	11.25%
20 years	11.75%
25 years	12.25%

(a) Compute the forward rate for year 2 based on yields specified, assuming a pure expectations hypothesis of the term structure of interest rates.

28. Assume that the current structure of forward interest rates is upward-sloping. Which will have a lower yield to maturity:

(a) A 15-year zero-coupon bond or a 10-year zero-coupon bond?

(b) A 10-year 5 percent coupon bond or a 10-year 6 percent coupon bond?

29. If zero-coupon U.S. Treasury bonds sell today at $955 for the one-year maturity and $910 for the two-year maturity, what are the one-year forward rates for years 1 and 2?

30. How does a valuation of am embedded option in a bond differ from a valuation of a listed call option on a stock or market index?

31. Why does volatility of interest rates become a prime consideration when valuing bonds with embedded options?

32. Explain how the binomial option valuation model is appropriate for valuing embedded options.

33. Outline the general procedure for valuing an embedded bond option.

34. Assume an unanticipated decline in intrest rate volatility, what would be the expected impact on returns for corporates vis-à-vis governments? Explain.

PART SIX

Portfolio Performance Analysis

The objective of portfolio performance analysis is to assess how well the investment plan is meeting its goals as well as the degree to which investment managers are adding value in carrying out the investment plan. In making the assessment, we need a clear statement of the plan's goals to provide a guideline around which results can be measured. To evaluate managers, we need an understanding and explicit statement of the critical elements of the investment process to develop a framework for judging where and to what extent portfolio managers have enhanced value for the plan.

A measure that is basic to the performance appraisal process is the rate of return earned on the assets employed over a period of time. This return should be time-weighted to adjust for any cash flows in or out of the plan over the period. This calculation becomes complex and tedious where there are significant flows of cash. Prior to the early 1970s, there was no standard for computing returns in the United States. Outside of the United States, even now, calculated returns do not meet the time-weighted or other standards in many instances.

Though managers can be evaluated by comparing rates of return earned over a period, we also need to consider risk. We have seen that there is a risk-return relationship that is basic to capital markets. In assessing whether a manager is adding value, we need to determine to what extent returns were more or less than commensurate with risk. Capital market theory provides an explicit framework—Security Market Line—and measure—beta and standard deviation—for making such risk adjustments to return.

Beginning in the mid-1960s and continuing on to the present, academics have developed, refined, and empirically demonstrated the application of capital market–based methods of assessing the performance of portfolio managers. Following along with this development, investment management consultants have integrated risk adjustment procedures into their appraisal system for evaluating the performance of managers in their comparison universes. Most recently, mutual fund performance evaluation services that report to a wide range of institutional and individual investor clientele are including capital market–based measures in their performance appraisal reports.

Because of the complexity of multimanager programs and the wide variety of special styles purchased by managers, there is a growing awareness of the need to evaluate more aspects of the investment plan and process. Furthermore, there is a growing awareness that factors beyond market risk can have a significant impact on the performance of a plan and its managers. Return attribution provides the framework for considering how various factors interact to generate the performance of a plan over time and how those factors are now being used extensively by major plan sponsors and their consultants.

To ensure that the relevant aspects of performance are evaluated, we need an understanding of those investment process aspects that are significant in determining return. In this sense, designing the performance evaluation, which is a review of the past, is the flip side of the forward-looking process of managing the critical aspects of the investment process. Correspondingly, this final section of the book might be considered both a review as well as a preview of the portfolio management process..

CHAPTER 15

![line]

Evaluating Portfolio Performance

INTRODUCTION

This chapter is concerned with evaluating portfolio performance, which will be illustrated from two complementary, yet distinct, viewpoints. One focus of performance appraisal is with respect to evaluating the major aspects of the investment process including (1) asset allocation, (2) weighting shifts across major asset classes, and (3) security selection within asset classes. This evaluation is often referred to as a process of attribution and is of prime importance to major plan sponsors, such as corporate and public pension plans, endowments, and foundations, that have responsibility for coordinating these many aspects. We illustrate this aspect of performance evaluation by way of a hypothetical medium-sized pension fund that undertakes a comprehensive investment program.

In comparison many investors are concerned with evaluating the productivity of a particular investment strategy or investment organization. Mutual funds offer a great variety of well-defined strategies for investing in stocks, bonds, and money market instruments and are popular vehicles for meeting the needs of investors. To illustrate this aspect of performance evaluation, we focus on that class of mutual funds offering common stock strategies. Here we concentrate on the special way that return is calculated for these and other types of funds, as well as the various ways that risk can be incorporated in the appraisal of fund performance. We first focus on this aspect of performance evaluation and then illustrate the method of return attribution in the second part of the chapter.

EVALUATING INVESTMENT STRATEGIES

This first portion of the chapter focuses on evaluating investment strategies. In this evaluation we cover the method of calculating returns and discuss appropriate measures of risk. We not only discuss methods of comparing relative performance based only on rate of return, but we also consider measures—known as composite performance measures—that consider risk as well as return. We further discuss ways of analyzing the productivity of two major methods of generating above-average performance: market timing and stock selection.

We use investment companies as a vehicle to illustrate the methods of calculating these portfolio performance measures. The data for these funds are publicly available, standard-

TABLE 15-1
Risk-return relationship for mutual funds

Fund objective	1957–1968 bull market			1969–1974 bear market		
	Range of betas	Average beta	Average quarterly return	Range of betas	Average beta	Average quarterly return
Growth (12)	0.99–1.25	1.13	2.36	0.97–1.25	1.12	(1.65)
Income-growth (15)	0.80–1.07	0.92	1.81	0.80–1.10	0.95	(0.93)
Balanced (11)	0.58–0.91	0.76	1.27	0.70–0.92	0.78	(0.56)
S&P 500		1.00	1.74		1.00	(0.85)

Source: James L. Farrell, Jr., and Fischer Black, "Mutual Fund Performance," Unpublished studies, 1969, 1975

ized, and representative of the investment experience of professional portfolio managers. In addition to providing a representative example of the activities of professional portfolio managers, investment companies are interesting to study because of their ready availability as viable investment vehicles for individual as well as institutional investors.

MUTUAL FUND OBJECTIVES

Mutual funds pursue a variety of investment objectives that also appear to be consistent with differing risk levels, whether measured in terms of total risk (standard deviation) or in terms of systematic risk (beta). The data in Table 15-1 illustrate this variety for a universe of 38 large representative mutual funds classified into three broad categories: 12 growth funds, 15 income-growth funds, and 11 balanced funds.[1] The table shows beta as a measure of risk as well as average quarterly returns earned over two time periods: 1957–1968 and 1969–1974. The earlier time period represents a period of generally rising stock prices—a long-term bull market—whereas the latter period represents a period of generally declining stock prices—a long-term bear market. Using these two time periods allows us to evaluate the risk-return relationship over two widely differing stock market episodes, as well as to appraise the consistency of the risk-ranking measures over time.

Note that the average beta within each of the three fund categories was in line with what might be expected; growth funds showed the highest risk, balanced funds showed the lowest risk, and income-growth funds showed intermediate risk. Furthermore, the risk measures for the categories displayed stability between time periods; note that the average betas of the three categories were relatively similar between time periods. Finally, the individual fund betas were generally close to the average for the category, as indicated by the range of betas within each category. The calculated beta values for the three fund groupings are in line with the riskiness that is implied by the investment objective of the fund category.

In addition, the data in Table 15-1 show the risk-return relationship for two time periods: 1957–1968 and 1969–1974. Note that in the earlier period of generally rising stock prices, high-risk growth funds provided the highest average return, whereas low-risk balanced funds offered the lowest. Conversely, during the latter period of generally declining stock prices, high-risk growth funds showed the greatest losses, whereas low-risk balanced

---

[1]John McDonald, "Objectives and Performance of Mutual Funds, 1960–1969," *Journal of Financial and Quantitative Analysis* (June 1974) generated results similar to these using a sample of 123 mutual funds.

funds suffered the least losses. As expected, high risk was rewarded the most during the bull market but penalized the most during the bear market; low risk was rewarded the least in the bull market but penalized the least during the bear market.

These data, in turn, have implications for evaluating the performance of funds with disparate investment objectives. For example, growth funds will be at a disadvantage during a bear market such as occurred during the 1969–1974 period but will be favored during a bull market period such as occurred between 1957 and 1968. Evaluating funds with such differing investment objectives on the basis of rate-of-return-only comparisons can lead to an overestimate or underestimate of the real value of the performance of a fund. The return earned over a period of time by a fund will be heavily dependent on the risk profile of the fund and the market environment encountered over that period.

Thus, we need to evaluate the return that the fund earned in the context of the risk that was undertaken. One approach to this evaluation is first to group funds in equivalent risk categories and then to compare returns. When evaluating funds across differing risk levels, we need to specifically adjust return for the riskiness of the fund. Composite risk measures provide such a mechanism, and we describe these and other aspects of the performance evaluation problem in the following sections.

CALCULATING FUND RETURNS

The first step in evaluating the performance of investment managers is to calculate the rate of return earned over the relevant comparison period. As before, return is defined to include changes in the value of the fund over the performance period plus any income earned over that period. Returns for investment portfolios, however, can be distorted by fund cash flows—in or out—during the interim between valuations. In particular, contributions to the fund during a period of rising markets will inflate the value of the fund and hence the calculated rate of return, but withdrawals will reduce the value and calculated return. Conversely, contributions to the fund during a period of falling prices will reduce the return, but withdrawals would inflate the return comparison. Thus, the method of calculating returns is the same as presented throughout this text, except that adjustments must be made for contributions and withdrawals of cash.

Panel A at the top of Table 15-2 illustrates this phenomenon for a hypothetical fund that experiences a cash flow at the middle of the year. Note that the fund has a value of $800,000 at the beginning of the year and that this value increases to $880,000 by midyear. With a cash inflow of $220,000 at midyear and further appreciation to the end of the year, the fund value at the end of the year is $1,320,000. The percentage change in fund value over the year, including the cash flow, would be 65% as compared with a change in value of 32% if there had been no interim cash flow.

Because the manager usually has no control over the timing of these flows, it is necessary to adjust for interim cash flows to properly evaluate the skill of the manager. One technique is to calculate a return at the time of each cash flow and then link (compound) these returns to derive what is known as a time-weighted return over the period of interest. Panel B of Table 15-2 illustrates that we adjust the return by separately calculating a return of 10% (880,000/800,000) for the first six months of the year, and a 20% return for the second six months after the receipt of the cash flow.

Linking or compounding these two six-month returns provides a time-weighted return of 32 percent that is the appropriate measure of return for the manager. That is,

TABLE 15-2
Calculating the rate of return

	Period	
	1st half	2nd half
Panel A:		
Beginning value	$800,000	$880,000
Cash flow	0	$220,000
Amount invested	$800,000	$1,100,000
Ending value	$880,000	$1,320,000
Change in value	10%	50%
Change in value over full year		65%
Panel B:		
Earned return per period	10%	20%
Time weighted return over		
periods 1 and 2		32%
Panel C:		
Units outstanding	800 units	1,000 units
Beginning unit value	$1,000	$1,100
Ending unit value	$1,000	$1,320
Change in unit value	10%	20%
Change in value over full year		32%

$$1.10 \times 1.20 = 1.32 - 1 = 32\%$$

A second way to adjust for cash inflows and outflows to the fund is to use the unit value method. When cash inflows occur, new units are issued, and when cash outflows occur, units are retired. As a result, the number of units change when cash flows occur, but the value per unit remains constant. Again using our hypothetical fund and assuming 800 units outstanding at the beginning of the year, the value per unit or net asset value would be $1000 at the beginning of the year and $1100 at June 30. With cash flow of $220,000 at July 1, 200 additional units would be issued so that the value per unit would remain $1100 at the beginning of the second half of the year. At the end of the year the total value of the fund would be $1,320,000, but the net asset value (NAV) would be $1320 because 1000 units are outstanding rather than the 800 at the beginning. The NAV of $1320 at the end of the year compared with the NAV of $1000 at the beginning of the year obviously results in a return of 32% for the year.

Mutual funds use the unit-value method so that cash flows result in changes in units, but not net asset value. As a result, evaluation of mutual fund performance can directly use beginning- and ending-period net asset values when calculating returns. The one period rate of return r_p for a mutual fund is then simply defined as the change in net asset value NAV, plus its cash disbursements D and capital gains disbursements C, and is calculated as follows:

$$r_p = \frac{(\text{NAV}_t - \text{NAV}_{t-1}) + D_t + C_t}{\text{NAV}_{t-1}}$$

This is the same as the holding-period formula that we have illustrated in prior chapters, the only difference being that explicit provision needs to be made for capital gains distributions.

Using this method, we calculated returns for a universe of mutual funds for the three-year 1993–1995 period, which are shown in Table 15-3. The funds shown in the table are 25 of the largest all-stock mutual funds with a history of performance over the full 1993–1995 period. These funds should be representative of the investment performance of large, stock-oriented mutual funds. Also shown is the return by the S&P 500 over the same period to provide a benchmark of performance.

Note that the funds are ranked from highest to lowest with respect to return earned over the period. Eleven funds had a higher return than the S&P 500, and fourteen funds had a lower return over the period. As noted before, however, a straight rate-of-return comparison in evaluating performance is incomplete. The differential return earned could have been due entirely to the differential risk exposure of the funds. The following sections describe some techniques for adjusting for risk and determining whether return earned is greater or less than expected for the fund given the risk incurred.

RISK-ADJUSTED PERFORMANCE

The comparisons in Table 15-3 provide a useful perspective on performance but are based only on rate of return. Because the differential return earned by a manager may be due to a difference in the exposure to risk from that of the index or typical manager, there would be merit in attempting to adjust the return for any differences in risk exposure. For this purpose, there are essentially three major methods of assessing risk-adjusted performance: (1) return per unit of risk, (2) differential return, and (3) components of performance. These methods are interrelated and evolve out of the sort of risk-return theory described in Chapters 2, 3, and 4 of this book.

Return per Unit of Risk

The first of the risk-adjusted performance measures is the type that assesses the performance of a fund in terms of return per unit of risk. The technique here is to relate the absolute level of return achieved to the level of risk incurred to develop a relative risk–adjusted measure for ranking fund performance. According to this method, funds that provide the highest return per unit of risk would be judged as having provided the best performance, and those providing the lowest return per unit of risk would be judged as the poorest performers.

Figure 15-1 is a risk-return diagram illustrating the reason that return per unit of risk is an appropriate standard for judging performance. The vertical axis represents return, and the horizontal axis represents risk, which for our current purpose we interpret in a generalized sense to represent either standard deviation or beta. The diagram shows the plots for three funds, designated A, M, and Z, where the fund M represents the market fund (say the S&P 500) and funds A and Z are hypothetical funds.

Note that fund Z provides the highest absolute return, fund A provides the lowest return, and fund M provides an intermediate return. Fund A, however, ranks highest in terms of return per unit of risk, fund Z ranks the lowest, and fund M ranks at an intermediate level.

TABLE 15-3
Mutual fund rate of return (1993–1995)

	Fund Name	Investment Objective	Total Returns, Annualized, 3 year
1	Fidelity Magellan	Growth	18.75
2	Brandywin	Growth	18.51
3	Fidelity Growth & Income	Growth and Income	18.28
4	Mutual Shares	Growth and Income	17.76
5	Fundamental Investors	Growth and Income	17.13
6	Washington Mutual Investors	Growth and Income	17.06
7	Fidelity Growth Company	Growth	16.62
8	Putnam Fund for Growth & Income A	Growth and Income	15.94
9	Scudder Growth & Income	Growth and Income	15.87
10	Vanguard/Windsor	Growth and Income	15.76
11	Affiliated	Growth and Income	15.73
12	T. Rowe Price Growth Stock	Growth	15.15
13	American Mutual	Growth and Income	14.64
14	IDS New Dimensions A	Growth	14.47
15	New Economy	Growth	14.38
16	Dean Witter Dividend Growth	Growth and Income	14.25
17	Growth Fund of America	Growth	14.13
18	Investment Comp of America	Growth and Income	13.45
19	Pioneer	Growth and Income	12.88
20	Amcap	Growth	12.54
21	Janus	Growth	12.39
22	Vanguard U.S. Growth	Growth	12.33
23	Nicholas	Growth	11.68
24	Dreyfus	Growth and Income	8.02
25	20th Century Growth Investor	Growth	7.15
	S&P 500 Index		15.34

Source: Homingstar, Chicago, Ill.

As shown in Chapter 3,[2] assuming that investors can borrow or lend freely at the risk-free rate return r_f, it is possible to attain any point along the line from r_f through the plot of fund A. Investors should prefer line (r_fA) by borrowing and lending by investing in funds M and Z, which is because the line r_fA provides a higher return at all levels of risk than the line r_fM, which, in turn, dominates the line r_fZ.

There are two alternative, yet similar, methods of measuring returns per unit of risk: (1) the reward-to-variability ratio developed by William Sharpe, referred to as the Sharpe ratio,[3] and (2) the reward-to-volatility ratio developed by Jack Treynor, referred to as the Treynor ratio.[4] The Sharpe ratio is simply the ratio of the reward, defined as the realized

---

[2]This process is directly analogous to the borrowing and lending mechanism used to construct the capital market line and which was described in Chapter 3. In this case, the investor constructs his or her own market line by borrowing and lending in combination with the most desirable portfolio and then by being positioned at the desired risk level to attain the highest return per unit of risk.

[3]William F. Sharpe, "Mutual Fund Performance," *Journal of Business* (January 1966), pp. 119–138.

[4]Jack L. Treynor, "How to Rate Management of Investment Funds," *Harvard Business Review* (January–February 1965), pp. 63–70.

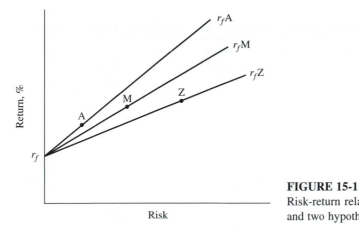

y-axis: Return, %

x-axis: Risk

Labels on lines: r_fA, r_fM, r_fZ

Points: A, M, Z

r_f

FIGURE 15-1
Risk-return relationship: market portfolio and two hypothetical portfolios.

portfolio return r_p in excess of the risk-free rate, to the variability of return as measured by the standard deviation of return (σ_p). The Treynor ratio is the ratio of the reward, also defined as the realized portfolio return r_p in excess of the risk-free rate r_f, to the volatility of return as measured instead by the portfolio beta (β_p).

$$\text{Sharpe ratio (SR)} = \frac{r_p - r_f}{\sigma_p}$$

$$\text{Treynor ratio (TR)} = \frac{r_p - r_f}{\beta_p}$$

The two performance ratios thus differ only in that one considers total risk as measured by standard deviation, but the other considers only market risk as measured by beta. Recall from the discussion in Chapter 3 that the standard deviation as a measure of total risk is appropriate when evaluating the risk-return relationship for well-diversified portfolios and when ranking portfolio performance. On the other hand, when we evaluate fully diversified portfolios or individual stocks, a relevant measure of risk may be the beta coefficient, as discussed in previous chapters.

The appropriate measure of return per unit of risk to use will, therefore, depend on the view held as to the relevant risk measure. For those investors where the portfolio being evaluated constitutes the total or predominant representation in the particular asset class, the total variability of return as measured by standard deviation should be the relevant risk measure. On the other hand, for some investors the portfolio being evaluated is only one component of the investor's representation in the asset class; for example, major pension plan sponsors generally, because of their size, use several managers within an asset class. For those investors employing a multimanager strategy, the beta coefficient may be the appropriate measure of risk.

Table 15-4 illustrates the calculation of the two return-per-unit-of-risk measures using the two hypothetical funds—A and Z—along with the market fund as a benchmark for comparison. Note that the market fund provided a 0.333 return per unit of standard deviation and exceeded the Sharpe ratio of 0.250 return provided for Z, but it was below the Sharpe ratio of 0.400 provided for fund A. According to the reward-to-volatility ratio, the market fund provided a return per unit of beta of 7, which again exceeded the Treynor ratio of 6 for

TABLE 15-4
Calculation of risk-per-unit-of-return ratios: market fund and two hypothetical funds

Fund	Return r_p, %	Risk-free rate r_f, %	Excess return $r_p - r_f$, %	Standard deviation σ_p, %	Sharpe ratio $r_p - r_f/\sigma_p$	Beta (β_p)	Treynor ratio $r_p - r_f/\beta_p$
A	8	2	6	15	0.400	0.67	9.0
M	9	2	7	21	0.333	1.00	7.0
Z	10	2	8	32	0.250	1.33	6.0

fund Z but was below the Treynor ratio of 9 derived for fund A. Using either measure, the ranking of the funds was identical: fund A the best, fund Z the worst, and the market fund an intermediate performer.

As a matter of fact, the ranking according to both measures—reward to variability and reward to volatility—will be identical when the funds under consideration are perfectly diversified or, for all practical purposes, when the funds are highly diversified.[5] The rankings of the two measures may, however, diverge as the funds being appraised are less highly diversified. For example, a poorly diversified fund that ranks high on the reward-to-volatility ratio compared with another fund that is highly diversified will rank less favorably and may, in fact, rank lower on the basis of the reward-to-variability ratio, because the less diversified fund will show relatively greater risk when using the standard deviation than the better diversified fund.

Differential Return (Alpha)

A second category of risk-adjusted performance measures is the type referred to as differential return measures, which are directly related to the discussion in Chapter 3 concerning the calculation of ex post security market lines. The underlying objective of this technique is to calculate the return that should be expected for the fund, given the realized risk of the fund, and to compare that with the return actually realized over the period. In making this comparison, we assume that the investor has a passive or naive alternative of merely buying the market portfolio and adjusting for the appropriate level of risk by borrowing or lending at the risk-free rate. Given this assumption, the most commonly used method of determining the return that should have been earned by the fund at a given level of risk is by way of the ex post alpha formulation:

$$N(\bar{r}_p) = r_f + \beta_p(r_m - r_f)$$

$$\alpha_p = \bar{r}_p - N(\bar{r}_p)$$

Note that the top formula is similar in form to the formula for the security market line (SML) that was described in Chapter 3. The differences are that the variables are expressed in terms of realized returns and risk rather than ex ante variables as would be appropriate for the SML and that $N(\bar{r}_p)$ represents expected return given β_p. The bottom formula shows

---

[5]Note that the hypothetical funds, though not perfectly diversified, are sufficiently highly diversified so that the relative ranking does not change as the measurement standard differs.

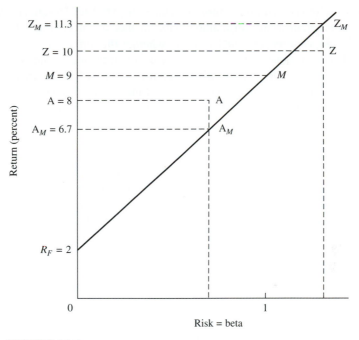

FIGURE 15-2
Differential return: funds A and Z.

alpha (α_p) as the difference between actual return and expected return. The equation is graphically represented as the line r_fM in Figure 15-2. Also shown in the figure are the two hypothetical funds—A and Z—from the preceding section that we can use to illustrate use of the equation for performance evaluation.

To evaluate the performance of fund A we would insert the appropriate variable from Table 15-4 into the formulas:

$$N(\bar{r}_p) = 2\% + 0.67(9\% - 2\%) = 6.7\%$$

$$\alpha_p = \bar{r}_p - N(\bar{r}_p) = 8.0\% - 6.7\% = 1.3\%$$

With this data, fund A would have been expected to earn 6.7 percent over the period, whereas it actually earned 8 percent as indicated in Table 15-4, thus providing a differential or risk-adjusted return of 1.3 percent. This difference is represented graphically as the distance A, A_M in Figure 15-2.

Similarly, we can evaluate the performance of fund Z by also inserting the appropriate variables from Table 15-4 into the formula

$$R_p = 2\% + 1.33(9\% - 2\%)$$

$$R_p = 11.3\%$$

Given this data, fund Z would have been expected to earn 11.3 percent over the period, whereas the fund actually earned 10 percent as indicated in Table 15-4, thus providing a differential or risk-adjusted return of -1.3 percent. This difference is presented graphically as the distance Z, Z_M in Figure 15-2.

This measure of risk-adjusted return, developed by Michael Jensen, is sometimes referred to as the Jensen measure.[6] In addition to this method of calculating differential return Jensen also developed a means of determining whether the differential return could have occurred by chance or whether it is significantly different from zero in a statistical sense, which is possible because, in practice, the Jensen measure is ordinarily derived by running a regression of monthly or quarterly returns of the fund being evaluated against the return of a market index over the relevant performance period. The regression equation usually takes the following form:

$$r_p - r_f = \alpha_p + \beta_p(r_M - r_f) + e$$

Note that the regression equation is the same as the previous equation, except that an intercept (alpha) term and an error term e have been added. The error term allows us to assess how well the regression equation fits the data—a low error indicating a well-defined relationship and a high error indicating a poorly defined relationship. The intercept term measures the extent to which the fund under evaluation gave an above-average or a below-average performance—a negative value indicating below-average performance and a positive value above-average performance.

The alpha value can in turn be tested by statistical methods for its degree of significance from a value of zero. The measure for this degree of significance is the t value, which is merely the alpha value divided by the error of the regression. When the alpha value is high and the error in the regression is low, the t value will be high, and when the alpha value is low and regression error high, the t value will be low. A t value in excess of 2 is strongly indicative that the performance, either positive or negative, is highly significant in a statistical sense; that is, there is a small probability that the performance results from chance. For the two hypothetical funds, the t value of $+2.5$ for fund A indicated that the performance was above average and significantly so in a statistical sense, whereas the t value of -1.0 for fund Z indicated that its below-average performance could have occurred by chance.

Comparison of Performance Measures

Table 15-5 demonstrates the calculation of risk-adjusted returns for the three-year period of 1993–1995 for a sample of 25 mutual funds, as well as for the S&P 500, which is the benchmark for the comparison. The mutual funds list includes those with assets over $2 billion, with 12 classified as having an investment objective of growth (G), and the other 13 classified as having an investment objective of growth with income (IG). The data is thus generally representative of the investment behavior of large, all-stock mutual funds over this performance period.

Note that the table shows the returns earned by the funds as well as the standard deviations and betas of the funds over the three-year period. It also gives the R^2 of the fund as a measure of the degree of diversification. The last three columns show the ratios of reward to variability, the ratios of reward to volatility, and the differential returns of the funds. The

---

[6]Michael C. Jensen, "The Performance of Mutual Funds in the Period 1945–1964," *Journal of Finance* (May 1968), pp. 389–416.

TABLE 15-5

Comparison of risk-adjusted performance measure for large all-stock mutual funds with the S&P 500, 1993–1995

	Fund Name	Investment Objective	Total Return Annualized 3 year	Std Dev 3 Yr	Beta 3 year	R2 3 Yr	Sharpe ratio	Treynor Ratio	Alpha 3 year
1	20th Century Growth Investor	Growth	7.15	11.99	1.06	52	0.29(25)	1.93(25)	−7.44(25)
2	Affiliated	Growth and Income	15.73	7.79	0.87	84	1.39(7)	12.22(8)	1.67(8)
3	Amcap	Growth	12.54	8.88	0.96	77	0.91(22)	7.75(22)	−1.93(23)
4	American Mutual	Growth and Income	14.64	6.83	0.77	85	1.43(5)	12.39(7)	1.73(7)
5	Brandywine	Growth	18.51	14.02	1	34	0.99(19)	13.41(3)	3.46(3)
6	Dean Witter Dividend Growth	Growth and Income	14.25	7.71	0.89	89	1.23(10)	10.28(14)	0.19(14)
7	Dreyfus	Growth and Income	8.02	8.68	0.97	84	0.45(24)	3.01(24)	−6.09(24)
8	Fidelity Growth & Income	Growth and Income	18.28	7.67	0.85	83	1.7(1)	15.51(2)	4.13(2)
9	Fidelity Growth Company	Growth	16.62	10.84	1	57	1.1(14)	11.52(10)	1.35(10)
10	Fidelity Magellan	Growth	18.75	11.13	1.05	58	1.23(10)	13.00(5)	2.8(4)
11	Fundamental Investors	Growth and Income	17.13	7.95	0.92	90	1.52(3)	13.08(4)	2.4(5)
12	Growth Fund of America	Growth	14.13	9.51	0.94	66	1(17)	9.61(17)	−0.36(17)
13	IDS New Dimensions A	Growth	14.47	9.87	1.07	78	1(18)	8.76(19)	−1.32(20)
14	Investment Comp of America	Growth and Income	13.45	7.51	0.89	95	1.17(13)	9.38(18)	−0.59(18)
15	Janus	Growth	12.39	7.33	0.83	87	1.07(16)	8.78(20)	−0.91(19)
16	Mutual Shares	Growth and income	17.76	7.87	0.79	68	1.6(2)	16.03(1)	4.34(1)
17	New Economy	Growth	14.38	10.45	0.96	56	0.94(20)	9.67(16)	−0.21(16)
18	Nicholas	Growth	11.68	8.25	0.87	76	0.88(23)	7.56(23)	−1.89(22)
19	Pioneer	Growth and Income	12.88	6.78	0.79	90	1.21(12)	9.85(15)	−0.03(15)
20	Putnam Fund for Growth & Income	Growth and Income	15.94	7.89	0.92	91	1.4(6)	11.78(9)	1.39(9)
21	Scudder Growth & Income	Growth and Income	15.87	8.42	0.94	82	1.31(8)	11.46(11)	1.16(11)
22	T. Rowe Price Growth Stock	Growth	15.15	8.51	0.93	80	1.22(11)	10.81(13)	0.59(13)
23	Vanguard U.S. Growth	Growth	12.33	8.52	0.89	74	0.92(21)	8.12(21)	−1.43(21)
24	Vanguard/Windsor	Growth and Income	15.76	10.12	0.97	61	1.09(15)	10.99(12)	0.86(12)
25	Washington Mutual Investors	Growth and Income	17.06	8.44	0.93	81	1.43(4)	12.86(6)	2.33(6)
	AVERAGE		14.59	8.92	0.92	75	1.14	10.39	1.31
	S&P 500 Index		15.34	1.31	0.00	1.00	1.00	7.84	10.24

Source: Morningstar, Chicago, Ill.

numbers in parentheses show the ranking of the individual funds according to each of the
three risk-adjusted return measures.

Note that the realized return of the funds ranges between 7.1% and 18.7%, with an
average of 14.6%, which was somewhat below that of the S&P 500 for the period. The
betas of the funds range between 0.77 and 1.07, with an average of 0.92, slightly lower than
that of the market as represented by the S&P 500. Note that the R^2 of the funds are all less
than 1, averaging around 0.75, and thereby indicating that the funds are less than perfectly
diversified. As a result the riskiness of the funds is relatively larger when measured by
the standard deviation than by the beta coefficient. Over the period, the average standard
deviation of the funds is 8.92%, 1.14 times the 7.84% standard deviation of the market.

The performance of the individual funds is consistent for alternative Treynor & alpha
measures, as can be seen by the fact that the performance ranking of the funds is fairly
similar with respect to both measures. For some less well-diversified funds with low R^2
values the ranking by the Sharpe measures differs significantly from that of the other two
measures. Using the reward-to-variability ratio, 8 of the 25 funds have a better ratio than
the market, but the reward-to-volatility ratio shows 14 of the 25 funds giving better risk-
adjusted performances than the market. On the basis of differential return, 14 funds show a
positive return, with four funds having t values (not shown) in excess of 2, thereby indicating
a statistically significant performance according to this measure.[7]

COMPONENTS OF INVESTMENT PERFORMANCE

The measures of risk-adjusted performance discussed in the previous section are primarily
oriented to an analysis of the overall performance of a fund. For some purposes it will be
useful to develop a more refined breakdown and assess the components, or sources, of performance. Eugene Fama has provided an analytical framework that elaborates on the three
previously discussed risk-adjusted return methods and allows a more detailed breakdown
of a fund's performance.[8]

Figure 15-3 is a risk-return diagram from the Fama study illustrating that framework of
performance analysis. The vertical axis, as is usual, refers to return, and the horizontal axis
shows risk measured in terms of both beta coefficient and standard deviation of return. Use
of these two risk measures allows us to evaluate the performance of the fund both in terms
of market risk and total risk. The diagonal line plotted on the diagram is the equation of the
security market line (SML), using the data from Table 15-4 in the previous section, a market
return r_M of 9 percent, and a risk-free rate r_f of 2 percent. It again provides the benchmark
for assessing whether the realized return is more or less than commensurate with the risk
incurred.

For purposes of illustration the data for the realized return ($r_A = 8$ percent) and market risk ($\beta_A = 0.67$) on hypothetical fund A, also shown in Table 15-4, are plotted on the

---

[7]Mutual funds as a group did somewhat less well than market over this period; however, the period of evaluation
is so short that it would not be appropriate to draw firm conclusions about the relative superiority or inferiority of
the funds.

[8]Eugene Fama, "Components of Investment Performance," *Journal of Finance* (June 1972), pp. 551–567.

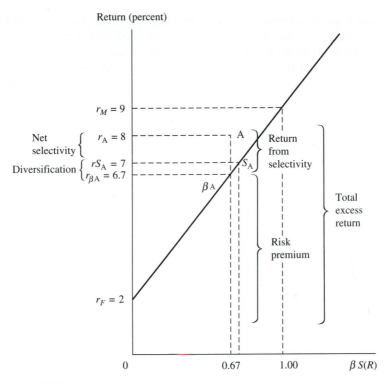

Return (percent)

$r_M = 9$

Net
selectivity $\left\{ \vphantom{\begin{matrix}r_A\\r\end{matrix}} \right.$ $r_A = 8$ A

Diversification $\left\{ \begin{matrix} rS_A = 7 \\ r_{\beta A} = 6.7 \end{matrix} \right.$

S_A

β_A

Return
from
selectivity

Risk
premium

Total
excess
return

$r_F = 2$

0   0.67   1.00 $\beta\ S(R)$

FIGURE 15-3
Decomposition of performance. (*Source:* Eugene F. Fama, "Components of
Investment Performance," *Journal of Finance,* June 1972, pp. 551–567.)

diagram and designated point A. The diagram shows that at the fund's market-risk level β_A,
it would have been expected to earn the return $r\beta_A = 6.7$ percent. This expected return is
composed of a risk-free component of 2 percent, shown as the distance from the baseline to
r_f, and a risk premium of 4.7 percent, shown as the distance between r_f and $r\beta_A$. The fund
actually earned a return of 8 percent, which was 1.3 percent greater than expected, shown
as the distance $r\beta_A$ to r_A. We can designate this incremental return as the return to stock
selectivity.

STOCK SELECTION

Using the following framework we can examine the overall performance of the fund in
terms of superior or inferior stock selection and the normal return associated with a given
level of risk:

$$\text{Total excess return} = \text{selectivity} + \text{risk}$$

$$r_A - r_f = (r_A - r(\beta_A) + r(\beta_A) - r_f)$$

$$8\% - 2\% = (8\% - 6.7\%) + (6.7\% - 2\%)$$

$$6\% = 1.3\% + 4.7\%$$

In striving to achieve above-average returns, managers will generally have to forsake some diversification, which will have its cost in terms of additional portfolio risk. We can use this framework to determine the added return that should be expected to compensate for this additional lack of diversification risk. We do this determination by first using the capital market line equation (CML) to determine the return commensurate with the total risk incurred as measured by the standard deviation. Again, using data from Table 15-4, the standard deviation of the market σ_m is 21 percent, the standard deviation of fund A (σ_A) is 15 percent, and risk-free rate and market return are the same as before. We can determine the normal return for fund A, $r(\sigma_A)$ using total risk as follows:

$$r(\sigma_A) = r_f + (r_m - r_f)\sigma_A/\sigma_m$$

$$= 2\% + (9\% - 2\%)15\%/21\%$$

$$= 7\%$$

The difference between this return of 7 percent and that expected when only considering market risk $r(\beta_A)$ of 6.7 percent is the added return for diversification, $r(\sigma_A) - r(\beta_A)$ or, in this case, $7\% - 6.7\% = 0.3\%$. In terms of the diagram, it is the distance $r(\beta_A)$ to $r(\sigma_A)$. The net selectivity of the fund then becomes the overall selectivity less whatever penalty or added return is needed to compensate for the diversification risk. The diagram shows that the net selectivity of the fund is the distance $r_A - r(\sigma_A)$. In terms of formulation the net selectivity can be shown as follows:

$$\text{Net Selectivity} = [r_A - r(\beta_A)] - [r(\sigma_A) - r(\beta_A)]$$

$$= (8\% - 6.7\%) - (7\% - 6.7\%)$$

$$= 1.3\% - 0.3\%$$

$$= 1.0\%$$

Because the diversification measure is always nonnegative, net selectivity will always be equal to or less than selectivity.[9] The two will be equal only when the portfolio is completely diversified, as would be indicated by an R^2 with the market of 1.00. By comparing the R^2's of funds we can obtain a quick indication of the degree of diversification risk incurred by a fund. Funds with high R^2's, say 0.95 and above, have relatively little diversification risk, but funds with relatively low R^2's, say 0.90 and below, have relatively large diversification risk.

To conclude this section we use the Fama components of performance framework to evaluate the mutual funds shown in Table 15-6. These are the same funds that we used in previous comparisons of risk-adjusted performance. Note that the table breaks down each of the funds' overall performance into that due to selectivity and the component due to risk. It further shows the expected return due to diversification, and from that derives the net selectivity of the fund (return from selectivity − diversification = net selectivity).

Note that all the funds, as would be expected, are less than perfectly diversified—R^2 less than 1.0—and as a result require added return to compensate for diversification risk.

---

[9] The Fama framework of analysis allows further and more elaborate comparisons. However, for our purposes, the one dealing with stock selectivity is most pertinent.

TABLE 15-6
Components of performance—large all-stock mutual funds (1993–1995)

	Fund Name	Investment Objective	(2) EXCESS RETURN	(3) RISK PREMIUM	(4) RETURN FROM SELECTIVITY	(5) DIVERSIFICATION	(6) NET SELECTIVITY
1	20th Century Growth Investor	Growth	2.05	10.85	−8.80	4.81	−13.61
2	Affiliated	Growth and Income	10.63	8.91	1.72	1.27	0.46
3	Amcap	Growth	7.44	9.83	−2.39	1.77	−4.16
4	American Mutual	Growth and Income	9.54	7.88	1.66	1.04	0.62
5	Brandywine	Growth	13.41	10.24	3.17	8.07	−4.90
6	Dean Witter Dividend Growth	Growth and Income	9.15	9.11	0.04	0.96	−0.92
7	Dreyfus	Growth and Income	2.92	9.93	−7.01	1.40	−8.42
8	Fidelity Growth & Income	Growth and Income	13.18	8.70	4.48	1.31	3.16
9	Fidelity Growth Company	Growth	11.52	10.24	1.28	3.92	−2.64
10	Fidelity Magellan	Growth	13.65	10.75	2.90	3.79	−0.89
11	Fundamental Investors	Growth and Income	12.03	9.42	2.61	0.96	1.65
12	Growth Fund of America	Growth	9.03	9.63	−0.60	2.80	−3.39
13	IDS New Dimensions A	Growth	9.37	10.96	−1.59	1.93	−3.52
14	Investment Comp of America	Growth and Income	8.35	9.11	−0.76	0.70	−1.46
15	Janus	Growth	7.29	8.50	−1.21	1.07	−2.28
16	Mutual Shares	Growth and Income	12.66	8.09	4.57	2.19	2.38
17	New Economy	Growth	9.28	9.83	−0.55	3.82	−4.37
18	Nicholas	Growth	6.58	8.91	−2.33	1.87	−4.20
19	Pioneer	Growth and Income	7.78	8.09	−0.31	0.77	−1.08
202	Putnam Fund for Growth & Income	Growth and Income	10.84	9.42	1.42	0.88	0.53
21	Scudder Growth & Income	Growth and Income	10.77	9.63	1.14	1.37	−0.23
22	T. Rowe Price Growth Stock	Growth	10.05	9.52	0.53	1.59	−1.07
23	Vanguard U.S. Growth	Growth	7.23	9.11	−1.88	2.01	−3.90
24	Vanguard/Windsor	Growth and Income	10.66	9.93	0.73	3.29	−2.56
25	Washington Mutual Investors	Growth and Income	11.96	9.52	2.44	1.50	0.94
	AVERAGE		9.49	9.45	0.05	2.20	−2.15
	S&P 500 Index		10.24	10.24	0.00	0.00	0.00

Source: Morningstar, Chicago, Ill.

The required return ranges from 0.70% to 8.07%, with an average of 2.20% for the sample of funds. After adjusting for diversification risk the funds on average showed a net return to selectivity of -2.15% with a high of 3.16% and a low of −13.61%. This return compares with an average gross return to selectivity of 0.05% with a low of −8.80% and high of 4.57%. The appropriate yardstick of performance—gross or net selectivity—will, of course, depend on whether the investor evaluates the performance of the fund manager as a single or multiple manager.

MARKET TIMING

The previous section focused on the capability of managers in generating superior performance by means of stock selection techniques. Managers can also generate superior performance by timing the stock market correctly—that is, by correctly assessing the direction of the market, either bull or bear, and positioning the portfolio accordingly. Managers who forecast a declining market can position a portfolio properly by increasing the cash percentage of the portfolio or by decreasing the beta of the equity portion of the portfolio. Conversely, a forecast of a rising market would call for reduction in the cash position or an increase in the beta of the equity portion of the portfolio.

One method for diagnosing the success of managers in this endeavor is simply to look directly at the way fund return behaves relative to the return of the market. This method involves calculating a series of returns for the fund and a market index over a relevant performance period and plotting these on a scatter diagram. For example, we could calculate quarterly returns for a fund and for the S&P 500 over, say, the 10-year period ending in 1983 and plot them on a scatter diagram. Given these plots, we could then fit a characteristic line that represents the relationship between the portfolio and the index and that allows for an analysis of market timing.

If the fund did not engage in market timing and concentrated only on stock selection, the average beta of the portfolio should be fairly constant, and a plotting of fund return against market return would show a linear relationship as illustrated in Figure 15-4a. If the manager changed the beta or cash position of the portfolio over time but was unsuccessful in properly assessing the direction of the market, the plotting would still show a linear relationship. The unsuccessful market timing activity would merely introduce an additional scatter to the plots around the fitted relationship.

On the other hand, if the manager was able to assess the market direction successfully and change the portfolio beta accordingly, we would observe the sort of relationship shown in Figure 15-4b. When the market increases substantially, such a fund has a higher-than-normal beta, and it tends to do better than it would otherwise. However, when the market declines, the fund has a lower-than-normal beta, and it declines less than it would otherwise. Therefore, the plotted points would be above the linear relationship at both high and low levels of market returns, giving a curvature to the scatter of points. To describe this relationship more properly, we need to add a quadratic term to the simple linear relationship:[10]

[10]Jack L. Treynor and Kay Masuy. "Can't Mutual Funds Outguess the Market?" *Harvard Business Review* (July–August 1966), pp. 131–136.

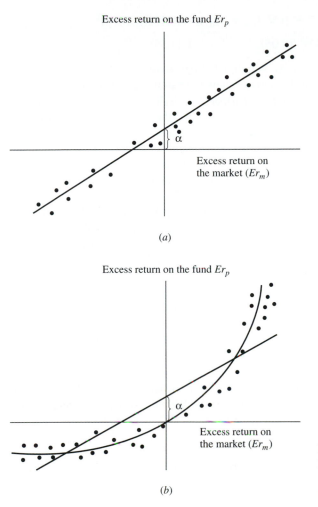

Excess return on the fund Er_p

Excess return on
the market (Er_m)

α

(a)

Excess return on the fund Er_p

α

Excess return on
the market (Er_m)

(b)

FIGURE 15-4
Fund returns vs. market return for
(a) superior stock selection and
(b) superior market timing.

$$r_p - r_f = a + b(r_m - r_f) + c(r_m - r_f)^2$$

where r_p = return of the fund
r_f = risk-free return
r_m = return on the market index
a, b, c = values to be estimated by regression analysis

To illustrate, we focus on the performance of a method of tactical asset allocation (TAA) pioneered by William Fouse, chairman of Mellon Capital Management. This organization uses TAA to manage several portfolios with over a billion dollars of assets and continues as one of the leaders in this investment specialty. Mellon Capital's Fouse method not only is representative of the sort of TAA approaches described in Chapter 11, but it also has the longest performance record, stretching back to 1973. Using quarterly data from 1973 to 1990 provides us with an extensive period to fit the quadratic regression. The following shows the estimated parameters from this regression:

$$r_p - r_f = 0.067 + 0.56\,[r_m - r_f] + 0.0125\,[r_m - r_f]^2$$

$$(0.542) \quad (0.05) \qquad\qquad (0.0035)$$

Note that the quadratic parameter (c value) is both positive at 0.0125, as well as sig-nificant with a t value of 3.6; standard errors are shown in parentheses below the parameter estimates. A significantly positive quadratic parameter is indicative of successful timing of the market over the period of analysis. Correspondingly, the estimated alpha parameter (intercept value) is not significantly different from zero and is indicative of neither value added to or subtracted from stock selection. This statistical result is reassuring as the orga-nization allocates assets across money market instruments and index funds of stocks and bonds. These passive asset class vehicles should, by construction, have no significant secu-rity selection component.

Figure 15-5 shows the plotted quadratic relationship for the 1973–1990 performance data. The figure indicates that the fitted curve becomes steeper as one moves to the right of the diagram and verifies that fund movements were amplified on the upside and dampened on the downside, relative to the market, which verifies that the fund manager was anticipat-ing market changes properly and that the superior performance of that fund can be attributed to skill in timing the market.

An alternative way to evaluate the changing beta of a portfolio is to fit two character-istic lines to the realized portfolio returns as illustrated in Figure 15-6. One line is fitted for periods when the market is up ($R_m > R_f$), and another line is fitted for periods when the market is down ($R_m < R_f$). A successful market timer should have a high beta during up markets and a low beta during down markets. Graphically, for the successful market timer the slope of the fitted characteristic line for up market periods will be greater than the slope of the fitted characteristic line for down-market periods. We can estimate this relationship

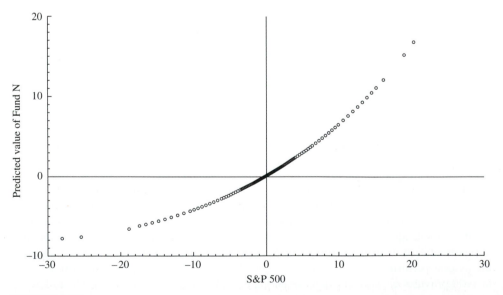

FIGURE 15-5
Relationship between fund and market.

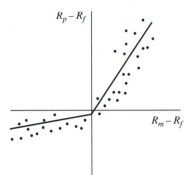

FIGURE 15-6
Dummy variable regression.

statistically by incorporating a dummy variable into the usual regression equation.

$$R_p - R_f = a + b[R_m - R_f] + c[R_m - R_f]D + e_p$$

In this equation, D is a dummy variable that is assigned a value of zero for periods when the market is rising ($R_m > R_f$) and a value of -1 for periods when the market is declining ($R_m < R_f$). As a result, the parameter (b) in the equation is representative of beta of this portfolio during periods of rising markets. For such periods the equation collapses to a simple formulation, because $D = 0$.

$$R_p - R_f = a + b[R_m - R_f]$$

The right-hand portion of Figure 15-6 represents the portion of the characteristic line fitted by this formulation, and the left-hand portion represents the portion during declining markets when $D = -1$ and the equation becomes the following form:

$$R_p - R_f = a + (b - c)[R_m - R_f]$$

Note that the slope in down markets is ($b - c$), and for a successful market timer the c parameter should be positive. As a result, successful market timing would be shown by a down-market slope ($b - c$) that is significantly less than the up-market slope (b). To illustrate this analysis, we again use quarterly data over the 1973–1990 period for Mellon Capital's Fouse method to estimate parameters in the dummy variable regression.

$$R_p - R_f = -0.78 + 0.80\,[R_m - R_f] + 0.52\,[D(R_m - R_f)]$$
$$(0.77)\quad(0.10)\qquad\qquad(0.17)$$

First, note that the alpha parameter (intercept value) is not significantly different from zero, and again it is comforting to find no confirming security selection capability where none is present. Correspondingly, the b parameter is significantly positive indicating an up-market slope of 0.80, and the c parameter on the dummy variable component is also significantly positive, again verifying market timing capability by the manager over the period of analysis. The plotted dummy variable relationship in Figure 15-7 illustrates that the slope of the characteristic line is substantially greater than the slope in down markets, indicating that the manager successfully reduced portfolio risk in anticipation of declining markets.

Table 15-7 compares parameters estimated for Mellon Capital's Fouse method from three types of regressions on the quarterly 1973–1990 data: (1) simple linear, (2) quadratic,

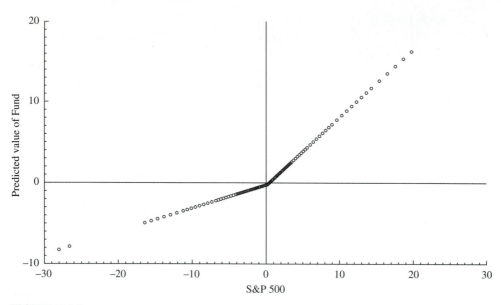

FIGURE 15-7
Relationship between fund and market.

and (3) dummy variable. First, both quadratic and dummy variable regression provide a better fit to the data as shown by higher R^2's than for the simple linear regression. In addition, the simple linear regression shows a significantly positive intercept value that might be interpreted (falsely) to represent superior stock selection capability. In contrast, both quadratic and dummy variable regressions with statistically insignificant intercepts—but other parameters (b, c, d) that are significant—clearly indicate that superior performance derives from market timing and not security selection.

Both methods of regression analysis—dummy variable and quadratic—provide similar and yet differing perspective in evaluating market timing capabilities. In each regression equation the value of the "slope" parameters provides an estimate of market timing capability. The quadratic equation differs in measuring how the portfolio beta fluctuates

TABLE 15-7
Market timing–comparative regressions

	Simple linear	Quadratic	Dummy variable
R_2	0.57	0.63	0.62
Intercept (a)	1.13	0.07	−0.78
(t value)	(2.3)	(0.1)	(−1.01)
Slope Parameter (b)	0.53	0.56	0.8
(t value)	(9.8)	(11.0)	(7.9)
Quadratic Parameter (c)		0.0124	
(t value)		(3.6)	
Dummy Variable Parameter (d)			0.52
(t value)			(3.1)

over many levels of the market, whereas the dummy variable equation indicates that the portfolio fluctuates between two values, depending on whether the market is above or below the risk-free rate. Graphically, we see from Figure 15-5 that the slope of the quadratic curve is continually increasing when moving from left to right, whereas the slope of the dummy variable equation increases from one value $(b - c)$ to a second value (b) when moving from left to right.

Cash Management Analysis

An alternative but complementary way to evaluate market timing is to simply analyze how the cash position of a fund or manager varies in differing market environments. Presumably, successful market timing would be shown by high cash positions during periods of market decline and low cash positions when the market is advancing. To evaluate market timing this way we need to assess what is the normal cash position of the fund, either directly from a stated policy or indirectly by calculating an average percentage cash position over time and using that as representative of a normal position. Deviations from the average would presumably represent commitments to either protect against market declines (above normal cash) or earn extra return from a rising market (below normal cash). For example, a study using this method to assess market timing for a sample of 56 large mutual funds showed that the average cash position was 8 percent and that this position varied from a low of 0 to 1 percent to a high of 18 to 20 percent over a 1958–75 period of analysis,[11] which implies that funds were generally willing to commit 10 percent of their assets in acting on market forecasts.

To specifically measure the degree to which variations in the cash percentage around the longer-term average have benefited or detracted from fund performance, two indexes can be constructed for the fund. The first index is based on the average cash-to-other-asset allocation experienced by the fund over the period of analysis. The second index is based on a quarter-to-quarter revision of the allocation percentages to match the actual quarter-to-quarter changes experienced by the fund over the period. In both cases the return on the cash allocation is assumed to be the return on Treasury bills, whereas the other asset allocation return is assumed to be the return on the S&P 500.

Note that both indexes are made up of two "market" portfolios (T-bill portfolio and S&P 500 portfolio), and they both disregard specific security selection. The difference in performance between the two indexes depends entirely on quarter-to-quarter allocations by the fund, which depart from long-term average allocations. The return of the actual allocation index, minus the return of the average allocation index, thus equals the gain or loss attributable to market timing. Table 15-8 uses hypothetical fund results to illustrate this method of market timing analysis.

The return on the S&P 500 was assumed to be 20 percent, but the T-bill rate was set at 5 percent for the quarter. Note that the return on the actual allocation index (Index 2), minus the return of the average allocation index (Index 1), equals the gain or loss from market timing. In this case, there was a net loss from timing of 1.8 percent (17.0% − 18.8%). The fund was more heavily in cash than usual in a rising market.

---

[11] James L. Farrell, Jr., "Is Marketing Timing Likely to Improve Performance?", paper presented at the Spring 1976 seminar of The Institute of Quantitative Research in Finance, Scottsdale, AZ.

TABLE 15-8
Hypothetical market timing results (one period)

	Index 1 (Average)			Index 2 (Actual)		
	Percent allocation	Return	Weighted return	Percent allocation	Return	Weighted return
Cash (T-bills)	8%	5%	0.4	20%	5%	1.0
Equities (S&P 500)	92%	20%	18.4	80%	20%	16.0
Total	100		18.8	100		17.0

Table 15-9 illustrates this method of measuring market timing success by showing the results of the analysis for one fund—Keystone K-2—from a study of the market timing activities of a sample of 56 mutual funds over the 1958–1975 period. Note the figure shows the year-by-year increment added or subtracted from fund performance along with an average for the full 1958–75 period, as well as two subperiods: 1958–1968 and 1969–1975. Market timing added 0.6 percent on average to performance over the full period and showed good consistency, with addition in 12 years and losses in only 4 years. The added increment, however, was greater in the latter 1969–75 period of more volatile markets than in the earlier 1958–68 period noted before (Chapter 11), which was more favorable to a buy-and-hold policy.

Keystone K-2 offers a good illustration because the fund was, in fact, actively engaged in market timing over this period of analysis, as shown both by significant changes in its cash position over time as well as by meaningful increments to performance. Subsequent investigation verified that the organization pursued such activity. On the other hand, the majority of funds in the sample showed little increment or decrement in performance from market timing, mainly because few funds showed major variations in their cash positions from a longer-term average. This lack of variation is indirect evidence that few funds aggressively engaged in market timing over the period of the study, and again the evidence is bolstered by observation of the investment behavior of these institutions.

TABLE 15-9
**Keystone K-2 cash management analysis
(1958–1975)**

Year	Incremental return	Year	Incremental return
1958	1.6	1969	1.1
1959	0.2	1970	1.4
1960	−0.2	1971	0.1
1961	0.6	1972	0.6
1962	−0.4	1973	0.0
1963	0.8	1974	4.7
1964	0.4	1975	−0.7
1965	0.0		
1966	0.5	1958–1968	Average 0.3
1967	−0.6	1969–1975	Average 1.0
1968	0.4	1958–1975	Average 0.6

Probability of Success

Another way of evaluating market timing success using this same type of cash management data is to assess the percentage of time that a fund moved the cash position correctly in anticipation of the direction of the market. It is important to segment market phases into bull and bear market periods when evaluating market timing using this percentage or probability-of-success analysis. Because bull market phases tend to predominate (historically about two-thirds of the time), a stopped-clock strategy of consistently predicting a bull market would result in an above-average degree of success. For example, over the 1957–1974 study period a stopped-clock forecaster predicting a bull market every quarter would achieve a 60 percent success rate, or the same as the occurrence of bull market quarters—43 out of 72 (60 percent) over the period. To adjust for this and other types of forecasting biases, the overall success rate for market timing can be assessed by combining the percentage of success in predicting a bull market (P_1) and a bear market (P_2) in the following formulation.

$$\text{Market Forecasting Success} = P_1 + P_2 - 1$$

Table 15-10 illustrates this way of assessing market timing success for several types of forecasters. For the stopped-clock forecaster (Case I) consistently predicting a bull market, the percentage of success for the bull phase would be $P_1 = 1.00$. However, in predicting bear markets the percentage P_2 would be zero, and the overall success rate would be 0. Correspondingly, a forecaster predicting a 50 percent chance of a bull market or bear market—forecasting (dart thrower) (Case II), $P_1 = P_2 = 0.50$—would also show a zero forecasting ability. At the other extreme the perfect forecaster (clairvoyant)—Case III—who predicts bull and bear markets with 100 percent accuracy, $P_1 = P_2 = 100\%$, the overall success rate will convert to 100 percent.

In Case IV our illustrative fund K-2 decreased the cash position in 35 quarters out of the total of 43 quarters of returns exceeding the T-bill return, correctly anticipating a bull market phase 80 percent of the time. Correspondingly, there were 29 quarters when the market failed to outperform the return on T-bills. The fund increased the cash position in 18 quarters, correctly anticipating a bear market phase 62 percent of the time. For the Keystone K-2 fund (Case IV) the success rate of $P_1 = 80\%$ for the bull phase and $P_2 = 62\%$ for

TABLE 15-10
Probability of market timing success

$\text{Market Forcasting Success} = P_1 + P_2 - 1.00$

where $P_1 = $ Percentage success predicting bull markets
$P_2 = $ Percentage success predicting bear markets

Case I:	Stopped-clock forecaster: $P_1 = 1.00$ and $P_2 = 0$
	Success rate $= 1.00 + 0 - 1.00 = 0$
Case II:	Dart-throwing forecaster: $P_1 = 0.50$ and $P_2 = 0.50$
	Success rate $= 0.50 + 0.50 - 1.00 = 0$
Case III:	Clairvoyant forecaster: $P_1 = 1.00$ and $P_2 = 1.00$
	Success rate $= 1.00 + 1.00 - 1.00 = 1.00$
Case IV:	K-2 mutual fund: $P_1 = 0.80$ and $P_2 = 0.62$
	Success rate $= 0.80 + 0.62 - 1.00 = 0.42$

the bear phase converts into an overall success rate of 0.42. This success rate is well above zero and provides confirming evidence of the capability of the fund managers in timing the market over the period.

RETURN ATTRIBUTION

The ultimate objective of an investment process is to accomplish the investment goals established by the investor. Performance evaluation aims not only at assessing the success of the investment process in achieving the overall investment goals but also at diagnosing the contribution of the individual elements that have made possible achievement of the overall goal. In turn, the performance evaluation should provide a feedback mechanism enabling the organization to emphasize those aspects of the process that are productive and downplay or reconstitute those that have been less than successful or have failed to contribute to the investment goal.

Because achieving investment goals is the basic aim of the investment process, identifying an explicit statement of these goals is a critical step in the evaluation of the process. As noted in the earlier sections of this book, setting and explicitly stating the investment objective is one of the first items that needs to be accomplished in portfolio management. We can best illustrate the goal-setting process by using a hypothetical pension fund, as managers of pension funds are confronted with as wide an array of investment problems as any other investors.

Table 15-11 shows the characteristics of our hypothetical pension fund. Note that the fund has a total asset value of $500 million, which approximates the size of a moderately large pension fund. The plan has a goal of investing in moderate-risk securities in order to earn a real return of 4 percent on assets; that is, the nominal return on assets less the inflation rate should be 4 percent. Because the market cycle is typically about five years as

TABLE 15-11
Setting goals for an investment fund

Fund type:	Pension fund
Fund value:	$500 million
Return goal:	4% real return
Planning period:	5 years
Risk to loss:	1/3 probability of not earning the return

Eligible assets and desired allocation:

Asset	Normal position, %	Allowable divergence, %
Domestic equities	60	±15
International equities	15	± 5
Japan	5	
United Kingdom	5	
Germany	5	
Fixed Income	25	±10
Long-term	20	
Short-term	5	

is its planning period, the fund has a goal of investing in moderate risk and earning this 4 percent return over any rolling five-year period. It expects to meet or exceed this goal at least two-thirds of the time. Alternatively, the acceptable risk in not reaching this goal is a shortfall one-third the time.[12]

The fund includes in its eligible list of assets both domestic and international securities. Among the eligible foreign national markets are Japan, the United Kingdom, and Germany. The fund has established a size limitation on securities of no less than $200 million in market capitalization to avoid the proliferation of an excessive number of individual small holdings. Corporate and government bonds, but not municipal bonds or preferred stocks, are eligible in the fund's investment universe. The fund—as is the case with pension plans in general— is not subject to tax, so tax-exempt securities are generally not of interest. Money market instruments such as Treasury bills and commercial paper are also eligible for purchase and serve as a reserve.

Table 15-11 also shows the asset allocation for the plan, which provides the most likely opportunity to meet the goal at the least risk. Note that the plan has a normal allocation of 60 percent domestic stocks, 15 percent international equities, and 25 percent fixed-income securities. These normal allocations provide the best opportunity for earning the objective return at the least risk over the longer term, again defined as the five-year planning period. The plan allows, however, the allocation to diverge from the normal allocations with the following ranges: ±15 percent for domestic stocks, ±5 percent for international equities, and ±10 percent for fixed-income securities. Generally, in return attribution we assume that the overall risk level is in line with the objective and thus focus on the return performance of the portfolio.

We will assume that the fund sponsor takes responsibilities in setting the longer-term allocation as well as in advising when and to what extent to shift the weights in the major asset classes. In managing the assets within the major asset classes we will assume that the fund uses outside professional money management organizations: (1) a management organization for domestic equities and (2) an international investment specialist for international equities. We will also assume that the fund uses the bond management division of a major financial institution to oversee the income portion of the fund.[13]

Table 15-12 illustrates the three major aspects of evaluating the performance of this hypothetical fund. First, we would want to determine whether our overall asset distribution (strategic asset allocation) was effective in meeting the longer-term real rate of return objectives. Second, we would want to assess the productivity of any changes in the weightings of the asset classes (tactical asset allocation) from its longer-run target; that is, we need to determine the incremental gain or loss from weighting the various asset classes differently

---

[12] An alternative way of expressing this idea is to say that the objective of a pension fund is to return at least as much as the actuarial rate. Another example of an investment objective for an institutional investor is that of an endowment fund with a goal of taking on sufficient risk to provide capital or income to meet the needs of the sponsoring organization.

[13] In managing pension assets, corporations vary in operating procedures, from managing the whole process internally—in-house management—to complete delegation of asset allocation, differential weighting, and security selection to an outside manager. The example here is a hybrid situation and may be illustrative of the typical sponsor-management relationship for pension funds.

> **TABLE 15-12**
> **Appraising fund performance**
> _____
>
> 1. Long-term goals: Evaluating the efficacy of the strategic asset allocation
> 2. Appraising tactical asset mix changes
> 3. Evaluating the performance of managers within major asset categories

than for the longer-run objective. Finally, we would want to analyze whether the managers of the differing asset categories—domestic equities, international equities, and fixed-income securities—were performing relatively better or worse through asset selectivity, than the appropriate benchmarks for the category.

LONG-TERM GOALS: STRATEGIC ASSET ALLOCATION

Recognizing risk and the possibility of an inflationary environment, many plan sponsors have stated their longer-term goals in terms of a real return on investment—nominal return less inflation rate. This strategy is in keeping with the necessity for pension plan assets to be sufficient to meet future pension liabilities, which will generally incorporate the rate of inflation experienced over the period. Generally, pension sponsors seem to be targeting this real return at the 4-percent level. The prime determinant of whether the plan will meet the real-return target at minimum risk over an intermediate to longer period of time—say, five to twenty years—is the effectiveness of the asset allocation.

Recall from previous chapters that the various asset classes behave differently over differing economic episodes. In particular, we noted that bonds perform well during periods of deflation, or disinflation, but suffer adverse effects during periods of inflation. Treasury bills provide returns in line with the rate of inflation, which has generally served as a hedge against inflation, especially in the postwar period. Common stocks perform most favorably during periods of strong real economic growth, but they show a mixed pattern as a hedge against inflation, especially over shorter periods. International equities might be expected to provide some protection against inflation, but they are subject to other political and economic risks. The objective of an asset allocation is to blend assets together so as to hedge against adverse economic changes (reduce risk) and at the same time provide the greatest opportunity for achieving longer-term rate of return.

Table 15-13 shows the returns earned on the various asset classes along with the rate of inflation experienced over the 1976–1980 period, which allows us to assess the real return earned on these assets over the period. Note that domestic common stocks showed high returns that were in excess of the 8.9 percent rate of inflation over the period. International equities also showed strong returns, especially in the early part of the period, and exceeded the rate of inflation for the overall period. Treasury bills tracked the annual rate of inflation and essentially showed returns about in line with the rate of inflation over the period. Finally, long-term bonds—as might be expected during a period of accelerating inflation—were unable to provide returns to offset the rate of inflation, showing a net real loss of 5 percent over the period (3.9 percent nominal return less 8.9 percent inflation rate).

Table 15-13 also shows the year-by-year return and average annual return over the full five-year period for a portfolio with a moderate-risk asset allocation in line with that of Table 15-11. Over the full five-year period the asset allocation resulted in an average annual return of 12.7 percent, exceeding the 8.9 percent inflation rate and providing a real return of 3.8

TABLE 15-13
Rate of return—asset classes and portfolio allocation, 1976–1980

	Asset allocation weight	1976	1977	1978	1979	1980	Annual average
Domestic stocks (S&P 500)	0.60	23.9	−7.2	6.6	18.6	32.4	14.1
International equities							
Germany	0.05	6.7	25.7	27.0	−2.1	−9.0	8.7
Japan	0.05	25.7	15.9	53.3	−11.8	30.2	20.7
United Kingdom	0.05	−12.4	58.0	14.7	22.2	41.1	22.3
Fixed-income							
Long-term	0.20	19.6	3.2	0.4	−2.1	−0.3	3.9
Treasury bills	0.05	5.1	5.1	7.2	10.1	11.6	7.7
Consumer Price Index		4.8	6.8	9.0	11.3	12.4	8.9
Return to portfolio allocation		19.5	1.6	9.2	11.7	23.1	12.7
Real return		14.7	−5.2	0.2	0.4	10.7	3.8

percent, which was essentially in line with the objective of 4 percent. At the same time, the return over the period was relatively stable—the real return was positive in four of the five years. The asset allocation for the hypothetical portfolio was appropriate for meeting the longer-term moderate-risk objective of the pension fund.[14]

APPRAISING ASSET-MIX CHANGES

A second dimension to analyze in appraising the performance of a fund is to assess the productivity of any changes in the weighting of the assets from the longer-run target asset allocation. In particular, we would be interested in assessing to what extent the fund has shifted classes from the longer-term target weightings and then measuring the effect of those shifts on return performance. For example, if the fund had been overweighted in international equities and underweighted in domestic equities over the period, we would measure what impact this shift had on performance as compared to a position held in line with the longer-term target.

To implement this, we first compare the return earned on the asset class to the return earned on the portfolio, assuming no change in the weighting from its longer-term target weighting. We would then simply multiply the differential return or loss on the asset class from that earned on the portfolio by the weighting divergence of the asset class. For example, if the portfolio manager had determined that the risk-return trade-off for long-term bonds was relatively attractive in a particular year and, therefore, overweighted bonds in the

---

[14]Be cautious in drawing firm conclusions about the success or failure of the asset allocation. Over periods as short as a year and even a period as long as five years, the risk profile of the overall market environment for asset classes will be a prime factor in determining achievement of the target return. During some periods, the market risk environment may be such that it is impossible to meet the target return—say, during a period of severe deflation. Any assessment should thus be made not only against the target return but also with the market environment in mind.

TABLE 15-14
Target and actual fund weightings, 1976–1980 (%)

Asset class	Target weight	Actual weight				
		1976	1977	1978	1979	1980
Domestic stocks	60	65	55	55	60	65
International equities						
Germany	5	5	10	5	5	5
Japan	5	5	5	10	–	5
United Kingdom	5	–	5	5	10	5
Fixed income						
Long-term	20	20	20	20	20	15
Treasury bills	5	5	5	5	5	5

portfolio by, say, −5 percentage points, we would multiply the 5 percentage points by the relative gain or loss in long-term bonds. If bonds had earned a higher return during the year than the overall portfolio, there would have been an overall gain to the weighting decision. On the other hand, if bonds had earned a lower return (shown losses) relative to the overall portfolio, there would have been a weighting loss.

Table 15-14 shows the longer-term target weights for the hypothetical fund, along with the actual weightings in these components, and allows us to evaluate the reweighting decisions of the fund year by year over the 1976–1980 performance period. Note that the fund overweighted domestic equities in 1976 and again in 1980 but underweighted this asset class in 1977 and 1978. Within the international asset class, the fund overweighted German equities in 1977, overweighted Japanese equities in 1978, underweighted U.K. equities in 1976, and overweighted U.K. equities in 1979. The fund held the weighting in the fixed-income class in line with the longer-term allocation, with the exception of a decision to underweight long-term bonds in 1980.

Table 15-15 shows the return added by these weighting decisions. Note that the weighting decisions in 1976—overweighting domestic equities and underweighting U.K.

TABLE 15-15
Performance attributable to nonstandard weighting, 1976–1980 (%)

Asset Class	Incremental return				
	1976	1977	1978	1979	1980
Domestic stocks	0.2	0.4	0.1	–	0.5
International equities					
Germany	–	1.2	–	–	–
Japan	–	–	2.2	1.2	–
United Kingdom	1.6	–	–	0.5	–
Fixed income					
Long-term	–	–	–	–	1.1
Treasury bills	–	–	–	–	–
Total	1.8	1.6	2.3	1.7	1.6

equities in the international sector—added 1.8 percent to overall performance; underweighting domestic equities and overweighting German equities added 1.6 percent in 1977; underweighting domestic stocks and overweighting Japanese securities added 2.3 percent to performance in 1978; overweighting U.K. securities and underweighting Japanese securities added 1.7 percent to performance in 1979; and overweighting domestic stocks and underweighting long-term bonds added 1.6 percent to performance in 1980. The fund thus showed a favorable return performance with respect to weighting decisions on both an overall and year-by-year-basis.

EVALUATING ASSET-CLASS MANAGERS

The third dimension to performance evaluation is assessment of the success of managers within individual asset classes: domestic equity, international equities, and fixed-income securities. In making this comparison we are essentially trying to evaluate the ability of the manager or managers to make individual security and industry selections. There are three types of comparisons: (1) comparisons with a market index such as the S&P 500 when evaluating the domestic equity manager, (2) comparisons with the performance of others specializing in the management of securities within the asset class, and (3) evaluation after adjusting for the influence of systematic factors.

Table 15-16 illustrates how we might use market indexes to evaluate the performance of asset-class managers. It shows the year-by-year and cumulative rate of return over the full 1976–1980 period for the asset-class market indexes. It also shows returns for hypothetical managers within each of the classes.[15] Returns in excess of the market index benchmark would be considered indicative of above-average performance, whereas returns below the index would be considered indicative of below-average performance.

Note that the domestic-equity manager provided superior return in each of the five years and an above-average return of 5.1 percent for the overall period. The international-equity manager outperformed the Japanese and German equity indexes for the overall period but earned a slightly below-average return against the U.K. index. The fixed-income manager provided superior return in four of the five years and outperformed the fixed-income index by 3.7 percent over the full period. On the basis of comparison with the market indexes, the individual asset managers appear to have delivered superior performance.

Furthermore, it is useful to compare the performance of individual managers against the performance of other managers within a particular asset class. For example, we would compare the fixed-income manager to other managers specialized in managing fixed-income securities. In this regard we would need to ensure that the managers in the comparison are, in fact, primarily engaged in the management of securities within the particular asset class; that is, we should make sure that the fixed-income managers are focused on fixed-income securities, that the domestic-equity managers are predominantly engaged in managing domestic equities, and that the international-equity managers are primarily concerned with managing international equities.

---

[15]The performance of domestic equities is actually measured by the return attributable to the implementation of the stock selection strategy described in Chapter 8. Measurement of the performance of the international equities manager is strictly hypothetical, whereas that of the bond manager is the actual performance of a bond management department.

TABLE 15-16
Asset-class managers performance, 1976–1980, (%)

Asset class	1976	1977	1978	1979	1980	Annual average
Domestic stocks						
Market index	23.9	−7.2	6.6	18.6	32.4	14.1
Manager	33.7	−2.7	13.6	21.4	34.2	19.2
Performance increment	9.8	4.5	7.0	2.8	1.8	5.1
International equities						
German market index	6.7	25.7	27.0	−2.1	−9.0	8.7
Manager	9.0	25.0	31.0	−1.0	−13.0	9.0
Performance increment	2.3	−0.7	4.0	1.1	−4.0	0.3
Japan market index	25.7	15.9	53.9	−11.8	30.2	20.7
Manager	26.5	13.2	55.6	−13.2	32.7	20.8
Performance increment	0.8	−2.7	2.3	−1.4	2.5	0.1
U.K. market index	−12.4	58.0	14.7	22.2	41.1	22.3
Manager	−15.3	55.0	17.3	24.0	37.5	20.9
Performance increment	−2.9	−3.0	2.6	1.8	−3.6	−1.4
Fixed-income securities						
Long-term bond index	19.6	3.2	0.4	−2.1	−0.3	3.9
Manager	17.7	3.4	3.1	6.2	8.0	7.6
Performance increment	−1.9	0.2	2.7	8.3	8.3	3.7

In making the comparison the usual method is to array the managers within an asset class from the one providing the highest return to the one providing the lowest return over a performance period and then to display the distribution as illustrated in Figure 15-8. This figure shows the return distribution for domestic-equity managers and fixed-income managers for the five-year period ending with 1980. It shows the median return earned by the universe of managers and a breakdown of the distribution into quartiles of manager per-

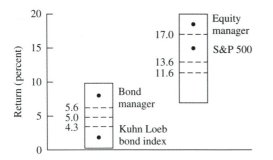

	Universe of bond managers	Universe of stock managers
25th percentile	5.6	17.0
Median	5.0	13.6
75th percentile	4.3	11.6
Market index	3.9	14.1
Manager	7.6	19.2

FIGURE 15-8
Relative performance—bond and equity managers, 1976–1980. (*Sources:* Frank Russell Company, Tacoma, Wash., and A.G. Becker Company, Chicago.)

formance. It also shows the ranking within the fund-manager distribution of the pertinent indexes—the S&P 500 and the Lehman Brothers–Kuhn Loeb bond index.

Note that the median fixed-income manager would have outperformed the bond index, whereas the median stock manager performed about in line with the stock market index over this period. There was, however, a wide dispersion around these average turns, especially in the case of the stock managers; this comparison is useful for placing the manager's performance in perspective. The wide dispersion of the stock returns is expected given the risk characteristics of equity as compared to debt. As for our hypothetical managers we can see that the performance of the bond manager was well into the first quartile of performance, as was the stock manager with respect to other domestic equity managers. The performance of both managers would, therefore, have been rated above average according to this measure.

MULTIFACTOR ADJUSTMENT

When returns are generated according to a multifactor process, we must further account for these differing factors to evaluate a manager's capability in security selection properly. In addition to a general market effect, which we discuss more extensively in the first part of this chapter, we might evaluate how attributes like the growth characteristics of securities in the portfolio impact performance. One way to assess the potential impact of growth on a portfolio is to calculate a weighted average of the projected five-year growth rates for companies in the portfolio and compare that to the weighted average growth rate of companies in the index as a measure of exposure relative to the benchmark average. Correspondingly, value is commonly considered to be the complement of growth; high growth is usually accompanied by higher valuation, and low growth is usually accompanied by lower valuation. In addition, many investors compare the weighted P/E of the portfolio to that of the benchmark as a way of assessing the valuation positioning of the portfolio.

Table 15-17 illustrates the exposure of a stock portfolio to the attributes of growth and value by comparing the distribution of the portfolio's weightings in five distinct growth rate and P/E segments to that of the benchmark S&P 500 index. Note that the portfolio is underweighted relative to the index in the lower two segments of growth but is overweighted in stocks growing at 12% or better. Correspondingly, the portfolio is underweighted in the two highest P/E brackets but overweighted in the lower three brackets. The portfolio is showing a somewhat anomalous configuration of exposure to high growth yet has a

TABLE 15-17
Portfolio positioning—growth and value

	Growth				Value		
Growth rate sectors	Index weight	Portfolio weight	Diff. weight	P/E sectors	Index weight	Portfolio weight	Diff. weight
(1) 0.0–8.0	17.2	5.5	−11.6	0.0–8.0	0.3	1.6	1.3
(2) 8.0–12.0	39.8	35.2	−4.7	8.0–12.0	6.2	12.3	6.1
(3) 12.0–16.0	24.6	29.9	5.3	12.0–16.0	22.2	31.0	8.8
(4) 16.0–20.0	13.9	18.5	4.6	above 16.0	64.2	50.2	−14.0
(5) above 20.0	4.5	10.9	6.4	n/a	7.0	4.9	−2.2

TABLE 15-18
Performance by sector (Dec. 31, 1992–Jan. 31, 1993)

	1	2	3	4	5	6	7	8
	Weights		Differential wt	Returns		Diff ret	Relative index*	Sect. sel. impact on portfolio
Industry sectors	Port	Index sector	(1 − 2)	Port	Index sector	(4 − 5)	(5 − $\sum$ 5)	(3 · 7)
Business equip. & serv.	0.0	2.6	−2.6	0.0	−2.5	2.5	−3.2	0.08
Capital goods	0.0	5.0	−5.0	0.0	1.7	−1.7	1.0	−0.05
Consumer durables	6.2	2.5	3.7	5.8	10.6	−4.8	9.9	0.36
Consumer non-durables	21.5	15.4	6.1	−1.6	−1.4	−0.2	−2.1	−0.13
Consumer services	5.3	3.5	1.7	1.0	6.0	−5.0	5.3	0.09
Energy	4.5	9.9	−5.4	−0.9	2.2	−3.1	1.5	−0.08
Financial services	15.0	10.6	4.4	3.6	3.5	0.1	2.8	0.12
Health care	10.6	9.9	0.7	0.4	−7.9	8.4	−8.6	−0.06
Multi-industry	5.1	1.9	3.3	−2.8	−2.1	−0.7	−2.8	−0.09
Raw materials	6.2	4.8	1.5	2.2	−0.6	2.8	−1.3	−0.02
Retail	3.2	8.4	−5.2	−2.8	−0.2	−2.6	−0.9	0.05
Shelter	3.8	2.3	1.4	8.3	2.5	5.9	1.8	0.02
Technology	6.4	7.2	−0.9	6.4	5.0	1.4	4.3	−0.04
Transportation	3.4	1.8	1.6	11.2	3.2	8.0	2.5	0.04
Utilities	8.9	14.1	−5.2	3.0	1.8	1.2	1.1	−0.06
Total				1.9	0.7	1.2		−0.25 = 0.92 (Stock Selection)

*Relative index relates how industry sector performed relative to total market index (sector return − total market index).

below-average *P/E*, which may be indicative of success in purchasing above-average growth at a reasonable valuation.

Many practitioners consider industry sector classification to be a significant factor impacting performance. The data in Table 15-18 comparing a stock portfolio to its benchmark S&P 500 index illustrate how to distinguish the impact of industry sector representation from individual stock selection. It shows a breakdown of the weighting of the portfolio and benchmark index into 13 broad industry sector classifications, as well as the differential weighting between the two. In addition it shows the index return for the industry sector, as well as the return earned by the portfolio sector holdings and return differential between the two. The manager of this portfolio generally has a strength in stock selection as compared to sector selection.

Sector weighting adds value to a portfolio when overweighted sectors outperform the market index and underweighted sectors underperform. However, as we would expect, sector weighting detracts from performance when underweighted sectors outperform and overweighted sectors underperform the index. In Table 15-18 note that the business equipment sector is underweighted in the portfolio relative to the index by 2.6% . Moreover, this sector showed a -2.5% return, thereby underperforming the total market index by 3.2% ($= -2.5\%$ sector return -0.7% index return). The underweighting of 2.6% added 0.08% to portfolio performance, which is simply derived as a product of the underweighting (2.6) and the relative sector underperformance ($-2.6\% - 3.2 = 8.32 \approx 0.08\%$). On the other hand, the underweighting in the capital goods sector (by 5.0%) detracted from performance (by 0.05%) as that sector outperformed the index by 1.0% ($= 1.7\% - 0.7\%$). Column 8 in Table 15-18 shows the impact of each sector selection on portfolio performance.

The last line of the table shows the total portfolio return compared to the S&P 500 return over the period of analysis: 12/31/92 to 1/31/93. Note that the portfolio outperformed the S&P 500 by close to 1.2 percentage points over the one-month period. The decomposition of incremental return, shown also at the bottom of the table, indicates that favorable stock selection was mainly responsible for the outperformance—comprising 0.92 of the total increment. Sector selection, though important to individual sectors, netted out to a much smaller increment of 0.25 of the total. The relatively greater value added from stock selection is consistent with the fact that the manager emphasizes stock selection as the way of achieving above-average performance over time.

Table 15-19 shows the results of evaluating stock selection after accounting for the potential impact of other factors such as beta, growth, *P/E*, and industry classification on performance. Note that stock selection was the major source of value added, regardless of

TABLE 15-19
Factor-adjusted performance (Dec. 31, 1992–Jan. 31, 1993)

Factor	1 Factor related	2 Stock selection	3 Incremental return (1 + 2)	4 Index return	5 Total return (3 + 4)
Beta	−0.01	1.17	1.16	0.73	1.89
Growth	−0.50	1.66	1.16	0.73	1.89
Value (*P/E*)	0.14	1.02	1.16	0.73	1.89
Industry Sector	0.25	0.92	1.16	0.73	1.89

which factor was considered for adjustment. With respect to individual factors, the analysis showed that both the growth positioning and industry classification factors detracted somewhat from performance, whereas the *P/E* adjustment and economic sector representation added somewhat to performance.

INFORMATION RATIO

Once we have adjusted for the systematic factors such as market, style, and industry classification, we obtain the return from stock selection. In our example, the differing adjustments showed that the manager's main source of value added to the portfolio over the month of evaluation was from active stock selection. Over time, however, the returns to stock selection, or other techniques for that matter, will fluctuate. These fluctuations represent the risk associated with the management activity; for active stock selection, the related risk is also known as residual risk.

In managing a portfolio, it is desirable that the residual risk be minimized while attempting to add value (alpha) to the portfolio. When residual risk is low, there is greater confidence that the alpha is sustainable, whereas high residual risk creates uncertainty about the significance of the value added to the portfolio. In order to increase confidence in the performance measurement, the objective should be to maximize the ratio of value added (alpha) to residual risk incurred. This ratio is known as the information ratio (IFR) and is simply

$$\text{IFR} = \frac{\alpha_p}{\sigma_e} = \frac{\text{Portfolio alpha}}{\text{Residual risk}}$$

For example, a manager who emphasized stock selection and averaged an annual alpha of 3.5% over time while incurring residual risk (tracking error) of 5% would have an information ratio of the following:

$$\text{IFR} = \frac{\alpha_p}{\sigma_e} = \frac{3.5}{5.0} = 0.7$$

Because returns increase with time but risk increases with the square root of time, confidence after n years is a function of the following:

$$\frac{\text{Portfolio alpha} \times \text{Time}}{\text{Residual risk} \times \sqrt{\text{Time}}}$$

By rearranging terms and using the definition of the information ratio (IFR) as α_p/σ_e, we can see that

$$\text{Time} = \text{function} \left[\frac{(\text{Confidence})}{(\text{Information Ratio})} \right]^2$$

Assuming that returns are normally distributed, we can use the standard normal distribution to establish confidence levels in terms of probabilities. Using a 95% probability and a 1.96 standard deviation above the mean of zero, we calculate that a manager with a 0.7 information ratio needs to sustain performance for a period of 7.8 years to reach that level of confidence.

TABLE 15-20
Years to verify performance, by information and ratio confidence level

| Information | Confidence level | | |
ratio	80%	90%	95%
0.5	6.6	10.8	15.5
0.6	4.6	7.5	10.7
0.7	3.4	5.5	7.8
0.8	2.6	4.2	6.0
0.9	2.0	3.3	4.7
1.0	1.6	2.7	3.8

$$\text{Confidence} = \left[\frac{1.96}{0.7}\right]^2 = 7.8 \text{ years}$$

At lower levels of probability, the number of years of sustained performance needed to reach the confidence level will be less. For example, using a 90-percent probability threshold, a manager with a 0.7 information ratio would need to sustain performance for 5.5 years to attain that level of confidence.

$$\text{Confidence} = \left(\frac{1.645}{0.7}\right)^2 = 5.5 \text{ years}$$

Table 15-20 illustrates the way that years needed to achieve a level of confidence varies with the information ratio and the desired probability level. We show three probability levels, including the 95% level, which is a standard level used by investment researchers as a high level of significance. Investors also consider probability levels of 90% and 80% quite satisfactory, and so we also include these in the comparison. We also show levels of performance excellence ranging from 0.5 to 1.0 as measured by the information ratio that encompasses managers that have achieved success. The 0.5 level is a threshold that monitored results indicate is representative of good performance on the part of managers, whereas a ratio of 1.0 is outstanding performance, attained by only a small minority of managers.

Note that the number of years to achieve a confidence level is lower as the probability threshold is lower. A manager with a 0.5 information ratio requires almost 16 years to be confident of the significance of performance at a 95% level but 6.6 years, or less than two market cycles, when the investor uses an 80% probability. Correspondingly, the number of years to achieve a given confidence level is lower as the manager's information ratio is higher. A manager with an information ratio of 1.0 (high degree of excellence) requires less than four years to be confident at the 95% level but less than two years at the 80% level.

In a sense, these results are discouraging. For investors demanding the highest level of statistical significance (95%), all but the most excellent managers require exceptionally long periods, ranging over several market cycles, to develop that level of confidence. When the probability threshold is less (80% or 90%), the time period is lower and more in line with conventional practice. Typically, investors will allow at least a full market cycle to evaluate a manager; a 3- to 5-year period is usually the norm. Correspondingly, investors will rarely take adverse action on managers, unless circumstances are exceptional, with only one or two years of performance data. As the table shows, even the most excellent managers need at least two years to attain confidence at the 80% threshold.

TABLE 15-21
Aggregate performance eveluation, 1976–1980

Activity	Five-year average
Asset allocation	12.7
Weighting asset classes	2.1
Selectivity	3.5
Aggregate performance	18.3
Consumer Price Index	−8.9
Real return	9.4
Target return	4.0
Performance increment	5.4

AGGREGATING RETURN COMPONENTS

To conclude this part of the chapter on performance evaluation we consolidate performance— asset allocation, weighting shifts across asset classes, and security selection within asset classes—into an overall performance evaluation for our hypothetical pension fund. Comparing these three aspects simultaneously allows us to determine the relative effectiveness of the individual components of the investment process. In addition, it allows us to assess the effectiveness of the process toward achieving the fund's overall investment goal of earning a real return at or exceeding the target return of 4 percent.

Table 15-21 shows the performance of the three main components of the investment process along with the net effect of these three individual aspects on the overall fund performance over the 1976–1980 period. Note that the table shows a building-up of performance, beginning with the basic asset allocation, then weighting, and finally security selection. The fourth line shows the net effect on the fund's return from all these activities, and the bottom line shows how the aggregate performance relates to the fund's goal of earning a 4% real return.

Note that all three components contributed to performance. The basic asset allocation essentially resulted in a return sufficient to meet the minimum target, as was previously indicated in this chapter. Weighting added an increment of 2.1 percent to return, and selectivity added another 3.5 percent. Each of the investment activities was thus productive, and the overall endeavor resulted in a performance incremental return of 5.4 percent, well in excess of the 4-percent target return. The performance evaluation of this hypothetical fund implies that it is productive and under control.

CONCLUSION

Evaluating historical portfolio performance is important to the investor in several respects. First, it enables the investor to appraise how well the portfolio manager has done in achieving desired return targets and how well risk has been controlled in the process. Second, it enables the investor to assess how well the manager has achieved these targets in comparison with other managers or, alternatively, with some passive investment strategy, such as an S&P 500 index fund. Finally, it provides a mechanism for identifying weaknesses in the investment process and for improving these deficient areas. In this sense, performance evaluation can be viewed not only as a way of appraising the worth of portfolio management but also as a feedback mechanism for improving the portfolio management process.

Though evaluating past performance is useful, we should be cautious about drawing overly strong conclusions from the analysis. First, the risk-adjustment measures currently available have some biases and deficiencies that can lead to a less than completely comprehensive consideration of risk-adjusted performance. Second, the market environment is so highly competitive that the edge possessed by even the best of management organizations is likely to be slight. Currently available performance measurement techniques are not likely to be powerful enough to clearly detect such a degree of superiority, at least over a relatively short time span. Finally, management organizations change over time; there is key personnel turnover, complacency can set in with success, the investment process can become stale, and the investment philosophy can change. All these factors mean that past results are not necessarily indicative of future prospects. Nevertheless, historical performance evaluation can serve as the starting point for estimating future prospects and, perhaps more importantly, can serve as a feedback mechanism for improving the ongoing portfolio management process.

SELECTED REFERENCES

Ankrim, Ernest: "Risk-Adjusted Performance Attribution," *Financial Analysts Journal,* March–April 1992, pp. 75–82.

—— and Chris Hensel: "Multi-Currency Performance Attribution," *Financial Analysts Journal,* March–April 1994, pp. 29–35.

Bailey, Jeffrey: "Evaluating Benchmark Quality," *Financial Analysts Journal,* May–June 1992, pp. 33–39.

——: "Some Thoughts on Performance-Based Fees," *Financial Analysts Journal,* July–August 1990, pp. 31–40.

Bank Administration Institute: *Measuring the Investment Performance of Pension Funds,* Park Ridge, IL, 1968.

Bookstaber, Richard, and Roger Clarke: "Problems in Evaluating the Performance of Portfolios with Options," *Financial Analysts Journal,* January–February 1985.

Bostock, Paul, and Paul Wooley: "A New Way to Analyze International Equity Market Performance," *Financial Analysts Journal,* January–February 1990, pp. 32–38.

Brenson, Gary, Jeffrey Diermeir, and Gary Schlarbaum: "A Complete Portfolio Benchmark for Pension Plans," *Financial Analysts Journal,* March–April 1986, pp. 15–24.

Collins, Bruce, and Frank Fabozzi: "Considerations in Selecting a Small-Capitalization Benchmark," *Financial Analysts Journal,* March–April 1991, pp. 27–36.

Cumley, Robert, and David Modest: "Testing for Market Timing Ability: A Framework for Forecast Evaluation," *Journal of Financial Economics,* September 1987, pp. 169–190.

Davanzo, Lawrence, and Stephen Nesbitt: "Performance Fees for Investment Management," *Financial Analysts Journal,* January–February 1987, pp. 14–20.

Dietz, P.O.: *Pension Funds: Measuring Performance,* The Free Press, New York, 1966.

——, H.R. Fogler, and D.J. Hardy: "The Challenge of Analyzing Bond Portfolio Returns," *Journal of Portfolio Management,* Spring 1980, pp. 53–58.

Fama, Eugene: "Components of Investment Performance," *Journal of Finance,* June 1972, pp. 551–67.

Fong, Gifford, and Oddrick Vasicek: "Fixed Income Performance Attribution," Institute for Quantitative Research in Finance, Spring Seminar 1994, Palm Beach, FL.

Grinblatt, Mark, and Sheridan Titman: "Mutual Fund Performance: An Analysis of Quarterly Portfolio Holdings," *Journal of Business,* July 1989, pp. 393-416.

——and ——: "Performance Measurement without Benchmarks: An Examination of Mutual Fund Returns," *Journal of Business,* January 1993, pp. 47–68.

Grinold, Richard, and Andrew Rudd: "Incentive Fees: Who Wins? Who Loses?," *Financial Analysts Journal,* January–February 1987, pp. 27–38.

Henriksson, Roy, and Robert Merton: "On Market Timing and Investment Performance," *Journal of Business,* October 1981, pp. 513–534.

——: "Market Timing and Mutual Fund Performance: An Empirical Investigation," *Journal of Business,* January 1984, pp. 73–96.

Higgs, Peter, and Stephen Goode: "Target Active Returns and Attribution Analysis," *Financial Analysts Journal,* May–June 1993, pp. 77–80.

Jensen, Michael C.: "The Performance of Mutual Funds in the Period 1945–1964," *Journal of Finance,* May 1968, pp. 389–416.

Kon, Stanley: "The Market Timing Performance of Mutual Fund Managers," *Journal of Business,* July 1983, pp. 323–348.

Kritzman, Mark: "Incentive Fees: Some Problems and Some Solutions," *Financial Analysts Journal,* January–February 1987, pp. 21–26.

Lehman, Bruce, and David Modest: "Mutual Fund Performance Evaluation: A Comparison of Benchmarks and Benchmark Comparisons," *Journal of Finance,* June 1987, pp. 233–265.

Leibowitz, Martin: "Goal Oriented Bond Portfolio Management," *Journal of Portfolio Management,* Summer 1979, pp. 13–18.

Martin, John, Arthur Keown, and James L. Farrell: "Do Fund Objectives Affect Diversification Policies?" *Journal of Portfolio Management,* Winter 1982, pp. 19–28.

Martin, Robert: "On Market Timing and Investment Performance," *Journal of Business,* July 1981, pp. 363–406.

Record, Eugene, and Mary Ann Tyron: "Incentive Fees: The Basic Issues," *Financial Analysts Journal,* January–February 1987, pp. 39–43.

Rennie, Edward, and Thomas Cowhey: "The Successful Use of Benchmark Portfolios: A Case Study," *Financial Analysts Journal,* September–October 1990, pp. 18–26.

Sharpe, W.F.: "Mutual Fund Performance," *Journal of Business,* January 1966, pp. 119–138.

Surz, Ronald: "Portfolio Opportunity Distributions: An Innovation in Performance Evaluation," *Journal of Investing,* Summer 1994, pp. 36-41.

Tierney, David, and Kenneth Winston: "Defining and Using Dynamic Completeness Funds to Enhance Total Fund Efficiency," *Financial Analysts Journal,* July–August 1990, pp. 49–54.

Treynor, J.L.: "How to Rate Management of Investment Funds," *Harvard Business Review,* January–February 1965, pp. 63–75.

Williams, Arthur: *Managing Your Investment Manager,* Dow Jones–Irwin, New York, 1990.

Williamson, Peter: "Performance Measurement," in Edward Altman (ed.): *The Financial Handbook,* Wiley, New York, 1980.

QUESTIONS AND PROBLEMS

1. What adjustment needs to be made in calculating the return on mutual funds as opposed to, say, the return on a stock or bond?
2. Explain the time-weighted return.
3. Explain why risk must be considered in evaluating performance.
4. Compare and contrast the two return-per-unit-of-risk performance measures. In what context is each best applied?
5. Explain the differential return performance measure as related to the capital asset pricing model.
6. Explain what is meant by net selectivity in the evaluation of stock performance.
7. Compare four methods of evaluating market timing capability.
8. How do you compute the net asset value of a mutual fund?

9. The net asset value of a fund was $20 at the beginning of the year, increased to $30 by the end of the year, and then declined to $27 the end of the second year. What was the return earned per annum, and what was the time-weighted return over the 2-year period?

10. A fund had a beginning-of-year asset value of $500,000 and end-of-year value of $600,000, at which time it suffered a cash outflow of $100,000. The value of the fund at the end of year 2 was $700,000. What was the time-weighted return over the 2-year period?

11. Refer to Table 15-4, and assume that all the data are the same except that fund A earned a return of 5% and fund Z earned 12%. Calculate the Sharpe ratio and Treynor ratio, and rank the performance of the three funds, including the market.

12. Assume again that fund A earned 5% and fund Z earned 12%. Calculate the differential return for the two funds, using the same risk data and market data as before.

13. Using the Fama framework of performance components, determine the selectivity, diversification return required, and net selectivity for fund Z.

14. Does a portfolio's ex post alpha measure gains and losses due to security selection, those due to market timing, or both? Explain.

15. Indicate and describe the three major aspects of performance that one should assess in evaluating fund performance.

16. Referring to Table 15-11, determine the year-by-year and five-year average return assuming the following asset allocations:
    1. Domestic equities, 55 percent
    2. German equities, 10 percent
    3. Japanese equities, 10 percent
    4. UK equities, 5 percent
    5. Long-term bonds, 15 percent
    6. Treasury bills, 5 percent

17. Using Tables 15-14 and 15-15, determine the year-by-year return to weighting assuming the following changes:
    1. UK equities overweighted by 5 percent and Treasury bills underweighted by 5 percent in 1976
    2. Domestic equities overweighted by 5 percent and Japanese equities underweighted by 5 percent in 1977
    3. Domestic equities overweighted by 5 percent and long-term bonds underweighted by 5 percent in 1978
    4. Japanese equities overweighted by 5 percent and Treasury bills underweighted by 5 percent in 1979
    5. Long-term bonds overweighted by 5 percent and UK stocks underweighted by 5 percent in 1980

18. Contrast performance evaluation based on index comparisons to that based on comparison to other peer groups (e.g., bonds versus bonds).

19. How can factor-based analytical routines be helpful in diagnosing the performance of individual managers?

20. What major attributes or factors do investors commonly consider when evaluating stock selection capability? What are the difficulties in implementing this approach?

21. What is the information ratio, and how is it useful in evaluating performance?

22. Assume a manager with a tracking error of 2% and an alpha value of 1.5%. What is the information ratio, and how many years would she need to sustain this performance to be 90% confident of its significance?

23. Assume that you have been asked to evaluate the performance of a common stock portfolio's manager during the past five years. If information on the objectives of the portfolio were not available to you, would this affect your evaluation in any way?

24. Contrast the following terms:
  (*a*) Dollar-weighted rate of return, time-weighted rate of return
  (*b*) Expected returns, realized returns
  (*c*) Portfolio beta, stock beta
  (*d*) Positive alpha, negative alpha
  (*e*) R_p, R_f, R_m
25. Given the following information:

Risk-free rate of return $= 5\%$
Total return, S&P 500 $= 11\%$

	Portfolios			
	A	**B**	**C**	**D**
Beta	1.0	0.8	1.8	1.4
Total return	13.1	10.0	17.1	16.0

  (*a*) Calculate the risk-adjusted performance of each portfolio.
  (*b*) Rank these portfolios in terms of risk-adjusted performance during the period

INDEX